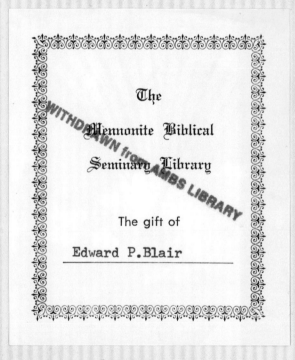

The ALEXANDRIAN LIBRARY
GLORY OF THE HELLENIC WORLD

The ALEXANDRIAN LIBRARY
GLORY OF THE HELLENIC WORLD

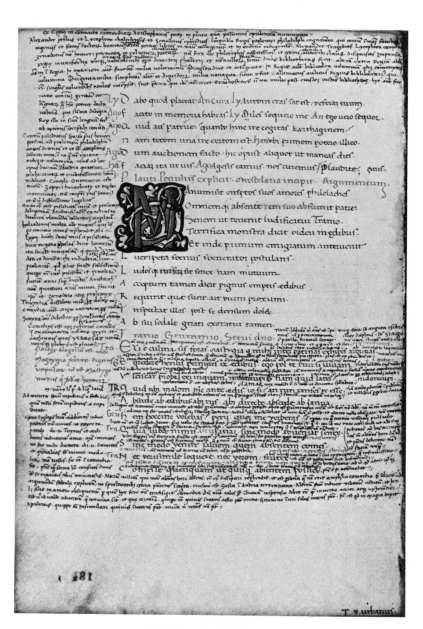

The Plautine Scholium

The
ALEXANDRIAN LIBRARY

GLORY OF
THE HELLENIC WORLD

*Its Rise, Antiquities,
and Destructions*

BY

EDWARD ALEXANDER PARSONS

AMSTERDAM – LONDON – NEW YORK

THE ELSEVIER PRESS

1952

SOLE DISTRIBUTORS FOR CONTINENTAL EUROPE:

Elsevier Publishing Company, n.v.

118 Spuistraat, Amsterdam-C.

FOR THE BRITISH COMMONWEALTH EXCEPT CANADA:

Cleaver-Hume Press, Ltd.

42a South Audley Street, London, W.I

Printed in the Netherlands

by Drukkerij Meijer, Wormerveer and Amsterdam

To

The Three Hearts

of the

du Chiron Coat of Arms

to which I have added

Auspice Deo Per Fidem et Laborem

Man must seek though he but partly finds; he must build, though it too shall be destroyed; he must live, though he shall surely die; he must strive for memory, though he shall be forgotten; and the deathless words of Solomon in Ecclesiastes thunder through the ages, even the vanity of wisdom hard pursued.

Man must seek though he but partly finds; he must build, though it too shall be destroyed; he must live, though he shall surely die; he must strive for memory, though he shall be forgotten; and the deathless words of Solomon in Ecclesiastes thunder through the ages, even the vanity of wisdom hard pursued.

PROEM

So glozed the tempter, and his proem tuned

PAR. LOST IX—549

DEEP in my study, as the outer world resounded with the havoc of war, or limped in slow recovery from its frightful toll, I thought I would write the history of the Alexandrian Library, itself the perfect victim of military madness and of the frenzy of the heart and soul of man.

At first it seemed a task of reasonable compass, but as the labor grew, the field ever broadened, and as the subject never flagged, the writer was confronted with almost an infinite investigation. He remembered the opinion of Mahaffy[1] against any attempt to remove all fault from your work, the professional advice of March[2] against too much recension, and above all the wise reflection of the great Persian scholar Dr. Browne[3]:

> But, "whoso desireth a faultless friend, remains friendless", says a well-known Eastern adage, and it is no less true that he who would write a flawless book writes nothing. I have admitted that I felt myself unprepared for so great a task; but I should have felt equally unprepared ten or twenty years hence, the subject ever widening before our eyes more rapidly than the knowledge of it grows in our minds. Even the most imperfect book, if it breaks fresh ground, may, though itself doomed to oblivion, prepare the way for a better.

The subject of this study has been curiously ignored alike by ancient and modern writers. Athenaeus thought there was no purpose in writing about it because it was in all men's minds, and the great Mommsen shows how little thought he gave to it when he makes Caesar reprove the Alexandrians for their foolish revolt which caused the destruction of their world renowned library. Unfortunately, it was not in all men's minds and fortunately

---

1. J. P. Mahaffy: *A History of Classical Greek Literature*, Preface to Vol. I.
2. G. P. March: *Lectures on the English Language.*
3. Edward G. Browne: *A Literary History of Persia*, London, 1929 (I–XI).

Caesar could never have uttered the rebuke, because it is almost certain that the Library was not destroyed in his time, and even if some books were burned neither Caesar nor his lieutenant, in their careful accounts of the incident, deigned to mention it.

A hundred years ago, the German scholars wrote preliminary monographs of much interest, such as Ritschl (1838), Parthey (1838), Klippel (1838); and since then their classicists have treated of the subject in Wilamowitz (1881), and in Kuiper, and in longer works, such as Bernhardy, Susemihl, Holm and Beloch. It has likewise had a place in the major and special works of French Hellenic scholars, as Bouché-Leclercq, A. Couat, and Alfred Croiset. The Italian studies by Lumbroso and Evaristo Breccia, and the Russian researches by Dziatzko and Rostovtzeff are distinguished. In England, Mahaffy, Sandys, J. B. Bury, Gilbert Murray, and Bevan have contributed of their learning, and likewise in America have John Williams White and Charles Burton Gulick[1].

The Alexandrian Library, certainly the greatest of all Antiquity and the greatest before the invention of printing, was perhaps potentially the most important ever collected. Because of the neglect in the annals of history and letters, we have only the existing fragments of original minor comments in the ancient authorities and mostly casual remarks af many modern writers out of which to attempt a restoration of the Alexandriana.

The Macedonian Ptolemy Soter, in an age of Hellenic Renaissance, found himself the sole ruler of the ancient empire of the Pharaohs with their mysterious gods, their eternal traditions and their teeming wealth. Ptolemy soon rose to the dignity of a great founder of empire. Militarily secure in his corner of the vast empire of Alexander, he laid the foundations of a dynasty of commercial prosperity and cultural grandeur which endured, in spite of most of his descendants, for three hundred years. Centuries after Ptolemy, Francis I, by no means a scholar, had the genius to gather the great artists at his court and thus helped to build the foundations of the French Renaissance. So the elder Medici, the merchant-banker, in a smaller though more brilliant field, as-

---

1. Of course, these names are neither exclusive nor preferential. A preface should not be a bibliography of the long list of international scholars to whom we are so much indebted.

sembled the genius of the age of the Italian Renaissance in Florence.

Now Ptolemy I, hardy Macedonian chief, a marshal of Alexander, courageous, yet shrewd, far seeing and ever governed by reflection and common sense, was indeed the forerunner of Francis I and the Medici. To his magnificent court, he invited the highest intellect of the age and founded in fair Alexandria the Hellenic Renaissance. He had the genius to discern that although armed might was necessary to maintain the state, it was the arts alone that could make the deathless fame for his House and Empire. So at Alexandria he gathered many of the poets, philosophers, scientists, and men of letters of the Hellenic world, and among those who accepted his gracious invitation was an Athenian scholar, ex-politician and man of the world, Demetrios of Phaleron. This was his great find. Demetrios suggested to him the foundation of the Museum and the Libraries and gathered the first hoard of manuscripts.

Thus we begin with the origin of the Alexandriana, its author, founder and first director.

The dramatis personae, the list of known librarians, is indeed small and, even within the first half dozen, controversial. Would someone but tell us when Zenodotus died, how much it would smooth our path. If the data for a reasonably full account of the Keepers of Books is meagre, so likewise is it difficult to ascertain the quantity, the quality, the contents of the great collections, their provenance, their authorship, titles and the authenticity of the manuscripts. And then the question whether the collections consisted of Greek books alone (without doubt the entire extant corpus of Hellenic literature) or also consisted of translations of important works in theology, history, art and science, of the non-Greek peoples: Egyptian, Babylonian-Assyrian, Hebrew, Phoenician, Syrian, and those of far India.

And how were they actually housed, how assorted, classified, and above all edited and catalogued? Of these vast labors we know little where we would know much.

The actual use of this vast treasure-house of learning by the writers and scholars of at least nearly seven hundred years, if not nine hundred and thirty-seven, is still a virgin field of intellectual inquiry.

The fate of the Alexandrian Libraries, of which some notion, more or less inaccurate, is known by most of us, is a fascinating, although at times provoking, field of inquiry.

The fate of the Libraries was undoubtedly that of the Phoenix, and the final book of this treatise is necessarily devoted to the destructions of the Alexandriana.

From Caesar to Omar, our journey shall be beset with many impediments, conflicting reports, and, most dreadful of all, long periods of profoundest silence. At stated eras we will behold the (apparently) complete destruction of the Library. Yet a few years later the phoenix-like institution appears to exist, if only to meet its next destruction. And this actually continues for some 686 years, if not for 937 years, when, unfortunately, the glorious phoenix certainly dies, never again to rise from its ashes.

And so this is an attempt, for the first time in English, to assemble the known materials and to essay the story of the creation and building of the libraries; the collecting, the division, the cataloguing and the editing of the books; and the amazing, phoenix-like existence for seven or nine centuries and the tragic fate of the fabulous University of Hellas, its Museum and Libraries.

CONTENTS

BOOK ONE

Books and Libraries in Ancient Hellas

BOOK TWO

The Founding of Alexandria

BOOK THREE

The Founding of the Museum and the Library

BOOK FOUR

The Destruction of the Library

BOOK ONE

Books and Libraries in Ancient Hellas

CHAPTER I

INTRODUCTORY

———————◆———————

A MONG the lost libraries of the world from those of Thebes and Nineveh to those of Baghdad and Louvain[1], none is so provocative as that of Alexandria.

> I should deceive the expectation of the reader if I passed in silence the fate of the Alexandrian Library[2],

writes classic Gibbon. And then he fails to satisfy our most reasonable curiosity.

The scholarly Mahaffy felt constrained to say:

> But in all that has so far been said in this chapter the reader will have noticed, perhaps with impatience, the omission of far the best known claim of Ptolemy and of his capitol to historic fame – I mean the foundation of the Museum or University of Alexandria, with its magnificent Library and scientific appointments[3],

and again, we are unsatisfied.

Yet how should we expect much from the modern scholar when the ancient sources are so meagre?

Take up the *Greek Anthology, Wreath of Meleager, Stephanus of Philippus*, or the *Cycle of Agathias* derived through Constantine Cephalas or Maximus Planudes, and not a verse commemorates the glory of the greatest Greek Library.

The book of Athenaeus, whom Sir Thomas Browne yclept a delectable author, was described by James Russell Lowell as "the somewhat greasy heap of a literary rag-and-bone picker", yet is now "in some respects... the most important work of later (Greek) antiquity", as is so well said by his most distinguished modern editor and translator, Dr. Charles Burton Gulick of Harvard, who so delightfully recalls, in the last line of the prefatory notice to his

1. History presents, as the prototypes of the barbarian destructions of Louvain, the havoc wrought by the Mongols (in the 13th century) and by the Tartars under Timur the Lame, the accursed (in the 15th century) on the great libraries of Baghdad.
2. Gibbon: Ch. Ll (Vol. IX, p. 182, edition Bury).
3. J. P. Mahaffy: *Greek Life and Thought from the Death of Alexander to the Roman Conquest*, London, 1896 (p. 206).

final volume, that the Abbé de Marolles in 1680 described *The Deipnosophists* as, "un ouvrage délicieux"[1]. Athenaeus, although he gives many pages to dances and dishes, to fish and cabbage, to pipes (musical), to feasts, to manners and customs proper and improper, cannot spare a few paragraphs for the Alexandrian Library.

In his important pot-pourri of the life of ancient Greece called *The Feast of the Learned*, Athenaeus described the host, Larensis, of this Dinner of Sophists, as a man who:

> Owned so many ancient Greek books, that he surpassed all who have been celebrated for their large libraries, including Polycrates of Samos, Peisistratus the tyrant of Athens, Eucleides, likewise an Athenian, Nicocrates of Cyprus, the kings of Pergamum, Euripides the poet, Aristotle the philosopher, Theophrastus and Nelius, who preserved the books of the two last named. From Neleus, he says our King Ptolemy surnamed Philadelphus, purchased them all and transferred them with those which he had procured at Athens and at Rhodes to his beautiful capital, Alexandria (Athen. 1–3).

Yet Athenaeus does not pause to tell us even a few of the titles or authors of some of the books which the fortunate Larensis possessed.

And later, when speaking of "fair Alexandria", Athenaeus quotes from Callixeinus[2] sixteen mortal pages of a description of a pleasure-dome (Pavilion) and of a processional in celebration of the Ptolemaeia in honor of the deified Ptolemy Soter and Berenice, in which their son displayed the incredible wealth of Egypt. Yet after this voluminous account of a Dionysiac or carnival pageant, Athenaeus adds less than four provocative lines:

> And concerning the numbers of books, the establishing of libraries, and the collection in the Hall of the Muses, why need I even speak, since they are in all men's memories?

How many pages of the general run of Athenaeus would we not

---

1. Athenaeus: *The Deipnosophists* with tr. by Charles Burton Gulick in 7 Vols., London, 1927–41 (Vol. I, p. XV). The text, spirited and courageous translation, and liberal notes (so lacking in many Loeb volumes) places this work of American classical scholarship in the van of the incomparable and indispensable Loeb Classical Library, now bravely approaching its 400th. volume.
As to the Abbé de Marolles, who could appreciate Athenaeus better than a Frenchman!
2. Callixeinus of Rhodes IV: *Description of Alexandria* (Athenaeus, V, 196–203; L.C.L. pp. 387–419).

give for a very few pages describing the contents of that "Hall of the Muses", the provenance of its collections, the arrangement of its rolls (books), the system of cataloguing, the rules for using the manuscripts, and the general management of the great Libraries of the Museum and the Serapeum[1].

From fragmentary ancient notices and meagre modern comment, one ventures, with some misgiving, to attempt to picture the Library of Alexandria.

The record-vaults and book-rooms of Asurbanipal had apparently commingled with their native Assyrian dust, and the sacred rituals and literary writing of Phaeronic Egypt which escaped the Persian barbarians had been secreted by the Keepers of Books of the Temple Libraries, when we are told by gossiping Aulus Gellius:

> The tyrant Pisistratus is said to have been the first to establish at Athens a public library of books relating to the liberal arts. Then the Athenians themselves added to this collection with considerable diligence and care; but later Xerxes, when he got possession of Athens and burned the entire city except the citadel, removed the whole collection of books and carried them off to Persia. Finally, a long time afterwards, King Seleucus, who was surnamed Nicanor, had all these books taken back to Athens[2].

The conclusion of this story is more than doubtful and in the historian of the House of Seleucus[3] we find no reference to the return of the library.

Of course, there were books and collections of manuscripts in Athens (and probably in other Greek cities) before the Persian War. The destruction of Athens was probably complete. Themistocles employed his genius in the material resurrection of the

---

1. Although Athenaeus has failed us in this regard, we should not forget our indebtedness to him, which was so well expressed by Donaldson:
The extent to which this one book has contributed to repair the ravages of time, and especially to save choise fragments from the wreck of the great Alexandrian Museum, in which Athenaeus pursued his studies, is shown by the test to which Schweighaeuser appeals, namely, that if we look into any collection of the fragments of Greek poets, we shall see how large a proportion is due to the *Deipnosophists*. K. O. Muller: *History of the Lit. of Anc. Greece*, III, 285.
2. Aulus Gellius: *Attic Nights*, Bk. VII–17–1 (L.C.L.), London, 1927 (Vol. II, p. 139).
3. Edwyn Robert Bevan: *The House of Seleucus*, London, 1902, 2 Vols. A perusal of this work will confirm how little the Seleucids and other successors of Alexander (with the exception of the Ptolemies) were concerned with the things of culture, and how they devoted their great energies and talents to the politics of empire and to arms.

capital. When the most splendid of all the intellectual ages was reached, when all of the arts flourished and many reached their most perfect development, when certainly the art of letters, verse and prose, at its ultimate height was setting the canons for all future efforts, in this time, under Pericles, there can be little doubt but that Athens possessed important private and public collections of manuscripts. The philosophical schools, the houses of Pericles and Aspasia and many others unquestionably had books (MSS.) and where there is more than one book, a collection is begun.

Although little reference has come to us of the libraries of the golden age of Greece, we must remember that on this subject the elder writers are mostly silent. The few accounts from the Hellenic-Roman times, when there was much travel and intercourse and more writers that have survived, are mostly of Athens.

There were libraries in Athens and in other cities of the Greek world before Plato and Aristotle, in spite of the remark of Strabo (13-1-54) that Aristotle was "the first man... to have collected books". If there were libraries or collectors, there must have been booksellers, in spite of the opinion of Boeckh[1] who was followed by many of the older classicists. Boeckh admits that there was a book market (τὰ βιβλία) in the Agora, at Athens, but contended that the books sold were blank books without writing. Our authority for the Book Mart is Julius Pollux of Naucratis who about 178 A.D. held a chair at Athens[2], and in one of his fragments (VII-210) he particularly sets forth that it was uncommon to use βιβλίον of unwritten books. Likewise Xenophon (Anabasis VII-5-14), referring to merchandise washed on shore from wrecked Greek vessels in the Pontus, says: "There were found great numbers of beds and boxes, quantities of written books." The story of Euthydemos, also from Xenophon (*Memor.* IV-2-1) is told in the next chapter.

Alexis, the gifted writer of the Middle (c. 372-270 B.C.) Comedy in a fragment of his play, *Linos*, in whose house Heracles is supposed to have been educated, represents Linos as having quite a comprehensive library:

---

1. Augustus Boeckh: *The Public Economy of Athens*, London, 1842 (p. 47).
2. Pollux: ed. Bekker, 1846 (IX–47 and VII–210), as quoted by Prof. Becker.

Go up and take whatever book from there you wish; then looking very carefully at the titles, quietly and at your leisure, you shall read. Orpheus is there, Hesiod, tragedies, Choerilus, Homer, Epicharmus, histories of all sorts.

But Heracles chose a book on Cookery (Athenaeus, IV 164-c). Dr. Hall reminds us[1]:

> The literature of early times in Greece was not composed in order to be read. It was composed for recitation in public or in private and consisted essentially of the spoken word (p. 25).

> The enthusiasm for Tragedy created a reading public, since but few Greeks could hope to see the masterpieces of the great dramatists performed in Athens. Thus an impulse was given to the production of books which ends in the growth towards the end of the fifth century of an organized book-trade with its centre in Athens (p. 27).

And so the noted rhetorician Aristeides (c. 117–c. 180 A.D.) says that the libraries of Athens were the finest in the world[2].

We are told that Ptolemy built a library at Athens (The Ptolemaeum), in which the boys partly contributed and used the books as they attended philosophical lectures in the gymnasium, and Cicero, in *De Finibus* (V–1–1), tells how he and his friends heard a lecture by Antiochus in this same School of Ptolemy.

We know that the Emperor Hadrian (117–138 A.D.), friend of Athens and patron of culture, built at Athens a magnificent institution, with colonnades of 100 columns of Phrygian marble, with a central building "adorned with a gilded roof and alabaster"[3], ornamented with statues and painting, in which was housed a great library, which later provoked the praise of St. Jerome[4].

1. T. W. Hall: *A Companion to Classical Texts*, Oxford, 1913 (p. 25).
2. Aristeides: Or. XIII, Fol. 1, p. 306, ed. Dindorf, Leipzig, 1829.
3. Pausanias: Bk. I (*Attica*) XVIII-9.
4. Eusebius (*Chronicon*, Vol. 2, p. 167, ed. Schone). See Frazer's notes to Pausanias, Vol. II, p. 185.

CHAPTER II

LIBRARIES OF OLD GREECE

N ow, who were these early Greek book-collectors so
casually mentioned by Athenaeus (1–3–a)?

a. Peisistratus (605–527 B.C.), well known tyrant of
Athens, was a noble and a man of culture. He built temples to the
gods, inaugurated the great festival of the Panathenaea, the
joyous processional of which was carved by or under Phidias on
the frieze of the Periclean Parthenon. He was a lover of music
and recitative and is said to have appointed a committee of
scholars (Onomacritus of Athens, Orpheus of Croton and Zopyrus
of Heraclea and a fourth whose name has not been deciphered)
to assemble the lays of Homer and to edit them. It has been
charged that at this time verses in praise of Athens were interpo-
lated[1]. However, this was the first critical attempt to arrange
the great epics. It is interesting to remember that Demetrios of
Phaleron, who suggested to Ptolemy the idea of the Alexandrian
Museum, was the last of the Attic critical Homeric scholars.

It is most reasonable to believe that a man of Peisistratus's
taste, who certainly affected learning and patronized men of
letters, should have had a collection of books to which he gave
access to the public and so justified that statement in Aulus Gellius that he established the first Public Library at Athens[2].

b. Polycrates (died 522 B.C.), tyrant of Samos, was a rougher
stone, although also a lover of the beautiful in art and letters and
a patron of literary men. By nature a true descendant of the

1. This is one of the weakest Homeric criticisms: John A. Scott: *Athenian Interpolations in Homer* (*Classical Philology*, VI, 419, Chicago, 1911).
2. Knowing the general freedom of Greek life, one cannot but feel that this was more truly a "public" library than that mysterious Hall of Books – a place of Healing for the Soul – entered through its door of beaten gold, on either side of which were carved the Ibis-headed Thoth, father of Letters, and the goddess Seshat, mother of Letters and President of the Room of Books (could the first librarian have been a woman!) and containing some twenty thousand papyrus-rolls, in the Ramesseum of Osymandyas, King of Kings, known in history as Rameses II. (See *The Library of Rameses the Great and Some of its Books* by Dr. Charles L. Nichols, Boston, 1909, a delightful paper read before the Club of Odd Volumes.)

Carian pirates, his romantic life and tragic end as told by Herodotus is one of the great narrative gems of that glorious saga book.

Ruthlessly and unscrupulously he ruled; he loved beauty ostentatiously, dined and wined and petted his poets, patronized learning, was lucky in all things, to the terror of his friend Amasis, King of Egypt, who when he heard of his unnatural success advised him to give up something which he held most dear. So Polycrates took his rare emerald signet-ring cut by the Samian artist Theodore, a gem beyond price, and cast it into the sea. Polycrates grieved for the sacrifice he had made. But shortly thereafter a poor fisherman making a catch of an unusually fine fish presented it to the King. When the fish was opened the ring was found within its belly. Polycrates took it as a good omen, but Amasis knew that Nemesis had turned down his offering. So luck pursued him till Nemesis struck. By a crude trick, he was lured to Asia by the satrap Oroetes and ignominiously put to death by "a mode not fit to be described" as old Herodotus tells. We believe that he was crucified[1].

Polycrates in the days of his power and wealth on the island of Samos, with Asia on his right hand and Greece on his left, with Egypt to the South, with his ships on many seas, was in a favored place to gather manuscripts (book-rolls) for and from the scholars whom he invited to his court and for his own love of splendor.

c. Nicocrates of Cyprus was a very early collector. This bald fact alone we are told, as we have of him neither date nor data.

d. Euripides (480–406 B.C.), the great tragic poet, was an ardent collector of books. Again, we know considerable about the eventful life of the dramatist who, born in Salamis during the naval battle, met his tragic end in Macedonia, torn to pieces by the hounds of his friend King Archelaus; who wrote 95 plays of which 18 (or 19) survive[2]; but we know nothing of his library. How keen is our curiosity to learn what rolls filled the armaria[3],

---

1. The immortal story has turned many a trick in *The Thousand Nights and a Night* and in other Eastern, as in Western, fable.

2. Euripides: *Tragoedie septendecim, ex quib. quaedam habent commentaria*, etc., Venetiis apud Aldvm mense febrvario M D III, 2 Vols. – the editio princeps, with leaves actually uncut, but this is something that would interest only a bibliophile.

3. The word is the Latin name for the cupboards or wall-cases which held the rolls in the small libraries of antiquity. Is not the tradition still honored in the Vatican?

or cases, of this skeptic, realist, and most modern tragedian of ancient Greece.

Euripides affords the first instance of a man of very limited means having a fine collection, and this may be attributed to his good fortune in having so intellectual and so faithful a servant as Cephisophon, who was an accomplished scribe, as his collaborator and friend.

Euripides was well known to his contemporaries as a man of books and learning. We may remember the scene in the *Frogs* of Aristophanes, who was highly prejudiced against him, where in Hades Aeschylus and Euripides debate their respective dramatic merits. And Euripides explains how "when first I took the art (of tragedy) from you" Aeschylus,... "I reduced and toned her down"... by "a dose of chatterjuice, distilled from books"[1]. Finally the elder tragedian challenges his younger rival that their verses be weighed in the scales (even as cheese is sold in the market-place, says the Judge Dionysus):

> Come! no more line for line! Let him bring *all*, His wife, his children his Cephisophon, And mount the scale himself, with all his *books*, I shall outweigh them with two lines alone[2].

e. The handsome and wealthy Euthydemus "had formed a large collection of the works of celebrated poets and professors"[3] when Socrates sought to rebuke him for his apparent self-sufficiency in knowledge.

"Tell me, Euthydemus," interrogated Socrates, "am I rightly informed that you have a large collection of books written by the wise men of the past, as they are called?"

"By Zeus, yes Socrates," answered he, "and I am still adding to it, to make it as complete as possible."

"By Hera," retorted Socrates, "I do admire you for valuing the treasures of wisdom above gold and silver. For you are evidently of the opinion that, while gold and silver cannot make men better, the thoughts of the wise enrich their possessors with virtue."

1. Aristophanes: *The Frogs*, 939 et seq. tr. by Benjamin Bickley Rogers: *The Comedies of Aristophanes*, London, 1902 (in his commentary on line 943, Mr. Rogers reminds us that "Euripides possessed one of the largest libraries in the ancient world" (Vol. V, p. 144, note), Sir Frederic G. Kenyon in *Books and Readers in Ancient Greece and Rome*, Oxford, 1932 (p.24), thinks that it amounted to "a few score rolls".
2. As tr. by J. E. Sandys: *A History of Classical Scholarship* (Vol. I, p. 54) 3rd ed., Cambridge, 1921; the italics *books* are ours.
3. Xenophon: *Memorabilia* (IV-2).

And in a short time through the merciless logic of the Socratic method, the Master reduced the poor bookman to fine dust. Yet the collecting of books (and we may assume the reading of them) had brought to our Greek bibliophile more wisdom than Socrates might have admitted, for Euthydemus gave up being an intellectual snob, if he ever was such, and became the constant, faithful disciple of the philosopher[1].

f. Eucleides, an Athenian, was perhaps the *archon eponymus* who gave his name to the year 403 B.C. We know nothing of his bookish flair.

g. Plato (427–348 B.C.), the philosopher of idealism, whose serene and sublime views on the invisible world and whose conception of God have exerted so profound an influence on scholarship, philosophies, and religion, was a collector of manuscripts. After the death of Socrates, Plato travelled extensively, at least in Magna Graecia, making three journeys to Syracuse. It is unreasonable to assume that in his sojourns in the cultured cities of that Greater Greece he failed to gather manuscripts of the writings of the amazing 5th century B.C. and records of earlier learning. We know that he sent a hundred minas to purchase three books *On the Pythogorean Doctrine* by Philolaus of Croton[2]. Indeed, Mr. Beriah Botfield, in his distinguished Introduction to his *Praefationes et Epistolae*[3] states that the library "of Plato the philosopher, whose collection was mainly formed by purchases at Tarentum in Italy from the heirs of its former proprietor Philolaus, another part being secured at Syracuse". One can hardly forget that the bookish men of the Italian Renaissance burned tapers before their divine Plato.

h. Clearchus (assassinated 353 B.C.), tyrant of Heraclea on the Euxine, was a pupil of Plato and of Isocrates. He is described as the mildest of men, but history records him as a cruel tyrant. He was a lover of books and "founded a library at the Pontic Heraclea in Bithynia before 364 B.C"[4].

1. The whole chapter of Xenophon (BK. IV-2) is interesting reading. I quote from E. C. Marchant's tr. (L.C.L.) Xenophon (London, 1923).
2. Diog. Laertius, VIII-15.
3. *Prefaces to the First Editions of the Greek and Roman Classics and of the Sacred Scriptures*, Cambridge, 1861 (p. XXXIX).
4. Memnon, native historian of Heraclea, author of one of the lost histories of antiquity (reported in Photius, *Myriobiblion seu Bibliotheca*, cod. 224). The quotation is from Sandys (*op. cit.* p. 86).

i. Demosthenes seems to have had a most select library, the better part of which consisted of manuscripts which he had copied with his own hand. And Lucian[1] refers to autographic manuscripts of the great orator as well as to eight beautiful manuscripts of Thucydides which Demosthenes had copied. One wonders if this was a memory exercise on the part of the orator, or whether he thus devoted his valuable time to copying Thucydides as gifts to his friends or for the purpose of sale. If he made so many copies of Thucydides, he may have made more of his own writings. We know that he is one of the four Greek prose-writers whose manuscripts have reached us in the best state.

j. Aristotle was the first to collect, to preserve, and to use the culture of the past. He was really a great collector and laid the foundation of literary history. A man of universal knowledge and of encyclopaedic interests, a pupil of Plato, he founded the Lyceum, and since his active nature induced him to walk as he taught, hence he was the Peripatetic philosopher. Aristotle had his own recension of Homer, different from that which we now possess, which corresponds more to that of Plato, or, should we not say to that of the vulgate. He was the tutor of Alexander, personally selected by Philip. He taught the future conqueror of worlds for three years. Alexander always respected his instructor and not only presented him with the vast sum of 800 talents but had collections made for and sent to him of the natural curiosities encountered by the Greeks in their conquest of Egypt and the kingdoms of Asia and the East. These extensive collections must have included manuscripts, at least Greek scripts from the cultured Hellenic cities of Asia Minor, and some oriental manuscripts from conquered cities, if only as rarities, which Aristotle must have had in his library like any modern collector who has writings in many tongues, most of them Greek to him.

We have every reason to believe that Aristotle had an extensive collection of books. We know that no individual collector ever had greater opportunity to bring together the manuscript records of human knowledge. These manuscripts may well have included written political records as well as literary scrolls. Just as speci-

1. Lucian: *The Ignorant Book-Collector*, 4 (L.C.L. by A. M. Harmon, London, 1921); or *The Works of Lucian of Samosata*, by H. W. & F. G. Fowler, Oxford, 1905 (Vol. III, p. 267).

mens of natural history were collected and sent to him, is it not reasonable that his pupils or reference scholars collected from many cities the material for his series of Constitutions of some 158 Greek communities, one of which was discovered in our time in a tomb at Akhmin, Egypt, written on four papyrus-rolls, *The Constitution of Athens*[1]?

This library consisted of an important collection of books made by a scholar of universal learning, together with the prodigious volume of his own writings, which the ancients ambiguously describe as 400 books, or 44 myriads lines, 445,270 lines according to Diogenes Laertius[2], which is supposed to represent at least three times again as much as all his extant works, to which we might add all the miscellanea and reference materials, which he and some of his pupils or scholars must have gathered during nearly a halfcentury of intellectual labors. The history of the peregrination of the Aristotle books is the first instance which I can recall where an attempt has been made to record the provenance of a library.

As Aristotle was failing in health, his pupils pressed him to name a successor. He was greatly embarrassed because he had two disciples above all the rest in learning and worthiness, Theophrastus of Lesbos and Eudemus of Rhodes.

"This wine I am drinking sits not well with my health," he remarked, "could you not fetch me some foreign vintage, say some wine of Rhodes and Lesbos?" His pupils at once "went, sought, found, brought" the desired wines to the master. Aristotle tested the wine from Rhodes, saying: "This is truly sound and pleasant wine." Likewise he drank of that of Lesbos, remarking: "Both are very good indeed, but the Lesbian is the sweeter." The tale is told by Aulus Gellius[3].

k. Theophrastus of Lesbos became the successor of Aristotle, who left him his library and the original manuscripts of his writings.

At his death, Theophrastus left the library and writings of Aristotle and his own library and writings[4] to his relative and pupil, Neleus of Scepsis.

Diogenes has preserved the will of Theophrastus:

1. Editio princeps, edited by Mr., now Sir, F. G. Kenyon of B. M. (January 30, 1891).
2. Diogenes Laertius: *Lives of Eminent Philosophers*, London, 1925, L.C.L., Vol. I, p. 475 (V-27), says 445,270 lines.
3. Aulus Gellius: *The Attic Nights*, London, 1927 (L.C.L.–Bk. XIII–5).
4. Dio. Laer. (V-50) says Theophrastus wrote in all 232,808 lines.

> Our property in Stagira I leave to Callinus, all my books to Neleus. But the garden and the pleasure-ground and the buildings attached to the garden I give all to those of my friends hereafter enumerated who desire to keep school and study philosophy together in them... on condition that no one shall alienate this property.

Here the story splits. One account would say that Ptolemy II acquired the collections from Neleus for the Alexandrian Library, the other, that Neleus kept the collections, which later were sold by his descendants to Apellicon, the wealthy book-collector of Teos, and that Sulla confiscated the Apellicon library which was at Athens and brought it to Rome.

The most reasonable view is that both stories are partly correct. We believe that Neleus sold to Ptolemy for a large sum the libraries of Aristotle and Theophrastus, but that he retained some, perhaps many, of the original manuscripts of the writings of the philosophers. These documents remained in the family of his heirs for many years. At the time when the Attalid kings of Pergamum were gathering a great library in rivalry of Alexandria, the descendants of Neleus, who were subjects of Pergamum, fearing the king would take the books from them, secreted the manuscripts in a cave. Years passed and the manuscripts were forgotten. In the first century before Christ, there lived one Apellicon of Teos, a Peripatetic philosopher, a man of large means and small character, who was an omnivorous acquirer of books, who was indeed a biblioklept, who had stolen books or records from the archives of various Greek cities, and who, discovered at Athens, had to fly for his life. During the tyranny of Ariston, who himself was a follower of Aristotle, Apellicon was allowed to return to Athens and was given command of the troops against Delos. Through incompetency he was surprised by the Romans and utterly defeated. He escaped and died.

Now this man had discovered the whereabouts of the Aristotle books and had acquired them, we hope honestly. They were in bad condition, having become moulded and partly rotted from the dampness of their hiding place. Apellicon attempted to publish the books, filling in the hiatuses with conjectures of his own. As he was utterly unfitted for this task, the text suffered mere mutilation and the labor of the future literary surgeon was proportionately increased.

Sulla, when he took Athens, confiscated the library of Apelli-con and carried it to Rome (B.C. 84). There Tyrannion, the learned freedman, sold copies of "Aristotle's books", and the antiquary Andronicus of Rhodes, the first of the great Aristotelian commentators, devoted much study and labor to the elucidation of the works of the last genius of the Greek classical age.

l. Strato of Lampsacus succeeded Theophrastus in the Lyceum. He was the head of the school from 286–268 B.C. Strabo[1] tells how Aristotle left his library to Theophrastus, who in turn left his and Aristotle's library to his nephew Neleus of Scepsis, who moved the books to his native place, leaving the school with "no books at all, with the exception of only a few, mostly esoteric works", and hence the early Peripatetic school declined. Yet Strato must have remedied this handicap because when he died he left a will leaving the school to Lyco, and stating: "I also give and bequeath to him all my books, except those of which I am the author"[2]. Strato was probably well to do, as his pupil Ptolemy II (Philadelphus) is said to have given him 80 talents. He was called to the Alexandrian court by Soter to finish the education of his son and heir, and it is most probably that Deme-trios of Phaleron suggested the choice of this tutor[3].

m. Mention may be made of later kings, tyrants, scholars and amateurs who collected books:

1. Perseus, king of Macedon:

It was only the books of the king (Perseus) that he (Aemilius Pau-lus) allowed his sons, who were devoted to learning, to choose out for themselves[4].

2. Mithradates, king of Pontus[5].

3. Hieron, tyrant of Syracuse, must have had great libraries in his palace; there must have been many dealers of manuscripts in his city. We do know that when he built the wonderful trans-port-ship, superintended by Archimedes, the mathematician, with all the luxuries of a transatlantic liner, indeed of an Italian liner with all its appurtenances of art, there was adjoining the

1. Strabo: XIII–1–54 (C. 609).
2. Diogenes Laertius: V–62.
3. Bouché-Leclercq: *op. cit.* I–130; Susemihl: *op. cit.* I–143, note.
4. Plutarch: *Aemilius Paulus,* 28–6.
5. Isidorus: *Etym.* VI–5–1.

room of Aphrodite, "a library large enough for five couches, the wall and doors of which were made of boxwood; it contained a collection of books, and on the ceiling was a concave dial," i.e., a vault (of the sky)[1]. The cabins of the ship had tessellated flooring portraying the entire story of the *Iliad*[1], and the ship was called *The Lady of Alexandria*.

n. When so little is known of public libraries, it is understandable that we know so much less of private collectors.

Erathosthenes: Strabo says:

> Why, Erathosthenes takes all these as matters actually established by the testimony of the men who had been in the regions, for he had read many historical treatises – with which he was well supplied if he had a library as large as Hipparchus says it was[2].

Strabo's last editor[3] notes that this was the library at Alexandria.

For proof that libraries were found in many towns and cities we have only to refer to the Fragments (Bk. XII–27–4) of Polybius, in which, in criticizing the historical methods of Timaeus, he remarks how easy it is for a writer who is indolent to make convenient research:

> Inquiries from books may be made without any danger or hardship, provided only one takes care to have access to a town rich in documents or to have a library near at hand[4].

o. Among the limited ancient bibliographical references to Greek towns may be mentioned:

For Athens, Pausanias speaks of the Ptolemaeum or gymnasium of Ptolemy[5]. The building included a library and lecture-room[5]. Again he describes great statues of Hadrian, a hundred pillars of Phrygian marble, gilded roof and alabaster apertures in sumptuous rooms, adorned with paintings and statuary, in which, he casually remarks, "are kept books"[6]. It is true that St. Jerome[7]

---

1. Moschion: apud: Athenaeus V-206 e to V-207 f; V-208 f.
2. Strabo: II–1–5.
3. Strabo: *The Geography of,* tr. Horace Leonard Jones (version J.R.S. Sterrett (L.C.L.), London, 1917 (I, p. 259, note).
4. Polybius (XII–27–4–5).
5. Pausanias (XVII–2); Frazer in his *Commentary* (II, p. 145), following the early ancient and modern custom, says: The founder was *probably* Ptolemy Philadelphus.
6. Idem (XVIII–9); Frazer: *Commentary,* II-185.
7. Eusebius: *Chronic.* II, p. 167, ed. Shöne.

is loud in praise of this wonderful library, and Aristides, the rhetorician, says Athens had the finest libraries in the world[1].

In pleasure-loving Corinth, even Dio Chrysostom was flattered when his portrait was placed in their library[2].

At the oracular shrine of Delphi[3], in the commercial Dyrrhachium of Illyria[4], and even in Patras, as Aulus Gellius tells:

> For in the library at Patrae I found a manuscript of Livius Andronicus of undoubted antiquity, entitled ᾿Οδύσσεια, in which the first line contained this word (insece) without the letter u[5],

in these very different places there were libraries.

Rhodes, in spite of the simple reference in Athenaeus (I–3b), was, after Athens, the book-market of Greece. There has recently been discovered a fragmentary inscription of a *Catalogue* of a library, of works on Politics and Rhetoric (with many new titles), probably of the celebrated University of Rhodes of the 2nd and 1st centuries B.C.[6].

Ephesus, although for proof we are reduced to inscriptional fragments[7], was a book-centre for Asia Minor.

Of Smyrna, after it was rebuilt by Antigonus and Lysimachus, Strabo[8] says it was a most beautiful city, "where there is also a library".

Soli, on the coast of Cilicia, Mylasa, in the plains of Caria, and the famous Halicarnassus, have at least a mention among the cities of the Hellenic East as having libraries.

This desultory sketch may be closed with a reference to a letter of the younger Pliny to the emperor Trajan in which he sought imperial advice on the curious legal question as to whether the emperor's statue could be placed in the same building with the dead. It involved the great Dio Chrysostom at Prusa, Bithynia:

> I have visited the spot myself where I saw your statue placed in a

1. Aristides (ed. Dindorf) - *Oration* XIII (I-336).
2. Dio Chrysostom: *The Corinthian Oration* (XXXVII–8).
3. Eph. Arch.,n 855–18.
4. C. I. L. III–607.
5. *Attic Nights:* XVIII–9–5.
6. J. U. Powell and E. A. Barber: *New Chapters in the History of Greek Literature* (2nd series), Oxford, 1929 (*Catalogue of a Library at Rhodes*), p. 83.
7. Inscription of Ephesus (Jahreshefte Österreichischen Arch. Instituts, 1898-1905), p. 67.
8. Strabo: XIV–1–37.

library; the alleged burial-place of Dio's wife and son is in a court-yard which is enclosed with a colonnade[1].

The emperor, true to his character, would not consider the charge and at once allayed the anxiety of his loyal governor and friend.

1. Pliny: *Letters* (X–81).

CHAPTER III

LIBRARIES OF NEW GREECE:
THE ATTALIDS OF PERGAMUM

THE extreme northwestern area of Asia Minor, bounded by the Aegean sea, the Hellespont, and the Propontic sea, was called Mysia. It was a well watered, mountainous country in which the Greeks and kindred people had early settled. It was the site of the most famous city of ancient story, Troy. From time immemorial its lofty hills and mountain-crags furnished safe strongholds for petty princelings and local chiefs, and the dense forest-slopes of Mounts Olympus and Ida offered refuge for robber-bands which often obtained rich pickings in the land that was the North Western Eurasian terminus or focal meeting-place for all the great trade-routes of Anterior Asia. Through Mysia the hordes of Xerxes marched in their attempt to conquer Greece, and, in reverse, Alexander the Great at the Granicus, a river in Mysia (B.C. 334), had signal victory over the Persians. Mysia was thus the springboard for Eurasian invasion and the beach-head for Asiatic conquest.

Along this highway of commerce and parade of phalanx and legion, many towns occupied the hilltops and trafficked with merchant or military adventurer as best served their interests

On a spur of the mountain-range in southern Mysia, encom-passed by two rivers (one flowing through the city, the other washing its walls), at an elevation of a thousand feet, overlooking a vast plain, with a magnificent view of the countryside as it descended some fourteen miles distant to the Aegean sea, was situated the citadel of the city of Pergamum.

We do not know its origin. Its people always claimed to be pure Greek, whether Arcadians who came under the Heraclides, or men of Epidaurus, we shall never know. As it had no early recorded history it must have been a place of little importance. It i s first mentioned by Xenophon in the *Anabasis*. It became known t hrough Lysimachus, one of the diadochi of Alexander the Great.

Lysimachus was of the great king's bodyguard. He was a man of much ability, always brave, a good soldier, a founder of cities. His all pervading vice was his love of money. As he grew old his true character developed in all its wickedness. He put his son Agathocles to death, murdered his son-in-law, and his many crimes alienated the allegiance of friends and followers. Though he died bravely in action, only his dog was faithful at his end.

Now Lysimachus had gathered a vast treasure amounting to some 9000 golden talents. He wished to secure it in a safe place under a trusty guardian. He selected Pergamum, perched upon its Mysian Hill, as a stronghold, a perfect place of safe-deposit. But in the selection of a guardian, he, unfortunately, like his great master and man of the Macedonians, was afflicted with an oriental taint. The Eastern kings have ever trusted their gold and their women to the care of those neutral creatures whose trust-worthiness rarely extended to their treasures of metal. Lysima-chus chose Philetaerus, of Tius in Paphlagonia, an eunuch, as a keeper of his wealth. The temptation was too great. True to form, Philetaerus, using as a veil some alleged ill treatment by Arsinoe, the wife of Lysimachus, and taking advantage of the domestic tragedies and political chaos in which Lysimachus was engulfed, faithlessly seized the hoard as his own (283 B.C.).

With the formidable position of the fortress-city and the stolen wealth of his master, Philetaerus actually founded a dynasty which for a hundred and fifty years played a notable part in diplomacy, art, and culture during the dying years of the silver age of Hel-lenic life. Born in infamy, it was queerly fated to end in little honor.

Its last ruler, Attalus III (138–133), has been described as "an incapable tyrant, who was fond of gardening and of making wax-figures" and who, considering Pergamum as his personal patrimony, seemed to take delight in preventing his illegitimate brother from succeeding to the kingdom by making Rome his heir.

But the world may be interested in what happened to the House of Attalus from the death of its infamous founder, the eunuch Philetaerus, to the short reign of the last of the house, Attalus III.

The steward of Lysimachus, with his master's wealth, had set up a feudal state. The crafty Philetaerus founded a money-power which he ruled with subtle prudence, bestowing his favor, with almost unerring judgment, upon the neighboring king or faction destined to Fortune's favor. As an instance of his adroit policy, he redeemed, at a great price, the body of Seleucus from the murderer Ptolemy the Thunderbolt, accorded it due funeral honors and sent the ashes, in a golden urn, to Seleucus's son Antiochus I, hoping thus to earn his favor. He raised Pergamum to a place of prominence. If not the actual guardian of the Hellespontine Gate between Europe and Asia, he could seriously oppose or greatly help the ambitious leaders in their military wayfaring. On his death at the age of 80 (B.C. 263) his principality was firmly established and was inherited by his nephew Eumenes I (B.C. 263–241).

Eumenes I defeated Antiochus I of Syria in battle near Sardis and preserved the wealth and kingdom received from his uncle.

A writer, Ctesiscles, in Athenaeus, says Eumenes died of drunkenness. He was succeeded by his cousin, another nephew of old Philetaerus.

Attalus I (241–197 B.C.) defeated the Gauls in battle, drove them from his domain, and considered this such a triumph as to justify his assumption of the name *Basileus*, a desirable title in the Greco-Macedonian age. Indeed, these successful struggles against the barbarous Gauls were a national movement which fired the imagination of the age with the names of Antigonus Gonatas, Antiochus Soter, and Attalus of Pergamum[1]. Although these great national struggles of the Greeks against the barbarians were to be commemorated in the plastic arts and to have abided to our time, it is unfortunate that nothing has survived in written eulogy in the greater art of letters, except unconvincing fragments of Callimachus and dark references in Lycophron.

Attalus I was a writer; a fragment has survived of his description of a mighty pine-tree over two hundred feet high. He was a patron of art in whose time the original school of Pergamene sculpture arose foremost in his century. He embellished his fortress-

---

1. Mahaffy: *Greek Life and Thought*: "These savages contributed more than they took away, by affording a standing example of brutality, of lawlessness and of indelible illbreeding" (p. 169). Mahaffy knew of the Turk and the Hun as a parallel. He was spared our towering examples of the Germans and the Japanese.

city with temples and public buildings. In politics he was pro-Roman. These Pergamene kings were diplomats, recognizing the indomitable rise of Rome. They were royal capitalists who protected Greek towns, erected fortifications, built ships, and furnished mercenaries to their neighbor states for money. They issued money, of which famous specimens survive, and, like the Medici, were princely bankers, having the hoard of Lysimachus which their uncle-founder had secured, as capital investment. They visited Greece; Polybius (22–11) records their purchase of Aegina for 30 talents, from which they brought treasures of archaic art; they displayed their wealth in Athens, and Pausanias described their dedicatory offerings on the Athenian Acropolis portraying the conquest of Athens over the Persians and of Pergamum over the Gauls. Arcesilaus, master of the Athenian Academy, was recipient of donatives from the money-kings and a poem in honor of Attalus I was perhaps a not indelicate quid pro quo.

Under Eumenes II (197–159), the splendor of Pergamum attained its greatest height. Politically, Eumenes continued pro-Roman, and after Rome's defeat of Antiochus the Great at Magnesia, 190 B.C., his kingdom spread over Mysia, Lydia, the two Phrygias, Pisidia, Pamphylia and Lycaonis. He, too, defeated the Gauls, and to commemorate his victory erected (166 B.C.) high above the agora, on a great platform on the slope of the acropolis, a marble altar to Zeus Soter. This colossal monument was decorated with a sculptured frieze in high relief depicting the contest between the Gods (the Greeks) and the Giants (the Gauls). Here Pergamenian art arose to great heights portraying the individual barbarian warrior in the anguish of defeat, yet with a sympathy worthy of the Greek spirit and genius. This is the most complete composition of decorative art which has survived from antiquity. It has no rival in Renaissance or modern times. German scholarship had rescued it from its tomb in Asia, restored and re-erected it as the archaeological glory of Berlin, where it now is probably but rubble, destroyed by the chaos aroused by the German terror which has descended upon the earth to a depth equal to the barbarism of all time.

And now the Attalids, having secured much peace through their wealth, having through policy or otherwise added many principalities to their kingdom, having won military victories of

considerable renown, which they commemorated by the erection
of beautiful temples and great monuments expressing their
gratitude to the immortal gods, had at last reached that stage of
culture which required only the true achievements of the highest
intellect to crown their civilization. The Attalids had visited
Athens, mother of Greek learning, and other great centers, they
had beheld Alexandria posing as the seat of culture of the Mace-
donian-Hellenic world. Pergamum itself was situated in a region
famous in Greek story, rich in Hellenic antiquity and the things
of civilization – why should they not make Pergamum take its
place with rival cities in the new Hellenic age? So it was decided
to make Pergamum a city of art and learning. Lacydes of Cyrene,
the head of the Athenian Academy, had been invited to Pergamum by Attalus I, but he shied, appreciatingly replying, "That
pictures should be viewed from a certain distance". Eumenes invited Lycon, the Peripatetic philosopher, but he, too, declined.
The schools of Plato and Aristotle having gently turned down the
princely invitations, the Stoics were more complaisant and seemed
willing to live in the shadow of a throne. Crates of Mallos in
Cilicia came and established himself in Pergamum. The Stoics
came, and so the Stoa accepted what the Academy and Lyceum
had declined.

Crates of Mallos became the head of the Pergamene school. He
was at least the founder of its school of grammar, and much effort
was expended in defending its system of anomaly against his rival
Aristarchus and the system of analogy of the Alexandrian school.
He was librarian of the Pergameniana and is thought to have
compiled its famous catalogues or *Pinakes* of prose and poetical
works. His miscellanea include commentaries, *On Hesiod*, *On
Aristophanes*, *On Euripides*, a work *On the Attic Dialect*, and perhaps
he wrote on geography and natural history. But his chief literary
labors were his studies in criticism and on Homer. As a good Stoic
he taught an allegorical interpretation of Homer, who thus employed his divine gift of Poetry to express his philosophical beliefs.
In this he was about as unsound as some modern interpreters of
Shakespeare. Crates was the author of two or three works on the
poet: certainly a *Critical Commentary*, perhaps *A Life*, and just
possibly a recension or *edition* of Homer. When Attalus went to
Rome, he took with him Crates and Stratius the physician. On

the Palatine hill, Crates fell into an excavation and broke his leg. The ensuing enforced inactivity was well spent, however; he gave critical lectures on literature and instilled a taste for pure learning among the Romans, and added much to the renown and prestige of his Attalid patrons.

Scholars and men of letters now repaired to Pergamum: the poets, Nicander, and Musaeus of Ephesus who wrote odes in honor of his royal patrons, Attalus and Eumenes; the philosopher Antigonus of Carystus, biographer, artist and writer, who has provoked an intriguing book of German classical scholarship[1]; and historians, Apollodorus the Athenian, who dedicated a work to Attalus II, and Neanthes, who as court historian wrote a *History of Attalus I*, now lost, and possibly lost at the time of Pausanias (2nd c. A.D.) who complained (I–VI–I) that "the age of Attalus and Ptolemy is so remote that the tradition of it has passed away, and the writings of the historians whom the kings engaged to record their deeds fell into neglect still sooner". Of course there were grammarians and critics; indeed a Pergamum school of Greek rhetoric and oratory arose, which taught the so-called Asiatic (or Mahaffy's Asianic) style. In science, Biton dedicated to Attalus his treatise *On Engines of War*, and above all the great Apollonius of Perge, who inscribed his important work *On Conic Sections* to Attalus I. In medicine, Pergamum was a health resort with cures, baths, and waters at its extensive Aschepion, to which the invalid pagan and imperial world resorted. Galen, perhaps the most celebrated ancient physician, was a Pergamenian (A.D. 129–199). Here he labored and thence went forth, as has been said, to cure the world.

With its political ascendance and as a center of art, Pergamum required only the establishment of an institution of learning to take its place with the older and newer cities of the Greco-Macedonian world, indeed to rival Alexandria. In the ancient world, as certainly in the modern ages, the foundation of such an institution was a collection of books.

Although Attalus I, patron of the Pergamene school of art, had collected some books and thus started a library, it was Eumenes II who was the father of the great Library of Pergamum. Under his reign, for the second time the Hellenic world was ransacked for

1. Wilamowitz: *Antigonos von Karystos*, Berlin, 1881.

manuscripts. The days of Demetrios of Phaleron were recalled, as the book-scouts of Pergamum tempted princes, cities, and individuals to part with their treasures. As the wealth of the Attalids could match that of the Ptolemies, the campaign must have been rich in individual contests of acquisition. Where originals were now more difficult to find and sometimes unprocurable, copies were made for the princely bibliotheke of the famous Mysian city. As Pergamum had started late to collect books, she must have spent more in proportion than the three early Ptolemies in their initial building of the Alexandriana. Again, most of the cream must have been gathered in the fabulous campaign of Demetrios for the first Ptolemy.

As the zeal of the Pergamene seekers for books grew apace, where the market was bare and unable to legitimately satisfy the ardent purchasers, spurious manuscripts and forged literary wares were foisted upon the royal agents, and it is probable that the Library of Pergamum had as ample a collection of faked *editiones principes* as some great modern libraries in the days of Wagenfeld, Vrain-Denis Lucas, and of Wise[1].

As a vast number of copies of manuscripts were required, huge stacks of materials, the papyrus-paper, had to be imported from Egypt. The authorities of the Alexandrian, who must recently have been often thwarted in their attempted purchases by the money-bags of young, progressive Pergamum, saw now their chance of weakening their presumptuous rival, and so the Egyptian government placed an embargo against the export of papyrus from Egypt. For the Attalid book-buyers, this was a serious setback. But they too were alive, ambitious, and resourceful, and so a medium that had been but partially used before, on account of the greater labor in manufacture and its resultant high costs, now *ex necessitate* was resorted to and put in high production. If the Pergamene could not have papyrus-paper, cheap, convenient, but fragile, he would have skin-paper, more costly, but more sumptuous and enduring. It is true that skin-rolls had been used in Egypt for a thousand years back (in the 4th Pharaonic dynasty, or about 1500 B.C.) and the Jews had employed skins in their synagogue-rolls of the Holy Scriptures, which medium of transmission had become a sacred tradition. It is thought that the

1. The University of Texas has perhaps a complete collection of these dubious curiosa.

keen business-instinct of the Phoenicians must have sensed the trade-value of the use of skins for writing, and we know that the Ionian Greeks and the peoples of Asia Minor employed parchments. A remarkable passage in Herodotus reads:

> Paper rolls also were called from of old "parchments" by the Ionians, because formerly when paper was scarce they used, instead, the skins of sheep and goats, on which material many of the barbarians are even now wont to write (Bk. V-58)[1].

Now Herodotus gave public readings of his *History* at Athens in 446 B.C. Ctesias of Cnidus (physician-historian, 4th cent. B.C.) declared that his sources for his *Persica* were "from the royal parchments".

All of this disposes of the claim made by Varro (reported by Pliny H.N. XIII–21) that parchment was an original invention of Pergamum, to which many good scholars have unwittingly subscribed[2]. But the claim in behalf of the Attalids was not made without verisimilitude. It must be admitted that in the reign of Eumenes II at Pergamum a great industry of manufacturing animal skins for the purpose of writing took place; whereas formerly the coarser skins of the sheep and goat were used, now a finer method of treating and preparing skins was devised and the finer texture of the skin of the calves and kids was employed, even, perhaps, the tender skins of the newborn or still born lambs or kids producing the so-called virgin or abortive parchment, or the amazing pure white vellum of immaculate quality[3]. What-

1. It may be well to remember that the early word for writing-skins was διφϑεραι not περγαμηνή.
2. S. Vailhé, as late as 1911 (*Cath. Encyc.* s.v. *Pergamus*): "parchment was discovered there."
3. The distinction in our language between *parchment* and *vellum* seems unsolvable. Perhaps our oldest reference is:

> That stouffe that we wrythe vpon: and is made of beestis skynnes: is somtyme called parchement, somtyme velem, somtyme abortyue, somtyme membraan. Parchement of the cyte: where it was first made. Velem: bycause it is made of a caluys skynne. Abortyue: bycause the beest was scante parfecte. Membraan: bycause it was pulled of by hyldynge fro the beestis lymmes (i.e. members).
>
> William Horman: *Vulgaria uiri doctissimi Guil. Hormani*, 1519 fo8ob.

If we assume that *parchment* is from the Greek; *velin*, French; *menbraria*, Latin; and that the omnivorous English has absorbed them all and uses *parchment* as a general term and *vellum* for the refinements of the product, we shall, I believe, go as far as our lexicons will allow.

Vide: W. Lee Ustick: *"Parchment" and "Vellum"* in *The Library*, 4th series, Oxford, 1936, Vol. XVI, p. 439.

ever may have been the technical advances in the process of manufacture, or in producing a better medium for the transmission of the knowledge and wisdom of the ages, Pergamum was from the 2nd century B.C. recognized as the center of production, if not the place of origin, of the finest animal skins for writing, and it was not long[1] before the skins were called, and known throughout antiquity and to our time, from the city of Pergamum Πεϱγαμηνή, Charta Pergamena: "paper of Pergamum", our parchment[2].

If we had courage, we would close this subject, suggestive of the slaughter pens, the smelling vats, and kindred things most unpleasant, even in the philosophy of poor Jack Cade:

> Is not this a lamentable thing, that of the skin of an innocent lamb should be made parchment? That parchment being scribbled o'er, should undo a man? (2 Hy. VI-2[3])

The crowning glory of Eumenes II, indeed of the House of the Attalids, was the founding and building of the great Library of Pergamum, which at the head of the Aegean, must have served the scholarship of the Islands, the Asiatic Greeks, and the Motherland of Hellas, and must have been a matter of irritation to her elder sister the Alexandrian who at the southern end of the sea was yet destined to be her Nemesis.

Attalus II (159–138 B.C.), putting aside the son of Eumenes, now actually succeeded his brother both to the kingdom and his

---

1. It is thought that the earliest use of the word pergamena, which has survived to our age, may be a passage in St. Jerome's *Epistles* and an edict of Diocletion (A.D. 301). Yet Mr. Ustick (quoted above) states: "Parchment, known in Europe as early certainly, as the second century A.D."

2. We are aware that the distinguished scholar John Williams White believed the tale of Pliny quite absurd, and though admitting that Ptolemy Epiphanes or Ptolemy Philometor may have imposed restrictions or an embargo on the export of papyrus and that some parchment may have been used for rolls written or copied in Pergamum, yet that both the libraries of Alexandria and Pergamum were originally of papyrus-rolls purchased in the book-markets of Greece (Vide: *The Scholia on the Aves of Aristophanes*, Boston, 1914, p. XXXVIII). This view is not irreconcilable with our text. However we are confident that in the heat of argument the great Hellenist's hand faltered when he wrote of the Alexandriana (in Caesar's time) being "set on fire" (p. XXXIX).

3. Even Hamlet had his fling:
Hamlet: Is not parchment made of sheep-skins?
Horatio: Ay, my lord, and of calf-skins too.
Hamlet: They are sheep and calves which seek out assurance in that. (Hamlet V –1)

widow Stratonice. It was he who formerly, having heard a report of his brother Eumenes's death, assumed his crown and took his spouse to wife. On the return of his brother and the discovery of the mistake, he surrendered both without further ado and there seems to have been no aftermath to the incident. Patience and persistence were rewarded, and this time Eumenes journeyed to the land of shades. We may thus well understand how Attalus assumed the sobriquet of Philadelphus. In political strategy, Attalus II was very successful in resisting the attack of Pharnaces, king of Pontus; in contributing his part towards the final defeat of the romantic Demetrius I of Syria; in the murder of Prusias II of Bithynia; and in the contest against Philip of Macedonia and the Achaeans. He was, as always, pro-Roman.

Culturally, Attalus supported the eminent position to which Pergamum had attained with its gardens of botany and of beasts, with the famous globe which had been erected in the palace of the king, with its patronage of art and letters and above all its renowned library to which he must have, like his predecessors, contributed his ample store.

With the death of Attalus II, the House of the Attalids came to an end. He was succeeded by his weak and incompetent nephew, who, unfitted as a ruler, frittered away the few years of his reign in the ominous art of brewing poisons[1] for the elimination of his relatives, as well as in the harmless hobbies of amateur gardening and modeling figures in wax. Attalus III (138 –133 B.C.) bequeathed the patrimony of the Attalids to Rome. Thus all the skill, effort, and achievement of his house for over a century and a half in building the brilliant and justly famed Kingdom of Pergamum were merged, with the surrounding countries, into the Roman Province of Asia.

It is true that Pergamum remained one of the so-called "free" colonies of Rome and was for many years a beautiful and famous city in the Roman East.

In Christianity it was one of the Seven Churches, but as a seat of the imperial cult and the Asian gods of the pagan pantheon, it is thought to be the place of "Satan's throne" in Revelations II 13[2].

---

1. B. G. Niebuhr: *The History of Rome*, London, 1844, Vol. I, p. 317.
2. W. M. Ramsay: *Letters to the Seven Churches* (1904).

The great library remained in Pergamum and was the resort of the scholars of the Hellenic-Roman world. We know that it continued intact for nearly a hundred years. In the nature of a collection of books, as in all things, not having diminished, it must have in some way increased. This mere assumption should extend to the amount and qualities of the accretions. We know that in 41 B.C. it was still a vast and noble collection of 200,000 rolls, perhaps mostly of parchment, or of papyrus and parchment rolls in indeterminate quantities, and certainly containing many priceless treasures of human genius. We know that the Library of Pergamum had its own great *Catalogues*, which merited praise, even in comparison with the famous Πίνακες of Callimachus and the continuation of Callimachus's *Catalogue* (Portraits) or commentaries thereon of Aristophanes of Byzantium. Unfortunately we are not certain of the names of the Pergamene bibliographers[1], although Crates of Mallos is thought to have done the biobibliographical work for the Library of Pergamum, in which lists if the prose writers are given prominence, the poets are not forgotten.

How curious that Pergamum, always pro-Roman, suffered most from Rome. The time came when the provincial city had to make a decision never exacted of royal Pergamum. When Caesar was killed, the Roman world fell into two mighty factions, Brutus and Cassius against Antony and Octavianus. The republicans lost at Philippi, and Antony and Octavianus, the victors, temporarily divided the world between them. Octavian took Rome and the West, and Antony the East. In his military wayfaring in Asia Minor, Antony came to Pergamum, that had supported the losing side, and was ripe for plunder. As always, Antony, the real victor at Philippi, needed money for his soldiers. After a triumphal progress through Greece, with his vast army, he descended upon the hapless cities of Lesser Asia. Pergamum was a model of the common disaster. Appian tells[2] how, assembling the Greeks and the surrounding inhabitants to Pergamum, Antony addressed them: "Your King Attalus left you to us in his

1. Athenaeus: VIII 336, d. (Speaking of a comedy by Alexis: *The Teacher of Profligacy*, Athenaeus says: "Certainly neither Callimachus nor Aristophanes has catalogued it, nor have even those who compiled the catalogues in Pergamum").
2. Appian: B. C. Bk. V, ch. 1, 4–5.

will, and straightway we proved better to you than Attalus had
been, for we released you from the taxes you had been paying to
him, until the action of popular agitators among us made these
taxes necessary... as allies of our enemies we should be obliged to
punish you... but we will relieve you from the heavier penalty...
We need money for our soldiers and will take nine years tribute
payable in two years."

The Pergamenes (B.C. 41) could do nothing, but comply.
Antony first demanded ten years tribute in one year, but was
prevailed to reduce the penalty to nine years tribute in two years.

The exact amount of the tribute we do not know or how soon
it was paid and with what property. It may well be assured that
he needed money, cash, for his soldiers as he frankly told them.

We know that he proceeded down Asia Minor making similar
exactions, when at Tarsus on the Cydnus in Cilicia he met
Aphrodite in the person of Cleopatra and that from then he was
the vassal of the Egyptian queen.

He took from Pergamum its far-famed library of some twenty
myriads of single manuscripts and gave it to Cleopatra. When
and how this greatest bibliophilic rape and gift in all antiquity
took place we do not know. Whether it was part of the original
tribute exacted by Antony before his own surrender to the
Egyptian; or levied because they had failed to pay fully in
amount and time; or in order to replace the books which may
have been lost at the time of the Alexandrian war during the
sojourn of the great Caesar, which loss we hope to show was
extremely doubtful; or whether Nemesis granted the green jade
god of jealousy the triumph for the Alexandriana over her
ancient rival; or whether Cleopatra, who was an intellectual,
greedily demanded this of her lover, who was not an intellectual,
and to whom it meant nothing, although to Pergamum it must
have been a cruel and perhaps additional exaction – of all this we
may never know[1].

But we do know that the books of the money-kings, luxurious

1. Lumbroso, *L'Egitto ai tempi dei Greci e dei Romani* (1895), denies the rape of the Pergamene Library. Modern scholarship supports Plutarch (Antony 58). Dziatzko
(Pauly-Wissowa) even speaks of the present remains of the eastern chamber of the
Library of Pergamum, showing traces of having been reconstructed, to be used for
other purposes, after the removal of the precious muniments for which it had originally been built.

art-patrons of Pergamum, were thus, *vi et armis*, added to the magnificent collections of the Alexandriana. Ruthlessly deprived of her greatest glory, the second library in all antiquity, the sun of Pergamum set. The state-slaves perfunctorily packed the precious parchments and papyri into bales which were transported by sea and land to her successful rival, and as the philosophic scholars of the Museum and the bibliographers of the Alexandriana opened the bundles and examined the rolls, they must have thought of the utter mutability of all human things.

And so, for us, the curtain falls upon the fabulous little Greek city-state, that at the Eurasian crossroads of history and commerce played for a little while so brilliant a part on the stage of the Hellenic-Roman world.

CHAPTER IV

LIBRARIES OF NEW GREECE:
THE SELEUCIDS OF ANTIOCH-ON-ORONTES

WHEN Alexander died, at Babylon, in the morning of his
life and glory, there was, among the host of his companions, no one able to assume his ample robe. There were
men old and young, brave and cunning, warriors and courtiers,
possessing many skills of mind and body, the Diadochi, who by
accident or through force became the heirs of his empire, if not
of his fame.

The youngest and physically the strongest of his generals was
Seleucus, an able soldier, a good administrator, a builder of cities,
a promoter of agriculture and trade, a patron of art, and a man
generally of a wise, prudent, and amiable character. With diplomacy, persistence, and courage he became the ruler of the greater
part of Alexander's empire, at least from the Mediterranean to
India. With consumate tact, he made real friends of the Ori-
entals and the Greeks. With Macedonian good sense, he recognized and was popular with the two great divergent elements of his
empire. With the war elephants of Chandragupta he conquered
Antigonus in Phrygia, in the great battle of Ipsus. With the
great Indian king on the Ganges, Seleucus maintained relations
through his ambassador Megasthenes, whose *Indica* fragments
are the sources of later Greek writers on India.

From East to West in his vast domain he founded innumerable
cities: Seleucia on Tigris (now nearby Baghdad), and some eight
others of the name; sixteen called Antioch, and founded or named
some twenty-eight others in honor of his father.

An outstanding feature of his genius was his remarkable
understanding of the relative merits of the East and West, an
attempt to justly appreciate the wonders of the fabulous East
and the glories of the Hellenic West.

He was the founder of a dynasty (312–65 B.C.) and gave his
name to an age and to a system of chronology, the Era of Seleu-

cus. In his seventy-fourth or seventy-eight year[1], as he contemplated the result of forty years of persistent effort and reasonable hope for the peaceful rule of practically the vast empire of Alexander, he was foully assassinated by the miserable Keraunus, the eldest son of the wise Ptolemy, the most greaceless and ungrateful scoundrel of the long line of Epigoni, as the second generation of the Great King's successors are called. The villain Ptolemy Keraunus actually sold the body of his victim for a vast amount of gold to the wily, fabulously rich Philetaerus of Pergamum, who, as related before, accorded the kingly relic magnificent funeral rites and sent the ashes to his son Antiochus, believing that he thus made a wise investment with the House of Seleucus for his own city-state, Pergamum, with its enormous wealth so dubiously obtained.

In beholding the ashes of his beloved father, Antiochus I must have thought of how kind, courageous, and self-sacrificing Seleucus had ever been to him, how he bestowed upon him half his empire and his young and beautiful queen Stratonice for whom Antiochus unfortunately had conceived an unquenchable passion.

Although the old Greeks and the West cannot view the affair but with disfavor, the story is one of the most romantic of the later Hellenic age.

In the political maneuvering of the post-Alexandrian princes, Seleucus takes to wife the sister of the brilliant, dynamic Demetrius, the beautiful princess Stratonice. His son and heir, Antiochus, apparently through no fault of his own or of the lady's, but solely through the wilfulness of Aphrodite's wayward son, falls desperately in love with the young queen. He tells no one. Consumed with the fatal secret he becomes desperately ill. Seleucus is in deepest distress, the court-physician Erasistratus is at his wit's end. The worried though clever medico can discover the presence of no known disease, indeed of no physical ailment. As it must be a malady of the mind or heart he watches for some outward sign to effect a diagnosis. His vigilance perceives that whereas the visits of the prince's family, men and women of the court, and others produce no particular effect on the patient,

1. Appian (*Syrian War* 6-3) makes him seventy-three; Justin (XVII–1–10) seventy-seven years.

when the Queen Stratonice visits the stricken prince, in spite of every effort to conceal his emotions, his fatal reaction is only too apparent to the competent physician who cannot be deceived. Erasistratus tells Seleucus his son is indeed stricken with an incurable disease, that he is in love with a woman whom he cannot have. The king cannot conceive of such a situation and insists on knowing. The doctor tells him it is his own (the doctor's) wife. The king pleads with his physician to make this sacrifice to save his son's life. The doctor bluntly asks would he, Seleucus, if the case were such, give up his wife Stratonice. The king calls upon the gods to witness that he would. Erasistratus tells the king the truth, and Seleucus, without upbraiding or complaint, surrenders his young queen. Antiochus and Stratonice are married amid the plaudits of court and army, and Seleucus gives them half his imperial domain, making them King and Queen of Upper Asia.

It is not an Arabian Night's Tale or a Boccaccian story; it is fully authenticated in Appian (*Syrian War*, 59) and Plutarch (*Demetrius*, 38). It is shocking to western morals, but only a cynic would impugn the motives of Seleucus, who erred through paternal affection and patriotic considerations.

In concluding this sketch of Seleucus Nicator, one cannot help but consider that if in the 42 years from the death of Alexander, Seleucus, his play-fellow and companion, with his considerable talents and fair character could have achieved so much, what might not the transcendent genius of Alexander, even with the defects of his character, have attained had he been accorded the precious gift of years.

The judgment of the historian Arrian[1] may be pertinent: "Seleucus was the greatest King of those who succeeded Alexander, and of the most royal mind, and ruled over the greatest extent of territory, next to Alexander."

After the decisive victory of Ipsus, Seleucus, in truth Nicator (the Conqueror), true to the genius of his master and the Macedonian kings, founded the city which for nearly a thousand years was to proclaim the fame of his house, and which he, in filial remembrance, called Antioch: Antioch the Golden, Antioch the Beautiful (Athen. 1–20), Antioch ἐπι Δάφνη, Antioch by Daphne.

1. Arrian: *Anabasis of Alexander*, VII-22-5.

The site selected by the king, with the help of the gods, in natural magnificence, for commercial expediency, for military security, for general adaptability, for municipal beauty, was second to no city of antiquity.

As the western littoral of Syria marches north, it strikes the southward coast of Asia Minor almost at right angles. Beneath this pocket, formed by the sea, about twenty miles from the coast, Seleucus in the spring of the 12th (11th) year of the Seleucidan era (300 B.C.) founded his city.

Amidst the confines of a hunting-park of the Persian kings, a little north of Baalbek, the ultimate fountains of the river Orontes arose and plunged now beneath the earth and then, arising in violence from its subterranean course, flowed nearly two hundred miles in a northerly direction, when it broke through Mount Taurus and Mount Lebanon, carving a magnificent gorge as it cut its way around heights of wondrous picturesqueness and compelling grandeur, from which it swept westward through a fruitful plain towards the Mediterranean, hard by Seleucus by the Sea, the port of the great Greek metropolis of Asia.

With the wooded slopes of the mountains, descending terrace after terrace, as a background, and upon which arose its citadel; in a luxurious valley of the river, now having overcome its rocky barriers, and on the east bank of the Orontes, Xenaeus, architect of Seleucus, built the city of Antioch, the Beautiful.

In a theatre of natural loveliness, the fatal gift of seismographic lands, amidst groves of oak and sycamore, arbors of olive, almond and fig and vineyards, where the scents of the narcissus, ilex, myrtle, and bay were wafted by the west wind, which tempered the extremes of temperature, and with an abundance of the sweet water of the Orontes, which enabled each house to have its fountain, it would seem that Antioch in basic advantages outrivaled her sister cities; Rome on its irregular hills, and Alexandria, flat and treeless by the sea.

The city arose in marble, constructed in all the sumptuousness of the Greco-Macedonian style. It followed the "gridiron" plan of Alexandria. Indeed, these Macedonian kings and their successors evidenced a prodigal display of resource and power, as they virtually dotted the classic East from the Mediterranean to India with magnificent cities: seats of power and government, residences of kings, fortresses of war, emporia of trade, and centers of vast populations, comprising varied races of the East and West who dwelt together in relative harmony.

The city, like Rome, was built on the east bank of the river; the Orontes, like the Seine, either naturally or artificially broadens as a lake in the midst of which was an island, like at Paris, upon which arose splendid palaces and public buildings. The city streets were broad, straight, colonnaded, and well paved[1]. Two of the streets were renowned in the ancient world for the symmetry and beauty of their porticos, and their structure suggests the plans of the two famous thoroughfares of Palarmo and the cities of Magna Graecia. In the center of the city was the Omphalos, proclaiming Antioch the center of the world.

For the quality and quantity of its water supply, the city was unexcelled. As a monument of this municipal necessity the immense Nymphaeum, a veritable temple of the water-nymphs, was erected near the Orontes, where from the hundreds of apertures perennial fountains flowed. Its handsome marble façade was embellished with numerous statues of gods and heroes embedded in niches. The art effects of this magnificent structure were crowned by an exquisite little temple consisting of a cella surrounded by columns upholding a monolithic dome, open on all sides and containing the far-famed statue of the *Tyche* or *Genius* of Antioch, the work of the sculptor Eutychides of Sicyon, pupil of Lysippus, the authorized portrait-sculptor of the great Alexander. The figure was that of a graceful woman seated on the rock throne of Silpius, crowned with the towers of the Tetrapolis, holding in her right hand the horn of plenty, while at her feet rises the river god Orontes, in the figure of a youth borne on the waves of the river as it rises from the caverns of the earth. Fortunately, a copy of this tutelary goddess of Antioch may be seen in the Museo Pio-Clementino, in the Vatican[2].

1. Athough Josephus (*Jewish War*, L.C.L., I-425), tells how Herod (with the design to flatter his Roman masters) lavished beneficent gifts dedicated to Roman greatness throughout the Near East; his bounty did not omit Antioch, where one of its greatest thoroughfares, through time and the dangerous nature of its soil, had fallen in decay:
    And that broad street in Syrian Antioch, once shunned on account of the mud, was it not he who paved its twenty furlongs with polished marble, and, as a protection from the rains, adorned it with a colonnade of equal length? Later the great artery running east to west was paved with granite by the Emperor Antoninus Pius.
2. Visconti: *Museo Pio-Clementino*, III-46.

All that Greco-Macedonian wealth and genius for city building, with a touch of oriental splendor which must have sprung from the artists and soil of Asia; all the desire of the princes of the House of Seleucus to make their western capital embody the perfect taste and beauty of old Greece, with some of the color and much of the luxury of Ecbatana and Babylon; all of Caesar's favor and imperial bounty of aqueducts, baths, circuses, and public monuments with which the Roman overlords sought to make the city an eastern Rome – these were some of the general features which, framed in a theatre of natural magnificence, proclaimed Antioch-on-Orontes as the "Golden" city of the East. It was indeed a Tetrapolis, each district with its separate wall, the whole perhaps protected by an outer wall.

The city boasted four distinct districts. Besides, it had a suburb, Heraclea, and a pleasant road led, five miles to the west, to the far-famed Paradise of Daphne with its cypress and laurel, indeed an exotic Grove of cedar and rare woods, fed by innumerable fountains of sweet waters, where the song of bird and the peaceful approach of tame animals enhanced the pastoral scene.

The reader may pardon a digression here, for an attempt to sketch this Pagan Paradise, this Oasis of Sanctuary, this Grove of Iniquity, which for many centuries affected the minds of men.

DAPHNE BY ANTIOCH

In the Villa Borghese at Rome, a marble of infinite glory wrought by Gian Lorenzo Bernini[1] in his eighteenth year (1616), still arrests the passer-by[2]. It is the Apollo and Daphne[3], bringing to life the very moment of which sweet Master Ovid tells:

> The winds bared her limbs, the opposing breezes set her garments a-flutter as she ran, and a light air flung her locks streaming behind her. Her beauty was enhanced by flight (*Meta.*, I-527).

1. Abbate Nicola Navone:
> O Bernin, Febo stesso a darti vanto
> Un di quei Lauri a la tua Fronte intreccia
> Ed in gioia e stupor cangia el suo pianto.

2. Many years ago, the writer on his first visit to the Villa Borghese saw this amazing work and on the margin of his Baedeker are the words: "A youthful masterpiece of eternal beauty". In spite of the criticisms he had and since has read, the personal judgment still is valid. He remembers a criticism: The young sculptor had dared to treat marble with the technique of the painter's art! So Keats, Shelley and Swinburne, too, have erred in their solemnities.

3. Stanislao Fraschetti: *Il Bernini*, Milano, 1900 (p. 26).

The best of the Roman poets have survived, although their Greek prototypes are lost; so, threading our way through Latin verse, we weave the story from *Metamorphoses*, Ovid's greatest bid for fame:

Apollo, god of light, Zeus's son, incurred the wrath of Cupid, who maliciously inflicted his godship with the fatal dart, and Phoebus experienced his first love – that for the beauteous Daphne, daughter of the river-god Penaeus. The wicked little son of Aphrodite did not fail to inflict the nymph with the opposite passion, to be, Diana-like, forever virgin. So the god of light, of eternal youth, and with the swiftness of the sun, pursued the lovely nymph, immaculate, borne by the ardent winds of fear, in the most exquisite love-race in story. Through vale and over hillock the radiant god pressed the chase.

> And as shee ran the meeting windes hir garments backwards blue,
> So that hir naked skinne apeerde behinde hir as she flue,
> Hir goodley yellowe golden haire that hanged loose and slacke,
> With every puffe of ayre did wave and tosse behind hir backe
> Hir running made her seeme more fayre.

But the unequal contest could not last:

> So that he would not let hir rest, but pressed at hir heels
> So neere that through hir scattred haire shee might his breathing
> feele
> But when she sawe hir breath was gone and strength began to fayle,
> The colour faded in hir cheekes, and ginning for to quayle,

With piteous cry she prayed her father, Penaeus, the river-god for help:

> Her sinews waxed starke,
> And therewithall about hir breast did grew a tender barke.
> Hir haire was turned into leaves, hir armes in boughes did growe,
> Hir feete that were ere while so swift, now rooted were as slowe
> Hir crowne became the toppe, and thus of that she earst had beene,
> Remayned nothing in the worlde, but beautie fresh and greene.
> Which when that Phoebus did beholde (affection did so move)
> The tree to which his love was turnde he could no lesse but love.
> And as he softly layde his hand upon the tender plant,
> Within the barke newe overgrowne he felt hir heart yet pant.
> And in his armes embrasing fast hir boughes and braunches lythe,
> He proferde kisses to the tree: the tree did from him writhe.

Well (quoth Apollo) though my Feere and spouse thou cannot bee,
Assuredly from this time forth yet shalt thou by my tree[1].

In Thessaly the Penaeus ran; at Delphi, Daphne delivered oracles,
of which even Homer used in his epics. These and many myths,
including the very laurel tree into which Daphne was meta-
morphosed, Seleucus took for his famous sanctuary consecrated
to Daphne, the first love of the great god Apollo.

To the southwest of Antioch, about six kilometers (less than
four miles), on a plateau almost square[2] was a dense forest of
cypresses of extraordinary height[3] and noble laurels[4], through
which ever flowed riverlets and brooks of sweet waters, from
innumerable natural fountains within the dank grove. It was a
region of exquisite beauty, where nature prodigally displayed all
the color, variety, witchery, wonder, suspense, and mystery of
her woodland kindgom.

In the middle of this paradise, Seleucus built the great temple
of Apollo and Daphne, whose glittering white marble was tempered by the Greek method of marble-painting, soft, in pastel-
tones. Bryaxis, the Athenian, who with Scopas and others was
a sculptor of the Mausoleum of Halicarnassus and who made the
Serapis of Alexandria, wrought the colossal figure of Apollo
in marble, with plates of gold and precious metals over wood,
which compelled the admiration of the beholder. The god was
portrayed as Master of the Muses, with Olympian harp, as
singing to all the world of the joy and beauty of life. Bryaxis may
have followed the Apollo of Scopas, which has been traced to
the so-called Palatine Apollo in the Vatican[5].

Here were baths, gardens of exotic foliages, preserves of rare
animals, porticoes, and colonnades. In clearings were belvederes
with masterpieces of Greek art and monuments to scions of the
Seleucidae. In a spot which seemed most favored in all this scene
of natural wonder was the far-famed bay-tree, the noble laurel

1. The XV Bookes of P. Ouidius Naso, entytuled *Metamorphosis*, tr. by Arthur Golding,
London, 1567 (Bk. 1–641 et seq. to 684).
2. Donald N. Wilbur: *The Plateau of Daphne* (in *Antioch-on-the-Orontes*), Princeton
University, 1938, Vol. II, p. 49.
3. Procopius: *Persian Wars*, II–14.
4. Even now the fertile and well irrigated site is luxuriant in olive and groves of fruit-
trees.
5. Adolph Holm: *History of Greece*, London, 1911, Vol. IV, note 10, p. 453.

which had possessed the beautiful body of the nymph Daphne, and which was to retain its attachment to Antioch six centuries hence in Ausonius: *Phoebeae lauri domus Antiochia*[1].

In time many buildings, temples, gymnasia, and lecture-domes were erected in the Sacred Grove.

The Romans added to the splendors of Daphne. Vespasian built there a theatre and is said to have erected before a gate of Antioch the bronze cherubim which Titus had found in the temple of Solomon[2].

The place for centuries was Sanctuary throughout the ancient world, and Onias, priest of the Temple of the Lord, did not hesitate to seek to keep "himself in a safe place at Antioch beside Daphne" (2 Mace., IV–33).

At first, the sanctuary was consecrated alone to the worship of Phoebeus Apollo and the chaste Daphne. But Daphne near Antioch was in Syria and the Syrians were a luxurious people, and the people of Antioch had the reputation of having all the vices of the Hellenic peoples together with an utter abandon to the soft life of the rich Orient. In a fragment of Posidonius[3] he tells:

> The people in the cities, at any rate, because of the great plenty which their land afforded, (were relieved) of any distress regarding the necessities of life; hence they held many gatherings at which they feasted continually, using the gymnasia as if they were baths[4], anointing themselves with expensive oil and perfumes, and living (in the assembly, common dining-rooms) as though they were their private houses, and putting in the greater part of the day there in filling their bellies – there, in the midst of wines and foods so abundant that they even carried a great deal home with them besides – and delighting the ears with sounds from a loud-twanging tortoise-shell, so that their towns rang from end to end with such noises.

A pampered citizenry undependable in public affairs, gay, frivolous, and with little morals in private life, soon made the famous Grove of Daphne a place notorious for all the extravagancies of Oriental religious pagan rites and orgies of Eastern

1. Ausonius: *The Order of Famous Cities*, XI–IV.
2. John Malalas: *Chronicle*, see Wilbur: *The Theatre at Daphne*, in *Antioch–on–the–Orontes* (II, p. 57).
3. Posidonius: *Histories* (Athenaeus, XII-527 f.).
4. It has been suggested that these were the prototypes of the stupendous Thermae of Rome, which attained the proportions of the Baths of Caracalla and Diocletion, etc.

cults. For it would seem that the clean-cut gods of Greece never set foot on Asian soil but to be defiled.

And so the mad king Antiochus IV, Epiphanes, introduced the worship of Zeus into Daphne's sanctuary, with a colossal statue of the Olympian, in ivory and gold in the manner of Phidias.

From all the classical world the men of leisure and wealth, and the frivolous, flocked to Daphne by Antioch, where continued revelry by day and night maintained a perpetual carnival of mad excitement and sheer debauchery.

Down the great road which led from the city-gate of Antioch to the Vale of Daphne, and which was bordered by sumptuous villas, rich pavilions of pleasure, monuments of art, and perennial fountains, a mighty throng of pilgrims, travellers from many lands, and city-folk, on foot, horse and chariot, made a continuous processional.

In emulation of the customs of Hellas, public games at Daphne were established, embodying some of the dignity and classic beauty of ancient Greece, more of the pomp and power of rising Rome, and most of the shameless abandon and mad orgies of the pagan East. The fame of these amazing festivals pervaded the Greco-Macedonian world, the regions of aspiring Rome, and the outer lands of Asia. Protagorides of Cyzicus actually composed a work in several books *On the Games at Daphne*, a fragment of which, on exotic musical instruments, has been preserved in Athenaeus (IV–176–b). The book is lost, but Posidonius of Apameia has left a longer account, and Polybius[1] in a fragment has given an extended description of the prodigious show.

The climax of these amazing spectacles may have been reached in the time (175–164 B.C.) of the Fourth Antiochus, surnamed Epiphanes (Illustrius), though he should be called Epimanes (the Insane). Long before Haroun-al-Rashid, with Arabian dignity and Moslem restraint, explored the byways of Baghdad in nocturnal adventures, Antiochus, in disordered toga, would slip away from his companions, visit the shops, the agora, the lowest taverns and the public baths, in the broad light of the sun, and there be guilty of the most unseemly conduct, ending his day, unannounced and unwanted, at the symposium of some unfortunate persons who would fly in disgust from the unbidden guest.

1. Polybius: Fragments of Book, XXX – 25 from Athenaeus V–194 and X, 439.

Now this king who gave prodigally, as well as to the unworthy as to the deserving, who was the great benefactor of the Olympieion at Athens and the Altar in Delos, hearing that the Roman, Aemilius Paulus, conqueror of Macedonia, was about to institute great games at Amphipolis to commemorate his victory, conceived the ambition to outdo the Roman by holding at Daphne games of unprecedented magnificence. Missions and heralds were sent to the cities and countries throughout the Hellenic and Mediterranean lands, inviting the world to come to Daphne by Antioch to the great games in honor of Zeus and Apollo, given (and they might have added "conducted") by the great king Antiochus Epiphanes of the Seleucids, at his royal capital in Syria.

THE GAMES AT DAPHNE[1]

The great games lasted thirty days. They opened with a processional along the highway leading to the Grove of Daphne. This spectacular display was intended to show the vast wealth, power, and glory of the Seleucidae. Along the great road, from palaces and villas, from buildings belonging to city-clubs and places of general amusement, and stretches covered with monuments and trophies of the House of Seleucus, throngs of visitors and Antiochians waited for hours to view the glittering array:

The van was brave companies of youth in chain-mail Roman armor, five thousand strong; then, Mysians, troops, also five thousand; then, Cilicians, light-armed soldiers, wearing gold crowns; Thracians to the number of three thousand; Gauls, five thousand; and then the great Macedonian contingent of twenty thousand men; ten thousand with shields of gold, five thousand with shields of silver and five thousand with shields of bronze;

A troupe of gladiators, some two hundred forty pairs, passed in review; then,

A thousand horses from Nisa;

Three thousand citizen soldiers with crowns of gold and silver and cheek-coverings;

A thousand "mounted companions", with trappings of gold;

A regiment of "Friends of the King" similarly accoutred;

1. This attempt at a description is based on the fragments of Polybius, Posidonius, and Protagorides in Athenaeus.

Picked horsemen, followed by the crack „Guard", a cavalry corps of a thousand men;

Heavy armed cavalry, men and horses in complete mail, about fifteen hundred;

The above wore surcoats of purple, embroidered with gold, with heraldic designs;

The chariots followed, a hundred drawn by six horses and forty by four horses; then,

The elephants, four and two drawing chariots and an Indian file of thirty-six elephants with sumptuous housings and richly caparisoned;

Ephebi, young men just of age, not wearing, however, the broad-brimmed hats and sombre mantles of their Athenian prototypes, but with golden crowns and to the number of eight hundred;

Fattened oxen and droves of fine cattle, the gifts of the sacred missions from friendly cities and countries; then three hundred sacrificial tables;

A forest of elephant tusks, some eight hundred, borne aloft by huge African slaves; and then, a special division of the pageant, a vast procession of sacred images and statues of the gods, demi-gods and heroes, some rare works of art, some gilded and some draped in garments of golden thread. All with legends inscribed on marble or painted on wood giving the name and traditional history or myths of the god or hero;

Allegorical figures of Night and Day, of Earth and Heaven, of Dawn and Noon were borne aloft;

Vast fortunes in gold and silver plate dazzled the beholders as one of the King's friends, Dionysius, his secretary, had one thousand of his personal household slaves carrying silver vessels, none weighing less than 1000 drachmae (c. 11 ½ lbs.), and six hundred of the royal slaves of the palace carried vessels of pure gold;

Two hundred women sprinkled the crowd with sweet perfumes from golden urns, and then a flood of litters of ivory and sweet woods, with gold and silver rests and magnificently furnished in cloths of damask and silks from Ind, containing beautiful women most richly attired;

And so, the processional, perhaps as yet in prodigal display unequaled in the world, wended its way to the sacred Grove of Daphne.

The first five days of the month of festival were devoted to athletic sports, many within the gymnasium, where the contestants and the spectators anointed themselves with oils of saffron, cinnamon, and nard, from fifteen huge golden basins, and finally the most precious of perfumed oils were lavishly supplied, the rare fragrances of fenugreek, marjoram, and orris.

Gladiatorial contests with all their ferocity of blood were held as these barbarous customs of Rome invaded the mild, aesthetic games of ancient Hellas.

Fights of many and various beasts were indulged, which displayed the curious and ingenious mind of the Orient in these primitive shows. Within certain portions of the park, actual hunts were held for courtiers, leaders of the armies, and privileged guest.

Finally great feasts were held at which 1000 and 1500 triclinia were spread with lavish expenditure and at these banquets whole beeves, calves, and sheep were served on vast platters of bronze and silver, and every sort of game and denizens of the sea on plates of gold. Graceful amphorae and the delicate vessels of Grecian ceramics held vintages of wines, rare, good, and common, as occasion served.

Professional musicians laid fingers to many instruments and castanets and tambourines; the pandura and the sweet single-pipe discoursed soft and rare melodies during the prodigious symposia.

The various details of the feast were ostensibly arranged by the mad king Antiochus who, as he had attempted to marshall the Great Processional, likewise flitted from couch to couch eating and drinking promiscuously with the guests and behaving most indecorously.

The dancers, with all the ecstasy of oriental rites, transcended the frenzy of Bacchic abandon or saturnalian revelry, and reached a crescendo, a pandemonium of orgiastic madness. The performers vanished. The great lights flared from gilded bashets held by "statued youths"; the great beams of the sweet wood of Lebanon extending from wall to wall of the banquet-hall, gave little aid to dissipate the fetid air, which was only seemingly dissolved as the female slaves burned gums of Araby in jeweled censers.

Ere the feasts were over, a troupe of mime-performers indulged in their usual lascivious bouts and catches. When they entered, they brought a mysteriously wrapped figure which they deposited in the center of the exhibition floor. At the sound of the symphony (a curious instrument used in the secret rituals) the covered figure sprang up wildly dancing naked before the feasters. It was the mad king who thus disgraced himself with the clowns of the mimes. And then (as Polybius most fortunately relates) "everyone departed in shame".

Yet the mad Antiochus was not the only scion of the House of Seleucus guilty of unpardonable excess, for Antiochus Grypus (the Hawk-nosed) when he celebrated the Games of Daphne held high carnival; fantastic festivals and prodigious displays, reaching the amazing performance of giving to each man uncarved meats, live geese, hares and gazelles. At his feasts he bestowed gold wreaths, silver vessels, slaves, horses, and camels. As his departing guest mounted his camel, he drank a farewell toast to the king, thus accepting all his gifts, the camel and even the attending slave[1].

Such was the prosperity and pomp of effete Syria. Perhaps only the Ptolemies and the Seleucids ever were guilty of these (almost peace-time) extravagances. Yet, such was the renown of the Grove of Daphne that many of the records of proud Antioch boldly read Αντιοχειάη ’επι Δάφνη, Antioch by Daphne.

The inhabitants of Antioch were mixed, some Greek and Macedonian, the Hellenic substratum, but the majority were Asiatics: Syrians, Phoenicians, Jews, peoples of Asia Minor and the more distant East. In manner and morals, they resembled the people of Alexandria and their reputation was that of a light, promiscuous, pleasure-loving, witty, turbulent, and unstable people. They experienced all the glories and all the terrors, human and natural, of a highly gifted, exuberant, fascinating, but undependable people of the Eastern Mediterranean.

The frivolity of Antioch had offended Hadrian, but to the unfortunate Julian, who tarried there in the autumn-winter of 361–362, it was "a prosperous and gay and crowded city in which there are numerous dancers and flute-players and more mimes than ordinary citizens, and no respect at all for those who govern"[2]. The Antiochians were tall, handsome, smooth-skinned

1. Posidonius, in Athenaeus, V-210-d
2. Julian: *Misopogon* (342-B).

and beardless; young and old cared not for righteousness but preferred "changes of raiment and warm baths and beds"[1]; "their love was for the witticism in anapaestic verse, for brazen spectacles, shameless women, boys who in their beauty emulate women, and men who have not only their jaws shaved smooth but their whole bodies too..."[2]; they sought the abandon of the theatre, the thrill of the racecourse instead of the serenity of the temples of the gods. This was the view of the poor, austere, unkempt, unshaven, pagan philosopher, who for a few months vainly attempted to stem the rushing and triumphant tide of Christianity. And yet the great St. Chrysostom in his homilies paints in varied colors the same picture of this joyous, thoughtless, and non-moral populace, as did his apostate brother in his self-accusing satire, the *Misopogon*.

Here Germanicus died (19 A.D.) and Trajan's life was in jeopardy during the earthquake (115 A.D.); yet Julian in his insincere praise of his cousin Constantius does not fail to extol his benefactions to Antioch:

> Her existence she does indeed owe to her founder, but her present wealth and increase in every sort of abundance she owes to you, since you provided her with harbours; ..... I need not stop to mention the porticoes, fountains, and other things of the kind that you consent to be bestowed on Antioch by her governors[3].

In Antioch Christianity almost arose; Peter and Paul taught, and the faithful were here first called Christians. Her soil is sacred with the blood of the martyrs, the seat of many synods; and for perhaps the unique distinction of a complete Catalogue of Bishops from the Apostolic age; although it was the birthplace of some of the most serious heresies of the early Church.

A new city, built in marble and stone, with imposing buildings, great monuments, forests of statues, with painted porches and all the sumptuousness of an age of wealth and luxury, must have tempted to her services a host of great architects, lapidaries, sculptors, painters and other artists. Where Greeks are in control or very prominent, there must be much talking, and where there is public speech, there are sophists, rhetoricians, orators and philoso-

1. Julian: *op. cit.* (342-D) and *Odyssey* (VIII–249).
2. Julian: *op. cit.* D 345 and 346.
3. Julian: *Panegyric in Honour of Constantius* (L.C.L., Vol. I, p. 105).

phers. At an Hellenic, or Greco-Oriental Court, fabulous with the spoils of Asia, the loot of Eastern empires, the present accumulation of the wealth of the East and West, there must be besides soldiers of fortune and men of government, courtiers and flatterers and men who precariously live by their wits, and where such are, they cannot speak alone in prose, but some must worship at the Muses' shrines. Poets and writers must have been abroad and the ambitious Seleucids could not have allowed in the south their great rival Alexandria to have a monopoly in the intellectual fields, much less could they have permitted the relatively insignificant Pergamum to their north to assume the role of city of learning and culture[1]. In spite of the paucity of records, Antioch at most periods of her centuries old existence presents the natural picture of an educated, cultured, art-loving, acquisitive people, consecrated, however, to a free and easy life in one of the great cities of history which care forgot.

Although it has been said that Antioch during the Seleucid era produced one philosopher, Apollophanes, a Stoic, and one writer, Phoebus, who wrote on dreams, this statement hardly presents a fair picture of a city where "a goodly number of Greek men of letters, philosophers and artists must always have been found at the king's table". Here Aratus of Soli, author of the astronomical poem, *Phaenomena*, which influenced Lucretius and Virgil and was translated by Cicero, lived at the court of Antiochus I, son of Seleucus, the founder. Here Aratus, in the true manner of late Hellenic (Alexandrian) scholarship, edited Homer's *Odyssey*. The king would have had him edit also the *Iliad*, but this he seemed unable to accomplish.

If there is a doubt as to Antioch-on-the-Orontes' being an intellectual center, a sole witness of archaeology should dispel the thought. In the splendid mosaics brought to light by the Expedition of the University of Princeton and its Associates, the art of the mosaicist, in illustrating the mythological cycles, most especially portrays scenes from Homer and Euripides, the two poets, foremost literary figures in Hellenistic and Roman times[2].

1. Holm: *op. cit.* IV, p. 315 (This scholar did not hesitate to declare: "This court of Antioch also endeavored to render services to literature.")
2. See the volumes of Antioch-on-the-Orontes, especially Kurt Weitzmann: *Illustrations of Euripides and Homer in the Mosaics of Antioch* (Vol. III, p. 233 et seq.), 1941.

But more intriguing still is the mosaic of Menander and Glycera representing the arrival of a letter from Ptolemy, king of Egypt, to Menander inviting him to Alexandria and his fabulous Court. It is this scene that the sophist, Alciphron, has seized and limned with consumate art in the imaginary letters between the great Attic master of comedy and his beloved mistress.

> I have received a letter from Ptolemy, King of Egypt, in which he intreats me, promising me right royally all the good things of the earth, and invites me to visit him... I wish you also to know what answer I have decided to make... May it be my lot, King Ptolemy, ever to be crowned with Attic ivy! to die and be buried in my own native land, and to join every year in the Dionysiac hymns at the altars! to be initiated into the mystic rites, to produce a new play every year upon the stage, now laughing and rejoicing, now in fear and trembling, and now victorious... by Bacchus and his ivy-wreaths, with which I would rather be crowned, in the presence of my Glycera seated in the theatre, than with all the diadems of Ptolemy: wrote Menander.

And Glycera:

> I would never believe that Menander would have the heart to leave Glycera in Athens and reign alone in Egypt, in the midst of such grandeur... For what would Athens be without Menander– What would Menander be without Glycera, who prepares his masks, puts on his costumes for him, and stands at the wings to give the signal for applause in the theatre, and to accompany it with her own. Then, may Diana be my witness! I tremble, then I breathe again, and clasp you in my arms, the sacred fount of comedy[1].

And the memorable story of Ptolemy's Letter has been recorded by the three arts, the sculptured Relief in the Lateran, the pic-tured mosaic of Antioch, and the delightful pages of the Greek sophist.

Of Antiochus II, who, according to gossip, was drunk every night, asleep in the morning, and ruled by the buffoon, Herodo-tus (forgive the use of the name!) and the dancer Archelaus, and finally poisoned by Laodice, the wife whom he had taken back, we know little. Much could not be here expected for the intellectual life.

The wars between the rival queens, Laodice and Berenice, the

1. Alciphron: *Letters*, Athens (pseudo), 1896, Bk. II, Ep. 3–4.

fraticidal conflicts of the House of Seleucus, bring us to the reign of Antiochus III (called the Great).

Little as we know of the librarians of the Alexandriana, still less do we know of the king's librarian of the Public Library of Antioch. It was in this reign that Antiochus the Great appointed Euphorion of Chalcis his *bibliotecarius*. A curious character was this Euphorion. Born in Euboea, B.C. 274–276, he became a citizen of Athens; unpreposing in appearance, sallow complexion, inordinately fat, and bandy-legged, he was notorious for his amours, which included the wife of a king; a poet, he yet accumulated great wealth. This Hellenic man of letters, poet-epic and elegiac, an epigrammatist, grammarian, and writer of history, celebrated throughout the Greco-Macedonian world, with Callimachus, Lycophron, Parthenius, as a leader in the Alexandrian school of thought and letters; who was to have his place in the *Wreath* of Meleager of Gadara, and to be imitated by great Roman poets to the neglect of their own versifiers and to thus incur the indignation of Cicero[1], was selected by Antiochus as librarian at Antioch.

We do not know what peculiar fitness he had for the post, but considering his known background and distinguished career, we may assume that, like Callimachus and Lycophron, he was well qualified for his honorable station. He died in Syria and was buried at Antioch.

True to the unfortunate absence of record, we know little or nothing of the Library at Antioch[2].

We do know that Hegesianax of Troas, who in his youth as a poor actor refrained from eating figs for fear that it would injure his voice, lived to become a man of letters and write a poem in honor of Antiochus, thus becoming officially a "Friend of the King".

Antiochus IV, in a great wave of intellectual enthusiasm, made Antioch for a brief moment the center of Hellenic culture and art. Papyrus dug out of Herculaneum tells how Philonides, an Epicu-

---

1. Cicero: *Tusculan Disputations* (III–19).
2. Joannes Malalas: *Chronicle of John Malalas*, Books VIII to XVIII, tr. by M. Spinka and G. Downey, Chicago, 1940 (p. 57), Bk. X–6. Yet even this writer in his *Chronicle*, with all of its errors and confusion, speaks of the public library with certainty, reporting a story of Claudius having deposited in the public library a description of the Trojan War found in the grave of a certain Diktys.

rean, with a troop of philosophers went to Antioch and converted king Antiochus Epiphanes. Doubtless the king was mad. To the end, the House of Seleucus sought to educate their sons at Athens and the seats of culture of Old Greece. Antiochus VIII, Grypus (Hawk-nosed) was an author. Antiochus XIII, practically the last of the House, when Pompey (64 B.C.) refused to recognize the throne of Seleucus[1], even the last Antiochus in the last moments of the sunset of his race, was library-minded, for he sought to use the property of Maron, an expatriate citizen of Antioch, to establish a temple of the Muses (a Museum) and a library. So that Antioch, like Alexandria, had at least two libraries and a Museum.

But the sun of the Seleucidae had indeed set, and the fatal defeat of Antiochus the Great at Magnesia (B.C. 190) bore its final fruit and Syria became a province of invincible Rome.

Antioch by Daphne – city of Libanus, city of Chrysostom, that had worshipped the pagan gods with ecstatic abandon and that had received the tidings of the followers of Christ with singular piety, once the proud mistress of Hellenic Asia, now the victim of nature and man's havoc, became a Turkish vilyat, now a Syrian village.

But for us, it will ever be difficult to forget that when Cicero[2] wished to extol the birthplace of his client Archias, he gladly said:

At Antioch, where he had been born of gentle parents, a place which in those days was a renowned and populous city, the seat of brilliant scholarship and artistic refinement.

1. For the poor claim of Philip II in 56 B.C. was ignominiously rejected by a Roman proconsul.
2. Cicero: *Pro Archia Poeta* III–5.

BOOK TWO

The Founding of Alexandria

Other cities are but the cities of the country around them;
Alexandria is the city of the world[1].

1. From lately discovered Hellenistic treatise (*Berlin Klass. Texts*, VII–13; ch. M.
Rostovtzeff (C.A.H.)

CHAPTER V

THE CITY OF ALEXANDRIA

A LEXANDER, having effected the easy conquest of Egypt, desired to receive the benediction of the god Ammon in the wastes of Lybia, so he sailed from Memphis down to the sea. Coming to Canopus, the westernmost mouth of the Nile, his boats rounded Lake Mareotis, and he disembarked[1].

And here the gods intervened, permitting the genius of Homer to appear to his faithful disciple in a vision of the night. He of hoary locks and venerable mien chanted:

> There is an isle
> Within the billowy sea before you reach
> The coast of Egypt, — Pharos is its name
> .... A sheltered   en lies within that isle[2].

On the mainland was the site of an old Egyptian fisher-village, quondam pirates' nest, perhaps an Egyptian outpost against the intrusion of foreigners, called Rhakotis. A tongue of land about two miles wide and several miles long between the sea and lake here formed the coast. On the south was Lake Mareotis, one of the many bodies of water which bestride the base of the great delta of the Nile (very similar to the lakes and waters in the delta of the Mississippi). On the north was the Mediterranean Sea in which was this long narrow island (Pharos) about a mile from shore, sheltering the land from the terrors of wind and wave and forming the bulwark for safe harbor. This was actually and ideally achieved by the natural feature of the land and an artificial work of man. From the shore line toward the east stretched out a long slender arm of land, the promontory Lochias, almost touching the island of Pharos. To the west was to be built a causeway (called the Heptastadium, i.e. 7 stadia, 4270 ft. long), the better part of a mile long from the mainland to the island of Pharos closing the bay toward the west and making the perfect harbor.

1. Arrian: *The Anabasis of Alexander*, tr. E. J. Chinnock, London, 1893 (Bk. III–1).
2. *Odyssey* (W. C. Bryant, tr. Boston, 1871), IV-354.

On the 25th day of Tybi (20th January 331 B.C.), when Alexander beheld this site[1], his genius at once sensed its topographical fitness for a great city[2]. With his usual quick thinking and prompt decision he decreed that here would be built the city that should perpetuate his name and fame. His enthusiasm mounting, he actually traced the boundaries of the new metropolis and pointed to the places where temples to the gods and public works should grace his city[3]. Dinocrates, his architect, who had accompanied Alexander on the Egyptian expedition, was instructed to draw plans for the building of a spacious and magnificent metropolis that, midmost of the civilized world, should be the veritable mistress of the trade of the East and the West and the center of the arts and intellectual endeavors of mankind. And from what we know of Dinocrates[4], his plans must have been grandiose, and in his usual attempt to excite the exalted imaginings of his ardent patron[5], he must indeed have promised him:

> The cloud-capp'd towers, the gorgeous palaces,
> The solemn temples——

And so by fiat the amazing son of Philip founded Alexandria (winter, 331–0 B.C.), which he himself was never to see, although his body, and we hope his spirit, became for at least seven centuries the divine guardian of its imperial splendors. After the conquest of Egypt (331 B.C.), Alexander appointed Cleomenes at least the Collector of Revenues for the province. Demosthenes[6]

1. The annual Foundation Festival of Alexandria was held on this date (25th of Tybi), hence legend assigns January 20, 331 B.C. as the natal day of the famous city (ch. Bevan, p. 7).
2. This view is ably supported by Hogarth (David D. Hogarth: *Philip and Alexander of Macedon*, New York, 1897, pp. 187–193), although Mahaffy (*Empire of the Ptolemies*, p. 11) lightly dismissed the selection of the site, as one that might have been chosen "anywhere else on the coast".
3. The city was to be of the "modern" rectangular type, with broad straight streets intersecting at right angles; in the style of the Milesian architect Hippodamus, whose work extended from the Asian coast to Magna Graecia, and who had made the crooked streets of Piraeus straight.
4. This was the Macedonian (Rhodian according to The Romance of Alexander) architect who boasted that he would shape Mount Athos into the figure of Alexander, with a city held in his left hand and a vast basin in his right which would receive all the rivers of the mountain (Vitruvius, Bk. II, pref.; and Plutarch: *Alex.*, 72). Have we not in our time ventured to shape one of the Black Hills into the figures of Washington, Lincoln, and Roosevelt I?
5. Candor requires reference to: Lucian: *Pro imaginibus*, 9.
6. Demosthenes: *Against Dionysodorus*, 1285 (7); Pseud.

ALEXANDER THE GREAT

Louvre, Paris

calls him "ruler of Egypt" and exposes his dishonest manipula-
tion of the grain-trade; Aristotle[1] calls him "governor of Egypt"
and recites instances of fraudulent conduct with merchants,
priests of the temple, and government-officials; and Arrian[2] says
he was "an evil man who had done many grievous wrongs in
Egypt".

Cleomenes was the first to commence the building of Alexandria, the building of which was at once begun. "King Alexander",
writes Aristotle, "had given Cleomenes command to establish
a town near the island of Pharos, and to transfer thither the
market hitherto held at Canopus." Undoubtedly he was the first
entrusted with the building of the city, and Justin[3] even calls
him one of the *architects* of Alexandria, along with Dinocrates[4].

Now as to what progress Cleomenes of Naucratis (who was not
satrap of Egypt, but nomarch of the Arabian district of Egypt
and receiver of the tribute from all Egypt) made we do not know.
But Alexander died shortly after (323 B.C.) and in the distribu-
tion of the empire Ptolemy obtained the satrapy of Egypt. Cleomenes was left as an officer under Ptolemy, who under a suspicion
that he was in sympathy with Perdiccas, had him put to death.
Cleomenes had amassed, doubtlessly dishonorably, the amazing
fortune of 8000 talents, which treasure came into the possession
of Ptolemy.

Dinocrates the architect laid out the city and erected some
of the principal buildings. Under Ptolemy Soter (first as satrap
to 305 B.C. and then as king to 283 B.C.) and under his son
Ptolemy II the city rapidly grew in imperial magnificence,
although it was lavishly embellished by almost every ruler of the
Ptolemaic line, the Hellenic kings who from little vantage-
ground on the edge of the coast of Egypt ruled that ancient land
and people from Alexander's death (323 B.C. – Ptolemy I) to
the ultimate triumph of Caesar's fortunate grandnephew Augustus (30 B.C. – Cleopatra).

1. Aristotle: *Oeconomica*, 1352a (16) to 1352b (25).
2. Arrian: *Anabasis of Alexander*, VII–23–6. It is true that Arrian most probably used
the *Memoirs* of Ptolemy, one of his two basic authorities, and that Ptolemy put Cleomenes to death.
3. Justin: XIII–4; also Mahaffy: *Empire of Ptolemies*, p. 10.
4. Even Weniger says Dinocrates the architect drew the plans, and Cleomenes super-
vised the work. Prof. Weniger: *Das alexandrinische Museum*, Berlin, 1875 (p. 11).

The ancients[1] tell us that the general ground-plan of the city was in the shape of a Macedonian chlamys or military cloak[2]. Its site was "washed by two seas", on the north by the Mediterranean, on the south by Lake Mareotis. It was built on a narrow sandy neck of land, consisting of low undulating hills, running obliquely from north-east to south-west for some three miles, with a slightly irregular width of about half its length, all within a fifteen mile circuit of the city walls.

The city embraced or was divided into ethnic regions:

1. The original Rhakotis, or native Egyptian quarter, in which was erected the Serapeum, considered the most magnificent public building, the Capitol at Rome alone excepted, in the ancient world.

2. The Brucheion or Royal Greek-Macedonian quarter occupied the entire front of the Great Harbor from the promontory of Lochias to at least the mole or causeway (the Heptastadium) which joined the city to the island of Pharos. In the Royal quarter dwelt the Greek-Macedonians and the many races and peoples of Europe and Asia who came to live in the city of Alexandria. Here were the offices of government, the marts of trade, and the great public buildings, above all the mausoleum (Soma) of the conqueror, the Great Museum with its far-famed Library and its adjuncts, such as the Theatre for lectures and readings, all connected by splendid colonnades of rare Egyptian marbles. Beyond, on the slender promontory of Lochias, amid gardens and groves of exotic trees, plants, and flowers, were palaces of the Ptolemaic kings, vast piles of buildings and estates, which extended to the heart of the Greek city.

3. The third district of the city, the Jewish quarter, was almost as large as the Greek or Royal quarter. It had its own walls, and here dwelt the vast population of Alexandrian Jews, not in ghetto, but practically in a city of their own, immediately governed by their own Ethnarch, having their own sanhedrin or

---

1. Plutarch: *Alexander*, 5-11; Strabo: *Geography*, 17-18.
2. The chlamys, the short oblong mantle, in length double its width, was originally the cloak of Macedonian and Thessalian hunters and soldiers, but became common throughout the Greek and Roman world. It is worn by riders in the Panathenaic procession on the Parthenon frieze of Phidias; Alcibiades wrapped his chlamys about his left arm in his last fight for life; the homely Spartan and the effete Roman emperor both affected this useful garment.

council and under their own laws. There were many quarrels between the Greeks and Jews of Alexandria and the privileges of the Jews were abolished, curtailed or restored (particularly by the Romans) with every political wind that affected this turbulent city.

The city is further described[1] as being divided into five sections bearing the first five letters of the Greek alphabet: Alpha, Beta (thought to have comprised the palaces of the Ptolemaic kings, the Museum, Library, and Soma of Alexander), Gamma, Delta (the Jewish quarter), and Epsilon. The location and use of three of these sections are unknown.

Within these three districts – Egyptian, Greek, and Jewish, or the five alphabetical quarters – the vast population divided into many groups or classes, chief of which may be distinguished: 1. a fabulous dissolute court of oriental luxury; 2. the Macedonian soldiery; 3. Greeks from the mainland and the islands of the Hellenic seas; 4. Afrasian Greeks of the littorals from Cyrene to Bithynian Chalcedon; 5. men of the Syrias and of all the states of Asia Minor; 6. Arabians, Babylonians, Assyrians, Medes, and Persians; 7. Carthaginians, Italians, Gauls; 8. Iberians and men from beyond the Pillars of Heracles, and from far-off Ind; 9. the intellectuals, scholars, poets, critics, scientists, artists of every vogue, and the dons of the Museum and the bookmen of the Library; 10. the merchants from all the world and local industrialists; 11. the Jews, numerous and important; 12. the mixed rabble, grading from political sycophants (non-Egyptian) to the common workman and laborer (mostly Egyptian); and, finally 13. from all the earth the vast horde of governmental and private slaves, the leper-mark of ancient civilization. Truly the so-called *Potters Prophecy*, which we have in some fragmentary papyri of the second and third century A.D., proclaimed the fact:

> This City was a universal nurse (pantotrophos), every race of men did settle in her[2].

Alexandria from its foundation was one of the world's most beautiful cities. More than seven hundred years had to elapse

1. Philo: *In Flaccum* (525),VIII–55, London, 1941. Philo says two of the quarters were called and mostly inhabited by Jews, but he does not give the letters; Josephus (*The Jewish War*, II–18–8) would restrict the Jews to the Delta-quarter.
2. Wilcken, in *Hermes*, XL (1905), pp. 544 ff. (apud: Bevan, p. 241).

before Rome could boast (under Augustus) of having been turned
from brick into marble. Alexandria was marble from birth. The
city was laid out on the most magnificent lines, with great
boulevards cutting at right angles and side-streets wide enough
for horses and chariots to course.

The city was cut into four unequal parts by two great avenues,
paved with squares of granite: one, the Canopic Way, with its
Mesonpedion, beginning at the Canopic Gate in the Jewish
quarter, ran over three miles from north-east to south-west,
through the Royal quarter and out through Rhakotis by the
Necropolis Gate, where in the West was the City of the Dead[1];
the other boulevard ran south-east to north-west from the Sun Gate
on or near the Mareotic lagoon to the Moon Gate at or near the
beginning of the Mole which connected the Royal quarter with
the Island of Pharos, or perhaps more easterly on the Great
Harbor. These great streets were over one hundred feet wide and
cut at right angles in the Brucheion, the Royal or Greek quarter.
On either side these avenues were flanked with stately marble
colonnades, fairways from sun and weather, through which
sheltered passages the din of many tongues provoked sonorous
sounds, as to-day may be heard in the covered streets of Bologna.

The centers of the streets were embellished with monuments, in
which the number of obelisks and sphinxes offered reasonable
flattery to the humbled pride of the conquered native Egyptians.

There were at least seven great streets running parallel to
and including the Grande rue Longitudinale, the length of
the city, something less than a thousand feet apart; and at least
eleven great streets running parallel to and including the street
of the Sun-Moon (Grande rue Transversale) at intervals of about
eleven hundred feet, the width of the city; and between these was
a series of secondary streets[2].

So solidly was the city constructed that even the ordinary
dwellings, as well as the better city residences, were built of
stone, without wooden floorings and timbers, with foundations of
masonry, upon which arose vaulted arches, enclosing cellars

1. This was the Grande rue Longitudinale of Saint-Genis, who says: "elle se dirige de
l'est–nord–est à l'ouest–sud–ouest." (Vide: À mémoire: *Description des Antiquités
d'Alexandrie et de ses environs*, by M. Saint–Genis, in the monumental: *Description de
l'Egypte*, Paris, 1818 (*Antiquités*, Vol. II, p. 57).
2. Mahmoud–el–Falaki: *Mémoire sur l'ancienne Alexandrie*, Copenhagen, 1872.

and cisterns connected with the waters of the Nile. The water thus conveyed became in time clear of mud and fit for domestic use. The very roofs of the houses were made of rubble or paved with stone[1]. This absence of wood in construction made Alexandria a city indestructible and more fireproof than any city of antiquity or most cities of modern times.

The lighthouse of Alexandria (Pharos), built by Sostratus of Cnidus.
3rd cent. B.C. (After Tiersch)

The great city spread over its three quarters on the mainland and the island of Pharos presented a glorious assemblage of marts of trade, factories of industry, of institutions of culture, and of the peoples of the known world. Immense docks bordered its two harbors (one on either side of the causeway called Heptastadium) where the ships of all nations made port[2]. Huge warehouses,

1. The author of the *Alexandrian War* confirms the above description.
2. Dio Chrysostom: *The Thirty–Second Discourse* (36), tr. H. Lamar Crosby, L.C.L., Vol. III–207:
Not only have you a monopoly of the shipping of the entire Mediterranean by reason of the beauty of your harbors, the magnitude of your fleet, and the abundance and the marketing of the products of every land, but also the outer waters that lie beyond are in your grasp, both the Red Sea and the Indian Ocean whose name was rarely heard in former days. The result is that the trade, not merely of islands, ports, a few straits and ithmuses, but of practically the whole world is yours. For Alexandria is situated, as it were, at the cross-roads of the whole world, of even the most remote nations thereof, as if it were a market serving a single city, a market which brings together into one place all manner of men, displaying them to one another and, as far as possible, making them a kindred people.

perhaps to the west of the Mole, stored the grain and products of the fertile valley of the Nile, ready for export to Greece and Rome. From the littoral, great steps of marble descended into the pellucid waters of the sea.

There were military establishments for the Macedonian and mercenary soldiers, barracks for the men, and arsenals for the implements of war; there were quarters, goodly slums we may be sure, for the sailormen with a Poseidonium for their offerings; there was a Gymnasium and a Stadium for relaxation and athletics; a Hippodrome for horse and chariot-races; theatres for lectures and public readings, and the open "Greek Theatre" for drama, where the spectators from their seats could see beyond the stage the little islet of Antirrhodus in the Great Harbor, and the burning torch of Pharos, one of the wonders of the ancient world. This great lighthouse, the prototype for all land signals for the sea, built by Sostratus the Cnidian, was five hundred ninety feet high and partly survived until the fourteenth century, when it succumbed to earthquake and the sea. The Theatre of Comedy was much patronized by the Alexandrians — that is some classic pieces, with much of even lighter vein, descending to vulgar buffoonery and indecent pantomime[1]; and the simple and fickle populace crowded the Marionette Shows, in which the great engineer Heron (like Leonardo at Milan for the Visconti) had to devise ingenious contrivances for the puppet-plays. There were temples of all the gods, particularly Greek and Egyptian, culminating in the mighty Serapeum where Greek and Egyptian could meet in common worship; there was the Panium, a curious shrine to Pan on the top of an artificial mound reached by a laborious winding path from which vantage-spot the teeming city could be surveyed; there were parks of wild animals and gardens of tropical plants; and above all, that which could be found in no other city of the ancient world, there were the Royal Museum and the Alexandrian Library.

No wonder that Achilles Tatius, the last of the early Greek novelists, with permissible hyperbole, particularly if he were an

---

1. Where there were mostly: Both mimes and dancers plying nimble feet. But how well Chrysostom, in *The Thirty–Second Discourse* (4): For the organ of hearing of a people is the theatre, and into your theatre there enters nothing beautiful or honorable, or very rarely; but it is always full of the strumming of the lyre and of uproar, buffoonery, and scurrility (III–175).

Alexandrian, describes this fair city in the opening of the 5th Book of his story of *Clitophon and Leucippe*:

> After a voyage lasting for three days, we arrived at Alexandria. I entered it by the Sun Gate, as it is called, and was instantly struck by the splendid beauty of the city, which filled my eyes with delight. From the Sun Gate to the Moon Gate – these are the guardian divinities of the entrances – led a straight double row of columns, about the middle of which lies the open part of the town, and in it so many streets that walking in them you would fancy yourself abroad while still at home. Going a few hundred yards further, I came to the quarter called after Alexander, where I saw a second town; the splendour of this was cut into squares, for there was a row of colums intersected by another as long at right angles. I tried to cast my eyes down every street, but my gaze was still unsatisfied, and I could not grasp all the beauty of the spot at once; some parts I saw, some I was on the point of seeing, some I earnestly desired to see, some I could not pass by; that which I actually saw kept my gaze fixed, while that which I expected to see would drag it on to the next. I explored therefore every street, and at last, my vision unsatisfied, exclaimed in weariness, "Ah, my eyes, we are beaten." Two things struck me as especially strange and extraordinary – it was impossible to decide which was the greatest, the size of the place or its beauty, the city itself, or its inhabitants; for the former was larger than a continent, the latter outnumbered a whole nation. Looking at the city, I doubted whether any race of men could ever fill it; looking at the inhabitants, I wondered whether any city could ever be found large enough to hold them all. The balance seemed exactly even.
>
> It so fortuned that it was at that time the sacred festival of the great god whom the Greeks call Zeus, the Egyptians Serapis, and there was a procession of torches. It was the greatest spectacle I ever beheld, for it was late evening and the sun had gone down; but there was no sign of night – it was as though another sun had arisen, but distributed into small parts in every direction; I thought that on that occasion the city vied with the sky for beauty[1].

To the exuberance of the Alexandrian novelist we would add an epitome of the sober geographer Strabo, who visited Egypt in the days of Augustus and lived in Alexandria (25–20 B.C.), where

1. Achilles Tatius: *Clitophon and Leucippe*, tr. S. Gaselee, London, 1917, L.C.L. (Bk. V–1–2).

it is most reasonably believed that he used the Alexandrian Library for his researches and for the quotations from many authors in which his *Geography* abounds.

His description begins as he enters the Great Harbor; on the right hand are the island and tower of Pharos, on the left the reefs and the promontory Lochias, with a royal palace upon it; on sailing into the harbor on the left are the inner royal palaces, continuous with those on Lochias, and groves with numerous painted lodges; in the harbor in front of a private artificial dock of the king, lies a small island, Antirrhodus, upon which is a palace and a small harbor. Above the royal dock lies the theatre; then the Poseidium, an elbow projecting from the Emporium; to this elbow of land Antony added a mole projecting into the water, and on its extremity he built a royal lodge which he called his Timonium where he intended to spend in solitude his last days. Then, the Caesarium, the Emporium, and the warehouses; and after these the ship-houses which extend to the Heptastadium. So much for the Great Harbor.

After the Heptastadium we come to the Harbor of Eunostus (to the west); above this, an artificial harbor called Cibotus and more ship-houses; then a navigable canal to Lake Mareotis; outside the canal there is left but a small port of the city, when we come to the suburb, Necropolis, with gardens, graves, and establishments for embalming of corpses; inside the canal, on the so-called Acropolis, in Rhakotis, the great Serapeum.

The city is full of public and sacred structures, the most beautiful is the Gymnasium, with porticoes more than a stadium in length; then the Courts of Justice in the center of the city; here, too, is the Paneium, a rocky hill, ascended by a spiral road, from the summit a view of the city. The broad street runs lengthwise from the Necropolis, past the Gymnasium to the Canobic Gate, and then one comes to the Hippodrome (beyond the walls); passing through the Hippodrome one comes to the settlements Nicopolis, where Augustus defeated the last remnant of Antony's followers, and Eleusis on the Canobic Canal, a lodging-place for shameless revelry, for those who would lead the "Canobic" life.

Alexandria contained most beautiful public precincts, and royal palaces, constituting one-fourth of the city; "there is building upon building"; all connected with one another.

"The Museum is also a part of the royal palaces; it has a public walk, an Exedra with seats, and a large house, in which is the common mess-hall of the men of learning who share the Museum."

The Soma also is a part of the royal palaces; this enclosure contains the burial-places of the kings and that of Alexander.

The happy advantages of the city: the only place in Egypt by nature well situated for commerce by sea with its good harbors, and commerce by land because the Nile conveys everything to it: "the greatest emporium in the inhabited world"[1].

And yet to all this we should add the salubrity of its climate and not forget that seeming military necessity had wrought the destruction of the far-famed city of Tyre, leaving the newly founded city of her conqueror undisputed mistress of the seas and roads of commerce as well as of the heart of all of the things of intellect and culture in the then known world.

In this famous city there were four monumental buildings which probably surpassed all others of their kind of which we have any knowledge:

THE SOMA[2]

Alexander died at Babylon, in the 114th Olympiad and in the archonship at Athens of Hegesias (13 June 323 B.C.). He was thirty-two years eight months of age according to Arrian. For a month his body remained practically neglected, while his generals sought to jockey each other in the game of world-politics. Finally his body was properly embalmed by skilled Egyptian and Chaldaean morticians. It was swathed in finest Sidonian linen and bound in malleable plates of gold so wrought as to preserve the beautiful contour of the Hellenic hero. Diodorus, the Sicilian[3], tells how they prepared a coffin of the size of the

1. Strabo: *The Geography* (XVII–1–8–16), tr. Horace Leonard Jones, Vol. VIII, London, 1932, with valuable notes, of the indispensable Loebs.
2. The manuscripts read *Soma*, i.e. *Body*. The Pseudo-Callisthenes: And Ptolemy made a tomb in the holy place called "Body of Alexander" and there he laid the body, or remains of Alexander (Gr. version: C. Muller: *Scriptores Rerum Alexandri Magni*, III–3–4; Jones's Strabo VIII–34). Dr. Ev. Breccia: *Alexandrea ad Aegyptum*, Bergamo, 1922 (p. 96, note) would justify both terms: το σῶμα was the corpse, the mummy, the *body* of Alexander; το σῆμα, the sepulchral building, particularly those erected by Ptolemy IV Philopator, in honor of all of his ancestors including Alexander.
3. Diodorus Siculus: *The Library of History*, XVIII–26–27.

body, also of hammered gold, with interstices filled with rare spices; it had a cover of beaten gold so wrought by the hammer and so exactly fitted as to set forth the true proportions of the body. A study of the text of this historian induces the belief that Alexander was embalmed in the Egyptian manner like some great Pharaoh of ancient Egypt. A funeral chariot or car of extraordinary ingenuity, constructed so as to meet the hardships of Asiatic roads, had upon it erected a superstructure of Hellenic-Oriental magnificence.

On a throne base covered with a Tyrian carpet of fabulous weave rested the magnificent sarcophagus of Pantalic marble, with episodes of the hero's life sculptured in relief by a master's hand whose genius had absorbed much of the impassioned activity of Scopas, tempered by the refined elegance of Lysippus, and pervaded by a magic sense of serenity, and play of light and shadow that was Praxiteles, over all of which was the delicate touch of the polychromatic coloring of ancient Greek art[1]. Within this marble chest reposed the imperial dead. Over the top was fitted a cover of gold, upon which was placed a robe of richest purple, gold embroidered, besides the arms of the king.

All this occupied the center of the funeral car and around and over it was built a mortuary chamber (rectangular, about 12 x 18 feet) in the form of an Ionic temple, with golden columns of that order supporting a vaulted roof of gold, covered with overlapping slabs embellished with precious stones. Around the chamber, beneath the roof, was a cornice of gold from which projected the heads of goat-stags like the water-spouts of Greek temples or the gargoyles of Gothic buildings. At each corner of the vaulted roof was a winged-Victory in gold. There were no cella walls to the temple-chamber, but instead a golden net which enclosed the interior of the structure, permitting the spectator to see the sarcophagus. The golden netting held long painted tablets, taking the place of an Ionic frieze, portraying, according to Diodorus[2]:

1. One could hardly imagine that the most heroic figure in the life of ancient Greece could have had a sepulchral shrine inferior to that which probably contained the body of one of his companions, which we may even now see in the Museum at Constantinople.
2. Diodorus: XVIII–26–6.

1. Alexander in his state-chariot, with his bodyguard, Macedonian and Persian;
2. the war-elephants following the king and his personal entourage;
3. cavalry in battle formation;
4. ships of war, alert for battle.

At the entrance of the chamber stood lions of gold, watchers of the imperial dead.

About the chamber, on a base topping the roof was a great golden crown in the form of a conqueror's olive-wreath, which in the sun's rays, as the huge car moved, gave the semblance of the lightning of Zeus. The mighty two-axled vehicle had Persian wheels shod with iron, with spokes and naves overlaid with gold, and axles terminating in golden lions' heads, with arrows in their mouths. Diodorus tells us that these axles were equipped with a curious device that protected the funeral chamber and its precious contents from shock, due to rough roads. The car had four lead poles, perhaps one in front of the other[1]; to each pole were four teams with four mules each, or sixty-four selected mules. Each had gilded crowns, golden bells on each cheek and collars of price. A special staff of engineers, roadmenders and mechanics accompanied the car, which was protected by a select body of soldiers, honored to render this last service to their great commander[2]. The execution of these labors occupied the better part of two years and the expenditure of enormous wealth.

The multitude from city, village, and countryside flocked to witness the magnificent processional[3]. With military pomp and pageantry the great funeral train journeyed from far Babylon up through Mesopotamia, over into Syria, down to Damascus, on its way to the Temple of Ammon in Libyan sands that the god might behold his divine son. Thence it was to be taken to the

1. H. Bulle: *Der Leichenwagen Alexanders, Jahrbuch der deutschen archäologischen Institute* 21 (1906), pp. 71 et seq.
2. Diodorus of Sicily, tr. Russel M. Geer (L.C.L.), London, 1947. To Diodorus and Dr. Geer I am indebted for much, without, however, their being responsible for this composite description in any way. Dr. Geer's translation and notes fully maintain the scholarship of the "indispensable Loebs".
3. This calls to mind those magnificent designs of Victor Adam, lithographed by Arnout, of the translation of the body of the hero of the people of France, particularly the plate: *Marche du Cortège Funèbre du Napoléon dans les Champs-Elysées*, Paris, Dec. 15, 1840.

ancient city of Aegae in Macedonia where Alexander was to rest with the kings of his royal race. But the final lap of this long mortuary procession was diverted by the shrewdness of Ptolemy, who at once realized the vast political significance of the conqueror's remains becoming the palladium of the city he had founded and to which he had given his eternal name. So Ptolemy with a respectable army met the bearers of the emperor and persuaded their leader to let him perform the last offices for the great dead. To Memphis he took the body, where it may have rested, until a great mausoleum was erected in the heart of the Brucheion or royal region of the city of Alexandria near where its most famous streets crossed at right angles. Here a precinct, sacred to the mighty dead, was set apart and surrounded by special walls. Within was erected the far-famed Soma, so called because it held the *body* of the most famous man yet known to history[1]. In the center of this burial-place of kings arose a mausoleum of indescribable magnificence. With rarest Greek and Egyptian marbles wrought by skilled Hellenic craftsmen, master builders and architects built this Dwelling-House for the mortal body and immortal spirit of the divine hero of their race in a supreme effort to harmonize the purity of fifth century art with the magnificent embellishments of fourth century architecture.

Within a spacious court defined by noble columns led down a flight of steps to the sepulchral ante-room, the Place of Lamentation where were performed the dignified, simple rites for the Grecian hero[2] and the more elaborate ritual for the oriental god[3]. At the end of this tomb-hall, in a recess, where in some temples was the image of the god, in a sarcophagus either as we have ventured to describe, or after the Macedonian manner in a sarcophagus perhaps bed-shaped, but wrought in the supreme

1. See Breccia: *op. cit.* p. 96, cited herein p. 63.
2. The Burial of Hector, *The Iliad*, XXIV–719–223:
    When they now to his famous palace had brought him, thereafter
    High on a bed of fret-work they laid him and seated beside him
    Minstrels to lead in a dirge; and mournful the requiem sounded.
    Dirges they sang, while women responsive added their mourning,
    White-armed Andromache for them began the loud lamentation.
                    (Tr. Wm. Benjamin Smith, New York, 1944.)
3. Breccia: *op. cit.* (96–98). Dr. Breccia believes that the sepulchre was underground, a greater temple built above. He considers as an established fact that the Soma was near the Mosque Nabi Daniel and that some actual vestiges of the funerary temple would be brought to light, if this spot was methodically explored (p. 100).

art of fourth century sculpture, the body of Alexander, in his golden winding-sheet, was interred. Above the sepulture proper arose a great Hall or Temple of white marble, of perfect Greek proportion, in which the builders seemed inspired by the ancient sense of Greek restraint in attaining the things of beauty. About this funerary temple were displayed mortuary objects and funereal furniture of greatest rarity and value, and here were celebrated public ceremonies of divine worship of Alexander, perhaps to appeal to both Greek and Egyptian.

Pleasure-ship of Ptolemy IV, built for his trips on the Nile.
Late 3rd cent. B.C. (After F. Caspari)

Like in all these Ptolemaic investigations, the question arises as to who built the Soma and brought the body of Alexander to his city. We believe this was done by Ptolemy Soter. Of course, there were most probably great embellishments made by Ptolemy II and his successors, notably by Ptolemy IV Philopater who seems to have rearranged the entire mortuary precincts. We know that Pausanias says the body remained in Memphis for forty years and was then transferred to Alexandria by Soter's son. We know how many writers, ancient and modern, are so prone to give all credit to the second Ptolemy. Yet all this is not consistent with the great efforts and the dangers incurred by Ptolemy Soter to obtain the body of his great commander, and having at great risks obtained the body, he was not the man to leave it in Memphis or elsewhere. His genius sensed perfectly the value of this precious relic to the capital city of the empire he had founded and every reason points to his completing his great accomplishment.

Dr. Bevan puts it well:

> Diodorus, Strabo, and other ancient authorities say that it was the first Ptolemy himself who placed Alexander's body in the *Soma* at Alexandria, where it still was in Roman times. Possibly this is the truth, and the fact behind the statement of Pausanias would then be simply that the body reposed for some years at Memphis, till the sepulchre at Alexandria was ready for it[1].

Around the mausoleum of the son of Philip were the tombs of Ptolemy Soter, possibly his half-brother, certainly his faithful friend, the able founder of the Greco-Egyptian dynasty and of his descendants the Ptolemies, whose sun set in the tragic life and death of Cleopatra. Both Cleopatra and Antony were buried near the Soma.

For many centuries this Soma or tomb-area of Alexander was the revered place of pilgrimage of the greatest and worse rulers and of men in every walk of life. Here came Caesar, and his fortunate grandnephew Augustus, who in his eagerness to examine the mummied form of Alexander incautiously crushed a part of the royal nose. Here came the emperor Severus who deposited within the tomb enclosure the sacred books of the ancient Egyptian religious scriptures and closed the place to casual visitors. Here his wicked son Caracalla, after depositing his personal jewels and imperial robes, massacred the youth of the city because of satirical references to his monstrous personality. Vespasian, Domitian, Hadrian, Aurelian, and other emperors of Rome visited the Soma and when the Moslems came under Amr iben el As in 642 A.D. it was said that the tomb still retained its original grandeur. Indeed Leo Africanus, the learned Arab of Granada, who was converted and baptised by his godfather pope Leo X, in his *Description* of Africa[2] quite freely declares:

1. Edwyn Bevan: *A History of Egypt under the Ptolemaic Dynasty*, London (1914), p. 19.
2. Leo Africanus: *The History and Description of Africa*, done into English by John Pory, 1600 (The Hakluyt Society), London, 1896; 3 Vols. Vol. III, p. 864.

Neither is it to be passed ouer in silence, that in the midst of the ruinous monuments of Alexandria there remaineth as yet a certaine little house built in forme of a chappell, and containing a sepulchre much honoured by the Mahumetans, wherein they affirme out of the authoritie of their Alcaron, that the bodie of the high prophet and king (as they terme him) Alexander the great lieth buried.

This, as late as circa 1500 could hardly be more than a legend of the Mausoleum that once crowned Alexandria, which according to Leo, was then "a citie decaying many yeeres together, was depruied of the ancient renowme and honour, and remained in manner desolate"[1].

A distinguished English classical scholar held views similar to Leo the African in a curious book, before Champollion, in which he attempted to show that a sumptuous Egyptian sarcophagus (now known to have been the outer stone coffin of an ancient Pharaoh) was the Tomb of Alexander[2].

But the truth probably is that the imperial remains and its magnificent mausoleum continued in practically its original splendor for seven centuries. So that when eight years after the destruction of the sanctuary of Serapis and the monuments of the pagan world (A.D. 391), he of the golden mouth, St. John Chrysostom, could have uttered more than rhetoric when in his zeal for the triumph of Christianity he cried out: "Where is now the Tomb of Alexander? Show me."

So the day came when the Heroön of Alexander, the Tomb of the hero *eponymous*, which, as the great heart of the metropolis, compelled the respect and admiration of mankind, had indeed vanished, provoking the words of another immortal young man:

Alexander died, Alexander was buried, Alexander returneth into dust.

THE MUSEUM

There it towered up, the wonder of the world, its white roof bright against the rainless blue; and beyond it, among the ridges and pediments of noble buildings, a broad glimpse of the bright blue sea[3].

1. Leo Africanus: *op. cit.* Book VIII, p. 861.
2. Edward Daniel Clarke: *The Tomb of Alexander: a Dissertation on the Sarcophagus brought from Alexander and now in the British Museum,* Cambridge, 1805.
3. Charles Kingsley: *Hypatia,* New York, 1895 (Vol. I, p. 23).

In the Brucheion, the Royal Greek center of the city, an amazing pile of white marble and stone was consecrated to the Muses. Here were statuary-halls, picture-galleries, lecture-rooms, and refectories for resident and itinerant scholars. Perhaps a hundred scholars lived under the generous patronage of the royal foundation: the Museum. Here, free from want and from taxes, they studied and labored, making researches into the history of the past and seeking to discover the secrets of nature. In verse and prose, they produced original work in letters and made lasting contributions to science. Above all, they collated the MSS., critically studied the texts, and through this exegesis, they issued recensions of Greek literature. And still more humbly, they copied manuscripts which they sold to those who had the desire and means of having books of their own. There was an archpriest of the Muses who nominally presided over the confraternity, although we believe the chief librarian of the king and of the Alexandriana was the most important personage of the intellectual entourage.

But the Museum, considered in its larger aspect as the University of Hellas, or rather of the Hellenic World, did not alone consist of sleeping-apartments, refectory or common hall for eating, or walks in cloisters or colonnaded shelters with seats for rest and contemplation, of theatres for lectures on philosophy or science, or for readings of the classic poets and historians, of botanical gardens and animal-parks for the study of flora and fauna, but above all it offered to its privileged fellows, or indeed to the scholarship of the world, the incomparable resources of the first real and greatest collection of intellectual materials or data ever assembled in antiquity: the Library of Alexandria.

Writing incidentally of the Museum-Library, Gregorovius says:

The Alexandrian school diffused a splendour over the civilized world which lasted longer than that shed by any university afterwards, whether of Paris, Bologna or Padua. Long after the creative power of Greek genius was exhausted, encyclopaedic knowledge and Greek sophistry were to be found in the Library and Museum of Alexandria[1].

1. Ferdinand Gregorovius: *The Emperor Hadrian*, London, 1898 (p. 238).

THE LIBRARY

A covered marble colonnade connected the Museum with an adjacent stately building, also in white marble and stone, architecturally harmonious, indeed forming an integral part of the vast pile, dedicated to learning by the wisdom of the first Ptolemy in following the advice and genius of Demetrios of Phaleron. This was the famous Library of Alexandria, the "Mother" library of the Museum, the Alexandriana, truly the foremost wonder of the ancient world. Here in ten great Halls, whose ample walls were lined with spacious *armaria*, numbered and titled, were housed the myriad manuscripts containing the wisdom, knowledge, and information, accumulated by the genius of the Hellenic peoples. Each of the ten Halls was assigned to a separate department of learning embracing the assumed ten divisions of Hellenic knowledge as may have been found in the Catalogue of Callimachus of Greek Literature in the Alexandrian Library, the far-famed *Pinakes*. The Halls were used by the scholars for general research, although there were smaller separate rooms for individuals or groups engaged in special studies.

Considering the date of its origin, at the close of the classic period of the world's greatest literature (Aristotle and Demosthenes died in 322 B.C.), when Athens, its mother, no longer afforded the means, power or genius necessary for its protection or preservation, the conception and building of this Library is an outstanding achievement in the intellectual life of man.

THE SERAPEUM

In the old Egyptian quarter, in Rhakotis, on a slight elevation[1], artificially enlarged, with a wealth of Egyptian marbles and rare materials gathered by the devotion of sacerdotal colleges, arose the Temple of Serapis. This was the most magnificent of all the buildings in monumental Alexandria, and dominated the metropolis, which it surveyed in all its quarters from its western coign of vantage. Here the Greco-Egyptian populace could worship at common altars, with a composite ritual, under an elaborate priesthood that could trace its spiritual succession from

1. Some writers as old as Aphthonius and as young as Parthey, have dignified it with the name acropolis.

the old priests of Zeus and the more ancient hierarchies of Osirus. This was the Serapeum of which Ammianus Marcellinus[1] declared:

> No description can do it justice, yet (it) is so adorned with extensive columned halls, with almost breathing statues, and a great number of other works of art, that next to the Capitol, with which revered Rome elevates herself to eternity, the whole world beholds nothing more magnificent.

Within its ample porticoes was housed the "daughter" library of Alexandria, the Serapeiana.

Alexandria was in fact *sui generis*, a city learned and gay, and we could hardly omit one of the rare bits of contemporary description surviving, that by the iambist Herodes:

> Egypt! There, think, is the temple of the Goddess (Arsinoe). Everything that is or can be anywhere, is in Egypt-riches, gymnasiums, power, comfort, glory, shows, philosophers, gold, young men, the precinct of the Brother-and-Sister Gods, the King, a liberal man, the Museum, wine, all good things heart can possibly desire, women too, more in number than the stars, and as beautiful as the goddesses who went to Paris for judgment[2].

In the autumn days of Athens, when the exquisite flowering of Attic culture felt the coming frost and Hellas seemed to have lived its amazing life and the golden book was about to close, there arose a radiant youth who seized the dying torch which he carried triumphant on three continents. In the center of the world he built by fiat a monument that for three centuries maintained in trade, in art, in science, and in thought Hellenic glory. And when Greece died as the Roman came, the mighty spirit of Alexander abided for still four hundred years.

The city of Alexandria was ever the symbol of the greatness of her founder, and it took a thousand years of the revolutions of men and the destructions of ages to effect the final ruin of that fabulous city that was the scene of both the triumph and the fall of pagan antiquity, and the rise and the disasters of the Christian faith, and which, in no flattering mood, provoked the dictum of Chrysostom:

> For your city is vastly superior in point of size and situation, and it is admittedly ranked second among all the cities beneath the sun[3].

1. XX–16–12.
2. Of course "Egypt" = "Alexandria", Herodes, I–23 ff. (tr. Bevan).
3. *The Thirty-Second Discourse* (36).

Various Plans or Maps of Ancient Alexandria
For those archæologically minded we append short cartographical
comments on interesting plans of ancient Alexandria

I. 1838

Plan in: *Das alexandrinische Museum* by
Dr. G. Parthey (Berlin, 1838).

A very early, yet interesting and satisfying plan.

Shows outlines of the city (the Macedonian chlamys), the long straight street (Canopic) from the Canopic Gate (running from N.E. to S.W.) to the Necropolis beyond Rhakotis; this street is cut at right angles by the great *cross*-town street from the *Sun Gate*, off of Lake Mareotis to the *Moon Gate* near the Heptastadium.

To the extreme N.E. (beyond which is the outer city, outskirts, beyond the walls) is the Hippodrome and the Jewish quarter beyond Lochias; then the large Brucheion quarter, ending (one feels most reasonably) at the great cross-town street running from the Sun to the Moon Gate (from near Lake Mareotis to the Heptastadium); and then Rhakotis with its frontage on Eunostus harbor and extending towards Lake Mareotis, having in this Rhakotis quarter in the section between the longitudinal (Canopic) street and Mareotis the elevated spot (an acropolis) on which is the Serapeum.

The Soma, and near it the Museum- (and) Library, are placed north of the Canopic Way but near it and a considerable distance from the water-front.

Note: This plan is drawn with proper regard, and the city shown in its true relations, to the ordinary cardinal points of the compass.

II. 1840

Plan in: *Histoire de L'École d'Alexandrie* by
M. Matter, Paris, 1840–1844 (in Vol. I,
1840) 2nd ed.

This plan shows the Grande Rue ("Canobus" (sic) Way) from the "*Canobus*" Gate to the *Necropolis*, cut or crossed at right angles by a great street running from the *Sun* Gate leading from Lake Mareotis, to the *Moon* Gate on the Great Harbor near (to E.) of the Heptastadium.

1. It places the *Soma* to the so-called (or indicated) north of the Canopic Way, very close to the great cross-street.
2. The *Museum* also placed to the *north*, but nearly a mile to the north-east from the Soma.
3. The quarter of the Greeks, *Jews* and Macedonians is queer-ly placed south of the Brucheion or that part of it south of Canopic Way; indeed most of this quarter is on the extreme south *on Lake Mareotis*!
4. The *Bibliotheque* is placed (with doubt) *on the Great Harbor*, with the *Theatre between it* and the *Museum*.

III. 1854

A sketch in: *Dictionary of Greek and Roman Geography*, ed. by Wm. Smith, Boston, 1854 (article by Wm. Bodham).

This sketch alone (doubtless following Parthey) has regard for the common cardinal points of direction, and at least is so printed, and has the two great streets:

from the Canopic Gate to the Necropolis Gate; and

from the *Sun* Gate (Lake Mareotis) to the *Moon* Gate on the Great Harbor.

It places the Library and Museum together; and near them the Soma; all *north* of Canopic Way.

(This sketch is mostly followed by the sketch printed in *Harper's Dictionary of Classical Literature and Antiquities*, ed. Harry Thurston Peck, New York, 1897, 1–57.)

IV. 1866

Mahmoud-El-Falaki (*Mémoire sur l'ancienne Alexandrie*, Copenhagen, 1872), at the command of the Khedive Ismail, labored faithfully in drawing his *Carte de l'antique Alexandrie et de ses faubourgs* (1866).

It is "a plan of the ancient town which has since been generally accepted and for which posterity owes him thanks" (Dr. Breccia). Of course, it is subject to many reservations, doubts, and changes,

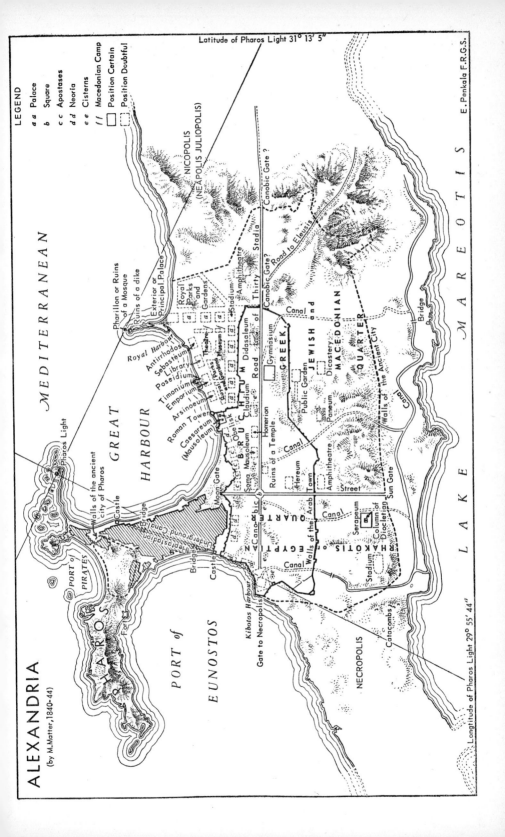

ALEXANDRIA
(by M.Matter, 1840-44)

LEGEND
a a Palace
b   Square
c c Apostases
d d Neoria
e e Cisterns
f f Macedonian Camp
□   Position Certain
▯   Position Doubtful

Latitude of Pharos Light 31° 13′ 5″

MEDITERRANEAN

NICOPOLIS
(NEAPOLIS JULIOPOLIS)

Pharillon or Ruins of a Mosque
Ruins of a dike
Exterior of Principal Palace
Royal Parks and Gardens
Royal Harbour
Antirrhodos
Sebasteum
Poseidium
Library
Timonium
Emporium
Arsineum
Roman Tower
Caesareum (Mausoleum)

Pharos Light
Castle
Walls of the ancient city of Pharos
Bridge

GREAT HARBOUR

PORT of PIRATES
PHAROS
Fort
Castle
Bridge
Heptastadium Underground Canal
Bridge
Moon Gate
Obelisk
Soma Mausoleum
Canal
Arabic Canal
Castle
Gate to Necropolis
Kibotos Harbour

PORT of EUNOSTOS

NECROPOLIS
Catacombs

B R U C H I U M
Didascaleum
Road of Thirty Stadia
Stadium
Amphitheatre
Theatre
Royal Gardens Museum

Gymnasium

Canobic Gate?
Road to Eleusis

GREEK and JEWISH and MACEDONIAN QUARTER

Canal
Dicastery
Paneum
Public Garden
Homerion
Ruins of a Temple
Canal
Hereum
Amphitheatre
Street
Sun Gate
Walls of the Ancient City

Canal
Canal
Bridge

Claudium

RHACOTIS or EGYPTIAN QUARTER
Walls of the Arab Town
Serapeum
Column of Diocletian
Stadium

LAKE MAREOTIS

E. Penkala F.R.G.S.

Longitude of Pharos Light 29° 55′ 44″

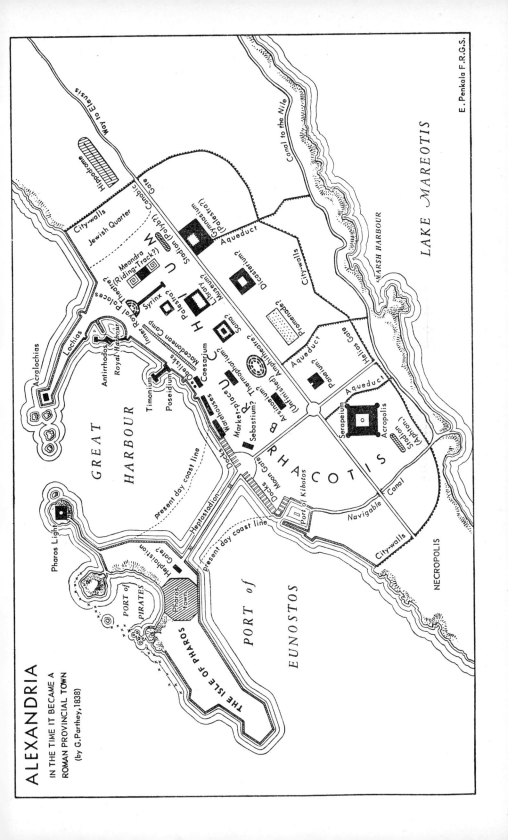

ALEXANDRIA

IN THE TIME IT BECAME A
ROMAN PROVINCIAL TOWN

(by G.Parthey, 1838)

E .,Penkala F.R.G.S.

Way to Eleusis

Hippodrome

City-walls

Jewish Quarter

Gymnasium
(Palestra?)

Canal to the Nile

Stadium (Polos?)

Meandra
(Riding-Track?)

Dicasterium?

LAKE MAREOTIS

Theatre?

Syrinx

Paisino?

Library

Museum?

Aqueduct

MARSH HARBOUR

Palaces

Macedonean Camp

Soma?

Acrolochias

Inner Royal Palaces

Amphitheatre?

Promenade?

City-walls

Lochias

Royal Harbour

Obelisks

Timonium

Poseidium

Caesarium

Thesmophorion?

Arsinaeum?
(unfinished)

Panium?

Aqueduct

Helios Gate

Antirrhodos

Warehouses

Market-
place

Aqueduct

GREAT

Docks

Sebastium?

R H A C O T I S

Serapeium

Acropolis

Stadium
(Aphrion)

Pharos Light

present day coast line

Moon Gate

HARBOUR

Heptastadion

Docks

Port of Kibotos

Navigable   Canal

City-walls

NECROPOLIS

Gate?

Hephaistion

present day coast line

PORT of
PIRATES

Pharos
Town

PORT of

EUNOSTOS

THE ISLE OF PHAROS

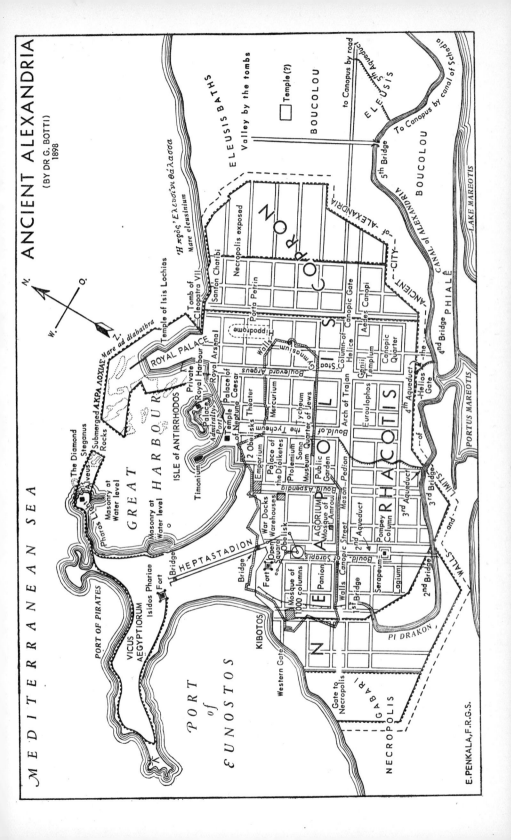

ANCIENT ALEXANDRIA

(BY DR G. BOTTI)
1898

MEDITERRANEAN SEA

N.

W.

O.

Z.

The Diamond
Steganus
Submerged ΑΚΡΑ ΛΟΧΙΑΣ Mare ad diabathra
Rocks
Masonry at Water level
Pharos
LIBUS
Alveus
Masonry at Water level
PORT OF PIRATES
VICUS AEGYPTIORUM
Isidos Phariae Fort
KIBOTOS

Mare ad diabathra

Ἡ πρὸς Ἐλευσῖνι θάλασσα
Mare eleusinium

Temple of Isis Lochias
Tomb of Cleopatra VII
Santón Chatibi

ELEUSIS BATHS
Valley by the tombs
Temple (?)

BOUCOLOU
to Canopus by road
ELEUSIS
5th Aqueduct
To Canopus by road
5th Bridge
To Canopus by canal of Schedia
BOUCOLOU

ANCIENT CITY of ALEXANDRIA
CANAL OF ALEXANDRIA
"ANCIENT"

ROYAL PALACE
Private Royal Harbour
Royal Arsenal
ISLE OF ANTIRRHODOS
Palace
Admiralty Port
Temple of Neptune Caesar
Palace of Caesar
Theater
Timonium
Emporium
2 Obelisks
Palace of the Dioiketes
the Tycheum
Soma Museum
Ptolemium
Public Garden
Boulevard Argeus
Mercurium
Tycheum Quarter of Jews
Boulevard Aspendia
Pedion
Meson Canopic Street
Bould of the
Bould of the Tycheum
Agora of Amrou
Mosque of Amrou
AGORIUM
Public Garden
Sarapis
Panion
Fort
War Docks
Open Square
Warehouses
Obelisk
Mosque of 1000 columns
Bridge
HEPTASTADION
Bridge

Hippodrome
Walls
Gymnasium
Stoa
Column of Helice
Aedes Canopi
Porta Petrin
Canopic Gate
Canopic Quarter
Necropolis exposed
Porta Petrin
Gymnasium
Templum
Genii
Arch of Trajan
Euorolophos
Helios Gate
Column of the Helios Gate
4th Aqueduct
4th Bridge PHIALÈ

NEAPOLIS
COPRON

RHACOTIS

Serapeum
Lagium
Serapeum
Pompey Column
1st Bridge
Walls Canopic Street
2nd Aqueduct
2nd Bould
3rd Aqueduct
4th Aqueduct
3rd Bridge
2nd Bridge
WALLS and LIMITS

PI DRAKON

GREAT HARBOUR

PORT of EUNOSTOS

Western Gate
Gate to Necropolis
GABARI
NECROPOLIS

PORTUS MAREOTIS

LAKE MAREOTIS

E. PENKALA, F.R.G.S.

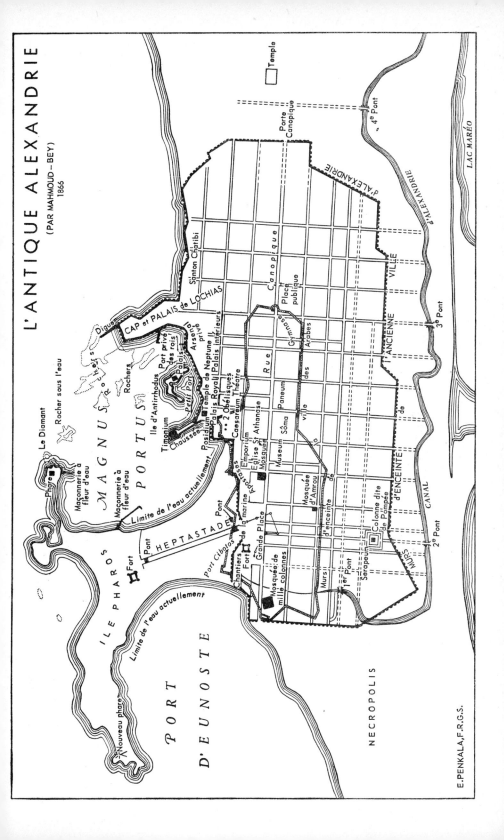

L'ANTIQUE ALEXANDRIE

(PAR MAHMOUD – BEY)

1866

Temple

E. PENKALA, F.R.G.S.

as are all the maps which have preceded his and, we fear, all those which have followed him.

His important contribution to the topography of ancient Alexandria was his arrangement of the streets intersecting at right angles in the form of a "gridiron". He said:

> I have discovered by means of excavations, eleven principal streets in the town of Alexandria, which cross the city from one side to the other, and seven streets which pass lengthwise through the city. The central street of the seven longitudinal streets is the Canopic street.

Dr. Breccia, after discussing the criticisms of Professor Noack, the disbelief of Mr. Hogarth, and his own doubts, however concludes:

> The *system* of streets established by El-Falaki may fairly correspond in its main lines to the *system* of streets in the ancient town. The plan which he drew up may be accepted as *approximate*, exception being made for the length of the roads towards the east, and for the position and direction of the main transversal street. (Ev. Breccia: *Alexandrea ad Aegyptum*, Bergamo, 1922, p. 76.)

The Museum and Soma are placed *south* of the Canopic Street.

V. 1888

Plan in: *L'ancienne Alexandrie* by Dr. Tass Neroutsos-Bey, Paris, 1888.

This plan places the great Longitudinal Avenue with its gate towards the extreme east, called Gate of Canopus, with an *inner* gate (doubtless at entrance of Brucheion) called Gate of the *Sun* or Eastern gate. At the west the *Longitudinal Avenue* terminates at the Gate of the Moon or Western Gate. There is an entrance on Lake Mareotis called Port du Lac, but apparently no gate or special entrance on the Great Harbor. There is a *Quarter of the Jews* beyond the Macedonian Camp, on the sea (Letter Delta), before you arrive at Eleusis and the Necropolis of the East (Jews, Christians, and Roman Army), coming from the west.

The *Soma*, the Museum, doubtfully placed next to it (and the Library not indicated) are placed *south* of the great Longitudinal Ave. The line of palaces beginning on Lochias are shown extending (separately) well into the Brucheion (restrictedly indicated) along the water-front.

VI. 1898

Plan by Dr. Giuseppe Botti (1898), curator of the Graeco-Roman Museum at Alexandria, who gives us the result of his researches and learning in a new Plan of the Town of Alexandria at the Ptolemaic Epoch, found in both J. P. Mahaffy (1898) and Edwyn Bevan (1927): *A History of Egypt under the Ptolemaic Dynasty.*

This plan is quite elaborate. It divides the city into Neapolis, Rhakotis, and Copron. The *Neapolis* extends from a line (sea to the Canopic Street) westward of Lochias, takes the whole front of the Great Harbor, passes the Heptastadium, and takes a good portion of the Harbor of Eunostus.

The *Rhakotis* is *south* of the Neapolis, occupying nearly the whole extent of the southern side of the Canopic Street, with its (Rhakotis) southern side taking nearly the whole of the city frontage on or towards Lake Mareotis.

The Brucheion is a narrow strip extending as a sort of continuation of the Lochias straight across the mainland, taking, apparently, the eastern ends of the Neapolis and Rhakotis. Within this Brucheion is placed the Hippodrome.

Between Brucheion (towards the west) in the midst of the Greek city is, extraordinarily, placed the *Quarter of the Jews.*

Beyond Brucheion (towards the east extending to Eleusis) is placed *Copron* without much definition as to its composition.

Following "the rectangular arrangement of the streets" of Mahmoud-El-Falaki, Dr. Botti, with essential changes, shows the city as crossed by the great longitudinal street (Canopic), which halfway in its course is designated Meson-Pedion; this street begins in the east at the Canopic Gate and terminates in the west at the Necropolis Gate.

Botti's plan appears to move this Canopic Way much further from the harbor-front, though he puts the *Soma* and *Museum* well to the *north* of the Canopic Street; the Soma in fact *next* to his Jewish quarter. The great cross-town streets are indicated and some named: from the east (named streets) we have:

1. Boulevard Argeus which runs from the *Helios* Gate on Lake Mareotis to *Selene* Gate on the Great Harbor, near the royal private harbor.

2. Boulevard of the Tycheum.

3. Boulevard Aspendia.

4. Boulevard of Sarapis, cutting across the Canopic Street leading to the great Serapeum in Rhakotis.

I do not find the Library indicated.

VII. 1922

Plan of Professor M. Bartocci in: *Alexandrea ap Aegyptum* by Evaristo Breccia, Bergamo, 1922·

This is an elaborate plan of Ancient and Modern Alexandria. The ancient names are superimposed over the modern topography. We do not find the ancient street indications as clear as in the preceding plans. The Brucheion as marked indicates a small area, apparently not including the Soma or Museum. The Museum (we do not find the Library) is much farther from the Soma than usual. The Neapolis appears smaller. The Jewish quarter (Delta) is more reasonably placed, similar to Parthay and Neroutsos-Bey. Rhakotis is west of the Neapolis, with a vast section on Lake Mareotis hardly designated and but partly charted.

This plan appears as a map of Modern Alexandria upon which are designated, in red, certain ancient sites based mostly upon archæological conclusions.

VIII. 1932

Ancient City of Alexandria, based on Maps of Mahmoud-Bey and A. M. de Zogheb in: *The Geography* of Strabo, tr. Horace Leonard Jones (L.C.L.), London, 1932 (Vol. VIII).

Here we have the ancient city: beginning *from the east*:

1. A vacant space which we may reasonably assume to have contained the *Jewish* quarter (Delta).
2. *The Brucheion* extending from eastward to Lochias, taking the whole water-front of the Great Harbor, and extending apparently slightly beyond the Heptastadium on the Eunostus Harbor.
3. Rhakotis, with the Serapeum.

The Canopic Street is shown, beginning from the Canopic Gate (presumably at the end of the Jewish quarter) to the *Gate of the Moon*, on the Harbor of Eunostus in the West. The *Museum* and *Soma*, not far apart, are placed *south* of the Canopic Street. The Gymnasium is placed to north of Canopic Way. We do not find the Library.

Note: The plan might have been extended, with more sites indicated, and we have grave doubts as to its *Moon Gate*.

IX.

Alexandria (Ancient and Modern) by
Admiral R. Massie Blomfield (1905).

This elaborate map is published by the *Bulletin de la Société Archéologique d'Alexandrie, No. 8* (Alexandrie, 1905). The ancient sites are printed in red, the modern in black.

It marks a small area to the N.E. from promontory of Lochias along the Great Harbor as *Brucheion*. The place where the stone scroll case (for the works of Dioscorides) was found is designated "supposed site of Library". I do not find the place of the Museum designated. Some distance to the east from the "Library" site, there is the legend: "supposed site of Soma". Both the Library and the Soma are on the south of the ancient Canopic Street (Modern Rosetta Street) from the Canopic Gate to the quays of Eunostus Port or West Harbor.

This map is the work of an enthusiastic and earnest amateur who has made many contributions to the study of ancient Alexandria from "observation at first hand".

However, the dictum of Dr. Breccia that "any plan of ancient Alexandria must be considered only as approximate, conjectural and provisional" still holds true.

X.

Map "Alexandria" from sketch
by D. G. Hogarth.

This sketch accompanies the *Report on Prospects of Research in Alexandria* by D.G. Hogarth and E. F. Benson, reprinted by the Society for the Promotion of Hellenic Studies, from the *Archæological Report of the Egyptian Exploration Fund, 1894–1895*.

Mr. Hogarth sketches the ancient authorities, is unable, as an archæologist, to follow the researches or approve the rectangular map of Mahmoud-Bey-El-Falaki, and believes that scientifically the work must be started *de novo*, from "the authorities and existing indications". He actually conducted test-borings, excavations and subterranean tunnelings, with negative results, and the following excerpts of the report fairly set forth his findings.

There is no Mediterranean site which so excites our curiosity as Alexandria.

"We know Alexandria to have been laid out on a rectangular plan." (Diod. Sic. XVII–52.)

Strabo gave an elaborate description of the monuments and buildings about the harbor-front, indeed a *coup d'œil* of one entering the Great Harbor in his day.

"The present port-town stands mainly on ground which has been gained from the sea, since the construction of Soter's *Heptastadium*, but such gain is balanced by the loss of the old coast-strip round the east of the Great Harbor, which, together with the island of Antirrhodus and most of that of Pharos, has subsided beneath the waves." "The modern city... in the last twenty years" has "covered more than the *center* of the Ptolemaic city". "So far as we can fix the topography of the latter, all its greatest buildings and monuments stood within the area covered now either by the inhabited quarters of Alexandria, or by the encroaching waves." The Emporium, the Poseideion, and the Timonium "must have been absorbed by the waves".

"I believe that in consequence of a general subsidence of the land, the water has risen considerably over all the Alexandrian area since the early ages of the city, and that Ptolemaic strata, when such exists, often would have to be sought now in bottom-mud, two or three meters below the mean water-level." "It is therefore a Roman, not a Greek city, which is to be excavated at Alexandria."

"As things stand at present, the site of no monument, except the Caesareum, is known certainly; and I doubt if any of the ancient charts, as accepted at present, can be relied upon." (Hogarth's Report, p. 28.)

BOOK THREE

The Founding of the Museum and the Library

CHAPTER VI

THE FOUNDING OF THE MUSEUM
AND THE LIBRARY
PTOLEMY SOTER AND DEMETRIOS OF
PHALERON

WHEN Alexander died, there was great confusion and jockeying for place among his commanders and companions. Formally, Philip Arrhidaeus, his feeble-minded brother, was made king. The real power was held by the Macedonian chiefs, and Perdiccas became supreme regent of the empire. Dr. Tarn[1] believes there was a deal between Perdiccas and Ptolemy, under which Ptolemy gave his support to Perdiccas, he receiving the satrapy of Egypt, and the funeral arrangements of Alexander were placed in charge of a Macedonian chief, named Arrhidaeus, not the king. Alexander died in June 323, and in about five months Ptolemy appeared in Egypt to take over the government.

Ptolemy was the son of Lagus who belonged to the soldier-farmer nobility of the country. Ptolemy's mother was a certain Arsinoe, who is said to have been related to the royal family[2]. There was a rumor that he was the son of the great Philip and halfbrother of Alexander. As a boy he was a page in the court, may have been educated partly with Alexander, and was always an intimate friend of the son of Philip, whom he followed in his great campaign throughout central Asia, into distant India, and was one of the seven bodyguards of the king. He was a man of much native ability, a competent commander, an able soldier, with a fund of common sense that made him carefully avoid the many temptations and courtier indiscretions so common among the intimates of Alexander. He was shrewd, ever looked ahead, and always played a safe game with consummate diplomacy in political matters. Yet withal, he seemed to be a robust, good-natured, genial man of the world who succeeded well in his

1. W. W. Tarn: *Journal of Hellenic Studies*, Vol. XLI (1921), p. 5.
2. Bevan: *op. cit.* p. 21.

dealings, both with men and women. He usually knew what he wanted and then quietly but quickly sought to attain his ends. He developed great political sagacity, and became easily the most successful of all the successors of Alexander. Wherever diplomacy served, he gladly resorted to it and used the military arm always cautiously and with apparent reluctance. Yet at the beginning, he had sufficient courage and boldness on taking possession of Egypt to act with prompt decision in most important matters that necessarily involved great risks.

He had been in Egypt but a short while when, perhaps according to understanding, Arrhidaeus appeared in southern Syria, after his long march with the great funeral car holding the body of Alexander. Ptolemy met the funeral train with a strong escort, took possession, and assumed the offices and ceremonies for the imperial dead. He took the body to Memphis, hoary seat of the ancient Pharaohs, where elaborate religious ceremonies were performed for the divine Alexander. Ptolemy knew full well that in taking possession of the body of the great king and intending to keep it as the greatest symbol of imperial authority, he had broken by this act with the powerful Perdiccas. Yet he took the chance, and by this step proved his capacity for greatness. He kept the body some time in Memphis until he erected in Alexandria the great Soma or sepulture for the imperial dead, which was to be the center of a burial-precinct for his house, destined to last for three centuries.

Having thus incurred the enmity of Perdiccas, he immediately seized the person of Cleomenes, whom Alexander had put in charge of the building of Alexandria and of the collection of the revenues and who was well known to be a friend of Perdiccas, indeed perhaps a spy for him on Ptolemy. Cleomenes was tried and executed, and 8000 talents, which he had accumulated dishonestly, according to Demosthenes, Aristotle, and Arrian, were taken possession of by Ptolemy.

And now a brief sketch of the military acts of Ptolemy will illustrate the quickness of his actions, competency of his judgment, and the success of his endeavors. A year had hardly passed since his taking possession of Egypt when he took Cyrene, which for more than a century had been a free Greek republic and the home of many illustrious men. Cyrene, as a neighboring land to the west, was a protection to his frontiers. By the spring of 321 (remember that Ptolemy came to Egypt towards the end of 323), Perdiccas with a great army came to punish and destroy Ptolemy. But Perdiccas failed to cross the eastern branch of the Nile and was assassinated in his own camp, and although the successful Ptolemy was offered the place of Perdiccas, he was too wise to accept it, being perfectly satisfied to be the ruler of Egypt. How well has Dr. Bevan said:

> Through the 40 years of struggle which followed between the great Macedonian chiefs – the men who had learnt war under Alexander –, Ptolemy, the son of Lagus, remained in his African province, safe as a tortoise in its shell, while armies marched to and fro across Asia and rival fleets battled in the Aegean[1].

In the incredible period of about two years since he took over Egypt as its satrap, Ptolemy had possessed the body of Alexander, disposed of Cleomenes, and beheld the defeat and death of Perdiccas, his most dangerous enemy.

For the next twenty years he engaged in many minor, routine military ventures and perhaps two major conflicts: Syria (southern) and Phoenicea were conquered, and perhaps Jerusalem seized on the Sabbath day – 319–318[2]. He occupied Cyprus (315 or 320), put garrisons in cities of old Greece, "protected" Aegean isles. In 305–4 old Antigonius came down with a mighty force[3] (army: 80,000 feet, 800 horse, 83 Indian elephants; navy: 150 vessels of war, 100 transports), but was defeated at Pelusium; and finally, Lysimachus, Seleucus, and Cassander won the decisive battle of Ipsus (summer 301) against Antigonius who was left dead on the field. The shrewd, diplomatic Ptolemy, who failed to appear and took no part in the fight, nevertheless claimed and retained his part of the spoils (Coele-Syria) which he occupied for the fourth time.

After Ipsus, Ptolemy diplomatically played the game now for one, now for another of the two *diodochi*[4] and the three *epigoni*[5].

1. Bevan: *op. cit.* p. 23.
2. Bouché-Leclercq thinks in 312, when Ptolemy, having temporarily lost Coele-Syria and Phoenicea to Antigonius (315), regained, at the Battle of Gaza, for he second time Syria-Phoenicea (312).
3. At least according to Diodorus.
4. Lysimachus, Seleucus, who with Ptolemy Soter were the remaining "successors" of Alexander then living.
5. Pyrrhus in Epirus, Cassander in Macedon, and Demetrius Poliorketes, the current *epigoni.*

After Ipsus he possessed practically Coele-Syria, Palestine, and Cyprus. After Ipsus, Ptolemy "engaged no more in war with any of the rival kings"[1].

This array of military activity is recorded in order to stress the point that the active genius of Ptolemy Soter during the short period of twenty-one years was able to lay the firm foundations of the Ptolemaic empire. During this time, this energetic man must have continued to build the great city that was the capital of his empire. That he had the undoubted genius to know what were the essential foundations of a world metropolis must be accepted as an ascertained fact. From the 20th of January 331 to the end of 323, Cleomenes of Naucrates, with Alexander's architect, must have done considerable to begin the building of Alexandria. With a man of Alexander's dynamic energy and insistence upon immediate results, Cleomenes, although he may have juggled with the intricacies of finance, would certainly never have ventured to lag in the building of the city for his exacting master.

From the end of 323 to 301, although much of Ptolemy's time was taken up with military affairs in building his empire, still he must have had considerable time to think, plan, and execute much in pressing forward the building of the city that was the seat of his own empire. We know that he had the political sagacity to appraise the enormous value of the body of Alexander to his city, to risk much to possess it, and to build the Soma to hold the reliques of the divine Alexander. Bevan remarks[2] that the reign of Ptolemy "was marked by one new creation, destined to have a future in the Greek world – the creation of a new cult". We know he was a good and successful soldier, his history proves his diplomatic skill; the employment of Timotheus, the Eumolped, expert in the Greek religious rites and Manetho, the Egyptian adept in the hoary mysteries of the religion of Egypt, who formulated the cult of Serapis, at whose shrine both his fellow Macedonian-Greeks and his subjects, the native Egyptians, could mutually worship, was a stroke of statecraft worthy of a great builder of empire. The building of the Serapeum, the second most magnificent architectural monument in the ancient world, was an achievement of the first order.

1. Bevan: *op. cit.* p. 36.
2. Idem: p. 41.

Yet this good soldier, able diplomat, astute ruler, creator of a new cult, builder of empire, has to his credit even greater claims to fame, achievements that not only effected the Hellenic world but which have placed all succeeding ages in his debt – the founding of the Museum and its handmaid, the Alexandrian Library. To set forth, as most reasonable, the proposition that at the "suggestion"[1], through the "inspiration"[2], from "the idea" arising "first in the brain of" [3], or "under the advice of"[4] Demetrios of Phaleron, Ptolemy Soter founded these institutions, is the purpose of this chapter.

> Ptolemy, upon whom, on Alexander's death, devolved the King-dom of Egypt, supplies us with the first great instance of what may be called the establishment of Letters. He and Eumenes may be considered the first founders of public libraries (p. 92).

> Ptolemy, however, prompted, or at least encouraged, by the cele-brated Demetrius of Phalerus, put into execution a plan for the formal endowment of literature and science (p. 94)[5].

Weniger:

> Ptolemy Soter... with the advice and assistance of the highly cultured Demetrios of Phaleron created the magnificent scientific institution[6].

Wilamowitz-Moellendorff:

> It must however be pointed out in just a word that Demetrios of Phaleron founded, like the peripatetic museum in Athens, the universal one in Alexandria[7].

Susemihl:

> From this influence [the peripatetic Demetrios of Phaleron] came without a doubt the beginning of the book collections[8].

1. White: *Aves.*, p. X.
2. Muller and Donaldson: *op. cit.* II-418.
3. Bevan: *op. cit.* p. 124.
4. Sandys: *op. cit.* p. 105; Mahaffy: *The Empire of the Ptolemies*, p. 92.
5. John Henry Cardinal Newman: *Rise and Progress of Universities* (in *Historical Sketches*, London, 1899, Vol. III, pp. 92–94).
6. Prof. Dr. Weniger: *Das alexandrinische Museum*, Berlin, 1875 (p. 9).
7. U. v. Wilamowitz-Moellendorff: *Antigonos von Karystos*, Berlin, 1881 (p. 29).
8. Franz Susemihl: *Geschichte der griechischen Litteratur in der Alexandrinerzeit*, Leipzig, 1891 (I, p. 6–7). Susemihl adds that the collections were continued in a grandiose measure by Ptolemy II "Philadelphus" through the actual founding of the two libraries.

Couat:

I have explained the feelings that urged Ptolemy Soter to found a
library; but this was not the work of a day... during the first part
of his reign, Ptolemy... was engaged in safeguarding his realm...
His later years were more peaceful. Once he had firmly established
his empire, Soter was able to devote himself more generously to
labours of peace. It was exactly at this time, in the year 290[1], that
the exiled Demetrius of Phalerum came to ask him for an asylum.
Demetrius had an active and fertile mind and knew all that was to
be known at that time... Ptolemy gave him a friendly welcome, and
profited by his knowledge and active mind by putting him in charge
of the library[2].

Bouché-Leclercq:

Demetrios of Phaleron was "the intimate adviser of Ptolemy"[3],
indeed "a man who had become indispensable to the king"[4]. "It
would seem that the Library dates back to the reign of Soter"[5].
"Posterity gladly forgets the royal weaknesses to take up the institutions which are the glory of the reign, the Museum and the Library
of Alexandria. One has seen above that the initiative in building
these praiseworthy creations belongs very probably to Demetrios

1. But Pauly-Wissowa: Demetrios Phalereus who went to Alexandria in 296–295;
Sandys (297); Mahaffy (probably, 306); Klippel (305).
2. Auguste Couat: *Alexandrian Poetry under the First Three Ptolemies* (tr. James Loeb),
London, 1931 (pp. 10–11). M. Couat adds: It is not "a formal office"; the library
"had still to be organized; no one was better fitted for that difficult task than Deme-
trius." Yet, "Ptolemy Philadelphus is regarded as their (Museum and Library)
founder. There is no document to prove it, but there is no mention anywhere of
Ptolemy Soter's having founded the Museum." M. Couat then quotes Callimachus
(Hymn IV–170):
And he shall know the ways of his father.
And then immediately adds: "An interesting passage in Plutarch (*Non posse suaviter vivi
secundum Epicurum*, 13–3) apparently contradicts this statement." Now the passage is:
    Ptolemy, who was the first to collect the Museum. What does it contradict? Not
the line from Callimachus. No one denies that Ptolemy II carried on the traditions
of his father, particularly that he added to the Museum and the Library many
scholars and valuable books. However, we are apt to forget that his son Euergetes
and his successors in turn did likewise. What Plutarch says is that *Ptolemy* (and it is
conceded that he means *Soter*) was the first to collect or bring together the Museum.
M. Couat himself interprets Plutarch as intending "to convey then that Soter had
begun to assemble books and scholars, and consequently, that he had conceived the
idea of founding the Museum." If this is so, then he was the founder, and it is quite
whimsical to insist that "his son "Philadelphus" was the founder". (Couat: p. 12,
note 2).
3. A. Bouché-Leclercq: *Histoire des Lagides*, Paris, 1907, I–119.
4. Idem: I–127.
5. Idem: I–129, note 3.

of Phaleron and to Ptolemy I. Philadelphus has only to follow or enlarge the first plans."[1]

John Williams White:

Hither (to Alexandria) also came Demetrius of Phalerum, orator, statesman and philosopher, who resided for many years in Alexandria as the king's intimate friend and counsellor. Ptolemy doubtless owed to Demetrius, fresh from Athens, the suggestion of the two foundations that made his city famous, the Museum and the Library[2].

Dr. Klippel's work[3], though it has passed the century mark, is, in spite of the many labors of his countrymen in this field, still the most charming treatise on our subject.

Demetrios's warm welcome to Egypt by the king, his faithful attachment for his native Athens, whose cultural institutions were deeply embedded in his heart and mind, helped immensely not only to strengthen Soter's sentiments for Attica, but also engendered in him the plan to make Alexandria a second Athens in the world of art and science. Of course, there is no definite proof for this contention in the ancient writers, yet there is no scarcity of inference in this direction[4]. If Demetrios used his influence with the king to help his friends and to draw educated and clever men from the upheaval of Greece to Alexandria, how can we doubt that this loyal son and benefactor of the Lyceum, this peripatetic philosopher, diplomat, and scholar, did not seize the opportunity to prepare for the king's guests a permanent place of abode, where they would be surrounded by the tools of their profession in such prodigal profusion, as to tempt the most indolent and fire the enthusiasm of the energetic to intellectual achievements. His position was secure, with access to the riches and the support of his royal patron whose noble aspirations he furthered.

Klippel believed that the founding of the Library may without hesitation be placed between 300 and 290 B.C.[5]

1. A. Bouché-Leclercq: *Histoire des Lagides*, Paris, 1907, I–217.
2. John Williams White: *The Scholia on the Aves of Aristophanes*, Boston, 1914 (p. X); see also his note pp. X and XI.
3. Dr. George Heinrich Klippel: *Ueber das alexandrinische Museum*, Göttingen, 1838.
4. Idem: p. 56.
5. Idem: p. 66.

Since that time Ptolemy Soter, with the help of Demetrios, worked on the enlargement of the Library till his death.

When we have now proven that the first Ptolemy must be accepted as the sole founder of the Museum, we still have to answer the question when this took place. That he started the Library before the Museum we have said before, but the foundation of the Museum must be placed in the years between 290–284, his death. Indeed no time in the long reign of the king was more favorable to the undertaking. An enduring peace had been well won and spread its benefits over the land[1].

We now propose to attempt to ascertain who was the founder of the Museum and, particularly, who was the founder of the Alexandrian Library.

A few preliminary elementary statements may be of value.

I. FOUNDER

The Oxford English Dictionary:

One who sets up or institutes for the first time; one who gives its first beginning to (an institution, etc.).

The Century Dictionary:

One who founds or establishes; one who lays a foundation or begins to build: as the founder of a temple or a city.
To found: To take the first steps or measures in erecting or building up; begin to raise; make a beginning of; originate by active means: as to found a city or an empire.

2. PTOLEMY

From the beginning the ruler of Egypt was *Pharaoh*. When the Hellenic monarchy was established in Egypt, the hoary tradition of merely giving the generic name of the king was preserved and generic *Ptolemy* took the place of generic *Pharaoh*. The Greeks and Romans were in the habit of referring to the Macedonian-Egyptian kings simply as Ptolemy[2].

These simple verbal references should be of real help.

---

1. Dr. George Heinrich Klippel: *Ueber das alexandrinische Museum*, Göttingen, 1838, p. 87. The student may examine some of the reasons assigned and arguments in favor of Ptolemy Soter as the founder of the Library and the Museum in pp. 77–87.
2. Does not Aelian (*De Naturae Animalium* (VIII–c–4) flippantly remark: "If you want to know which Ptolemy is referred to, go and ask him."

PTOLOMY SOTER

After a Silver Tetradrachme

In the meager references to the Museum and to the Library, in the classical writers which have survived, we find little reward for the most painstaking inquiry. That a general knowledge of these institutions was assumed is a reasonably admitted inference. That no single extant writer has treated the subject with fullness or the slightest regard to accurate consideration is the chief difficulty which confronts the investigator at every turn.

The possible work of Callimachus *On the Museum*[1] and the book of Aristonicus, distinguished Homeric critic and rival of Didymus, who wrote *On the Alexandrian Museum*, are hopelessly lost.

Herondas, the writer of mimes, who lived in the later part of the reign of Ptolemy II, has but a word: *The Museum*, which he mentions as one of the sights of the city. He does not mention the Library; and old Timon of Phlius (c. 230 B.C.) vents his satire on "the bird-coop of the Muses" (the Museum).

Strabo (c. 64 B.C.–19 A.D.) mentions the Museum but not the Library, although his latest editor has properly inferred that Strabo was indebted to the Library for his numerous excerpts from ancient writers.

It is curious that probably the first extant ancient writer who has treated the Library to some extent was the pseudo Aristeas. As one of the chief palpable errors of Aristeas, who was copied *in extenso* by Josephus and, with individual modifications, by most of the Christian writers, was the convenient assignment to Ptolemy II (whom we have all up to now erroneously called "Philadelphus") of the credit for all the literary, art, and cultural achievements of his predecessor or successors, it may be well to consider this matter now.

As the biblical writers thought it sufficient to merely state that *Pharaoh* did this, so many Greek and Roman writers felt that they had fulfilled their obligation by affirming the actions of *Ptolemy*. However, some writers, with a sense of accuracy, referred the incident or achievement to more than one *Ptolemy* (i.e. to Ptolemy I and/or Ptolemy II; or to the early Ptolemies), and, finally, some boldly selected *his* Ptolemy to which he assigned all achievements. As Ptolemy II had a long, prosperous and brilliant reign,

1. Whether this was a sub-title of the *Pinakes* or an independent work on the Museum we do not know.

in which he greatly added to the material embellishments of Alexandria, and in which he continued, in a grandiose way, the entertainment of artists, scholars, and scientists of the Museum at his luxurious court and made fabulous additions to his animal parks and botanical gardens, as well as great purchases of manuscripts for the Library founded by his father, at the suggestion and through the labor of Demetrios of Phaleron, it seemed easy, at least to a writer like Aristeas, to save himself the trouble of too much research and investigation, and to give all the glory to the fortunate and luxurious patron of learning and the easy life, indeed the Sun-King of the sunland of Egypt, Ptolemy, the son of Ptolemy, the soldier-founder of empire.

And, as much as we know, the first writer, guilty of specious error, it was quite understandable for later writers to copy. And so the error grew into more plausibility with time. With time, indeed, it had every appearance of a fact, and good men, ancient and modern, accepted it without further to do.

Herr Schmidt puts it well:

> In as much as Demetrios was persona non grata with Philadelphus, we must attribute at least the plan of the library to Ptolemy I, if Demetrios, as the ancient writers assert, was connected with it. If most witnesses designate Philadelphus (Ptolemy II) as the founder of the library this may well be a simple error which could easily happen through omission of the surname [i.e. Soter] in as much as the literary interest of the second king and his sister-wife Arsinoe were more widely known[1].

It is well to remember that the apparent interest of the Christian writers in the Alexandrian Library was due to their deep interest in the Greek translation of the Old Testament, the Septuagint, with all its glamorous traditions. Now these authors are arranged to show how generally the name Ptolemy was employed. As many of the authorities mention Demetrios of Phaleron as prominent in this great work, and as this view is controversial, we quote at the outset the opinion of one of the wisest commentators on this subject, Dr. Swete:

> If Demetrius took part in the inception of the LXX, he must have done so in the reign of Soter. This is not in itself improbable. He

1. F. Schmidt: *Die Pinakes des Kallimachos* (Berlin, 1922), p. 32.

had taken refuge in Egypt as early as B.C. 307, and for many years had been a trusted adviser of the first Ptolemy; and it is not unlikely that the project of translating the Jewish Law was discussed between him and the royal founder of the Alexandrian Library, and that the work was really due to his suggestion, though his words did not bear fruit until after his death[1].

And Bernhardy:

The name of Demetrios stands so embedded in tradition that Church history connects him with the translations of the Bible which was supposed to have been made by the king's order[2].

Let us see how the tradition has come down from Aristeas and the historians through the ecclesiastical writers, remembering the apt comment of Sir Frederick Kenyon:

Tradition is a bad master, but is a useful guide and the scholar must teach himself not to be afraid of it. It is by no means always to be accepted, but it should always be scrutinized with respect; and it should be realized that the early Christian centuries were not wholly credulous, not deficient in critical ability[3].

We start with:

a. *The Letter of Aristeas*, purporting to be by a Greek of the court of Ptolemy II (285–247 B.C.), tells the story of the Greek translation of the Pentateuch of the Old Testament. Most critics believe it to be an apologetic work by a Hellenistic Jew[4], a piece of propaganda-writing to magnify the Jewish people, their laws, and institutions. It has been attacked from the early sixteenth century[5] to the present time. It was written between 200 and 63 B.C.[6] Dr. Thackeray's summation against its credibility may be used. It is not a contemporary record of Ptolemy II; his historicity is unreliable, he being guilty of gross inaccuracies and anachronisms, and thus we doubt him in places where he is

1. Henry Barclay Swete: *An Introduction to the Old Testament in Greek*, Cambridge, 1902 (p. 19).
2. G. Bernhardy: *Grundriss der griechischen Litteratur*, Halle, 1892 (I-557).
3. Sir Frederick G. Kenyon: *The Bible and Modern Scholarship*, London, 1948.
4. Dr. Ralph Marcus in the ed. of Josephus (L.C.L.),Vol.VII, p. 8.
5. Vide: Chapter *Non–Greek Books*, of this work.
6. Schurer and Sir George Adam Smith (200 B.C.); Ralph Marcus ("sometime in 2nd century B.C."); H. St. J. Thackeray (120–80 B.C.); Wendland (96–63 B.C.); Gratz and Wellrich date it in early imperial times, but this is, in our judgment, untenable.

the only authority; and above all he was a Jew masquerading "under a heathen mask". In favor of Aristeas, Prof. Lumbroso[1] has well shown that "there is not a court title, an institution, a law, a magistracy, an office, a technical term, a formula, a remarkable turn of language in this letter, there is no piece of evidence of Aristeas concerning the civil history of the epoch, which is not found registered in the papyri or the inscriptions and confirmed by them". Not only are his references to Alexandrian life and customs and to the etiquette of the court impeccable, but his description of Jerusalem is vivid and accurate. We now know that his references to Hecataeus of Abdera are worthy of respect, and it hardly sounds reasonable to disregard his references to Theopompus and Theodectis, of whom we know so little.

But to our mind there are two insurmountable hurdles that his critics have failed to make:

1st. Why, if he was a Jew endeavoring to disguise himself as a Greek, did he take the name of a Jewish historian (Aristeas) of the second century, when there were hundreds of good Greek names which he might have assumed; and

2nd. What earthly reason, being a Jew, did he have for making Demetrios of Phaleron the hero of his story. For after an introductory address to his brother Philocrates to whom *The Letter* is supposed to have been written in order to tell his story of the deputation to Eleazer, the high-priest of the Jews, he at once proceeds to give the origin of the scheme in these words:

> Demetrius of Phalerum, as keeper of the king's library, received large grants of public money with a view to his collecting, if possible, all the books in the world; and by purchases and transcriptions he to the best of his ability carried the king's purpose into execution. Being asked once in my presence, about how many thousand of books were already collected, he replied: "More than two hundred thousand, O king; and I will ere long make diligent search for the remainder, so that a total of half a million may be reached. I am informed that the Jews also have certain laws which are deserving of transcription and a place in thy library." "What is to hinder thee then," replied the king, "in this task? For all the necessary means are at thy service." And Demetrius answered: "Translation is also required. For in the Jews' land they use a peculiar script..."

1. Lumbroso: *Recherches sur l'économie politique de l'Egypte sur les Lagides*, p. XIII.

And when the king had learnt all the facts, he gave command that a letter should be written to the high-priest of the Jews, in order that the proposal [of Demetrius] above mentioned might be carried into effect[1].

Then Demetrios draws a Memorial concerning the transcription of the Jewish books; he rendered every servility to the seventy-two (the famous LXX) Jewish scholars who are to translate the Hebrew text into Greek; he personally, after three days, leads the savants over the Heptastadium to the island of Pharos, where he holds a session with them in a magnificent hall erected for the purpose; they agree upon the details of the work which is to be transcribed under the direction of Demetrios; and when the work was ended, "Demetrius assembled the Jewish people on the spot where the translation had been made and read it through to the whole assembly in the presence of the translators, who received another great ovation from the people in recognition of the great services which they had rendered. And they gave a similar reception to Demetrius and requested him to have a copy of the whole Law transcribed and to present it to their rulers"; and the proceedings were brought to the king, and he rejoiced and held converse with Demetrios concerning the Law and why the Greek writers had not mentioned it. And when the king heard the explanation of Demetrios he "ordered that great care should be taken of the books, and that they should be guarded with proper awe".

Throughout the text the king is called *Ptolemaeus*, although from the mention of his father in several places in *The Letter*, we know that Ptolemy II is meant.

Now assuming that the writer was a Jew, with the perfectly reasonable desire to exalt his own people and their divine writings, what possible reason could he have had for "building up" Demetrios of Phaleron. He could have had but one motive, and that was that he found ample and perfectly sound authority recording the achievements of Demetrios in making the great book collections, and his work in advising old Ptolemy in founding the Library and Museum and even initiating or suggesting the translation of the Hebrew books.

If it is said that all this falls to pieces because it is said to have

1. *The Letter of Aristeas*, tr. H. St. J. Thackeray, London, 1918 (p. 23).

taken place under the second Ptolemy, we answer that the facts narrated in *The Letter* took place mostly under Soter. The outstanding figure of the brilliant statesman-scholar, Demetrios, who in his second spring had been able to achieve such fine intellectual feats, attracted the talents of the pseudo-Aristeas, and he did not hesitate to give him his full meed of renown. But what of Ptolemy? Why Ptolemy was the king and whether it was the first or second meant little to many writers. It may be (the truth of course we will never know) that he, like many, gave the credit to the easy-going, splendor-loving, fortunate son of the great founder. But certain it is that *The Letter of Aristeas* kept alive the record and tradition of Demetrios's work which many subsequent writers will carry on, paying little attention as to under which Ptolemy it took place, some placing it in the time of Soter, others in that of his son, and some in that of both.

The record of later writers, Jewish, Christian, and Pagan, some in a chronological order (prefixing the list with some ancient Jewish records):

b. Megillath Taanith (The *Roll of Fasting*):

> On the seventh day of Tebeth (= Dec.–Jan.) the Law was written in Greek in the days of King Tolmai, and darkness came upon the world for three days[1].

c. Masseketh Sopherim (*The Tractate of the Scribes*, I, 7–10[2] (8th–9th cent. A.D.):

> It happened once that five elders wrote the Law in Greek for King Tolmai; and that day was a hard day for Israel, like the day on which Israel made the golden calf, because the Law was not capable of being interpreted according to all its requirements.

> Again, it happened to King Tolmai that he assembled seventy elders and placed them in seventy cells... and they wrote out for him the Law by itself. But they altered thirteen passages in it[3].

d. Talmud of Jerusalem (Palestinian Talmud[4]):

> Thirteen passages were altered by the Wise for King Tolmai.

1. *Anecdota Oxoniensia*, Semitic Series, Vol. I, pt. VI, *Mediaeval Jewish Chronicles*, II, Oxford, 1895.
2. Joel Muller, ed., Leipzig, 1878.
3. These Hebrew references are all taken from Dr. Thackeray: *op. cit.* pp. 89–96.
4. Megilla, I-71d (See Mechilta on Exod. XII-40).

e. Babylonian Talmud[1]:

> Rabbi Jehuda said the permission of our Rabbis as to writing in Greek extends only to the book of the Law, and that because of what happened in the case of King Tolmai. And they wrote for him "the short-footed one" and they did not write for him "the hare" [hâarnebeth] because of the wife of Tolmai, whose name was Arnebeth, lest he should say, "The Jews have mocked me by introducing the name of my wife into the Law."

f. Aristobulus (Pseudo-Aristobulus[2]), *On the Mosaic Law*, a fragment reported by Eusebius; said to be addressed to Ptolemy Philometor (182–146 B.C.); its claim to such antiquity disputed by some critics:

> Evident that Plato was a follower of our code of laws... For before the time of Demetrius of Phalerum, before the dominion of Alexander and of the Persians, a translation had been made by others of the narrative of the leading forth of the Hebrews, our fellow countrymen, etc....

> But the complete translation of the Law and all its contents was made under the king surnamed Philadelphus, thy ancestor, who displayed the greatest zeal, while Demetrius of Phalerum busied himself with the necessary arrangements.

g. Philo Judaeus (fl. A.D. 39). His account founded on Aristeas[3]. In his *Life of Moses* (II, 29–31), he expresses much adulation for Ptolemy II and says:

> In all the qualities which make a good ruler, he excelled not only his contemporaries, but all who have arisen in the past... To put it shortly as the house of the Ptolemies was highly distinguished, compared with other dynasties, so was Philadelphus among the Ptolemies. The creditable achievement of this one man almost outnumbered those of all the others put together, and, as the head takes the highest place in the living body, so he may be said to head the kings.

> This great man, having conceived an ardent affection for our laws, determined to have the Chaldean translated into Greek, and at once dispatched envoys to the high-priest and the king of Judea, both

1. Megilla, 9a.
2. Eusebius: *Preparation for the Gospel*, XIII-12.
3. Philo: *On the Life of Moses*, II-29–37 (L.C.L.), tr. F. H. Colson, London, 1935 (Vol. VI, p. 463–7; see appendix, p. 605).

offices being held by the same person, explaining his wishes and urging him to choose by merit persons to make a full rendering of the Law in Greek... Under inspiration, wrote, not each separate scribe something different, but the same word for word, as though dictated to each by an invisible prompter[1].

h. Flavius Josephus (37–c. 100 A.D.):

Demetrius of Phalerum, who was in charge of the king's library, was anxious to collect, if he could, all the books in the inhabited world, and if he heard of, or saw, any book worthy of study, he would buy it; and so he endeavoured to meet the wishes of the king, for he was very much devoted to the art of book-collecting. Now, when Ptolemy once asked him how many tens of thousands of books he had already gathered together, he replied that the present number was about two hundred thousand but that within a short time he would assemble some five hundred thousand. He added that he had been informed that among the Jews also there were many works on their law, which were worthy of study and of a place in the king's library, but, being written in the script and language of this people, they would be no small trouble to have translated into the Greek tongue[2].

i. Justin (c. 103 – c. 165 A.D.):

Now when Ptolemy, the king of the Egyptians, was forming a library and endeavoured to make a collection of all men's writings, he heard tell, among the rest, of these prophecies, and sent to Herod who was then king of the Jews with a request that the books of the prophecies might be transmitted to him. And King Herod sent them, written in their native Hebrew tongue of which I have spoken. But, since the Egyptians were unacquainted with the things written therein, he sent yet again and requested him to dispatch men to render them into the Greek language. This was done and the books remained with the Egyptians and are there to this day[3].

j. Pseudo-Justin:

Ptolemy, king of Egypt, formed a library in Alexandria and collected books from every quarter and filled it. Then, learning that certain ancient histories written in Hebrew characters had been preserved with scrupulous care, and being desirous to know what was written therein, he sent to Jerusalem for seventy wise men, who

1. Philo: *On the life of Moses*, II–VII–37.
2. Josephus: *Jewish Antiquities*, tr. Ralph Marcus (L.C.L.), London, 1943 (XII–12–14).
3. Justin: *Apology*, I–31.

were familiar with the speech of both Greeks and Hebrews, and bade them translate the books... So he bestowed many presents upon them and bade them return to their own country; the books, as he was like to do, he held to be divine and laid up in his library.

These things which we declare unto you, men of Greece, are no myths nor fictitious history. We ourselves have been in Alexandria and have seen the traces, still preserved, of the cells in the island of Pharos, and have heard this story... from the inhabitants, who have had it handed down as a tradition of their country. You may learn it from others also, and chiefly from those wise and distinguished men who have written of it, Philo and Josephus, but there are many others besides[1].

k. Irenaeus (c. 120–140 – end 2nd cent. A.D.):

For before the Romans possessed their kingdom, while as yet the Macedonians held Asia, Ptolemy, the son of Lagus, being anxious to adorn the library which he had founded in Alexandria with a collection of the writings of all men, which were [works] of merit, made request to the people of Jerusalem, that they should have their Scriptures translated into the Greek language. And they — for at that time they were still subject to the Macedonians — sent to Ptolemy seventy of their elders, who were thoroughly skilled in the Scriptures and in both the languages, to carry out what he had desired[2].

l. Clement of Alexandria (160–215 A.D.):

They say that the Scriptures, both of the Law and of the prophets, were translated from the Hebrew tongue into Greek under King Ptolemy, son of Lagus, or, as some assert, under him who was surnamed Philadelphus, Demetrius of Phalerum displaying the greatest zeal in this undertaking and carefully supervising the details of the business. It was in the days when the Macedonians were still masters of Asia that the king was fired with the ambition to adorn the library which he had founded in Alexandria with all manner of writings, and among other requests asked the men of Jerusalem to translate the prophecies in their keeping into the Greek tongue[3].

m. Tertullian (160–240 A.D.):

The most erudite of the Ptolemies, whom they surname Philadel-

---

1. Pseudo-Justin: *Exhortation to Greeks*, 13.
2. Irenaeus: *Against Heresies*, Bk. III–XXI–2. The entire passage of Irenaeus is also quoted in Eusebius: *Ecclesiastical History*, V–VIII–11–15.
3. Clement of Alexandria: *The Stromata* or *Miscellanies*, Bk. I–XXII: *On the Greek Translation of the Old Testament*.

phus, and one who was most deeply versed in all literature, when in his passion for collecting books he was, I suppose, emulating Pisistratus, among other records whose title to fame was due to their antiquity or some curious lore, besought the Jews also for their own literature, of which they were the sole possessors, in its native tongue. This he did on the suggestion of Demetrius of Phalerum, the most eminent philologist of his time, to whom he had entrusted the superintendence of the volumes... You have confirmation in this in what Aristaeus has stated. Thus the king left the records in Greek and accessible to all. To this day the libraries of Ptolemy are shown in the Serapeum with the actual Hebrew documents[1].

n. Anatolius (fl. 270 A.D.):

The famous Aristobulus, who was enrolled among the Seventy who translated the holy and divine Scriptures of the Hebrews for Ptolemy Philadelphus and his father; he also addressed to those kings books in which he expounded the meaning of the Mosaic law[2].

o. Eusebius (260–c. 339):

God... providentially ordained that the predictions about... the Saviour... should, by means of an accurate version deposited in public libraries, be revealed to the world and come to light. It was King Ptolemy into whose heart He put it to fulfil this task, in preparation, it would seem, for the impending time when all nations would participate in these blessings.

The story is told by Aristaeus, a man of exceptional erudition, who moreover took part in the events which happened under the second Ptolemy, surnamed Philadelphus. For it was in his reign and through his zeal that the translation of the Jewish Scriptures was produced and deemed worthy of a place in the libraries of Alexandria[3].

p. S. Cyril of Jerusalem (b. before 318 – d. after 386):

One of those who reigned over Egypt, Ptolemy Philadelphus, being a king very fond of learning, while collecting the books that were in every place, heard from Demetrius Phalereus, the curator of his library, of the Divine Scriptures of the Law and the Prophets and

1. Tertullian: *Apology*, 18.
2. Anatolius: *The Canons on the Pascha*, in Eusebius: *Ecclesiastical History*, VII-XXXII-17.
3. Eusebius: *Preparation for the Gospel*, VIII-1.

judged it much nobler not to get the books from the possessors by force against their will, but rather to propitiate them by gifts and friendship... sent to Eleazer, who was then High-Priest, a great many gifts for the Temple here at Jerusalem, and caused him to send him six interpreters from each of the twelve tribes of Israel for the translation[1].

q. Chrysostom (347–407 A.D.):

The Seventy may justly be deemed more trustworthy than the rest of the translators. The others translated after the coming of Christ, continuing to be Jews, and might with justice be suspected of having spoken rather from enmity and of obscuring the prophecies of set purpose. But the Seventy, in that they approached their task a hundred or more years before the coming of Christ and were so many, are above all such suspicion, and by reason of their date, their number, and their agreement may well deserve the greater credence[2].

r. Epiphanius (c. 320 – c. 403 A.D.):

Now the successor of the first Ptolemy and the second of the kings of Alexandria was, as we said, Ptolemy surnamed Philadelphus. He was a lover of all that is beautiful and of literature, and built a library in that same city of Alexander in the Bruchium socalled (now an uninhabited district in the said city), which he placed under the charge of one Demetrius the Phalarene. Him he bade collect the books in existence in every quarter of the world, and he wrote letters importuning every king and governor on earth to send ungrudgingly the books (that were within his realm or government); I mean the works of poets and prose writers, orators and sophists, physicians, professors of medicine, historians, and so on. One day, when the business was proceeding apace and the books were being assembled from all quarters, the king asked his librarian how many volumes had (already) been collected in the library. He made answer to the king and said: "There are already fifty-four thousand eight hundred, more or less. But I hear that there is still a great mass of writings in the world, among the Ethiopians and Indians, the Per-

---

1. S. Cyril of Jerusalem: *Catechetical Lectures*, IV–34 (tr. Edwin Hamilton Gifford, D.D. The Canon of S. Paul's says in a note:
It is generally admitted that "the whole Law" (the Pentateuch) was translated into Greek at Alexandria in the reign either of Ptolemy Soter (323–285 B.C.) or his son Ptolemy Philadelphus (285–247 B.C.) "under the direction of Demetrius Phalereus, curator of the king's library" (pp. 26–27).
2. Chrysostom: *Homilies on St. Matthew*, V-2.

sians and Elamites and Babylonians, the Assyrians and Chaldaeans, among the Romans also and the Phoenicians, the Syrians and them of Hellas... There are, moreover, with them of Jerusalem and Judaea certain divine books of the prophets, which tell of God and the creation of the world and contain all other teaching that is for the general good. Wherefore, O king, if it is thy Majesty's pleasure to send for these also, do thou write to the doctors in Jerusalem, and they will send them to thee."

The account of Epiphanius is entirely without restraint. He gives full run to his gift of narration and omits no incident that may add to the embellishment of his tale, which we have epitomized:

> The seventy-two were shut up from morn till eve on the isle of Paros, in six and thirty cells; at even they would cross over in thirty-six skiffs to the palace of the king and feast with him; they slept in thirty-six bed-chambers; two in each compartment with two attendants to cook and wait upon them; and shorthand writers for their convenience; there were no windows in their cells, which were lit from skylights in the roof; thus they lived under lock and key and translated. To each pair one book was delivered i.e. Genesis to one pair, Exodus to another pair, and so on; then each pair when finished received another book, so that each book of the Scriptures was translated thirty-six times. The translators were seventy-two, six from each of the twelve tribes of Israel. (And Epiphanius gave all of their names.) When the work was completed, the king took his seat on a lofty throne and thirty-six readers sat at his feet, one reader recited and the rest diligently attended; there was found no discrepancy between the translations by "a marvellous act of God".

And concludes Epiphanius:

> And so the books were rendered into Greek and deposited in the first library which was built in the Bruchium[1].

s. St. Jerome (345–420 A.D.), whose spiritual greatness has survived the centuries, and whose humanity is so pleasantly remembered, in letters, when he confessed:

> Many years ago for the sake of the kingdom of heaven I cut myself off from home, parents, sister, relations, and, what was harder, from the dainty food to which I had been used. But even when I

1. Epiphanius: *On Weights and Measures*, 3–11.

was on my way to Jerusalem to fight the good fight there, I could not bring myself to forego the library which with great care and labour I had got together at Rome[1].

And remembered in art, when we view the famous engraving of Dürer[2], even St. Jerome in one of his passionate outbursts says:

I know not who was the first lying author to construct the seventy cells at Alexandria, in which they were separated and yet all wrote the same words, whereas Aristeas, one of the bodyguard of the said Ptolemy, and long after him Josephus have said nothing of the sort, but write that they [the translators] were assembled in a single hall and conferred together, not that they prophesied[3].

And again, Jerome:

It is not my purpose, as snarling ill-will pretends, to convict the LXX of error, nor do I look upon my own labour as a disparagement of theirs. The fact is that they, since their work was undertaken for King Ptolemy of Alexandria, did not choose to bring to light all the mysteries which the sacred writings contain, and especially those which gave the promise of the advent of Christ, for fear that he who held the Jews in esteem because they were believed to worship one God would come to think that they worshipped a second[4].

With a brief reference, to refresh our memory, to the pagan writers, we will close this list of authorities. Plutarch says that Ptolemy (meaning Soter) brought together the Museum; Athenaeus that "Philadelphus surpassed many kings in wealth, and devoted himself with enthusiastic zeal to all his establishments, so that he surpassed all others in the number of his ships as well" (V–203 d), and later Athenaeus says: "And concerning the number of books, the establishment of libraries, and the collection

1. St. Jerome (*Letter* XXII–30), tr. F. A. Wright (L.C.L.), London, 1933.
2. *St. Jerome in his cell*, the celebrated engraving on copper of 1514. A slight pen-sketch of the early woodcut was in the Ambrosiana, forerunners of the famous copper-plate. See Moriz Thausing: *Albert Durer, His Life and Works*, London, 1882 (Vol. I-73); Dr. Friedrich Nuchter: *Albrecht Dürer*, Ansbach, 1911 (p. 71).
3. Jerome: *Preface to the Pentateuch*. For this and most of the references from the Rab-binical writers to here, I am indebted to H. St. J. Thackeray.
4. Jerome: *Preface to the Book of Hebrew Questions* in *Lib. of Nicene and Post Nicene Fathers*, 2nd series, Oxford, 1893 (VI–486). Jerome was right in the main in correct-ing the LXX by the Hebrews. He was not aware that there are various readings in the Hebrew itself and that these may sometimes be corrected by the LXX which was made from older MSS.

in the Hall of the Muses, why need I even speak, since they are in all men's memories?" (V–203 e.) Ammianus, in a chapter full of all sorts of errors, yet speaks of "700,000 books, brought together by the unremitting energy of the Ptolemaic kings" (XXII–16). Vitruvius has the amazing statement that the Attalid kings established a fine library at Pergamum. "Then Ptolemy, moved by unbounded jealousy and avaricious desire, strove with no less industry to establish a library at Alexandria after the same fashion" (Bk. VII, Preface, 4). The *Ptolemy*, however, that Vitruvius must refer to according to the context of his immediate text was Ptolemy III (Euergetes).

A consideration of the Plautine scholium of Tzetzes has been reserved for separate treatment in the following chapter.

A resume of the foregoing authorities discloses that some writers attribute the foundation of the Museum-Library to Ptolemy Soter, some to Soter and his son Ptolemy II, and some to Ptolemy II. We shall remember how loosely the ancient writers use the name merely of Ptolemy in referring to the Hellenic rulers of Egypt. Again not one authority denies or throws doubt on the important part played by Demetrios of Phaleron in the founding of the Museum and Library. Here is a tradition persistent and practically unbroken, save for a few writers upon which might be made an attempt to advance an *argumentum e silentio*. Nearly every authority gives credit to Demetrios; a few are silent; none disputes the point. A tradition such as this, we believe, should be accorded most respectful consideration, particularly when it is the case of a private individual, a scholar, persistently credited with a creative work for which he was so perfectly fitted by education, qualification, taste, environment, and all the circumstances of the time. We believe, from the limited sources at our command, that it is a reasonable conclusion, that in the dynamic age of the new Hellenism, the vast wealth of Egypt and the power of Ptolemy (Soter) soon converted the plans of Demetrios of Phaleron into two institutions that lasted for nearly seven hundred or a thousand years. This follower of Aristotle, pupil and friend of Theophrastus, had all the necessary background and the talent to seize the opportunity to suggest to Ptolemy the nature, scope, and details of the institutions of the scheme, and the king, soldier, and founder of empire had the wisdom to approve the plans of Demetrios. No greater ideal was ever conceived in antiquity nor one that so quickly bore fruit.

Thus the Museum and Library were founded[1].

1. Long after the above was written, the latest word, by a ripe scholar, in the latest book (April, 1949), sets forth on the subject:

Beyond doubt the foundation of the Library at Alexandria marks an epoch in bibliographical history. It appears to have been founded in connection with the Museum, by Ptolemy I, under the direction of Demetrius of Phalerum, but greatly extended by Ptolemy II, whom some regarded as the real founder. (See *The Oxford Classica Dictionary*, Oxford, 1949 – s.v. *Libraries* by F. G. Kenyon.)

CHAPTER VII

THE PLAUTINE SCHOLIUM FROM TZETZES

C IVILIZATION has few miracles to compare with the transmission of ancient learning on frail papyrus or tougher parchment. If men first sang or chanted or prophesied, if when letters came they were first used as a source of preservation or as a memory-tab, if men preferred to listen to the shout of the dithyrambist, the chant of the rhapsode or the eloquence of the orator, and if "books" were *heard* but not *read*, in good time all this changed to the normal use of manuscripts. As genius of the first order passed, the scholar took over, and recensions of the works of literature were made, and texts were emended in an attempt to restore corrupted words or passages. The scholars were indefatigable and wrote huge commentaries on the classical writers of verse and prose. These were separate books. But the critical editor, after employing the resources of recension and emendation, provided still further help for the earnest reader by the uses of glosses, scholia, and short or longer (broken or continuous) commentaries. The gloss might suggest the correction of a word or phrase, the scholium generally was a short or longer comment on the adjoining text, taken from some authoritative commentary, and the commentary could be a set interpretation of the work occupying the margins (lateral, top, and bottom) of the text of the manuscript; in some cases, if not actually swallowing the text, at least furnishing a frame on three sides, formidable, and often of great value[1].

Now a scholium is usually a short marginal note, explaining a difficult passage, or criticizing or interpreting the text or the author's treatment of his theme; or again it may be a comment quite remote from the adjacent text which the scholiast in some way thinks is germane. The scholium was usually written by a philologist, grammarian, or professional writer. Sometimes,

---

1. Papyrus manuscripts are rarely surrounded by marginal notes (scholia or commentaries) as is the case in later vellum codices (Vide: F. W. Hall: *A Companion to Classical Texts*, Oxford, 1913, p. 13; Wilamowitz-Mollendorff: *Herakles*, 1899.

The Plautine Scholium
(A Fragment)

however, the scholium was the note of an individual owner of the manuscript. Often, and this was the importance of the marginal notes, the scholium was an excerpt from an authoritative source, sometimes the opinion of a known original authority, sometimes the dictum of an apparently ancient but unknown scholar.

And so literary technicians have labored through the ages, at least from the era of Alexandria, to explain the dubious phrase, to excise the corrupt passage and to present for future readers a clear and reasonably authentic original text of the ancient classics. But in addition, the curious mind of scholarship could not fail to set forth matters of literary or historic interest, and so the extant scholia is a mine of most valuable, important, and sometime dubious information from which modern scholarship must attempt to extract the grains of gold to be used in reconstructing some important or fascinating institution, person, or era of the past.

In the library of the old Collegio Romano, a fifteenth century parchment codex of Plautus, containing fifteen of his plays, was being examined in 1819 by the classical scholar F. Osann, when he discovered a curious scholium concerning the Alexandrian Library, on the page of the manuscript where the final six lines of the *Poenulus* occur and on which the *Mostellaria* begins with its Argument and the first ten lines of the play[1]. The scholium gave as its authority a certain Caecius in his Commentary on the Plutus of Aristophanes.

Osann communicated his discovery to Meineke. That is the beginning of the history of the scholium. Meineke published it in *Quaest. Scen. Spec.* (III, p. 3); in 1830 in *Rheinisches Museum* (IV, p. 232). W. Dindorf identified Caecius with Johnnes Tzetzes, the Byzantine scholar of the twelfth century. Although Cramer[2] does not "quite accept the identification of Cecius" as Tzetzes, the conjecture of Dindorf has met with most modern approval[3]. H. Keil in 1847 published *The Prolegomena to Aristophanes* by Johnnes Tzetzes, from a codex ("Cod. Ambrosianus C. 222 sup.

---

1. We give the number of lines as actually written by the copyist in the manuscript, although in early printed editions, such as Aldus, 1522, the number of lines embodying this text is thirteen, and in the late edition, 1924, Nixon (L.C.L.) it is fifteen lines.
2. J. A. Cramer: *Anecdota graeca e codd. manuscriptis Bibliothecae Regiae Parisiensis*, Oxford, 1839 (Vol. I, p. 3).
3. A. W. Mair: *Callimachus and Lycophron*, London, 1921 (pp. 9–10).

4 mai bombycinus, saec. XIII, qui olim Georgii Merulae fuit")
in the Ambrosiana, Milan, in *Rheinisches Museum*, VI (1847). The
latest editions of *The Prolegomena* are those of Nanck[1] and Kaibel[2].
Now all this means that the scholiast states that he obtained
his information from Caecius; that Caecius = Johnnes Tzetzes;
that *The Prolegomena to Aristophanes* by Tzetzes has been sought and
that a comparison of the scholium with the two or three versions
of *The Prolegomena* should satisfy reasonable scholarship that the
source or at least the greater part of the scholium is based on Tzetzes.

The Latin text of the scholium was published by F. Ritschl
in 1838[3] and with emendations in 1866[4].

THE PLAUTINE SCHOLIUM FROM CAECIUS

(Tzetzes) reads as follows:

From the commentary of Caecius on the comedies of Aristophanes, on the "Plutus", which we may interpret as "Wealth".

Alexander of Aetolia and Lycophron of Chalcis and Zenodotus
of Ephesus at the request of King Ptolemy, Philadelphus by surname, who wonderfully favored the talents and the fame of
learned men, gathered together the poetical books of Greek
authorship and arranged them in order: Alexander the tragedies,
Lycophron the comedies, and Zenodotus the poems of Homer
and of other illustrious poets. For that king, well acquainted with
the philosophers and other famous authors, having had the volumes sought out at the expense of the royal munificence all over
the world as far as possible by Demetrius of Phaleron (and other
counsellors), made two libraries, one outside the palace, the
other within the palace. In the outer library there were 42,800
volumes; in the palace library 400,000 mixed volumes and
90,000 single volumes and digests, according to Callimachus, a man of the court and royal librarian, who also wrote the
titles for the several volumes. There was also, as one who makes
the same statement, Eratosthenes, not so much later the custodian

1. Nanck: *Lexicon Vindobonense*, St. Petersburg, 1867 (Appendix).
2. Kaibel: *Comicorum Gr. Frag.*, Berlin, 1899 (p. 18 ff.).
3. Dr. Friedrich Ritschl: *Die alexandrinischen Bibliotheken unter den ersten Ptolemaern*,
Breslau, 1838 (pp. 3–4).
4. Dr. F. Ritschl: *Opuscula philologica*, Leipzig, 1866 (Vol. I, pp. 124–25).

of the same library. These learned volumes which he was able to obtain were of all peoples and languages; and the king caused them to be translated into his own language, with the utmost diligence, by excellent interpreters. Now Pisistratus, 200 years before Ptolemy Philadelphus and with all the more ingenious care, gathered into the volumes that now exist the poetry of Homer, which previously had been scattered, using for this divine purpose the industry of four very famous and learned men: namely, Coneylus, Onomacritus of Athens, Zopyrus of Heraclea, and Orpheus of Croton. For before that time Homer was to be read in separate pieces and with great difficulty. And after the care of Pisistratus and the diligence of Ptolemy, Aristarchus attended still more carefully to the perfecting of the collection of Homer, Heliodorus says many things absurdly to the contrary, which Tzetzes reproves in a long refutation. For he (Heliodorus) says that Homer was thus assembled by 72 learned men appointed to this task by Pisistratus, who (i.e. the 72) indeed approved the industry of Zenodotus and Aristarchus, preferred to all others. Which is obviously false, since there were more than 200 years between Pisistratus and Zenodotus, and Aristarchus was younger by four (and█) years than both Zenodotus and Ptolemy[1].

We will print the scholium, line for line, with brief critical comment.

SCHOLIUM

Text: Alexander of Aetolia and Lycophron of Chalcis and Zenodotus of Ephesus at the request of King Ptolemy, Philadelphus by surname, who wonderfully favored the talents and the fame of learned men, gathered together the poetical books of Greek authorship and arranged them in order: Alexander the tragedies, Lycophron the comedies, and Zenodotus the poems of Homer and of other illustrious poets.

Comment: Correct. Referring, of course, to matter following the reign of Ptolemy Soter.

Text: For that king, well acquainted with the philosophers and other famous authors, having had the volumes sought out at the

---

1. This translation was made by Dr. Ernest H. Wilkins, the distinguished medieval and renaissance scholar, former president of Oberlin College.

expense of the royal munificence all over the world as far as possible by Demetrius of Phaleron (and other counsellors), made two libraries, one outside the palace, the other within the palace.

Comment: That king could not be Ptolemy II, but was almost without doubt Ptolemy Soter. Merely another (of many) instances giving all credit to Ptolemy II, like to Lorenzo di Medici or Louis XIV.

Text: In the outer library there were 42,800 volumes; in the palace library 400,000 mixed volumes and 90,000 single volumes and digests, according to Callimachus, a man of the court and royal librarian, who also wrote the titles for the several volumes.

Comment: Correct. (The outer library was the Serapeum; in the palace library was the great Alexandriana in the Brucheion.)

Text: There was also, as one who makes the same statement, Eratosthenes, not so much later the custodian of the same library.

Comment: Significantly correct, for Eratosthenes was "not so much later" (than Callimachus) "the custodian of the same library"; he was doubtlessly his successor, with the possible interposition of Apollonius of Rhodes.

Text: These learned volumes which he was able to obtain were of all peoples and languages; and the king caused them to be translated into his own language, with the utmost diligence, by excellent interpreters.

Comment: The king, Pharaoh, Ptolemy, generic names of Egyptian kings. In this instance, the king may be Ptolemy Soter, Ptolemy "Philadelphus", or some other Ptolemaic king. We hold with Dr. Swete that it was probably Soter.

Text: Now Pisistratus, 200 years before Ptolemy Philadelphus and with all the more ingenious care, gathered into the volumes that now exist the poetry of Homer, which previously had been scattered, using for this divine purpose the industry of four very famous and learned men: namely, Coneylus, Onomacritus of Athens, Zopyrus of Heraclea, and Orpheus of Croton.

Comment: Doubtlessly essentially correct, even if our extant sources start with Cicero (*De Or.* III-137) and Pausanias, VII-26-13. See further comment on similar passages in Tzetzes.

Text: For before that time Homer was to be read in separate pieces and with great difficulty.

Comment: May be correct.

Text: And after the care of Pisistratus and the diligence of Ptolemy, Aristarchus attended still more carefully to the perfecting of the collection of Homer, Heliodorus says many things absurdly to the contrary, which Tzetzes reproves in a long refutation.

Comment: Essentially correct as to Pisistratus; Ptolemy II had Zenodotus edit Homer. Aristarchus, of course, much later, correct. Rest, as to Heliodorus, unimportant.

Text: For he (Heliodorus) says that Homer was thus assembled by 72 learned men appointed to this task by Pisistratus, who (i.e. the 72) indeed approved the industry of Zenodotus and Aristarchus, preferred to all others.

Comment: Of course incorrect, but of no importance.

Text: Which is obviously false, since there were more than 200 years between Pisistratus and Zenodotus, and Aristarchus was younger by four (and ■) years than both Zenodotus and Ptolemy.

Comment: Quite unimportant, although there were just about 200 years between Pisistratus's death, 527 B.C., and the supposed date of Zenodotus's birth, c. 325 B.C. Aristarchus was younger than Zenodotus by four (and an hundred and one) years if he (Aristarchus) was born c. 220. Ptolemy (Philadelphus) was at least 17 years younger than Zenodotus and so Aristarchus was 88 years younger than Ptolemy Philadelphus, who, indeed, died (247 B.C.) 27 years before Aristarchus was born!

The translation of *The Prolegomena* or *The Prooemia to Aristophanes* by Tzetzes, which we believe is the source of the Plautine scholium, is based on the third form of *The Prolegomenon*, printed in Kaibel[1]. The three forms are designated as Pb, Ma (a very brief summary) and Mb. As the scholium is much closer to the third form than to the other two, we give a translation of this Mb form. It is thought that Kaibel in a note on this third form did not accept the conjecture of Dindorf or the identification of

1. Kaibel refers to Ritschl: *Opusc.* I–5; and to Karl Dziatzko: *Rheinisches Museum*, 46, 349.

other scholars, as to the source of the scholium; yet the more the matter is considered, the sounder becomes the attribution.

If Tzetzes is the source of the Plautine Scholium, the authority of Tzetzes would prevail in cases of clear conflict, although it is possible that the scholiast had access to other sources now unknown.

The translation of Tzetzes is as follows:

THE PROLEGOMENA TO ARISTOPHANES

by Johnnes Tzetzes (Kaibel: Mb. 1-28-34).

(28) Under the royal patronage of Ptolemy Philadelphus, Alexander of Aetolia edited the books of tragedy, Lycophron of Chalcis those of comedy, and Zenodotus of Ephesus those of Homer and the other poets. (29) That Ptolemy, the king I spoke of, was really the most philosophic and divine soul, and desired everything fine – sights, deeds, and words. Through Demetrius of Phaleron and other councillors, he collected the books at royal expense from all over and housed them in Alexandria in two libraries. The public library had 42,800 books; the private library of the court and palace had 400,000 unsorted books, and 90,000 single, sorted books, as Callimachus states, who was a young man of the court and catalogued the books after they were edited. (30) His contemporary Eratosthenes was entrusted by the king with the important post of librarian. The work of Callimachus and Eratosthenes took place a short time after the collecting and editing of the books (as I said) – even within the lifetime of Ptolemy Philadelphus himself. (31) Once all the Greek books and those of every foreign nation – Hebrew included – were collected, then that generous king, who was a river flowing with gold and emptying it through seven mouths, had the foreign books rendered into Greek script and language by scholars to whom the original language was native and who also spoke perfect Greek. For example, the Hebrew works were done by seventy-two Hebrew translators who were experts in both languages. (32) Aside from translating the foreign books, he had the Greek books edited, as I said before: those of tragedy by Alexander of Aetolia, comedy by Lycophron, the other poets by Zenodotus of Ephesus and in particular the Homeric books, which had at the instance of

Pisistratus been put together by these four wise men – Epicon-cylus, Onomacritus of Athens, Zopyrus of Heraclea, and Orpheus of Croton – 200 years or more before Ptolemy Philadelphus and the edition of Zenodotus. (33) So at the time of Pisistratus, the Ho-meric writings, which circulated in separate pieces, were put together by these four wise men and became books. At the time of Philadelphus, as I said, they were edited. After Zenodotus, they were again edited by Aristarchus, who came fourth or fifth after Zenodotus. (34) That foul and odious Heliodorus, who does not know what foolery he is sporting, gets it all mixed up and makes a goulash out of the facts. He is crazy to say that under Pisistratus Homer was put together and edited by the Seventy-two (sc. rabbis!) but the arrangement and the edition of Zenodo-tus and Aristarchus were approved over all others. Still he in-fluenced me, while I was still young, just growing my first beard, to talk this way when I expounded Homer. So did several other highfalutin' fellows who have their heads in the clouds. Without examination I took their word for, oh, one expression, instead of verifying the facts from the material in the ancient manuscript. I made a fool of myself following them; but after it happened to me once or twice because of my youth, I took a lesson from grief[1].

TZETZES

Text: (28) Under the royal patronage of Ptolemy Philadelphus, Alexander of Aetolia edited the books of tragedy, Lycophron of Chalcis those of comedy, and Zenodotus of Ephesus those of Homer and the other poets.

Comment: Correct. Referring to time following Ptolemy Soter.

Text: (29) That Ptolemy, the king I spoke of, was really the most philosophic and divine soul, and desired everything fine – sights, deeds, and words.

Comment: Usual praise of Ptolemy II or Louis XIV.

Text: Through Demetrius of Phaleron and other councillors, he

---

1. This translation was made by Mr. Saul Levin, a Hellenist of the Society of Fellows, Harvard University.

collected the books at royal expense from all over and housed them in Alexandria in two libraries.

Comment: "He" could *not* mean Ptolemy II, but Ptolemy Soter. As soon as Ptolemy II became king, *he* banished Demetrios and probably caused his death.

Text: The public library had 42,800 books; the private library of the court and palace had 400,000 unsorted books, and 90,000 single, sorted books, as Callimachus states, who was a young man of the court and catalogued the books after they were edited.

Comment: Doubtlessly correct.

Text: (30) His contemporary Eratosthenes was entrusted by the king with the important post of librarian.

Comment: What *king*? Not Ptolemy II who died 25th January, 245 B.C. *Eratosthenes* was called by Ptolemy Euergetes to Alexandria from Athens, where he had sojourned many years, in c. 235 B.C. and became librarian under Ptolemy Euergetes who died c. 222 B.C. and also under Ptolemy Philopater (222–205).

Text: The work of Callimachus and Eratosthenes took place a short time after the collecting and editing of the books (as I said) – even within the lifetime of Ptolemy Philadelphus himself.

Comment: Partly true for Callimachus, and indeed up to the word "books". Not possible for Eratosthenes who returned to Alexandria about 235 B.C., ten years after death of Ptolemy "Philadelphus", certainly under Ptolemy Euergetes. Dziatzko (Pauly-Wissowa, II, p. 412) remarks that the words of Tzetzes or the scholium Plautinian are not quite in order. "Die Worte des Tzetzes oder des Schol. Plaut. sind übrigens an dieser Stelle nicht in Ordnung." (III-412.) Merely another of the many examples of giving Ptolemy II credit for all things.

Text: (31) Once all the Greek books and those of every foreign nation – Hebrew included – were collected, then that generous king, who was a river flowing with gold and emptying it through seven mouths, had the foreign books rendered into Greek script and language by scholars to whom the original language was native and who also spoke perfect Greek.

Comment: Could convey a part truth, but requires elaborate consideration of the whole question of the translation of the Pentateuch (the Septuagint).

Text: For example, the Hebrew works were done by seventy-two Hebrew translators who were experts in both languages.

Comment: The old legend of Aristeas, often treated in this treatise.

Text: (32) Aside from translating the foreign books, he had the Greek books edited, as I said before: those of tragedy by Alexander of Aetolia, comedy by Lycophron, the other poets by Zenodotus of Ephesus and in particular the Homeric books, which had at the instance of Pisistratus been put together by these four wise men — Epiconcylus, Onomacritus of Athens, Zopyrus of Heraclea, and Orpheus of Croton — 200 years or more before Ptolemy Philadelphus and the edition of Zenodotus.

Comment: First part repetition of the facts. Second part doubtlessly essentially correct. Even the chronology: if Pisistratus died in 527 and Zenodotus was born about 325, there was almost exactly 200 years between them. Ptolemy II ("Philadelphus") was born 308 and died 245 B.C.

Text: (33) So at the time of Pisistratus, the Homeric writings, which circulated in separate pieces, were put together by these four wise men and became books.

Comment: Doubtlessly essentially correct; as to the names of three of the "wise men", one, Epiconcylus, is hopelessly corrupt; as to their execution of the literary commission, the tradition has provoked, as usual, much Homeric controversy.

Text: At the time of Philadelphus, as I said, they were edited.

Comment: By Zenodotus? Correct.

Text: After Zenodotus, they were again edited by Aristarchus, who came fourth or *fifth* after Zenodotus.

Comment: They were certainly edited by Aristarchus, who was the *fifth* or sixth after Zenodotus.

LIST OF LIBRARIANS AFTER ZENODOTUS:

First List: 1. Callimachus of Cyrene
2. Eratosthenes of Cyrene
3. Apollonius of Rhodes
4. Aristophanes of Byzantium
5. Aristarchus of Samothrace

We believe this was what Tzetzes considered quite correct. However, for those who think so much of Oxyrhynchus Papyrus (1241), of which Tzetzes knew nothing, Aristarchus would still be the *fifth* after Zenodotus if we omit Callimachus, and this list would be:

Second List: 1. Apollonius of Alexandria
2. Eratosthenes
3. Aristophanes of Byzantium
4. Apollonius the "Classifier"
5. Aristarchus of Samothrace

But for those who will not accept this fragment of papyrus (Ox. P. 1241) without study or proper exegesis, with such scholars as Dr. Beloch, we would still find Aristarchus fifth:

Third List: 1. Callimachus
2. Eratosthenes
3. Aristophanes of Byzantium
4. Apollonius the Eidograph
5. Aristarchus

It is only when Dr. Beloch is willing to allow Apollonius of Rhodes a place on the list that the position of Aristarchus becomes sixth. (Vide p. 160 of this work).

Text: (34) That foul and odious Heliodorus, who does not know what foolery he is sporting, gets it all mixed up and makes a goulash out of the facts.

Comment: Of no importance.

Text: He is crazy to say that under Pisistratus Homer was put together and edited by the Seventy-two (sc. rabbis!) but the arrangement and the edition of Zenodotus and Aristarchus were approved over all others.

Comment: Of no importance.

Text: Still he influenced me, while I was still young, just growing my first beard, to talk this way when I expounded Homer.

Comment: This is Tzetzes, that "copious, careless, quarrelsome, Byzantine polymath", as he is described by his latest biographer (Dr. P. B. R. Forbes in *The Oxford Classical Dictionary*, s.v. *Tzetzes* (Oxford, 1949). It is well known that this scholar was extremely inaccurate, due perhaps to his separation from his library. "Nevertheless, he preserved much valuable information from ancient scholarship."

Text: So did several other highfalutin' fellows who have their heads in the clouds.

Comment: Personal to Tzetzes.

Text: Without examination I took their word for, oh, one expression, instead of verifying the facts from the material in the ancient manuscript.

Comment: Important for the admission of Tzetzes, that he merely took someone's word for some of his statements, *instead of verifying the facts from the material in the ancient manuscript,* showing that he did have access to good sources.

Text: I made a fool of myself following them; but after it happened to me once or twice because of my youth, I took a lesson from grief.

Comment: Personal to Tzetzes.

Any general survey of the texts of the scholium and of Tzetzes should lead to the following reasonable and probable conclusions: that Tzetzes had access to good sources, perhaps to Callimachus, Eratosthenes, or their contemporaries, or certainly sound sources derived from them; that in spite of his admitted carelessness in not consulting the original manuscripts, and the unavoidable misfortune of his being separated at times from his books, he is guilty of very few errors in his *Prolegomena*, indeed, if we examine his *Prooemia* line for line, there is but *one* serious and, in our judgment, most obvious error, his obsession that his favorite Ptolemy II (called "Philadelphus") was the presiding genius over all matters, many of which we believe took place in the days of his father Soter, and some with certainty in the days of his son, Ptolemy III, Euergetes, after his (Ptolemy II's) death. Giving Ptolemy II full credit for everything he did, and merely removing the name "Philadelphus" from assignments impossible for chronological reasons or for the most reasonable and sound traditions that have survived, which together with admitted authenticated facts form not only the history of the Museum and Library of Alexandria, but most of the history of the Ptolemaic dynasty – with this reasonable single correction, Tzetzes has become a primary authority on the origin and growth of the Alexandriana.

And especially remembering Dziatzko's critical observance that the words of Tzetzes or the scholium Plautinian are not quite in order (Pauly-Wissowa, II, p. 412) we would venture an emendation of Tzetzes or an arrangement of his text according to our best traditional and historical remains.

TZETZES, AS EMENDED AND REARRANGED

Through Demetrius of Phaleron and other councillors, he [Ptolemy Soter] collected the books at royal expense from all over and housed them in Alexandria in two libraries. The public library [the Serapeum] had 42,800 books; the private library of the court and palace [the Alexandriana in the Brucheion] had 400,000 unsorted books, and 90,000 single books, as Callimachus states, who was a young man of the court and catalogued the books after they were edited.

Under the royal patronage of Ptolemy "Philadelphus", Alexander of Aetolia edited the books of tragedy, Lycophron of Chalcis those of comedy, and Zenodotus of Ephesus those of Homer and the other poets. That Ptolemy, the king I spoke of, was really the most philosophic and divine soul, and desired everything fine – sights, deeds, and words. Once all the Greek books and those of every foreign nation – Hebrew included – were collected, then that generous king, who was a river flowing with gold and emptying it through seven mouths, had the foreign books rendered into Greek script and language by scholars to whom the original language was native and who also spoke perfect Greek. For example, the Hebrew works were done by seventy-two Hebrew translators who were experts in both languages. Aside from translating the foreign books, he had the Greek books edited, as I said before: those of tragedy by Alexander of Aetolia, comedy by Lycophron, the other poets by Zenodotus of Ephesus and in particular the Homeric books, which had at the instance of Pisistratus been put together by these four wise men — Epiconcylus, Onomacritus of Athens, Zopyrus of Heraclea, and Orpheus of Croton — 200 years or more before Ptolemy "Philadelphus" and the edition of Zenodotus. So at the time of Pisistratus, the Homeric writings, which circulated in separate pieces, were put together by these four wise men and became books. At the time of "Philadelphus", as I said, they were edited. After Zenodotus, they were again edited by Aristarchus, who came fourth or fifth after Zenodotus. His [i.e. Callimachus's] contemporary, Eratosthenes, was entrusted by the king [Ptolemy III, Euergetes] with the important post of librarian. The work of Callimachus and Eratosthenes took place a short time after the collecting and editing of the books (as I said) even within the lifetime of Ptolemy [i.e. the work of Callimachus in the lifetime of Ptolemy II, "Philadelphus", and   Ptolemy III, Euergetes; and that of Eratosthenes in the lifetime of Ptolemy III, Euergetes, and Ptolemy IV, Philopator]. (The concluding part of the *Prolegomena*, from "That foul and odious Heliodorus", to the end is entirely unimportant.)

A reasonable appreciation of the *Prolegomena* of Tzetzes and the Plautinian scholium, whether the latter was derived wholly or in part from the *Prolegomena*, or if the scholium is in no way derived from Tzetzes, but is an independent scholium founded on an unknown author, Caecius, in any event shows that they are founded upon an early and sound source and justifies the essential facts disclosed in the traditions and accounts preserved in the authorities who deign to mention the Alexandrian Museum and Library, from the pseudo-Aristeas, through the few Greek and Roman classical writers to nearly all the fathers of the Church.

From these sources we may reach the reasonable conclusion that the Museum and Library were founded by Ptolemy Soter at the suggestion and through the labors and genius of the experienced academician, scholar, and statesman, Demetrios of Phaleron. Ptolemy II, Soter's son, enthusiastically followed his father in collecting books and scholars, as did, in his turn, his own son Ptolemy III, Euergetes. Indeed, most of their successors, good and bad, had some interest in culture, and we believed did something for the great Alexandrian Hellenic University, which, existing nearly three centuries in an age still Hellenic, was to survive for a longer period in an age entirely Roman.

It may not be out of place to conclude this chapter with an account of the rediscovery of the original manuscript of Plautus, containing the scholium, after its probable loss for nearly a century.

The desire to find the manuscript was originally prompted by a wish to check the corrupt words or passage in the copy of the scholium printed by Ritschl, the mysterious "phzxa" or the more hopeless "XXX".

It was well known that Osann had found the scholium on the margin of a fifteenth century manuscript of Plautus, designated 4. c. 39, in the Collegio Romano. This was in 1819.

Osann sent the beginning of the scholium to the young philologist, Johann Meineke, and Friedrich Ritschl published a text of the scholium, with emendations, yet with a curious hiatus. How long the Plautus manuscript remained in the Collegio Romano we do not know. We did know that it was a parchment codex of the fifteenth century, containing fifteen plays of Plautus and that it was designated 4. c. 39. We also know the exact place or page in the manuscript where the scholium occurred.

Now the Collegio Romano occupied a large edifice built by Ammanati at the end of the sixteenth century under the Popes Gregory XIII and Sixtus V. It had an important library, where Osann fortunately found the scholium. In one of the tragic historic episodes to which the eternal city has been subject for over two and a half millennia, in 1870, the House of Savoy and the republicans took the City of Rome. They took the Collegio Romano, and the library became the Biblioteca (Centrale) Vittorio Emanuele. The matter seemed quite simple; we would examine the manuscript there. Through the gracious courtesy of a distinguished scholar[1], a search was made for me in the Biblioteca Vit. Emanuele, where two paper codices of Plautus, both of the fifteenth century, were found. The first has 101 leaves (marked V.E. 975) and contains seven of the plays of Plautus; the second has 208 leaves (V.E. 365) and contains six of the plays. Both manuscripts were acquired after 1870 and, of course, were not the object of our search. We next sought the Vatican Library and after a difficult search there found a parchment codex with the following designation:

> Vat. Lat. 11469, Codex membranae. in 4.° Ms. Saec. XV cum pluribus adnotationibus inter lineas et in margine. Constat foliis scriptis 250 – Dono di Pio X.

Although we were seeking a parchment from the Jesuits' Library (Collegio Romano) marked 4. c. 39, a parchment codex containing fifteen plays, this codex was on parchment and had fifteen plays of Plautus, but all of its former provenance was missing. However, it was the manuscript we were seeking, and the scholium from Caecius (= Tzetzes) on the Alexandrian Library was found on the verso of page 184 between the end of the *Poenulus* and the beginning of the *Mostellaria*.

The Plautine page with the scholium is reproduced by special permission of Cardinal Mercati, librarian of the Vatican Library, as a frontispiece of this treatise, in the interest of scholarship.

---

1. I am again indebted to Dr. Evaristo Breccia for all of these researches which he so kindly made for me and which resulted in the rediscovery of the original Plautine codex with the Alexandrian scholium.

CHAPTER VIII

THE PERSONNEL OF THE ALEXANDRIAN LIBRARY

THE wisest, certainly the most successful of the successors of Alexander, was the first Ptolemy whom we correctly call Soter. He founded an empire that lasted three centuries; within that empire he built a city that for seven hundred years was a wonder of the earth; and within that city he established a unique institution of culture, The University of Egypt (The Museum-Library) which for that time and probably for over nine hundred years was the intellectual luminary of the world.

This rugged Macedonian mountaineer, reared among the children of chieftains and the king's son, was the possessor of varied talents. To his native military ability, he added the characters of diplomat and statesman, and from his early years must have had a leaning towards things of culture which he might well have developed through his association with Alexander. That he had a certain flare for learning is amply shown when as soon as he had laid the foundations of his House and Empire and as the great city was rapidly arising in splendor around him, he sensed the lasting quality of its true greatness as the intellectual center of the ancient world. The world must not only look to Alexandria as the seat of power and social order, as the mart of trade and commerce, as the possessor of great wealth, but in this city in the center of the civilized world must be the treasury of learning and science, the place that men must seek who want to know. With the energy he had given to statesmanship, diplomacy, and arms to create the Hellenic empire in Egypt, he now sought by every means to lure the poets, philosophers, scientists, and men of learning to come and abide with him in his fair, wealthy, and luxurious Greek city in the land of ancient knowledge, wonder, and mystery.

In this, like in most efforts, he was successful. It is true he could not get the philosophers Theophrastus to leave Athens nor

Stelpo to leave Megara, nor Menander, the great master of the New Comedy to forego his luxurious life in Athens and the Piraeus, even for the fabulous life and career offered at the court of Ptolemy. But few could resist the call to an easy life, rich with the varied opportunities of the amazing city. If Theophrastus would not come, Strato, his pupil and successor, came; if Menander would not leave Glycira, Philemon, his popular rival, came at least later for a time to Alexandria. A stream of intellectuals eagerly responded to the gracious invitation of the Ptolemies. Many men of the highest rank, such as Euclid, the mathematician; Herophilus, the anatomist and physician; the philosophers Theodorus, Diodorus the Carian, Hegesias of Cyrene; from Cyrene the great Callimachus and Eratosthenes; Hecataeus of Abdera; indeed, a host came from the African mainland, the islands, Asia Minor, and the motherland of Hellas, many of these after the time of Soter.

As Alexandria was an entirely new city, she had, of course, no native intellectuals, in fact she had no natives of any sort, except the Egyptian inhabitants of the old fishing-village, Rhakotis. As she needed government officials, the Macedonian-Greeks came to embrace the opportunity; as she needed soldiers they came from all the soldier-markets of the Mediterranean; as she required trade, the merchants, capitalists, and businessmen flocked to get in on the "ground-floor"; the irresistible call went forth that here where were being assembled the greatest gathering of men, there were required, in large and permanent values, all the things that men would need or desire. Ptolemy's wish to make his city a seat of learning required indeed a different approach. Here again his good fortune and his good judgment did not fail. Among the men who came from the Greek motherland, was an extraordinary person, rich in many experiences both of victory and defeat, a man of letters, but also a man of the world, a philosopher, yet also a politician, a man who had drunk from many a kalix of high power and super luxury, yet who had, both before and after, eaten of coarse cheese and drunk the dregs of the last vintage – Demetrios of Phaleron. And what is more important still, he was a man that Ptolemy Soter thoroughly understood, whom he trusted and made his companion and friend. In the leaden period of his life Demetrios had possessed temporary power and cheap renown, and had little to look backwards to with pleasure. Now in the last but golden days of his life he could associate with kings as companion and friend, and he was able to suggest and bring about the crowning glory of Ptolemy Soter, as well as to achieve his own lasting personal renown.

As we shall often meet the known leading scholars who in building the first great library laid the foundation for all subsequent ideas and systems in bibliography, it would seem proper that we recall at least the known famous *dramatis personae* of the Alexandrian Library.

I. DEMETRIOS OF PHALERON

Though from an humble stock, undoubtedly
Was fashion'd to much honour from his cradle.
He was a scholar, and a ripe and good one;
Exceeding wise, fair-spoken and persuading:
Lofty and sour to them that loved him not,
But to those men that sought him, sweet as summer.

HY. VIII–4–2

ATHENS – HIS POLITICAL CAREER

At Phaleron, one of the three ports of Athens, Demetrios was born ca. 354–348 B.C. He was the son of Phanostratus. Whatever may have been his humble origin[1], he received the liberal education of an Athenian youth of the upper class. Amidst the shady walks of the Lyceum, as the pupil of Theophrastus, the favorite disciple and successor of Aristotle, he imbibed the practical wisdom of the Peripatetic school. He must have often heard the great Master himself[2]. Here he was taught the serene ethics of the Lyceum: a calm, moderate, rational view of life. From careful observation of the reality of things and systematic inquiry into the origins and experiences of life, we should know ourselves and

1. Diogenes Laertius: *Lives of Eminent Philosophers*, V-76: "He was one of Conon's household servants, according to Favorinus in the first book of his *Memorabilia*." As Conon died (probably at Cyprus c. 392 B.C.) about forty years before the birth of Demetrios, it is just possible that his father could have held this humble station. So Aelian: *Var. Hist.*, XII-42, and the learned translator of Athenaeus says he was the son of a slave.
2. So Pauly asserts (Pauly-Wissowa, IV–2818).

to ourselves be true, pursuing the good and beautiful and rejecting that which is evil and imperfect. Aristotle, the carefully chosen tutor of Alexander, was the most practical of men and Theophrastus was perhaps not out of step with his master, when he dedicated some of his writings to Cassander. It is reasonable to assume that the finer, as well as some of the practical aspects of the character of Demetrios took root in the philosophical school where he was the companion, and later the patron of Deinarchus, the last, if the least, of the ten Attic orators, and of Menander, the supreme master of the New Comedy. The acts of friendship shown by Demetrios, when he had great power, to these early associates of his studies, is a happy augury if not a confirmation of his character.

He early entered public life, beginning his career between his twenty-fourth–thirtieth year (c. 324 B.C.), displaying high talent as a public orator.

His brother Himeraeus was an ardent member of the anti-Macedonian party, active in the Lamian war, and like Demosthenes and Hyperides against the cause of Alexander and his successors. After the victory of Antipater, Demosthenes killed himself, and Hyperides and Himeraeus were torn from the sanctuary of a temple in Aegina and put to death. Demetrios who greatly loved his brother offered divine rites in the privacy of his home, thinking of how Patroclus appeared to Achilles[1]. His enemies raised a hue and cry of sacrilege, and Demetrios went to Peiraeus to stay with Nicanor, through whom he met Cassander. Demetrios was a member of the party of Phocion, the party of peace and conciliation. Phocion was condemned by the Athenians to drink the hemlock, an act described by Holm as[2] "one of the darkest stains on the fair fame of Athens".

Cassander, son of Antipater, was one of the most ruthless of the *epigoni*, faithless and cruel, yet "the wisest head in the world's councils"[3]; a great lover of art who could recite Homer by heart; truly a man of the age of despots, or shall we say of the early Renaissance. He appointed the brilliant young Athenian his vice-roy

1. Carystius of Pergamum: *Notes* (Bk. III); Athenaeus (XII–542–f); Pauly-Wissowa (s.v. *Epiphaneia*), Suppl. IV-304.
2. Holm: *op. cit.* IV-26.
3. W. W. Tarn (in C.A.H., Vol. VII, p. 78).

or governor of Athens. "His choice of the Phalerean Demetrius," says the great historian of democracy[1], "appears to have been judicious."

At the outset of his political career it is just that we quote the wise and liberal opinion of Niebuhr[2]:

> It was unfortunate for Demetrius, that his position was connected with the servitude of his country; but his conscience was free, for, although he was then still young, he did not surrender his country to the Macedonians... But he lived for the circumstances by which he was surrounded.

The same scholar declared[3]:

> The fact of Demetrius being governor of Athens was a very fortunate circumstance for the city.

He administered the affairs of Athens for ten years (317–307 B.C.) with ability, moderation, and considerable success. It must be remembered that the Athenians at no time were easy to govern; that in the most favored period of their extraordinary history they were perhaps the most difficult problem for government: the most gifted of the children of men, the creators of earthly beauty, with an art appreciation beyond all those who have ever lived, loquacious, litigious, the supreme individualists of time, who in the serene contemplation of soul, in thought, in word, and in the visible aspect of things, attained to unknown heights.

This was the difficult task of Demetrios, in the autumn days of Athens. That he ruled Athens for ten years with moderation and without disaster is an achievement. True, he governed Athens somewhat as a princely autocracy, and the shade of Pisistratus might have hovered over the Acropolis, as Demetrios foreshadowed the rule of the Medici in Florence. But it should not be forgotten that he kept from his fellow citizens the daily reminder of foreign domination. He kept the Macedonian garrison in distant barracks at Munychia; he had no troops to accentuate his power; his detractors speak of his strolling in the streets of Athens; he tried to eliminate the presence of force, save in the administration of the law. He, at least, was always an Athenian,

1. George Grote: *History of Greece*, 2nd ed., London, 1857 (Vol. XII, p. 489).
2. B. G. Niebuhr: *Lectures on Ancient History*, London, 1852 (Vol. III, p. 84).
3. Idem: VII, p. 80.

DEMETRIOS OF PHALERON

Florence

one of their own. His fellow citizens voted him 360 statues (some on foot, some equestrian, and some in chariots) in unique appreciation of his public service, which, allowing for the usual modicum of sycophancy, must have reflected some shadow of personal esteem. He did attempt to impose some laws of a sumptuary nature, such as the regulations of the number of guests at a feast, and the regulations of funerals by limiting their expense and directing that they should be held before daylight. These were, of course, unpopular, and doubtless, like all sumptuary laws, unenforceable.

A man of his temperament and talents must have contributed much to the cultural life of Athens. We knew he celebrated sumptuously the Panathenaic festivals and gave great games. He brought back the ancient recitatives of the rhapsodists and the theatre of Athens again heard the exquisite renditions of the Homeric poems[1].

Under his administration an important census was taken which according to Ctesicles[2], reported:

> 21,000 citizens
> 10,000 metics
> 400,000 slaves

Boeckh[3] resolves this, adding the women and children, into:

> 90,000 citizens
> 45,000 resident aliens
> 365,000 slaves
> _____
> 500,000 total population

Clinton[4] makes the estimate 527,660, as he says that in spite of the many inconveniences of an ill-balanced democracy, Athens "in the days of Demetrius Phalereus is found with as large population, and a trade as extensive as it possessed in the days of Pericles". Although Athens now had no allies, or rather subject states, and only export, import, and personal or indirect

1. Athenaeus: 620 B.
2. Ctesicles: *Chronicles*, Bk. III; Apud: Athenaeus: VI–272–b.
3. Auguste Boeckh: *The Public Economy of Athens*, 2nd ed., London, 1842 (pp. 35–36).
4. Hy. Hynes Clinton: *An Epitome of the Civil and Literary Chronology of Greece*, Oxford, 1841 (p. 292).

taxes from which to draw, Demetrios is praised for having increased the state revenues, which Duris of Samos[1] places at 1200 talents. These revenues were used for administrative maintenance of the state, maintaining the garrison, embellishing the city with public buildings, paintings, etc.[2] and giving expensive games, and finally for ample allowance for the up-keep of his own princely state.

It is, indeed, concerning the last item of expense that the yellow press of antiquity, the imperial writers of anecdota, have indulged their love for sensation and their conscienceless abuse of freedom of expression. In order, however, not to suppress anything that is said by the ancient authors of this distinguished man, I report their salacious gossip, as an example of the age-old effort of the vile tribe of scribblers to destroy the prominent, the worthy, or the great.

Demetrios is thus represented as a dilettante, an orator who invented a new type of speech, a philosopher, who dyed his hair blonde, rouged his cheeks, and anointed his person with Eastern salves. Meticulous in his dress, the *arbiter elegantiarum* of his age, in the bright light of day, strolls down Tripod street, seek-ing to allure the handsome idle youths who frequent this famous way. He, who was used to a meal of olives and country cheese, has now become a gourmet. He has purchased Moschion, the most celebrated chef who, in his royal kitchens, with unlimited resources of fish, fowl, meats, and viands of many places and seasons, improvises daily feasts beyond the dream of Macedonian quantity and Cyriote and Phoenician quality. So bountiful indeed are the repasts and so prodigal the service that Moschion, the cook, who receives what is left of the meals as his perquisite, has from this item alone been able top urchase three apartment-houses and to himself become a debauchee. And these Greco-Oriental feasts are held in the luxurious palace of the governor, in vast dining-halls, whose cedar beams prolonged the soft harmony of cithara until the moon hides her face in the morning-light, and upon the revellers' sweet perfumes fall, as professional

---

1. Duris: *Histories*, Bk. XVI; Apud: Athenaeus: XII-542 c. 1200 talents, very roughly $ 1,200,000 or nearly a million and a half dollars, but even this gives a poor idea of its true value and purchasing-power.
2. Klippel: *op. cit.* 54; Pauly: in Pauly-Wissowa, IV-2824.

dancers exhaust patterns of the human form. The mosaic floors, exquisite in floral design, glisten in the flickering light of the dying scented woods in the great bronze torchères or flambeau-baskets in the halls.

But our Sybarite must plumb the nadir of it all, and he must not only, like some Eastern potentate, European king, or Athenian gentleman, have many mistresses, but his palace must be the resort of courtesans, and we are even told of the terms of endearment by which he permitted himself to be called by Lampito, the Samian courtesan[1]. Of course, all this is very non-Athenian and smacks of the more vulgar imperial times.

Finally, it is alleged that in the great processional of the Dionysia, which he marshalled as archon (399–8 B.C.), the chorus sang a dithyramb in honor of Dionysius, by Castorion of Soli, in which Demetrios is praised and of which but two lines survive:

The archon above all others noble, in beauty like the Sun,
Celebrates thee with honours divine[2].

The states of ancient Greece, once the homes of individual freedom and national liberty, were now, like all the countries of the Eastern Mediterranean, pawns in the hands of the *diadochi* and the *epigoni*, the successors of Alexander and their progeny. In 307 B.C., Demetrius, son of Antigonus, "a brave, handsome, and able man, and a man of the world into the bargain, like his namesake of Phalerum"[3] took the Piraeus, and the Athenians received their new master with open arms. He declared they were "free"; they hailed him and his father as kings and gods.

Demetrios of Phaleron proceeded to the camp of the invader on behalf of Athens, but the personality of the son of Antigonus and the delusion of the people that they were going to be free and their desire for change made the task of the hero-invader most simple. Demetrios of Phaleron was banished and went with an escort to Thebes.

Demetrius, son of Antigonus, with Asiatic servility, was hailed by the light and frivolous populace as a hero, deliverer, and as

1. Athenaeus: XIII-593 f.
2. Idem : XII-542 e.
3. Holm: *op. cit.* IV-43.

a god, and so was his father. Altars were erected to them, sacrifices in their honors held. In the great Panathenaea, where the peplos of the goddess is carried in procession, the images of Demetrius and Antigonus were woven with those of the gods[1]. The final infamy of the Athenians was their invitation to their heroic voluptuary to be the house guest of Athena, where in the opisthodomos of her temple, Demetrius, son of Antigonus, resided, unashamed, with his courtesans, in the space behind the great statue of the chaste, dread goddess. A people who had thus desecrated the Parthenon, Temple of the Maiden, may well have destroyed the statues of Demetrios of Phaleron, all save one[2]. They passed a degree condemning Demetrios, their fellow citizen, to death, and now turned to worship Demetrius, the stranger.

Demetrios of Phaleron's work in Athens was finished. He was an exile in Thebes; he may have gone to Macedonia. For some time, perhaps for ten years, the career of this able, active, dynamic thinker, scholar, and statesman is unknown.

We submit the following as the fair verdict of history, as to his difficult task of governing Athens for ten years, spring 317 to spring 307 (Niese):

Grote:

His administration is said to have been discreet and moderate[3].

Thirlwall:

Yet in one very important point he continued to the last to deserve praise: his administration appears to have been quite free from the stain of cruelty: he continued it seems, to exercise his authority mildly, even after he had become conscious that the people were weary of it[4].

Sandys:

For a period of ten years (317–307) he ruled with distinction at Athens as Regent for Cassander[5].

And finally:

1. But the wrath of the gods caused a whirlwind to tear the peplos to pieces.
2. Pauly: Pauly-Wissowa, IV-2819. The statue on the Acropolis, probably the portrait given by Verro, was made from this.
3. Grote: *op. cit.* XII-489.
4. Thirlwall: *op. cit.* VII-358.
5. Sandys: *op. cit.* p. 101.

Leake:

> At no period was Athens more happy and secure than when Demetrius of Phalerum, supported by a Macedonian garrison, administered its affairs[1].

HIS CAREER IN LITERATURE AND SCHOLARSHIP

If the position of Demetrios of Phaleron in politics is open to discussion and the subject of some controversy, his place as a man of letters seems quite secure. He was a ripe and good scholar. Diogenes Laertius was of the opinion that "in learning and versatility he has no equal"[2]. In learning he had many peers and some superiors; in versatility he had but few. He wrote on every subject from Love to Legislation and from Homer to Ptolemy. When his failing sight was restored he wrote in gratitude, *Paeans to Sarapis*, which were sung for six centuries. In criticism, he wrote: *On Homer, On the Iliad, On the Odyssey*; in belles lettres: *On Rhetoric* (where he may have told the story of Demosthenes's correcting his impediments of speech on the sea-shore, which Demetrios is thought to have heard from Demosthenes himself)[3]; essays: *Of Fortune, Of Marriage, Of Old Age*; in philosophy: *An Exhortation to Philosophy*; legalistic writings: *Of Legislation at Athens* in 5 books, *Of the Constitution of Athens* in 2 books, *Of Law*; in politics: *On Politics*; in government: *On Peace, On Military Matters*; in biography: *Aristides, Aristomachus*; in miscellanea: *Anecdotes*, and the curious *Of the Beam in the Sky*. In history Demetrios must have been quite important. If Ephorus was the first to write history from the muniments (monumental and papyrus documents), Demetrios likewise seems to have written a *History of Athens* from the documents, in which he drew up a careful *Fasti* of the Archons. Indeed Niebuhr ventures the opinion that Plutarch in his life of *Solon* is never so trustworthy as when he is following the critical judgments of Aristotle, Demetrios, and

1. Wm. Martin Leake: *The topography of Athens*, London, 1841 (I-19) and also, ch.: Schlosser, Droysen, Schwarcz (*Die Demokratie*, Leipzic, 1882), Wilamowitz (*Antigonos von Karystos*, p. 184). Holm: *op. cit.* IV, p. 60, and Johann Gustav Droysen (*Geschichte des Hellenismus*, Hamburg, 1836, p. 429) are the other way.
2. Diog. Laertius, V-80; V-77.
3. A fragment of an inscriptional catalogue of a Library at Rhodes has lately been discovered containing several (some new) titles of the works of Demetrios. (Powell & Barber: *New Chapters in the History of Greek Literature*, Oxford, 1929, p. 83.)

Philochorus[1]. In oratory, he was the foremost representative of the "intermediate" style, perhaps with the "minimum of force, with the maximum of charm", and with a diction "marked by a placid smoothness", "lit up by the stars of metaphor and metonymy"[2]. Cicero when asked "Did Demetrius of Phaleron speak pure Attic?" replied: "To me at least his orations exhale the very fragrance of Athens"[3]. Such was "the distinguished Demetrius of Phaleron, the most elegant, to my thinking, of all that school"[4]. Cicero is said to have modeled his style on that of Demetrios. At least he was the last of the great Attic orators and would have been one of the Ten, if the three Kings could have been four![5]

Demetrios made a collection of Aesop's *Fables*, the text of which has had so painful a transmission to our time, from Greek to Latin, to Syriac, back to Greek; from verse to semi-prose or prose.

But of all of Demetrios's writings, we would have wished to have survived his *Autobiography* or *On the Ten Years of my Supremacy*, or his *Letters*, particularly the latter which may have illuminated many an incident in his most interesting life, the link between the golden and the silver ages.

He was the last figure of the great Attic period of letters, or shall we say the first of the Alexandrian age.

It was this extraordinary man, old in varied learning, rich in experiences of power and chastened through the vicissitudes of life, that about the year 297 B.C. [6], Ptolemy Soter had the good fortune to induce to come to live in Alexandria. Of all the distinguished men, poets, philosophers, scientists, philologists, who accepted the invitation of Ptolemy to come to the Ptolemaic court and bask in the royal comforts, the brilliant life, the amazing intellectual advantages of the fabulous Greek city of Egypt, none could compare in services to the king, to the glory of his reign, or to the things that should renown Alexandria, with the handsome, cultured Athenian man of letters and man of the world, Demetrios of Phaleron.

1. Niebuhr: *Lectures on Ancient History*, London, 1851 (Vol. I–283).
2. Sandys: *op. cit.* I-102.
3. Cicero: so in *Brutus*, 285 (L.C.L.).
4. Cicero: *De Oratore*, 95 (L.C.L.).
5. Niebuhr's witticism.
6. Mahaffy, 307–306 B.C.; Sandys, 297 B.C.; Pauly-Wissowa, 296–295 B.C.; Auguste Couat, 290 B.C.

It is easy to understand how this man of many gifts soon became the companion, adviser, and friend of Ptolemy, his true friend, not a "friend of the king" in courtier wise. And this position he maintained with honor, dignity, character, and courage throughout the whole life of Ptolemy Soter. How close he was to the king cannot better be shown than that he not only selected the books for the king to read, but in doing this he did not hesitate to persuade his royal patron to study works on liberal government and such matters "which the friends of kings dare not advise" them to read[1]. So intimate was he with the king that he discussed with him the delicate question of the royal succession and bravely advised Ptolemy to follow the rule of custom and to choose his eldest son Keraunos, as his successor. But the sweet persuasion and brilliant logic of the courtier crumbled before the powerful influence of the age-old subtlety of feminine orientalism, and the king, remembering the mild yet compelling intercession of his beloved Berenice, was faithful to her wishes and to her son, although his younger, whom we call Ptolemy "Philadelphus", and to whom he left the great Ptolemaic succession[2]. The fact that Demetrios had advocated an unsuccessful aspirant to the throne in no way interrupted his continued friendship with the old king, yet it ultimately cost him his life. While Soter lived, Demetrios's position was secure, but as soon as the king died (283 B.C.[3] Ptolemy II, perhaps out of respect for his father, did not publicly take his life, yet immediately removed him from the headship of the Museum and Library and banished him to Busiris, near Diospolis, Upper Egypt. There he was bitten by an asp and died. Whether the serpent that stung Demetrios was he who now wore his father's crown, we shall never know[4]. In arid Upper Egypt he slept far from his native surf-sounding Phaleron[5].

1. Plutarch: *The Apophthegms of Kings and Great Commanders.*
2. Sotion: *Successions of Philosophers*, in the *Epitome* of Heraclides, reported by Diogenes Laertius V-79.
3. Ernest Meyer: *Untersuchungen zur Chronologie d. erst. Ptolemy* (1925), pp. 16, 67. He perhaps died in June or July 282. See Bevan: *op. cit.*
4. The words of Laertius, his biographer: "Somehow, in his sleep, (he) received an asp-bite," might justify a suspicion.
5. There is a legend that when the first Ptolemy died, Ptolemy II did not know of the advice that Demetrios had given his father and that he was allowed to hold his position as head of the library, but that later a concubine of the young king told him the story and that then Demetrios was exiled. Valckenaer (de Aristobulo Jud.); apud G. Parthey: *Das alexandrinische Museum*, Berlin, 1838 (pp. 69–70).

In spite of his unhappy end it was in Egypt that Demetrios attained imperishable renown. Leaving, if not expelled, from his homeland of Greece where democratic freedom had died in the temple of Poseidon, on the isle of Calauria, on 13th October 322 B.C., and realizing that whatever political talents he might possess were no longer available to his countrymen ever as a palliative, Demetrios responded to the generous call of Ptolemy and set his face toward the new-born capital of Hellas. To Alexandria he brought and wisely employed the distinguished resources of his scholarship and cultured life, knowing that in that field alone he could use the pent up and dynamic forces of his active intellect. He beheld the influx of poets, philosophers, and scientists responding to the invitation of the king; he was aware that Ptolemy in obtaining the most detached portion of Alexander's empire could reasonably look forward, in Egypt, to centuries of security for his dynasty; he saw a gay, frivolous, but industrious people, at the cross-road of the world, with the twin-trade of the East and West poured into their lap; he could not but know of the fabulous wealth of this vast productive land and its millions of workers, all of which was funnelled through the mighty city which was building up around him in permanent stone and marble. What could he do that would save the gold from the dross in the mighty vortex of life that was milling actually within his sight in the greatest human center in the world? Could not the residuum of it all be preserved by men of thought, by men of art, and by men of letters? His crucial years had been passed amid the groves and walks of the Lyceum; that he had been a devoted scholar at its altars was evidenced by his versatile literary labors and his distinguished intellectual career; and that his loyalty to his alma mater had been honorable was attested when in the days of his power, he had secured a house and garden for his teacher Theophrastus[1]. This was after Aristotle's death and it has been thought[2] that this property, as an estate, included the original foundation of the Peripatetic school. It is more probable that Theophastus, having become the successor of Aristotle, that this property, perhaps in addition and adjoining or connected with the Lyceum,

1. Diog. Laertius: V-39.
2. Muller and Donaldson: *A Hist. of Lit. of An. Gr.*, III-9–10.

was obtained from or through Demetrios and that together it was left by Theophrastus as the philosophical college (the Lyceum). One remembers how much attention in his will[1] Theophrastus gives to the word *Museum*. First his executors must "finish the rebuilding of the *Museum* with the statues of the goddesses", etc. "Next to rebuild the small cloister adjoining the *Museum.*" Indeed the word *Museum* appears in the early days of Hellas. The Muses were ever the particular patrons of arts and letters, they were the goddesses of the varied forms of beauty which graced the intellectual life of Greece. On Mount Helicon their temple stood; the porch of the house of Pythagoras at Metapontium was called the Museum[2]; the name suggests the Platonic brotherhood and their common cult in the "groves of Academe"[3]; there was a Museum at Stagira[4]; and certainly a Museum was the cult-chapel of the Lyceum of Aristotle, and Theophrastus was ever devoted to the idea. Demetrios, a distinguished pupil of Theophrastus, was familiar with the genesis and historical development of the word and its peculiar fitness for the time[5].

These matters resolved themselves in the active, practical and talented brain of the distinguished refugee. He was aware that the Lyceum was the product of democratic Athens, one of the finest flowers of free Greece. He was aware that he was a guest at a court of monarchy, where favor flowed from the hands of royalty. With his cosmopolitan mind, however, he visioned what the royal favor, if properly directed, could accomplish, especially when backed by the limitless wealth of Egypt. He suggested to Ptolemy Soter the establishment of the University of Egypt, where would be gathered the intellectual luminaries of Hellas: a Museum, true temple of the Muses, a meeting-place where the scholars of the earth should forgather to fix the canons of letters and to extend the scientific horizons of man. Here too, there should be

1. The *Will of Theophrastus* in Diogenes Laertius V-51 et seq.
2. Diog. Laer.: VIII–15.
3. Sandys: *op. cit.* I–106.
4. Pliny: *Nat. His.*, XVI–133.
5. Indeed how well Dr. W. S. Ferguson of Harvard in *C.A.H.*, Ch. I, puts it:
At Athens when he speaks of "the right of philosophers to teach had been forbidden in the reaction that followed Demetrius of Phalerum's attempt to make the city an ideal state on the Peripatetic model"; and at Alexandria: "At the court of the Ptolemies such favourites of fortune were Demetrius of Phalerum, founder of the Museum and benefactor of Athens"; et seq.

food and lodging and living-rooms for the workers in the vine-yards of thought, in the form of refectories, sleeping-lodges, and assembly-halls. There should, in this treeless sun-land, be cloisters, colonnades broken at intervals by *exedrae* where the dons might walk as they discoursed (how could a peripatetic think of less!) and might also rest in the ample alcoves of the *exedrae*. Yet in all these arrangements there was no provision for the actual tools of learning. Hence was to arise the Alexandriana, handmaid to the Museum, indeed its natural complement – Carlyle would have said the true University itself –, a treasury where were to be assembled, assorted, edited, and preserved all the extant wisdom, knowledge, and information of Hellas, together with some of the visions, learning, and experiences of the non-Greeks, with whom the vast conquests of Alexander had thrown the Hellenic world in such intimate contact as to excite its native curiosity. How could the now acquisitive Greek-Macedonian behold the great cities and gigantic monuments of Asia and Africa without desiring to know something of the written records of these de-parted yet fabulous civilizations?

Demetrios was not a dreamer, he was a thinker and a man of action. He suggested to Ptolemy Soter the founding of the Alexan-drian Library and made the first great collection of manuscripts. Ptolemy Soter "profited by his knowledge and active mind by putting him in charge of the library"[1]. He certainly was the King's Librarian or the Director of the Library, or Keeper of the Books, which he had collected. ,,Cette bibliothèque, créée par Soter... eut pour premier directeur Démétrius de Phalère, ancien gouverneur d'Athènes en exil et l'un des écrivains éminents de ce temps"[2].

Dr. Couat argues that he had no formal office, although he states:

It (the Library) had still to be organized; no one was better fitted for that difficult task than Demetrius. On his recommendation Ptolemy bought, among other works, everything that had been written on the art of government..... Such were the beginnings of the Library. If we can trust various ancient statements, it harboured no

1. Auguste Couat: *Alexandrian Poetry under the First Three Ptolemies* (tr. Jas. Loeb), London, 1931, p. 11. Dr. Couat is for the assumption, although he admits there is no proof, that Ptolemy II founded the library.
2. Arthur Rhoné: *Résumé chronologique de l'histoire d'Egypte*, Paris, 1877, p. 35.

less than 200,000 volumes at the end of Ptolemy Soter's reign, and Demetrius, whom the king questioned on this subject, flattered himself with the hope of having 500,000 in his charge[1].

"During the reign of Ptolemy Soter... Demetrius of Phaleron gave the first impulse toward the founding of public libraries in the Egyptian capital (c. 295 B.C.)." "The foundation of the Great Library in particular was probably due in the first instance to Ptolemy Soter, acting under the advice of Demetrius."[2]

The tendency to ascribe to Ptolemy II all the great achievements in Alexandria, except the foundation of the Empire itself, includes crediting him with the foundation of the Library and the Museum. We believe both to be the work of Ptolemy Soter and Demetrios of Phaleron[3]. Ptolemy II without doubt kept up and greatly advanced these institutions, as did practically all the Ptolemaic rulers. The collections in the library almost of necessity must have grown from reign to reign. Ptolemy II's main intellectual interest was in zoology[4], yet as a well educated man, we would assume that even amidst his luxurious life, this "magnificent voluptuary" had time for art and literary appreciations, and that whether he was a bookman in the real sense we may never know, but we feel sure that he was an interested patron of art and of the knowledge to be found in manuscripts.

The view that Demetrios of Phaleron and Ptolemy II together founded the Museum was ably refuted by Kuiper[5] many years ago. He shows how these two men, Demetrios and Ptolemy, the son of Soter, were naturally opposed and could hardly have been closely associated in this great intellectual movement, and above all, that the very name and structure of the Museum were suggestive of the Lyceum and a Peripatetic philosopher, which should confirm Demetrios as its founder[6].

1. Auguste Couat: p. 11.
2. Sandys: *op. cit.* I-105.
3. Wilamowitz-Moellendorff: *Antigonos von Karystos* (Berlin, 1881), p. 291; Franz Susemihl: *Geschichte der griechischen Litteratur in der Alexandrinerzeit* (Leipzig, 1891), I-6-138; J. P. Mahaffy: *The Empire of the Ptolemies* ((London, 1895), p. 91; Edwyn Bevan: *A History of Egypt under the Ptolemaic Dynasty* (London, 1927), p. 124.
4. Diodorus: III-36-3f.
5. K. Kuiper: *Proceedings of the Utrecht Society of Letters for 1894.*
6. It was here that Mahaffy's (*op. cit.* p. 92, note) enthusiasm mounting, he ventures that as Ptolemy with his fleet was hovering near the Greek coast in 307 B.C., Demetrios, after his fall from power and the capture of Athens by his namesake, the

And so, Mahaffy: "The famous Museum at Alexandria, which has also been ascribed by many to the second king, but which was certainly the work of Soter, aided by the advice of Demetrius of Phaleron."

Indeed, we believe it was the *work* of Demetrios of Phaleron, under the patronage and aegis of Ptolemy Soter, the king.

II. ZENODOTUS OF EPHESUS

Zenodotus of Ephesus was appointed librarian by Ptolemy II, "Philadelphus", probably when Demetrios of Phaleron was dismissed. A pupil of Philetas, the elegiac poet, grammarian, and tutor of Ptolemy II, Zenodotus was essentially a grammarian, critic, and recensionist, and his work as such will be noted later.

The date of his birth has been placed between B.C. 325 and 320. We know he flourished certainly after 282, the date of the death of Ptolemy Soter.

The date of the death of Zenodotus is unknown.

He is called the first librarian or director of the Alexandrian Library. This can only be so on the assumption that Demetrios, who may have come to Alexandria between 307 and 296 B.C.[1] and who ended his career not later than 282 B.C., may have devoted his entire effort to the collecting or gathering from all places and sources of the vast material, to which free public access was had at the beginning of the reign of the second Ptolemy, after the appointment of Zenodotus. At most, he could have been the first "public" librarian of the Alexandriana; but the first royal or "king's" librarian was Demetrios, whose genius and labor built the foundation of the great library[2].

son of Antigonus, may then have accompanied Ptolemy Soter to Alexandria. This would account for the unexplained loss of ten years by this forceful and energetic man.

1. This chronology is based on F. Ritschl: *Die alexandrinischen Bibliotheken* (Breslau, 1838, pp. 89–90). I have taken these dates like Dr. Donaldson's note in his continuation of *A History of the Literature of Ancient Greece*, by K. O. Muller (London, 1858, Vol. II, p. 421). Sir John E. Sandys: *A History of Classical Scholarship* (London, 1921, p. 101) says "in 297, (Demetrios) left for Egypt". Pauly-Wissowa gives 296–295; and Mahaffy probably as early as 306 B.C.

2. The distinction "public", "royal" or "king's" librarian is quite invidious, as they were all appointed by the king, to whom the Museum and Library both belonged. This should satisfy the meticulous scholars who hesitate to conceed the librarianship of Callimachus, because the Plautine scholium uses the phrase "aulicus regius bibliothecarius".

If there were on the marble walls of the Alexandrian Library the names of the illustrious men who directed its labors (like there is on the marble walls of our Library of Congress) the failure to place at the head the name of Demetrios of Phaleron would have been one of the supreme injustices of the history of literature.

III. ALEXANDER OF AETOLIA

Alexander of Aetolia (b.c. 315 B.C.), poet and grammarian, lived most of his life in Alexandria. He was one of the seven poets included in the Alexandrian tragic *Pleiad*. He was selected by Ptolemy II to compile a list and to form a collection of the entire extant body of tragic and satyric plays, and in this capacity, at least, had an office in the Alexandrian Library.

Mahaffy says: "Alexander the Aetolian, one of the men who organized the Library for the second Ptolemy."[2]

Holm records him as librarian succeeding Zenodotus. "The Library was entrusted to him (Zenodotus) along with Alexander the Aetolian and Lycophron, and while the former arranged the tragic poets and the latter the comic ones, Zenodotus had Homer and the other poets under his special care."[3]

Notwithstanding these views, we believe that Alexander the Aetolian was at the most an assistant librarian or associate of Zenodotus[4]. For some unknown reason the Aetolian later left Alexandria and sought Aratus of Soli at the court of Antigonus Gonates at Pella, c. 276[5].

Of his literary labors, one title of his tragedies survives, *The Diceplayers*, two elegies (*Apollo* and *The Muses*) and a few other fragments[6].

1. It may be remembered that Ausonius (Epistles, XIII-29; L.C.L. II-45), with more than poetic license, described Zenodotus as "he who gathered the mangled limbs of sacred Homer", an honor that antiquity, at least traditionally, assigned to Pisistratus.
2. Mahaffy: *Greek Life and Thought, op. cit.* p. 261.
3. Holm: *op. cit.* IV-438 (also Ch. IV-318).
4. Symeon Magister (562), the Byzantine writer, ventures to allot twelve assistant librarians to the official family.
5. Bouché-Leclercq: *op. cit.* I, p. 224.
6. J. U. Powell: *Collectanea Alexandrina* (1925); E. A. Barber: s.v. *Alexander of Pleuron in Aetolia* (Ox. Class. Dic., 1949).

IV. LYCOPHRON OF CHALCIS

Lycophron of Chalcis in Euboea was a "maker of tragedies", poet, and grammarian, of whose life we know little. He was adopted by Lycus, the historian, reputedly an enemy of Demetrios. He was of the constellation of the seven tragic poets in the Alexandrian *Pleiad*, and is credited with the obscure, curious poem, *Alexandria* (or *Cassandra*), which has excited the interest of various men before and since the brilliant English statesman, Charles James Fox.

Like many of the Greek intellectuals of his age, he was drawn by its glamorous lure to Ptolemaic Alexandria. He may have written dull tragedies and obscure verse, yet he is credited with the cleverness of writing an anagram which interpreted Ptolemy, as sweet as honey, and Arsinoe, as violet. He soon was with the influential Museum group, and he was allotted the comic muse. As a result of these bibliographical labors, he wrote his treatise *On Comedy*, in not less than nine books.

We do not know the dates of his birth (c. 330–320 B.C.) nor death, although Ovid (*Ibis*, 531–32) says that he was shot by an arrow[1]; neither do we know exactly when he came to Alexandria[2]. Holm[3] names him as librarian after Alexander of Aetolia. However, we do not believe that he was ever librarian, but rather, like Alexander the Aetolian, an assistant or special librarian or associate, if not the colleague, of old Zenodotus.

Of his literary labors, Suidas gives twenty tragic titles, and Tzetzes says he wrote forty-six or sixty-four tragedies.

A fragment alone survives:

While death is far away
   Sad hearts are fain to die;
But when the latest wave
   Of life draws nigh,
We fain would live, for life
   Knows no satiety[4].

He wrote *Menedemus*, a satyric drama.

1. Utque cothurnatum cecidisse Lycophrona narrant.
   Haereat in fibris fixa sagitta tuis.
2. It is probable that he came to Alexandria after the dismissal of Demetrios of Phaleron (B.C. 283), who was an enemy of the historian Lycus of Rhegium who had adopted Lycophron.
3. Holm: *op. cit.* IV–318.
4. Translation of A. W. Mair (*Callimachus and Lycophron* (L.C.L.), London, 1921, p. 481.

V. CALLIMACHUS OF CYRENE

Now we come to probably the third of the great librarians or directors of the Alexandrian Library – Callimachus of Cyrene. Of his tenure of office there is much controversy, but of his position as the dominant figure in the Alexandrian intellectual world there should be none. The winds of controversy have not yet abated, as to the question of his librarianship of the Alexandriana.

Ritschl, Muller, and Donaldson, Leonhard Schmitz in Smith's *Dictionary of Greek and Roman Biography and Mythology*, Messrs. Brown and Tedder in the *Britannica*, Bevan[1], Auguste Couat[2], and A. Bouché-Leclercq[3] made him the successor of Zenodotus (i.e. the third librarian). Holm places him a probable fifth, that is, after (Demetrios), Zenodotus, Alexander, and Lycophron. Smith's *Dictionary* says:

> It was formerly believed, but it is now established as an historical fact, that Callimachus was chief librarian of the famous library of Alexandria[4].

But Dr. A. W. Mair[5] has grave doubts and Dr. George M. Bolling[6] will risk his classical reputation on but four names, viz.: Zenodotus, Eratosthenes, Aristophanes, and Aristarchus. Dr. Bolling takes his stand with those who believe that Callimachus and Apollonius Rhodes seem chronologically impossible.

The authoritative Pauly-Wissowa-Kroll[7], although it states that Zenodotus was followed by Callimachus, expresses grave doubts, stating that they do not find outside of the scholium of

1. "The second Librarian was perhaps the poet Callimachus of Cyrene." (Bevan, p. 126.)
2. Auguste Couat: *Alexandrian Poetry under the First Three Ptolemies* (tr. James Loeb), London, 1931, p. 50.
3. A. Bouché-Leclercq: *Histoire des Légides*, Paris, 1903; Vol. I, pp. 224–5.
4. Smith's *Dictionary*: *op. cit.*, s.v. *Callimachus*.
5. Dr. A. W. Mair: *Callimachus* (L.C.L.), says: "Suidas tells us he was a teacher in Eleusis, a suburb of Alexandria; afterwards he was introduced to the court of Ptolemy Philadelphus, in whose service he continued – apart from occasional excursions – till his death circ. 235 B.C." As Ptolemy II died January 27, 245 B.C., this is impossible, but it indicates the time of his service under Ptolemy III (Euergetes).
6. *Catholic Encyclopedia*, s.v. *Alexandrian Library*.
7. Pauly-Wissowa-Kroll: *Real-Encyclopädie der klassischen Altertumswissenschaften*, s.v. *Alexandrinische Bibliotheken* (Vol. III, p. 410).

Tzetzes anything concerning his activity as head of the library, an activity which, notwithstanding his large literary, historical, and bibliocarian labors, seems to be impossible for chronological reasons. Reference is made to W. Busch[1] by Dr. Dziatzko. Sir, John Edwin Sandys, likewise, thinks it "improbable".

The question is difficult, mostly on account of the poverty of our sources.

That Callimachus was for his time a universal scholar, the Father of Bibliography, the greatest bookman of his age, would not alone justify the inference that he was the king's director or chief librarian; on the contrary, his peculiar fitness for the office might quite humanly work against him.

A purely critical examination, as we have undertaken in chapter VII of this work, seems to disclose that the scholium[2] founded on the *Prolegomena of Aristophanes* by the Byzantine Tzetzes (12th century A.D.), discovered on a manuscript of Plautus in the Collegio Romano, in 1819, by F. Osann, is the sole authority that has come down to our day naming Callimachus as librarian. The cautious Dr. A. W. Mair notes that the words: "aulicus regius bibliothecarius", do "not necessarily imply that he was the Chief Librarian". Again we repeat what we said under "Zenodotus of Ephesus" (p. 138). The distinction between king's, royal, or public librarian or library is indeed invidious. They were all the appointees or servants of the king (in Roman days, of Caesar), and all the libraries were the king's. Even in *The Letter of Aristeas* (and it must be remembered that whatever may be the opinion as to the historicity of this document, "the author, it must be admitted, is thoroughly conversant with the technical and official language of Alexandria and the court")[3], when Ptolemy is reported to have written to the High-Priest, Eleazar, that it is his will that the Jewish Law be translated into Greek, he is doing this so that "these writings also may find a place in our library with the other *royal* volumes"[4].

If the scholiast meant that Callimachus was the librarian of the great library, then we should accept the statement as

1. Busch: *De bibliothecariis Alex. qui feruntur primis*, 1884.
2. See Chapter VII of this work.
3. H. St. J. Thackeray: *The Letter of Aristeas*, London, 1918 (Introd., p. XI).
4. *Letter of Aristeas: op. cit.* d. 38 (p. 31).

the best available authority and one probably founded on the original writings of Callimachus and Eratosthenes or some other ancient and good source. Unfortunately, the Alexandrian Library is taken for granted by the ancient writers, and little is recorded about its personnel and management. Among the foremost difficulties are our lack of knowledge on three points:

   a. When did Zenodotus die?
   b. When did Callimachus die?
   c. When did Eratosthenes leave Athens to go to Alexandria at the call of Ptolemy Euergetes?

It is thought that Zenodotus was born in 324 or 325 B.C. He was certainly librarian from 283 (282) B.C. (the death of the 1st Ptolemy). Suidas says that he was tutor of the children of Ptolemy Soter and that he lived under the first Ptolemy. Of course he lived under both Soter and Ptolemy II, who made him "the first superintendent of the great Library at Alexandria, in which office he was succeeded by Callimachus"[1]. We do not know the date of his death, but if he lived as long as his patron, Ptolemy II, he would have died 246 B.C., about the age of seventy-seven years, and been librarian for about thirty-six years. Of course, he may have died sooner or lived longer. There are some who place his death ca. 245 (Bevan) or even as late as 234. Dr. Gulick gives ca. 260 as the probable date of Zenodotus's death, and this accords with Beloch. It is this date to which we are most inclined.

Now Suidas gives reason to infer that Callimachus survived Zenodotus. He is very definite in stating that Callimachus survived to the time of Ptolemy, surnamed Euergetes (B.C. 247–221).

There is every reason to believe that Callimachus stood high in the esteem of Ptolemy II who called him from obscurity to the Museum and whose genius as a bookman was apparent to all and whose intellectual, if not political, power drove Apollonius, the Alexandrian, to Rhodes. It would seem most reasonable that on the death or retirement of Zenodotus this brilliant man should become librarian[2]. Susemihl does not hesitate to express his considerate reasoning on the side of Callimachus:

1. Smith: *op. cit.* s.v. *Zenodotus.*
2. Dr. Donaldson, in his Continuation of K.O. Muller's *A History of the Literature of Ancient Greece* (London), Vol. I, p. 419, says: "This encouragement of literature was carried on with still greater earnestness by Philadelphus, who had celebrated Callimachus for his librarian."

That Callimachus was the director rests only on weak testimony, but all of the information about these things is so insufficient, and on the other hand the essential probability for this subscription is so great that we are forced, even lacking all outside proof, simply by scientific deduction to believe it[1].

As to the standing of Callimachus with Ptolemy Euergetes (B.C. 247–221), the successor of Ptolemy II, the famous incident of the hair of Queen Berenice should alone suffice. The new King Euergetes immediately on taking the throne of his father was plunged into the Syrian wars against Antiochus, Seleucus, and his traitorous brother. The Queen vowed to the gods that if they permitted her husband to return safe, she would cut off a lock of her beautiful hair and dedicate it in the temple to the gods. Euergetes returned safe and victorious, and the Queen sacrificed her tresses to the gods, whereupon the court-astronomer Conon placed the *Coma Berenices* in the heavens as a new constellation and the court man of letters, Callimachus, made immortal the story in verse, which unfortunately has come down to us only in the paraphrase of Catulus.

We believe that Zenodotus died before Callimachus, more probably in the reign of Ptolemy II (d. 246), and Callimachus succeeded him. Is it not reasonable to believe that when the son of the second Ptolemy (Euergetes) came to the throne, that he continued the great scholar in his post as librarian, which he held until his death (about 240 or 235)?

Callimachus may have been succeeded by Eratosthenes when he was called from Athens by Euergetes, or, more probably, by Apollonius of Rhodes, who may have returned to Alexandria on the death of Callimachus[2].

There is nothing chronologically impossible about this. It lacks the precision of many Ptolemaic dates, yet it is sound in reasonableness and violates no known system of time. Considering the uncertainty of chronological data, or rather the lack of chronological data, concerning the Alexandrian scholars, it would seem unnecessary to deprive Callimachus of his bibliothe-

1. Susemihl: *op. cit.* I, p. 341.
2. See further consideration of this assumption in our examination of the *Oxyrhynchus Papyrus 1241* (p. 153).

cariate post in the great library, which had been the scene of his most assiduous intellectual labors, solely because there is not more evidence of his tenure.

And yet after all the foregoing, a stray scrap of papyrus from the dust-heaps of Oxyrhynchus has been thought to upset the ordered line of Alexandrian librarians upon which scholars have labored, every now and then, for over a century. As these fragments appear not only to effect the tenure of Callimachus, but also to produce a new figure in the succession, and other matters concerning our subject, we have thought it well to discuss it fully at the close of this Chapter[1].

VI. ERATOSTHENES OF CYRENE

All agreed that Eratosthenes of Cyrene succeeded either Zenodotus or Callimachus. But now the *Oxyrhynchus Papyrus* (1241) claims that Eratosthenes succeeded Apollonius of Rhodes.

Eratosthenes of Cyrene was the most distinguished of the pupils of Callimachus. He was one of those omnivorous scholars: mathematician, geographer, astronomer, grammarian, chronographer, historian, philologer, philosopher, and even a poet. He has a claim as the founder of astronomy, and he was probably the founder of physical geography and certainly the father of geodetic science.

He was born in c. 275 B.C. His masters were Ariston of Chios, the philosopher, Zenodotus of Ephesus, and Callimachus. M. Alfred Croiset writes:

> After a long sojourn in Athens, he was recalled by Ptolemy Euergetes to Alexandria, when he was about forty years old, to direct the famous library after Callimachus's death[2].

He died at eighty years from enforced starvation, after losing his eye-sight and becoming satiated with life (c. 196 B.C.).

He wrote on innumerable subjects in prose and verse. His labors must have been prodigious.

1. p. 153.
2. Alfred and Maurice Croiset: *Histoire de la littérature grecque*, Paris (V, p. 121); G. H. Klippel: *Ueber das alexandrinische Museum*, Gött., 1838 (p. 139), says he was called to Alexandria between 228–226; Sandys gives c. 335.

But above all, he founded two sciences, Chronology and Geography.

In Chronology he stated for the first time that the historic age began with the Olympiades; that preceding ages were unknown, although he separately delved into the chronology of the Egyptian dynasties. He arranged dates of all important literary, as well as political events, and lists of the victors of the Olympic Games. His establishment of the Trojan era as 1183 or 1184 B.C. was classical in ancient times and has been considered with deep respect by modern writers.

In Geography his great achievement was in discovering a correct method of ascertaining the circumference of the earth, which he calculated "by comparing the distance from Alexandria to Syene with the corresponding arc of the meridian". His result was some 250,000 stadia (it should have been 216,000 stadia) but was the most accurate to the modern age of science. His Geography was furnished with a Map upon which, for the first time, was found a system of parallels of latitude. His great mathematical and other scientific treatises are lost.

He wrote *On the Old Attic Comedy*, a great critical work[1], and, of course, like a good scholar of the Museum, he wrote *On Homer*.

How these Alexandrians call to mind the men of the Renaissance! Eratosthenes was one of those of universal learning and broad scholarship in many fields, deserving the sobriquet, that was pleasantly given him, of Beta, or Number Two, the primary number being reserved it is thought for divine Plato. It was also said that his enemies jeered at the universality of his learning as indicating a certain mediocrity, and hence called him Beta.

If Pythagoras was the first to receive the title of *philosopher*, Eratosthenes was the first scholar in all the world to be named philologer[2], which has been so happily described as one possessing the knowledge of the known. He was indeed "the greatest man of learning of the whole Ptolemaic age"[3].

We crossed a curious epitaph of our scholar, also preserved by Baron Bunsen, which we like to think was done in gratitude for the pioneer labors of Eratosthenes in Egyptological research:

1. Bernhardy: *Eratosthenica*, Berol, 1822, pp. 203–237.
2. Bernhardy: *op. cit.* p. XIV; see Donaldson: *op. cit.* III-507.
3. Gilbert Murray: *op. cit.* 387.

Gently ages stole o'er thine eyes, no enervating pangs had unmann'd
thee,
When at the summons of Fate, musing of loftiest themes,
Calmly thou sanks't to repose, Eratosthenes. Nor did Cyrene
Offer thy ashes a tomb deep in her rocky abode,
Ageaus' Son; but belov'd in the arms of the stranger thou sleepest,
Close by the edge of the shore, Proteus' primaeval domain[1].

VII. APOLLONIUS OF ALEXANDRIA

Apollonius of Alexandria[2], known to succeeding ages as Apollonius of Rhodes, was a pupil of Callimachus.

Unlike most of the Museum dons, he was a native, yet he early ran amuck against the powerful, strongly entrenched hierarchy of scholars that ruled that Alexandrian Museum and Library, and driven from his perhaps ungrateful city, he found a hospitable haven at Rhodes where, in its learned schools, he attained high fame and happiness. Yet the fires of Pharos finally lured him back to his homeland, where in the reign of Ptolemy III, Euergetes (B.C. 247–221), he was recalled or returned; here he may have finally read his *Augonautica* with success and here we believe he became the librarian of the Alexandrian Library, succeeding Callimachus on his death.

Two anonymous *Lives* from a lost original, an account in Suidas, and fragments in earlier writers, indicate for our native Alexandrian scholar a most vigorous, colorful, and ultimately triumphant career.

Pupil of the omniscient Callimachus, whose slightest word was *ex cathedra* and who taught the new, modern Hellenistic doctrine that Homer and the epic writers were dead giants of an age that was past, proper objects of critical and exegetical study, but impossible, and against the spirit of the times, to attempt to imitate. It was an age of wide-flung Hellenic activity, of scientific investigations, and of the beginning of solid scholastic learn-

1. By Dionysius of Cyzicus in Brunch: *Analect*, II-255; tr. by Baron Bunsen in his *Egypt's Place in Universal History*; cf. *Greek Anthology*, Book VII, *Sepulchral Epigrams*, 78.
2. Or of Naucratis, according to Aelian and Athenaeus. From the two "Lives" of Apollonius in the Scholia he is said to have been an Alexandrian by birth. It was certainly a slip of the classical scholar in (L.C.L.) Ovid: *The Art of Love and other Paeans* (p. X) to say: Apollonius, "though a native of Rhodes was apparently a citizen of Naucratis".

ing, in which highly polished bits of prose and verse were served up to a sophisticated public by the pundits of the Museum – The University of Neo-Hellenism. These dainty morsels, clever works in studied prose and faultless verse, were the short, bright, smart, *little* books, desired by the Alexandrian Age and of which the master Callimachus had himself contributed perhaps several hundred, and were heralded as the modern vogue, an advance over the obsolete, ponderous *big* book of the ancient epos[1].

Now Apollonius, although he may have derived much from the teaching of Callimachus, would not follow the master on this great point. Indeed, he was a lover of the ancient wisdom and the heroic songs of Homer; and the epic bards were still for him the foremost expression of human utterances, embodying the forms of perfect beauty. Not only did the pupil refuse to follow his master's teaching, but he, who had also the urge to write, wrote an epic poem in the old classical manner to prove that the forms and modes of great literature were ageless and deathless. With little temerity, he took his stand, and with the *Argonautica* challenged his teacher to the fray.

We do not know who was more to blame in this famous quarrel, whether the pupil was too forward or the master too severe, but we do know that it developed into a contest without quarter. Apollonius defied the Museum clique to read his poem and was driven from the field. The rebellious young poet had small chance against the entrenched officialdom of the University. He was condemned, bitterly denounced, vilely lampooned by Callimachus himself, who compromised his dignity by besmirching his opponent pupil in the poem called *The Ibis*. In impotent despair, Apollonius left his native city and went to Rhodes, an island famed for its schools and culture, and there, while attaining citizenship and much renown, improved and polished his epic poem on the search for the Golden Fleece.

Our present interest in him is that he became one of the early librarians of the great Library. As in the case of his master Callimachus, former distinguished classicists throw doubts upon

1. One cannot think of this famous literary controversy without remembering that Edgar Allan Poe contended that there had never been a long *poem*, merely long works in *verse*, interspersed now and then with outbursts of poetry.

his claim because of supposed chronological difficulties. We all know how meager are the fragments of the lives and how uncertain are the chronological data concerning the scholars of the Museum and the Library. It is thought that Apollonius would be too old to have become librarian upon the death of Eratosthenes in 196–193 B.C. Now we know that Eratosthenes, though he lived to about eighty years, became tired of life, that he became blind and died of voluntary starvation. It may be that like Ritschl believed he gave up his office on the approach, or during these fatal years of physical, if not mental, decay. Yet still Apollonius would have been too old. It seems more reasonable to believe that Apollonius preceded Eratosthenes, succeeding Callimachus, with a few years of librarianship.

It has been well said[1]: "It is rather arbitrary to take away the bibliothecariate of Apollonius, which is clearly asserted by Suidas, on account of chronological calculations which are themselves uncertain."

Even the story of his being buried with or next to his old antagonist Callimachus may be reconciled if we assume that the Alexandrian scholars were buried within the sacred precincts of the Muses and that in a tomb or burial-place reserved especially for the librarians, Apollonius, having actually died before Eratosthenes, was indeed buried next to Callimachus.

But a most curious end of this short notice of his life is that whereas most scholars doubted his librarianship and as great an authority as Herr Susemihl declares without reservation against him[2], the discovery of the *Oxyrhynchus Papyrus* (1241) has compelled, at least, a new consideration of his claim[3].

VIII. ARISTOPHANES OF BYZANTIUM

With Aristophanes of Byzantium we reach the pleasant stage where we find a scholar whose librarianship is admitted by the whole classical world.

His career in connection with the Library was regular. He was the pupil of Callimachus and of Eratosthenes, the third and

1. R. C. Seaton: Apollonius Rhodius – *The Augonautica* (L.C.L.), London, 1912, p. VII.
2. Susemihl: *op. cit.* I-341.
3. This document (*Oxyr. Pap. 1241*) will be fully examined at the end of this Chapter.

fourth or fifth librarians. He was the teacher of Aristarchus, who in his turn, by universal consent, succeeded his master as librarian (my seventh or eight bibliocarius).

A story is told by Vitruvius[1] as to his rise to fame and the headship of the Alexandrian Library.

In the days of King Ptolemy[2], at a celebration of the public literary "games" in honor of Apollo and the Muses, the intellectual athletes presented original compositions, mostly in verse, in competition for the Prize of Letters.

The judges were seven in number, presumably learned scholars of the Museum. On this occasion the king had appointed six and wanting the seventh he sent for the "Governors of the Library" and asked for a suggestion. They offered the name of Aristophanes, a scholar whom they had observed daily for a long time, sedulously pouring over the manuscripts, studying, and reading in the Library. So the king appointed Aristophanes.

The contest was held and six of the judges, deferring to the applause of the audience, were for awarding the prize in response to the public appeal, in which the king joined. But Aristophanes staunchly opposed the award to the indignation of everyone, and insisting upon his judgment when allowed to speak, denounced the composition of the favorites as pure plagiarisms, and leading the doubtful Ptolemy and his fellow judges to the *armaria* or book closets or cupboards in the Library, he produced the papyrus rolls containing the original works which had been copied by the contestants. Thus confronted, they confessed. "They were condemned and dismissed in disgrace, while Aristophanes was raised to high office, and became librarian."

In spite of this good story, he was of a mature age (probably sixty) when he was appointed Keeper of the Library. If he were born B.C. 257–250 and died c. 180, he was librarian for some fifteen years.

It has been definitely stated that Aristophanes came to Alexandria in his youth with his father, who was a soldier, and that after studying under "all of its greatest teachers, devoted himself

1. Vitruvius: Bk. VII, preface.
2. This is a good story, but I cannot bring myself to localize it to the time of Ptolemy Euergetes (246–221 B.C.), although so placed by such eminent scholars as Samuel Sharpe and Frank Granger. Aristophanes was librarian ca. 195–180 B.C. Euergetes died 221 B.C.

to the study of philology, and was appointed librarian in 195 B.C. at the age of sixty-two"[1]. However, it is thought that he gave up his librarianship before his death, and that Alexandria had become "so incongenial that Aristophanes strove to escape in old age to Syria"[2]. The Pergamene prince Eumenes II (197–159 B.C.) is said to have invited him to Pergamum to be director for the great Attalid Library. When Ptolemy Epiphanes (205–182 B.C.) heard of it, he threw him in prison[3]. In resigning or surrendering the librarianship he anticipated the similar steps to be taken by his own successor Aristarchus. One of their predecessors, Eratosthenes, when his health failed, had also probably resigned.

The contributions of this omnivorous scholar Aristophanes to the science of grammar and the art of letters are of the first rank and will be treated in discussing the great work of the Alexandrian scholars in fixing the canons of literature. (See Chapter XII.)

IX. ARISTARCHUS OF SAMOTHRACE

Aristarchus of Samothrace, pupil of Aristophanes, by universal consent, was the successor of his master. At least this was the general belief until the discovery of *Oxyrhynchus Papyrus* (1241), when another "Apollonius" (i.e. the Eidograph) arises to plague the Ptolemaic investigator. Dr. Beloch assigned the Eidograph or "Classifier" to the period 180–c. 160 B.C. and Aristarchus to c. 160–131. If Aristarchus were born circa 220 B.C., he was about sixty when he became librarian; if he were born c. 202–200 B.C., according to Beloch[4], he would be about forty years old.

We do not know when he left Alexandria. If it were in the reign of Ptolemy Physcon (145–117 B.C.), who had been one of his pupils, it might have been in the beginning of this tyrant's reign; yet Beloch raises the point that if he were fleeing from Ptolemy (Physcon) Euergetes II (145–116 B.C.), he would hardly have gone to Cyprus, which was a firm dominion of Physcon's[5].

1. J.W. White: *The Scholia on the Aves of Aristophanes*, Boston, 1914, p. XVIII (referring to von Wilamowitz: *Herakles*, I (1889), p. 137).
2. J. P. Mahaffy: *Greek Life and Thought, op. cit.* p. 545.
3. Suidas, ap. Susemihl, I-431; cp. II-669, referred to by Sandys.
4. Beloch: *op. cit.* par. 270.
5. Beloch: *op. cit.* par. 270.

It is more likely that Aristarchus accompanied his old pupil (Euergetes II) when he was driven out of Alexandria (131–130 B.C.)[1].

However, Aristarchus, now about seventy-seven years old, the age of his master Aristophanes, finding himself exhausted with his scholarly labors, hopeless as to the state of society in which his career unfortunately had been cast, suffering from an incurable dropsy, starved himself to death. He died at Cyprus a little before Ptolemy (Euergetes II) returned to Alexandria.

It is curious that this Ptolemy (Physcon), disgusting monster as he appears to have been, aspired to the intellectual life. He wrote a critique on Homer's *Odyssey* and a large work in 24 books about *Historical Monuments*.

It is important to remember that Klippel[2] tells us how urged by Aristarchus, he supported the enlargment of the Library, and that though it is true that all of his predecessors, as well as successors, did much or something for the Library, his efforts were outstanding.

Indeed after the time of Ptolemy VII (Euergetes II – "Physcon", 145–116 B.C.), the vast wealth of Ptolemaic Egypt was largely used to bribe Rome. So, materially, the Museum-Library suffered. As the liberal sums spent on culture dwindled, it was impossible to maintain the amazing intellectual importance of these institutions as they had been conducted under the early Ptolemies. The dons were drawn into the political vortex, and those not so inclined were silent. The zest to produce the things of culture was permanently interrupted. The members taught more and sent their pupils throughout the world. They devoted less time to research, and the institution changed from a college of research into a university of learning. This change was completed under the emperors.

Aristarchus was the most famous of all the Alexandrian critics, indeed the prince of all the critics of antiquity, and some believe that we read his recension of Homer at the present time. Indeed he was a critic alone and wrote only in line with his scholarship.

With his tenure, the line of the known great librarians of the Alexandrian Library came to an end, and provoked the

1. Rostagni: *Atti. Accad.*, Torino, 1914–15, p. 264.
2. Klippel: *op. cit.* p. 160.

remark of Gilbert Murray: "Zenodotus, Callimachus, Eratos-thenes, Aristophanes of Byzantium, and Aristarchus were the first five librarians; what institution has ever had such a row of giants at its head?"

X. THE UNHERALDED FEW

There must, of course, have been able men from that date but with only two or three fragmentary notices, history has been unkind to their memory.

Out of the sand-heaps of Oxyrhynchus, an ancient city site in Upper Egypt, west of the Nile, on the edge of the Libyan Desert, about 130 miles from Cairo, two English classical scholars, Dr. Bernard P. Grenfell and Dr. Arthur S. Hunt, have found treasures richer than gold, fragments, new and old, in verse and prose, of the literature of ancient Greece and muniments of the civil and governmental life of Greco-Egyptian civilization.

Among their many wonderful finds, a scrap of papyrus was found in 1903-4, which has excited the interest of students of the Alexandrian Library. It is true that the paucity of documents on this subject greatly stresses the smallest find, and it is equally true that many scholars have quietly ignored the papyrus. Yet some distinguished Hellenists have given it such importance that a full examination of the source is to be expected here.

The document is Papyrus 1241 of the Oxyrhynchus Papyri[1]. It has been honored by the title of useful-learning-*Chrestomathy*. It appears to have consisted of at least six consecutive columns. The script is uncial of perhaps the first half of the second century and was put together "under one of the earlier Emperors". Of the first column only the ends survive and the last column is broken vertically. The four central columns though damaged are in quite a good state. The work consists of historical and mythological lists 1. of famous sculptors, statuaries, painters, and grammarians; 2. of Alexandrian librarians; and 3. of persons who initiated various acts of war, the inventors of instruments of combat and the establishment of the rules of conflict. Who made these lists we do not know. Whether by a scholar or by some student,

1. B. P. Grenfell and Arthur S. Hunt: *The Oxyrhynchus Papyri*, Part X, London, 1914 (X-99).

whether they were made seriously for permanent use, or for any exercise, or merely for personal amusement, we likewise have no knowledge. The first list, that of the artists, is practically lost; the second list, that of apparently the librarians, is entirely mutilated as it is found at the end of Column I and in good state in Column II, where it occupies 20 ½ lines.

The entire fragment has received the learned, careful, and expert editing of Dr. Hunt with the brilliant assistance of Prof. V. von Wilamowitz-Moellendorff. Nothing has been left undone in learned thoroughness for the elucidation of this document.

The end of Col. I is undecipherable. The editor says that the name of "Zenodotus of course preceded towards the end of Col. I". Anyone has the equal right to say that towards the end of Col. I the following names were found:

Zenodotus – Callimachus,

or the names of

Demetrios – Zenodotus – Callimachus.

Now Col. II which is decipherable reads:

Col. II–1–21

The son of Sillius, of Alexandria called the Rhodian, disciple of Callimachus; he was also the teacher of the first king. He was succeeded by Eratosthenes, after whom came Aristophanes son of Apelles of Byzantium and Aristarchus.Then Apollonius of Alexandria called the Eidograph, and after him Aristarchus son of Aristarchus of Alexandria, originally of Samothrace; he was also the teacher of the children of Philopator. After him Cydas (λογχοφορων) of the Bodyguard (or of the spearmen). After under the ninth king there flourished Ammonius, Zenodotus, Diocles, and Apollodorus, the grammarian.

The above is all that is said, for immediately after the word "grammarian", the author commences to make a list of military information and never returns to our subject.

Nothing can show the ephemeral nature of these jotting down of names than the fact that nowhere does the name Alexandrian Library or Museum appear or is the name librarian ever mentioned or indicated, nor indeed is the name of "Apollonius" (i.e.

of Rhodes) ever mentioned, and the condition of the last line
of Col. I is sufficiently shown to preclude the assumption that
the name "Apollonius" occurred therein.

Now the papyrus itself (Col. II) is well preserved and as
written is full of errors:

1. Admitting as sound that "The son of Sillius" was Apollonius the Rhodian, he was hardly the disciple of Callimachus. He
was his deadly enemy. He had been his pupil.

2. Apollonius of Rhodes could not have taught the first king
(Ptolemy Soter). Dr. Hunt says that πρωτον is an obvious error
for τριτον (hence Euergetes I). But it is doubtful even as to this
assumption, that Apollonius was the tutor of Euergetes. Zenodotus was certainly the teacher of the children of Ptolemy II
("Philadelphus"). If it is argued that Euergetes had more than
one teacher, Apollonius may have been the second tutor, although
the custom seemed to be for one to succeed the other, as Philetas
and later Strato did for "Philadelphus". Apollonius could not
have followed Zenodotus, as when Zenodotus died c. 260, Apollonius retired to Rhodes.

3. Aristarchus is named as succeeding *both* Aristophanes of
Byzantium and Apollonius the Eidograph.

4. Aristarchus was not the teacher of the children of Philopator.
Dr. Hunt says this error should be corrected to *Philometor*.

5. "Under the *ninth* king." Dr. Hunt says that if Euergetes II
is meant, that he was either called the *seventh* or *eighth* king.

The view taken by some of this fragment of papyrus is that
it reverses the whole tradition as to Apollonius of Rhodes leaving
Alexandria as a result of his quarrel with Callimachus and that it
decides that Callimachus never was librarian, and assumes that
Callimachus worked in the Library under Apollonius as a mere
cataloguer. A fine scholar has taken this view:

The chief figure in Alexandrian Poetry was Callimachus; yet his
supremacy was far from being undisputed. If, as now seems probable, Apollonius succeeded Zenodotus as Chief Librarian, Callimachus at the zenith of his career was faced with the opposition of a
man who was officially his superior. That Apollonius had once been
Callimachus' pupil and that he had laid the works of his teacher
under contribution for his own, only made matters worse. The end
came soon after Euergetes' accession (246 B.C.). Apollonius lost

his post and left Egypt, an event jubilantly celebrated by his rival at the end of his Hymn to Apollo[1].

Why should the able Euergetes have dismissed his teacher, as Dr. Hunt suggests he was, in his above correction of *Ox. Papy. 1241*? (See our second error in the Papyrus.)

We believe that Dr. Hunt, after having done everything he could to make the most out of *Oxyrhynchus Papyrus 1241*, as was his editorial duty, felt that he should state toward the end of his introduction to the fragment:

> It is possible that after all the tradition is correct which represents Apollonius as having returned to Alexandria and become librarian comparatively late in life[2].

It would seem to be unsound historically to reverse the position of Callimachus in the Alexandrian scene, to ignore how he came to devote his great talents to the composition of the *Pinakes*, to dethrone him from the intellectual supremacy he held in the Ptolemaic age; as well as to entirely refute Suidas, as well as to refuse credence to the second Life of Apollonius (Westermann Biogr. 50) that at the end records the tradition that he finally returned to Alexandria and became librarian, and to do all this in order to give some importance to this scrap of papyrus, itself full of errors, and probably the innocent if not careless jotting of some student, without research, for his own convenience, never expecting that in some two millennia scholars would by it correct all their previous views.

But Dr. Beloch[3] has fully studied the true value of this fragment. Although we have used his labors freely in the following pages, together with our own studies of the Papyrus, Dr. Beloch is not to be charged with any statement unless it is specially attributed to him.

Now Dr. Hunt says that Apollonius may have become the

---

1. E. A. Barber in *C. A. H.*: s.v. *Alexandrian Literature* (VII, p. 274–5; and p. 253). If the learned Doctor is correct, who was librarian from 246, when "Apollonius lost his post" to 235 (230) B.C., when Eratosthenes came from Athens at the call of Euergetes, most probably at the death of Callimachus? We can think of no other successful candidate than Callimachus.
2. *Oxyrh. Pap.*, Vol. X, p. 101.
3. Karl Julius Beloch: *Griechische Geschichte*, Leipzig, 1927 (2nd rev. ed.), Vol. IV, pt. 2 (pp. 592–599).

teacher of Euergetes about 270, *not* earlier, because the marriage of "Philadelphus" and Arsinoe did not occur before 285 B.C. His retirement to Rhodes may be placed with Knaack[1] about 260 B.C. But as we have shown, was not Zenodotus the teacher of the children of "Philadelphus" about 270?

Now comes the difficulty impossible to solve: If Callimachus and the men of Cyrene (which would connect with the marriage of Berenice and Euergetes) were now in control, why did not Callimachus become librarian on his putting his rival out? But the Papyrus says no, Apollonius of Rhodes was succeeded by Eratosthenes. But unfortunately Eratosthenes was then not more than 15 years old. Everyone knows that at about 235 or 230 B.C. Euergetes called Eratosthenes from Athens to be librarian. In this dilemma as to what became of the librarianship from 260 to 235, the distinguished scholar, Dr. Wilamowitz, rushes to the rescue and suggests that the office of librarian remained in abeyance during the lifetime of Apollonius of Rhodes. But here Dr. Hunt will not follow his colleague; he realizes that this imaginary interregnum cannot be considered, and Beloch says it is so unlikely that it hardly needs mention. It is here that Dr. Hunt so justly exclaims:

> It is possible that after all the tradition is correct which represents Apollonius as having returned to Alexandria and become librarian comparatively late in life[2].

Dr. Beloch labors the point:

> In order to maintain this anonymous scrap of papyrus which itself makes no claim to authority or show of scholarship, we must throw Suidas and the two Vetae, and the tradition, to the dogs, for they say that Apollonius wrote the *Argo* as a young man, that it was turned down by the critical clique of the Museum, that Apollonius left for Rhodes, where he lived long, became famous, rewrote his epic, and returned late in life to Alexandria, filling the librarianship (after Callimachus and *before* Eratosthenes). After Callimachus's death, it was most reasonable for Apollonius to return to his native city, and if he had been a teacher of Euergetes, it was most reasonable (almost poetic

---

1. G. Knaack: c.v. *Apollonios* (71), in Pauly-Wissowa: *Real–Encyclopädie*, II-126–34.
2. Dr. Hunt in *Oxyrh. Papyri*, X-101.

justice) for his pupil to thus honor him. He served but a few years and could well have been buried in the Librarians' Campo Santo in a patio within the library pile, next to his teacher and old antagonist, Callimachus.

It is curious that since the discovery of the Papyrus List the librarianship of Apollonius has become even more complicated and that of Callimachus logically advanced. We have not too many alternatives to select.

1. If Zenodotus was librarian to about 260 and according to the Papyrus Apollonius *must* succeed him, we have to imagine that he held it but for a few days, for Apollonius did go to Rhodes (whence his very name), and his retirement to Rhodes is fixed by Knaack about 260 (to which Dr. Hunt agrees). Now there was not the slightest circumstance to mar the friendship of Ptolemy II ("Philadelphus") for Zenodotus. Did he not make him the tutor of his children and at the beginning of his reign, when Demetrios was exiled, did he not appoint Zenodotus as librarian? But there is nothing to indicate any friendship on the part of Apollonius toward Zenodotus; just the contrary, as we have even mention of a work he wrote entitled *Against Zenodotus*[1]. This is hardly the man Ptolemy II would have appointed to succeed his old friend.

But further, Eratosthenes could not have succeeded him (even though the Papyrus says he did) because he, Eratosthenes, was then only 15 years old and did not come to Alexandria until 230–235. The only reasonable solution is that this was the date of Callimachus's librarianship (c. 260–c. 235 (or 240). How one remembers Susemihl's dictum that without the authority of the Plautine Scholium, the very circumstances of the times make for Callimachus's librarianship.

2. If you believe that Apollonius retired to Rhodes about 260 and that Callimachus became librarian and died about 240 (or 235), what more reasonable for Apollonius's return and appointment then by his pupil, Euergetes. Now it has been contended that there was very little difference between the ages of Callimachus and Apollonius. If that is so, it is again reasonable that Apollonius held the post but a short time when he too passed.

1. E. A. Barber in *Oxford Classical Dictionary* (1949) s.v. *Apollonius* (1). We do not know the date of this tract against Zenodotus.

3. If you reject both above possibilities, then there is the old story of Apollonius returning indeed in his extreme old age and, when Eratosthenes retires, becoming librarian. But as Eratosthenes was librarian to 195, Apollonius (if he was born as early as 300 B.C.) would have been 105 years old!

This third possibility could only take place if we are all wrong as to the birth of Apollonius and if he were a much younger man than his teacher, Callimachus, but it would take many years to reduce this to reasonableness and of course would deprive Apollonius of a tutorship of Euergetes who was born between 284–277 B.C.[1]

The writer, having spent years in the labyrinth of Ptolemaic chronology and having come forth perhaps but little wiser than when he went in, is inclined to believe in the second possibility. Beloch, who has made a serious study of this episode, has indeed practically argued Apollonius of Rhodes out of court. He does, however, in a final note (p. 599) conceed that Apollonius may find a place between Callimachus and Eratosthenes (c. 230–c. 240 B.C.).

As the contest over the *Oxyrhynchus Papyrus* (1241) centers primarily around Apollonius of Rhodes, and indirectly affects Callimachus, we have endeavored to bring some order out of this chaos. The substantial positions of Zenodotus, Eratosthenes, Aristophanes of Byzantium, and Aristarchus are not much affected. The almost unknown[2] other Apollonius called the Eidograph we have not disturbed, leaving him where he is probably meant to be placed by the writer of the *Lists* in the Papyrus. He is called by Dr. Hunt the Classifier. We might suggest that he had been Head Cataloguer, and in the unsettled conditions of the times was promoted to librarian.

Dr. Beloch, one of the latest, most distinguished and satisfying of the Hellenists who have studied this subject, has, according to his historical method, given a Table of Librarians of practically the first two centuries of the Alexandriana, which, with the insertion of Apollonius of Rhodes (which insertion he allows, though he does not himself make it), I shall adopt as the tentative Table of Librarians for this treatise.

1. Klippel: *op. cit.* p. 144, it is true, says Apollonius died in the reign of Ptolemy V (Epiphanes), 203–181 B.C. But so *did* Eratosthenes (c. 195).
2. Cf. *Etym. Magn.* 295–52; *Schol.* Pindar, *Pyth.* II init.

THE ALEXANDRIAN LIBRARY

TABLE OF DIRECTORS – LIBRARIANS

	From	To
Demetrios of Phaleron		282 B.C.
Zenodotus of Ephesus	282	c. 260
Callimachus of Cyrene	c. 260	c. 240
*Apollonius of Rhodes	c. 240	c. 230
Eratosthenes of Cyrene.	c. 230	195
Aristophanes of Byzantium	195	180
Apollonius the Eidograph.	180	c. 160
Aristarchus of Samothrace	c. 160	131

*This would even conform with the Papyrus, and is the only reasonable place for Apollonius of Rhodes, if he must be included among the librarians.

It is true that the Papyrus mentions one more apparent librarian: Cydas of the Spearmen (λογχοφορων) as is given by Dr. Hunt[1], who states that he has not found another use of this military term in Egypt. Dr. Barber calls him "one of the Bodyguard"[2] and ingeniously suggests that Cydas was merely a political appointment of the infamous Ptolemy Physcon. If this be so, even the bad Physcon has had some followers in succeeding ages.

This ends the consideration of *Oxyrhynchus Papyrus 1241*.

In the Temple of the Paphian Aphrodite, in the village of Kuklia, a Greek inscription was found in the excavations on the island of Cyprus (1887–1888)[3]. It is on a pink pedestal (broken) and the following comment has been made by the scholars:

> From the character of letters and offices mentioned, certainly Ptolemy VIII, Soter II (Lathyrus); [is the king] he reigned in Cyprus 117–88, and till 81 over the whole kingdom. Probably Onesander obtained his office [librarian] in Alexandria after his patron's return to Egypt in 89.

How long Onesander of Cyprus served we do not know.

In the first century A.D. there was apparently a short succession:

1. *Oxyrh. Pap.* X, p. 108.
2. C.A.H., Vol. VII, p. 253.
3. *Excavations in Cyprus, 1887–1888* – E. A. Gardner, D. G. Hogarth, M. R. James, R. Elsey Smith (*The Journal of Hellenic Studies*, London, 1888 (Vol. IX, p. 240).

Chaeremon of Alexandria, Stoic philosopher, grammarian, and historian, was the author of a *History of Egypt*, a work *On Hieroglyphics*, and possibly one *On Comets*, and a work on grammar. Josephus violently attacks his credibility (*Contra Apion.* cc. 32–33) and Martial, in an epigram (XI–56), treats him with pitiless contempt. Yet, he must have been a person of some importance, for Porphyry says that Origen in his secular studies, "used also the books of Chaeremon the Stoic" (Eusebius, *Ecclesiastical History*, VI–19), and he was also the teacher of Dionysius of Alexandria and later a tutor of Nero.

Chaeremon was chief librarian at Alexandria, although it has been thought that as he was called Keeper of the Sacred Books, that may have meant that he was the librarian of the Library of the Serapeum only. However, there is nothing to show that the Library of the Serapeum was a theological library, and not, like the "Mother" Library of the Museum, a general collection.

Dionysius, son of Glaucus, of Alexandria, pupil of Chaeremon, in the manner of the original tradition, succeeded his teacher as librarian of Alexandria. He flourished in the time from Nero (d. 68) to Trajan (d. 117) and seems to have been secretary to the emperors and to have served on embassies. He was the teacher of the grammarian Parthenius. Of his activities at the Library, of course, we know nothing.

The loss of the very names as well as the biographies of the many men, who, for at least over 500 years (say from the death of Aristarchus 143 B.C. to the destruction of the sanctuary of Serapis 391 A.D.), presided over the vast and varied collections in the Halls of Books at the Museum and at the Serapeum, many of whom must have been men of learning and ability, is one of the great tragedies of the early history of bibliography.

Particularly should we have liked to have known the librarian who beheld the first invasion of the sacred precincts of the Alexandrian Library, when the daring and ambitious Cleopatra permitted the statesman and bibliophile Caesar to remove from the Library some of its greatest treasures. We earnestly hope that he who helplessly beheld the rape of the Library (and in a few days perhaps the fatal destruction of these manuscripts so taken in the fire on the wharves or warehouses of Alexandria) by Julius Caesar in 47 B.C., lived to see the one great accession of books when the Queen's last Roman lover gave her the library of Pergamum (41 B.C.), itself acquired by Antony through the ruthlessness of war.

Many other epochs in the long history of the Alexandriana excite the imagination of the student of letters and of bibliography, but the fires of man's incredible barbarity and stupidity have raised a pall beneath which he buried the joyous dreams and profoundest thoughts of humanity, together with the visages and characters of their temporary earthly guardians.

CHAPTER IX

THE COLLECTING
OF THE BOOKS OR MANUSCRIPTS:
THE GREEK BOOKS

T HE wealth and power of the Ptolemies, backed by the mighty name of the deified Alexander, gave to their agents a special opportunity as they ransacked the four quarters of the Hellenic, Mediterranean, and Asian cities, towns, and countrysides for literary manuscripts and records of every kind. Manuscripts were acquired in every way, honestly and otherwise, by private purchase or unscrupulous force, and when it became known that there was a ready market for books at Alexandria the forerunners of all the great modern purveyors of books must have flocked to this queen city of Egypt to exchange many a precious document for the talents of the Ptolemies.

Particularly do we learn that large purchases were made from Athens and Rhodes, reasonably, the book-marts of that time. I have often thought that Magna Graecia and the great Greek cities of Asia Minor, which enveloped like a cloak the heart of old Greece, must have contributed of their ample stores.

From Neleus, pupil, relative, and heir of Theophrastus, was bought for a large price the famous library of Aristotle and the personal collection of Theophrastus with some of the manuscripts of the writings of these celebrated men. Neleus, who inherited all these treasures from Theophrastus, retained, I believe, many of the personal manuscripts of Aristotle and Theophrastus which centuries after were acquired by Apellicon and later were taken by Sulla to Rome.

Among the devious ways of acquiring manuscripts should be mentioned the embargo which was quietly placed on books. At this great port, where ships came from all the known world, vessels were searched and books or manuscripts when found were confiscated. Copies were made and given to the rightful owners with some other compensations if not too much trouble was made, but the originals were retained for the Library.

Curious it is that in the early years of the Library we get some faint references or mental glimpses of these Books of the Ships, and somehow we have thought that they were kept as a separate collection.

The famous story is told by Galen of how under Ptolemy III (Euergetes), the original autograph or authentic manuscripts of Aeschylus, Sophocles, and Euripides were obtained from Athens and how the Ptolemies, realistic book-hunters that they were, kept the priceless muniments of the Attic drama and willingly forfeited the sum of fifteen talents which had been deposited for their safe return.

Or let the story be told of the man who made this possible:

It should be remembered that it was Lycurgus, one of the Attic orators, who for twelve years, in the corrupt age of Philip and Demosthenes, controlled the treasury of Athens with impeccable honesty. This illustrious man was an aristocrat, the portraits of whose ancestors were actually painted on the walls of the Erechtheum on the Acropolis. His grandfather had suffered death for Athenian liberty under the Thirty Tyrants. He was a pupil of the schools of Plato and Isocrates. Inheriting wealth, he lived with becoming simplicity; he erected a great armory and arsenal for the soldiers and built four hundred galleys, as well as a gymnasium, a stadium, and a theatre. He revered the gods to whom he built temples in which he stored vessels of gold and silver, the result of his honorable administration of the public revenues. He encouraged the religious festivals, promoted the public theatre, and rendered to letters a unique and abiding service which would have made not only his fellow-citizens but succeeding ages his debtors. There is hardly a Greek to whom he may be compared. The mention of Roman Cato as a compeer by a brilliant modern classical scholar[1] is hardly tenable. Lycurgus was eminently superior to Cato in his personal and private character. It is always difficult to forget that the great censor was a slave-trader of the most offensive sort.

The special service rendered by Lycurgus to the Muses was the preservation in their original integrity of the plays of the great Attic tragic trio – Aeschylus, Sophocles, and Euripides. Like the works of Shakespeare and of his fellow-dramatists the texts

1. Gilbert Murray: *A History of Ancient Greek Literature*, N.Y. 1897 (p. 360).

of these supreme dramatic poets were becoming corrupt through the careless scribes and actual interpolation of actors:

> Before the invention of the press, this was a serious evil, as it endangered the very existence of the original works. To remedy it, Lycurgus caused a new transcript or edition to be made by public authority, in many cases probably from the manuscripts of the authors and to be deposited in the State archives. The value of this edition was proved by its fate. It was afterwards borrowed by one of the Ptolemies to be copied for the Alexandrian Library and fifteen talents were left at Athens as a pledge for its restitution. The king, however, sent back the copy instead of the original, and forfeited his pledge (not to mention his honour)[1].

When we consider what has been done in less than two generations by the great wealth and sound judgment of the Houses of Morgan and Huntington in an age of keen competition, we may attempt to visualize what the Ptolemies, with equal wealth and greater power, in an age of military force, were able to achieve in launching a new enterprise, the building of the great Libraries of Alexandria. The plural is used because there were two libraries at Alexandria, the greater or "Mother" Library directly connected with and housed in one of the pile of buildings (in the Hall of the Muses) adjoining the Museum in the Greek quarter and the smaller or "Daughter" Library near or in the porticoes attached to the great Temple of Serapis in the Rhakotis or Egyptian quarter.

As the result of this, relatively the greatest campaign of book gathering of which we have any knowledge, an immense number of manuscripts was assembled, embodying, it seems reasonable to assume, the entire body of Greek verse and prose then extant.

The Greek and Latin writers give various figures as to the number of books (rolls or scrolls) in the libraries of Alexandria, but it should be remembered that they refer mostly to different periods of time. Also we should note that a papyrus roll rarely represented a complete work in prose or verse. It is also true that a papyrus roll might contain more than one short work.

---

1. See the able account of this great Athenian in Connop Thirlwall: *The History of Greece* (Vol. VII, pp. 153–165), London, 1855. We miss much in our age by not reading this fine work by the Bishop of St. David's.

What may we sift out of the classical records of the past as to the governance of the Museum and the collections of the Library, which constantly suggest considerations of the foundations of these two institutions?

Demetrios of Phaleron (c. 354–283/2 B.C.) came to Egypt sometime after 307 B.C.[1] and soon became the companion, the friend, and the adviser of Ptolemy Soter. The king, in spite of his labors in building Alexandria and in the administration through arms and diplomacy of his empire, seems to have desired to make his city not only the center of the world in commerce but also in culture. Demetrios appeared on the scene at the propitious time, won the confidence of the king, and set his active mind to work. His keen intellect, calling up his early academic experience, logically conceived the idea of The Hellenic University in Alexandrea ad Aegyptum. No greater ideal was ever conceived in antiquity nor one that so quickly bore fruit. In the dynamic age of the New Hellenism, the vast wealth of Egypt and the ample power of Ptolemy soon converted the plans of Demetrios into two historic institutions that for the next seven (686) or nine hundred (937) years were to be the repositories of Hellenic learning. Too much of a realist to attempt to build within the royal compound of the new monarchical city a Lyceum or Academy which he well knew required democratic soil nourished by springs of freedom, he thought that at least he might use the little cultural symbol found in most of the free schools of Athens and other philosophic centers of Greece. That was the museum (Μουσεῖον), a small building or shrine to the Muses with statues of the goddesses and later of the founders of the school. In his own Lyceum, the Museum most probably housed the Library of Aristotle, the greatest personal collection yet gathered, which had been enlarged by his own master Theophrastus. This was the germ and here was the title of the first institution: The Museum. In keeping with the new city, it was to be a great building connected with the Palaces by a colonnade and public walk, broken by an exedra[2] with seats[3], where the scholars "who take delight in stud-

1. Mahaffy suggests: "As Ptolemy and his fleet were on the Greek coast during 307 B.C., Demetrios may have accompanied the king back to Egypt." (*The Empire of the Ptolemies*, p. 92, note.)
2. Suidas: s.v. ἐξέδρα.
3. Strabo (17–1–8; c. 794). Jones (L.C.L.).

ies can engage in disputation"[1], and all within the royal quarters, the Brucheion. Within the Museum building was a refectory, "the common mess-hall of the men of learning who share the Museum"[2], and rooms for the scholars and cells for study. It was to be a College, which we, with our little knowledge, have likened to some of the English colleges, such as Queen's at Oxford[3]. It was to house the poets and men of letters, the scientists and scholars who were invited to Alexandria as Fellows of the Museum and permanent guests of the king[4]. As a true Temple of the Muses the Museum was under the presidency of a priest, appointed by the king (in Roman times by Caesar); he was perhaps the hierarch of Serapis or the chief priest or an assistant of the hierarch of the divine cult of Alexander, soon to have added that of the reigning king and queen as "saviour gods". It is probable that his supervision was merely administrative and had little to do with the scholars. We remember here the remark of the great scholar, Cardinal Newman, concerning the *Studium* or University of Alexandria:

> Over the Library a dignified person presided, who, if his jurisdiction extended to the Museum also, might answer to a medieval or modern chancellor; the first of these functionaries being the celebrated Athenian who had so much to do with the original design[5].

There was some property held in common by the members of the Museum who were probably also recipients of a regular stipend from the royal treasury, and they may have participated in further royal endowments. They were free from regular duties to the state and from taxes. It is thought that the Fellows were not required to teach or perform tutorial labors, but had their leisure to devote to studies and experiments. Indeed the general opinion prevailed that they were liberally compensated and well treated, hence the gibe of old Timon of Phlius:

1. Vitruvius: *De Architectura* (5–11–2).
2. Strabo (17–1–8).
3. Mahaffy: *op. cit.*: "in the foundation of Queen's College, and appears in the modern history of All Souls, Oxford" (p. 95, note).
4. Bouché-Leclercq (*op. cit.*), believes that Ptolemy seems to have relied upon Demetrios to invite to his new capital the distinguished men most capable of implanting there the culture of letters and sciences (Vol. I, p. 128).
5. Newman: *op. cit.* Vol. III, p. 96.

In the thronging land of Egypt,
There are many that are feeding,
Many scribblers on papyrus,
Ever ceaselessly contending,
In the bird-coop of the Muses[1].

Of course the bird in the gilded cage lacks the one greatest right of the creature, his personal freedom. The members could read and study what they pleased, they could write, lecture, debate, and converse as the spirit moved them, but it is only reasonable to assume that those whose only happiness is to destroy existing institutions, those who denounced monarchy and could live only amid the tumult of democracy, those who would preach against the king and criticize his court and its way of life, that these rugged characters found little comfort in the Museum. And so tales (anacdota) are told of how the Greeks were scandalized by the marriage of Ptolemy II and his full sister, the indomitable Macedonian princess Arsinoe[2], and how Sotades of Maroneia indecently satirized the royal couple, was imprisoned, perhaps escaped and was apprehended by the king's admiral Patroclus, and was finally thrust into a leaden jar which was thrown into the sea. Again, when Zoilus of Amphipolis, the scourge of Homer, read his *Homeromastix* before Ptolemy, he was rebuked by the king, who refused him assistance, saying that as Homer had supported so many men[3] for centuries, Zoilus could well maintain himself[4]. And, in a lighter mood, we hear how Sosibius of Sparta, the grammarian, noted for his subtleties, had boasted to the king that he had solved a serious problem in Homer

1. Few writers have resisted quoting the version of Sir John Sandys: Timon of Phlius: *On the Alexandrian Museum* (ap. Athenaeus, 22d).
2. It was this Arsinoe who was called *Philadelphus* during her lifetime as inscriptions prove. (W. Dittenberger: *Orientiz Graeci Inscriptiones Selectae*, Leipzig, 1905, I, p. 648.) Ptolemy II was never called "Philadelphus", but Ptolemy son of Ptolemy (ch. Bevan, p. 56).
3. The writer remembers how some years ago George Herbert Palmer (whose *Odyssey* of Homer has been read by every schoolboy in America) so quaintly confided to him, that for many years he had "lived on old man Homer".
4. Vitruvius (*Praef.*, VII) says that this took place after the time of Aristophanes of Byzantium; and in the next paragraph says some report he was crucified by Philadelphus; others stoned at Chios, or again, thrown on a burning pyre at Smyrna. However, it is most probable that Zoilus the critic and Zoilus the rhetorician were one and the same person and that he lived before the time of Ptolemy II (ch. Sandys: *op. cit.* I, p. 108).

by merely changing the position of one letter. Later when his stipend fell due, he went to collect it and was told by the stewards that he had received it. He complained to the king, who sent for the rolls and examining them said the stewards were correct. "Your name is on the rolls, Sosibius," said Ptolemy. As Sosibius denied it, the king said, "Look, "marvelous solver of problems", here are recorded the names Soteros, Sosigenous, Bionos, Apolloniou." Scanning them the king said, "If you take the *so* from Soteros, the *si* from Sosigenous, the first syllable from Bionos and the last from Apolloniou, you will find your name on the rolls by your own fantastic notions." "Not by others, but by thine own feathers art thou caught."[1]

These stories were told to illustrate how the scholar of the Museum had to be the courtier at Court. And yet the chief labor of the Fellows of the Museum-Library was to assort the great mass of manuscripts containing the corpus of Hellenic letters, to discover a true text, to edit with critical apparatus the classic works in verse and prose; and for the scientists by thought and experiment to actually extend the frontiers of science for the benefit of mankind. There was nothing here that could offend the despot or disturb the most sensitive ruler.

Yet with these few thoughts as to the structure, the constitution, and customs of the Museum, and these popular anecdotes, it is singular how little we actually know of this famous institution. We have no certain knowledge of its origin, constitution, or history. Aristonicus, a distinguished Homeric critic and scholar, who was an Alexandrian and lived at the end of the first century B.C., is said to have written a book *On The Museum*. His work is lost. As a native of Alexandria, living at the time of the very apogee of the Library (from its origin under the first Ptolemy, Soter, to the acquisition of the Library of Pergamum under the last of the Ptolemies, Cleopatra), this misfortune may be considered as second only to that of the loss of the *Pinakes* of Callimachus[2].

And so the plans of the Museum had been worked out and the

1. Athenaeus (XI–493–494).
2. Cf. Mahaffy, a valuable authority on the subject of the Museum-Library, who was constrained to remark: "The whole modern literature on the subject is a literature of conjectures." (*Op. cit.* p. 92.)

ideal realized. Yet bread and wine and lodging were not enough. The members of the Museum must be furnished with the tools of learning. Old Carlyle's dictum was to be found correct two thousand years before he was born: The true University is a collection of books.

Demetrios now suggested and planned the second great institution, complementary to the first, The Alexandrian Library.

In our attempt to picture the Museum we think of *a building*, a structure of stone and marble, a work of architectural art equipped with all convenient appurtenances for the use and comfort of the scholars who are to assemble, labor, and live there.

In our attempt to visualize the Library we think of the *contents*, the manuscripts, their quality and quantity, and then secondarily of the facility of housing them, their assortment and accessibility! Of course they must have a building in keeping with the Museum or collegiate or royal palace pile and it should be furnished in every way to house, segregate, and protect its precious contents. It must have contents, otherwise it would be but an empty cage. The great achievement was thus the collecting of the manuscripts which we believe Demetrios first began.

1. Josephus, the Jewish historian of the first century of our era, tells us how Demetrios of Phaleron collected the first 200,000 rolls[1].

The authority of Josephus was Aristeas in his famous *Letter*[2]:

And so it would appear that in the incunabular years of the Alexandrian Library, in the days of the first Ptolemy, the zeal of the far-flung book hunt (the first of any record) had yielded a return of 200,000 rolls, perhaps unsorted and unarranged, but the basic material for the bibliographical labors of the great bookmen of the days of Ptolemy II and his successors.

2. Our chief authority[3] is doubtless the famous Latin scholium,

1. Josephus: *Jewish Antiquities*, L.C.L., tr. H. St. J. Thackeray and Ralph Marcus (Book XII-2–1), London, 1943; also *Letter of Aristeas*, tr. H. St. J. Thackeray, 1928. (Aristeas ap. Eusebius, *Praep*. VII, p. 350 a.)
2. *The Letter of Aristeas*, II–9–11 (p. 23).
3. I.e. if we assume a. that Caecius is the Byzantine scholar, Johnnes Tzetzes (c. 1110–1180); b. that the scribe who wrote the Plautine Scholium copied correctly from Tzetzes; and c. that the prose works of Callimachus (and those of Eratosthenes and Aristophanes of Byzantium) were extant in the 12th century and actually used by Tzetzes.

on the margin of a 15th century MS. of Plautus, discovered in 1819, in the Collegio Romano, by the classical scholar Osann. This tells us that Caecius (Johnnes Tzetzes) in his *Commentary on Aristophanes* informed us that the number of rolls was as follows: In the inner or main Library (in the Brucheion or Royal Greek quarter) at the Museum:

400,000 unsorted rolls,
90,000 segregated rolls, arranged in order[1].

In the outer Library (in the Rhakotis or Egyptian quarter) in the precincts of the Serapeum:

42,800 segregated rolls, arranged in order[2].

Such would appear to be the state of the Library in the time of Callimachus (died c. 235 B.C.).

3. Aulus Gellius (2nd century A.D.) who wrote for his children *The Attic Nights*, and Ammianus Marcellinus who wrote, about 390 A.D., *Roman History*, a continuation of Tacitus, both referring to the supposed destruction under Julius Caesar, speak of the vast collection; Gellius:

An enormous quantity of books, nearly 700,000 volumes, was either acquired or written (i.e. copied from other MSS.) in Egypt under the kings known as Ptolemies[3].

4. Ammianus:

In this (Serapeum) were invaluable libraries, and the unanimous testimony of ancient records declares that 700,000 books, brought together by the unremitting energy of the Ptolemaic kings, were burned in the Alexandrian war, when the city was sacked under the dictator Caesar[4].

1. John Edwin Sandys, in *A History of Classical Scholarship*, 3rd ed., Cambridge, 1921, p. 110–111, says (from Tzetzes, ap. Susemihl, I–342): 400,000 volumes, including several works in each volume (roll); 90,000 separate works.
2. Idem: p. 111 says: 42,800 volumes, "which were probably comparatively modern MSS. with each roll complete in itself". A. W. Mair, in *Callimachus and Lycophron* (L.C.L.) quoting from the *Prolegomena to Aristophanes* of Johnnes Tzetzes, says: Wherefore the number (of books) in the outside library was 42,800; in that within the Court and Palace the number of "mixed" books was 400,000, of "simple and unmixed" books 90,000 (*Callimachus and Lycophron*, London, 1921, p. 10).
3. Aulus Gellius: *The Attic Nights*, London, 1927, Bk. VII-17–3,L.C.L.).
4. Ammianus Marcellinus (L.C.L.), tr. J. C. Rolfe, London, 1937, Bk. XXII–16–13. Interesting note by learned translator. The Libraries however had probably 532,800

Whatever was the extent of the destruction in the time of Julius Caesar, 47 B.C. (which will be fully treated later), we know that Antony after the fall of Pergamum (41 B.C.) gave the great collections of the Attalids to Cleopatra and that they numbered some 200,000 books (simple and unmixed manuscripts).

5. Paulus Orosius of Braga, Portugal, the theologian and Christian historian, who wrote his universal history, *Historiarum adversus paganos, libri semptem,* at the suggestion of his friend St. Augustine (early 5th century), speaks of 40,000 rolls.

6. Seneca (c. 4 B.C.–A.D. 65) refers to 40,000 rolls – *Quadraginta milia librorum Alexandriae arserunt*[1]. He probably meant just this and was referring to the number of books (volumes, *burned,* and not to the number *in the Library*). But much more of this later. These various statistics would indicate that the Library's extent was not less than 700,000 MSS. in the first century B.C. before the alleged removal and destruction of some volumes under Caesar. It may be a vain though curious conjecture to consider the value and contents – the number of the books – of the Library *after* the supposed destruction of some books which Caesar intended to send to Rome, as well as *after* the acquisition of the 200,000 rolls, on vellum or parchment (pergamena-Pergamum) and papyrus from the royal library which was the pride of the Attalid kings.

Yet it must be assumed, as common-place, that once the collecting of manuscripts was begun by Demetrios of Phaleron in the big way in which he commenced to build the Alexandriana, that further acquisitions continued throughout the succeeding years under every librarian worthy of the name, in every reign, under every government, doubtless in various and unequal quantities and values, but still ever growing. This constant stream, whether rivulet or river, of acquisition during two hundred fifty years from Demetrios to Cleopatra, starting with Demetrios's magnificent assemblage of 200,000 to the acquisition of another 200,000 rolls from Pergamum, to which must be added the accumulated efforts of the intervening two centuries, would justify an assump-

MSS. in the time of Callimachus (d. c. 235 B.C.); we have no way of knowing what they numbered at the time of the battle of Pharsalia, but all natural probabilities are that they then exceeded that amount. Dr. Rolfe well says: "The damage done by Caesar has been greatly exaggerated."

1. Seneca: *De Tranquillitate Animi,* IX–5.

tion that the vast collections attained an apogee of nearly a million rolls.

We are apt, in considering the contents of the Alexandrian Library, to think only of all the Greek books in verse and prose from Homer to Demosthenes and Aristotle, the pure classic age. This has caused a distinguished German Hellenist to remark that there would not be sufficient writers and works to make the great totals that we have been contemplating, but that is perhaps not giving due credit to the large number of various editions or copies of the innumerable writers, and to the necessary duplicates, but, above all, that is forgetting that the Alexandrian or later Hellenic age during three centuries produced an enormous body of verse and prose and endless commentaries and books on books, as well as the records of amazing discoveries in the sciences. Such were the poets and their schools or followers: Philetas (elegiac), Callimachus (lyric), Lycophron (tragic), Apollonius and Euphorian (epic), and Theocritus, Bion, and Moschus (idyllic). Such were the writers of prose and pure scholarship: Demetrios, Zenodotus, Alexander the Aetolian, Aristophanes of Byzantium, and Aristarchus. Such were the men of science: Eratosthenes, Euclid, Archimedes, Conon, and the great Hipparchus of Nicaea. No age of Greek thought and genius has contributed so much to pure science, as the Alexandrian. It is not only Delambre[1] who has acknowledged our debts to the great cultural institutions and the patronage of the Ptolemaic princes, which enabled or encouraged the great Greek thinkers of antiquity to create at least the foundations of much of our modern science.

> And Alexandria may thus claim, in addition to its services in furnishing warehouse-room for the literature of Greece, and mustering a troop of careful editors and commentators, the distinction of having encouraged the first beginnings of the greatest of inductive sciences. It is only to be regretted that we have so often saved from the ruins of the library the results of scholastic industry and ingenuity, instead of those efforts of original genius which have left their impress on the intellectual world[2].

It is probably most true that a great volume of written manuscript of this age was the result of scholarly research, critical study,

1. Jean Baptiste J. Delambre: *Hist. de l'Arts anc.*, I-185 et seq.
2. Muller and Donaldson: *op. cit.* II, p. 515.

the formulation of literary apparatus for ancient classics, and the assembling and rearranging the accumulated knowledge of the past and present. It is likewise true that it was not only in the sanctum of the Museum or the rooms of the Alexandriana that scholars reduced their labors to papyrus. Throughout the Hellenic world men thought and wrote, and a vast output of publications issued from the private studies or professional scriptoria of Athens, Rhodes, Cos, the other island cities, Antioch, Pergamum, Tarsus, Nicaea, Byzantium, and the literate Asian littoral, Syracuse, Cumae, and the seats of Magna Graecia, of Pella and the mountain towns and inland cities.

All the manuscripts of these "modern" Greek writers must, in the lifetime or after the death of their authors, have found their way to the great Libraries of Alexandria, and thus have added to their immense store.

And so by common accord we must feel that a contemporary Catalogue of the Vellum-Papyrus Books of Pergamum and of Callimachus (the lost *Pinakes*), Lists or Tables of the Papyrus Rolls of Alexandria, including all these "modern" additions, would be worth more to the cause of pure scholarship than the discovery of a Livy "whole".

But the ambition of the Ptolemies after collecting the physical remains of all the Greek wisdom, knowledge, and information, the most important, certainly the most brilliant, ever produced by man, was still unsatisfied. They had been told of the wonderful Scriptures, or Laws of the Jews; they had seen the pictographs of the Egyptians, which seem barbarous and crude to the scientific Greek; and they had wondered at the cryptic cuneiform of the Assyrians and the marvelous mural histories in technicolor at Babylon; all holding under strange linguistic keys hidden, perhaps esoteric, knowledge and wisdom, which easily excited the imagination of the most curious of peoples – the Hellenes.

As the whole body of Greek learning was now assembled, or an attempt made to bring it together at Alexandria, the Greek, ever eager for knowledge, looked to the New Hellenic countries and those under Macedonian rule for their original history, literature, and philosophy in their original tongues.

CHAPTER X

THE COLLECTING
OF THE BOOKS OR MANUSCRIPTS:
THE NON-GREEK BOOKS

A s the Greek came into contact with the two great empires of the ancient Eastern world, in the East, the Assyrian, the heir of most ancient Babylon, and predecessor of Persia, and in the South the hoary Egyptian, the Hellenic curiosity sought to understand the language, history, and culture of Egypt and Assyria.

Sir Flinders Petrie believes that the Alexandrian Library contained translations in Greek of many books in other languages, such as Egyptian, Hebrew, Punic, etc., but Mr. Bevan protests that no Greek writers show any knowledge of these translations[1]. Should we not say that very few Greek writers extant, if any, have much to say concerning the non-Greek books in the Alexandriana, as likewise how few Greek authors or ancient writers extant have anything much to say concerning even the Greek books of the Library.

Now the Greeks had also often met in Asia Minor, and especially in Alexandria (where they had a vast quarter of the city to themselves), a race of men not numerous but distinctive, self-centered, exclusive, religiously proud to the degree of snobbery, with souls supremely contemplative of Divinity, whose vision lifted the eternal veil, yet with brains sharp, keen, and ever alert for commercial gain – these people, self-sufficient, must possess Laws, a philosophy or religion that should be interesting even to the sophisticated Greek.

THE SACRED WRITINGS OF THE JEWS

So the legend is told by Aristeas[2], a supposed official at the court of Ptolemy "Philadelphus".

1. Bevan: *op. cit.* p. 125, note.
2. Whether Aristeas was a Greek as he himself records (Pseudo *Letter of Aristeas to his brother Philocrates*, written about 200 B.C.; editio princeps (Simon Schard, Basil,

We give the succinct description of this document by H. St. J. Thackeray, whose admirable translation we shall use throughout this work[1]:

> The document known as the Letter of Aristeas purports to be a contemporary record, by a Greek holding a high position at the court of Ptolemy Philadelphus (285–247 B.C.), of the translation of the Hebrew Pentateuch into Greek, undertaken at the instance of the royal librarian, Demetrius of Phalerum. The familiar name "the Septuagint", by which the Greek Old Testament as a whole came to be known, owes its origin to the story here told of the seventy-two translators of the Law. The narrative is communicated in the form of a letter from Aristeas to his brother Philocrates. Aristeas claims to have been a member of the embassy sent from Alexandria to Jerusalem to obtain a copy of the Law and the services of a company of Palestinian translators.

Demetrios of Phaleron in reporting to the king[2] the great progress made in gathering books for the Alexandrian Library reminds Ptolemy that there are many books of Law among the Jews worthy of the great collection; that these books are written in Hebrew characters unknown to the Greeks; and that these books of Law are "full of hidden wisdom, and entirely blameless, as being the legislation of God; for which cause it is, as Hecateus of

1561)); or a *Cyprian* (Wm. Smith (ed.), *Dictionary of Greek and Roman Biography and Mythology* (London, 1867), Vol. I-293); or an *Egyptian* (A. Vander Heeren: in *Catholic Encyclopedia*, s.v. *Septuagint*); or a *Persian* noble (Kirsopp Lake in his tr. Eusebius: *The Ecclesiastical History* (London, 1926), Vol. I, p. 461, note. – L.C.L.), is of little consequence as the authenticity of the *Letter* has been doubted since the days of Luis Vives, of the University of Louvain (1492–1540) and apparently completely destroyed by Humphry Hody, Oxford, in 1684. Whoever the writer of this letter was, he was most probably an Alexandrian *Jew* (i.e. an Hellenistic Jew). Yet Prof. Mahaffy does not hesitate to affirm: "The course of recent criticism, starting from the researches of Lumbroso, has tended rather to rehabilitate the authority of this much decried author. His knowledge of the Egyptian Court seems good, and we now know that the books of Moses were translated as early as the fourth Ptolemy. I am therefore disposed to give credit to his general statement, though many details are of course fabricated." (Mahaffy: *Greek Life and Thought*, 2nd ed., London, 1896, p. 508). He adds: "Successful forgeries are, however, usually exaggerations of real facts" (*op. cit.* p. 522). Sir John Sandys (*op. cit.* pp. 108 and 110) also cites *The Letter of Aristeas*. This *Letter* is translated into English by H. St. J. Thackeray (rev.), 1928; and R. Tramentano's *La Lettera di Aristea a Filocrate*, with translation and commentaries, 1931, is a most important edition.

1. *The Letter of Aristeas*, tr. H. St. J. Thackeray (London, 1918), p. VII.
2. Most reasonably to his patron, Ptolemy Soter, certainly not to his Nemesis Ptolemy "Philadelphus".

Abdera says, that the poets and historians make no mention of
it, nor of those men who lead their lives according to it, since it
is a holy law, and ought not to be published by profane mouths"[1].
But let Aristeas or the original text of *The Letter of Aristeas*
tell the story:

"I (Demetrios) am informed that the Jews also have certain laws
which are deserving of transcription and a place in thy library."
"What is to hinder thee, then," replied the king, "in this task? For
all the necessary means are at thy service." And Demetrius answered, "translation is also required. For in the Jew's land they use
a peculiar script (just as Egyptians have their system of letters)
and speak a peculiar language. It is commonly thought that they
use the Syrian language, but this is an error; it is another dialect."
And when the king had learnt all the facts, he gave command that
a letter should be written to the high-priest of the Jews, in order that
the proposal above-mentioned might be carried into effect.

(II–10–11.)

The king emancipates the Jewish captives and slaves in Egypt
and orders Demetrios to make his report on the state of the
Library.

THE LIBRARIAN'S MEMORIAL

"To the great king from Demetrius.— In obedience to thy order,
O king, that the books which are wanting to complete the library
should be added to the collection, and that those which are defective should be duly repaired, I have expended great care upon these
matters and now submit a reference to thee. The books of the
Jewish law with some few others are wanting. They are written
in Hebrew letters and in the Hebrew tongue, and have been interpreted somewhat carelessly and do not represent the original text,
according to information supplied by the experts, because they
have never received a king's fostering care. It is necessary that these
books too should in an emended form find a place in thy library,
because this code of laws, in that it is divine, is full of wisdom and
faultless. For this reason authors, poets, and the mass of the historians have abstained from any mention of the books aforesaid and
of the men who have lived (and are living) in accordance with them,
because the views presented in them have a certain sanctity and
holiness, as says Hecataeus of Abdera. If then it be thy good pleas-

1. Flavius Josephus: *The Antiquities of the Jews*, Bk. XII, ch. 2 (XII–38).

ure, O king, a letter shall be written to the high-priest at Jerusalem, bidding him send six elders from each tribe, men of the highest repute and versed in their country's law, in order that we may test wherein the more part agree, and so obtaining an accurate translation may deposit it in a conspicuous place in a manner worthy of the undertaking and of thy gracious will. Fare ever well!''

King Ptolemaeus writes a Letter to Eleazar the High-Priest setting forth:

Now since we desire to confer a favour not on these only (the Jews in Ptolemy's army or those who may become attached to the Court), but on all Jews throughout the world and on future generations, it is our will that your Law be translated from the Hebrew tongue in use among you into Greek, that so these writings also may find a place in our library with the other royal volumes. (II-d-38.)

Eleazar replied granting the request and said:

We selected six elders from each tribe, good men and true, whom we are also sending with a copy of the Law.

The names of the Translators are given, a description of the royal presents, an account of the journey of the Greek Mission to Judaea with an eye-witness's vivid description of Jerusalem, Eleazar's Apology for the Jewish Law, the reception of the Translators at Alexandria, their entertainment, banquet in their honor, the questions of the king put to his learned visitors and their replies to the royal questioner.

After three days Demetrios took the Translators apparently by the Heptastadium to a magnificent house on the island of Pharos:

And so it came about that the translation was accomplished in seventy-two days, as though this coincidence had been intended.

And when the work was ended, Demetrius assembled the Jewish people on the spot where the translation had been made and read it through to the whole assembly in the presence of the translators, who received another great ovation from the people in recognition of the great services which they had rendered. And they gave a similar reception to Demetrius and requested him to have a copy of the whole Law transcribed and to present it to their rulers. And after the reading of the rolls the priests and the elders of the translators and some members of the Jewish community and the rulers of the people stood up and said, "Forasmuch as the translation has been well and piously executed and with perfect accuracy, it is right that it should remain in its present form and that no revision should take place." And when all had assented to these words, they bade them, in accordance with their custom, pronounce an imprecation upon any who should revise the text by adding to, or in any way transposing, or omitting ought from, what had been written; and herein they did well, to the intent that the work might for ever be preserved imperishable and unchanged.

When word of these proceedings was brought to the king, he greatly rejoiced, for it seemed that his purpose had been securely attained. The whole work was read through to him, and he was greatly astonished at the spirit of the law-giver. And he said to Demetrius, "How is it that none of the historians or poets ever thought of mentioning such great achievements?" And he said, "Because the Law is holy and has been given by God; and some of those who did essay to do so were smitten of God and desisted from their attempt." For he said that he had heard Theopompus tell how when he was too rashly intending to introduce into his history some of the incidents from the Law which had previously been translated, his mind was deranged for more than thirty days; and when the disorder abated he besought God that the cause of the misfortune might be made plain to him; and when it was shewn him in a dream that his desire to disclose divine truths to common men was misguided, he desisted, and thereupon recovered his reason. "I have been informed too," he added, "by Theodectes, the tragic poet, that when he was intending to introduce into one of his plays something recorded in the Book, he was afflicted with cataract of the eyes; and, suspecting that this was the reason for his mishap, he besought God's mercy and after many days recovered his sight."

Although the story as told by the pseudo-Aristeas is quite romantic, "it must not be hastily inferred that it has no historical basis", as Dr. Swete[1] so judiciously concludes.

That the writer was an Hellenistic Jew, that he was seeking to glorify his exalted religion, there can be little doubt. That he followed an existing tradition is more than probable. If we only knew his authorities, we would be in a position to separate

1. Henry Barclay Swete: *An Introduction to The Old Testament in Greek* (Cambridge, 1902), p. 15.

the skeleton of facts from much of the fantastic tinsel with which he has adorned his tale. But what is certain is that he has been quoted or followed by Jewish and Christian exegetes, by more than a dozen Christian fathers, as well as by Josephus, Philo, and Aristobulus, all of whom repeat the substance of his account, with the usual modifications, omissions, and changes, some indeed adding embellishment to embellishment, and a few apparently correcting errors or assuming a critical attitude. Now it is only reasonable to assume that some of the later writers must have known or had access to his authorities, and had the story not been substantially true, it would have been denounced long before St. Jerome.

Irenaeus (c. 130-c. 200 A.D.), an Asian, arch-bishop of Lyons, who had heard the preaching of the martyr St. Polycarp, the disciple of St. John, is reported by Eusebius[1] as saying:

> Ptolemy, the son of Lagus, being very anxious to adorn the library, which he had founded in Alexandria, with all the best extant writings of all men, asked from the inhabitants of Jerusalem to have their Scriptures translated into Greek. They, for they were at that time still subject to the Macedonians, sent to Ptolemy seventy elders, the most experienced they had in the Scriptures and in both languages, and God thus wrought what he willed. But Ptolemy, wishing to make trial of them in his own way, and being afraid lest they should have made some agreement to conceal by their translation the truth in the Scriptures, separated them from one another and commanded them all to write the same translation. And this he did in the case of all the books. But when they came together to Ptolemy, and compared each his own translation, God was glorified and the Scriptures were recognized as truly divine, for they all rendered the same things in the same words and the same names, from beginning to end, so that even the heathens who were present knew that the Scriptures had been translated by the inspiration of God.

The books of the Hebrew Law were translated at Alexandria, most probably by Alexandrian Jews in the third century B.C., possibly in the days of Ptolemy II[2]. That the *Pentateuch* was

---

1. Eusebius: *The Ecclesiastical History*, Bk. V–VIII–11–12 (L.C.L., ed. Kirsopp Lake), London, 1926.
2. H. St. J. Thackeray: *The Letter of Aristeas*, London, 1918 (p. XV, Intro.): "The Greek *Pentateuch* goes back at least as far as the middle of the third century B.C."

then translated was the opinion of the author of Aristeas's *Letter*, of Josephus, and of Philo Judaeus.

It is reasonable to assume that the Laws were placed in the great collection by the curious minded Macedonian-Greeks ruling Hellenic Egypt.

Within about a century (at least before 130 B.C.) the Prophets, and the *Historical Books of the Old Testament* followed the *Law* and the Hebrew Scriptures, the far-famed *Septuagint*, The LXX[1], now were completely embalmed in the eternal language of Hellas.

In the life of the intellect, in the eternity of the Spirit, this was one of the greatest moments.

The infinite beauty, the sublime wisdom, and the awful judgments of the Hebraic cosmos transmuted into Greek, became the most ancient translation of the *Old Testament*. As Hebrew had long ceased to be a living tongue, the *Greek Version of the Scriptures*, this *Septuagint*, was read in the synagogue of the Jews of the Dispersion not only in Alexandria, but throughout the Greek-speaking world, and spread even into the Holy Land, where it was recognized as an authoritative text. Through it the Macedonians, Greeks, and later the Greco-Romans were able to know, through Hebrew theology, of the wondrous Promises of God to Man. Hence the lands of the Gentiles were being prepared for the rich sowing of the Glad Tidings, the Gospel of Jesus Christ. The world-language of the Greeks, in which the Alexandrian Philo and the Palestinian Josephus wrote their philosophies and histories, became the mother tongue of Christianity in its appeal to mankind. When the *New Testament* appears, we see

1. *The Septuagint* (The LXX):

a. The Aldine edition, (commenced by Aldus Manucius) and actually published at Venice, 1518. Really the *editio princeps*.

b. The Complutensian, *printed* at Alcalá (Spain) in 1514–18, but not *published* until 1520, when it appeared in the *Polyglot* of Cardinal Ximenes.

c. Codex Alexandrinus, one of the six exemplars on vellum: *Vetus Testamentum Graecum e Codice MS. Alexandrino* (with Letter of Cyril and volume, *Prolegomena et Notae*), published by H. H. Baber, 6 vols., London (Ricardi & Taylor), 1816–1828, also *Novum Testamentum Graecum e Codice MS. Alexandrino* (C.G. Woide), London (Joannis Nichols), 1786, one of seven exemplars on vellum.

d. Codex Vaticanus (B): *Bibliorum S.S. Graecorum Cod*. Vat. 1209, Cod. B, denuo phototypice expressus, jussu et cura praesidum Bibliothecae Vaticanae, Milan, (Hoepli) 1904–1906 (in 3 vols.) – "This most important of Biblical MSS." (Swete, *op. cit.* p. 127).

that Apostles, Evangelists, and the sacred writers, have freely used the *Septuagint* as the chief source for quotations from and references to the Old Testament, and for four centuries (to A.D. 400) the Fathers and the Church drew from this fountain of primal wisdom (from which all ancient versions of the *Old Testament*, except the Syriac, were derived) and many considered the *Version* inspired. The nomenclature of the early Church was Greek. *The LXX* is still the official text of the Greek Church. It has even been used exigetically and critically for an understanding and correction of the Hebrew text itself[1]. The temptation to quote a few lines, from the Preface of The English Bible (1611) is irresistible:

> It pleased the Lord to stirre up the spirit of a Greeke Prince (Greeke for dicent and language), even of Ptoleme Philadelph, King of Egypt, to procure the translating of the Booke of God out of Hebrew into Greeke .... Therefore the word of God, being set foorth in Greeke, becometh hereby like a candle set upon a candlesticke, which giveth light to all that are in the house, or like a proclamation sounded foorth in the market place, which most men presently take knowledge of; and therefore that language was fittest to containe the Scriptures, both for the first Preachers of the Gospel to appeale unto for witnesse, and for the learners also of those times to make search and triale by[2].

But as the crowning glory of its divine mission to humanity the Apostles, Galileans all, who, before the miraculous gift of tongues, knew no Hebrew, made their chief references to the *Old Testament* in the words of *The LXX*. And finally it is believed that in the time of Christ, the people of Palestine were bilingual and spoke Aramaic and Greek and that Christ had at least these accomplishments.

The parents of Jesus were most orthodox. He lived with them the greater part of His life in Galilee. In the synagogue of Nazareth the Greek Version (*The Septuagint*) appears to have been generally read. Here we cannot forego recording the immortal scene in Luke IV–18 (for which I quote the latest of modern

---

1. Of course the text of the Hebrew Scriptures was established in the 6th century A.D. by the Massoretes (*op. cit.* Vander Heeren).
2. *The Holy Bible*, conteyning the Old Testament and the New, newly translated out of the Originall Tongues. Imprinted at London by Robert Barker, Anno Dom. 1611.

versions, *The New Testament*, translated from the Vulgate Latin by Mgr. Ronald A. Knox, New York, 1944):

> Then he came to Nazareth, where he had been brought up; and he went into the synagogue there, as his custom was, on the sabbath day, and stood up to read. The book given to him was the book of the prophet Isaisas; so he opened it and found the place where the words ran: The Spirit of the Lord is upon me; he has anointed me, and sent me out to preach the gospel to the poor, to restore the broken-hearted; to bid the prisoners go free, and the blind to receive their sight; to set the oppressed at liberty, to proclaim a year when men may find acceptance with the Lord. Then he shut the book, and gave it back to the attendant, and set down. All those who were in the synagogue fixed their eyes on him, and thus he began speaking to them. This scripture which I have read in your hearing is to-day fulfilled.

The apposite comment of Bishop Walton is indicated:

> Here we see that the words of the Evangelist differ from the Hebrew text, while they exactly agree with the Greek interpretation (*The Septuagint*); whence, it appears, one may infer that our Lord used the Greek version in the Synagogue, and afterwards explained it to the people in the vernacular tongue (Syriac).

And again:

> But the greatest authority has been added to this version (*The Septuagint*) because it was used by Christ and His Apostles, etc. (*The Hexaglot Bible*, ed. E. Riches de Levante).

Christ in His chief reference to the *Old Testament* uses the words of *The LXX*; hence it seems most reasonable to believe that Jesus, as a child, was taught from manuscript rolls and verbal lessons of his native rabbins, the *Old Testament* from the Greek Version, *The Septuagint*[1].

And so the amazing scroll, up to that time the *Book of Books*, silently found its potential place amid the treasury of Hellenic learning from Homer to Aristotle, destined, in time, to survive all empires and all cultures, and to maintain its prophesies in eons yet to come, when the memory of the Alexandriana shall have faded from the earth.

1. E. W. Grinfield: *An Apology for the Septuagint*, London, 1850.

MANETHO AND THE EGYPTIAN LITERATURE

Perhaps before Manetho, the *Calendar of Sais* was translated into Greek; we know that Greek writers at various times wrote of the Wonders and Mysteries of Egypt. Their works are unfortunately in the vast necropolis of literature among the lost books of the world.

In the days of Ptolemy Soter (323–283 B.C.) and of his son Ptolemy "Philadelphus" (B.C. 285–246), the first two kings of the famous Greek dynasty of Egypt, there lived an Egyptian of the priestly caste named Manetho. He called himself "high-priest and scribe of the sacred shrines of Egypt, born at Sebennytus and dwelling at Heliopolis".

Manetho appears[1] to have been the Egyptian priestly-adviser to Ptolemy Soter, associated with the king's Greek spiritual counsellor Timotheus, the Eumolpid (priestly family of Eleusis, consecrated to the famed Eleusinian Mysteries), and they had much to do with the inauguration of the cult of Serapis, where Greek and Egyptian might worship together. It was near or in the porticoes of the great temple of this god (the Serapeum) in the Rhakotis quarter of Alexandria, that the smaller or "Daughter" Library was housed with some 42,800 selected or simple rolls.

Manetho, as an Egyptian priest of high rank, was a man of culture, indeed a man of letters, and he wrote in Greek works on Egyptian history and religion, transmitting to the Hellenes much of the sacred learning and historical chronology of the ancient Egyptians hitherto concealed in the hieroglyphical writings of that venerable people.

Manetho's qualifications for the role of interpreter of ancient Egypt to the Greek has been brilliantly described[2]: "As a Heliopolitan priest" he "was without doubt acquainted with the sacred tree in the great Hall of Heliopolis, the tree on which the goddess Seshat, the Lady of Letters, the Mistress of the Library, wrote down with her own hand the names and deeds of the rulers. He did nothing more than communicate to the Greek world what

1. Plutarch: *Isis and Osirus*, ch. 28.
2. Richard Laqueur, in Pauly-Wissowa-Kroll: *Real-Encyclopädie*, quoted by Dr. W. G. Waddell in his *Manetho*, London, 1940, one of the great volumes of the "indispensable Loeb".

the goddess had noted down. But he did so with the full sense of the superiority which relied on the sacred records of the Egyptians in opposition to Herodotus whom he was contradicting".

There is an old Egyptian glyph or sculpture showing the goddess with Thoth and Atum writing inscriptions on the leaves (the most primitive form of writing) of the Sacred Tree[1]. It was most fitting that Manetho, which may mean "Beloved of Thoth" or "Truth of Thoth", should be the interpreter of his country's sacred and hoary past to these new-comers, these eager and inquisitive Greeks.

Yet Manetho had sources even beyond the inspired notes of the goddess Lady of Letters, because he had access to the vast recorded materials then existing in Egypt: in Temple Libraries, in Palace records, the papyri rolls of the sacred books, the liturgies and formulae for the living and the dead; the annals of the Kings of Egypt kept through the ages by the priestly scribes; the rolls inscribed with the economic records of temples and estates, as well as the poems and prose literature of Egypt. In monumental records there were the vast remains of Palace and Temple sculpture, and historical and religious wall inscriptions in the abodes of the gods, man, and the dead, not to mention *stelae*, tablets, and statues of the kings and gods replete with hieroglyphical writings.

Particularly we know he could have consulted such primary sources as:

a. *The Royal List of Abydos* (cut on the dim corridor wall of the temple of Seti I at Abydos) with its series of 76 kings (Manes to Seti I).

b. *The Royal List of Karnak*, originally 61 kings (Manes to Tuthmosis III) (This was in the Louvre.)
a and b furnish the royal traditions of Upper Egypt.

c. *The Royal List of Sakkara* (in Cairo Museum), originally 58, now 47 kings (from Miebis of the 1st Dynasty).

d. The famous *Turin Papyrus* (Turin Museum), an hieratic papyrus written on the *verso* of an ancient document of the time of Rameses II (c. 1200 B.C.) with records of the king written on the *recto*. "It contains the names of kings in order, over 300, when complete, with the length of each reign in years, months, and

1. Dr. W. G. Waddell: *Manetho, op. cit.* p. XII.

days."[1] The classical world is still waiting for a definitive edition of this great historical record[2].

c and d furnish the royal traditions of Lower Egypt.

e. *The Palermo Stone* (Museum of Palermo), with list of kings of greatest antiquity, and dating from the 5th Dynasty[2].

With this background Manetho is said to have written eight works:

1. *The Aegyptiaca* or History of Egypt.
2. *The Book of Sothis*.
3. *The Sacred Book*.
4. *The Epitome of Physical Doctrines*.
5. *On Festivals*.
6. *On Ancient Ritual and Religion*.
7. *On the Making of Kyphi* ("a kind of incense").
8. *Criticisms of Herodotus*.

Modern criticism has cut the number of the above works to two or at most three:

a. *The History of Egypt* (which may have included 8).
b. *The Sacred Book* (which may have included 5–6–7).
c. *An Epitome of Physical Doctrines*.

The Book of Sothis is rejected as not being by Manetho.

But the most important fact is that all of the works of Manetho are *lost!*

We have fragments of fragments which have come down the hard road of classical literary transmission of ancient records to our times.

As an example of this tortuous course let us see what happened to his principal work the *Aegyptiaca*.

a. In the Jewish historian Josephus (37–c. 100 A.D.) are preserved some extracts from the original work, together with passages which show that "the efforts of Jewish apologists (who sought by the *Egyptian History* of Manetho to secure the traditions of the origin and antiquities of the Jewish people) account for much rehandling, enlargement, and corruption of Manetho's

1. Dr. W. G. Waddell: *Manetho, op. cit.* p. XXII.
2. We hope the *Papyrus* and the *Stone* have escaped the havoc of the world's most destructive war.

text, and the result may be seen in the treatise of Josephus, *Contra Apionem*[1].

b. An *Epitome* of Manetho's work, not by Manetho, was made very early. It too is lost.

Fragments of this *Epitome* are preserved principally by the Christian chronographers who sought to harmonize the chronology of the Bible with the records of the oriental empires.

Sextus Julius Africanus wrote a *Chronicle* (from the beginning of the world 5499 B.C. to Elagabalus, 217 or 221 A.D.) in 5 books.

But the important *Chronicle* of Africanus is also lost. Fragments of Africanus are preserved in Eusebius, also in Syncellus, Cedrenus, and in the *Paschale Chronicon*. Now the original Greek text of Eusebius is lost. We have a part of it from the Greek text quoted in Syncellus and we have an *Armenian Version* of the whole of Eusebius (5th century A.D.) and a *Latin Version* of Eusebius made by St. Jerome in the 4th century.

To sum up this intricate trail:

a. From a good Josephus we get excerpts from the original Manetho and some "pseudo-Manethonian" passages.

b. From the Latin and Armenian versions of Eusebius and the passages of Eusebius quoted by Syncellus we get the lost Greek original of Eusebius in which were passages of Manetho which Eusebius himself transmits, but Eusebius is held "responsible for unwarranted alterations of the original text of Manetho"[2] as well as of the extracts which the lost Greek original of Eusebius transmitted from the lost Greek original of Sextus Julius Africanus.

c. Besides Josephus, Africanus, and Eusebius, a writer, George the Monk (800 A.D.), who is known in literature as the Syncellus, wrote a *World History* (from Adam to the emperor Diocletian) in which he quoted Manetho "as transmitted by Africanus and Eusebius, and as handed down in a corrupt form in the *Old Chronicle* and the *Book of Sothis*, which had been used by the chronographer Panodorus (400 A.D.)"[3].

---

1. Dr. W. G. Waddell (*op. cit.* p. XVI) to whom we are continually indebted in this business of Manetho.
2. Idem: *op. cit.* p. XVII.
3. Idem: p. XVII.

d. Finally there are short excerpts to be found in Plutarch, Theophilus, Aelian, Porphyrius, Diogenes Laertius, Theodoretus, Lydus, Malalas, the Scholia to Plato, and in the *Etymologicum Magnum*[1].

From all of this melange a corpus of Manetho has been evolved! Opinions differ as to the value of the work of the Egyptian priest.

François Lenormant[2], still a great name when we first collected books on the ancient world, most favorably writes:

Of all the Greek writers who have treated of the history of the Pharaohs, there is only one whose testimony has, since the decipher-ing of the hieroglyphics, preserved any great value, a value which increases the more it is compared with the original monuments; we speak of Manetho, once he was treated with contempt; his veracity was disputed; the long series of dynasties he unfolds to our view were regarded as fabulous. Now all that remains of his work is the first of all authorities, for the reconstruction of the ancient history of Egypt.

Next to the monuments in importance, says classic Mariette[3], in his *Aperçu*, "comes the Greek history of Egypt written by Manetho, an Egyptian priest, about B.C. 250; and were the book itself in existence, we could have no more trustworthy guide."

And Samuel Sharpe:

The correctness of Manetho's list of Kings, which runs back for fifteen hundred years, is shown by our finding the names agree with every Egyptian inscription with which they can be compared. But what little there is in it beyond the names would seem to be built on rather uncertain tradition[4].

In Brugsch-Bey's great work we find:

The national historian of this period was Manetho, an Egyptian who was well acquainted with the Greek tongue, and was ordered by Ptolemy Philadelphus to write in that language the history of

1. Dr. W. G. Waddell: p. VII.
2. François Lenormant and E. Chevalier: *A Manual of the Ancient History of the East* (Phila., 1871, I, p. 196).
3. Auguste Mariette: *Outlines of Ancient Egyptian History* (tr. Broderick), N.Y. 1892 (p. 2).
4. Samuel Sharpe: *The History of Egypt* (London, 1885), Vol. I, p. 326.

his native land. He appears to have been both a scribe and a high-priest, and thoroughly well versed in the language and literature of his country, as the monuments often afford confirmation of many of his statements. If only the *Book of Manetho* were yet extant, the writing of a history of Ancient Egypt would be comparatively speaking a light task; but the manuscript itself perished, along with other priceless documents, in the burning of the great library at Alexandria[1].

Everyone knows the praise bestowed upon Manetho by the illustrious Bunsen[2] and the learned Richard Lepsius.

Manetho of Sebennytus (a city in the Delta), is the author whose works possess by far the greatest amount of value and importance to our subject of any that have come down to us from the Greeks... from him alone have we derived anything like certain knowledge regarding the chronology of the history of Ancient Egypt[3].

In our day, Mr. Flinders Petrie[4] says:

The classical authority for these lists (of the Kings of Egypt) is all derived from various copyists and extractors who worked on the great Ptolemaic compilation of Manetho.

It is perfectly true that Canon Rawlinson[5] believed that Manetho's scheme of chronology as we have it, is untrustworthy and that even if we had the original work "before us in its entirety we could derive from it no exact or satisfactory chronology".
And we remember that our own Dr. Breasted[6] said:

A more or less arbitrary and artificial but convenient subdivision of these epochs, beginning with the historic age, is furnished by the so-called dynasties of Manetho... The value of the work was slight, as it was built up on folk-tales and popular traditions of the early kings.

1. Henrick Brugsch-Bey: *Egypt under the Pharaohs, a History derived entirely from the Monuments* (London, 1891). New, revised and condensed edition, p. 442.
2. C. C. J. Baron Bunsen: *Egypt's Place in Universal History* (London, 1867), Vol. I, p. 78 et seq.
3. William Osburn: *The Monumental History of Egypt* (London, 1854), Vol. I, p. 180.
4. Wm. Flinders Petrie: *A History of Egypt from the Earliest Times to the XVIth Dynasty*, New York, 1895 (p. 16).
5. George Rawlinson: *History of Ancient Egypt* (London, 1881, p. 9).
6. James Henry Breasted: *A History of Egypt from the Earliest Times to the Persian Conquest*, New York, 1905 (p. 13–14).

Perhaps the more just view is expressed by Dr. Griffith[1], Reader in Egyptology at Oxford:

Notwithstanding all the defects, the fragments of Manetho have provided the accepted scheme of Egyptian dynasties and have been of great service to scholars ever since the first months of Champollion's decipherment.

And finally, Dr. Hall states fairly:

In fact, Manetho did what he could; where the native annals were good and complete, his abstract is good; where they were broken and incomplete, his record is incomplete also and confused[2].

And in the *Cambridge Ancient History*[3]:

So far as we are able to check Manetho from the contemporary monuments, his division into dynasties is entirely justified. His authorities evidently were good. But unhappily his work has come down to us only in copies of copies.

The considerable fragments of it, preserved by Josephus and other writers, gave Europe almost all the substantial information it had about ancient Egypt till the 19th century, when scholars discovered the key to the old Egyptian writing[4].

The importance of Manetho is well expressed by Dr. Waddell of Fuad el Awal University, Cairo, his last able redactor:

The significance of Manetho's writings is that for the first time an Egyptian was seeking to instruct foreigners in the history and religion of his native land[5].

And so records of Egyptian history and literature found a place in the Library of Alexandria.

BEROSSOS AND THE BABYLONIAN LITERATURE

The conquest of the oriental kingdoms of Asia and of Egypt by Alexander the Great led to the permanent introduction of Hellenic civilization and the establishment of the Greek language

1. Francis Llewellyn Griffith: *Encyclopaedia Britannica* (11th ed.), s.v. *Manetho*.
2. H. R. Hall: *Ancient History of the East* (p. 14).
3. H. R. Hall: *Cambridge Ancient History* (I, p. 260).
4. Bevan: *op. cit.* p. 85.
5. W. G. Waddell: *op. cit.* (XXVI).

throughout the East. Native scholars sought to bring to these somewhat arrogant Greeks an account of their own history and antiquities, the genealogies of their ancient gods and the achievements of the heroes of their race. So Manetho, the Egyptian priest of On (Heliopolis), wrote his *Aegyptiaca*; so Menander, of "those Phoenicians who wrote their histories in Greek"[1], of Tyre wrote the *History of Tyre*; and so Berossos, a priest of Bel-Marduk of Babylon, who wrote the *Chaldiaca* or rather the *Babyloniaca* or history of Babylonia.

We know little of Berossos's life, except the facts of his priesthood, and his reputation for extraordinary learning and uniform veracity. A contemporary of Alexander the Great, he lived under Antiochus I, Soter (280–261 B.C.) to whom he dedicated his *Babyloniaca*.

"He was a Chaldean, and no doubt an astronomer or astrologer," says Niebuhr[2]. If this be sound and we may believe Vitruvius and the elder Pliny, our Babylonian was not only the historian of his race, but also an astronomer widely known, who established a school at Cos, taught at Athens, earning there a statue with a tongue of gold, erected in the gymnasium. He invented the semicircular sundial[3]; and his optical theory of the conflict of the rays of the sun and moon "anticipated Young's discovery of the absorption of light by interference"[4]. Tatian correctly calls Berossos "the most learned historian of Western Asia"[5]; and his master, Justin Martyr, declares that the Babylonian Sibyl who prophesied at Cumae was his daughter. Now though the oracles of the *Sibylline Books* doubtlessly came to Rome from Cumae, they came in the days of Tarquinius Superbus, the last of the kings of Rome (c. 500 B.C.). Berossos lived between 356 and 261 B.C. Old Justin Martyr visited Cumae (Kyme) about the middle of the 2nd century of our era, and must have been impressed by many mysterious aspects of the place. Even to-day, the traveller (for such were the impressions of the writer) who explores its vast subterranean passages and provocative remains, cannot but feel the spirit of the great Sibyl

1. George Rawlinson: *History of Phoenicia* (London, 1889), p. 72.
2. Berthold George Niebuhr: *Lectures on Ancient History*, Vol. I, p. 15 (London, 1852).
3. Vitruvius (London, 1934, L.C.L.), Book IX–8.
4. Idem.: Vol. II, p. 228, note.
5. Gabriel Oussani, in *Catholic Encyclopaedia*, s.v. *Berosus*.

who provoked the voice of Virgil[1] and the brush of Michelangelo.

Be these matters as they may, Berossos, the Babylonian wrote in Greek, with great learning and truth, the history of Mesopotamia in 3 books (I from the Creation to the Flood[2]; II from the Flood to Nabonassar; and III from Nabonassar to Alexander the Great and to Antiochus I, Soter).

He wove a vast picture of the primitive world from the painted walls of the temple of Bel at Babylon which depicted the monstrous fauna of primeval times, and he studied the cuneiform records in the libraries of the departed Kings of Babylonia.

> The materials of this history, written in Greek, he professes to have derived from ancient Babylonian chronicles and inscriptions preserved in the temple of Bel at Babylon, and there is every reason to believe in the truth of his assertion, as most of his statements, notwithstanding the manifold and unconscientious handlings which his work underwent at the hands of later Greek and Roman writers, show a remarkable agreement with the cuneiform records and inscriptions found in the libraries and temples of Babylonia and Assyria[3].

But this precious work is, like Manetho, among the lost books of the world.

Like Manetho we have only fragments of Berossos's work which have come down to us by the tortuous way of Abydenus (perhaps a scholar of Berossos, who wrote a book *Assyriaca*, a history of Assyria, also lost); of Apollodorus; and Alexander, surnamed Polyhistor on account of his great learning, a Greek or Phrygian freedman of Lentulus in the days of Sulla, whose works are also lost. Fragments of these fragments have reached us through Nicholas of Damascus, the friend of Herod, through Josephus, Athenaeus, Sex. Julius Africanus, Eusebius, and George the Syncellus.

1. W. Warde Fowler believes that the Sibylline Oracles found their way from Erythrae to Cumae. Smith-Wayte-Marindin: *A Dictionary of Greek and Roman Antiquities*, 3rd ed. (London, 1891), s.v. *Sibyllini Libri*.
2. In his account of the Flood, the Deity commands Xisuthrus (Noah). "He therefore enjoined him to write a history of the beginning, procedure, and conclusion of all things; and to bury it in the City of the Sun at Sippara." (Isaac Preston Cory: *Ancient Fragments*, London, 1832, p. 27. My copy is the Pickering edition. There is a later one edited by E. R. Hodges, 1876.)
3. Gabriel Oussani: *op. cit.* (II, p. 514).

THE NON-GREEK BOOKS 193

How well says Layard[1], pioneer classic archæologist of the Chaldean-Assyrian world:

In his time the walls were probably still covered with the painting representing the ancient deeds of the people. We know from Scriptures how carefully public records were kept in Babylon, even those of the Assyrian empire existing after the Persian occupation. (Ezra, c. IV) The traditions or history, preserved by Berosus, may therefore be presumed to have been generally current in his time, among the Babylonians. Moses of Chorene calls him a most learned Chaldean.

Berossos was indeed "a man every way qualified"[2] for the great work to which he devoted his life, the elucidation of the history of the great empires of Asia to the Hellenic-Macedonian peoples. His great importance is justly recognized by the historian of Bactria[3] which country Heeren[4] calls "one of the cradles of infant civilization".

Mr. Rawlinson[3] says:

Berosus, the Chaldean priest who wrote a great history of Babylonia, Media and Persia about the time of Alexander the Great, probably preserved a mass of information which would have thrown light on the early history of Bactria.

Unfortunately, this "mass of information" contained in the great history of Berossos is lost.

But these records of Chaldea, Babylonia, Media, Persia, Bactria, and the histories of the empires of Asia written in Greek, must have found their place in the Library of Alexandria.

It was the curious coincidence that Berossos, the Babylonian priest of Bel-Marduk at Babylon wrote in Greek, in 3 books, his *Chaldiaca*, which he dedicated to his Greek sovereign, Antiochus I, and that Manetho, the Egyptian priest of On or Heliopolis, at Alexandria wrote in Greek, in 3 books, his *Aegyptiaca*, which he dedicated to his Greek sovereign, Ptolemy, that led M. Ernest Havet[5] to doubt the existence of these two Greek-writing foreigners whose lives and works presented such an unusual parallel.

1. Austin Henry Layard: *Nineveh and its Remains* (3rd ed.), London, 1849; Vol. II, p. 222, note.
2. William Palmer: *Egyptian Chronicles* (London, 1861), Vol. II, p. 302.
3. H. G. Rawlinson: *Bactria, The History of a Forgotten Empire* (London, 1912), p.XVI.
4. A. H. L. Heeren: *Manual of Ancient History* (Oxford, 1840), p. 22.
5. Ernest Havet: *Mémoire sur les écrits qui portent les noms de Manethon* (Paris, 1873).

MISCELLANEA, OR MINOR FOREIGN WRITERS

These writers, mostly historians, I have classed as minor because we have unfortunately only limited fragments of their works found mostly in the Jewish (such as Josephus) and Christian (such as Eusebius) apologists.

Of these lost books and their writers we may mention:

1. Menander of Tyre, or Ephesus or Pergamum, who wrote *A History of Tyre* or *A History of Phoenicia or The Acts of the Greeks and Barbarians under the Tyrian Kings*.

2. Dius who wrote *A History of Phoenicia* of which a considerable fragment concerning Solomon and Hiram is found in Josephus.

3. Hypsicrates, who wrote an *Account of Phoenicia*, in Phoenician, translated by a certain Asitos or Laetos.

4. Theodotus, likewise a Phoenician historian before Josephus, translated by the same Greek.

5. Philostratus, who wrote *On Phoenicia* and *On India* and is known especially as having written on the Siege of Tyre.

6. Hieronymus of Candia, under Antigonus, given by Kenrick[1] as one of the "historians of Phoenicia (who) are all known to us under Greek names".

7. Mochus, a Phoenician historian mentioned by Athenaeus[2] and possibly another writer by the same name of Sidon to whom Strabo[3] attributes the atomic theory.

Many of these writers it is believed had access to the public records of the great cities of Tyre and Sidon and their preservation would have furnished a valuable primary source for the very important history of Phoenicia.

8. Sanchuniathon. Among the lost writers of Phoenicia no one is so wrapped in mystery or so much a subject of legend as Sanchuni-

1. John Kenrick: *Phoenicia*, London, 1855, p. 169.
2. Athenaeus (III, p. 126–a).
3. Strabo (XVI, p. 757).

athon. First there is the doubt whether this is the name of a person or rather the formula for "the God Sakkun has given", i.e. for the designation of the body of *Sacred Books of the Phoenicians*. If, on the one hand the name represents that of an ancient Phoenician scholar, we are told that he lived before the Trojan war and that one Philo of Byblus who lived in the time of Nero, claimed to have translated from the Phoenician originals the mythological writings of Sanchuniathon who is said to have interpreted the sacred esoteric learning "from the mystic inscriptions on the "sun pillars" which stood in the Phoenician temples".

But the writings of Philo are also lost and in spite of the brave array of works attributed to him by Suidas and others, the literary remains of Philo of Byblus consist of a fragment from the supposed cosmogony of the mythical Phoenician sage, Sanchuniathon.

One could hardly leave the name of Sanchuniathon without remembering the greatest classical hoax of which we know. Over a century ago (in 1835) a young German scholar, Friedrich Wagenfeld, in his 25th year, a brilliant Hellenist, announced the amazing discovery, through a Portuguese friend from a monastery, Santa Maria de Meninhao, between the rivers Minho and Duero, of the whole nine books of Philo Byblius's translation of the supposed *Phoenician History* of Sanchuniathon. He actually deceived one of the world's foremost oriental and classical scholars, Dr. G. L. Grotesfend, whom he induced to write a preface to an Epitome of the famous work of Sanchuniathon. The fact that almost won the praise of modern scholarship was that the young scholar was able from the few fragments in Eusebius (Praeparatio Evangelica) to actually compose a complete work of history with all the usual and reasonable legends, tales of the gods, description of Cosmos, etc. Learned men fussed about the new data, snatched as it were from oblivion, and wrote profound articles and commentaries to maintain their respective views. In a short while the bubble burst, and the forgery was denounced. But young Wagenfeld stuck to his guns and in 1837, in the spring, published the whole of the supposed Greek version of Philo Byblius (even with a Latin translation on the opposite pages): Sanchuniathonis Historiarum Phoeniciae libros novem Graece versos a Philone Byblio edidit Lati-

naque versione donavit Fr. Wagenfeld, Bremae 1837, ex officina Caroli Schunemanni[1].

THE INDIAN MISSION

Finally from the far East, from mysterious India, came the
last foreign knowledge, learning, and wisdom to the Alexandrian
Library.

What the land of Ind was to the adventurous Elizabethans
and the men of the Renaissance, the fabled domains on the banks
of the Indus and Hyphasis were to the daring and intrepid
Macedonian-Greeks. Alexander's invasion of India put an end
to an era of that ancient country and out of it arose a new order.
The genius of the son of Philip had destroyed the mighty Persian
empire, heir of imperial Asia and venerable Egypt. So too, in
India, Alexander put an end to the smaller kingdoms, as the
last of the house of Nanda succumbed, and India was ready for
empire when Alexander died. The "successors" were too busy
seeking their own aggrandizement and too far from home to make
a real effort to preserve the eastern terminus of the conquests of
the great warrior. So out of the native earth, as it were, from a
low caste, arose a leader, who, with his hand against the law, had
lived in the jungle, a guerilla-fighter who espoused the cause
of the Macedonian invader and who finally became heir to the
Indian inheritance. Chandragupta was his name. Of course, the
Hindu legends tell that a lion, finding him asleep in the jungle,
licked him in friendly acknowledgment of his regal destiny, and
the war-elephant he rode was wild, untrained, yet it knelt to
receive his royal master. The Greek writers tell that Chandragupta never forgot his obligation to the Hellenic hero whose
meteoric genius had so changed the Indian scene. So Alexander
was worshipped by Chandragupta among his native gods. As a
young man he had beheld with admiration the great Macedonian
warrior. Proscribed by the reigning king, Chandragupta lurked
in his jungle lair, from whence he sprang like the Bengal beast
on some devoted city which he sacked or conquered at his will.
He followed the example of the Greek conqueror in greater ways

1. My copy (IV and 205 pp.) has the page of Errata. See also J. A. Farrar: *Literary
Forgeries*, London, 1907 (p. 191 et seq.).

and finally became the ruler of The Panjab, not from the Indus to the Hyphasis, but of India from the Indus to the Ganges and on to the Bay of Bengal.

The jungle marauder left a vast kingdom to his son, Bindusara, whose son was the great Asoka, and as the third generation, true to form, Asoka was a gentleman.

Now these three Indian rulers, Chandragupta, Bindusara, and Asoka, had frequent contact through the Macedonian successors of Alexander with the Hellenic or Macedonian-Greek world. Chandragupta, ardent pupil of the military greatness and worship-er of the genius of the divine Alexander, had at his court the ambassador of Seleucus, Megasthenes, of whom Dr. Schwanbeck[1] declares: "the work of Megasthenes – in so far as it is a part of Greek literature and of Greek and Roman learning – is, as it were, the culmination of the knowledge which the ancients ever acquired of India."

Deimachus of Plataea was ambassador to the court of Bindusara. It was the King Bindusara who wrote a letter to Antiochus, asking for the price of one of the rich wines made by Greek process; for the price of the dried figs for which Asia Minor has ever been famous; and for the price of "a teacher of Greek learning, a "sophist" – to which the Greek ruler somewhat faceitiously replied:

> We shall send you, to be sure, the dried figs and sweet wine, but it is against the law in Greece to sell a sophist[2].

But the House of Ptolemy was not to be outdone by the rival Syrian kings, and we find that Dionysius was sent by Ptolemy II as his ambassador.

"We may presume," wisely concludes the historian of *The House of Seleucus*[3] "that Hindu envoys were likewise to be seen at the Seleucid and Ptolemaic courts even before Asoka sent his missionaries."

And now there occurred one of the unique epochs in the spirit-ual history of man.

1. Dr. E. A. Schwanbeck of Bonn: *Megasthenis Indica*, Bonn, 1846; Vide J. W. McCrindle: *Ancient India as described by Megasthenes and Arrian*, Calcutta, 1926, p. 27.
2. Athenaeus (XIV–652e–653a) quoting Hegesander. (frag. 43, F. H. G. IV, p. 421).
3. Bevan: *op. cit.* Vol. I, p. 297.

Asoka, grand-son of the jungle outlaw, the "man of blood and iron", was carefully reared in the three accomplishments, training for the body, knowledge for the mind, and wisdom for the spirit.

Early in his life he had experience in the art of government, when his father, Bindusara, sent him as vice-roy of the frontier province of north-western India. Here in its capital of Taxila, one of those fabulous cities of the East, in the midst of Hindu art, the learning of the Indian schools was imparted to the youth of the great Brahmin families and the fortunate of the upper castes. In this Athens of north-western India, Asoka sat among his pundits, when each sought to impart to his imperial prince the glories and wonders and truths of his particular school.

This western province had beheld the lightning flash of Macedonian conquest which it actually welcomed and of which it certainly retained some of the dynamic vigor and perfect sense of beauty of the Hellenic visitation. It must not be thought, however, that the ancient Hindu civilization receded before the Greek; it merely felt the faultless touch of Grecian genius. Like a coat of wonderful weave, native to be sure, it was shot here and there with magic threads of Olympian looms. But the old India was hardly impaired and the venerable Hindu traditions were preserved in the manners and customs of the land. How well is this put by the biographer of Asoka[1] when he says that the Greeks "noted with interest, and without disapprobation, the local customs, which included polygamy, the exposure of the dead to be devoured by vultures, and the sale in open market of maidens who had failed to secure husbands in the ordinary course".

Asoka, through assiduous study, profound contemplation, and tireless labor became not only a great king, but a great man. As a hard-working ruler he has been compared to Philip II; as the establisher of Buddhism, to Constantine; and as the preacher of the teachings of Gautama, to Saint Paul. In legend and native lore he equals the western myths of King Arthur, Charlemagne, and Alexander.

He reluctantly made war, which he abhorred, and for having sinned in that regard, he endeavored to make amends during the rest of his life. His practical piety is illustrated by his solicitude for the well being of man and beasts: the banyan tree planted to

1. Vincent A. Smith: *History of India* (N. Y. 1906), Vol. II, p. 131.

give them shade, the wells dug to supply water, the caravanserai erected for their shelter. And he, who with his spiritual mentor Upagupta sought the spot where the great Gautama was born in the Lumbini Garden, in the foothills of Nepal, where he erected the famous pillar, still *in situ*[1], did not fail to place markers on the roads to assist the humble wayfarer. His establishment of hospitals for animals and his zeal in their behalf should entitle him to the honor of father of the S.P.C.A.

Perhaps the most interesting feature of his administrative genius was his system of proclamations throughout his vast domains. From the Himalaya mountains to Mysore in the Deccan, from the Sea of Arabia to the Bay of Bengal, high on some rocky ledge above the public road, deep in some cave, on the walls of a sacred shrine, cut on Monumental Pillars, in the vernacular dialects (*i.e.* in Prakrit, related to the literary Sanskrit and the Pali of Ceylon, yet intended to be understood by all the people), more than thirty of these stone-engraved Edicts proclaimed to all Asoka's subjects his governmental policies and his just way of life.

After his conversion by Upagupta, he became the royal apostle of Buddhism, making of the teachings of Gautama a world religion. He summoned all the kings and people to receive the Four Truths and to follow the Eightfold Path (*right* belief, will, word, deed, life, effort, thought, and self-withdrawal) and engraved on the everlasting rocks a record of his spiritual mission. The famous "fourteen edicts" of Asoka were inscribed on the Rocks of Girnar, Kalsi, Shahbazgarhi, and Mansehra.

These rescripts on morality written by King Devanampriya (Asoka) were proclaimed to all mankind:

"No living being must be killed and sacrificed. Even animals shall not be killed in future." (1st Rock-Edict: Girnar.)

Two kinds of medical treatment established, for men and for cattle. (2nd Rock-Edict: Girnar.)

Obedience to mother and father; liberality to friends; moderation in expenditure and in possessions. (3rd Rock-Edict: Girnar.)

1. Recorded by himself on the Rummindei Pillar.

"The sound of drums has become the sound of morality." (4th Rock-Edict: Girnar.)

"He who starts performing virtuous deeds accomplishes something difficult." "For sin is easily committed." (5th Rock-Edict: Girnar.)

Reporters are posted everywhere (with instructions) to report to me the affairs of the people at any time, while I am eating, in the harem, in the inner apartment, even at the cowpen, in the palan-quin, and in the parks. For I consider it my duty (to promote) the wel-fare of all men. (6th Rock-Edict: Girnar.)

In times past kings used to set out on pleasure-tours; now tours of morality (were undertaken) visiting the aged and supporting them, the people of the country receiving instruction in morality.(8th Rock-Edict: Girnar.)

Proper courtesy to slaves and servants, reverence to elders, gentle-ness to animals, liberality to Brahmanas and Sramanas; these, and other virtues are called the practice of morality. (9th Rock-Edict: Girnar.)

King Asoka does not think that either glory or fame conveys much advantage, except that in the present time and in the future men may be induced by him to practice obedience to morality. (10th Rock-Edict: Girnar.)

The King honors all sects; concord alone is meritorious. (12th Rock-Edict: Girnar.)

But even one who (practices) great liberality (but) does not possess self-control, purity of mind, gratitude, and firm devotion, is very mean. (7th Rock-Edict: Kalsi.)

In the 13th Rock-Edict: Girnar, *envoys* are mentioned, but the inscription is defective, as is that of Mansehra. In the 13th Rock-Edict: Kalsi, it is complete, as is that of Shahbazgarhi, and reads:

Even those to whom the envoys of Asoka do not go, having heard of the duties of morality, the ordinances (and) the instruction in morality of Asoka, are conforming to morality and will conform to (it).

And before the above, the pertinent part, for us, of the inscription reads:

And this (spiritual conquest) has been won repeatedly by Asoka both [here] and among all (his) borderers even as far as at (the distance of) six hundred yojanas, where the Yona king named Antiyoga (Antiochus II, 261–246, is ruling) and beyond this Antiyoga (where) four – 4 – kings (are ruling), (viz. the king) named Tulamaya, [= Ptolemy II, B.C. 285–246], (the king) named Antekina [=Antigonus Gonatas of Macedonia (276–239)], (the king) named Maka [= Magas of Cyrene (c. 300–250)], (and the king) named Alikyashudala [=either Alexander of Epirus (272–c. 255) or Alexander of Corinth (252–c. 244)][1].

And so this was the summons:

Open your ears ye kings, the Redemption from death is found!

made to the warlike Alexander (II of Epirus) and Antigonus Gonatas (of Macedon)[2], to the drunken Antiochus (II, Theos), to the art-loving book-patron Ptolemy II ("Philadelphus"), and to the gourmand and luxury's own Magas, King of Cyrene, who died a victim of fatty suffocation!

It would seem that Asoka, Buddhist "monk" and ruler of India, sent his missionaries to these great Hellenic courts and that in the streets of Alexandria, the towns of Epirus, and the throne-cities of Asia, the tall, dark, tonsured Hindu scholar-priests were noted amid the Greek and the motley crowds.

What actually took place, what wisdom of the East was imparted and how (particularly at Alexandria) we know not. Yet it is only reasonable to assume that the curious minded Hellene made some record of this unusual visit and its significance, and that record, whether of Hindu pundit or Hellenic scribe, was placed in the Alexandrian Library together with the other foreign or barbaric learning, along with the books of Manetho, Berossos, and the Semetic peoples – even the Sacred Scriptures of the Jew, the histories of the Phoenicians, and such other non-

1. *Corpus Inscriptionum Indicarum* (New ed., edited by E. Hultzsch), Oxford, 1925, Vol· I, p. 48; also Beloch: *Griechische Geschichte*, 3-2-105; Bevan: *The House of Seleucus*, I-298; Vincent A. Smith: *Asoka*, 1901, p. 131; Lessen: *Ind. Alt.*, II-255.
2. The new edition of *C.I.I.* must be correct in substituting Antigonus Gonatas, for old Antigonus.

Hellenic knowledge, most of the record of which has vanished with the years.

It is true that the writer is interested in discovering what muniments of learning the Indian scholars brought to and what they may have left in Alexandria. Yet on this subject modern scholarship seems completely silent, and our almost quixotic efforts among Hindu pundits were unfortunately as barren[1].

We are aware that the historians of Ptolemaic Egypt seem to be interested, not in what India brought to Egypt, but in what way, if any, Ptolemaic Egypt may have influenced, financially and economically, the governmental structure of the empire of Chandragupta, particularly since the late discovery of the *Arthashastra* of Kautilia, which is a political treatise, setting forth conditions quite similar to those of Egypt under the Ptolemies, such as the regulation of the great state monopolies – "oil, salt, and mines" – and their organization.

However, as Dr. Rostovtzeff[2] says, the chronological controversy of the date of the Arthashastra must first be decided before we may assess the obligation of the Indian empire to that of the Ptolemies. For us the important point is the apparent intellectual intercourse between India and Alexandria. If that is once proved, and it is shown that Egypt contributed to the governmental structure of the Indian empire, we will have better reason to believe that at least a modicum of Hindu learning and wisdom was reciprocally left with the Hellenic city and naturally

1. The writer personally discussed this intriguing question with Sir Girja Shanker Bajpai, K.C.S.I. Hon. R. H. Hadow, C.M.G., M.C. of British Embassy, graciously directed inquiries to the Indian Embassy in Washington and to the Foreign Office Librarian to seek from the India Office and other repositories of learning for any known source. A scholar of the Dept. of Coins and Medals, British Museum, knows of no record of any such intercourse. The Embassy of India referred us to Dr. Tara Chan, Vice-Chancellor, Allahabad University, and Prof. Dr. K. A. Nilakanta Sastri, University of Madras, who wrote: "There is no tradition or record of this mission in Hindu annals, except the statement of Asoka in his Rock Edict XIII, that he sent his agents to preach his religious and moral tenets to beyond the Kingdom of Antiochus, where four Greek kings were ruling, "Turumaya, usually identified with Ptolemy II, among them," and adds the interesting note: "It has sometimes been suggested that Theraputae, a set of Alexandrine monks were really of Buddhist origin, on the view that their name is derived from Thereputa, son of Thera, the common name for a Buddhist monk. The use of the suffix *puta* for describing a tribe or a group is not otherwise unknown. There is so far as I know no further proof of this mission, its nature or its work."

2. M. Rostovtzeff: *Ptolemaic Egypt* in C.A.H., Vol. VII, p. 154, Cambridge, 1928.

found its way amidst the fragments of foreign wisdom in the Alexandriana.

And now I am about to commit the fault of Athenaeus in saying: Would you know what were the *collections*, what were the *books* contained in the Alexandrian Libraries?

Why, they were all the extant writings of the Greek peoples from Homer to the age of the Ptolemies and to the end of the ancient pagan calendar and beyond to the seventh century A.D., and they were the writings of the non-Greeks, particularly of the East, which had forced their way into that exquisite mode of human expression, the language of ancient Hellas.

The Alexandrian Library was not only the largest and most important collection of Greek books that ever existed, but, in the days of its greatest glory, it was the greatest library in all the world before the invention of printing.

CHAPTER XI

THE CLASSIFICATION AND CATALOGUING
OF THE MATERIAL ASSEMBLED

T HE vast number of manuscripts gathered by Demetrios of Phaleron and his early successors were mostly bundles of writings forming high piles in the warerooms of the Museum. The first task was to assort the mass. This must have been a tremendous labor. Imagine a modern library or large collection of books, with most of the title pages removed, without preface or introduction, without name of author or work, with no chapter headings and, of course, with no description at the top of pages, but beginning solely with the writer's text. Of course, some manuscripts had labels or syllabi, and some books had author-protection, such as: "Herodotus of Halicarnassus, these are the researches of"; or "Thucydides, an Athenian, wrote the history of the war in which the Peloponnesians and the Athenians fought against one another". But all books, particularly the poems and shorter miscellanea, did not have such perfect *incipit*. Many of them had to be worked out, and the mixed volumes must have required additional effort. Even in the time of Callimachus (d. c. 235 B.C.), the assortment had been only roughly completed. In the scholium on the margin of the MS. of Plautus in the Collegio Romano, so important in the investigation of this subject, we are told that:

In the Inner or Main Library (in the Greek or Royal quarter of Alexandria) there were:

> 400,000 mixed rolls
> 90,000 single rolls
> ——————————
> 490,000 rolls

In the Outer Library ("The Daughter" Library, in the Egyptian quarter) connected with the Temple of Serapis, there were 42,800 single rolls.

By a single roll we should understand such as contained only one work of an author, or if the work were extensive, one book of the work. Such were the *Iliad* and the *Odyssey*, which Zenodotus is credited with having divided into 24 books each, not only to have an equal number of books as there are letters in the Greek alphabet, but to have each book under 1000 verses so that it would comfortably take a roll of reasonable size[1]. Gradually the mixed rolls ceased. Thus in the late Library of Pergamum which Antony gave to Cleopatra, the single rolls must have been in the majority, as no mixed ones are mentioned, and at Herculaneum hardly any mixed rolls have been found. Yet we should not forget that the works of the philosopher Antisthenes were preserved in 10 mixed volumes at least until the time of Diogenes Laertius (3rd cent. A.D.), and that this arrangement of volumes is thought to have come from Callimachus and the Alexandrian Library[2].

But to resume, in the two libraries there were over a half million rolls (actually 532,800) of which 400,000 or nearly three-fourths were mixed volumes at the time of Callimachus. These mixed rolls must have contained many duplicates, some mutilated and damaged copies, and of course, an indeterminate number of good mixed manuscripts (such as Antisthenes?), collections of shorter works of authors, and purely miscellanea of verse and prose. The 132,800 single rolls were apparently the cream of the mass. Be this as it may, it would appear that the great work of Callimachus and the early cataloguers must have been with the 132,800 single rolls in the Museum and Serapeiana and with some of the mixed rolls. Again, although the exact number of rolls can hardly be insisted upon, we are reasonably sure of the vast labor involved in merely assorting or separating these huge collections, which had to be unrolled and examined in all states of preservation.

It would be interesting to know whether the rolls were assorted into divisions according to the form or kind of writing, by era of

1. Large rolls were the rule in pre-Alexandrian times. The moderate roll was started in Athens in the IVth century B.C. It was, however, an innovation and not the general form.
2. Susemihl, Franz: *Geschichte der griechischen Litteratur in der Alexandrinerzeit*, Leipzig, 1891 (I-343). However, although he was accused of being a "prolific trifler" and certainly wrote many works, they may have been short (one of his volumes contains 11 separate works); hence the rolls may have been only of a reasonable size.

the script, or by authors or subject matter. As we hear a great deal about the earliest scholars of the Museum or Library devoting themselves to the poets and perhaps afterwards to the philosophers, it is reasonable to assume that all the writings were first assorted as to verse or prose, a standard still abiding in our times. We know that the vast poetic literature of the Greeks was at once separated into Epic and non-Dramatic works, and the Drama, which we believe was divided into Tragedy (including satyric plays) and Comedy. Zenodotus probably assorted and catalogued or rather made lists of the epic and other poets (non-dramatic), Alexander the Aetolian of the tragedies and the satyric drama, and Lycophron of the comedies (of their work in editing these writings we are reasonably assured), and we do know that the great work of cataloguing, in general, was performed by Callimachus and embodied in his celebrated *Pinakes*.

THE PINAKES

It may not be certain that the bibliographical scribes of Ashurbanipal[1] and Callimachus of the Alexandriana were the first cataloguers, yet, as far as we know, they were the pioneers in this essential department of library science. Here we are concerned only with Callimachus and must endeavor to eke out, with the fragments of his fragments and the passing hints of ancient writers, some faint pattern of his great work, the *Pinakes*. It was common in later centuries for men of letters, like Cicero, to call for the Index Tragicorum of the Library of Lucullus (Hortensius fr. 9) or for Seneca to advise Lucilius to pick up the Index Philosophorum in his search for a cram in philosophy (Ep. XXXIX), but in early Ptolemaic years the field was indeed untilled.

Out of the dust of *Oxyrhynchus* has come the conclusion of the poem of Callimachus, *Aitia* (IV–1):

O thou who didst assist at the birth of the Graces and who didst

---

1. Bezold: *Catal. of the Cuneiform Tablets*, British Museum, 5 (1899), p. XXIX. The Assyrian enthusiasts believe that in Nineveh we have the forerunner of the Alexandriana, and that Callimachus followed the technical library rules which have been found in the Library of Ashurbanipal. S. Bezold: Pauly–Wissowa, II-1762; Clark: *Care of Books*, p. 2; Dr. Victor Gardthausen: *Die alexandrinische Bibliothek*, Leipzig, 1922 (p. 8).

bring to birth my Queen, not with lying lips did the minstrel call thee of perfect excellence and of perfect fulfilment; Hail to thee and do thou come with prosperous weal. Hail, greatly hail to thee also, O Zeus! do thou save all the house of our kings! and I will visit the haunt of the Muses on foot[1].

The gifted Hellenist, the late Dr. A. S. Hunt, remarks that Callimachus here "takes a formal fare-well of poetry, and declares that he will now devote himself to prose. The poet must then at this time have had in view a large and important prose work; and it is natural to suppose that he was here alluding to his Πίνακες, a kind of literary encyclopaedia, which is said by Suidas to have extended to 120 books and must have occupied the author during a long period".

"At any rate the present passage is in thorough accordance with view of Wilamowitz (*Textgesch. d. gr. Bukoliker*, pp. 173–4; cf. Götting. Nachr., 1893, pp. 745–6) that the practical activity of Callimachus is to be assigned to the prior part of his career, and that his appointment at the Alexandrian Library turned his energies into another channel"[2].

That the literary luminary of his age should have deserted the winged horse, Pegasus, even for a time, for the pedestrian role of bibliography is one of the curiosities of scholarship. A true son of the Hellenic Renaissance, he was both a poet and a scientist and brought to all his great work:

broadest knowledge, fine taste, not mere intelligence, but inner warmth, and a little dry slightly ironic humor, but above all a proper evaluation of his own capacity as well as the limitation of his time[3].

We know that during the time of Zenodotus his two associates, Alexander the Aetolian and Lycophron the Chalcidian, the first on the tragedies and satyric dramas, the second on the comedies, had expended much scholarly labor. They had assorted, corrected, revised, and edited the dramatic writers, and, although their work was of a high order of literary, critical exegesis, it necessarily involved the drawing up of lists of the authors and their plays and thus served as a good foundation for the

1. Callimachus: *Aitia*, IV–I (L.C.L.); A. W. Mair: *op. cit.*
2. Grenfell and Hunt: *Oxyrhynchus Papyri*, Vol. VII, p. 18 (No. 1011).
3. Wilhelm von Christ: *Geschichte der griechischen Litteratur*, München, 1920, II-125.

future cataloguer. But their work was essentially that of critical recension and not the making of a catalogue. If these labors were performed for the scenic works, Zenodotus was doing a similar job for Homer and the non-dramatic poets and for these last must have drawn up necessary lists of authors and their works. All of these labors must have been helpful to Callimachus and his staff, when Callimachus started his great woık, the *Pinakes*, which was bio-bibliographical Tables of the corpus of Hellenic verse and prose, from the beginning to his day, and as found in the Alexandrian Libraries.

Now the titles of the works of Callimachus have come to us from the list in Suidas, and from other sources. In Suidas we have three arresting titles:

1. *The Museum.* About which we know nothing. This lost work, most probably a monograph on the great Museum, must have contained valuable information. Its loss, like that later of Aristonicus, *On the Museum of Alexandria*, is deplorable.

2. *Table and Register of Dramatic Poets chronologically from the earliest times.* This is thought by A.W. Mair[1] to be a sub-title or chapter of the *Pinakes*. Dr. Gardthausen[2] however thinks that there were two works by Callimachus on the *pinakes*, one a sort of catalogue of which the above was at least a part, being the *Pinax* on the Dramatic Poets, the other an elaborate Handbook of Literary History in 120 books. This the work from which all the fragments have come that are now extant, and that have been used by Bentley, Schmidt, and Schneider[3]. Schneider believes that the *Pinakes* was not a catalogue but a History of Literature written by Callimachus, and based on the catalogues of Zenodotus and his associates. We would assume also, if this were correct, that Callimachus used his own materials, certainly for the prose writers. If this wcre so, Callimachus would be the father of Literary History, if not the father of Bibliography. It seems, however, most reasonable to assume that the *Pinakes* was, even as in Suidas, where it is set forth to be: Tables of literature, the authors and their writings. Or as more fully set forth:

3. *Tables of all those who were eminent in any kind of literature and of their writings*, in 120 books[4]. This last was, without doubt, the famous

1. *Callimachus and Lycophron* (L. C. L.), London, 1921 (pp. 11–12).
2. Dr. Victor Gardthausen: *Die alexandrinische Bibliothek*, Leipzig, 1922 (p. 6).
3. *Callimachea* (2–297).
4. Mair: *Callimachus and Lycophron, op. cit.* pp. 11–12.

Pinakes. The title *Pinakes* means tablets, which were above or on the book-lockers (or armaria) or possibly attached to the walls of the storerooms (stacks?). These tablets carried the name of the authors; whether also the names of their works is doubtful. The authors were arranged in the division of their type of literature, which was thus kept together, perhaps in separate halls[1]. Each division was at least one *pinax;* collectively they gave the title *Pinakes.*

Into how many divisions, classes or *pinakes* the entire body of Greek literature was divided we cannot tell.

As the fragments of Callimachus are small in number and content, Schmidt believes we are bound to scrupulously adhere to tradition. His principle of division of subjects is shown from quotations. Unfortunately we have only three of the main divisions:

1. *Ῥητορικά* – Oratory (Fr. 2 – Fr. 4 – Callimachus).
2. *Νόμοι* – Laws (Fr. 5 – Callimachus).
3. *Παντοδαπὰ συγγράμματα* }– Miscellanea (Frs. 6-7 – Callimachus)[2].

These three classes have come to us through Athenaeus, who perhaps helps us with two more, History and Philosophy; however, Diogenes Laertius more directly confirms "Philosophy" (Diog. Lae. VIII–86).

There were doubtless lists in post-Callimachian times. Hermippus of Smyrna, disciple and probably co-worker with Callimachus, wrote a great biographical work (*Βίοι*), perhaps grounded on the *Pinakes.* Aristophanes of Byzantium, who was to be one of his successors in the Library, actually issued a revised edition, or rather an original work, on the *Pinakes,* and his contemporaries and successors for some generations knew the full list of classifications. However, men in after years made lists doubtlessly from library catalogues, if not from the great prototype itself. The Lists of Proclus (*Christomathie*) and Cicero are mere poetic divisions; Dionysius of Halicarnassus (*On Imitation,* II) and Quintilian (*Institutes,* X) are mixed; Quintilian gives some seven of the ten divisions of his list to the poets; Hesychius of Miletus in perhaps an epitome of his *Ονοματολόγος*

1. Fr. Schmidt: *Pinakes des Kallimachos,* Berlin, 1922, p. 48.
2. Idem: *op. cit.* (pp. 49–50).

has an intriguing division, Medicine; and finally the two *Tables*, one of the Bodleian (with fifteen divisions) and the curious *Canones Coisliniani*, a manuscript of a list of authors, in the order of their classes of literature, which evidently was taken from library indices, has sixteen divisions[1].

How many main classifications Callimachus made we do not know. Susemihl thought there were two divisions for the poets (one for the epic and all other non-dramatic poets, and one for the dramatists); a third division was for the lawgivers; four others for philosophers, historians, orators and rhetoricians; and a division for miscellaneous writings, and that these were fairly proven. That there were other divisions was quite probable.

The arrangement was:

Dramatic writers, in chronological order.

Demosthenes, according to subjects.

Pindar and possibly other lyric writers, according to place or subjects.

Theophrastus, alphabetical.

Miscellanea, of necessity, alphabetical[2].

Schmidt believes that the Drama was divided into two main divisions:

1. Tragedy (with satyr plays) whether or not by the same author.
2. Comedy[3].

It would seem more probable that instead of two main divisions for the Drama, there might naturally have been two subdivisions: a. Tragedy (with satyr plays) and b. Comedy.

What seems certain is that there were more main divisions than have come down to us. An attempt to arrange the various genre of writings, with a Procrustean method, may be ventured:

I – Epic and other non-Dramatic Poetry.

II – The Drama.

III – Laws (Athenaeus, XIII–585b).

IV – Philosophy (Diog. Laet., VIII-86; Athen., VI–252c).

V – History (Athenaeus, II–70b).

VI – Oratory (Athenaeus, XV–669e).

VII – Medicine.

1. Schmidt: *op. cit.* p. 52.
2. Susemihl: *op. cit.* I, 339.
3. Schmidt: *op. cit.* p. 51.

VIII – Mathematical Science.
IX – Natural Science.
X – Miscellanea (Athenaeus, VI–244a)[1].

Of the above classifications only three (Laws, Oratory, and Miscellanea) are *pinaces* fragments and five (Laws, Philosophy, History, Oratory, and Miscellanea) have Callimachian reference. The others await the fortunate find of further or fuller fragments, for confirmation or refutation.

Under these or more main classifications, Callimachus gave the name of the author, place of birth, name of his father, his teachers and education, his nickname or pseudonym, a short biography, the titles of his works (if none, a title was provided), comment on their authenticity, and finally a stichometric note giving the first words of the work (often the ancient title) and the exact number of the lines of the MS. (of each work and of all of the authors's writings). The last was an important bibliographical detail, used to control the size of the manuscript and to ascertain the compensation of the scribe, as well as for general reference.

From fragmentary hints, casual comments, the general and special studies of classical scholarship, we venture a slight account of the system of Callimachus under some of his leading classifications. The alphabetical system seems to have been followed with some exceptions. Even in an exception, the alphabetical method may have been followed under sub-groups. The Romans adopted this system from Alexandria as would appear in the list of the twenty-one genuine plays of Plautus[2]. This system is found in Suidas, Diogenes Laertius and Greek writers, and in extant Greek antiquities on this subject.

a. Epic and other non-dramatic poets:

Under *Homer*, of which there may have been over a thousand rolls in the Library, the arrangement may have been 1. Homer, the genuine work; 2. the works attributed to him or the doubtful poems, with a critical note on their authenticity *vel non*.

Under *Hesiod:* the same method was employed.

Under *Pindar:* a sub-group was created for each *place*.

Under *Simonides:* the grouping was in accordance with type of subject (*i.e.* sports, etc.).

1. Mair: *op. cit.* p. 12.
2. Schmidt: *op. cit.* p. 74, note 21.

Minor poets: it is thought Callimachus catalogued each poem.

b. The Drama:

Each author had the usual short bio-bibliographical account, with didascalic notes.

Susemihl believed the dramatic authorswere arranged chronologically[1]. Sandys also declared that in the Drama the order was that of date, and the dates of production of the Attic plays were given[2]. As to the chronological method we have the authority of Suidas's title of one of Callimachus's works or a chapter of part of the *Pinakes:*

Tables and Register of dramatic poets chronologically from the earliest times.

Schmidt thought that with some small exception, not explainable, the alphabetical system seemed to have been followed, and he cited as to *Tragedy:*

Taking the dramatic writers as an example, because they wrote in only one genre, we have:

1. The famous catalogue of Aeschylus's tragedies, of which the alphabetical order is undoubted. It is remarkable to note that they do not separate the satyric plays from the tragedies and that no attention is paid to the continuity of the trilogies, but all are treated alphabetically.

2. There is no such catalogue for Sophocles.

3. For Euripides we have the curious antiquity, the seated figure of the poet (in the Louvre), holding in his left hand the mask of tragedy, and on the background of the monument, we have thirty-six of Euripides's plays alphabetically set forth[3].

4. The Peiraeus Stone has a different arrangement[4].

5. In Suidas's account of a tragic poet Timesitheus, only known through him, we have the alphabetical arrangement[5].

6. In Suidas's catalogue[6] of the tragedies of Lycophron, the order is alphabetical[7].

1. Susemihl: *op. cit.* I, p. 339.
2. Sandys: *op. cit.* I, p. 123.
3. Winkelmann: *Monum. inediti*, 168, p. 225; Gardthausen, *op. cit.* p. 94, for cut; see *I. Gr.*, ed. Kaibel, XIV–1152.
4. Wilamowitz: *Anat. Eurip.*, p. 138; see Gardthausen, *op. cit.* p. 93, for cut.
5. Schmidt: *op. cit.* p. 71 et seq.
6. Suidas: s.v. *Lycophron*.
7. Schmidt says (p. 73) meticulously alphabetical; Mair (p. 481) says "in a roughly alphabetical order". Both are correct because the Greeks did not always regard the letter or letters following the initial.

For Comedy:

For the writers of comedy we have:

1. A similar list to the Aeschylean tragedies in the *Novatische* list (Kaibel, R. E. II-972).

2. In Suidas the eleven plays of Aristophanes, which have come down to us, are alphabetically arranged.

Although a distinguished classical scholar of our time has said that were it not for the Alexandrians we might not have Homer, it is certain that the labors of the scholars of the Museum-Library have enabled us to have texts of the three greatest tragic writers and the greatest comic writer of antiquity, readable and relatively free from error. Perhaps the finest critical and exegetical efforts of the Alexandrian school were lavished upon the drama. Not all of this precious work has survived, but much remains, and the profound study of modern scholarship has revealed glimpses of the deft recension of these faithful preservers of letters. To Alexander of Aetolia and Lycophron must have fallen the first hard task of judicious selection from the mass of various manuscripts; Callimachus, brilliant poet and man of letters, must have embellished their work and may have written some of the hypotheses; and Aristophanes, ὁ Γραμματικός, must have devoted much of his grammatical genius to what may have been the final elucidation of the plays. He is credited with many of the prose arguments to comedies and tragedies, which are thought to be based on the *Pinakes* of Callimachus. The metrical (iambics, elegiacs) hypotheses, as we have them, he hardly would have written[1].

Dr. White in one of the most fascinating technical books ever written[2], in two intriguing passages, visions the profound study devoted to Aristophanes by the great master of rhythmic and metric:

> Aristophanes of Byzantium raised the whole question of metrical form by his investigation in colometry, of which the results were

1. B. B. Rogers, *The Comedies of Aristophanes*, Vol. I: *The Acharnians* (p. LIX), thinks it "may be a libel to attribute" these doggerel to Aristophanes (London, 1910). Vide: J. D. Denniston, s.v. *Hypotheses* in *Ox. Clas. Dic.*; Cohn: Pauly-Wissowa: II-998; and Korte, *Hermes*, XXXIX (1904), 481–98, who believes Symmachus, who compiled "the second variorum edition" of the poets, was the author of the Arguments to Aristophanes.
2. John Williams White: *The Scholia on the Aves of Aristophanes*, Boston, 1914.

published in his colometrical editions of Pindar, and probably the tragic dramatists and the poet Aristophanes... No doubt the great Library furnished him texts of some of the lyrics that he was investigating with the music still written above the solid lines of texts, but probably it was lacking in the case of most of the odes, for the booksellers eliminated it early (p. XLIX).

Whether Aristophanes, in his text edition of the poets, wrote the lyrics in cola or not cannot now be determined. Nobody else is so likely to have introduced this useful method of writing; it certainly is not to be attributed to Heliodorus (p. XIX).

c. Laws:
Our authority:

Callimachus has recorded it in the third "tablet" (pinax) of his *Rules* (Laws) citing the beginning of it as follows: "The *Rule* here written down is equal and fair for all" – three hundred and twenty-three lines[1].

d. Philosophy:
We have no fragments of Callimachus but some detailed lists belonging to Hermippus of Smyrna, who was perhaps his pupil and most probably one of his assistants in the Library working on the *Pinakes*. If a list goes back to Hermippus (middle 3rd cent. B.C.) then we can assume that he derived it from Callimachus and from the *Pinakes*. Hermippus was a scholar and became a distinguished writer, author of an important biographical work[2], *Lives of Philosophers, Historians and Poets*, doubtlessly founded on the short biographies in the *Pinakes* which he enlarged to full length portraits, thereby producing an original work read and quoted until the times of the emperors.

The famous alphabetical list of the writings of Theophrastus in Diogenes Laertius goes back to the *Pinakes* by way of Hermippus, although it cannot be definitely proven that this alphabetical order was used for all of the peripatetics, as difficulty arises as to the arrangement of Aristotle[3].

1. Athenaeus: XIII-585b. The last, as Dr. Gulick remarks, is a stichometric note convenient for librarians and booksellers, and refers to Birt. *Ant. Buchwesen*, 162 ff., 168, 337.
2. Schmidt: *op. cit.* p. 88.
3. Idem: *op. cit.* p. 88.

And then we have the case of Antisthenes (c. 446–366 B.C.), the Socratic, in which we have an edition of his works in ten volumes. This elaborate edition (Diog. Laer. VI–15), in which each roll contains several works, is not alphabetically arranged, yet Susemihl[1] says that it in all probability comes from the Alexandrian Pinacography.

Diogenes Laertius[2], who tells us that Epicurus wrote 300 rolls, and who enumerates the best of them, does not give an alphabetical list.

And so we have other lists in Diogenes Laertius and in other writers perhaps for other purposes, such as the list of Democritus's writings arranged by Thrasylus, dividing them in four categories (Ethical, Physical, Mathematical, Literary and Musical) and a division on the Arts, and a special division entitled: The following fall under no head. This division is alphabetically arranged[3].

"Under the circumstances," wisely remarks Herr Schmidt, "it seems impossible to form a certain judgment regarding the arrangement of the philosophical writers in the *Pinakes*"[4].

e. History:

For the historians we have still less material. We have no fragments, no long lists of books, probably due to the fact that the old historians did not write numerous works, certainly nothing comparable to the lyrical writers or the orators. The few lists that we have are alphabetically arranged[5]. There is, however, an apposite reference in Athenaeus (II–70b):

Hecataeus of Miletus, in the *Description of Asia* (granting that this book is a genuine work of the historian, since Callimachus[6] ascribes it to Nesiotes; whoever then the author may be).

It is curious to note that many of the early and greatest historians did not have regular titles to their works: *cp.* Herodotus, Thucydides, etc.

f. Oratory:

In the orators every speech was noted and every speech was

1. Susemihl: *op. cit.* I-343.
2. Diogenes Laertius: X–26.
3. Idem IX–46.
4. Schmidt: *op. cit.* p. 88.
5. Vide: Suidas and Schmidt: *op. cit.* p. 86.
6. Schneider: *Frag.*, 100d, 10.

given a title. Callimachus seems to have divided the orations according to their purpose: Official (State-Political), Professional (Matters of Law), and Civic, ornate speeches for various occasions.

The arrangement of Demosthenes's speeches is generally attributed to Callimachus. He does not seem to decide on the genuineness of the orations of Demosthenes, yet our edition of the greatest orator contains exactly what Callimachus declared Demosthenic[1].

Dionysius of Halicarnassus wrote a monograph *On Dinarchus* in which he takes issue with both the catalogues of Alexandria and Pergamum. He may have used other lists than the *Pinakes*[2].

g. Medicine:

Schmidt says that there was unquestionably a pinax of Medicine. In the list of Hesychius it was No. 7[3]. Hesychius wrote a work called *Pinakes*. He used examples of Callimachus's classifying writers according to their genre. His work was the source of the lists in works written centuries later and which in turn were later enriched by clerical and profane authors and must have served Suidas for his Lexicon in the tenth century in which his lists have come down to us.

h. Mathematical Science:

In those classifications of literature, which have not come down to us, mathematical or pure science must have claimed a main division of knowledge in the great catalogue of Callimachus, as well as in the *Pinakes* of Aristophanes of Byzantium.

i. Natural Science:

It has been said that the Museum was not a hot-bed of philosophical controversy, but rather an academy of specialized knowledge, especially medicine, the natural sciences, and philology[4], so that Natural Science must have been considered.

j. Miscellanea:

The miscellaneous authors were arranged alphabetically[5]. The mass may have been divided into subjects, and each of these groups was treated alphabetically.

1. Schmidt: *op. cit.* pp. 85 and 101.
2. See Callimachus: Fr. 16.
3. Schmidt: *op. cit.* pp. 52 and 57.
4. Christ: *op. cit.* II, pp. 17 and 19 et seq.
5. Susemihl: *op. cit.* p. 339.

There is a good Athenaeus reference (VI-244a):

There is even a book by Chaerephon (a parasite) recorded by Callimachus in his *Table of Miscellany*[1]; he writes as follows: Writers on dinners: Chaerephon; dedicated to Pod'. And then he subjoins the beginning of it, "Since you have often bidden me" (and adds the size) "in three hundred and seventy-five lines"[2].

It would seem that not far from *Writers on Dinners*, in Miscellany division of the *Pinakes*, Callimachus must have had a subdivision on Cook Books, where he had an alphabetical list of authors on the subject of Pastry Cooking (the baking of cookies)[3].

Thus the *Pinakes* was the first great library catalogue of western civilization, just as *The Bible* of Gutenberg was the first great printed book; it contained, in original form, the essentials of all the modern systems worthy of the name, and earns for its author the title of Father of Bibliography. Thus, as in all intellectual efforts, the Greeks fixed the canons of cataloguing, which have been incorporated, more or less, in our Library of Congress, European, and other systems. However, the *Pinakes* was more than a catalogue. It was the work of the foremost man of letters of his age. He could not treat even a purely scientific subject as the *Pinakes*, giving merely the names of authors and their works with technical information, of the whole corpus of Greek literature from Homer to Callimachus in the Alexandrian Library, without imparting to his work the rich stores of his scholarship, and thus the first world catalogue of knowledge became also the first literary and critical history of Hellenic literature, and also earned for its author the title of Father of Literary History.

It may be assumed that Callimachus in the *Pinakes* undertook to sort the Greek literary wealth as found in the Royal Alexandrian Library, with self imposed limits; the work stands somewhere between literary history and catalogue, perhaps closer to the latter. There could be no question of detailed scientific treatment of each individual author and of each of his individual works. That was precluded by the enormity of the task. Callimachus recognized that a systematic scientific work covering the field

1. Schneider: *Frag.*, 100d, 8.
2. This is an important fragment of *The Pinakes*, preserving the exact method of Callimachus, at least under his Miscellanea.
3. In Fr. 7 (Schmidt: *op. cit.* p. 59).

of Greek literature was only possible after inventory of stock available[1]. He made that inventory and opened the golden gates of learning for generations, may centuries, of scholars who followed him.

The proof of the importance of this great work lies in the fact that the least that can be said of it is that it was a work according to the principles of Aristotle, who taught that the material had first to be collected before being wrought into forms of art. Out of the *Pinakes* arose contemporary and later schools of biographers, the learned Hermippus and the scientific Sotion, who did so much to make the importance of Diogenes Laertius. Chronologers and descriptive writers found the *Pinakes* a mine of ready information. A veritable flow of critical research writers and specialized workers tapped the 120 volumes of the *Pinakes* for their writings. Even the great Eratosthenes doubtlessly used the *Pinakes* for his important book *On Comedy*, as well as for his geographical works. So Lysandius of Cyrene, *On Iambic Verse;* Euphorion, *On the Melic Poets;* and Istrus of Cyrene, who came to Alexandria with Callimachus and who wrote a historical Description of Famous Cities.

Aristophanes of Byzantium, one of the giants of the Museum, felt he should issue a revised *Pinakes*. It was, of course, an original work by an original thinker, and though based on the *Pinakes* of Callimachus, Aristophanes reserved his scholar's privilege of disagreeing with the master and no doubt added much to the cause of learning. His labors, too, are lost.

That the original *Pinakes* is lost is a major disaster to learning. We repeat we would rather have the priceless 120 volumes of Callimachus even than a "Livy whole"[2].

1. Schmidt: *op. cit.* p. 99.
2. Just as this work goes to the publishers (1951), the last volume of Paulys Real-Encyclopädie der klassischen Altertumswissenschaften, Vol. XX-2, Pigranes bis Plautinus (1950), was received containing the article Πίναξ by Regenbogen. It is with keen regret that we record our inability to study this important contribution on this interesting, if intricate, phase of our subject and report upon its learning and deductions for the benefit of the reader.

CHAPTER XII

THE EDITING OF TEXTS AND FIXING THE
CANONS OF LITERATURE

T HE division of all literature into its integral groups was a reasonably simple act of orderly scholarship, requiring of course a general knowledge of the field of letters. After this rough division or assortment had been made, it became necessary to proceed with an examination of the vast or meager number of manuscripts of each work of every author to ascertain the most ancient, purest or best text extant. If by rare good fortune, the original autographic text of a work had survived, this of course would form the authentic text of that particular work. If a copy known to have been transcribed from a lost original by some reliable scribe or noted scholar was found, that would become the canon of the work, with an authentic text of a high order. If a number of manuscripts survived of unknown dates by unknown scribes, a higher order of critical judgment and exegetical skill was required to select a text which was to be canonical. Fragments of poetical writings and parts of prose works where the authorship was in doubt or not indicated presented problems calling for an expert in that particular form of expression. And so examples of possible situations might be pyramided to dizzy heights, calling into play the finest critical judgment supported by much patient care and long profound study.

When we consider the vast mass of manuscripts obtained by every method from the Mediterranean, Hellenic and Greek-Macedonian worlds, the muniments of the whole body of Greek letters, in which must have been found some real *editiones principes*, many fine copies, many different versions in every condition of preservation, many fragments, important, provocative, or hopeless, all written on fragile papyrus or other delicate media; when we consider this avalanche of information, learning and wisdom poured before the fellows of the Museum and the scholars of the Library for their critical treatment, we can in some measure realize the mighty task undertaken and performed by the Silver Age of Hellas for the enlightenment of all future time. These enormous labors of textual criticism and literary preservation and probably reconstruction of an entire literature, the greatest yet known, constitute our imperishable obligation to the Alexandrian Scholar Age.

Assorting, editing, cataloguing were processes so closely connected, that one must have followed the other, and often been contemporary efforts[1]. They must have first assorted the books, yet even during this work the editing could have commenced. It is certain that such elaborate and complete cataloguing as is suggested by the *Pinakes* or *Tables* of Callimachus could only have been made after a considerable amount of the editing had been done. It is also reasonable to assume that it is the best text which he catalogued.

When at last the first stage of greatest pressure of the founding of the Museum and Library and the assembling of its first great hoard was over, at the beginning of the reign of Ptolemy II, the time had been reached for the director and his assistants of the Museum-Library to undertake the vast and arduous labor of serious critical editing.

Zenodotus, who became at least the first director under Ptolemy II, assigned to himself the enormous task of editing Homer and the epic poets, as well as the lyric and all other poets, except the dramatic writers.

For Homer he employed the comparison of many manuscripts as the basis of his work. Suidas thought he was the first Homeric editor. He probably divided the *Iliad* and *Odyssey* into 24 books each[2], and spurious verses were marked with the obelus. It is true that he condemned lines as describing actions which he thought unsuited to the gods or heroes and is sometimes wrong. However, "he is sometime right, while his great successors, Aristophanes and Aristarchus, are wrong" and Sandys also thought:

> His recension of Homer was the first recension of *any* text which aimed at restoring the genuine original[3].

1. Hence it was difficult to decide whether to place Chapter XI before or after the present Chapter.
2. See page 205; also Susemihl I-343.
3. Sandys: *op. cit.* pp. 120–121.

Sir Richard Jebb[1] has summarized his critical merits:

> In the dawn of the new scholarship, he appears as a gifted man with a critical aim, but without an adequate critical method. He insisted on a study of Homer's style; but he failed to place that study on a sound basis. The cause of this was that he often omitted to distinguish between ordinary usages of words and those peculiar to Homer. In regard to dialect again, he did not sufficiently discriminate the older from the later Ionic. And, relying too much on his own feeling for Homer's spirit, he indulged in some arbitrary emendations. Still, he broke new ground; his work has a great repute; and to some extent, its influence was lasting.

Zenodotus made a recension of Hesiod's *Theogony* and worked on the texts of Anacreon and Pindar[2].

To Alexander the Aetolian was assigned the tragic writers and the satyric plays. Alexander was a tragic poet in his own right and was, or was to become one of the seven Alexandrian *Pleiads*. Lycophron had the comic writers.

However, a fair idea may be formed of the immense task of classical critical exegesis by briefly considering only one writer. Of Aristophanes, the greatest of all writers of Comedy, who Suidas says wrote fifty-four plays, various texts of at least thirty-six plays were extant in the Alexandrian Library. Most of all the great scholars of the Museum and Library had contributed to the vast labors: Demetrios had gathered the first batch of manuscripts; Zenodotus had assigned to his colleague, Lycophron, the classification and arrangement of the comic poets, and Lycophron wrote the earliest work *On Comedy*, in 11 Books, even if its fragment gives a poor impression of his scholarship[3]; Callimachus in his great Index (the *Pinakes*, in 120 Books) had certainly described numerous MSS. of all extant texts of Aristophanes; Eratosthenes was the author of a famous work *On the Old Comedy*, in 12 Books; Euphronius, a poet of the Pleiad, wrote a *Commentary on Aristophanes*.

The Aristophanic text, like many of the texts of other great writers and certainly of authors of theatrical pieces, must have been in a state requiring the attention of literary surgeons. Care-

---

1. Jebb: *Homer*, p. 92.
2. Susemihl: *op. cit.* I-330–334; Christ: *op. cit.* 428; and Sandys: *op. cit.* I-121.
3. Idem: *op. cit.* I–274; see Strecker: *De Lycophrone*; Sandys *op. cit.* I–122.

less scribes, where nearly every copy may have been by a different hand, written at a different time; interpolations (like in the case of Shakespeare) by actors and managers, changes by owners of separate manuscripts; even, it is possible, corrections or changes by the author himself, and many other conceivable tamperings with the text, honest and dishonest, created a vast field of critical labors. Of course, different copies even had variable texts. The cataloguers described them as they found them, with the succinct comments of Callimachus, yet there was the necessity for a thorough study of the text and a truly critical edition.

Aristophanes of Byzantium, librarian of the Alexandriana, undertook this task and edited an edition of the poet. We believe Aristophanes of Byzantium wrote a *Commentary* on the poet; he certainly wrote a book *On Masks* (or *Comic Roles*)[1] and we know that his pupil Callistratus was the author of such a *Commentary*. Finally, Aristarchus, the last of the known great librarians, whose prodigious output of critical commentary (some 800 rolls according to Suidas) entitles him in place of Gibbon, to the epithet "voluminous", amid his labors wrote a *Commentary on Aristophanes*[2].

And yet all this is but the merest sketch of the infinite labors of many scholars of the Museum and of the Library, on the innumerable text of the vast body of Greek poetical and prose literature gathered by Demetrios and his successors.

Perhaps it was for the dramatic poets and lyric poetry that the greatest service for posterity was rendered by the critical scholars of the Museum. These texts probably reached the Alexandrian age in greater degree of variety, corruption and confusion, due to their transitory and occasional nature. Eccentric texts, indeed, must have been numerous, in spite of Athenian labors and Lycurgus's great effort in behalf of the supreme tragic masters. Hence we believe that in this field work of the first order was done to establish a text, to assemble its words and language structure in glossaries and studies, to illustrate their special meaning, and generally to write commentaries on the subject matter of the poem or drama[3].

1. Athenaeus, XIV–659a.
2. Vide: J. W. White: *The Scholia on the Aves of Aristophanes* (Boston, 1914). Dr. White writes: "Whether Aristophanes, in his text edition of the poet, wrote the lyrics in cola or not cannot now be determined. Nobody else is so likely to have introduced this useful method of writing." (p. XIX.)
3. E. A. Barber: *Alexandrian Literature* (Ch. VIII, Vol. VII, p. 254), *C.A.H.*

But an adequate description of the critical process employed in formulating the final texts of the Greek writers would indeed require a separate treatise[1].

To the grammarian's knowledge of the tradition, history and examples of the origins and structure of the language, the scholar's knowledge of the general field of literature, the special-ist's study of an individual author or of a school of expression or of a mode of verse or prose style, must be added a free, unbiased, critical attitude, a reasonable, sound, and enduring judgment.

Painstaking care in minutely comparing text with text, an investigation of the author's time, place and flare, the relative authenticity and provenance, when known, of the manuscripts: these are but a few of the many intricate labors required of the true critic or recensionist.

A complete history of these vast intellectual labors may never be attained. Yet we do know the names of some of the great specialists and have some account of their important work. That there were pre-Alexandrian critics and recensionists in earlier days and throughout the golden age of Greek letters is well known.

I have often thought of what we owe to those men who devote their lives that other men might read clean copy!

THE ALEXANDRIAN CANON

It is a far cry from the scholars of the Alexandrian Museum-Library to the members of the Grolier Club. Between these more than two thousand years, scholars have ventured to select the best. Sir John Lubback in a lecture at the Working Men's College announced his *Best Hundred Books*, which provoked the eccentric, abusive, if not silly criticism of Mr. Ruskin, who entered the list through the medium of the open discussion started in the *Pall Mall Gazette*. That fussy, erratic genius assured us that as to Grote any head-clerk, if he had the vanity to waste his time on it, could write a better book; and as to Gibbon, that he lacked imagination, logic, picturesqueness or wit, and wrote "the worst

---

1. Indeed of many volumes. A great American Greek scholar, Dr. J. W. White, writing only on the *Scholia* of *one* of the plays of Aristophanes (*The Aves*), most proper-ly required 434 pages.

English that was ever written by an educated Englishman"[1].
It was logical that men such as the Alexandrian scholars who
had taken upon themselves the enormous task of discovering the
authentic texts of the world's greatest literature and arranging
it for future ages should, having as it were between their hands
the destinies of books, have been tempted to choose the very best
in verse and prose to be preserved for posterity. It was natural,
therefore, for them to draw up lists of the most distinguished
writers in each genre and to set up some sort of *Canons*. Of course,
such selections could only be of value in a general way, as the
individual preference and prejudice of the scholar making the
list could not be entirely avoided. Before Alexandria, men had
considered Aeschylus, Sophocles and Euripides as the greatest
tragic writers and Homer as the greatest epic writer, if not the
greatest of all writers, and these, perhaps individual, preferences
had a public approval. But it was apparently reserved for the
scholars of the Museum-Library to select in their literary labo-
ratory the foremost writers and to construct lists or canons of
their selection. We do not know just what they did. The learning
of Ruhnken, Montfaucon, Cramer and Usener, with the antiquarian resources of the Bibliotheca Coisliniani[2] and the saving
good sense of Sandys, have eked out lists probably reflecting the
original selections. There has been much discussion collaterally as
to whether the lists were for scholars only or for the adult world,
and Susemihl says that there is no reason not to believe that
Aristophanes engaged in this aesthetic judgment purely for its
own sake[3] and reminds us that he compares Menander to Homer.
It would seem reasonable that the Canons were to serve all
purposes. They could be used by the teachers of youth, and serve
likewise as recommendations for the reading public as well as for
the scholar's study.

That Aristophanes of Byzantium drew up lists of the greatest
writers, at least of the poets, there is reason to assume. If the
authoritative weight of the powerful Aristarchus approved the
selection, it seemed then to have the force and authority of a

1. John Ruskin: *The Works of John Ruskin*, edited by Cook and Wedderburn, London,
1909, *Arrows of the Chace*, p. 582 and 586.
2. Now among the antiquarian treasures of the Bibliothèque Nationale.
3. Susemihl: *op. cit.* I, p. 445, note.

canon. Unfortunately, little has survived to maintain or to set forth the honored names of the Alexandrian Canon. It would seem that the two Alexandrian scholars did not record the names of living writers. However these, as we shall see, were doubtlessly added later.

Of documents there are 1. a list from a manuscript of the tenth century from Mount Athos (the Codex Coisliniani, 387), published by Montfaucon (*Bibl. Coisl.*, p. 597); and 2. a late MS. in the Bodleian, with variations, published by Cramer (*Anec.* IV, p. 196).

Of ancient writers we have the suggestive passages of Quintilian[1] in his tenth book:

a. Apollonius is not admitted to the lists drawn up by the professors of literature, because the critics, Aristarchus and Aristophanes, included no contemporary poets. (X–1–54.)

b. Of these (the elegiac poets), Callimachus is regarded as the best. (X–1–59.)

c. Of the three writers of iambics approved by the judgment of Aristarchus, Archilochus will be far the most useful... (X–1–59.)

d. Of the nine lyric poets Pindar is by far the greatest. (X–1–61.)

e. There follows a vast army of orators. Athens alone having produced ten remarkable orators in the same generations. (X–1–76.)

And most apposite:

The old school of teachers indeed carried their criticism so far that they were not content with obelising lines or rejecting books whose titles they regarded as spurious, as though they were expelling a supposititious child from the family circle, but also drew up a canon of authors, from which some were omitted altogether. (I–IV–3.)[2]

These and a few other references, particular to at least four epic poets: Homer, Hesiod, Antimachus and Panyasis, uncle of Herodotus, are the basis for the labors of Ruhnken and others in their efforts to reconstruct the Alexandrian Canon. These passages reasonably indicate some sort of list or canon, at least for the

1. Quintilian: *Institutio Oratoria*, X–1–54–76.
2. Quintilian.

poets. Ruhnken believes the canon included writers of verse and prose. Bernhardy[1] will only support the poets and that for school purposes.

As for the orators[2] there has always been a popular vogue for the "ten". Susemihl does not agree to limiting the canon to poets[3]. The canon of the orators is also regarded as not being of the Alexandrian Museum, but of the Pergamene school (c. 125 B.C.)[4]. It has also been assigned to voluminous Didymus or to Caecilius of Calacte[5].

Whoever may be the author, it seems that there was a canon of orators.

As to the historians the difficulty grows. Usener (p. 136) says that in the Pergamum Library there was a statue of Herodotus[6] and assumes a similar recognition in the Alexandriana, but Susemihl with reason remarks that even if this were so, it would not prove an Alexandrian Canon of Historians. However, he does not wish to decide[7]. Probably, with equal significance, the writer remembers that there is a statue of Herodotus in the Library of Congress!

If the historians are difficult, a canon of the philosophers presents even a greater problem.

And yet, as difficult as is the situation, and as meager the proofs, it would seem that there was an Alexandrian Canon. It is true the material for the poets is more ample, yet the scholars of the Museum could hardly reject the two great divisions of letters and have ignored the master-pieces of prose in Oratory, History and Philosophy.

1. Bernhardy: *op. cit. Gr. Lit.* I-185–8.
2. Ruhnken: *Hist. Crit. Orat. Gr.*, pp. 94–100; Opus I-385–392.
3. Susemihl: *op. cit.* I, pp. 444–7.
4. In his introduction to the *Pseudo-Plutarch: Lives of the Ten Orators* (Plutarch's *Moralia*, Vol. X, p. 342, L.C.L.), H. N. Fowler says:
At some time in the second century before Christ ten Attic orators were selected, probably by Apollodorus of Pergamum, as the orators whose speeches were most worthy of preservation and study, and this "Canon" of the Ten Attic Orators was generally accepted.
Cf. Brzoska: *De canone decemoratorum Atticorum*, 1883.
5. See Sandys: *op. cit.* 130–131, whose epitome, as usual, is most admirable. Also Susemihl: I, 444, 521 and II, 484 and 694.
6. As there were of Homer, Alcaeus, Timotheos of Miletus (See Pauly–Wissowa: s.v. *Pergame Library*, under *Bibliotheken*).
7. Susemihl: *op. cit.* I-447, note.

We believe the Canon was added to in subsequent periods to conform to the opinion of the time. Hence Callimachus and Philetas could well have been added after their deaths. So Apollonius of Rhodes, Aratus of Soli and certainly the Sicilian Theocritus, who had the friendship of the Ptolemies and the suffrages of succeeding ages, and Polybius the historian, who died half a century after Aristophanes of Byzantium.

The following tentative list is the one revised by Usener[1], printed in Sandys[2], to which we have added the names of Apollonius, Aratus and Theocritus, which had been added by the ancients to the list sometime between the age of Aristarchus and the age of Strabo, as the names of Philetas and Callimachus had been added to the elegiac list. We have also ventured a canon of philosophers.

CANON ALEXANDRINUS

POETRY:

Epic: Homer – Hesiod – Peisander – Panyasis – Antimachus – Apollonius of Rhodes – Aratus – Theocritus.
Iambic: Semonides – Archilochus – Hipponax.
Tragic: Aeschylus – Sophocles – Euripides – Ion – Achaeus.
Comic (Old): Epicharmus – Cratinus – Eupolis – Aristophanes – Pherecrates – Crates – Plato.
Comic (Middle): Antiphanes – Alexis.
Comic (New): Menander – Philippides – Diphilus – Philemon – Apollodorus.
Elegiac: Callinus – Mimnermus – Philetas – Callimachus.
Lyric: Alcman – Alcaeus – Sappho – Stesichorus – Pindar – Bacchylides – Ibycus – Anacreon – Simonides.

PROSE:

Orators: Demosthenes – Lysias – Hypereides – Isocrates – Aeschines – Lycurgus – Isaeus – Antiphon – Andocides – Deinarchus.
Historians: Thucydides – Herodotus – Xenophon – Philistus – Theopompus – Ephorus – Anaximenes – Callisthenes – Hellanicus – Polybius.

1. *Dion. Hal. de Imitatione*, p. 130, reprinted in Peterson's Quintilian X, p. XXXVI.
2. Sandys: *op. cit.* p. 131.

Philosophers: Pythagoras – Socrates – Plato – Xenophon – Aristotle – Theophrastus – Pyrrho – Epicurus – Zeno – Carneades[1].

There are other lists:

Tragic Poets (first class): Aeschylus – Sophocles – Euripides – Ion – Achaeus – Agathon.
Tragic Poets (second class) or *Tragic Pleiades:* Alexander of Aetolia – Philiscus of Corcyra – Sositheus – Homer the Younger – Aeantides – Sosiphanes or Sosicles.
Poetic Pleiades: Apollonius of Rhodes – Aratus of Soli – Philiscus – Homer the Younger – Lycophron – Nicander – Theocritus.

1. Harry Thurston Peck in his admirable *Harper's Dictionary of Classical Literature and Antiquities*, New York, 1897, ventured four names only, two of the Academy, Plato and Xenophon, and for the Peripatos, Aristotle and Theophrastus. He also included Aeschines.

The scholars of Alexandria were mainly but not exclusively concerned with the verbal criticism of the Greek poets, primarily with that of Homer.

Sandys I–144.

But for the patronage of the Ptolemies and the labours of devoted students in the Museum, Homer, for instance, might have wholly perished, and we might know nothing of Aeschylus ... We still owe Alexandria a great debt.

Dr. Thomas Ethelbert Page (A Letter to James Loeb).

CHAPTER XIII

HOMER

To take up one author, the most important it is true, should we not, with Quintilian, exclaim: With Jove let us begin[1]. So we take up Homer, "model and inspiration of every department of eloquence", and attempt to sketch, if not the genesis, at least the critical descent of the epic texts.

The early rhapsodes in Ionian towns, through Aegean islands (Chios, Delos, Cyprus) in Attica, in Sicyon, at Syracuse and towns of Magna Graecia, recited in parts, consecutive or selective, the epic tales of the Homeric poems. Their audiences became the first crude critics of a traditional text, as well as judges of the professional minstrel's histrionic gifts of presentation of the song he stitched together.

In the Silver Age of Greek letters, its ostentatious capital was Alexandria. The early galaxy of illustrious men of the Museum and the Library were not only scholars but men of letters: Philetas, Lycophron, Alexander Aetolus, Aratus, Callimachus, Apollonius Rhodius, Eratosthenes (a universal genius, in the Aristotelian or Renaissance sense), Timon of Phlius, Rhianus, Herondas, Euphorion, not to mention Theocritus and Demetrios of Phaleron and others. There were scholars and scientists: Euclid, Apollonius of Perga, Archimedes of Syracuse, Hero of Alexandria, Hipparchus of Nicaea, Claudius Ptolemaeus, Nicander, and others who came to the schools of Alexandria. There were philosophers of the Academy, the Lyceum and the Stoa galore. Besides many artists and intellectual specialists, there were men particularly attached to the Museum and Library, who were not men of letters, but who were men of learning, and to whose labors succeeding ages are more indebted than to all the poets and purely literary men of Alexandria. Such were Zenodotus, Aristophanes of Byzantium, Aristarchus, Ammonius, Aristonicus, Didymus, and possibly Sym-

1. Quintilian (X–1–46) quoting Aratus in his *Phaenomena* 1.

machus. To these should be added perhaps Demetrios of Phaleron and certainly Lycophron, Alexander Aetolus, Callimachus and Eratosthenes. Of all these, not excluding Callimachus, compiler of the great Catalogue (*Πίνακες*), Aristophanes of Byzantium and Aristarchus of Samothrace are outstanding.

As a consideration of the poetry and literary labors of the Alexandrian age is not within the scope of this treatise, we are compelled to forego the allurement of comment here, and confine ourselves to the prosaic presentation of the real work of genius performed by the Alexandrian scholars in collecting, preserving, editing, annotating, illuminating and publishing the Greek classic texts. As an example we will take, as we have said, the work of one Greek author, and roughly sketch the genesis and important mile-posts of its journey or transmission to our time.

In the intellectual development of man (in which the most gifted of all peoples are no exception) poetry, of course, preceded prose. Song and music preceded poetry, and the dance, physical, doubtless artistic, was probably the earliest method of general cultural communication.

In the far-time, amid the dark forests of Thessaly and Thrace, in the sloping valley of Thessalian Mt. Olympus, dwelt a Greek people (Pierians they have been called), who had well advanced from mimicry and dance through music to song. In time, Lucretius tells how by imitating the birds men learned to sing:

Next step by step they learnt the plaintive melodies which the reed pipe gives forth tapped by the players' fingertips, – the pipe discovered amid pathless wood and forests, amid the solitary haunts of shepherds and the peace of the open air[1].

So song resounded in grove and clearing.

Now it was the Linus song (*Αἴλινος*), where a youth of faultless form represented perhaps the soft beauties of spring devoured by the summer heat, or the autumn song personifying not the harvest but the planting of the seed in the dark bosom of earth, both plaintive laments, where, even in the song of the vintage, the men and women, in rhythmic steps, utter the final melancholy cry: *αἴ λινε*.

1. Lucretius: *De rerum natura*, V–1385 (tr. W. H. D. Rouse, in L.C.L.), London, 1943.

Then the loud paean, song of hope and courage, as well as victory, would ring out on great occasions and at high festivals, with its interjection, when they cried ἰή παιῆον, ἰή παιῆον! In goodly city with towers and seven gates of gold they:

Were bringing home a bride to her husband on a well-wheeled car, while the bridal song swelled high and the glow of blazing torches held by handmaidens rolled in waves afar. And these maidens went before, delighting in the festival; and after them came frolicsome choirs, the youths singing soft-mouthed to the sound of shrill pipes, while the echo was shivered around them, and the girls leading on the lovely dance to the sound of lyres. Then again on the other side was a rout of young men revelling, with flutes playing; some frolicking with dance and song; and others laughing all in time with the flute players as they went along[1].

And then, the final notes of the Threnos, or lamentation for the dead, as the body is laid on the couch of death, or borne in the cold grey dawn to the sepulchre, or as the all consuming flames of the pyre resolve to its primal state the form of the beloved. This dirge, which may first have been heard in Thracian or Thessalian wood, or glen, has survived in the perfect scenes of death:
Of Achilles, where:

The Muses, nine in all replying to one another with sweet voices, led the dirge[2].

Of Hector, the supremest example:

High on a bed of fret-work they laid him and seated beside him Minstrels to lead in a dirge; and mournful the requiem sounded. Dirges they sang, while women responsive added their mourning. White-armed Andromache for them began the loud lamentation[3].

Out of these wild parts came the first singers, whose names we have, with habitats of wide range, of whom we know so little, except the persistent traditions that link their name and fame with the early cults of Apollo, Dionysus and Demeter. Olympian Orpheus was the first singer of the heroic age, and his tragic fate

1. Hesiod: *Shield of Heracles*, 270 et seq. (L.C.L., tr. Hugh G. Evelyn-White), London, 1914.
2. Homer: *The Odyssey:* (XXIV–60), tr. A. T. Murray, L.C.L., London, 1919.
3. Homer: *The Iliad* (XXIV–720), tr. Wm. Benjamin Smith & Miller, New York, 1944.

must have evoked in music and in song the sad story of the loss of his beloved Eurydice, as well as hyms connected with the rituals of the worship of Dionysus, Demeter, and the powers of the nether world. Eumolpus, also called a Thracian, must have been likewise attached to the worship of these deities, as, for centuries in historical times, his descendants (the Eumolpids) were the chief priests in the Sacred Mysteries of Eleusis; Musaeus, a disciple of Orpheus, also called an Eumolpid; and Pamphus and the Bakides there were, all inspired singers of the gods, whose revelations have been lost.

Out of these primitive songs and mystic singers, there grew single ballads chanting the stories of heroes and heroic exploits. In time these multiplied, transmitted solely by memory's threads. The shepherd, to relieve the tedium of his simple lot, improvised strains of harmonious sounds. The ambitious youth, in his village, sang to his fellows rhythmic words in praise of gods and men. Then, Greek genius, gathering many of these wayward songs, commenced, in guilds of minstrelsy, to give them poetic forms and in chant and recititive purveyed them professionally to rich and poor. In agora or market-place, on market-days or days of festival, in a sequested nook on the slope of a hill, the humble minstrel chanted the deeds of heroic gods and men, just as to this day in some unspoilt Mediterranean lands his Arabic brother narrates the Arabian tales. In festive halls of warriors and kings, the rhapsodes recited in heroic lays the glorious exploits of their ancestors, both gods and men. All of these steps took generations, nay centuries, to evolve, and it was indeed a far cry from the first shepherd's imitative strain of the lark to the perfect curtain of Homeric song.

As the mists arose from the Greek lands, we discover not only the primitive, if not autochthonic, Pelasgians, but the three great tribes, the Aeolian, the Ionian and the Dorian, which, vital and fluid, pressed one upon the other causing displacements of populations and cultures and vast tragic migrations of peoples beyond the seas. These human seismic movements finally subsided into the formal sites of the Greek states as we find them in the first clear days of Hellenic history.

Whether the tribes came by two routes: by land from the north through Thessaly, and by sea, from the East, from Asia, from some ancestral Aryan, Phrygian, Greco-Italic homeland, may never with certainty be known[1].

At least three Hellenic dialects did service for these tribal groups, Aeolic, Ionic and Doric. More primitive forms of speech may have existed, but when the Greeks emerge in the hard light of history the Ionian and Dorian languages possess the field. The Aeolic, of course, still survived and is admitted to form the supposed earlier substratum in Homer, and a modern scholar[2] has had the courage and learning to transpose the supposed more ancient parts of Homer back to an assumed Aeolic original. There is something slightly ironic in the view that all the Greeks were Aeolians, except those who were Ionians and Dorians and that whatever in language or dialect was not Ionic or Doric was necessarily Aeolic.

Duncker (and Holm agrees) even says: "that the existence of an Aeolian dialect was asserted merely because they wished to contrast all the Greek dialects with the decidedly more developed ones of the Dorians and Ionians."[3]

To these national dialects we should add a fourth, the so-called "Epic", an artificial form, if you will, that was certainly never spoken by Aeolian or Ionian. It is the language of the epos, the language of the Homeric poems. It was a high, exalted, poetic norm woven by singers and poets from songs and poems and in the course of time and in the hands of later poets and minstrels or reciters it became "a "large utterance", rhythmic and emotional, like a complicated instrument for the expression of the heroic saga"[4], as it flowed from the fountains of the Muses into the myriad streams of dactylic hexameter, the oldest and "Homeric" verse of Grecian prosody, which may have been invented by the priests at Delphi for Apollo's oracular pronouncements and which became a common vehicle for religious song.

In Thrace, whence the worship of the Muses was derived, the mystic chants of the priests, the songs of early singers, the lays of the primitive poets, were slowly spread throughout northern Greece. Perhaps in the old Aryan-Phrygian homeland, certainly

1. Among those who favor these prehistoric wonderings, may be mentioned Curtius, Duncker and Holm.
2. Dr. August Fick of Göttingen.
3. Holm: *op. cit.* (note 5, p. 73, Vol. 1).
4. Murray: *Lit. of Ancient Greece*, p. 23.

in Hellenic settlements on the mainland of Asia and adjacent
isles, the early Greeks cultivated the arts of music and song, and
in the centuries' course, the song in honor of the gods, the lays
in praise of warrior or heroic king took shape and were gradually
perfected as poetic utterance, until a body of poetic narratives
was created, rich in character and incidents and endowed with
the native imaginative genius of the Hellenic race. With the
increase of songs and singers, schools or guilds arose, from whence
professional reciters, as well as the original poets or singers, who
to the body of a popular narrative would "stitch" in verses for
their particular convenience or such as would harmonize with
some great or festive occasion. In such an age (as indeed in every
age) the minstrel took from the general mass what he thought he
would require.

At last there arose from these brotherhoods of minstrelsy,
from these guilds of rhapsodes, from these schools of poesy, a
singer gifted beyond all men in magic utterance, true son of the
morning, in whom alone, in amplitude and quality, the Muses
had implanted the divine sense of beauty. In genius transcendent,
unique, selective, he took what he required from wherever found,
but taking transmuted it into perfect forms of sound and thought,
just as the greatest of those who were to follow him, Shakespeare,
was to do.

Men called him Homer. With certainty we know nothing of
his life. His maternal ancestors may have come from Achaean
Greece, rich in memory of the glories of Mycenae. His paternal
ancestors may have come from Attica, and during the Ionian
migration or later sought asylum in Asia Minor at Smyrna. Here
his father may have married an Aeolian woman from Cyme,
for which there is a thread of legend, though it is difficult to
forget that the great Aristarchus said Homer was an Athenian,
and Gladstone[1], Monroe[2] and Leaf[3] agree that the argument for
the origin of the poems in continental Greece is unanswerable.

Ihne[4] records that Athens as metropolis of the Ionians could

1. Wm. E. Gladstone (Vide: *Studies on Homer and The Homeric Age*, 3 Vols., Oxford, 1858).
2. D. B. Monroe: in *English Historical Review*, I, p. 43.
3. Walter Leaf: *The Iliad*, London, 1886 (Vol. I, p. XXV).
4. W. Ihne: (referring to Bekker, *Anecdota*, Vol. II, p. 768) in his article *Homerus* in Smith *Dic. of Gr. & R. Biog. & Myths*, Boston, 1867 (Vol. II, p. 500).

claim Homer as a citizen. Again, Smyrna was originally founded by Ionians from Ephesus, who were expelled by Aeolians from Cyme, who in turn were driven out as the city became permanently Ionic. Thus Smyrna, the meeting-place of Aeolian and Ionian, may have been singularly destined to present to the world its supreme singer.

The contribution of Aeolia to the Homeric corpus was indispensable. The Aeolians were the depositaries of the treasury of Trojan legend. Their people had the leadership and played the largest part in the Trojan War; they had, therefore, original and continuous recollections of the exalted heroes and amazing exploits, from their original European, Grecian, Achaean and Mycenian homeland.

After achieving the apogee of fame and glory, they had fled themselves from the ruthless invaders of their Achaean cities practically to the land of Troy herself; their knowledge had come unbroken through the generations, perpetuated by the stream of epic lays by which their minstrels had preserved the wondrous story of their race in the golden days of the heroic age. The Aeolians had the storehouse of material for the great Homeric adventure. But the genius, not only to assemble the best that had been done by other men, which may indeed have been considerable in quality and quantity, but to create living heroes of flesh and blood who, in perfect theatre, enact scenes of universal life that have compelled the admiration of nigh three thousand years, this the Aeolians may not have had.

The Ionic race now made its supreme contribution to the Greek genius, in the person of Homer, who whether partly Aeolian, or with a slight Aeolian strain, or full Ionian, yet had profound knowledge of the Aeolic language, literature and art. From these cultures he took what he thought he needed (how little or how much we shall never know), and wove them, now turned by him to strands of gold, with immortal genius and divine art, into the great body of his original design and thus wrought for all time, the *Iliad* and the *Odyssey*.

Perhaps after exhausting what Smyrna and its school had for him, he went to Chios, an Ionian isle famous for poets as well as for figs and wine. Here in its noted guild of minstrels, he may have labored, composed or completed his epics. Certainly these

Homeridae, this school of singers or poets or minstrels or rhapsodes, claimed descent from Homer and the custodianship of the Homeric traditions and they perhaps wrote some of the post-Homeric epics and hymns. It is in the hymn *To Pythian Apollo*, that to the question who is the sweetest singer, we read:

He is a blind man, and dwells in rocky Chios: his lays are ever more supreme.

And now, the Homeric Questions:

The Homeric Questions which have engaged the labors and talents of innumerable scholars, in many lands, begin with the propositions: Did Homer ever live? To which follows: If Homer livid did he compose both the *Iliad* and the *Odyssey*, or did he only write the *Iliad* and another (unknown) poet the *Odyssey*? If Homer never existed, who wrote the immortal epics, or how have they come into being and when and where? How were they transmitted to our time? What is their real significance?

For nearly two centuries this, the most important literary controversy known, has challenged the knights of the pen and the brotherhoods of books, to an enduring conflict which has actually lasted for a century and a half, during which time the soldiers of letters, of Germanic, Latin and English breeds, have continued to battle with valor and with a pertinacity truly Homeric, in order to maintain or destroy the classical tradition and thought of at least two thousand years. In the conflict all the ingenuities of mind have been exploited if not exhausted. Everything has been thought and said. There are no new weapons to create. We can suggest nothing new, though we may be able to gather these conflicts of learning and attempt to assimilate or "stitch" them together in an Homeric way, saving, were it possible, the best fruit of each and welding them into a pattern agreeable to our individual though humble viewpoint, to which we have arrived after a sincere endeavor to behold the vast intellectual field.

It is important to remember, that out of all this din, fuss and controversy, there has been a precious gain to true scholarship, in the intensive study to which the poems, verse by verse, their language structures, word by word, and all the traditions and conceivable circumstances of their being, have been subjected, even though they may have had to experience infinite tests, as each scholar, in his individual crucible, has tried to separate the immortal mass into its elemental parts in order to prove his particular theory. Yet the practical results are that more pains-taking and brilliant scholarship has been devoted to these poems than to any other work of pure literature.

Only to solve even the first question, prodigious learning and the study and research of many lives have been devoted to an attempt to wring from the faltering oracles of antiquity the simple answer as to whether Homer ever lived.

Yet Solon, Pisistratus, Pericles, Herodotus, Thucydides, Plato, Aristotle and Aristarchus and indeed all antiquity never doubted the physical existence of the poet who they believed wrote the *Iliad* and the *Odyssey*.

And so, the second question, the Homeric authorship of the epics, was practically the universal belief of the poets, philoso-phers, thinkers, scholars, and the people of the classic ages. It is true that after the creative ages of Greek literature, in the time of later Greek scholarship, a small critical group advanced the opinion that the two poems were written by two different poets. They were called Chorizontes, the "separaters". Their influence must have been small, as they seemed to have been dismissed by such simple statements as that of Longinus, who naively tells us that the *Iliad* was written by Homer in his early years and the *Odyssey* in the poet's old age[1]. It is true that Aris-tarchus wrote a book (now lost) against the skeptics and de-stroyed them. Prof. Mahaffy attaches great importance to Aris-tarchus's having thus taken notice of the novel theory, and takes his place beside the Chorizontes, when he says:

> Until, therefore, some new evidence is produced, which is well nigh impossible, there seems no reason whatever for assuming the *Iliad* and the *Odyssey* to be the product of a single mind[2].

We know that the great Mr. Grote argued for a dual authorship, and some continental critics, chopping the *Odyssey* into its sup-posed integral parts, can conjure a greater number. Yet to assume that two poets of equal genius, living at or at about the same time, were the authors of two epics of a quality surpassing all such

1. Dionysius Longinus: *On the Sublime*, PX I–IX.
2. J. P. Mahaffy: *His. Gr. Lit. op. cit.* I, pp. 61 and 81.

other works of men, that one was called Homer and was known to all in the Athenian, Alexandrian and Roman ages, that the other poet's name was unknown, indeed had never been sought and that such attribution would not have alike amazed the genial mind of old Herodotus or the cold intellect of Aristotle, to assume all this "stands not within the prospect of belief". The verdict of antiquity, the opinion of Holm and other Germanic scholars, the consistent belief of an historical line of English classical scholarship, would seem to justify the conclusion of Prof. Bury, that if the tide has not definitely turned, "there is at all events an increasing number of critics who believe in an original unity of authorship and design". After all, it is most reasonable to believe that the author of *Hamlet* and *Lear* was also the author of *Winter's Tale* and the *Tempest*.

And so for centuries a living Homer and a single authorship sufficed. But the modern age, in which man has endeavored to investigate all things and in turn to deny all things spiritual, mental and physical, could not be expected to except Homer.

The French scholar Casaubon[1] and the English scholar Bentley[2] had doubts and misgivings, as did also Perrault[3] and Hedelin, who were French, and the Italian Vico[4]. But the seventeenth century brought forth *Conjectures académiques* of the Abbé d'Aubignac. This work was first published in 1715. He maintained that Homer never existed; that the epics were a collection of perhaps forty separate lays brought together first by Lycurgus in the 8th century and rearranged by Pisistratus in the 6th century. Then Robert Wood argued that writing was unknown in Homer's time, in his *Essay on the Original Genius of Homer*, 1769, and finally the recovery of the great body of Alexandrian criticism found in an ancient scholia in a Venetian manuscript in San Marco at Venice, published by the French scholar Villoison, the discoverer of the great Marcian codex of the *Iliad* (Venice, 1788), set the perfect stage for the sensational *Prolegomena ad Homerum* (1795) of Friedrich A. Wolf, who has been called "the father of modern Homeric criticism", but who was probably

1. Casaubon and Menage *ad Diogenes Laertius*, IXO13.
2. Richard Bentley: *Remarks on a Late Discourse of Freethinking by Phileleutherus Lipsiansis*, 1713 (or 1737).
3. Charles Perrault: *Parallèle des Anciens et des Modernes*, 1692 (Vol. III, p. 33 seq.).
4. Giambattista Vico: *Il Vero Omero* (in Opera di Vico, Milan, 1836, Vol. V-437-497).

its foster-father, as Prof. J. B. Bury has shown in his valuable, conservative and brave chapter on Homer in *Cambridge Ancient History*[1]. His summation on the theory of Wolf is as follows:

> About 950 B.C. Homer, a poet of genius, composed a number of songs on the Trojan war, other poets followed him and added new pieces. These songs were handed down orally by reciters (rhapsodes) and on their lips underwent considerable change. They were first written down at Athens in the time of Pisistratus, and further changes were made by learned critics who revised them. The greater part of the songs may be attributed to Homer himself, but it is impossible to distinguish them from the rest. The apparent unity of design which has deceived the world is due to the artifices of compilers and editors (diasceuasts)[2].

During the 19th century the fires of controversy never abated. Hermann (1832) evokes from the body of the epics two original poems: the *Wrath of Achilles* (from the *Iliad*), the *Return of Odysseus* (from the *Odyssey*). The encrusting lays are said to be the work of later, or added singers. The skepticism of Lachmann, after a comparative study of the old German epics, led to the belief "that he has found so many inconsistences and contradictions that he distinctly asserts the plan of the *Iliad* to be the afterthought of a clever arranger and not an original feature in the poem"[3]. Under the fierce light of his examination he discovers eighteen separate lays. After a century of much learning and infinite labor, the modern school of Chorizontes or expansionists, have added to their cause the elaborate work of Wilamowitz-Moellendorff[4]. The theory may be expressed: that the original *Iliad* of Homer consisted of Books I–VII (i.e. to v. 321); Books XI–XV; Books XVI–XXIII (i.e. to v. 256); and a concluding part of the poem ending with the death of Achilles, now lost. Much might be said against the assumption that the work of a great poet that has weathered twenty-five to twenty-eight centuries should be free from inconsistences, contradictions, and mental or literary lapses.

---

1. Prof. J. B. Bury: in *Cambridge Ancient History* (Vol. II, ch. XVIII, pp. 502 et seq.), London, 1940 (1926). We have ventured this opinion in spite of the strictures of Dr. Arnold J. Toynbee (*A Study of History*, Vol. I, p. 4, London, 1934, on the "synthetic histories" ..."in course of publication by the Cambridge University Press").
2. *Cambridge Ancient History*: *op. cit.* II, p. 503.
3. J. P. Mahaffy: *A History of Classical Greek Literature*, London, 1895 (I-49).
4. U. von Wilamowitz-Moellendorff: *Die Ilias und Homer*, Berlin, 1916.

We merely would recall Holm's[1] remarks in this connection:

> But what right have we to look upon Homer as merely the author
> of certain sections of the *Iliad*? For antiquity, Homer was the
> representative, first of the whole epico-cyclic poetry, and then of the
> *Iliad* and the *Odyssey*. For us he either has no existence whatever,
> or he is the author of the finest passages in the *Iliad* and *Odyssey*.
> But there is no reason why we should credit him only with frag-
> ments of the *Iliad*. To pick out fragments of this kind, to call
> Homer their author, and then to say that other passages which do
> not correspond [in the judgment of the critics] in language, etc., are
> not Homeric - for this there is no justification.

How hard it is to forget Shakespeare, to which a similar process of
disintegration has and will ever be a matter of little importance.

As to the original language of the poems and the language
vehicle in which they are extant, the authorities hold many
theories.

August Fick devoted great learning, much labor and ingenuity
to this question.

Two distinct dialects are embalmed in the present text of
Homer: the Aeolic, known in its later stages in Sappho and
Alcaeus, and the Ionic, known in its later stages in Herodotus.
The poems were originally composed in Aeolic and then trans-
literated into Ionic.

Upon this Prof. Mahaffy[2] declared:

> I will not here make myself responsible for more than one of his
> (Fick's) conclusions, and that the greatest of them – I mean, the
> transliteration of the older Aeolic lays into an Ionic dress, which
> lets the older forms show through here and there, as evidence
> beyond dispute.

Yet Dr. Leaf's[3] comment is compelling here:

> While not admitting that the Aeolic into which he (Fick) converts
> the poems is in any way to be regarded as the original dialect, I
> believe that his proof that the poems were not originally in an Ionic

1. Adolph Holm: *History of Greece* (I, p. 165, note 9), London, 1894. Of course Holm's
comment referred to Wilamowitz-Moellendorff's: *Homerische Untersuchungen*, Berlin,
1884.
2. Mahaffy: *History of Classical Greek Literature, op. cit.* I-75.
3. Walter Leaf: *The Iliad*, London, 1886, Vol. I, pp. XII and XV. The writer almost
added that he quoted from Walter Leaf's autographed copy to Ernest Myers.

form will be found to hold good. The original Epic dialect was Achaian and past recovery for us. We can only say that this Achaian seems to have been nearly akin to several dialects which we know in their later forms, notably the Asiatic Aeolic and to the Cyprian which, as is well known, leads us to Arcadia. Whether or no the poems passed through a state of Asiatic Aeolic, or were transformed from Achaian to Ionic, it is beyond our power to say; but that such a change of dialect has been made Fick has almost proved; to have done so is a notable service to the Homeric question, however little he may satisfy us by the actual dress in which he clothed them.

And Gilbert Murray postulates an "Epic" dialect which "as it stands, it is no language, but a mixture of linguistically incongruous forms, late, early and primeval". It is "a language that no Ionians, Dorians or Aeolians ever spoke" yet "a "large utterance", rhythmic and emotional, like a complicated instrument for the expression of the heroic saga. It is a dialect conditioned at every turn by the Epic metre; its fixed epithets, its formulae, its turns of sentence-connections, run into hexameters of themselves"[1].

But Homer or no Homer, a single, two or a dozen authors, or no distinctive authors at all, or a school, commission or individual "arrangers" or compiler, or what soever we will, the fact is presented that two epic poems of the highest order, have come down to us from at least the sixth century before Christ, and we are interested in their wondrous wayfaring adown the ages for over twenty-five centuries. The transmission of sacred and classical literature is one of the most curious chapters in the history of letters.

We first hear of Homer through a legend of Lycurgus in Plutarch[2].

The law-giver on a visit to Crete:

made his first acquaintance with the poems of Homer, which were preserved among the posterity of Creophylus;... he eagerly copied and compiled them in order to take them home with him.

This Creophylus of Chios or Samos was an epic poet reputed to have written the *Oechalia*. He appears to have been the friend, hardly the teacher or son-in-law of Homer. Legend would make

1. Gilbert Murray: *op. cit.* pp. 23 and 24.
2. Plutarch: *Lycurgus*, IV-4.

him the first link connecting Homer and the Homeric poems; that he entertained the poet in his house; was one of the first Homeridae, preserved the poems and handed them down through his posterity, from which Lycurgus copied them to take to Sparta. This legend can play many pranks; Plutarch may have followed the historian, Ephorus (4th century B.C.)[1]. Holm says[2] that Lycurgus became acquainted "in Chios with Homer, whose poems he brought to Greece". Of course he meant the poems, and yet as he places Lycurgus in the first half of the ninth century, he could have been a contemporary of Homer[3]. Is there not the Cretan tradition which places Homer in the time of the poet-statesman Thaletas (670–40) with whom Lycurgus conferred in Crete?[4] Again Holm says "in Chios". The writer hastily referring to Plutarch first thought he meant Asia (i.e. Asia Minor), but assumes Crete to be correct. Plutarch does not mention "Chios". Finally Plutarch closes the paragraph with a certain tone as of knowledge:

> These epics already had a certain faint reputation among the Greeks, and a few were in possession of certain portions of them, as the poems were carried here and there by chance; but Lycurgus was the very first to make them really known[5].

Here we would like to interpolate a few words as to the date of Homer. Of course the chronology is as varied as everything concerning his life and works. You may choose from Philostratus (c. 1159 B.C.) to Theopompus (c. 683 B.C.).

Famous selections were:

Eratosthenes	c. 1083 B.C.
Aristotle	c. 1043 B.C.
Aristarchus	c. 1043 B.C.
The Athenian tradition	c. 1043 B.C.
Herodotus	c. 854–830 B.C.

Contemporary of Ionian migration; 140 years after the war.

All computations were post Troic. Herodotus, the first account concerning the date of Homer, placed him 400 years before his own time. Now the acme of Herodotus was about 454–430 B.C.,

1. Sandys: *op. cit.* p. 20.
2. Holm: *op. cit.* 1–176–177.
3. Henry Fynes Clinton: *An Epitome* (of the *Fasti Hellenici*), Oxford, 1851 (69).
4. Mahaffy: *op. cit.* 1, 24.
5. Plutarch: *Lyc.*, IV-4.

making the acme of Homer about 854–830 B.C. or 329 years after the fall of Troy (c. 1183 B.C.). Clinton, from whom most of these computations are taken, preferred the date sanctioned by Aristotle (1043 B.C.); Sandys takes a floruit for Homer of c. 700 B.C.; Prof. Bury about 950 B.C.

If we were compelled to choose, we would take the date of Herodotus, the middle of the ninth century B.C. (c. 850–830 B.C.).

If the legend of Lycurgus that in his travels he met with Homer or at least with the poems through Creophylus or some Homeridae, must be assumed as mythical, the Homeric traditons concerning Solon and the Pisistradae rest on firmer ground and should not be so lightly considered. Of course, as in all Homeric questions, the critical forces are valiant and numerous on either wing.

The ancient extant authorities:

a. Dieuchidas (4th century B.C.), *Megarian History*, says:

Solon did more than Pisistratus to throw light on Homer[1].

Dieuchidas of Megara, the historian, was like his fellow-citizens an enemy of Athens, yet he knew that both Solon and Pisistratus had done something for the poems of Homer.

b. Pseudo-Plato[2]: *Hipparchus*:

Your fellow-citizen Pisistratus's son Hipparchus of Philaidae, who was the eldest and wisest of Pisistratus's sons, and who among many goodly proofs of wisdom that he showed, first brought the poems of Homer into this country of ours, and compelled the rhapsodes at the Panathenaea to recite them in relay, one man following another, as they still do now.

c. Cicero, in *De Oratore*[3] says:

He (Pisistratus) is said to have been the first person who arranged the previously disordered books of Homer in the order in which now we have them.

Gilbert Murray comments: "Cicero's statement about the recension by Pisistratus seems to be derived from a member of the Pergamene school, whose founder, Crates, was hostile to

---

1. Dieuchidas: *Megarian History* (Book V), in Diogenes Laertius, I–57.
2. Plato: *Hipparchus*, tr. W. R. M. Lamb (L.C.L.), London, 1927 (228 B).
3. Cicero: *De Oratore*, III–34–137.

Aristarchus. It is quite possible that the latter tended to belittle a
method of explanation which was in particular favor with the
rival school"[1].

d. Josephus[2]:

He (Homer) they say, did not leave his poems in writing. At first
transmitted by memory, the scattered songs were not united until
later; to which circumstance the numerous inconsistences of the
work are attributable. (A vast controversial literature on this point.)

e. Plutarch[3]:

Most writers say that the fame of Homer favoured the contention
of Solon; for after himself inserting a verse (*Iliad*, II-557) into the
Catalogue of Ships, he read the passage at the trial (i.e. the arbitra-
tion between the Megarians and Athenians after their war).

f. Pausanias:

But they allege that when Pisistratus collected the scattered verses
of Homer which were preserved, some here, some there, in oral
tradition, he or one of his associates[4] changed the name (*Iliad*, II-
573) in ignorance.

g. Aelian[5] states that Pisistratus collected the Homeric lays, and
so created the *Iliad* and *Odyssey*.

h. Diogenes Laertius[6]:

He (Solon) has provided the public recitations of Homer shall
follow in fixed order ("in succession"): thus the second reciter
must begin from the place where the first left off.

i. Suidas[7] says "that the various lays of *Iliad* were composed by
Homer separately, and that the task of putting them together into
one epic was afterwards accomplished by many hands, but chiefly by Pisistratus".

j. Eustathius[8] speaks of "the *Iliad* as a continuous and harmonious
whole which had been put together by learned men at the command of Pisistratus".

1. Murray: *Greek Literature, op. cit.* p. 12.
2. Josephus: *Contra Apionem*, tr. H. St. J. Thackeray (L.C.L.), London, 1926 (I–12).
3. Plutarch: *Solon*, X.
4. Pausanias: *Achaia*, VII–26–13.
5. Aelian: *Var. Hist.*, XIII–14.
6. Diogenes Laertius: *Lives of Eminent Philosophers*, tr. R. D. Hicks (L.C.L.), 1–57.
7. Suidas: s.v. *Homer* (see: J. C. Frazer: *Commentary on Pausanius*, IV–180).
8. Eustathius: *Commentary on the Iliad and Odyssey*, ed. Stallboum, 1825–30.

k. Tzetzes[1]:

Pisistratus edited the scattered poetry of Homer two hundred years before Ptolemy Philadelphus, with expert care in those books which are still in existance, using for his divine work the diligence of four most famous and learned men, that is, Concyli, Onomacritus the Athenian, Zopyrus of Heraclea and Orpheus of Crotona.

And so from the fourth century B.C. to the end of the twelfth century A.D. classical and subsequent writings are still extant concerning Solon's and particularly the Pisistratids' intimate connection with the poems of Homer.

Yet the Pisistratids' Homeric labors are rejected by many modern scholars: Ludwich[2], Flach[3], Wilamowitz-Moellendorff[4], Lehrs[5] among the Germans, and among the English Grote and Gilbert Murray who says:

The whole commission has a fabulous air, and smacks of the age of the Ptolemies rather than the sixth century[6].

On the other hand, the account about Pisistratus has been accepted by many scholars, some in a limited sense, as Sir John Sandys: who held that the story need only imply the restoration of a unity[7] which in process of time had been gradually ignored.

Among the Germans who accept the Pisistratid tradition are, of course, Wolf, and Lachmann, both of whom believed that the *written* Homer actually dates from Pisistratus. Ritschl[8] even separates the work of Solon and Pisistratus: Solon regulated the order of the *presentation* by the rhapsodes correcting their license as to reciting from separate books; Pisistratus, however, with his literary assistants, settled the order of the parts of the poem, binding each together, with some corrections and some interpolations, but all these parts had been composed by one poet and originally designed as a whole.

1. Tzetzes: *Prolegomena on Aristophanes*.
2. Ludwich: *Aristarchs Hom. Textkritik*, 1885 (II–390).
3. Flach: *Peisistratos und seine literarische Thätigkeit* (1885).
4. Wilamowitz-Moellendorff: *Hom. Uuntersuchungen*, 1884 (235 seq.).
5. Lehrs: *Aristarchus*, 1862 (p. 434 seq.).
6. Murray: *Greek Literature, op. cit.* p. 11.
7. Sandys: *His. Class. Sch., op. cit.* p. 21 and notes.
8. Ritschl: *Die Alexandrinischen Bibliotheken*, p. 67–70.

K.O. Muller[1]:

And we are still indebted to the regulator of the contest of rhapsodists at the Panathenaea (whether it was Solon or Pisistratus), for having compelled the rhapsodists to follow one another, according to the order of the poem, and for having thus restored the great works, which were falling into fragments, to their pristine integrity.

Ernest Curtius[2]:

Pisistratus assembled at his court a number of learned men, whose duty it was to collect copies, compare the text, decide upon the true reading, exclude improper interpolations and fix the Epos as a great whole, as a national Hellenic document in a form that might be generally accepted as valid.

Adolph Holm[3]:

Athens on account of the revision undertaken by Pisistratus was even mentioned as a birth-place of Homer.

Among English scholars, we may select:
Connop Thirlwall[4]:

The traditions relating to the new forms which the Homeric poems assumed in the age and through the influence of Pisistratus, had appeared to Wolf one of the main props of his hypothesis. These traditions have been recently confirmed by the discovery of a scholion of Plautus..... The undertaking of Pisistratus has been variously interpreted: sometimes as merely a new edition of the *Iliad* and *Odyssey*, executed by means of a collation of manuscripts, which exhibited great variations, though each contained an entire work: at other times as a collection of the various epics which composed the Cycle, most of which was by some traditions attributed to Homer.

Prof. Mahaffy[5]:

There seems little doubt of the fact, hinted at by Pausanias and Plutarch, but explicitly stated only in later scholia that not only did Pisistratus and his son Hipparchus take every pains to circulate the

1. K. O. Muller: *A History of the Literature of Ancient Greece*, London, 1858 (Vol. I–85). Still an important work.
2. Dr. Ernest Curtius: *The History of Greece*, London, 1868 (Vol. I, p. 371).
3. Adolph Holm: *The History of Greece*, London, 1894 (Vol. I, p. 162).
4. Connop Thirlwall: *History of Greece*, London, 1855 (Vol. I, p. 513, appendix).
5. J. P. Mahaffy: *A History of Classical Greek Literature*, London, 1895 (Vol. I, p. 28).

old epics by establishing or encouraging musical and poetical contests, at which recitations took place, but that there was even a sort of literary commission appointed to re-arrange and edit the poems. It is asserted that the version or edition of the poems which they sanctioned rapidly superseded all others; that it was the archetype from which the well-known *city-editions* were long afterwards copied and we know that these were the oldest and most trustworthy materials which the Alexandrine critics used.

Sandys (p. 21) in saying that "this view has been recently gaining ground", states that Dr. Leaf[1] believes that:

An official copy of Homer was made in Athens, in the time of Solon and Peisistratus.

J. B. Bury[2]:

It was probably towards the end of his reign that Pisistratus and his son Hipparchus took in hand the work of arranging and writing down the Homeric poems... At the instance of Pisistratus, some men of letters undertook the task of fixing definitely the text of both poems, and wrote them down in the old Attic alphabet... We may say that the Pisistratean revision of Homer was the beginning of literary criticism in Europe. Some liberties indeed were taken with the text; a line or two were added, a line or two may have been omitted, for the sake of the political interest or vanity of Athens.

William Mure[3]:

The simple fact that the remaining mass of Epico-Homeric poems were collected by Pisistratus under, whatever title, can hardly admit of doubt...

The establishment of a public library by Pisistratus... perhaps the best authenticated fact of his literary labours...

He was the founder, as Zenodotus, with whom he is compared by Tzetzes, was the director of a public library. His "collection and arrangement" of the "Poems of Homer" for his Athenian Institute may therefore, in the general spirit of the tradition, safely be understood in the same comprehensive sense as that of his Alexandrian

1. Dr. Walter Leaf: *Iliad*, 1900 (p. XIX). I have quoted this way because my copy of Dr. Leaf *Iliad* (2 Vols., 1886) does not say this.
2. J. B. Bury: *A History of Greece*, London, 1911 (p. 198).
3. William Mure: *A Critical History of the Language and Literature of Ancient Greece*, London, 1850, Vol. I, pp. 215–216.

successor for the shelves of the Museum. The whole series would not only be required for the Athenian library, but must have formed the most bulky portion of its contents.

Mr. Edmonds[1]:

The Athenian Age, of which the morning-star is Solon, rises with Peisistratus and his son Hipparchus. To one or the other of these we perhaps owe the first recensions, if we may so call them, of Homer and Hesiod, and Peisistratus is said to have collected the first library.

And finally:

Mr. Allen[2]:

It is unnecessary for me to state the arguments or to take a decided position.

If Solon or Pisistratus did establish any text of Homer, that text can have been no other than the κοινή, and however inferior the direct evidence for their achievement may be, we have the only real proof that can be given *in tali materia*, agreement with later conditions. If Pisistratus were reputed father of the κοινή it is natural that we find no mention of him in the scholia... We are informed explicitly that Aristarchus thought Homer an Athenian; the Attic edition to him therefore was not one among the κατὰ πόλεις but the κοινή itself. In his silence in regard to the κοινή is included silence upon its origin and its putative author. While therefore I do not find it necessary to assert the authenticity of the Pisistratean legend, I find that it agrees with all the conditions, and that the omission to notice it in the scholia is no impediment to its probability.

This Attic edition might well be called the editio princeps of Homer, and that there is not much extant comment upon it might well be due to at least two causes: the paucity of bibliographical information extant in current writers, and the indifference or reluctance of a democratic people to accord their fellow-citizen (perhaps because he was a prince-dictator) the honor (the Homer of Pisistratus), that two imperial peoples so freely gave to the genius of Justinian and Napoleon in the Codes which bear their names and which to this day form the basis of the civil laws

1. J. M. Edmonds: *Elegy and Iambus* (L.C.L.), London, 1931 (Vol. I, p. 25).
2. J. W. Allen: *The Nature of the Ancient Homeric Vulgate* (*The Classical Review*, Vol. XV, pp. 7–8, 1901).

of a large portion of the civilized world. So, the Attic edition of Homer, which would seem to us to be the editio princeps, is most certainly the vulgate of the poems.

We all know that the verification of every position in the history of the past lacks much of the completeness that we would like. But the vast mass of lost ancient records has not prevented the patient scholar from putting together the broken fragments of antiquity or even suggesting a reasonable explanation for the missing parts.

Now the first reference extant to mention the name of Homer is that of Callinus of Ephesus, the elegiac poet who lived about 690 B.C. Would it not be absurd to say that no one had mentioned Homer before Callinus! Of course, many early references are lost.

We, who have ventured upon this treatise, know how few references not only are extant, but how few writers apparently have written about the Museum and Library of Alexandria[1].

In creative periods of art, very little is written about the creation or the creator. Taking the Attic edition of the scholars of Pisistratus as the first known critical labors for an ordered Homer (although there may have been many editions before this time), we find that the tribe of commentators were early in the field, and that from nearly 600 B.C. (time of Solon, 594 B.C. archon; d. 560 B.C.; and the Pisistratids, 560–510 B.C.) to Zenodotus (c. 285–c. 234 B.C.), over 300 years, we have extant or reference to, commentators, critics, editors, and miscellaneous quoters[2]. Indeed, in ancient Greece, at least since Solon, as in modern times, if every generation did not have its edition of Homer, many cities had their special recensions and it would seem that many personal editions or texts existed.

Without further ado, it may be well to mention the texts of Homer, public or "official", individual or private; the commentaries, the comments upon and quotations from the poems, by the writers of prose and verse, which certainly formed part of the

1. Aristonicus of Alexandria, who wrote critical commentaries on Homer, Hesiod and Pindar, was the reputed author of a work *On the Museum in Alexandria*, most unfortunately lost. (Photius: Bibliotheca 104 B 40 f; Suidas; Athenaeus, XI–481D.).
2. "These citers of the important or the curious are not to be lightly considered. Next to the originator of a good sentence is the first quoter of it." Emerson: *Quotation and Originality*.

vast Homeric material which must have been embedded in the body of Hellenic learning and literature, all of which formed part of the data for the study and interpretation of the critical doctors and literary analysts of the Alexandrian Museum.

The list must have included, at least, the following:

Even before the era of Pisistratids, we have extant:

1. Callinus (c. 690 B.C.), first reference to have come down to our day. He speaks of Homer as the author of the epic *Thebais*, and is reported by Pausanias (IX–9–5).
2. Semonides of Amorgus (c. 640), who said[1]:

> But there is one saying of the man of Chios which passes all: "As the passing of the leaves is, so is the passing of men."

This is the earliest quotation extant from Homer.

Homer had been imitated, followed or alluded to by, at least:

3. Hesiod, the epic poet (c. 700 B.C.). Noted in the Scholia as having knowledge of the *Iliad*.
4. Alcman, the melic poet (c. 657 B.C.).
5. Archilochus, the iambic poet (c. 650 B.C.).

Was Herodotus alone the constant imitator of Homer? No: Stesichorus and Archilochus imitated him more than Herodotus; but Plato more than all of them, who from the copious Homeric fountain has drawn a thousand rivulets to cherish and improve his own productions[2].

6. Stesichorus (c. 640–555 B.C.). His works extant in the Alexandrian Library filled 26 Books[3]. He was nearest to a rivalship with Homer[4]. And Homer has been imitated and followed "in fact in all the older poets", says Mahaffy.

Later by:

1. At least so ascribed to Semonides of Amorgus by Wilamowitz and Gilbert Murray. J. M. Edmonds, however, in his *Lyra Graeca* (L.C.L.), Vol. II, London, 1924, gives it to Simonides of Ceos. I have used both Gilbert Murray and Mr. Edmonds in this connection of the translation from Stobaeus, *Anthology* (cf. *Iliad*, VI–146).
2. Longinus, *On the Sublime* (XIII, p. 112 of Dr. Wm. Smith's *Dionysius Longinus*, London, 1819).
3. *Lyra Graeca*, II (L.C.L.), now we have scarcely 98 fragments, some of but one word, and some a bare reference.
4. Quintilian: *Inst. orat.*

7. Simonides of Ceos (c. 556–468 B.C.), "who beat all the youth of Iolcos of the vineyards in throwing the spear across the eddies of Anaurus: for these have Homer and Stesichorus sung to the peoples"[1].

8. Pindar (518–443 B.C.). Comments on Odysseus and places Homer's birth at Chios or Smyrna.

9. Bacchylides (c. 507–430). Refers the birth-place to Ios.

10. Pythagoras of Samos (582–500 B.C.). In his Dantean adventure in Hades, he is reputed to have seen "the soul of Homer hung on a tree with serpents writhing about it, this being (his) punishment for what (he) had said about the gods"[2].

11. Xenophanes of Colophon (c. 530 B.C.), who accused "Homer and Hesiod (as having) imputed to the gods all that was blame and shame for men"[3].

12. Aeschylus (525–456 B.C.), according to Athenaeus[4] called his tragedies "slices from the great banquets of Homer". Homer at least furnished the theme for six of the tragedies and a satyric play.

13. Theagenes of Rhegium (c. 525 B.C.), one of the earliest of the critics, who sought an allegorical interpretation of Homer. Mahaffy thought[5] he was the first critical writer on the *Iliad* known to the Greeks. Dr. Leaf called him the first commentator on Homer.

14. Heraclitus of Ephesus (c. 500 B.C.), the philosopher. This difficult man said:

> Homer deserved to be chased out of the lists and beaten with rods, and Archilochus likwise[6].

15. Sophocles (496–406). Mahaffy quotes that Sophocles "copied the *Odyssey* in many dramas" and that the populace acclaimed him the tragic Homer.

16. Gorgias (c. 485–380) of Leontini. Composed an *Eulogy of Achilles*, an *Encomium of Helen* and a *Defense of Palamedes*.

17. Protagoras of Abdera (c. 482–411). A sophist who provoked

1. Edmonds: Simonides (in *Lyra Graeca*, II–317).
2. Diogenes Laertius (VIII–21).
3. Sixtus Empericus: *Math.* IX–193 (See: Sandys).
4. Athenaeus: 347 e.
5. Mahaffy: *His. Gr. Lit.*, p. 30.
6. Diogenes Laertius: IX–1.

the comment of Gilbert Murray: "After all, the Sophists are the spiritual and intellectual representatives of the age of Pericles; let those who revile them create such an age again"[1].

18. Prodicus of Ceos (fl. 435 B.C.), like Protagoras, Hippias and other sophists of the age of Pericles, gave to Homer the labors of scientific study[2].

19. Stesimbrotus of Thasos (c. 450), a sophist. The hater of the Empire and the Democracy, who libeled Pericles. He wrote a work *On Homer*, which is lost, title unknown. A contemporary of Cimon, he was praised by Plato and Xenophon and quoted by Plutarch.

20. Democritus of Abdera (460–357 B.C.), who certainly wrote a *Study of Homer* or the earliest Homeric Glossary, of which we know nothing, although he is referred to by Dion Chrysostum (Or. 53), and Clemens Alexandrinus (Stromat. VI–18).

21. Anaxagoras of Clazomenae (fl. 450). Like Metrodorus of Lampsacus, he was an allegorical interpreter of Homer.

22. Alcibiades (c. 450–404 B.C.). This enfant terrible:

> Once, as he was getting on past boyhood, he accosted a school-teacher and asked him for a book of Homer. The teacher replied that he had nothing of Homer's, whereupon Alcibiades fetched him a blow with his fist, and went his way. Another teacher said he had a Homer which he had corrected himself. "What!" said Alcibiades, "are you teaching boys to read when you are competent to edit Homer? You should be training young men"[3].

23. Isocrates (436–338 B.C.), rhetorician. In his *Panathenaic*, written in his ninety-fifth year, he promises to speak again on Homer, but the time never came.

24. Alcidamas (432–411) of Elaea (in Aeolis, Asia Minor), pupil of Gorgias, perhaps the first whose moral courage prompted him to politically advocate the abolition of slavery. He wrote *On the Odyssey*, which he calls "a fair mirror of human life"[4].

25. Licymnius of Sicily (5th cent. B.C.), a pupil of Gorgias, teacher of Polus, perhaps an expositor of Homer[5].

1. Murray: *op. cit.* 164.
2. W. Ihne (s.v. *Homerus*, in *Smih's Dic. of Gr. Biog. and Myth.*).
3. Plutarch: *Alcibiades*, VII.
4. Aristotle: *Rhetoric*, III–3–4.
5. Sandys: *op. cit.* p. 29.

26. Hippias of Thasos (c. 5th cent. B.C.), one of the earlier Greek grammarians, who occupied himself with explanations of obscure and difficult passages in Homer and with difficult politics which cost him his life. The method of his execution is one of the hiatuses of Lysias (*Against Agoratus*, VIII–54).
27. Ion of Ephesus (5th cent. B.C.), a rhapsode, a contemporary of Socrates. He wrote *A Commentary on Homer*. His name is perpetuated in the title of one of Plato's most interesting dialogues. He himself declared that he could speak about Homer better than anyone else[1].
28. Hippias of Ellis (c. 430 B.C.), a sophist. Contemporary of Socrates, he published the List of Olympian Victors and was one of the great sophistic figures of the age of Pericles.
29. Demosthenes (383–322 B.C.). "Like every great Greek writer" Demosthenes "is said to have imitated Homer". However, he certainly was not influenced by the poet as were Aeschines and Lycurgus, who both quote passages, quite different from our text.

Recensionists, "editors", and quoters from varied and unknown versions:

A. THOSE OF PERSONS

30. Lycurgus (c. 850–776 B.C.). Doubtless a myth. Plutarch tells[2] that in Crete Lycurgus made his first acquaintance with Homer among the posterity of Creophylus, that he copied and compiled the poems in order to take them back to Greece and that "Lycurgus was the very first to make them really known". Sandys suggests that Plutarch's source may have been the historian Ephorus (4th cent. B.C.).
31. Solon. Mahaffy asks:

Did the arrangers of Solon's and later day only restore the original order, or were the elements of these works lying in their original disorder and confusion when Onomacritus, or Theagenes, or Antimachus brought them into unity, thus creating an *Iliad* and an *Odyssey* which had never before existed?[3]

1. Sandys: *op. cit.* p. 29 and 31.
2. Plutarch: *Lycurgus*, IV.
3. Mahaffy: *op. cit. Hist. Gr. Lit.*, I-22.

32. Pisistratus (560–527 B.C.), or
33. Hipparchus, his son (d. 514 B.C.), or
34. Onomacritus of Athens and his Commission of
35. Orpheus of Croton, and
36. Zopyrus of Heraclea, and
37. a fourth commissioner whose name is unknown.

Did Onomacritus sift the vast body of epic material? Did he (and the literary commission) gather the outstanding lays into the *Iliad* and the *Odyssey*, or did he or they collect the older existing "editions" or manuscripts and effect a Pisistratian edition, an Attic recension, the Vulgate text, the Κοινή itself?

38. Euripides (480–406 B.C.). The last of the masters of Greek tragedy was not only a man of letters and collector of manuscripts, among the servants of whose household was the celebrated amanuensis Cephisophon, whom the enemies of the poet inferred collaborated with his master. Euripides was, like all of the Greeks, a student of Homer; at least, his *Cyclops*, the sole surviving example of the satyric drama, was probably founded on Book IX of the *Odyssey*, and titles of his plays extant and lost are suggestive of the Epic Cycle. He was a collector and doubtless had several different manuscript versions of Homer.

39. Antimachus of Colophon (Ionia) (fl. 464–410), was an epic poet, pupil of Stesimbrotus of Thasos, Homeric critic, who edited an "edition" of Homer and who is mentioned twelve times in the Venetian *Scholia* on the *Iliad*.

40. Plato. There is talk of a *Plato's Homer*. We believe it is a mere phrase. Of course Plato must have learned Homer by rote at school: the texts were part and parcel of the Library of the Academy; he imperceptibly used them in his teaching; his quotations of the text were so noted, as to provoke Ammonius to write a book *On Plato's Citations from Homer*; and, as it has been so beautifully expressed: "The words falter on his lips," as he said[1]:

I must speak out.... though a certain love and reverence for Homer that has possessed me from a boy would stay me from

1. Plato: *The Republic*, Book X–595 B. (L.C.L., Dr. Storey).

speaking. For he appears to have been the first teacher and
beginner of all these beauties of tragedy. Yet all the same we must
not honour a man above the truth,

and with philosophical courage Plato excluded his beloved
poet from his ideal Republic. As has been said, Plato's
quotations agree with our text.

41. Aristotle. In his treatises *On Poetry*, Aristotle highly praises
Homer, as "pre-eminent in the serious style of poetry, as the
foremost model of epic poetry and as unequalled in diction
and thought". Literary criticism may be found in the *Poetics*,
in which work he drew up a list of Homeric Problems still
preserved in fragmentary state[1]. In the *Rhetoric*, numerous
illustrations are pointed from Homer. He quoted frequently
from the poems, yet his quotation is strangely different from
our text. He is reputed to have prepared an "edition" of
Homer for his pupil Alexander, yet the writers do not
quote from it and no one wrote a book on Aristotle's
Quotations from Homer, as did Ammonius on the Homeric Citations in Plato. His text "had been lost when the
school of Alexandria began its labours"[2].

42. Alexander's Iliad of the Casket. The story is told by Plutarch[3].

He (Alexander) was also by nature a lover of learning and a lover
of reading. And since he thought and called *The Iliad* a viaticum
of the military art, he took with him Aristotle's recension of the
poem, called the *Iliad* of the Casket, and always kept it lying with
his dagger under his pillow, as Onesicratus informs us.

And later he placed the *Iliad* in a small coffer, the most precious
object found among the Persian treasures of Dareius.

And according to Strabo[4]:

He (Alexander) was fond of Homer; at any rate, we are told of a
recension of the poetry of Homer, Recension of the Casket, as it is
called, which Alexander, along with Callisthenes and Anaxar-
chus, perused and to a certain extent annotated, and then deposited in a richly wrought casket which he had found amongst the
Persian treasures.

1. Sandys: *op. cit.* p. 35–37.
2. Mahaffy: *op. cit. Gr. Lit.*, I-31.
3. Plutarch: *Alexander*, VIII and XXVI.
4. Strabo: *Geography*, XIII–1–27.

But Dr. Monro (Od. 418) concludes: "The Iliad of the Casket may safely be dismissed as a picturesque legend." It may be of interest to record that when Gibbon commenced to correct the second edition of his history, his autograph marginal notes on his own copy, which may be read in the British Museum, on page 7, state:

> Late generations and far distant climates may impute their calamities to the immortal author of the *Iliad*. The spirit of Alexander was inflamed by the praises of Achilles; and succeeding heroes have been ambitious to tread in the footsteps of Alexander.

43. Demetrios of Phaleron (c. 354–c. 283), last of the Attic orators, summoned by the First Ptolemy, who laid the foundation of the Museum and the great Library, had access to the manuscripts which Plato bequeathed to the Academy[1]. Demetrios wrote both: *On the Iliad* and *On the Odyssey*.

44. Philemon, author of a *Recension of Homer, A Commentary on Homer*, is quoted in the Scholia of the *Codex Venetus*.

45. Sosigenes. Dr. Allen assures us that his date is unknown.

And as we approach the threshold of the Alexandrian era of criticism and enter the very halls of the Museum and the Library we find:

46. Rhianus. Scholars speak of his private recension. At least he wrote a *Commentary on Homer*. Zenodotus "was succeeded by a recension executed with taste and judgment by the epic poet Rhianus"[2].

47. Zenodotus (324/320–x B.C.), pioneer and first important editor of Homer.

48. Old Timon of Philus (c. 320–230), who certainly did not make a recension or "edit" Homer, must have his little say. He started life as a stage-dancer, became a skeptic philosopher, poet, lampoonist, made a fortune, settled at Athens, and lived 90 years. Aratus sought him and asked how he could get a good text of Homer: "You can if you get hold of the ancient copies, and not the corrected copies of our day."[3] The famous

1. Grote: *Plato*, Ch. VI.
2. Sandys: *op. cit.* I–211.
3. Diog. Laert.: IX–113.

conversation may have taken place when Timon visited the Macedonian Court (c. 276 B.C.) and the "rash emendation, against which Aratus is warned" doubtlessly referred to the recent edition of Zenodotus[1].

49. Aratus of Soli, Cilicia (d. at Pella before c. 239), was a reckless corrector of the texts, and apparently did not take his friend's advice. Aratus resided for a time at the court of the son of Seleucus, Antiochus I (Soter) and there edited an edition of the *Odyssey*. The king urged him to make a recension of the *Iliad*, which he apparently, perhaps for the best, failed to do.

50. Apollonius Rhodius. Also inferred that he was not a careful recensionist.

51. Callimachus who catalogued the hundreds of Homeric manuscripts in the Alexandrian Library in his *Pinakes*.

52. The great Aristophanes of Byzantium. His Homeric labors are treated at the close of this Chapter.

53. Aristarchus, the supreme critic of antiquity. His Homeric labors are treated at the close of this Chapter.

Editions and Recensions:

B. THOSE OF PLACES

The state or city, "official", editions of:

54. Massilia.
55. Chios.
56. Argos.
57. Sinope.
58. Cyprus.
59. Crete.
60. Aeolis.
61. Ptolemaic papyrus fragments, from the find of Flinders Petrie, 1891 (publication of Mahaffy), M. Jules Nicole, the Grenfell and Hunt fragments, to our time, and numerous other fragments.

Such were some of the "eccentric" texts or editions which we know or hear of, and which we have reason to believe were

1. Aratus: tr. G. R. Mair (L.C.L.), London, 1931, p. 361.

numerous. Their contents show marked variations and consider-
able divergences, as may be noted in the quotation of Pseudo-
Plato and especially those of Aeschines in his speech Against
Timarchus 149–150.

62. The Pisistratean, Attic, Athenian edition, *The Vulgate.*

C. WRITERS FROM HERODOTUS TO THE
ALEXANDRIAN AGE

To this material must be added the Quotations to be found
in pre-Alexandrian writers "from Herodotus downward", which
Prof. Arthur Ludwich[1] has collected and arranged with his
fine scholarship. In making use of his labors, we have retained
the convenient alphabetical list of writers, and have added only
their dates or floruit, with a word as to their vocation or principal position in life, as a sort of *Greek Who's Who,* which may
be convenient for some readers. The numbers of lines of Homer
attributed to each author are given as set forth in the researches
of Prof. Ludwich.

Verses

63. Aeschines (c. 390–314 B.C.). Orator   .   .   .   32
64. Antisthenes (fl. 366 B.C.). Cynic philosopher .   .   6
65. Aristophanes (c. 448–380 B.C.). Comic poet   .   .   9
41. Aristotle (384–Aug. 322 B.C.). Philosopher   .   .   93
43. Demetrios of Phaleron (c. 354–d. after 283 B.C.). Man
     of letters   2
66. Dicaearchus (d. 285 B.C.). Peripatetic philosopher .   4
67. Diogenes of Sinope (412–323 B.C.). Cynic philosopher   14
68. Diosorides (436–338 B.C.). Stoic philosopher .   .   2
69. Duris (fl. c. 352–324 B.C.). Historian   .   .   .   2
70. Ephoros of Cumae (fl. 408–333 B.C.). Historian   .   6
71. Heracleides of Pontus (fl. 360 B.C.). Philosopher .   21
72. Herodotus (484–425/408 B.C.). Historian.   .   .   12
73. Lycurgus of Athens (c. 396–323 B.C.). Orator .   .   6
74. Metrodoros of Lampsacus (d. 414 B.C.). Philosopher   6

1. Arthur von Ludwich, *Die Homervulgata als voralexandrinische erwiesen* (Leipzig, 1898)
pp. 71–133.

75. Phalaecus (contemporary of Alexander). Epigrammatist 2
76. Pheidias (c. 500–432 B.C.). Sculptor . . . 3
77. Philomelus of Euonymaea (fl. 287 B.C.). Skeptic
philosopher 2
40. Plato (c. 430–347 B.C.). Philosopher . . . 209
78. Pyrrho of Ellis (c. 360–270 B.C.). Skeptic philosopher 2
79. Sophocles (496–406 B.C.). Tragic poet . . . 2
80. Theophrastus (371–c. 287 B.C.). Philosopher . . 4
81. Theopompus (fl. 412–305 B.C.). Historian . . 2
82. Thucydides (c. 460–c. 400 B.C.). Historian . . 2
83. Timaeus (c. 352–c. 256 B.C.). Historian . . . 4
84. Xenocrates (396–314 B.C.). Philosopher . . . 3
85. Xenophon (c. 426–354 B.C.). Philosopher . . 14
86. Zenon of Citium (Cyprus) (333–261 B.C.). Philosopher 2
87. Zoilos (He was "eminent before the rise of Demosthenes and continued to write after the death of
Philip".) (336 B.C.) (Clinton, p. 485). Grammarian 4
Total 470

The above list is ten lines less than that of Prof. Ludwich's
(i.e. 28 instead of 29 writers); because we have omitted
Pythagoras (c. 582–500 B.C.), who of course was dead
before Herodotus was born.

The number of verses credited to him by Prof. Ludwich is 10
Prof. Ludwich's total 480

The above 78 source items were accessible to the School of
Alexandria, who sought, gathered, segregated, studied, critically
analyzed and edited the texts of the classical writers which have
become standard texts for our day. Of the 78 items listed, about
9 were of Places and about 69 of Persons. Yet we must assume that
this was but a part, perhaps a small part, of the mass of source
materials accessible to the Ptolemaic scholars.

Henry Fynes Clinton in his *Fasti Hellenici*[1] had enumerated

1. I have used Henry Fynes Clinton: *An Epitome of the Civil and Literary Chronology of Greece*, Oxford, 1851 (p. 154 and 255 et seq.).

some 296 literary names of poets, philosophers, historians, orators
and men of letters who flourished from the tyranny of Pisistratus
to the reign of the second Ptolemy ("Philadelphus"). The brave
list is as follows:

Tragic Poets	42
Comic Poets (Old Comedy)	52
Comic Poets (Middle Comedy)	35
Comic Poets (New Comedy)	20
Poets (non-Dramatic)	22
Philosophers	46
Historians	47
Orators	32
Total	296

Of the above array of nearly 300 writers from Pisistratus to the
Ptolemies, 296 according to count, only 18 are found in Prof.
Ludwich's list (11 of whose names are not mentioned by Clinton)
and likewise only 18 of Mr. Clinton's list are included in the list
of the writer, which list contains at least 32 names not in Clinton's
list, including 21 not in either Prof. Ludwich's or Mr. Clinton's
lists.

Mr. Clinton lists 296
Prof. Ludwich lists(29) additional names not in Clinton   11
The present author's list, say 76 or 77 names (of which
8 or 9 are pre-Pisistratean, and 68 post-Pisistratean), of
which names after Pisistratus 29 are in Ludwich's list
and 18 in Clinton's, leaving names in neither Clinton's or
Ludwich's list, that is additional names of about . . 21

328

To which may be added the few pre-Pisistratean names, say   9

Total   337

These numerical data present a picture of the fabulous stores
of rich materials existing at the time when Demetrios had first
collected the myriads of rolls, which Zenodotus and his associates
assembled and assorted and which Callimachus, the first bibliographer, catalogued in his famed *Pinakes*.

As the School of Alexandria opened in the Museum, with its
handmaiden the great Library, rich with the accumulated

manuscripts containing the vast body of Greek letters and learning, the scholars, critics, exegetes, recensionists and the literary
canonists had the labors of over 300 writers, in prose and verse,
in thousands of rolls together with numerous anonymous manuscripts, or recensions or "editions" of the text of the author, to be
studied and re-edited in the light of the principles of criticism
which were taking final shape in the critical schools. This vast
material, and how much more it may have been we shall never
know, was at the disposal of the first great scientific Homeric
scholarship.

Homer was the Bible of the Greeks, the common textbook of
her elementary schools, the public recitative for political and
State ceremonial and functions, and the elementary foundation
on which was erected the amazing superstructure of Hellenic
letters bequeathing to the ages wisdom, knowledge and information, in the noblest forms of language, art and beauty.

The early creative ages of art and thought ended with the
Golden Age of Athens. When Demosthenes and Aristotle died the
curtain fell upon the greatest creative epoch of the intellect
of man. The vast treasures of the mind were left to be examined,
arranged, interpreted and appreciated by an era of wealth,
culture and scholarship. The Age of Alexandria attempted to
assemble and marshal this great inheritance and to transmit
their important labors to the recurrent centuries. Logically
Homer received the first and perhaps the greatest attention.
All men who wrote or thought in Greek have contributed imperceptibly or visibly to the massive monuments of the *Iliad* and
the *Odyssey*. Every poet, writer, or scholar of the Museum made
his contribution, great or small, towards the preservation, elucidation and perfection of the old epic master of Hellenic genius.

In the schools of the Museum three scholars have indelibly
etched their names on the massy fabric of the epics: Zenodotus of
Ephesus and one of his pupils Aristophanes of Byzantium, and
one of his pupils Aristarchus of Samothrace.

I. ZENODOTUS OF EPHESUS

Zenodotus of Ephesus (c. 325–c. 234 B.C.) was the pioneer in
Homeric critical scholarship. In the morning of the vast critical

labors of the School of Alexandria when the poets were divided among the Museum experts, and the tragic and satyric poets were assigned to Alexander of Aetolia, and the comic poets to Lycophron of Chalcis, the associates, if not the colleagues of Zenodotus, he, Zenodotus, an epic poet himself, retained the epic poets, and the initial task of the recension of Homer fell to his lot. Suidas says he was the first editor of Homer; certainly he was the earliest critical editor of the Homeric poems known to us. He was an able scholar as well as a man of letters. He had for his material the manuscripts of the poems, personal and local, that had for three centuries served the purposes of the people and the schools, together with the vast array of auxiliary authorities in the verse and prose of most of the literature of the Greeks down to his time. According to our limited knowledge we have indicated most of the names and places of these sources. We know, however, that the corpus of written Hellenic literature and knowledge, both in quality and quantity, greatly exceeded not only the writings now extant, but much of which we probably shall never know.

These authorities he must have examined, and certainly he studied and compared the various manuscripts of the Homeric poems, and, with his best critical acumen, compiled an *Homeric Glossary* and finally the first critical recension of the poet based on an attempt to restore the true and genuine *Iliad* and *Odyssey*. This is the first edition of any classical author in which it was sought to restore the original text. He marked the spurious lines with the marginal obelus and made the well known division of the poems into 24 Books, naming them after the Greek alphabet.

Succeeding scholarship has found much criticism of his method and its application, and we are told:

In his *Glossary*, he may have guessed at the meaning of words.

In his recension of the texts of the *Iliad* and the *Odyssey* he may have:

> Condemned lines which he deemed inconsistent with the text, such as those ill-suited to the gods or heroes described; inserted verses of his own to complete the sense; blended several verses into one; confused grammatical constructions; failed to fully distinguish the dialects in the poems, etc.

And yet it should be remembered that our little knowledge of his criticisms is derived solely from context in the Homeric Scholia (Venetus A)[1].

Yet Sir Richard Jebb[2] says:

> In the dawn of the new scholarship, he appears as a gifted man with a critical aim, but without an adequate critical method... relying too much on his own feeling for Homer's spirit, he indulged in some arbitrary emendations. Still, he broke new ground; his work had a great repute; and to some extent, its influence was lasting.

Pioneer editor of Homer, he is entitled to our respect and grateful appreciation.

II. ARISTOPHANES OF BYZANTIUM (C. 257–C. 180 B.C.)

We now enter the domain of pure scholarship. The poet-scholar, the prose literary-scholar and even the universal genius in Aristotelian, or rather Renaissance sense, has passed. Instead we have the serious student of philology, the skillful scholarly surgeon capable of dissecting the works of other men, of removing the extraneous or corrupt parts, restoring the corpus to nearly its pristine state and preserving it for the future. The creative age has passed and is followed by an era of art-assembling, correcting, and preservation. There was important work to be done and no workman more competent than Aristophanes of Byzantium, who as a lad came to Alexandria and spent a long life in the Museum and Library (he did not become Librarian until 195 B.C. when he was 62 years old) where he was to lavish an amazing fund of erudition on the improvements of the classics, their recension and preservation.

"It must not be forgotten," as a great modern scholar[3] has so well said, "that systematic commentaries on "classical" authors were the invention of the scholars of Alexandria. The methods of literary, textual and exegetical criticism that these scholars originated have been of permanent value. It is sheer self-complacence that would lightly esteem the service that they rendered to posterity, sheer prejudice that fails to find in the extant scholia to classical authors, however mutilated and

---

1. Sandys: *op. cit.* p. 120.
2. Sir Richard Jebb: *Homer*, p. 92 f.
3. Dr. John Williams White: *op. cit.* p. XXV.

abbreviated, indubitable remains of their handiwork and satisfactory exemplification of their method."

Taught by the greatest scholars of his age, Zenodotus, and especially Callimachus and Eratosthenes, and himself the teacher of Aristarchus, foremost critic of Antiquity, Aristophanes's contributions to human learning were of the first order.

He formulated a definite system of punctuation and accentuation; he invented many of the diacritical marks; to preserve the true pronunciation in a changing Hellenic world, he may have invented the accents; he originated new symbols for use in textual criticism; and probably wrote introductions to the comedies of Aristophanes, although probably not the author of some of the metrical hypotheses.

He edited the *Theogony* of Hesiod, the poems of Alcaeus, Anacreon, the first collected edition of Pindar, probably editions of Aeschylus, Sophocles and Euripides together with introductions to these and to Aristophanes which we now know in the abridged form of Arguments. The works of Plato he divided into trilogies.

He wrote a work on or a continuation of the famous *Pinakes* of Callimachus, the great *Catalogue* of the Alexandriana[1].

His miscellanea included: *On Comic Roles*, or *Masks*, *On Courtesans*, *On Proverbs*, all suggestive of his keen interest in the comic poets.

He was the father of lexicography, and fragments of his great *Lexicon* have been found in a MS. at Mount Athos.

He edited the *Iliad* and the *Odyssey*, using his new symbols for textual criticism. His edition was an advance on Zenodotus and that of Rhianus. He shows an independence in retaining or rejecting some of the labors of Zenodotus. It is thought that he, too, had an Alexandrian view of scenes of life in the poems rather than one of Homeric simplicity suited to a primitive heroic age[2].

As was natural for the bibliographical mind and for a critical, rather than creative, age in letters, the men of the Museum and Library had from the beginning formed *Lists* of poets and prose writers in the various divisions of their work. One would think that the famous *Pinakes* of Callimachus first pointed the way.

---

1. Athenaeus (IX–408 f.) who speaks of the *Commentaries* of Aristophanes on the *Portraits* of Callimachus, that is *Portraits of men distinguished in every branch of knowledge, and their writings*; Aristophanes Byz. Nauch (Halle, 1848), p. 251.
2. Sandys: *op. cit.* 126–131.

As the vast quantity of writings were assembled in the Library, its scholars with critical acumen sensed the danger to the purity of the language of so vast and unequal a mass of literature. With their sense for order and appreciation of standards they naturally felt that from the thousands of rolls the best should be garnered and separated from the common mass. Like Sir John Lubbock and most of us who view the threatening miles of shelves of books, they felt that the contents of the armoria or book-presses, the vast quantity of rolls, should be reduced to a reasonable number of "musts", hence the so-called Alexandrian canon[1].

III. ARISTARCHUS OF SAMOTHRACE
(c. 220/200 – c. 145/131 B.C.)

The last of the great librarians and the foremost critical scholar of antiquity was Aristarchus. He was the pupil, the collaborator and successor of his master Aristophanes[2]. His own school was celebrated for the number and fame of his pupils. Forty are mentioned by Suidas, and the names of at least twenty-two are known. Ammonius was his successor and faithful defender, and Dionysius Thrax (c. 166 B.C.), though a severe critic of Aristarchus, had his portrait painted with the figure of Tragedy emblazoned over his heart. Of his royal pupils there was Philopator Neos, the son of Ptolemy Philometor (181–146 B.C.) on whose murder by his uncle Physcon (Euergetes II), Aristarchus is thought to have fled to Cyprus where he died. However, Beloch and Rostagni believe he accompanied Physcon (Euergetes II) who was also his pupil, when Physcon was driven out of Alexandria (131–130 B.C.), and that he died in Cyprus before Physcon's return.

Aristarchus was a prolific productive scholar, editing recensions of the poets Alcaeus, Pindar and Anacreon, and writing commentaries on Hesiod, Archilochus, Aeschylus, Sophocles, Aristophanes and at least one prose writer, Herodotus[3]. His works filled 800 rolls[4]. His chief fame, in ancient as well as in modern times, rests on his Homeric labors. It is true he was heir to all the patient

1. See Canon Alexandrinus – Ch. XII for treatment of this subject.
2. See Ch. VIII, sec. IX for his succession as result of the discovery of *Oxyrhynchus Papyrus* (1241).
3. Sandys: *op. cit.* 130.
4. Suidas: s.v. *Aristarchus.*

study and accumulated researches of Zenodotus, Aristophanes, and the mighty scholars of the Alexandrian schools. In addition, he had the pre-Alexandrian "editions" or recensions of Places and Persons, together with the comment of the range of Greek literature from Pisistratus to the Ptolemies. Although Zenodotus, Rhianus, Aristophanes, and others had certainly broken the ground, initiated the work and made important progress, yet it was reserved for Aristarchus to formulate the more perfect method of critical study and with his meticulous scholarship to apply this method to the recension of the Homeric corpus and the elucidation of its text. His method was founded on exact knowledge and profound scholarship. A consummate grammarian, who had covered the field of language, with a special genius for the Homeric vocabulary, he employed with fine restraint, in his critical apparatus, the following principles: a deep respect for manuscript authority; a painstaking study of the words and language of Homer, from which study he did not resort to arbitrary changes and never omitted lines of the text, avoiding in emendation the appearance of "mere conjecture". He physically marked the text with: a. the obelus (–) to indicate a spurious line; b. the diple (>) to denote something notable in language or matter; c. the asterisk (*) for a verse wrongly repeated elsewhere; d. the stigme or dot for suspected spuriousness[1]; and other critical symbols. He noted likewise differences between his text and those of his predecessors, Aristophanes and Zenodotus.

With it all he taught that it was safest to rely upon the author's own interpretation, and he himself avoided a parade of learning.

As a result of his critical method and its practical application, a recension of The Iliad and The Odyssey crowned a galaxy of editions of the poets by the Alexandrian school. Its success or the devotion to meticulous accuracy of its author induced Aristarchus to issue a second recension or edition. Unfortunately, they are both lost, and the ingenuity of a distinguished German and of an American scholar has suggested that they were burned in the supposed fire of Caesar's visit[2].

Our knowledge of Aristarchus's scientific labors in Homeric

1. See Sandys: op. cit. 132, etc.
2. White: op. cit. XXXVII.

criticism has come to us down the precarious road of transmission of ancient letters.

From an Epitome of the works of four scholars we have derived most of our information:

1. Didymus (c. 80–41 B.C. to c. 10 A.D.), the man of "iron bowels", a writer of prodigious productivity who is accredited with 3500 books, wrote: *On the Aristarchean Recension*;

2. Aristonicus of Alexandria wrote: *On the Signs of the Iliad and Odyssey*;

3. Herodian (time of Marcus Aurelius), wrote: *On the Prosody and Accentuation of the Iliad*; and

4. Nicanor of Alexander wrote: *On Homeric Punctuation*, in 6 books.

An epitome of these works was made in the 3rd century A.D., and they are preserved in the famous manuscript, Venetus A, of the 10th century, containing the *Iliad* only, in the Library of San Marco, Venice[1].

With this limited data scholarship is able to "practically establish a text *according to Aristarchus*" which is believed would satisfy the exacting demand of the scholars of the Museum.

One would imagine that the recognition of the critical leadership and merited fame of Aristarchus as the foremost critic of all antiquity, an opinion which has survived to this day, would have enabled his work to have easily relegated all other crude, ancient or eccentric copies to the discard and that the Aristarchean text of Homer, crowned by the Museum, representing the most brilliant critical mind of the Alexandrian school, would have become not only the received text of its time, but would have been recognized as the standard text during Alexandrian, post-Hellenic, Roman, Mediaeval and Modern times. Yet the contrary has been its fate. Strange as it may seem, and in spite of the papyrus finds and publications of Mahaffy, Jules Nicole, and Grenfell and Hunt, the common text of Homer was and is not that of Aristarchus or the other scholars of the Alexandrian or other schools, but it is the old, common text of the fourth and fifth centuries, the vulgate.

On the whole the nature of the evidence is undeniable, and shows

1. See Murray: *op. cit.* p. 16.

beyond dispute that the text of the fourth and fifth centuries was essentially the same as ours; that is to say that the vulgate existed as far back as the fifth century[1].

For those who delight in the statistics of letters, it has been mathematically worked out, to illustrate how much our text of Homer is the vulgate and not Aristarchean or Alexandrian, that at least 60% of noticed passages are of the ancient vulgate:

Known readings	Number	left no trace	found in all mss.
Aristarchus	664	1/5 to 1/6	some 66
Aristophanes	81	46	2
Zenodotus	385	259	4

And yet the foregoing should not leave an impression of the futility of the labors of scholarship or that the particular work of the Alexandrians was of little moment in the intellectual life. On the contrary, within the Museum and the Library was the heart of pure scholarship. Here arose and were developed the true sciences of knowledge: the study of philology, the rules of exegesis, the art of literary criticism, the canons of literature, the science of bibliography. From all the known world were gathered the muniments of information, knowledge and wisdom of the most gifted of the races of man: the crude accumulations of experience, the prose master-pieces of science and history, the divine works of philosophy, the songs of eternal beauty, all these and more, complete or in fragments, were poured into the receiving rooms of the Museum-Library, there to be assorted, ordered, studied, edited, annotated by commentary, catalogued, and published for the enlightenment and gratification of mankind.

Blessed be the memory of Callimachus, of Zenodotus, Eratosthenes, Aristophanes, Aristarchus or whoever it was who in the Alexandrian Library labored on the mass of Hellenic prose and verse, enabling us to-day to read old Homer in 24 books, the nine books of Herodotus, the dialogues of Plato, and above all to read clean copy.

1. See T. W. Allen: *Ludwich's Homervulgata*, in *The Classical Review*, Vol. XIII (1899), pp. 39–40.

BOOK FOUR

The Destruction of the Library

CHAPTER XIV

CAESAR'S VISIT

ERHAPS the greatest miracle in human existence is the transmission of the thoughts and the record of the actions of
man by means of letters on papyrus and parchment.
The brittle and frail paper of Egypt and even the tougher
skins of Pergamum seem fragile media indeed on which to
confide the precious knowledge and wisdom of the ages. Ready
victim of the accidents of nature, fire, water and the other elemental forces, of the destructive damp, the mischievous rodent and the
ubiquitous worm, the manuscript would appear to have small
chance of survival. And when to this is added man's own contribution to the destruction of his own muniments, which contribution so far outstrips all the evil done by nature, the wonder
grows that anything considerable could have survived the dual
ravage of soulless nature and barbaric man.

In the intellectual life, the crowning example of this is the
tragedy of the Alexandriana.

By the end of the fourth century before our era, that incomparable flowering of the intellect which we may call Greek culture had reached its last great stage, as both Aristotle and Demosthenes died B.C. 322[1]. A year before, Alexander died, but he
had designated a place that should bear his name and control the
spirit of his age. His reputed half-brother Ptolemy built Alexandria, which became not only the emporium of the world but also
the center of learning and of art. If the ages of great literature
had past, the age of preserving the wonderful productions of
Greek genius in the past had now been reached, and the Ptolemies founded the first university, the Museum with its Library
where for the first time were assembled the extant writings in
verse and prose of the greatest literature yet known.

The Age of Alexander, the Hellenistic epoch, was the Silver
Age of the life of Greece. Into the old Greek civilization, which,
having attained the highest reaches of the human intellect, now

1. Both were born 384 B.C.

rested from its labors, was poured the young, fresh, vigorous, acquisitive Macedonian. Rough they were, these Macedonians, barbarians (i.e. Greek barbarians) if you will, yet possessed of teeming energy and the spirit of the conquistadores. Conquerors of known Asia, they built in the center of their world a city of marble, with wide, straight streets and magnificent public edifices, and within a short period potentially the largest city in the world. Center of power, of wealth and of commerce, they would also make it the center of culture. Like a young, new people, they must do all this on a grand scale. They had the wisdom to send to old Greece, to Mother Athens, for that re- markable man Demetrios of Phaleron, who, although he had some of the vices, had many of the virtues and much of the genius of classic Greece; indeed, how well he would have found a place in the most dizzy days of the high Renaissance.

Coming to Alexandria under the patronage of Ptolemy Soter, it is remarkable how quickly this philosopher-politician, who was essentially a man of letters, adjusted himself to the surround- ing Hellenic-Macedonian life. He doubtless suggested and organized the Museum as well as the great Library, whose first, vast collections he certainly made. And he did all this in what we would now call the true spirit of the new order, with singular speed and a determination to achieve regardless of cost or method. In an incredibly short time, less than ten or twelve years[1], he had collected 200,000 rolls and laid the vast foundation of the Alexandrian Library.

When Ptolemy II "Philadelphus" (B.C. 283) became sole ruler, he had this splendid start. In the time of Callimachus (d. B.C. 235) there were in the "Mother" Library in the Museum and in the "Daughter" Library at the Serapeum at least 532,800 rolls. In the first century B.C. it had reached 700,000 rolls, and naturally was growing fast or slow throughout the years accord- ing to the circumstances of the time.

It may never have reached a million, but it had certainly passed seven tenths of the way when Julius Caesar came to Egypt in B.C. 48, when in 47 apparently the first chapter in the

1. Demetrios went to Egypt probably 306 B.C. (Mahaffy), 297 (Sandys), 296–295 (Pauly-Wissowa), and certainly ceased his labors at the death of his friend and patron Ptolemy Soter (B.C. 283).

tragic story of the destruction of the Alexandrian Library begins.
For nearly two and a half centuries (295–48 B.C. or 285–48
B.C.) the Alexandrian Library[1], founded by the line of Ptolemaic
kings, through the labors of Demetrios, Zenodotus, Alexander the
Aetolian, Lycophron, Callimachus, Eratosthenes, Apollonius
Rhodius, Aristophanes of Byzantium and Aristarchus and many
whose names have not survived, was recognized as the greatest
treasury of learning yet known to the world. During all these
years, under good or bad rulers of the great Hellenic city of
Egypt, and many of them were very bad, the library had grown
until now (48 B.C.) it would seem that it had reached its ultimate
glory. Its 700,000 manuscripts represented the only great collection of the extant information, knowledge, and wisdom of the
ancient classic world and it was in many respects the most important collection ever made. It had escaped all the elemental
dangers of nature and all the vicissitudes of ages of war, when
Caesar came to Alexandria.

Caesar, flushed with the victory of Pharsalus, precipitously
pursued his rival. Through Greece he hurried, tarrying at Athens
long enough to remind, with pleasant irony, the Athenians that
(partisans of Pompey as they had been): "How often will the
glory of your ancestors save you from self-destruction."[2] At
Ephesus, where he saved the treasury of the Temple of Diana
from the grasp of Balbus, he heard that Pompey was reported
to have been in Cyprus. With haste he left Asia Minor for Egypt,
arriving at Alexandria. He hesitated in the roadstead, when the
assassin brought to his ship the head and the signet-ring of
Pompey, who had been murdered by order of the eunuch
Pothinus and those in control of the young king Ptolemy. He
turned with horror from the sight. Whether he was to sail away
or tarry awhile in Egypt was the momentous question pressing
for immediate decision.

Three very dissimilar motives may have possessed the mind of
Caesar at this moment:

1. Political. Ptolemy Auletes ("the flute player"), the last king

1. One may remember that the British Museum was founded in 1753 and, not yet
two centuries old, has already been subjected to a rain of fire in the Battle of Britain
(1940).
2. Appian of Alexandria: *The Civil Wars*, II–13.

of Egypt, a wretched descendant of the great Ptolemy Soter, illegitimate by the Macedonian law, legitimate by the Egyptian
law, had fled to Rome seeking the aid of the leaders of the Roman
Senate. He had been lavish with his bribes and is said to have
promised Caesar 17,500,000 denarii (about three and a half
million dollars) for his influence. Of course he had not paid, and
Caesar now, as almost always, needed money. He would take
ten million denarii in full settlement, and this seemed the time
to exact payment from the fabulous coffers of Egypt.

2. Diplomatic. He heard of the dispute concerning the will of
the late Ptolemy Auletes, who had left his kingdom to his elder
daughter Cleopatra (16–20 years) and his son Ptolemy (10 years).
He had appointed the Roman people guardian of his son. The
Roman Senate had made Pompey his tutor. Pothinus, head of
the palace clique, had possession of the young Ptolemy and of the
kingdom; Cleopatra had fled to Syria, but early exhibiting her
wonted vigor, had raised an army, with which she had reached
the borders of her country when Pompey was murdered and
Caesar arrived. Caesar knew that for over a century and a half
the dynastic troubles of the royal house of Ptolemy had been
adjusted by the leaders of Rome. If such a role were proper for a
Lepidus or Scipio Africanus, certainly Caesar should not shrink
from the responsibility. He at once decided that he should, as the
representative of Rome, settle this present dispute pontifically, if
not judicially.

3. Personal. Caesar, an intellectual and scholar of the first rank,
had a traveler's desire to visit the city of marble, its palaces,
public buildings, great University and far-famed Library, its
boulevards and colonnades, the most spacious and magnificent in
all the world; indeed, what better time than the present to see:

> The memorials and the things of fame
> That do renown this city.

And so Caesar made the precarious decision and landed at
Alexandria with his small force of 3200 legionaries and 800 horses.
He took possession of the palace. He took the king with him and
announced that he would decide the dispute between the king
and his sister. In a short while, Cleopatra presented herself either
from out of a carpet or bedroll, or certainly on the carpet in

Caesar's study[1]. Why not assume that Caesar gave most careful attention to the case? Certainly he decided according to the terms of the will, upon sound juridical principles, that there should be a joint sovereignty of Cleopatra and Ptolemy. Although the Alexandrians had favored Pompey, he treated them fairly. He demanded no war indemnity but did require the payment of ten million denarii, as we have above noted. Yet he lingered in Alexandria. He had only a small contingent; he sent to Syria for reinforcements, but the winds were unfavorable for sailing from Egypt, and we are sure that Herr Mommsen and Mr. Froude would admit no other reason for Caesar's failure to leave Egypt. However, a storm was indeed brewing.

In the meanwhile he must have visited the famous sights of this extraordinary city, with his guard and doubtless with Cleopatra as his gracious host and most competent guide. The Palaces of the Ptolemaic kings with their accumulation of wealth of the centuries and with the residue of the vast spoil of the Assyrian, Babylonian, and Persian empires, not to mention the native ancestral treasuries still abiding in Egypt; the great harbors, east and west, divided by the Heptastadium, the long causeway, connected by two bridges, giving access to the two basins, the whole linking the city proper with the island of Pharos which protectively spread its dazzling white rocky mass between the city and the elements of the sea, and whose eastern extremity was capped by the mother and eponym of all lighthouses, the far-famed Pharos, one of the seven wonders of the Ancient World; its two harbors whose great commercial emporium included docks and vast structures to store the grain brought from the Nile valley and held for export, and many other warehouses; the Temple of Serapis (dual god of Greek and Egyptian) on its hill in the old Egyptian quarter, in architectural splendor rivaled only by the Capitol at Rome; all of these he must have seen.

Yet there were at least two other sites which he would be ex-

1. This dramatic appearance of Cleopatra is quite historic. When Caesar came to Alexandria, she was beyond the frontier of Egypt with the army she had collected (like Cleopatra IV in 113 B.C.) against her enemies, the palace-cabal, Pothinus, Achillas, and Theodotus. Bevan (p. 363) puts it perfectly: "For Cleopatra the difficulty was how to get from the frontier to Caesar without being murdered by the palace-gang on the way." So her faithful slave, Apollodorus the Sicilian, conveyed her by boat to Alexandria, and smuggled her, hid in an Eastern bedroll, into the palace.

pected to especially visit with emotions worthy of the philosopher and statesman, the lover of learning and books.

In the heart of the Brucheion, the Greek-Macedonian quarter of the city, one of the pile of royal buildings was the Soma, or Mausoleum of Alexander the Great. The first Ptolemy had taken from Perdiccas his greatest treasure, the body of the son of Philip. Embalmed by the eastern masters of this art, swathed in malleable plates of gold, in a golden casket, the body of Alexander was placed in a Hall built of the most precious Egyptian marbles by Greek master-builders. Around this central shrine, the descendants of the Lagidae had erected wondrous mausoleae for their abiding-place within the shadow of the great heroic dead. Although one of the decadent scions of Ptolemy had rifled the golden encasement of the conqueror, the body had been perfectly preserved in a glass or thin transparant alabaster covering. For nearly three centuries then and for more than four yet to come, this relic of human greatness had been and was to be the Mecca of curious and thoughtful travelers. Now men of renown, of alien bloods, from countries perhaps unknown, had made this pilgrimage, yet all other visit spale into insignificance when we imagine this scene, when the foremost man of action in all antiquity was confronted by the mortal remains of his only possible rival or superior. It was a rare moment, unique in the human history of the psychologyofgreatness.

So imperial Caesar stood, contemplative, beside the remains of the divine Alexander. Slowly he turned away, led by his fair guide, from the scene of eternal death to the scene of eternal life. For as the life of the body passes quickly and all men's craft and art can retain its remains but transiently, ere it disappears forever, so the life of the spirit, the glorious children of man's brain, gossamer, intangible dreams, visions, impressed on the most fragile media, become visual and vocal for all peoples and all time.

They left the enclosure of the Mausoleum, the Soma of Alexander and the Ptolemaic kings, where the delicate hand of Greek restraint had softened the awful solemnity of Egyptian genius in erecting the sombre and nigh eternal mansion of the dead.

Caesar and Cleopatra stepped into the graceful, light city chariot of the queen, whose Etheopian out-runners cleared the way through the early morning press of the usual turbulent Alexandrian crowd, and Caesar's small personal guard were watchful of their precious charge. The road along the great boulevard, the most magnificent thoroughfare of any city of antiquity, which longitudinally from the Canopic Gate to the Gate of the Necropolis cut the city in northernly and southernly halves, was over three miles in length and more than one hundred feet in width. Through the center, there ran almost a spina, rich in obelisk, sphinx, and symbols of old Egypt, with statues, tripods and stelae, in bronze and marble, monuments of Hellenic art.

The way was short, yet their minds may have reverted to the gay symposium of the night before, in fact of that very day, as the gods of the morning were contending with shades of night ere the feast was over, and only the old, tireless energy of Caesar could have provoked this morning-tour of the sights of Alexandria.

ONE OF CLEOPATRA'S FEASTS

Since Cleopatra had assumed the role of royal hostess to Caesar, she had given him many rare and sumptuous feasts, exquisite in their appointments, with viands of the fabulous Alexandrian cuisine (on which gossip Athenaeus has squandered hundreds of pages which might have been devoted to the Alexandriana) and wines of rare vintages, all with an oriental magnificence, tempered with Greek taste, that outshown anything this blase man of the world had seen in provinces, in kingdoms, or in eternal Rome. The ingenuity of the queen seemed limitless as hostess, for on this night she planned for Caesar a most particular entertainment. Court feasts and official dinners had been frequent, routs and debauches attaining heights of pagan sensuality had been held; and many a wondrous tête-à-tête at which the Egyptian Aphrodite gained such victories over the unconquerable Roman as might have changed the pages of history. Yet this night there was a different appeal.

On a lofty terrace of the great palace entirely encrusted in rare marbles, in the midst of a peristyle whose columns of white marble were in perfect Greek proportion, and which were festooned with fine stuffs lately brought by caravan from the unknown east, was spread a sumptuous feast.

Everything was there to excite the eye and to tempt the appetite of the exquisite gourmet (of whom the chief guest was a noted exemplar), fish and fowl and meats in wondrous manner cooked, with sauces unknown to Braillet-Savarin and yet undiscovered by the masters of French kitchens, the teeming things of earth, vegetable and fruit, paid willing tribute, and fantastic creations of the confectioner's art added quaint joy to the feast. The cellars of Alexandria were the finest in the world. And all were served in vessels and on plates of gold and in high crystal chalices of fabled price. The tables were dexterously spread with flowers and an alluring odor of perfumed spices kissed the nostrils of the guests. Household slaves, meticulously trained, served with the awful perfection of an ancient regime.

On either side of the terrace, bronze torch-bearers held the pleasant smelling-woods, the flames of which gave light to the midnight festival. The view from the terrace embraced the entire city, and the tables were most carefully arranged with this consideration. To the left spread the great Greek or Royal quarter, the Brucheion, with vast buildings of white stone and marble, with its two great thoroughfares cutting the city into four unequal parts (from the Sun Gate on Lake Mareotis, to the Moon Gate on the Great Harbor or near the beginning of the Heptastadium, and from the Canopic to the Necropolis Gate, from north-east to south-west); beyond in the Rhakotis or Egyptian quarter, arose the amazing Serapeum; and further beyond was the City of the Dead. Eastward of the palace district, was the vast Jewish quarter, and beyond, the Hippodrome. To the front of the feasters was the Great Harbor with the promontory of Lochias continuing to the right and the island of Pharos with its connecting Mole completing its frame in the west.

On the docks and in the harbor, twinkles of light might be seen, but at the extremity of the island the perpetual fire of the great tower (the Pharos) flamed in the heavens. And above all spread, diamond starred, the faultless sky, the ebony dome of Egypt.

The guests had all arrived before Caesar and Cleopatra entered and occupied the place of honor, a slightly raised dais, over which was spread a formal tapestry depicting the Rape of Helen of Troy. The guests were not the courtiers of the House of Ptolemy, the military or official members of the government, nor were they Caesar's close military entourage. There were a few exceptions, of course, from all these groups. The guests were the literary men and men of art of the great cosmopolitan Hellenic city – poets, historians and scientists; they were faint representatives of Demetrios, Callimachus, and Euclid. Above all, there were the leading scholars of the Museum and bibliographers and librarians of the Alexandrian Library. The Master of the Keepers of Books of the great Library had been specially placed near to Caesar.

The Queen was in radiant good form, marvelous to behold and memorable in wit and repartee and every now and then evincing a scholarship of high order and a cultural judgment unsurpassed by any woman of her age.

Cleopatra was in the heyday of her fabulous life. Crowned with imperious youth, her genius had just won for her the throne of the Ptolemies, and the infinite witcheries of her feminine arts had conquered the affection of the foremost man in all the world. Supreme beauty she may not have had, such as Helen, whose face alone could launch a thousand ships, or Phryne, whose form divine alone could control the judgment of men, but she possessed more than just beauty of face and perfection of form.

Of Macedonian-Greek blood, perhaps tinged with some oriental strains, Cleopatra was small of statue, with a poise of sheer dignity, a body lithe and ever falling into motions of supreme grace; with a charm of manner and a sense to please baffling description; with a mind informed, quick and brilliant; with a wit subtle and gay, but ever sure to please; and above all, hers was the supreme gift of woman divine, a voice soft and resonant like magic sounds of many stringed instruments[1]. To these compelling fascinations there must be added accomplishments in all the arts of Aphrodite, a knowledge of Hellenic philosophy and culture, a heart teeming with the zest of life, and eyes from whose liquid beds flashed a soul of indomitable courage and limitless ambition. The heir of the Ptolemies may have had hair of a Titian stain[2]. Such was Cleopatra in the perfect flower of her youth.

1. The lyre of Orpheus or the flute of Pan could not have affected the imagination like the divine voices of Julia Marlowe or Viola Allen.
2. My friends Dr. Bechtel of Tulane and Will Durant are not in accord with me: Dr. Bechtel insists she was a brunette, but Will Durant is in favor of a probable blond (*Caesar and Christ*, New York, 1944, p. 187).

Caesar had accomplished fifty-three years. Though he had led a life of political hardship, of military labor and peril, a personal career as a man of society with many intrigues and scandals to his discredit; although he had always been a student of man and his history, a scholar, indeed a man of letters, a lover of books as well as of women, he was still in athletic form, a graceful, handsome, slightly bald man of splendid manners and compelling personality. He was a moderate gourmet, who ate most carefully and drank with perfect discretion.

As the daring, youthful votary of Aphrodite and disciple of Aspasia, Cleopatra was flattered that he loved her; as the *arbiter mundi*, Caesar was flattered by his conquest.

The feast was on. A few of the well-known figures who may have been there were: Dioscorides, the queen's private physician, a man whose medical labors survived almost to the modern age and who was reputed to have kept a *Diary* in which was recorded the daily personal life of his celebrated patron; Photinus, the mathematician; the empirical doctor Serapion; the voluminous Didymus, the critic, with 3500 mortal rolls to his credit, a residuum of which survives in his Scholia on the *Iliad* and *Odyssey*; and the famous Sosigenes, foremost astronomer of the age, a peripatetic philosopher who was to be Caesar's chief aid, when in 46 B.C., the master of the world, in his office as *pontifex maximus* was to reform the calendar, which was to serve western civilization until the Bull of Gregory XIII (February 24, 1582) was to make relatively correct our system of time.

Caesar discoursed with the Greek philosophers and seemed especially interested in a sage deeply learned in the Egyptological ideology and the mysterious cult of old Egypt and the modern Egypto-Grecian rituals.

Turning from religion and philosophy to science, he would know from whence mighty Nilus rose, not hesitating to say that the discoverer of the original fountains of the great river would be greater than the mere military conqueror of mankind.

The conversation, brilliant and varied, ever drifted back to the subject of letters and their wonderful preservation in the manuscript rolls of the great repositories of learning, the greatest and mother of all, the Museum with its fabulous Library.

A few minor poets and literary men were there, but the

JULIUS CAESAR

Museo Vaticano, Rome

mentioned names show how the Museum had been even from
the beginning a scientific group rather than a body of great
writers in verse or prose, and one in which the historian was
rarely present. Indeed, the conversation had stressed the rise
and importance of science and the decline of pure letters, the
common index of a practical age, and between Caesar and
Sosigenes some significant discourse covering the confusion of the
current reckoning of time, when Cleopatra gaily interposed,
calling on her Master of the Keepers of Books of the great
Library, who was a bibliographer of note, to tell her guest of
some of the treasures of the Alexandriana:

> Divine Caesar, *arbiter mundi*, who I have no doubt will yet regulate
> the course of the heavens, and who is himself a great writer, a
> lover of learning, a collector of books, is it of this he would hear, in
> our own Alexandria, seat of the culture of the world?

And so, the Master of the Keepers of Books ventured:

> Of course Demetrios, under Soter, was the true founder of the
> Library, and we have always believed that some old Homeric
> manuscripts in the Epic Section are originals of the commissioners
> of Pisistratus; Aristotle's books were bought by king Ptolemy for a
> high price, but we know that we were deceived and that only a part
> of the *Omnia Opus* was delivered to us and that later the balance
> found its way to Rome. But we scored in the matter of original
> official copies of the manuscripts of the great Attic tragic trilogy. It
> is true we forfeited a goodly sum, but we have the *editiones principes*
> of Aeschylus, Sophocles and Euripides.

And Caesar laughed. "After all," he rejoined, "it was Greek
against Greek, and the Greek won."

And then the heads of the Ten Sections adroitly boasted of
their wares. "The Sappho papyri are the most complete extant
and some of the scrolls have an eerie provenance," put forth the
young Keeper of the Lyric Section, himself a minor poet. In
History, in which the Alexandrian period was not over blessed,
the custodian talked of an ancient Herodotus, which from internal evidence might have been used by the famous raconteur in
his Attic readings, and certainly was traditionally from Thurii,
or at least from Magna Graecia. "Not only Herodotus," some one
cried, "but we have perfect texts of Aristophanes, Plato, Iso-

crates, Demosthenes, to mention just a few." An old scholar
of the Museum added:

It is not alone in collecting and preserving the rolls of older times,
but in editing and arranging all the ancient writers in accordance
with modern views of literary division, and grammatical usage, to
make them in fact accessible not only to scholarship but an agreeable temptation for the general reader; this was the real achievement, the great glory of the Alexandrian Museum and its Libraries.

The night waned, the last cups were drunk, Caesar and Cleopatra
left the banquet board, and the principal guests, the scholars,
literati, dilettanti, of intellectual Alexandria departed in the
early morning hour for their respective abodes.

This scene lingered in the mind of Caesar as the chariot stopped
at the main entrance to the Museum. He was keenly interested
in this great seat of learning and in its time-honored provisions
for the care of scholars and the advancement of learning. In a
short while he found himself in the Hall of the Muses, the great
"Mother Library" of the Museum or University, the far-famed
Alexandriana, the wonder of the world.

A number of bibliographers, each an expert in his field, were
on hand to find in the lockers, or cabinets, the most celebrated
rarities of the collection, some few of which had been mentioned
at the symposium the previous night.

Caesar, for the nonce, ceased to be the statesman, soldier,
dictator of the world. With almost the enthusiasm of youth his
quick mind and glittering eyes assumed a distinct facet of his
wonderful personality. He was the student, the scholar, the
seeker of knowledge, the lover of books. The men of the library
were busy answering his keen questions, amazed at his fund of
bibliophilic learning and the sincere interest he evinced. The
observant Cleopatra was delighted and never for a moment
changed her role: to please, at any price, her lover, the master
of the world. As his enthusiasm mounted and the desire of
acquisition gleamed from his eyes, the subtle adept of the masculine heart and mind knew just when to strike. Unerringly she
read his thoughts and offered him some precious manuscript
which he was examining. He declined with due propriety, but
she insisted the books were hers, she had so many, she forced

them on him, until he, feeling that he had paid sufficient respect to the proprieties, entirely gave way, and before long orders were given for the packing of hundreds of items of the great collection. The Queen was obdurate; he must accept them, and he, the first glow of modesty over, fell into the delightfully gay adventure as he visioned these wondrous rolls in his Villa beyond Tiber. If the Queen was in high spirit of generosity, and Caesar in the most delightful receptive mood, the state of mind of the Keepers of Books and the Master of the Library was one of greatest alarm and sorrow. How much he regretted having boasted of particular treasures at the symposium, and as the orders of Caesar, joyfully approved by the Queen, for more and more of the fine manu-scripts or book-rolls came, clear and fast consternation reigned among the poor bookmen; a veritable panic seized the faithful guardians of the Alexandriana. For them it was a ruthless inva-sion of the Latin barbarian, before whose pitiless power they stood in awful helplessness as the Queen seemed to revel in her reckless mood of gifts for Caesar. So there was no resistance to the mounting cupidity of the Roman bibliophile or the insistance of the Queen that he should take as bountifully of her book-store as he wished, and more. After hours the agony of the visit was spent, the final orders given for a considerable number of the books to be packed and sent without delay to the docks, from whence they would be shipped to Rome.

As Caesar and Cleopatra left the Alexandriana, a pall of grief and helplessness enveloped the place and personnel. The orders had to be carried out. It is hoped that the custodians of the Library early enough in the fateful visit detected the danger they were running and refrained from showing many a valuable roll which they would have been proud to have exhibited to a visitor, but hardly to one with designs upon their most dear books. It is also reasonable to believe that in so vast a collec-tion the selection having to be made mostly by the officials of the Library, they were faithful to their charge and did not give the best copies where it could reasonably be avoided.

The awful ordeal was experienced. The books were carefully packed and sent to the docks, and the officials prayed to Serapis that they should never again have such a royal visit.

What numbers of books and what quality of rolls were taken

from the collection can never be known. After their destruction, it was to the interest of the guardians of the Library to exaggerate the loss and certainly to conceal from further depredations the remaining treasures, which must have been of goodly quantity and quite reasonably their greatest.

For the darlings of the gods, the last few days had been the heyday of their amazing lives. The Queen in the happiness and realization of vaulting ambition was in the seventh heaven of delight, and Caesar, perhaps never so well cared for, was having a glorious holiday after the anxieties and labors of his public career.

But ominous clouds were gathering, and the storm broke with cataclysmic violence.

Alexandria rose against Caesar and the Queen. The regular army, composed of Macedonians, expatriate legionaries, some soldiers of Pompey, many ex-slaves, and international cut-throats, but with all over 20,000 strong, under Achillas, the military commander, marched on the city, the greater part of which they occupied, and stormed the Palace where Caesar was virtually besieged and with difficulty held his own. Pothinus, the eunuch, prime minister of the Ptolemies, Arsinoe, the sister, and the young King Ptolemy, were dangerous hostages within the palace. The water-supply became contaminated; wells had to be dug. The army of Caesar (originally 3200 men, 800 horses) was too small to overcome the aroused populace of the Egyptian city and an army five times that of the Roman visitor. But in the harbor the large Egyptian fleet which had been raised for Ptolemy was a definite menace against the arrival of reinforcements sent for by Caesar, and an immediate danger to the few ships of the Roman. In this situation of extreme peril, Caesar acted with characteristic genius and experienced personal good fortune. As he did not have the means of capturing, manning, and maintaining the Alexandrian fleet, he decided to destroy it by fire. This daring plan was successfully carried out and the fleet was burned, but the burning ships, drifting into piers, or themselves being in docks, communicated the fire to wharves and harbor installations of the city, starting a serious conflagration which destroyed not only the vessels of the Alexandrian navy, but the warehouses and buildings on and near the water-front and the cargoes of imports and exports on the docks. Had Alexandria not been so well built of stone and marble with very little wood used in construction, the fire might have been even more catastrophic.

Caesar, surmounting every danger, was finally victorious and escaped, through his genius and luck, perhaps the most ominous episode of his career.

As we are interested in the fire resulting from the burning of the ships, I have attempted to review all the ancient, and the most important of the modern authorities.

I.

Our first authority should be Caesar in *The Civil Wars*. Achillas, the military commander of the Alexandrian forces, with 20,000 men, not counting the rabble of Alexandria, and 2000 horses, was attempting to secure the larger part of the city. Although he had failed to penetrate the Palace which Caesar had made his citadel, his forces were fighting in the streets and, more important, a serious battle was being fought at the port, where "the enemy was attempting in great numbers to seize the warships", some 72 in number, most of them splendid vessels fully equipped for Pompey's service and all celebrated craft of the Alexandrian navy which Seneca seemed so delighted to praise (Ad Lucilium, LXXVII–1).

If these ships were secured by Achillas, the harbor and seaboard would be lost, and Caesar's ships cut off from supplies and reinforcements. Caesar felt his safety depended upon the event, and "Caesar gained his purpose":

> He burnt all those ships and the rest that were in the docks, because he could not protect so wide an extent with his small force, and at once he embarked his men and landed them on Pharos.
>
> (*Civil Wars*, III-111.)

In the street fighting in the town "neither side was beaten".

It is to be noted Caesar says nothing about a great conflagration, merely reporting the burning and destruction of the ships. There is not a word about the destruction of the Museum, the Library, or the Books.

II.

After reciting the above events, Caesar concludes the last book (III) of *The Civil Wars* with the sentence: "This was the beginning of the Alexandrian war."

Now *The Alexandrian War,* written probably by Hirtius, a friend of Caesar, evidences a desire to continue the narrative where Caesar ends. The author of *The Alexandrian War* goes into much detail as to methods of defense, and in treating of the necessity of having an open space or clearing between the Palace and the small part of the city held by him from the greater part of the city held by the enemy, Caesar was compelled to actually batter down houses by inserting holes in the walls and using his batter-ing-rams to demolish the buildings in order to have open ground before his defensive positions. Why did he go to such trouble? Why did he not burn these impeding structures? How complete is the answer:

> He could not effect this purpose by burning the town, for Alexandria was nearly safe against fire, because the houses were built without wooden floorings and timber, and were formed of masonry with vaulted arches, and roofs were made of rubble or paved[1].

And again:

> Almost the whole city of Alexandria was excavated and contained cellars which were connected with the Nile. By these means, water was brought into private houses, and gradually in a certain time the water became clear and the mud subsided[2].

When we consider the foundations of the great city, from its beginning built of marble or stone, with wide streets and broad thoroughfares, the most magnificent in antiquity; its buildings built with ample space between them, interspersed with gardens, and often connected, it is true, by colonnades of stone and marble; when we know that the permanent character of its structures had been maintained until Caesar's day and that its houses, built of stone, had stone or paved floors and roofs with an entire absence of wood or timber, with Nile water lapping every house, we have indeed a picture of the most indestructible or at least most fire-proof city in all the ancient world[3].

The author of *The Alexandrian War* makes no mention of the destruction of the Museum, the Library, or the Books.

1. George Long: *The Decline of the Roman Republic,* London, 1874, Vol. V, p. 251, The Alexandrian War.
2. Long: *op. cit.* Vol. V, p. 253, note: Auct. B. Alex. 4.
3. The point herein stressed did not fail to impress the author of the *Alexandrian Library* (Dziatzko) in *Real Encyclopädie* of Pauly-Wissowa, Vol. III, pp. 409-414.

III.

Cicero (106–43 B.C.), the most distinguished man of letters of his age, contemporary opponent of Caesar, whom he survived, could hardly have failed to recount, somewhere, somehow, the appalling disaster to scholarship through the destruction of the Alexandriana, victim of the heady ambition of Caesar in his mad career for pleasure and power – had it occurred. It is just inconceivable that Cicero would have remained silent on such a subject.

IV.

Strabo (c. 64 B.C. to 19 A.D.), the Greek geographer, was in Egypt from 25 to 20 B.C., only 22 years after Caesar's visit. He wrote an extensive description of Alexandria (Book XVII). As an eye-witness, he most carefully described the harbor front of the city, building by building, yet he does not place the Museum (or Library) near the harbor. He could not have omitted such a situation had it existed. Yet he seems eager to tell, when speaking of the island of Pharos that:

> Divus Caesar devastated the island, in his war against the people of Alexandria, when they espoused the party of the kings.
>   (XVII–C. 1–6.)

He speaks of the Museum as a part of the palace pile, of its having a public walk, a place with seats, a Hall for the men of learning, etc.

He does not mention that but twenty-two years before, the Museum or its Library was destroyed by fire under "Divus Caesar".

In the probably latest edition of Strabo (L.C.L., edited and translated by Sterrett and Jones), London, 1917, we read:

> In 25 and 24 B.C. he (Strabo) is in Egypt, and accompanies Aelius Gallus up the Nile, proceeding as far as Syene and the frontiers of Etheopia (2.5.12). At that time he was 39 years old. He was still in Egypt when Augustus was in Samos in 20 B.C. (14.1.14). He was then 44 years old. Accordingly he lived for more than five years in Alexandria, and we may infer that it was in the Alexandrian Library

that he made from the works of his predecessors those numerous excerpts with which his book is filled. (Vol. I, p. XX–XXI.)

Using the Library, as it is only reasonable to assume he did, it is unthinkable that he would not have complained of the absence of some valuable authority, due to the recent "fire".

Strabo, a Greek, keenly aware of the significance of the Museum in the intellectual life of the Hellenic-Roman world, could hardly have failed to record the recent destruction of the Museum or Library.

Strabo makes no mention of the destruction of the Museum, the Library, or the Books.

V.

Titus Livius (59 B.C. to 17 A.D.) of Padua, whose *History of Rome* in 142 books (of which 107 are lost) was the monumental narrative of Rome's stupendous records from the foundation of the city to the principate of Augustus, or the death of Drusus (9 B.C.), fails here to help.

Unfortunately Book CXII of Livy, which treated of the flight of Pompey to Egypt and the entire sojourn of Caesar in Alexandria, is lost. This is particularly a major loss to the history of our inquiry, as Livy lived in the perfect period to acquire the facts. He was 15 years old when Caesar was murdered (44 B.C.) and outlived Augustus by three years (17 A.D.). We do not know what, if anything, Livy might have reported about the Museum, the Library, or Books, or of their partial or complete destruction. The epitomes are silent.

However, Seneca says (*De Animi Tranquillitate*, IX–5) that Livy referred to the Alexandrian Library as *elegantiae regum curaeque egregium opus*.

VI.

A famous scion of the Cordovan family of Seneca seems to be the earliest extant authority referring to the destruction of the books.

In 49 A.D. Seneca (4 B.C. to 65 A.D.), the philosopher, returned from his Claudian banishment and was made tutor to the vicious youth Domitius, who was to become the infamous emperor Nero. He had been selected for the dubious post by the more infamous Agrippina, mother of Nero, wife and poisoner of Claudius, a woman whose incredible wickedness had plumbed the depths of incest and murder.

Seneca at this time of his eventful career was juggling with conscience, common ambition, and the desires of the intellectual life. It was the psychological moment for him to write *De Animi Tranquillitate*. It was his intellectual "out", an examination of the ways of attaining that which he so much desired, the tranquility of mind.

In this work (IX–5) written 96 years after the alleged event, we read:

> Quadraginta milia librorum Alexandriae arserunt; pulcherrimum regiae, opulentiae monimentum alius laudaverit, sicut T. Livius qui elegantiae regum curaeque egregium id opus ait fuisse.

It was Seneca's reference to Livy's praise of the Alexandriana that provoked Gibbon's retort: "a liberal encomium, for which he (Livy) is pertly criticized by a narrow stoicism of Seneca (*De Animi Tranq.*, c. 9), whose wisdom on this occasion deviates into nonsense"[1].

The chain of comment is continued by Mr. Merivale[2] who would gently twit Gibbon, whom he calls "a modern devourer of large libraries", for his severe rebuke of Seneca. We are on the side of Gibbon.

A careful study of the statement of Seneca, which is, as far as we know, the first time the destruction is mentioned by anyone, and certainly the earliest extant account, since there is no evidence of a lost description, should lead to a reasonable solution of the inquiry. Seneca wrote:

> *Forty thousand books were burned at Alexandria*; let someone else praise this library as the most noble monument to the wealth of kings, as did Titus Livius, who says that it was the most distinguished achievement of the good taste and solicitude of kings[3].

1. Gibbon: *op. cit.* Ch. LI.
2. Charles Merivale: *History of the Romans under the Empire*, 4th ed., New York, 1896 (Vol. II, p. 259, note).
3. Seneca: *On the Tranquility of Mind* (IX–5), L.C.L. (tr. John W. Basore), London, 1932. The italics are ours.

What is it that Seneca clearly sets forth in this narrative? Certainly it contains two statements:

1. He asserts that the 40,000 books were burned at Alexandria.

2. That Livy considered the Alexandrian Library the most noble monument to the wealth and wisdom of kings.

Now the first statement is very definite as to the *thing*, the *quantity* and the *place*. *Books* to the number of 40,000 are burned at *Alexandria*. There is nothing said as to *time* and no mention of *Caesar*.

Then let us assume that Seneca *meant* to say that 40,000 books were burned at Alexandria *at the time of Caesar's visit* (48–47 B.C.). And let us further assume that he drew his information nearly 100 years after the occurrence from contemporary Livy (from Book CXII, now lost).

Any further assumptions would be more than uncritical. To attempt to assert that Seneca meant to say (which he did not) that not only 40,000 manuscripts were burned at Alexandria during Caesar's time, but that also the great Library of Alexandria, containing at least 700,000 MSS., or probably a million books, was destroyed, is to violate the canons of true criticism, as well as the dictates of common judgment.

It is well that we carefully note how definite Seneca is about the quantity of books destroyed, 40,000. Now if we assume that he followed Livy (which assumption gives his statement its only authority), Livy's lost Book CXII must have stated that 40,000 manuscripts burned. In subsequent writers, common exaggeration or carelessness must be responsible for other amounts[1].

VII.

Lucan (39–65 A.D.), grandson of Seneca, the rhetorician, and nephew of Seneca, the philosopher, was also a man of letters and a scion of this distinguished intellectual family of Spain. Like his family, his life (in his case, too young a life) was early con-

---

1. Even Dr. Basore, the last editor of Seneca's *Moral Essays* (L.C.L., Vol. II, p. 246), London, 1932, writes: "The extent of the loss is variously given, but in no authority is the estimate placed so low." What "estimate"? We trust Seneca followed Livy. If not, his statement has less value than we are willing to accord to it.

sumed in the vortex of Roman imperialism. In intellect he was precocious, in character his fundamental weakness sunk to dishonor. He wrote an epic poem, *Pharsalia*, in ten books. He was for the republic, pro-Pompeian, and Caesar was Satan in his "Republic Lost". In the last (Xth) Book of his best and sole surviving work, which probably was called *De Bello Civili*, the young poet describes Caesar's sojourn in Egypt. Apparently he never lived to finish this tenth book, but he did complete his description of the burning of the ships and the spread of the conflagration.

> He (Caesar) ordered brands steeped in resin to be hurled at the sails of the crowded ships; and the fire coursed swiftly along the ropes of tow and the decks running in the wax, till the rowers' benches and the towering yards blazed up together. Soon, the ships, almost half-consumed, sank beneath the surface, and soon the assailants and their weapons were swamped. Nor did the fire fall upon the vessels only: the houses near the sea caught fire from the spreading heat, and the winds fanned the conflagration, till the flames, smitten by the eddying gale, rushed over the roofs as fast as meteors that often trace a furrow through the sky, though they have nothing solid to feed on and burn by means of air alone. The calamity for a time called off the crowd. (X–491–505.)

Now, of course, this is a poetic description, the usual poetical license of the rush of fire as fast as meteors, yet not one word of the burning of books or libraries.

Lucan hated Caesar more than anyone (except Alexander the Great in a general way and, I assume, Nero personally at the end, for his own dear life); so furious and unfair were his headlong attacks upon Caesar, that Macaulay, an admirer of Lucan, is provoked to write: "Caesar, the finest gentleman, the most humane conqueror, and the most popular politician that Rome ever produced," is by Lucan represented as "a bloodthirsty ogre"[1].

Now everyone will admit that Lucan would have joyously sung of anything to the discredit of Caesar, and would never have omitted so wonderful an opportunity for wide sympathetic condemnation as the story that Caesar in setting fire to the ships recklessly destroyed the world-famous Library of Alexandria and the Museum! Why did he not use this glowing artistic spec-

1. Lucan, in L.C.L. ed., tr. by J. D. Duff (London, 1928, p. XIII).

tacle which in his fervid, poetic hands could have shown the satanic Caesar, in ruthless ambition, burning the veritable heir-looms of the intellectual world, the awful pall of the disaster obscuring the eternal light from the Mediterranean lands, as Caesar rushed madly on his career for fame?

He could have had two reasons for the omission: either he did not know of it, if it happened, which is incredible; or he did know of it and considered the accidental burning of some books too insignificant. Under no view, could he have known that the great Alexandrian Library was destroyed under Caesar, and have omitted to tell it to all posterity[1].

We must remember that in his poem, Lucan had finished the description of the burning of the ships, and had turned to other quite insignificant incidents, before he had his veins opened in the warm bath of death:

Bidden[2] while singing of battles and with lofty utterance solacing the mighty dead to plunge in Lethe's rushing stream.

So Lucan, also, makes no mention of the destruction of the Museum, the Library, or of Books.

VIII.

If Plutarch (c. 46–120 A.D.) wrote his famous *Lives* after his return to his native Chaeronea and after Trajan's death (117 A.D.), he therefore wrote the *Lives of Pompey, of Caesar*, and *of Antony*, over 150 years after the events in which we are chiefly interested.

We always think of Plutarch as having made good use of the Bibliotheca Ulpia, which Trajan founded at Rome and named after the illustrious Tyrian Ulpian, whose labors as a Roman jurist were to form so large a part of the *Digest of Justinian*.

He must have derived much information from the collection of Latin and Greek rolls in the imperial foundation, and as he says that it was late in his life that he devoted himself to Latin

1. The thought that he was silent due to a kind of patriotic shame is quite exploded by Bouché-Leclercq: *op. cit.* II-199 (note).
2. By "the impious, frenzied tyrant" (Nero): Statius: *Silvae*, II–VII–100 (Statius tr. by J. H. Mozley (L.C.L.), London, 1928).

studies, it follows that he must have frequented the Ulpiana in the years before he returned to Boeotia. He must have used the Alexandriana when he was in Alexandria, as well as the libraries in Athens and other Greek cities. He bravely used the works of other men and quotes from some 250 writers, one third of whose works are among the lost books of the world.

When he wrote the *Lives*, it would appear that the story of the burning of the library or of books in Alexandria, under Caesar had gone the rounds of some of the writers.

How valuable it would be if we could definitely learn who first told of the burning or destruction, and when and where. From our present knowledge it was Seneca.

In one breathless chapter (*Caesar* **XLIX**) the inimitable biographer tells the story:

Of Cleopatra's obtaining access to Caesar secreted in the bed-sack, of her captivating the conqueror by her boldness and infinite charm, of the attempted reconciliation of the queen with her young brother Ptolemy, of the feast given by Caesar in celebration, of the discovery by Caesar's barber of the plot against him by Achillas the general and the eunuch Pothinus, the prime minister of Ptolemy, of Caesar's promptness in putting Pothinus to death, as Achillas raised the Alexandrian army in a grievous and dangerous war against the small forces of Caesar; of the three perils of the campaign: first, the shutting off of the Nile water from Caesar's part of the city; second,

> When the enemy tried to cut off his fleet, he was forced to repel the danger by using fire, and this spread from the dockyards and destroyed the great library;

and thirdly, the battle for Pharos, of Caesar's desperate adventure in springing into a small boat from the mole connecting the city with the island of Pharos, the sinking of the boat, his swimming, amidst flying missiles, in the sea, holding aloft papers in one hand, of his escape, of little Ptolemy going over to the enemy, of Caesar marching out of the city against him, his defeat and death, when the indefatigable Roman:

> Leaving Cleopatra on the throne of Egypt (a little later she had a son by him whom the Alexandrians called Caesarion), he set out for Syria.

In this marvelous condensation of narrative there may be some errors and omissions in the sequence of historical events, but the picture is sure, with all the main incidents boldly sketched but few details, particularly in the one item of special importance to us, the supposed burning of the Library.

The true situation was that Caesar could not afford to let the returned ships prepared for Pompey and other Alexandrian vessels fall into the hands of Achillas. He had himself too few men to attempt to man them, so he had them set afire. The wind blew the ships into the docks, where some of the ships were burned, and the fire consumed some of the water-front property. How many buildings on the water-front were burned we do not know. However, the Library was not situated on the water-front, but in the midst of the Museum structures, all built of stone, certainly fireproof for the age, and must certainly have occupied a place removed from the commercial buildings of the harbor-front.

It is true that Plutarch says "and destroyed the great library", and that would infer the library building itself. How much we would like to know his authority for his passing statement.

His latest editor or translator[1] notes:

The destruction of the library can have been only partial.

We venture the belief that the library *building* was not destroyed and that if anything was burned it was an unknown quantity of *books* from the library waiting to be shipped to Rome.

IX.

Lucius Annaeus Florus (fl. 81–96 A.D. and after): *Epitome of Roman History*, derived largely, although not solely, from Livy, has been a much read book throughout the centuries. It has a certain felicitous sweep of narrative, marred by some rhetorical shortcomings and, more unfortunately, by many historical, chronological, and geographical errors.

Now the very MSS. describe this work as an Epitome of Livy. Certainly he makes every use of Livy, and the great work of the Paduan was then completely extant. In describing the Alexan-

1. Bernadotte Perrin: *Plutarch's Lives* (L.C.L.), Vol. VII, p. 560.

drian War and Caesar's danger in being immediately surrounded in the palace by the hostile Egyptian arms and the Alexandrians, Florus says that Caesar resisted his enemies:

> First of all, by setting fire to the neighboring buildings and docks he kept the missiles of his assailants at a distance; then he made a sudden sally and occupied the peninsular of Pharos[1].

Now although we know this to be a poor description of what took place, yet the author mentions the fire, but not a word is said about the burning of the Museum, the Library, or of Books.

X.

Suetonius (70–160 A.D.) in his first of the *Lives of the Caesars*, the Deified Julius, which he published (119 to 120 A.D.), and which he crowds with tales and gossip, wherever possible, mostly scandalous, and who, although he was not an historian and hardly a biographer, yet particularly affected the spectacular or bizarre incidents, says nothing of the burning of the Alexandrian Library, or of the Museum, or of Books. And yet one would easily imagine that Suetonius would, had he known of it, told of Caesar desiring to carry a Library from the Alexandriana in his Egyptian (or Alexandrian) Triumph![2]

XI.

Aulus Gellius (c. 123 to 169 A.D.) wrote, on winter-nights at Athens, the *Noctes Atticae*, a sort of potpourri of comments or notes on history, biography, antiquities, philosophy, grammar, criticism, law, and other topics. He quotes from 275 named authors, Greek and Roman, many of whose works are now lost. At the end of the VIIth Book of his *Attic Nights*, he says:

> At a later time an enormous quantity of books, nearly seven hundred thousand volumes, was either acquired or written (*i.e.* copies from

1. Florus: *Epitome of Roman History*: Book II–XIII (L.C.L.), tr. E. S. Forester, London, 1939.
2. Dr. Paul Graindor in his *La Guerre d'Alexandrie* (p. 53), says that Suetonius, according to Livy, states precisely that 40,000 or more probably 400,000 volumes of the library of the Ptolemies were destroyed. We know of no such statement by Suetonius (See more fully appendix to Ch. XIV, no. 13, Graindor).

other MSS.) in Egypt under the kings known as Ptolemies; but these were all burned during the sack of the city in our first war with Alexandria, not intentionally or by anyone's order, but accidentally by the auxiliary soldiers. (B VII–17.)

Unfortunately for us, he does not give his authorities.

This Chapter 17 is full of inaccurate or very doubtful statements. In the paragraph before the one quoted above, Gellius says that Xerxes, when he took possession of Athens, burned the entire city except the citadel and "removed that whole collection of books" of the Athens Public Library "and carried them off to Persia. Finally, a long time afterwards, King Seleucus, who was surnamed Nicator, had all these books taken back to Athens." We would like this to be true.

Now as to the paragraph on the Alexandrian Library, we know that his military information was incorrect; that Alexandria was not sacked, that all the military measures of Caesar were defensive, and that in no offensive action either on the part of the Alexandrian Army or of Caesar was any attempt made to sack the city. And who indeed were these "auxiliary soldiers" who accidentally burned *all* the 700,000 rolls? Dr. Rolfe, the last editor of the *Nights*[1] hastens to note:

> By no means all of the Alexandrian Library was destroyed at that time, and the losses were made good, at least in part, by Antony in 41 B.C.

XII.

Appian of Alexandria (95–165 A.D.) wrote *The History of the Romans* from Aeneas to 35 B.C., in 24 books, 11 of which have come down nearly complete, along with fragments of some of the other books.

In Book II of *The Civil Wars* (Ch. XIII–90) he described the Alexandrian War. His account is brief, thin in fact, yet he mentions many romantic incidents including the apocryphal journey up "the Nile with 400 ships, exploring the country in company with Cleopatra and generally enjoying himself with her".

1. John C. Rolfe: *The Attic Nights* of Aulus Gellius (L.C.L.), London, 1927, Vol. II, p. 138.

Appian says "various battles took place around the palace and on the neighboring shores". Yet Appian does not mention the burning of the Museum, of the Library, or of the Books. Appian was an Alexandrian; he must have known the facts about a matter so momentous for his native city.

He is supposed to have consulted the Court Journals at Alexandria, most probably in the Alexandrian Library, about 160 A.D. (Praef. 10.)

XIII.

Dion Cassius (born c. A.D. 155 to 164; died c. 235), a Bithynian, son of a Roman senator and probably grandson of "golden mouthed" Dio Chrysostom, wrote (A.D. 200–222 or 229) a *Roman History*, from Aeneas to 229 A.D., on which he labored at least 22 years, longer than the time devoted by Gibbon to his immortal work. Dion wrote in Greek in 80 books of which about one third are extant (Books 34 to 60) mostly, complete, together with many fragments of the others.

Dion modeled his work after Thucydides; he was a rhetorician at heart, and although he claimed to have read everything about his subject (the history of Rome from its foundation to A.D. 229), he appears to have ignored important Latin authorities for his treatment of the Civil Wars, including at least the *Commentaries* of Caesar, and the same treatment seems to have been extended to the histories of Sallust. He was very unfriendly to Caesar. He speaks of Caesar selecting "a safe place" to harangue the Alexandrians, of his being possessed with "a great fear". His account is long, confused, and inaccurate in spots, yet he does say that Achillas led the army against him and that after many battles by day and by night many places were set on fire with the result that the docks and storehouses of grain and also of books, which were said to be of great number and excellence, were burned. (Dion: XLII-38.)

Nothing is said here about the burning of the ships. A long time after, after the death of Achillas, and under Ganymedes, the eunuch, Dion has the Alexandrians attack the Romans, burn some of their ships to the water's-edge and tow others away. Caesar, after watching for his chance, "suddenly sailed into the harbor, burned a large number of vessels and disembarking on Pharos, slew the inhabitants of the island"[1].

There is nothing here said about the fire from the ships attaching the docks and water-front buildings and spreading to adjoining structures or installations.

It is curious to note the importance given to Dion on this subject. I quote only from recent advocates of Caesar's burning the Library:

a. S. B. Mon. Kyrillos Macaire:

> Dion Cassius who wrote in the second half of the 2nd century said: The fire, started by order of Julius Caesar, took on proportions and spread to the neighboring buildings, destroying not only the docks, several buildings and provisions of wheat, but also the collections of books, and it is said that these books were numerous and very valuable[2].

b. M. Magdi Bey:

> I begin by establishing that the eminent orator His Blessedness Kyrillos Macaire knew as well as we that the great Library, called the principal, founded by Ptolemy Soter, was burned in the year 48 B.C. by Julius Caesar, who set fire to his fleet in order to rescue it from the revolting Alexandrians. The burned fleet thus spread the fire to the buildings of the Museum and the great Library[3].

c. Dr. Graindor:

> It is true that Dion Cassius speaks only of the burning of "the warehouses of grain and books", but nothing prevents these "warehouses" from designating in particular the part of the library where the books were stored[4].

d. J. Staquet:

There is no believer in the burning of the Library by Caesar to equal Dr. Staquet, whose enthusiasm mounts to eloquence, and whose eloquence permits him to conjure up a conspiracy of silence without parallel in human annals. Dr. Staquet says:

1. Dion: Bk. XLII-40-3 (L.C.L.), Ernest Cary, after H. B. Foster, London, 1916, Vol. IV, p. 177.
2. S. B. Mon. Kyrillos Macaire: *Nouvelle Étude sur le Serapeum*, Bulletin de la Société Khédiviale de Géographie, VIIe série, no. 8, Le Caire, 1911.
3. M. Magdi Bey: *Observations on the Fate of the Alexandrian Library*, Bulletin de la Société Khédiviale de Géographie, VIIe série, no. 10, Le Caire, 1911.
4. Dr. Paul Graindor: *Op. cit.* p. 56.

I hope to convince the reader of the culpability of Cleopatra's lover... One should not have an unlimited confidence in the veracity of the Commentaries... Caesar desired to hide the truth... Without question his sorrow was immense... In writing his memoirs, he must have stopped just before engraving the word burned on his tablets... Could he hope that his silence alone would prevent the diffusion of the truth. No, but he had enough power to prevent its being publicly proclaimed. And he was momentarily successful... Besides, during the Alexandrian war, who were the credible witnesses?... Cleopatra? It is superffuous to consider it. Achillas and Pothinus? One can easily see what fate would have been reserved for them. [Fate had already settled the matter! They were both dead, one killed by order of Arsinoë, the other by order of Caesar!] The scholars of the Museum? They formed an integral part of the court of the Ptolemies... Later, perhaps fifteen years later, after Cleopatra's death, would they venture to prattle? [But did anyone prattle?] Ninety per cent of the Roman soldiers were illiterate... The population of Alexandria was just as ignorant... One recalls an event which, at the time, raised the indignation of the entire world, I mean the burning of the Library of Louvain. And nevertheless? How many Belgian citizens would be able still to cite the name of the incendiary? [Query: How many Belgian citizens to-day would be so ignorant as not to know that the Library of Louvain was burned by the Germans? Could one citizen of Louvain be found so dense?] However a day came when the tongues loosened. Titus Livius, still a partisan of Pompey, spoke. The greater part of his work is lost. [*When* did Livy speak, if he spoke at all? Certainly not much sooner than about fifty years after the supposed event (see note on Livy[1]); and *what* did he say? Seneca, the first and only authority, writing ninety years afterwards, says: "Forty thousand books were burned at Alexandria", and then Seneca adds: "Let someone else praise this library as the most noble monument to the wealth of kings, as did Titus Livius, who says that it was the most distinguished achievement of the good taste and solicitude of kings". Now this is all that we can possibly *know* as to what was said by Livy. To imagine that he said that

1. Livy (59 B.C.–17 A.D.) began his immense work about 27 B.C. It was in 142 books. If he worked to the end, he would have written a little over 3 books a year. The Bk. CXII would certainly fall after the first year A. D. It is worthy of note that none of the abridgments, *Epitomes* or the so-called Periochae, or the numerous writers who copied him, ever mention that Livy said that Caesar destroyed the great Alexandrian Library. And, remember that Livy was an admirer of the Republic, a Pompeian as well as a great historian without fear, who would have recorded the destruction of the Library if it had taken place.

Julius Caesar burned the great Alexandrian Library in the Alexandrian War is as unscientific as to imagine that Livy said that Caesar during the Alexandrian war burned the docks and warehouses of grain and books, some forty thousand valuable books from the Alexandrian Library which were stored on the harbor-front. Had he said the first, Seneca would have noted it, had he made the second statement, Seneca might not have bothered with its details.] He [Seneca] and Titus Livius before him, speak of the library of the Ptolemies as a thing no longer existing in their time. [We cannot to subscribe this. We know that the Library of the Ptolemies existed long after the death of both Livy and Seneca.] Proceeding from this instant — without the least concern regarding the identity of the sources — the accusations are more or less categorical. The historians who do not declare Caesar guilty of destroying the work of the first Ptolemies are those who rapidly pass over the episodes of the Bellum alexandrinum. I admit that Dion Cassius should be placed apart. According to him, it was not the great Library which was burned, but warehouses of goods and books which were located on the shore of the sea[1].

So much for Dion.

XIV.

Athenaeus (fl. 228 A.D.) of Naucratis, in Egypt, a Greek gentleman, a man of letters, a prodigious reader, who was at least a gourmet, in the third century of our era, without art and with little literary skill, wrote the delightful and important *Deipnosophistae*, the *Sophists at Dinner*, or *The Feast of the Learned*. He probably wrote at Rome after 228 A.D.

As a work illustrative of ancient manners, as a collection of curious facts, names of authors and fragments, which, but for Athenaeus,

1. Yet the learned scholar desperately clings to his thesis. He contends that this passage of Dion Cassius has at last been ,,corrected" by the Byzantine chronicler Zonaras in the 12th century. Zonaras compiled a book which he himself called *Epitome of History*, in which he drew largely from Josephus and Dion Cassius. Zonaras copied, sometimes literary, much from Dion, and Dr. Staquet says that Zonaras did not believe that warehouses containing grain and books were burned and corrected his source, simply writing instead: "When Caesar set the fleet on fire, the great library burned." We do not choose to argue that any writer, copying from a source a thousand years old, has the authority to "correct" a perfectly clear, unambiguous and reasonable text of the original work. The Byzantine Zonaras could put what he pleased in his own book, he could not "correct" the text of Dion Cassius. J. Staquet: *J. César à Alexandrie. L'incendie de la bibliothèque*, *Nova et Vetera*, XII, 1928 (p. 169).

would utterly have perished; in short, as a body of amusing antiquarian research, it would be difficult to praise *The Deipnosophistae*
too highly[1].

The erudition of Athenaeus, although a little too gastronomical,
covers the widest fields of life and letters. In gathering his mountain of curious lore he must have used the Alexandriana, as well
as the great collections at Rome, including the *Bibliotheca Ulpia*
founded by Trajan, in which were preserved many official records
of inestimable value, including the *libri elephantini* with leaves
made of sheets of ivory on which were recorded the *Senatus
Consulta*, concerning the emperors. In his work, Athenaeus
writes or quotes from over 1200 works of nearly 800 writers. Of
these amazing references, many are known solely through the
pages of Athenaeus. It would seem most unreasonable to assume
that Athenaeus, a Greek of Egyptian birth, who knew Alexandria,
its Museum and great Library intimately, should not have known
of the destruction of the Library during Caesar's visit. His silence
is formidable against a belief in the legend.

XV.

Ammianus Marcellinus (c. 330 A.D. to end of IVth Century) was
born at Antioch and was member of the imperial bodyguard. At
the close of his life he retired to Rome and wrote in Latin a
Roman History (from A.D. 353–378) in 31 books, of which the
first 13 are lost. This *History* was a continuation of the history
of Tacitus.

Ammianus was a man of high character, a loyal Roman and a
philosophical historian, whom Gibbon called his "accurate and
faithful guide, who has composed the history of his own times
without indulging the prejudices and passions which usually
affect the mind of a contemporary".

In Book XXII (Ch. XVI–12) he describes the lofty temple of
Serapis, with its splendid pillared halls and beautiful statues,
"that next to the Capitol, of which the ever-venerable Rome
boasts, the whole world has nothing worthier of admiration".
And then he immediately writes:

1. G. E. L. Cotton: in Smith's *Dictionary* (s.v. *Athenaeus*), Boston, 1867.

In it were libraries of inestimable value; and the current testimony of ancient records affirms that 70,000 volumes, which had been collected by the anxious care of the Ptolemies were burnt in the Alexandrian war when the city was sacked in the time of Caesar the Dictator[1].

This is a prize example of what little attention was paid to the history of the Alexandrian Library by the ancient writers. So honest a man as Ammianus appears to tell us that in the Serapeum there were inestimable libraries carefully gathered by the Ptolemies and that in the time of Caesar 70,000 volumes were burned.

Now we know that there was a most valuable library (the "Daughter" Library) attached to the Serapeum, and we certainly know that whatever took place as a result of the burning of the ships by Caesar in the great harbor the fire never extended to Rhakotis, the distant Egyptian quarter to the west of the great Greco-Macedonian city, and that the temple of Serapis was situated on an acropolis in this Rhakotis or Egyptian quarter of Alexandria.

If, however, there is a desire to divide the paragraph and make it set forth two distinct statements, we then have:

1. The statement of the fine collections of the Serapeum, which we should assume to be correct; and
2. the statement that in Caesar's time, when he *sacked* Alexandria, 70,000 volumes were burned.

There is no inference that the great ("Mother") Library, the Alexandriana connected with the Museum, in the Greek (Brucheion) quarter was burned, but that 70,000 *books* were destroyed. Indeed there is no apparent knowledge on the part of Ammianus that the Alexandrian Library ever existed.

It may be unnecessary to add that Caesar did not sack Alexandria and that the great city of stone and marble relatively suffered little material damage by the incident of his visit.

Indeed, it would appear that Ammianus's 70,000 *books* were but a reasonable exaggeration of Seneca's 40,000. Seneca wrote about 49 A.D., Ammianus about 390 A.D.; the increase is not so unreasonable.

1. Ammianus Marcellinus: *The Roman History*, tr. C. D. Yonge (XXII–XVI–13), London, 1894.

However, we must remember that Ammianus does not say that the Alexandrian *Library* was burned, but the 70,000 *volumes* were destroyed.

XVI.

Orosius (c. 380–some date in 5th cent. A.D.), the Christian historian of Braga, friend of St. Augustine and St. Jerome, who journeyed to the East about 415 A.D., wrote a history of the world (from the Creation to 417 A.D.), *Historiarum adversus paganos libri septem* – the first universal history written from a Christian standpoint.

> According to the historian Orosius (c. 415 A.D.) the flames (from Caesar's fire) spread to the shore, where 40,000 volumes *happened* to be stored up in the adjacent buildings[1].

It was these books, probably stored for shipment to Rome for account of Caesar, that burned, if any were destroyed.

It is most curious to reflect that all this business of the burning of books started with Seneca, the philosopher (49 A.D.), who definitely states that 40,000 *books* were burned; and that the record ends with Orosius (415 A.D.), who likewise speaks of 40,000 *volumes*, and gives further details. By neither Seneca or Orosius is the destruction of the Museum or the Alexandrian Library mentioned.

In following the legend or fact of the burning of the books from the fatal burning of the ships by Caesar (47 B.C.) to the writing of Ammianus of his history (390 A.D.) and Orosius (5th century), we have attempted to examine the extant ancient writings of the times, and have particularly analyzed the 16 writers who might have had some knowledge of the incident.

A final summary is interesting: of the 16 writers, 10, Caesar himself, the author of the *Alexandrian War*, Cicero, Strabo, Livy (as far as we know), Lucan, Florus, Suetonius, Appian, and even Athenaeus apparently knew nothing of the burning of the Museum, of the Library, or of Books during Caesar's visit to Egypt; and 6 tell of the incident as follows:

1. Seneca (49 A.D.), the first writer to mention it (and that

1. Sandys: *op. cit.* p. 112.

nearly 100 years after the alleged event), definitely says that 40,000 *books* were burned.

2. Plutarch (c. 117 A.D.) says that the fire destroyed the great Library.

3. Aulus Gellius (123–169 A.D.) says that during the "sack" of Alexandria 700,000 *volumes* were all burned.

4. Dion Cassius (155–235 A.D.) says that storehouses containing grain and books were burned, and that these books were of great number and excellence.

5. Ammianus (390 A.D.) says that in the "sack" of the city 70,000 *volumes* were burned.

6. Orosius (c. 415 A.D.), the last writer, singularly confirms Seneca as to *number* and the *thing* destroyed: 40,000 *books*.

From these authorities, modern scholars, treating the matter in the same limited, casual, and incidental fashion as had the ancient writers, permitted their extensive histories to carry a few lines on this, to us, important subject.

PRO

1. Gibbon:

> I shall not recapitulate the disasters of the Alexandrian library, the involuntary flame that was kindled by Caesar in his own defense, or the mischievous bigotry of the Christians who studied to destroy the monuments of idolatry[1].

And in a note:

> The *Old* library of the Ptolemies was *totally* consumed in Caesar's Alexandrian war[2].

2. Niebuhr:

Who most picturesquely compares Caesar's situation in Alexandria with that of Cortez in Mexico, and says:

> The insurrection became at last general; the palace was set on fire, and the library, which had been founded under Ptolemy Philadelphus, was burned to ashes[3].

3. Mommsen:

1. Gibbon, ed. Bury: *op. cit.* (Ch. Ll–Vol. IX–184).
2. Idem (Note: Ch. XXVIII–Vol. V–85).
3. B. G. Niebuhr: *The History of Rome*, Vol. V., p. 74.

After describing the ultimate triumph of Caesar in the Alexandrian war in which the foremost man in all this world had fought against the city rabble, Herr Mommsen says:

> Caesar, pointing to their city severely devastated of its granaries, of its worldrenowned library, and of other important public buildings on occasion of the burning of the fleet, exhorted the inhabitants in future earnestly to cultivate the arts of peace alone, and to heal the wounds which they had inflicted on themselves[1].

Of course, Caesar never made such a speech, and one would not believe this reference without turning to the amazing page in Mommsen's history.

4. Samuel Sharpe:

> The fate of the Alexandrian library still requires our attention. The first great library of that name, collected by the Ptolemies and placed in the Museum in the quarter of the city called the Bruchium, was burnt by the soldiers of Julius Caesar[2].

5. Smith's Dictionary:
William Bodham Donne:

> The library of the Museum was destroyed during the blockade of Julius Caesar on the Brucheium[3].

6. George Long:

> Dion Cassius states that the dockyard was burnt, and the corn warehouses and the library which contained a large number of very excellent books. The library was that of the Museum, which was in the Bruchieum. Caesar does not mention the destruction of the library. It was an accident of war. The ships which were fired had been drawn up on the shore and the flames spread to the adjoining houses and the Museum[4].

7. Encyclopaedia Britannica (11th ed.):

> The library attached to the Museum at Alexandria is said to have contained at the time of its destruction in 47 B.C. as many as 700,000 rolls (Aul. Gell., Vol. VII–17–3)[5].

1. Theodor Mommsen: *The History of Rome*, Vol. IV, Pt. II–431, London, 1866.
2. Samuel Sharpe: *The History of Egypt*, Vol. II–378, London, 1885.
3. Smith's *Dictionary of Greek & Roman Geographie* (s.v. *Alexandria*), Vol. I–97, Boston, 1854.
4. George Long: *The Decline of the Roman Republic*, Vol. V–245, London, 1874.
5. E. R. Bevan (s.v. *Hellenism*, Vol. 13–239).

When Caesar set fire to the fleet in the harbor of Alexandria, the flames accidentally extended to the larger library of the Brucheum, and it was destroyed[1].

8. Seyffert's Dictionary:

The best part of the Library of the Museum of Alexandria was burnt down at taking of the town by Caesar[2].

9. Susemihl:

Die grosse Bibliothek brannte schon 47 im Kriege Caesars ab[3].

10. Daremberg and Saglio:

After the fire which started during the battle which Caesar was compelled to wage against the Alexandrians, the conflagration spreading from the flaming area reached the Museum collection which was destroyed at least in great part. Parthey nevertheless, assembling on this point the accounts of several authors, maintains with plausible argument that the palace, remote from the port, was not affected, and that, if the books were destroyed, this was due to the fact that they had been moved previously, perhaps for the purpose of being transported to Rome[4].

11. Dr. Paul Graindor[5]:

Dr. Graindor in his learned *La Guerre d'Alexandrie* treats of the burning of the ships and rallys to the support of those writers who believe that at this time the great Alexandrian Library was destroyed.

His fine scholarship generously admits that the majority of modern historians deny the burning of the great library and consider that the fire was concerned with books temporarily stored in warehouses on the harbor-front, which were going to be transported to Rome or which appertained to the book-trade (p. 54).

1. H. R. Tedder and James Duff Brown (s.v. *Libraries*, Vol. 16–546. But the authors hasten to add a note of Parthey, assigning topographical reasons for doubting this story).
2. Dr. Oskar Seyffert: *A Dictionary of Classical Antiquities*, London, 1906.
3. Susemihl: *Geschichte der gr. Litt. in der Alexandrinerzeit*, Leipzig, 1891, Vol. I, p. 344.
4. M. F. Rabiou, in Ch. Daremberg et Edm. Saglio: *Dictionnaire des Antiquités Grecques et Romaines* (s.v. *Bibliotheca*), Paris, 1877.
5. Dr. Paul Graindor: *La Guerre d'Alexandrie*, Le Caire, 1931.

Now Dr. Graindor says that the majority of modern historians do this "in spite of the formal texts of Plutarch, Suetonius and Aulus Gellius". What are these „textes formels" of these ancient authors?

a. Plutarch, 150 years after the event, is the first author to say that the fire "spread from the dockyards and destroyed the great library". (*Caesar*, XLIX.)

b. Aulus Gellius, nearly 200 years after the event, says:

> At a later time an enormous quantity of books, nearly seven hundred thousand volumes, was either acquired or written (*i.e.* copies from other MSS.) in Egypt under the kings known as Ptolemies; but these were all burned during the sack of the city in our first war with Alexandria, not intentionally or by anyone's order, but accidentally by the auxiliary soldiers. (B. VII-17.)

This statement can hardly be said to be free from error. Caesar never sacked Alexandria and who were the auxiliary soldiers?

Aulus Gellius, however, was not an historian. He was a well-to-do, educated man who wrote for his children a potpourri of famous things he had read or heard in pleasant conversations with his friends. He called the work *Attic Nights*. There are many good quotations in his book, and no one tries to point out his numerous errors. His last editor, Dr. Rolfe, commenting on the very passage about the fire, hastens to note: "By no means all of the Alexandrian Library was destroyed at that time." (See p. 299 of this work.)

c. Suetonius:

Dr. Graindor quotes Suetonius as stating precisely, according to Livy, that 40,000 or more probably 400,000 volumes of the library of the Ptolemies were destroyed (p. 53) and again refers to the formal texts of Suetonius (p. 54), and again the citation by Suetonius (p. 56-57) that the burned books were really those which had been collected by the Ptolemies.

We do not know of these formal texts and citations of Suetonius. The only reference given to Suetonius by Dr. Graindor is a long note (p. 53):

> (6) Suet., *Tranq. an.*, IX, 5 (ed. Hermes): quadraginta [cod. A(mbrosianus): XL. quadringenta (Pincianus)] milia librorum Alexandriae arserunt; pulcherrimum regiae opulentiae monimen-

tum alius laudaverit sicut T. Livius, qui elegantiae regum curaeque egregium id opus ait fuisse [-Liv. fragm. 40 (Hertz)]. D'après les chiffres cités par les autres sources, la lecture quadringenta paraît s'imposer. Elle est due à un humaniste dont les *Castigationes*, parues à Venise, en 1536, reposent sur la tradition manuscrite.

Now the above text is not from Suetonius, but from Seneca's *De Tranquillitate Animi* (IX-5), and it says:

Forty thousand books were burned at Alexandria; let someone else praise this library as the most noble monument to the wealth of kings, as did Titus Livius, who says that it was the most distinguished achievement of the good taste and solicitude of kings.

The above is the translation of Dr. John W. Basore, latest editor of Seneca (L.C.L.), who based his text on the edition of Hermes, Leipzig, 1905.

Now this is the very first text to refer to the burning of books at Alexandria, and that ninety years after the supposed event, and it does not mention Caesar, Ptolemy or The Alexandrian Library. Assuming, for the sake of argument, that Seneca meant that *Caesar* was responsible for the burning of the books, and that Seneca further meant that Livy said Caesar was the cause of the burning of 40,000 books at Alexandria, with all these admissions without evidence, there is still not the slightest word that the great Alexandrian Library in the Brucheion, a part of, or next to the Museum, at that very time having over 700,000 volumes, was destroyed. Forty thousand volumes may have perished in the fire on the docks, where Dion Cassius says that storehouses of grain and books were destroyed. The juggling of *quadraginta* milia (40,000) and *quadringenta* milia (400,000) in the texts of Orosius can be of little help, as Orosius, writing over 400 years after the alleged event, was proverbially unreliable. The bare statement of Plutarch, without details, in the midst of a rapid fire description of many incidents, cannot be taken literally. Gellius who raises the quantity to 700,000 evidences a confusion worthy of Ammianus, when he speaks of Alexandrian affairs. Dion Cassius, who hated Caesar, says explicitly that *storehouses* of grain and books were burned. Suetonius in his life of Caesar says nothing.

Certainly 40,000 valuable volumes should satisfy those who believe in the burning.

One must regret the almost anti-Caesarianism of Dr. Staquet[1] who, admitting that Dion did not say the great Library was burned, but storehouses of grain and books which were located on the seashore, exclaims: "Je crois également qu'il [Caesar] a tout fait pour cacher la vérité!"

CONTRA

For more than a century, many scholars who seem to have given the matter more than passing attention are inclined to the view that the Museum and the Alexandrian Library were not destroyed during Caesar's time.

1. Friedrich Wilhelm Ritschl[2].
2. Parthey[3].
3. Pauly-Wissowa[4]:

From the article on the Alexandrian Library (under *Bibliotheken*) in Pauly-Wissowa, we note the author's complete comments on the burning of the Library in the time of Caesar. It will be noted that the writer first talks of "the burning of the books"; later of "the greater part of this library went up in flames in the year 47, during the war between Caesar and Pompeius, which would mean that the rolls were in the neighborhood of the harbor; we may assume that the books had been moved at this particular time from their usual place"; and finally, "in 47 B.C., the largest part of the collection burned, Caesar intended to transport it to Rome".

At the time of Caesar before the burning of the books Gell. VI-17 and Amn. Marc. XXII-16, 13 deserve more credence with seven hundred thousand rolls than Senec. de tranq. an. 9 and Oros. VI-15, 31 with the number four hundred thousand.

When according to Oros. VI-15–31, the greatest part of this library went up in flames in the year 47, during the war between Caesar and

1. J. Staquet: *J. César à Alexandrie. L'incendie de la bibliothèque, Nova et Vetera*, XII, 1928 (p. 169).
2. F. W. Ritschl: *Die alexandrinischen Bibliotheken*, Breslau, 1838.
3. Parthey: *Alexandrinisches Museum*, 1838.
4. Pauly-Wissowa: *Real-Encyclopädie* (s.v. *Alexandrinische Bibliotheken*, by Dziatzko (Vol. III-1, 409–414), Stuttgart, 1897.

Pompeius, which would mean that the rolls were in the neighborhood of the harbor, we may assume that the books had been
moved at this particular time from their usual place (compare for
this Oros. Quadringenta milia librorum proximis forte aedibus
condita exussit), probably for the purpose of shipping them to
Rome (Parthey 32f).

This opinion is supported in Auct. b. Alex. (incendio fere tuta est
Alexandria, quod sine contignatione ac materia sunt aedificia
et structures ac fornicibus continentur tectaque sunt rudere aut
pavimentis) which, could not have been said by the author if the
books had burned at that time within their own building. Plutarch
Caes. 49 does tell of the fire spreading to the library and Cassius
Dio XLII-38 probably refers to the library building itself (as LIII-1;
s.o. Bd. II, S. 184), but those may be erroneous deductions from
the knowledge that together with the νεώριον also books have
burned.

In 47 B.C., the largest part of the collection burned. Caesar
intended to transport it to Rome not so much to show the
people the completely new spectacle of a captured library in the
triumph (Parthey 32) but rather in fine understanding of the
importance of such basic literary collections.

That Dziatzko did not believe that the library building proper
burned, that is the great Alexandriana, next to the Museum,
which itself was a part of the Palaces, situated in the heart of the
Brucheion, is shown by his constant references to "the burning
of *books*", to "*part* of this library" where rolls were in "the neighborhood of the harbor", and that "the largest part of the collection burned", which "Caesar intended to transport to Rome".

And further in his article as to the location of the library, he
says:

The library did not lie near the harbor, as Strabo (XVII–794)
described the buildings in that neighborhood without mentioning
either the library or museum.

And further:

Excavations of more recent times (Neroutsos-Bey: *L'anc. Alexandrie*,
Paris, 1888, Ch. 2, p. 7) give good reason for the belief that the
Museum was located just about in the middle of the new part of
town, in the Western half of the city.

And it is reasonably certain that the Library was attached to or adjoined the Museum.

4. Charles Merivale:
In a note, he says:

> The conflagration reached the shore and consumed a large portion of the celebrated library of the Ptolemies. Seneca asserts that *four hundred thousand* volumes perished (De Tranquill. 9). Comp. Dion XLII-38[1].

5. James Anthony Froude:
Mr. Froude, who seems quite embarrassed about the whole Alexandrian incident, with his hero associating with a "loose girl", just omits to talk about the unfortunate library incident[2].

6. George Melville Bolling:

> In 47 B.C. Caesar was compelled to set fire to his fleet to prevent it falling into the hands of the Egyptians. The fire spread to the docks and the naval arsenal, and destroyed 400,000 (sic) rolls. It is most probably from the statement of the author of the Bellum Alexandrinum, that Alexandria was built in such a way as to be safe from a great conflagration[3].

(Here again we have the 400,000 instead of the 40,000 volumes. See our discussion under Merivale.) Of course, Caesar did not

1. Charles Merivale: *History of the Romans under the Empire*, 5th ed., London, 1864 (Vol. II, p. 326, note). But Seneca, we believe, did not say that 400,000 (quadringenta milia) volumes were burned, but 40,000 (quadraginta milia) volumes were burned at Alexandria. The difference between *quadringenta* (400) and quadraginta (40) will explain the use of the words "a large portion of the celebrated library" by Merivale and "the greatest part of the library" used by Dziatzko (referring to Orosius) in the classic Pauly-Wissowa.
I have followed the L.C.L. ed. of Seneca (London, 1932, Vol. II, p. 246), ed. by John W. Basore, who followed the text of Hermes, Leipzig, 1905, and which had long previously had the benediction of Sir John Sandys (*His. Clas. Scholarship*, 3rd ed., London, 1921, p. 113), who notes that *both* Orosius and Seneca say quadraginta. See Sandys (*op. cit.* pp. 112 and 113, notes).
The amount of 40,000 is reasonable and explains much. Caesar could hardly in so short a time, even with the avidity of a bookman, have taken 400,000. Certainly 40,000 would have made a goodly show in his triumphal procession, and it would certainly form the foundation for a great, new library at Rome. And the argument might be extended.
2. J. A. Froude: *Caesar, A Sketch* (London, 1896).
3. George Melville Bolling in *The Catholic Encyclopedia*, New York (s.v. *Alexandrian Library*).

set fire to *his* fleet, but to *their* (the Alexandrians', the enemy's) fleet.

7. J. B. Bury:

In his edition of Gibbon[1]:

This Library (the great Library of the Brucheum) is said to have been burnt down when Caesar was in Alexandria (but see Mahaffy, *Egypt under the Ptolemies*, p. 454)[2].

8. J. P. Mahaffy:

Had these (the ships equipped for Pompey) passed into Alexandrian (i.e. Achillas's) hands, Caesar was blockaded by sea and land, and probably lost. In this extremity Caesar was obliged to set fire to the ships, and with it the naval arsenal was burnt. A far greater disaster is said to have ensued. The famous Library, situated close to the dockyards, took fire and was burnt. As Caesar only urges the necessity of his action, and its success as regards the ships, we cannot tell the amount of the collateral loss. But possibly his silence implies that the worst had happened. If he had set his soldiers to save what they could from the flames, it is more than likely that he would have said a word on the subject. On the other hand, his silence is no satisfactory denial of what is recorded by several other credible authorities. *Still I am disposed to consider the whole story a fabrication.*

9. Sir Paul Harvey:

In 47 B.C. when Caesar was in Alexandria, some 40,000 volumes which were stored near the Arsenal, perhaps with a view to their shipment to Rome, were accidentally burned. It is improbable that the library itself was destroyed[3].

1. Bury's *Gibbon* (note 3 Appendix, for Ch. 37 of Gibbon).
2. Mahaffy's work is *The Empire of the Ptolemies*, p.454, London, 1895. The italics are ours. It is proper to note that within a very short while Mahaffy wrote another work: *A History of Egypt under the Ptolemaic Dynasty*, London, 1898, p. 242, where, after a short account of the Alexandrian War, he says:
Meanwhile Caesar was obliged to burn the fleet in the harbour, which he could not man, or even save from the enemy; and in the conflagration a great quantity of books (papyrus rolls) in stores beside the quay was destroyed. This accident of the seige produced no impression whatever on contemporaries, even such as Cicero, whose correspondence of those years are extant. Strabo, who saw Alexandria in the next generation, and who gives us a general description, says not a word on the subject. By and by, in Seneca's day, people had come to believe that the great library had been burned. The general silence of contemporaries is to my mind conclusive against the occurrence of so terrible a catatrophe to letters.
3. Sir Paul Harvey: *The Oxford Companion to Classical Literature* (s.v. *Alexandrian Library*), Oxford, 1940.

10. Jones (editor of Strabo).

11. Rolfe (editor of Gellius).

12. Perrin (editor of Plutarch's Lives) in the Loeb Classical Library.

All hold the same view that the Library was not destroyed.

13. Will Durant:

> When Caesar saw that the fleet would soon fall into the hands of his enemies, he ordered it burned; in the fire an uncertain portion of the Alexandrian Library was consumed[1].

14. John William White:

It is proper that we should pause before stating our conclusion on this somewhat vexed problem, to give a summary of Dr. White's lucid description of the supposed incident, his rapid, almost advocate's marshalling of the authorities, and his ingenious, if not unique, conclusion.

This is a summary of his conclusions:

Were some of the original accumulations of books of the Alexandrian Library or the great Library totally destroyed when Caesar in 47 B.C. (as is commonly admitted) was put to the necessity of burning the ships in the harbor?

Caesar himself says nothing. Caesar was library-minded, he was a man of letters; his silence would seem incredible if he had been the cause, however innocent, of so irreparable a loss.

Plutarch's brief account agrees with Caesar's, but he adds that the Library was destroyed.

Cassius Dion says the "repository of the books was burnt".

Gellius, writing at the end of the second century, states in positive terms that the fire was accidentally kindled, and he gives the number of the volumes both in the great Library and in the Serapeum and says that they were *all* burnt, but we know that the library of the Serapeum was not affected. Gellius discredits his own statements.

Ammianus Marcellinus, two centuries later, is even less creditable; he says both libraries were burnt, but his knowledge of them is so vague and untrustworthy that he places them both in the Serapeum.

Seneca (the first of our authorities) does not mention Caesar

---

1. Will Durant: *Caesar and Christ*, New York, 1944 (p. 187).

and says that 40,000 books were burned. This number of books
that Seneca here says were burnt is far below that mentioned
by any other authority and, what is more important, far below
that which we know the great Library must have contained at
this time. Seneca was in error; he was thinking of his contempt
for many books, and this amount would have seemed to him a
generous amount for a library.

Orosius (5th cent. A.D.) introduces new and significant
details. Parthey concluded from his words that Caesar had had
the books removed from the library, and brought provisionally to
buildings (on the dock?) in which they were burnt, with the
intention, perhaps, of carrying them to Rome and exhibiting
them in his triumph.

Caesar, we know, had public libraries in mind and had called
Varro to his aid. But Alexandria was then seething with the
hostility to Caesar, whose force was small, and Pompey's party
still had a powerful fleet afloat. It would have been extremely
difficult, if not impossible, in times so troubled as these, either to
transfer 400,000 papyrus rolls from the Library to the dock or to
transport them so great a distance across the sea. The most recent
advocate of this view silently adopts the reading *quadraginta
milia* (40,000) in the clause quoted from Orosius, quadringenta
milia (400,000). This reading is against the best tradition of
Orosius's text. Besides, Orosius has no standing as a historian,
and Casaubon declared that no dependence could be placed
on his statement unless corroborated by some other trustworthy
writer.

As to the exact location of the Library, we are perplexed by
our ignorance. Strabo states that the Museum was in the royal
quarter of the town where the palaces of the kings were situated.
Scholars agree that the Museum and the Library were near one
another. Dion implies that the fire spread to the north-east along
the shore of the Great Harbor and then to the Library, but neither
Library nor Museum can have been on the shore, for Strabo gives
an enumeration of all structures along the shore from the promontory of Lochias to the Heptastadium and mentions neither of
them. We reach the conclusion that the Museum and Library
were somewhere in the northern part of the city not far from
the shore of the Great Harbor.

Now the total destruction of the Library would imply a general conflagration at this time in this part of the city, but this supposition is excluded by Caesar's statement, by that of the author of *The Alexandrian War* (that the town was built of stone and marble, without wood and practically fireproof.) These contemporary accounts are confirmed by Strabo who came to Alexandria 23 years later and gives the only complete description of the city that is still extant. *The Museum was then intact.*

These various considerations justify the conclusion that Plutarch's and Dion's statement that the Library was "destroyed" or "burnt" should not be interpreted literally.

Caesar's silence would seem incredible. Cicero, who studied at Athens and Rhodes and knew the East, would have felt the loss deeply, but there is no mention of it in his voluminous writings.

Strabo's silence also is intelligible on the assumption that the Library may have been seriously damaged, but had not burned down and had been repaired.

And so, the Library was in the track of the fire, but presumably at its limits; it must have been a large building, covering a great area, if it housed 500,000 or 600,000 papyrus rolls and contained workrooms for students and staff; the damage done to the building may have been great and the loss of books serious, but it is improbable that both building and books were destroyed[1].

15. Sir John Edwin Sandys:

At this long last, after careful consideration of all the authorities ancient and modern, we are constrained to believe that the story of the burning of the Alexandrian Library is either a myth or legend as Mahaffy believed, growing out of the remark of Seneca, or at most a partial loss as best set forth by Sandys:

> In 47 B.C., shortly after the death of Pompey, the conflicts between the Roman soldiers and the Egyptians in the streets of the city compelled Caesar to set the royal fleet on fire to prevent its falling into the hands of the Egyptians. The naval arsenal was burnt. According to the historian Orosius (c. 415 A.D.), the flames spread to the shore, where 40,000 volumes happened to be stored up in the

1. J. W. White: *The Scholia on the Aves of Aristophanes*, Boston, 1914 (pp. XXXI to XXXVI).

adjacent buildings. The phrase used by Orosius has led to the conjecture that these volumes, having been removed by Caesar from the Library, were temporarily stacked in certain buildings near the harbor with a view to their being shipped to Rome as part of the spoils of conquest; and that the burning of these books led to the legend of the burning of the Library. It is not at all probable that the Library itself was at this time consumed by fire. The author of the *Bellum Alexandrinum* expressly states that, as even the private houses of the citizens, including the very floors and roofs, were built entirely of stone, Alexandria was in general safe from the risk of a conflagration. Writing about 80 A.D., Plutarch in his *Life of Caesar* implies that the flames spread from the fleet to the docks and from the docks to the Library; and early in the 3rd century, Dio Cassius describes the arsenal and the stores of corn and of books as having perished in the flames; but these accounts seem less probable than the suggestion that it was not the Library itself, but only those of the books which had been transferred to buildings near the harbor, that suffered destruction[1].

16. Edwyn Bevan:
It would be unjust to omit Mr. Bevan's concise statement:

It was on this occasion that some warehouses near the Harbour, containing corn and papyrus rolls (books probably prepared in Alexandria for export), caught fire, and a large number of precious volumes – 40,000, Livy says – were destroyed. This probably gave rise to the legend, current a few generations later, that the great Alexandrian Library had been burnt[2].

1. Sir John Edwin Sandys: *A History of Classical Scholarship*, Cambridge, 1921 (p. 112).
2. Bevan: *A History of Egypt under the Ptolemaic Dynasty* (London, 1927), p. 364. Also Arthur Weigall in his well known work: *The Life and Times of Cleopatra*, new & rev. ed., New York, 1926 (p. 108) says:
In this conflagration some of the buildings on the quay near the harbour appear to have been burnt, and it would seem that some portion of the famous Alexandrian library was destroyed; but the silence of contemporary writers upon this literary catastrophe indicated that the loss was not great, and, to my mind, puts out of account the statement of later authors that the burning of the entire library occurred on that occasion.

CHAPTER XV

MINOR IMPERIAL DEPREDATIONS
TRAJAN (98–117 A.D.)

FROM the early days of the city the Jews had formed a substantial part of the population of Alexandria. They had their own quarter that was almost a Jewish city, their own ethnarch and minor officials. They spoke Greek and had translated their Holy Scriptures into Alexandrian Greek in order that their children, generations of Alexandrian-born Jews, might follow their venerable worship of God. They were probably difficult to get along with as were the average Macedonian-Greeks of Alexandria, yet they did live side by side to each other in relative peace. But since the dreadful catastrophe of the Jewish War, the destruction of Jerusalem, the utter desecration of the Temple of the Lord, the massacres and enslavement of their people and dispersion of their race to the three quarters of the world, it was most natural that of those who escaped from Palestine, many came to Alexandria. Many of these were zealots within whose hearts burned the deathful fires of hatred for their conqueror and of hope for revenge against their Roman masters. These Jews who had so greatly suffered aroused their more conservative brethren, who had enjoyed for years the Roman peace, to strike down the oppressor of their people, and finally, in the closing days of Trajan's life, the Jews of the East revolted. Unfortunately, the fanatical element carried the day, and the Jews of Alexandria plunged into the hopeless struggle. They had certain early successful encounters; the Roman prefect seems to have been shut up within the city wall (i.e. probably those of the Greek quarter), and although many were killed on both sides and the historic shrine dedicated to the murdered Pompey was destroyed, the troops of Trajan came to the rescue and, as was inevitable, the rebellion was completely suppressed.

Though the loss of life and attendant suffering were considerable, no monument, except the funeral chapel of Pompey, was destroyed.

Thus the first of the minor imperial depredations, with which the frivolous Alexandrians cannot be charged, left the Museum and the Library apparently untouched.

CARACALLA

The son of Septimius Severus, an African, and Julia Domna, a Syrian lady, Marcus Aurelian Antoninus – Caracalla, as he is known in history –, dishonorer of his father and mother, fratricide, murderer of Papinian, the great jurisconsult, and thousands of helpless and innocent men and women, one of those incredibly savage beasts that stalk through the pages of history, particularly in the records of the Roman empire, succeeded his father, who died at York, England, February 4, 211 A.D. He soon treacherously murdered his brother Geta and reigned alone for some six hectic, erinnyes-driven years, when he was murdered (217 A.D.) under most ordinary circumstances.

Lavish bribes to the army gave him a few years of infamous life; his pride was assuaged by the building in unparalleled magnificence of the Thermae Antoninianae (the Baths of Caracalla) with its architectural and engineering wonders and the wealth of its marble statues and objects of art. But his restless, evil spirit urged him to leave the capital, where the wraith of his brother and some 20,000 hapless victims of his blood-lust met him at every turn. He journeyed through the provinces, through Thrace and Lesser Asia, crowning his career of horror with the massacre of the citizens of Alexandria and the pillage of their city.

All the world knew that he had murdered his brother; scandal, we hope in gross exaggeration, reported that he wanted to marry his mother. In lighter vein, he was known to dress like Achilles, and to affect great admiration for Alexander, though his physical height was much below the two heroes; he had introduced a Greek phalanx in the army, and all of these eccentricities had travelled before him to the East. He announced he would visit the tomb of his beloved Alexander and worship at the shrine of the great god Serapis.

The Alexandrians were notoriously a people of free speech, and reckless follies and wildest tumults were not uncommon on many occasions. They had the keenest sense of humor, and their outbursts of witticism often reached the heights of bitterest satire with which they amused themselves in the theatre as well as in the streets and public places. Their jests had reached the black-hearted prince that ruled the Roman world and he meditated and planned his dark revenge.

The thoughtless people hailed his coming with great preparation and joy. The Emperor entered at night, between a procession of torches[1], to the soft sound of pipes and the clash of cymbals; the air was freshened with the odor of incense, the way strewn with flowers, and the grateful populace acclaimed their Prince in joyous shouts of welcome. They furnished him with hecatombs for sacrifice. He visited the Soma of Alexander, on whose tomb he reverently deposited his scarlet robe and personal precious jewels. Then he left for the Serapeum and he ordered all the youth of the city to form in military array according to their age and size, as he proposed to form an Alexandrian phalanx. He went through their ranks praising their athletic perfection as they assembled on the plain naked and unarmed. He slipped away to give the fatal signal to his troops, that had been, unnoticed, gradually approaching the array of the devoted Alexandrian youth. On the sudden order of this imperial fiend, his troops rushed upon the naked and defenseless Alexandrian youth and slew them mercilessly, as the ditches of the Nile ran blood into its muddy channels.

In the Temple of Serapis, he stood watching his handiwork, and then he dedicated to the god the sword with which he had murdered his brother Geta[2]. His soldiers plundered the hapless population of their movable property. He built a wall lined with forts, fully garrisoned, dividing the royal quarter from the rest of the city, and he ordered that Alexandria should be broken up into villages. Apparently there was no fire, and the substantial building of the city again saved Alexandria as probably it did in Caesar's time.

The houses of the citizens and the merchants' shops were looted, but we have no reason to believe the Alexandrian Library greatly suffered during this direful visitation.

Spartianus[3], the biographer, calls him "the most cruel of

1. One thinks of the description of the novelist Achilles Tatius (see Ch. V, p. 61, of this work).
2. Herodian (IV); Dion (LXXVII).
3. Aelius Spartianus, in *The Life of Antoninus Caracalla, Historiae Augustae*, Vol. II, p. 29 (L.C.L.), London, 1924.

men", and Gibbon: "But Caracalla was the common enemy of mankind."[1]

Nothing illustrates the resilience, the recuperative power of the Museum and the great Library better than this dreadful visitation of the beast Caracalla. Although officials and members of the Museum were cruelly treated, the Museum deprived of its revenues and the fellows of their allowances, and foreign members expelled, it was but a short time when, as Dr. Bidez so well remarks in his delightful chapter:

> After this first alarm the reading-rooms of the city libraries [The Alexandriana and its branch at the Serapeum] recovered sufficient quiet for the Egyptian Athenaeus of Naucratis to be able to devote his leisure to the scrutiny of more than 1500 works and to draw from them the material for the essays in his *Deipnosophistae* in fifteen books.

We to-day can find entertainment in the diverse episodes in the literary life of the past of which Athenaeus's compilation enables us to form a picture[2].

GALLIENUS

The people of Alexandria were ever their worst enemies. Basically a Greek-Macedonian stock with infiltrations of many peoples from the Hellenic East and some from the Roman West, a cosmopolitan population uncontrolled and uncontrollable, they brought down upon their devoted city most of its disasters and ultimately its final ruin.

Whatever their composition, the Alexandrians in the ancient world, like the Parisians in the modern ages, were a type *sui generis*. Industrious, clever, brilliant in crafts, in commerce and in the arts and sciences; argumentative and controversial beyond all other men in matters of the intellect, particularly in philosophy and theology; children of faction, zealots of division, at least in politics, they attained to a refinement of almost atomic disunion. Possesssing all social graces, they were a joyous, light, intellectual people with almost a fatal gift of humor. The dark side of the

1. Gibbon: Ch. VI (1–174; Bury).
2. J. Bidez: *Literature and Philosophy in the Eastern Half of the Empire* (in *C.A.H.*, Vol. XII, p. 620).

picture is that their proneness to faction let their personal
quarrelsomeness and their keen wit sink to ribaldry and unforgiv-
able irony.

And so this people, who but fifty years before (211 A.D.) had
paid so dreadful a price for their love of ridicule, under the
insensate Caracalla, now in the reign of Gallienus (265 A.D.)
seem again to have provoked their evil destiny.

It would be easy to attempt a portrait of the son of Valerian,
who will never be forgiven for having abandoned his father and
emperor to the ignominious servitude of Sapur the Persian. The
pages of Trebellius Pollio in his *Lives of the Two Gallieni* in the
Augustan History, though not without prejudice, afford ample
material.

Only pedantry however would fail to simply quote Gibbon:

> It is difficult to paint the light, the various, the inconstant character
> of Gallienus, which he displayed without constraint as soon as he
> became the sole possessor of the empire. In every art that he attempted
> his lively genius enabled him to succeed; and, as his genius was
> destitute of judgment, he attempted every art, except the important
> ones of war and government. He was a master of several curious
> but useless sciences, a ready orator, an elegant poet, a skillful
> gardener, an excellent cook, and most contemptible prince.
>
> (Ch. X .[1])

Now in the reign of Gallienus, in restless Alexandria a petty
quarrel between a slave and a soldier, as to the relative merits
of a pair of shoes, led to the usual riot. As a result, L. Mussius
Aemilianus, a Roman prefect of Egypt, was constrained to assume the imperial power. As far as we know, he was an able
soldier who had held the frontiers of Egypt for the empire as far
as beyond Thebes in Upper Egypt. Seizing the vast granaries of
Egypt, he threatened the corn supply of Rome and the empire,
and held for a while a great power.

Gallienus is reported by his enemies to have said when he
heard of another usurpation: "What! We cannot do without
Egyptian linen." However, he sent his general Theodotus against
the rebels and Aemilianus was besieged in the Royal quarter of
Alexandria. The conflict must have been severe, as Eusebius tells[2]

1. In spite of some modern attempts at rehabilitation, this is still the best portrait.
2. Eusebius: *The Ecclesiastical History* (Vol. II–VII, 21 and 32), L.C.L., London, 1938.

how many lives were saved from starvation in the siege by the help of the Christian presbyters. But Aemilianus was defeated, taken prisoner and, like Vercingetorix and Jugurtha, strangled.

The siege had been severe; much property must have been destroyed, and the city must have suffered much, according to the testimony of Dionysius, after St. Cyprian the most eminent Christian bishop of the third century. He was bishop of Alexandria (247–264/5), and returning to his charge in 261/2 A.D., he beheld the chaos left by the siege of the city by Theodotus against the imperial pretender Aemilianus. He declared that the great street, which separated the Brucheion (i.e. the one which we assume ran from the Sun Gate on Lake Mareotis to the Moon Gate on the Harbor or at the Heptastadium) from the western part of the city, was so impassable with rubble and debris that it was "harder to traverse and more impassable than the great and trackless desert through which Israel journeyed for two generations". And then he described the dreadful visitation of the plague, after War and Famine and the usual other Horsemen of the Apocalypse, which struck about 250 A.D., Alexandria being one of the first inflicted:

> The air made foul by vile exhalations, the dews discharged from corpses rotting in all their constituent elements; the dread and fears of the people, the bodies cast in the roads half-dead; corpses unburied for fear of contagion.

In his narrative of the horrors of pestilence, the bishop almost takes a place with the classic descriptions of Thucydides, Boccaccio, Orosius, and Defoe.

Yet with it all, no one, pagan or Christian, deigned to speak of the Museum or the Library. It is true that they do not mention the palaces of which we feel sure they would have spoken, had they been destroyed.

In the absence of a single reference, we may assume that the Museum-Library was probably not fatally affected.

CHAPTER XVI

MAJOR IMPERIAL DEPREDATIONS
ZENOBIA

I N the midst of the Syrian desert, from time immemorial, an oasis rich in palms and the waters of cool fountains arrested the weary caravans laden with the rare spices, silks and jewels of the East, as they journeyed from the Persian gulf to the great cities of western Asia and the capitals of the Mediterranean littoral. The origin of its name is obscure: Tadmur may suggest an Assyrian or Arabian source, as Palmyra, its name in fame, exhibits a union of Greek and Latin. Early it became the abode of enterprising desert chiefs who attended to the needs of the passing caravans; soon through the allurement of trade and wealth, the heads of great families became princely merchants, who not only dealt with the caravan masters as their equals, but who themselves launched great trains of transportation. With opulence the city grew in population and estate, with marble temples to the sun, its most natural deity, with fine boulevards, great storehouses for goods, and rich palaces, indeed the very metropolis of the sands, occupying its pleasant site of abundant waters and delightful shade, surrounded, as by a wall, by the burning waste of the desert, and fortunately protected by great distances from interfering neighbors.

From the rich trade pouring in from Cathay and Ind, and the successful merchants returning with the wealth of the West, Palmyra reaped her full share. Her people were prosperous, her great nobles dwelt amid oriental luxury, tempered by the dignity and refinements of Greek manners and learning. Her yeomanry furnished an ample force of skillful and formidable archers and the famed ancestral horsemanship of her chiefest people readily supplied a cavalry force noted for its splendid accoutrement, famous mounts, and the dexterity of their riders. These forces sufficed for the protection of the city, its fame, and wealth. Thus, the city-state possessed all things necessary to its own well-being. It did not possess political aggrandizement and fame. It had beheld the armies of Assyria, Persia, and the eastern empires pass to great victories and to utter defeats. It had beheld the armies of imperial Rome come and go; it had played an important role with these armies. Thus, the Palmyrenes felt that they could do great things themselves. The temptation to military glory caused them to ignore their experience and overpowered their better judgment.

The time was indeed ripe for such error. The Persian monarchy was erratic and had lost its awful power. The empire of Rome, throughout its civilized domain, was the constant theatre for pretenders to the imperial dignity. In the period of twenty-four years, at least thirty persons sought to be emperor. The world was in tumult.

In these times, Odenathus[1], scion of one of the great families, was Prince of Palmyra. He was not only a distinguished noble, a man of lineage and wealth, but a brilliant soldier, and on the perilous waters of political greatness in which he had embarked, he was a statesman and ruler of renown. With his own archers and cavalry and the remnants of Roman army corps, he attacked and defeated Shapur at the gates of Ctesiphon. He restored Roman prestige in the East. He, himself, obtained great fame. Rome bestowed upon him every possible honor, short of making him emperor. He most probably almost touched the imperial diadem. However, he never broke with Rome. In a short time, at the pinnacle of his fame, he was foully murdered, together with his son, by his nephew (or cousin). No figure in the East, in any way connected with Rome, within the orbit of his short career, presents such a character of distinction, ability, nay true greatness, as that of the mighty sheik[2] of the East, the Prince of Palmyra.

Odenathus married Zenobia, one of the greatest women in history. Indeed her fame, unfortunately, has dimmed the splendor of his career. She was a patrician, who did not need the claim of descent from Cleopatra. Like the last of the Ptolemies, she was of singular beauty, although her skin was slightly brown, either from desert descent or from her custom to ride as well as march in the van of her armies in the flaming lands of Helios.

1. We use his western appellation as more suited to our eye and ear.
2. The title, too humble for his greatness, was, I believe, given by A. Alföldi (*C.A.H.*).

328   THE DESTRUCTION OF THE LIBRARY

Like the last of the Ptolemies, she was a woman of courage, rare quality of mind, whose cultural attainments included the useful knowledge of the Latin, and a mastery of the Greek, Arabic, and Egyptian languages. Unlike the last of the Ptolemies, she was a woman of highest character. Her virtue was equalled only by her ambition and fitness for rule. With almost masculine energy, she followed the hardy pleasures of the chase and the exacting hardships of war. On foot, on horse, in the field or in council, she was ever the distinguished sovereign earning the love of her people, the respect of her neighbors and allies, and the dread of her enemies. For Odenathus she was his active partner in all of his enterprises, and when he was murdered, she promptly avenged his death[1] and took over the government of "their" empire with masculine ability and strength. Indeed, in the short period of their amazing careers, they had through the genius of arms and diplomacy gathered an empire in the East containing rich cities and provinces from Bithynia in the north-west to Mesopotamia in the east and Egypt in the south.

The complicated skein of happenings in Egypt, in which we are interested, has been attempted to be worked out by the science of numismatics, where the considerable and varied output of imperial and pseudo imperial coinage is used to bolster a dubious and defective literary tradition.

1. Papyri show that by September 260 Macrianus and his son Iuietus were recognized in Alexandria and other parts of Egypt.

2. After the defeat of Macrianus in Illyricum and Iuietus was

---

1. Thebellius Pollio in his *Tyranni Triginta* under his life of *Odaenathus* and his life of *Zenobia* does not report the slightest suspicion that Zenobia had any part in her husband's death. It is true that in his life of *Maeonius* he states that "it is said, however, that previously he had entered into a conspiracy with Zenobia" (XVII). Pollio, moreover, has left his opinion of the Queen and of the wretch Maeonius; of Maeonius, he says: "But Maeonius, too, was a filthy fellow." Of Zenobia, he says: "She was held to be more brave than her husband, being, indeed, the noblest of all the women of the East." But, of course, the sentence of Pollio had been observed by modern historians: Gibbon (Ch. XI, p. 85, note; ed. Bury): "Some very unjust suspicions have been cast on Zenobia, as if she was accessory to her husband's death." Dr. Alföldi, who, as far as I remember, does not even mention Pollio's gossip, does refer to a tradition (Johann. Antioch. frag. 152, 2 (F.H.G. IV-599) that the instigator was the Emperor Gallienus, through Rufinus, governor of Roman Arabia, who considered it a political act in the interest of Rome. (Alföldi, *op. cit.* (*C.A.H.*), XII, p. 176.) Since Gibbon, it would seem to have been ignored by writers. We are aware of a contrary view by the writer in *The Oxford Classical Dictionary*, s.v. *Zenobia*.

killed by Odenathus, the allegiance to Gallienus was resumed by Alexandria.

3. The Alexandrian mob, "like madmen and fools", were led by the most trivial matters, as when the slave of the chief magistrate was killed by a soldier over a dispute as to who had the better sandals, a riot ensuing, and Aemilianus the prefect was forced to assume the purple[1]. Certainly the city split into two factions; there was much fighting and bloot-letting as told by Bishop Dionysius. Aurelius Theodotus put down the revolt for Gallienus, and Aemilianus, according to Pollio, was strangled in the ancient Roman fashion, like were Jugurtha and Vercingetorix.

4. Later a Moorish officer named Memor staged a revolution which was likewise suppressed by Theodotus, who was named prefect of Egypt.

5. Since the suppression of the above revolts, there was much anti-Roman sentiment, which together with the usual turbulent attitude of the Alexandrian populace led to a serious revolution joined by many of the local council. The revolt lasted for years, the rebels being besieged in the Brucheion quarter, where they were reduced to starvation and surrendered in autumn 268 B.C[2].

6. In February 270, Tenagino Probus, prefect of Egypt, returning to Alexandria from quelling a revolt at Carthage, was confronted by the Gothic pirates who were invading the islands of the Aegean, like their kinsmen had done the lands of Dacia. These locust swarms had reached Cyprus, and the danger being imminent, he took to the sea to subject their piratical fleets.

It was during his absence that Zabdas, commanding an army of Zenobia, composed of some 70,000 men, defeated the weak Roman army. Probus hastily returned, repulsed the Palmyrene forces, but was killed through the treachery of the party in Alexandria who were in favor of Palmyra[3]. Here again the attempt was made to treat the conquest of Egypt by Zenobia as a friendly act to Rome: the coins were struck with the portrait of Vaballathus, the son of Zenobia, on one side and the bust of Aurelian on the other; the corn-ships were dispatched to Rome.

1. Pollio: *Tyranni Triginta* (*Aemilianus*, XXII).
2. A. Alföldi: *The Crisis of the Empire* (A.D. 249–270), *C.A.H.* (Vol. XII, p. 161 sq.), Cambridge, 1939.
3. *Ox. Class. Dic.* s.v. *Museum*.

But the famous Queen of the East and the great Roman emperor were fast reaching the dread moment of destiny.

After Odenathus's death Zenobia took the title of Βασίλισσα although she cherished the doubtful title of Queen of the East. Her son was dux Romanorum and Lord of Palmyra. She could have had little respect for those before Aurelian, who daily contended for the empire. She and her husband had preserved, nay, advanced the prestige of Rome in the East and assumed the position of almost equality with the reigning emperors. When Aurelian came to power, it was hard for Zenobia to step down yet there was room for but one on the imperial throne and her pretensions were inconsistent with the solidarity of the empire. Aurelian, with his accustomed promptness and vigor, marched against her. Her forces failed at Chalcedon, Aurelian took Ancyra and Tyana, city of Appolonius the pagan seer, and likewise Antioch and Emesa. He granted the cities fair treatment, employed the desert tribes to supply the army, defeated or bought off the Persian succor, had constant reinforcements from Syria, Palestine and Egypt, and laid siege to the city of Palmyra. Zenobia too was indefatigable in her activities for defense[1]. The city was well supplied with food and weapons of war. Did not Aurelian write a Letter to Rome:

> The Roman people speak with contempt of the war which I am waging against a woman. They are ignorant both of the character and of the power of Zenobia. It is impossible to enumerate her warlike preparations, of stones, of arrows, and of every species of missile weapons. Every part of the walls is provided with two or three balistae and artificial fires are thrown from her mile long engines[2].

Aurelian offered surrender terms which were rejected. However, the siege was becoming critical, foreign aid did not arrive and Zenobia, desperate, left Palmyra on her fleetest dromedary with a small group for the East to seek help. But through treachery or the Roman espionage she was captured at the Euphrates and returned a captive of the emperor. The city surrendered, Zenobia was tried by Aurelian and is reported to have put the blame on

1. The rapid enumeration of points in the campaign are those of Dr. Bury in his appendix V to his edition of Gibbon.
2. Flavius Vopiscus: *The Deified Aurelian*, XXVI – 3. We have not attempted to change the version of Gibbon.

her advisers. The sublime Longinus met his fate as a philosopher and the world of the end of the third century lost the great Hellenic intellect. The city afterward revolted and was destroyed by Aurelian.

Zenobia, although led in Aurelian's Roman triumph, was pardoned, and he assigned to her a villa at Tibur where, after her amazing early career, she led the life of a Roman matron.

Zenobia throughout history, ancient and modern, has justly had the highest reputation for courage and virtue.

Only a few months ago have we noted an author who attacked her character, involving her in the plot of the assassination of her husband. We hope the somewhat elaborate note in this section has justified the almost uniform belief that the statement in this regard was pure slander.

But the sole remaining reflexion against her character, and it is serious and has been accepted and has been best stated by Gibbon:

> But as female fortitude is commonly artificial, so it is seldom steady or consistent. The courage of Zenobia deserted her in the hour of trial; she trembled at the angry clamours of the soldiers, who called aloud for her immediate execution, forgot the generous despair of Cleopatra, which she had proposed as her model, and ignominiously purchased life by the sacrifice of her fame and her friends. It was to their counsels, which governed the weakness of her sex, that she imputed the guilt of their obstinate resistance; it was on their heads that she directed the vengeance of the cruel Aurelian[1].

Among these friends was the great Longinus, of whom Gibbon generously adds that his fame will survive that of the queen who betrayed, or the tyrant who condemned him.

Now on what grounds have we to make this charge against this otherwise most virtuous queen.

Now the authorities are:

1. Flavius Vopiscus, biographer of Aurelian.
2. Tribellius Pollio, biographer of Zenobia.
3. Zonaras, the distinguished Byzantium historian, who wrote his *Annales* in 18 books from creation to A.D. 1118.

1. Gibbon: *op. cit.* Chapter XI (p. 9).

4. Zosimus, who wrote *The Decline of the Empire* about 425 A.D.

1. Flavius Vopiscus[1] who gave a long account of Aurelian's campaign against Palmyra and also an account of her capture, and even tells that "there arose a terrible uproar among all the soldiers, who demanded Zenobia for punishment". Aurelian, however, deemed it improper to put a woman to death.

Nothing is said of her betraying her friends and counselors.

2. Tribellius Pollio[2], who wrote the lives of the thirty pretenders to the imperial throne, who wrote a biography of Odenathus, of his assassin Maeonius (in which he tells the slander of Zenobia being involved in her husband's death and shows that he himself did not believe it) and finally a biography of Zenobia, reports a Letter of Aurelian to the Roman Senate in which Aurelian, who was the best possible witness in all the world, says:

> Nor would I have spared her life, had I not known that she did a great service to the Roman state when she preserved the imperial power in the East for herself, or for her children. Therefore let those whom nothing pleases keep the venom of their own tongues to themselves.

This certainly gives the true reason for sparing her life, the justice of Aurelian. She did not need to betray anyone. Besides, Aurelian probably knew all the facts and although he cruelly executed the counselors it was, after all, and according to the times, the usage of war.

3. Zonaras, the Byzantine does not mention the occurrence of the betrayal of her friends by Zenobia.

4. Zosimus, alone, does.

Now Zosimus was a pagan, an official in the employ of the younger Theodosius. He wrote a work (about 425 A.D., in six books) *The Decline of the Empire*. He was an inveterate foe of Christianity and all its works and freely blamed the fall and destruction of paganism and the decline of the empire upon Christianity. It is curious the opinion of scholarship upon his value or authority as an historian. Bentley[3] speaks of Zosimus with great contempt;

1. *The Scriptores Historiae Augustae*: Vopiscus: *Divus Aurelianus* (ed. and tr. David Magie (L.C.L.), London, 1932, Vol. III–XXX–1).
2. *Scrip. Hist. Aug.*: Pollio; *The Thirty Pretenders* (L.C.L.), London, 1932 (XXX–8).
3. R. Bentley: *Remarks upon a Late Discourse of Freethinking* (P XII, p. 21).

Tillemont[1] calls him a "bad authority"; Gibbon: "In good policy we must use the service of Zosimus without esteeming him or trusting him." It is true Dr. Harold Mattingly speaks well of him. However, Dr. Mattingly will not follow him in his certain misstatement as to the death of Zenobia:

> According to Zosimus (I-59) Zenobia died by illness or by voluntary starvation; this conflicts with the general tradition and should be rejected[2].

Certainly it is in conflict with the general tradition as well as the positive authority of Aurelian himself in Pollio's biography, and although it destroys a colorful story, it does a great injustice to a woman rightly celebrated in history for her fame and virtue and should be rejected.

Most recently T. J. Haarhoff in his article *Museum* in *The Oxford Classical Dictionary* writes:

> By far the most famous Museum was that of Alexandria, founded by Ptolemy Soter c. 280 B.C., on the advice of Aristotle's pupil, Demetrius of Phalerum... Suidas gives the last member of the Museum as Theon, the father of Hypatia (c. A.D. 400).

Dr. Haarhoff also tells us that the Museum "was destroyed, probably by Zenobia, in 270, but seems to have resumed its activities"[3].

If this is correct, it is another example of the remarkable vitality of the Museum-Library to be able to recover from disaster and continue its amazing mission.

AURELIAN (270–275 A.D.)

Aurelian was the son of a peasant-farmer on an estate of a Roman Senator, Aurelius, at Sirmium in Pannonia. He arose, by merit, from a common soldier through every rank to commander, duke, or guardian of a frontier.

A consummate soldier, an inflexible disciplinarian, he was most competent to unite the empire again under one head, a

---

1. Tillemont: *Hist. dec. Emp.* (11, p. 212).
2. H. Mattingly: (*C.A.H.*) *The Imperial Recovery* (XII, Ch. IX–1).
3. *Ox. Class. Dic.*, s.v. *Museum*, by T. J. Haarhoff. Also see Müller–Graupe, in Pauly–Wissowa, s.v. *Museion.*

condition that had not been obtained for at least two decades.

On the death of Claudius, he was proclaimed emperor by his legions. He put down every pretender to the throne and defeated every enemy of the empire, both in the east and west – Gauls, Goths, Vandals, Germans, and other barbarian peoples, and the famous Zenobia, Queen of the East (Palmyra).

He reigned about four and a half years and was on his way again to the east to avenge the blot on the Roman military escutcheon, to punish the Persians for their treatment of Valerian, when he was treacherously murdered near Byzantium.

He may have been Rome's best soldier since Caesar; he was the restorer of the empire, he was without the common vulgar vices of most of his predecessors; he was stern and put down mercilessly corruption in government; he no doubt considered himself just, he could be generous and magnanimous, yet he was by temperament a man devoid of culture and at heart a tyrant who could most cruelly decree the slaughter of thousands of Christians because they would not bow to his intolerant will, and it was only due to his unexpected violent death that the Church was spared a major persecution.

After his victory over Zenobia and the Palmyrene empire of the East, and as he was proceeding to the West to settle with the last imperial pretender (Tetricus), his program was interrupted by the report that a revolt had broken out in Egypt where one Firmus, a rich merchant, had seized the government. This Firmus was said to be a native of one of the Seleucias, but whether a Greek, Egyptian, or Semite is unknown. He trafficked throughout the East, even to India, and his luxury indulged in the use of glass windows in his palace.

We assume that one of his industries was the paper or papyrus trade, although we are constrained to record that the biographer, Vopiscus[1] would have us believe that his was a bookman!

> He owned so many books that he used often to say in public that he could support an army on the paper and glue.

Personally, he was a huge creature, with prominent eyes, curly hair, swarthy skin, and a scarred brow. His strength was prodig-

---

1. Flavius Vopiscus of Syracuse (in the *Historiae Augustae*) in Lives of the minor pretenders, Firmus etc. (L.C.L., Vol. iii), iii-VI.

ious, and his capacity for food and drink placed him in the class of the famous gourmanderie, as he consumed an ostrich in a day and could outdrink any of Aurelian's generals and yet remain sober.

This man seemed to have had connections with the Blemmyes and Saracen tribesmen, and in the summer of 272 to have marched on Alexandria, seduced the fickle populace, and proclaimed himself ruler of Egypt. If he did not assume the imperial purple, for a few days he enjoyed the fatal gifts of power.

Aurelian, with his usual vigor and promptitude, marched on Alexandria, immediately put down the revolt, captured the hapless Firmus, whom he considered a brigand and whom with his violent temper he crucified, announcing to Rome that the grain supply would be resumed immediately. The Emperor then immediately left for Italy.

Now all accounts make of this revolt a minor incident, promptly if not easily suppressed.

Vopiscus[1] says:

Without delay Aurelian turned back against him (Firmus), and there also his wonted good fortune did not abandon him. For he recovered Egypt at once and took vengeance on the enterprise, violent in temper, as he always was.

And Vopiscus[2]:

Aurelian in his message to the Roman people:
Firmus, that brigand in Egypt, who rose in revolt — we have routed and seized and tortured and slain.

Zosimus[3] does not even mention the name of Firmus.

Gibbon describes Firmus as leading his disordered multitude into Alexandria, adding:

Such troops were a feeble defence against the approach of Aurelian; and it seems unnecessary to relate that Firmus was routed, taken, tortured, and put to death[4].

Dr. Sharpe[5]:

Firmus fixed his government at Coptas and Ptolemais — but he either

1. In his *Life of the Deified Aurelian* (p. 257).
2. In his *Life of Firmus*, etc.
3. Zosimus: I-61, 1.
4. Gibbon: Ch. XI.
5. Samuel Sharpe: *The History of Egypt*, II-234, London, 1885.

never conquered Alexandria or did not hold it for many months – as for every year we find coins bearing the name of Aurelian. Firmus was at last conquered by Aurelian in person, who took him prisoner, and had him tortured and then put to death.

Had Firmus raised the Roman legions in rebellion, he would have been honored with the title of a rebel emperor; but, as his power rested on the Egyptians and Arabs, Aurelian only boasted that he had rid the world of a robber.

Now there is another account of this interlude.

Zabdas, with an army of 70,000 had conquered Alexandria for Zenobia, who placed the victory to the credit of Aurelian and herself. But as the "Empire of the East" was threatened by the advance of Aurelian, Zabdas left Egypt with probably the greater part of his army and hurried to the defense of his sovereign. We know he died heroically before Palmyra in one of the forlorn sorties of the siege. About this time, either before or after the defeat of Zenobia, Firmus a wealthy merchant, with the help of Blemmyes tribesmen, established himself in Alexandria not so much as emperor but as representative of "what was left of the cause of Zenobia"[1] or for account of the opponents of Aurelian. Mr. Mattingly[1] says:

> Aurelian moved at once against this new enemy, besieged him at Bruchium and forced him to commit suicide.

Now all of these accounts are of little significance for the subject of our inquiry, the history of the rise and destruction of the Alexandrian Library, and certainly would find no place in this work were it not that Ammianus Marcellinus of Antioch, a historian most highly praised by Gibbon and extolled by subsequent writers for truthfulness and accuracy, wrote in the sixteenth chapter of the XXIIth Book of his *Roman History*:

> But Alexandria herself, not gradually (like other cities), but at her very origin, attained her wide extent; and for a long time she was grievously troubled by internal dissensions, until at last, many years later under the rule of Aurelian, the quarrels of the citizens turned into deadly strife; then her walls were destroyed and she

1. H. Mattingly: in *C.A.H.* (Ch. *The Imperial Recovery*), Vol. XII, p. 305.

lost the greater part of the district called Bruchion, which had long been the abode of distinguished men[1].

Now this paragraph, fifteen of Chapter XVI of Book XXII of Ammianus, which is quoted in extenso, is one paragraph of twenty-four in this Chapter, all on Egypt.

Candor compels us, in spite of the reputation of Ammianus for historical accuracy, to point out that this Chapter XVI on Egypt is full of inaccuracies.

In the second paragraph, we pass as trivial:

As to Thebes, with its hundred gates, there is no one ignorant of its renown.

In the third paragraph, he says:

That the noble city of Pelusium was founded by Peleus the father of Achilles.

Pelusium, whether the Avaris of Bunsen[2] or the Philistine town of Lepsius[3], was the key of Egypt where all invaders negotiated for the valley of the Nile. It was a hoary city before Sennacherib or the rise of the Greek hero or the formulation of his legends.

In the ninth paragraph, he says:

Cleopatra erected a lofty tower in the harbour, which was named Pharos, from the spot on which it was built.

Now Arrian (VII) says Alexander commanded Cleomenes to build a lighthouse on the island of Pharos.

In the reign of Ptolemy Soter, the architect Sostratus of Cnidus probably commenced the erection of the lighthouse eponymus of the world (one of its seven ancient wonders), and certainly under Ptolemy "Philadelphus" the great tower was finished and dedicated "To the gods Soteres" (i.e. Soter and Berenice, the parents of the second Ptolemy).

In the tenth paragraph, he says:

1. Ammianus Marcellinus: *The Roman History*, XXII–16–15, tr. J. C. Rolfe (L.C.L.), II-303. Also Ammianus Marcellinus: *The Roman History*, XXII–16–15, London, 1894.
2. C. C. J. Baron Bunsen: *Egypt's Place in Universal History*, Vol. III, p. 121, London, 1859.
3. Lepsius: *Chron. de Egypte*, I, p. 341.

This same queen built the Heptastadium, remarkable alike for its great size and for the incredible speed with which it was constructed for a well-known and sufficient reason.

This was the famous Heptastadium joining the island of Pharos to the mainland and forming the two harbours of Alexandria, which of course, was not built by Cleopatra.

In the tenth and eleventh paragraphs, he says:

That Pharos was liable to tribute to the Rhodians and that Cleopatra being a wily woman induced the farmers of the revenue to come to the city on the mainland to celebrate some holiday and that during that time she completed the Heptastadium in seven days[1].

In the thirteenth paragraph, he says:

In this (the Serapeum) were invaluable libraries, and the unanimous testimony of ancient records declare that 700,000 books, brought together by the unremitting energy of the Ptolemaic kings, were burned in the Alexandrine war, when the city was sacked under the dictator Caesar.

Now Alexandria was never "sacked" by Caesar; there were no *libraries* in the Serapeum, but there was the well-known one library (the "Daughter Library") connected with the Temple of Serapis, and it is certain that the burning of the ships at the time of Caesar's visit never in any way touched the Serapeum and the temple area, as they were situated on an Acropolis in Rhakotis or the Egyptian quarter. No wonder that on this particular text Dr. White says:

Ammianus two centuries later, is even less credible (than Gellius)[2].

And so we come to the fifteenth paragraph:

But Alexandria herself, not gradually (like other cities), but at her very origin, attained her wide extent; and for a long time she was grievously troubled by internal dissensions, until at last, many years later under the rule of Aurelian, the quarrels of the citizens turned into deadly strife; then her walls were destroyed and she lost the greater part of the district called Bruchion, which had long been the abode of distinguished men.

We are aware that the traditional reputation of Ammianus for accuracy, doubtless well-deserved but certainly not in what he

1. The story as well as its application to Cleopatra is absurd.
2. J. W. White: *op. cit.*, p. XXXIV.

calls "this long digression" (ch. 16 of Bk. XXII), has met with
approving adoption by Dziatzko, in Pauly-Wissowa[1], who says
that under the rule of Aurelian the greater part of the Bruchion
was almost destroyed (272 A.D.).
And Sir John Sandys:

> In the time of Aurelian (272 A.D.) the larger part of the region of
> Alexandria in which the library was situated was laid waste (Amm.
> March. XXI–16–5) and it may be conjectured that this was the
> date when the Library suffered most damage; for late in the follow-
> ing century, we find a rhetorician of Antioch, Aphthonius, assign-
> ing a special importance to another Library identified as that of the
> Serapeum[2].

And yet, everything said above by Sir John Sandys might perhaps better apply to the "destruction" under Diocletian, at which
we now arrive, where again the many-times destroyed Alexandriana exhibits her singular tenacity for existence.
But Dr. Butler is doubtlessly correct when he writes:

> The destruction wrought in this quarter (the Bruchion) by Aurelian
> was no doubt great but probably it has been exaggerated; and it is
> unlikely that the ruin would have been left unrepaired[3].

DIOCLETIAN (284–305)

Diocletian, whose parents had been slaves, provoked the rhetoric
of Gibbon.
As the reign of Diocletian was more illustrious than that of
any of his predecessors, so was his birth more abject and obscure.
He was well-educated, became a scribe, but soon, through
merit in the army, arose to Governor of Maesia, consul and
commander of the imperial guard. When Numerian, son of the
emperor Carus, was murdered at Chalcedon, Diocletian was
proclaimed Emperor (Sept. 17, 284).
His character was a mixture of many elements. He began his

1. Pauly-Wissowa, op. cit. Vol. III, pt 1, p. 410.
2. Sir John E. Sandys, op. cit. p. 113, referring to Aphthonius: Progymnasmata c. 12
(1–107 Walz.)
3. Alfred J. Butler: The Arab Conquest of Egypt, Oxford, 1902 (p. 371); and he seems
to place little credence in Ammianus, adding that "John of Nikiou [end of the 7th
century] proves conclusively that the area of the city had not shrunk in the manner
alleged."

reign with a show of mildness as he put down all opposition without the usual murders of his adversaries, prescriptions, and
confiscations; he ended his reign, at his abdication (May 1, 305),
with the dreadful edict for the destruction of Christianity, the
tenth, the last, and most terrible of the persecutions of the Church.
Although doubtless a good soldier, his best talents were in statecraft, in which he in some way suggests Augustus. He, at once,
introduced radical changes in the structure of the empire; the
Principate became an absolute monarchy and he courageously
took as an associate a military companion, a crude, rough, able
soldier, but an ignorant man, named Maximian, who with himself were Augusti, and he further divided the imperial responsibility by creating two Caesars, Galerius and Constantius, two of
his generals. These four administered the vast Roman Empire
with much harmony for twenty-one years. Italy and Africa and
probably Spain were assigned to Maximian; Britain and Gaul
to Constantius, Galerius on the Danube protected the Illyrian
provinces; and Diocletian retained Thrace, and the countries of
Asia and Egypt.

In 305 Diocletian, whether through philosophic choice or evil
pressure on the part of Galerius, abdicated and retired to a great
imperial estate near Salona, in Dalmatia, his native country, on
the Adriatic Sea. He played with building and gardening, leading
the country life of a great Roman noble, and here he resisted the
temptation to return to imperial rule as so gracefully told by
Victor, when Diocletian serenely wrote to Maximian that if he
could but see the lovely cabbages he was raising he would not
ask him to return to the troubles of empire.

In November, 303, Diocletian went to Rome and with Maximian celebrated the last of the great historical spectacles, the
Roman Triumph. It should be recalled that none of the four
administrators of the Roman world deigned to live in Rome;
indeed in this reign the imperial sun was very definitely setting
for the city of Romulus.

Whatever benefits the greater portion of the Roman Empire
enjoyed during the greater duration of Diocletian's reign, the
ancient land of Egypt unfortunately failed to derive its share of
peace and prosperity. It is true the fault was Egypt's. At the far-
distant frontier, at the First Cataract of the Nile, the native

Egyptians and the various tribes were constantly in revolt. The natural turbulence of the mixed Greek-Macedonian population of Alexandria was more than augmented by the fanatical Egyptian natives who hated all foreign people; so that the Roman prefects were permitting their soldiers to salute them with the imperial title on the slightest occasion. Under these conditions rebellion flickered and blazed forth in Upper and Lower Egypt. Galerius appears to have led an army through the Thebiad; Diocletian besieged and utterly destroyed the cities of Coptos and Busiris. Finally the Great Rebellion in Egypt culminated with the disaffection of Alexandria in favor of perhaps one only vaguely numismatically known as L. Domitius Domitianus, and immediately thereafter most certainly in favor of Achilleus. Egypt again revolted.

Diocletian returned to Egypt, where he found the resistance so serious that he was compelled to employ against the devoted city all the destructive instruments of war in an eight months' siege beginning in July 295. Securing his own camp against sallies of the Egyptians, Diocletian surrounded the city with a trench and a wall and then cut off the water supply. Although the city would have surrendered to the mercy of the Emperor, it experienced all the terrors of being taken by storm. Thousands of the citizens were slaughtered by the ruthless soldiers and a large part of the city burned. The disaster to the city would have been even greater, we are told, had not the conqueror's horse stumbled on entering Alexandria, which Diocletian's humanity interpreted as a command of the gods to mitigate the terrors of the capture. The Alexandrians erected his statue on top of a column of great antiquity which had been used by a Roman prefect as a signal for sailors, and which for centuries has beguiled the credulity of travellers as Pompey's Pillar. It has been said to bear the legend: To the most honored emperor, the Saviour of Alexandria, the unconquerable Diocletian.

Now in the sack of the city much damage must have been done to movable and immovable property. The Alexandrian Library must have suffered a considerable, if not a major, loss. We are told nothing about it, but considering the easy and short campaign of Aurelian and the difficult and long siege of Diocletian, we are inclined to the belief that the Brucheion must have suffered much

under Diocletian. There were only some twenty-four years
between the capture by Aurelian (272) and that by Diocletian
(296); from the two sieges the buildings of the city must have
suffered greatly. Ammianus's statement (Bk. XXII, ch. XVI–15)
in a chapter of errors, in which he speaks so vaguely and with
apparently little knowledge, might, if essentially correct, apply
equally, if not more probably, to Diocletian than to Aurelian.
Under which alternative the comment of Aphthonius, rhetorician of Antioch, cited by Sir John Sandys, would equally apply.

But one thing is certain, that in the time of Diocletian books
were still extant in Alexandria, in spite of the military violence of
Aurelian and Diocletian. After order had been secured in Alexandria, Diocletian caused a diligent search for:

> All the ancient books which treated of the admirable art of making
> gold and silver, and without pity committed them to the flames;
> apprehensive as we are assured, lest the opulence of the Egyptians
> should inspire them with confidence to rebel against the empire[1].

And then Gibbon is guilty of one of his greatest logical and
philosophical errors as he extols Diocletian, whose act he says
"instead of being condemned as the effect of jealous tyranny,
deserves to be applauded as an act of prudence and humanity".

The same intolerant approval might thus be accorded Omar in
the final destruction of the Alexandrian books; the same to every
puritan or other religious zealot; the same to the wretched Hitler
who burned the Jewish books.

But the chief point for our inquiry is that if there were books
in Alexandria on alchemy – the pseudo works of Pythagoras, of
Solomon and of Hermes, the curiosae of ancient letters – there
were certainly books of poetry, history, literature, science, and
art. They apparently were not burned by the intolerant Diocletian, and, after all the destruction of 350 years, still abode in the
city of the Ptolemies.

And all this provokes the pleasant, reassuring thought of the in-
destructability of the destructible media of the transmission of
man's thoughts on God, himself, and all his works. You may burn
the manuscript, the book, even the author thereof, but the writing

1. Gibbon: *op. cit.* Vol. II, p. 163, referring to John Antioch in *Excerp. Valesian*, p. 834
(F. H. G. IV, p. 601). Suidas (s.v. *Diocletian*).

abides through the ages to await certainly the sober rejection or approval of mankind.

Again the Alexandriana (at least its great branch at the Serapeum) calmly awaits its next destruction.

CHAPTER XVII

THE FALL OF PAGANISM

In the reign of Tiberius Caesar, on Friday, the fifteenth day of Nisan, in Jerusalem of Judea, took place the most momentous event in time.

And Plutarch relates[1]:

In the reign of Tiberius Caesar, Epitherses, a schoolmaster and a man of integrity, journeying to Italy, reported that in the evening, as their ship was becalmed and drifted near the isles of Paxi, not far from Corcyra, a mighty voice was heard across the waters, crying: *The great god Pan is dead.* And then was heard a dreadful noise, as of great lamentation.

The matter was bruited about Rome, and Tiberius inquired of his wisemen as to who was Pan, and they answered the son of Mercury and Penelope. And so the rustic god who for centuries had inhabited the mountain slopes of Arcady and who typified the simpler and the frailer spirit of paganism was chosen as the symbol, as the demons of the deep, announced the death of *all* the gods[2].

The Christians invaded the empire in the first century. Peter and Paul were martyred at Rome. The fires of hell burst forth in Nero's day, the Church was buried in the catacombs, but deathless arose in the resurrection under Constantine. But the living spiritual faith in Christ could not abide the frivolous myths and idolatrous rites of the ancient but dead gods. And yet incense arose from the temples of Jove, and the long train of animal sacrifice prevailed in shrine and grove. However, the empire could not continue half Christian and half pagan. All the efforts of Greek and Roman sophists and learned sectaries of the gods, who agnostically strove to retain the ancient forms and symbols under which the Greeks had conquered the intellectual, and the Romans the

---

1. Plutarch: *De Defectu Oraculorum*, XVII.
2. "Pan.Ce dieu occupe dans le panthéon hellénique une place à part," says J. J. A. Hild in his fine article s.v. *Pan* in Daremberg et Saglio: *Dictionnaire des Antiquités Grecques et Romaines* (Paris).

material world; all the strivings of the ubiquitous neutral who would preserve both true and false, all the wishes of the mostly inarticulate, ignorant, superstitious masses, the rustics who clung to the customs and usages of their ancestors, to the simple, colorful, joyous, and sometimes improper festivals and amazing spectacles of the olden faith; all failed before the patient, persistent, skillful, untiring zeal of the Christian leaders, bishops, presbyters, catechumen and the laity, men and women, who, after centuries of persecution, through faith and courage, had now attained to power and who unconditionally sought the extirpation of the pagan religions.

As the Church had gone through the fires and experienecd all the horrors of ten ruthless persecutions, so the sacrifices, the idols and the temples of the gods must now be destroyed.

In the time of Theodosius (375–395), called the Great, the Church triumphed, and the edicts went forth for the destruction of paganism. Theodosius was the last to rule the undivided empire and "the Roman world was never again united"[1].

The three most important cities of the empire were still: Constantinople, that as Byzantium had a proud antiquity to which were now added the splendors of the imperial capital; Rome, whose dying glories had not yet affected her fabulous past, now under a representative of her sovereign; and Alexandria, ever the turbulent, attractive metropolis, guardian of the granary of Egypt, the meeting place of merchants and the restless seat of controversy, human and divine.

In Constantinople, the Edicts contra Paganism were administered under the eye of the Palace where diplomacy often softened the harsh, rigid letter of the law. In Rome, the see of Peter and the real seat of the Church, although serious local contests might be fought for the personality of the Papacy, a spirit of moderation generally prevailed. But in the city of Alexandria, of the Ptolemies and now of Theophilus, the fires of fanaticism enveloped the place as a pall which only violence and blood could assuage.

Ptolemy Soter, perhaps of the blood of Alexander, true builder of Alexandria and founder of the Greco-Macedonian dynasty that for three centuries ruled Egypt and excited the fatal envy of all the world, including imperial Rome; Ptolemy Soter who, as a

1. Andrian Fortesque: *Cath. Encyc.* (s.v. *Theodosius* 1).

realist had made his capital the commercial heart of the East and West; who, as an intellectual, had consecrated it as the seat of learning, the omphalos of the world's culture; and who, as a master in statecraft, knew that he must spiritually unite his Macedonians with the ancient, mysterious, stubborn, changeless Egyptians over whom he hoped to rule, earnestly sought for a cult at whose altars his widely different subjects might in unison worship. Ptolemy Soter was a genius when it came to selecting men to achieve his vast ideals; himself a soldier, his experience military, he used many a trusted follower of Alexander to maintain his military supremacy; but when he would control the intellect of men, he sent for Demetrios of Phaleron who created the Museum and its fabulous Library, and so, when he would control the spiritual faith of men, he chose, with the assistance of his faithful Demetrios[1], as his Greek spiritual adviser Timotheus, the Eumolpid, ancestral adept in the Eleusinian Mysteries, and, as his Egyptian spiritual adviser, Manetho, "beloved of Troth", priest of Heliopolis, the Egypto-Greek historian, whose labours have for over two thousand years excited the curiosity of those who have thought of Egypt, and the discovery of whose original text would outvie the finding of a Livy "whole".

Timotheus and Manetho, doubtless with Greek and Egyptian mystagogues and temple exegetes, formulated the Serapic cult: a Black-sea Plutonian god, Hades, who with a dominant Zeus serenity would satisfy the easy-going Greeks; and much of Osiris-Apis (Userhapi), and earth-old mysteries of Isis, Anubis, Harpocrates, and the Egyptian pantheon[2], who should satisfy the exacting Egyptian worshipper. In the composition, we believe the Egyptian won and many of the occult ceremonies in the crypts of the Serapeum and in the darkly lit Hall of the god, perhaps portraying some esoteric doctrine of death, judgment, hell and heaven, the eschatology of ancient Egypt, and much of this must have been "Greek" indeed to the Alexandrians, who

1. "The creation of the cult was marked by the introduction of the worship into Alexandria and, according to tradition, was accomplished through the assistance of Demetrius of Phaleron, the Eumolpid Timotheus, and Manetho." Demetrius is the first important witness of the power of Serapis, as he wrote his *Paeans* in gratitude for the restoration of his sight. *The Oxford Classical Dictionary*, s.v. *Serapis* by Thomas Allen Brady.
2. See M. Georges Lafaye's study, in Daremberg and Saglio: *op. cit.* (s.v. *Serapis*).

were, however, willing to pay tribute to the native conquered race in the measure of a joint deity.

The cult created, Ptolemy dreamed of a colossal statue of Pluto at Sinope[1] which he felt sure must be a figure of the new Greco-Egyptian god. He described its whereabouts, and his emmissaries "stole away the statue", and so in 286 or 278 B.C. Eusebius[2] says:

Serapis came to Alexandria and became resident there.

The statue was said to be by Bryaxis (c. 372-312 B.C.), a famous Athenian sculptor who, with Scopas, Leochares and Timotheus, adorned the Mausoleum.

A cult, so skilfully devised, aimed to bring together two peoples so fundamentally different, a great idol of the new-found god, wanted but a temple to enshrine the deity and house his sacerdotal rites and priests. So the Ptolemaic kings (Soter and, later, "Philadelphus") built the Serapeum. The building, one of the wonders of the world, was said to have been designed by Parmenion, an architect, employed in much of the building of ancient Alexandria[3].

The site selected was in the Western, Egyptian part of the city in the old district of Rhakotis. A slight elevation of ground was artificially raised to a great height and leveled to form a vast foundation of underground stone walls, forming crypts, cells, long corridors, labyrinthine ways, rooms of various size and vast halls supported by granite columns. In this subterranean world were rooms of bare stone for general storage, where were stocked the scented woods for the flambeaux and fires of the temple; laboratories for manufacturing the incense, where the odor of nard, frankincense, myrrh, rare gums of Araby, and spices of the unknown East overpowered the sense of smell; depositories for the ceremonial utensils, the instruments of sacrifice and all the intricate paraphernalia of religious rites; robe-rooms for the sacerdotal vestments and the garments of many orders of priesthood, of acolytes and lesser servants of the god, male and female; chambers for meetings of temple author-

---

1. Manetho (Plutarch: *Isis and Osiris*, Ch. 28).
2. Jerome says 286 B.C.; Eusebius, in Armenian version of the *Chronicle*, says 278 B.C. (See Waddell: Manetho: *op. cit.* p. XIII).
3. *The Oxford Classical Dictionary* calls him Parmeniscus.

ities and priestly confraternities; chapels for special contemplation and ascetic worship; cells and dungeons for recalcitrant worshippers, and those guilty of sacrilege and offenses against the god-head; lodges for religious brotherhoods; vast cryptic halls for the mysteries and esoteric rites of the deity; vaults for the more precious gold and jeweled vases and the endless implements of worship; extensive bakeries and kitchens and cellars of wine, with small halls for symposia and long refectories for the numerous functionaries and servants of the temple; stalls or stables for the sacred and sacrificial animals; and arsenals, well-stocked with weapons, for the guardians of the enormous accumulated wealth and vast extent of properties of the great god Serapis.

On this foundation was built by the first Ptolemaic kings, a building oriental in its splendor and size, yet sufficiently tempered by the refining sense of grace and beauty, so characteristic of Greek art, that Ammian sincerely exclaims that:

> The Serapeum which, although no description can do it justice, yet is so adorned with extensive columned halls, with almost breathing statues, and a great number of other works of art, that next to the Capitolium, with which revered Rome elevates herself to eternity, the whole world beholds nothing more magnificent[1].

From the great thoroughfare which divided Alexandria and ran from the Canopic gate to the gate of the Necropolis, from the Jewish through the Royal-Greek, and Egyptian quarters, as this splendid way crossed at right angles the equally amazing street terminating at the Sun and Moon gates, and as it, the Street of Canopus, entered Rhakotis, the old Egyptian section of the city, it connected with a wide street that ran to the base of the elevation of the temple-area. From this base, a flight of one hundred marble steps which grew inward in ascent, and which on either side were flanked by a row of sphinxes, the traditional man-headed lion of ancient Egypt ascended to the vast platform of stone where, at the top of the steps, entrance was had to the sacred precincts, through the propylaeum formed by two sentinel rows of huge red granite columns; the entrance to this citadel, acropolis or vast temple-area being closed by massy gates of

1. Ammianus Marcellinus, XXII–16–12.

ornamental bronze. Here was also a chariot road according to Aphthonius.

The great temple-area was a quadrangular[1] platform of white stone, an oblong 500 cubits long by 250 wide. From the propylaeum or entrance base of the area red granite columns marched in double row, forming a series of spacious porticoes, with roofs of copper gilt, all surrounding a vast rectangular court, at the center of which arose a colossal column from which, within a circle of copper, astronomical observations may have been made by Eratosthenes, the universal scholar, by Hipparchus of Nicaea, and by Claudius Ptolemy (2nd cen. A.D.), who doubtless owed much to Hipparchus, an Alexandrian astronomer, who controlled the scientific geographical thought for ages, indeed until the time of Copernicus (d. 1543)[2].

Within the porticoes were rooms for various uses, and especially some of which were depositories for manuscripts, bookrooms open to those who would read and study. Within the temple-area, not *in* the temple, were these Halls of Books housing the famous "daughter" collection or outer Library of the Alexandriana. Originally a carefully selected library of 42,800 rolls, in the time of Callimachus (d.c. 235 B.C.), or of duplicates from the great overflow of the "mother" Library within the Greek (Brucheion) quarter, it must at some time have grown to over 100,000 manuscripts in the ordinary growth of centuries. If, as some think, here were lodged the Library of Pergamum, then it was a collection of some 300,000 rolls.

The accounts of the destruction within the Royal-Greek quarter (*i.e.* the Brucheion) which I have classed major and minor are uniformly unsatisfying. If any of these depredations ever reached the Museum or Library, proper, and were of devastating extent, some of the precious contents must still have been saved, and unless the "mother" Library was rebuilt or restored, these manuscripts must, naturally, have found their way to the "daughter" or Library of the Serapeum, and have thus augmented its stores. Did these cabinets or halls, in the prostyle porticoes

1. "The general plan of the arrangement is quadrilateral," says Dr. Butler, who made a careful study of the statements of Aphthonius and Rufinus as well as the works of Dr. Botti: *Colonne Théodosienne* (pp. 24 seq.) and *L'Acropolis d'Alexandrie et le Sérapeum*. The measurements are from Mas'udi.

2. Copernicus: *De orbium coelestium revolutionibus Nurimburgae* (1543).

of the Serapeum, hold this great collection or its residium in the dark days of the pagan gods? They were certainly the libraries visited or mentioned by the rhetor Aphthonius.

Beyond this splendid introductory ensemble of prostyle porticoes and court, on the remaining greater part of the vast base of white stone, the temple rose in sheer magnificence with a façade of granite columns from Syene, around whose shafts, in colored glyphs, were pictured the stories of the gods whose mythic streams had wrought the incarnation of the great god Serapis.

Seven stone steps led to an open pillared vestibule, crowned by a dome of deep green basalt, on which was sculptured the celestial history, according to the astronomical wisdom of the Alexandrian Museum.

Colossal doors of massy bronze, whose panels depicted the birth, and death, and resurrection of Osiris, the cult of Userhapi, the Osiris-Apis, enclosed the grand entrance into the fabulous Hypostyle Hall, whose vast central aisle, sentineled by massive sculptured, painted columns, ascending to the dim vaults above, produced on the beholder an overpowering sense of architectural grandeur, dominating the little figures of worshippers who walked below. On either side of the great central aisle were double rows of columns, of lesser heights, all upholding the roofs of solid stone, enclosing the temple. Mural paintings covered the sides of the Hall and the walls to the right and left of the great portal, with endless scenes of the reigning Osiris-Isis (or Serapis-Isis) in the persons and sacerdotal portraits of the royal Ptolemaic-Pharaohs, Soter and his Berenice, "Philadelphus" and his sister-wife Arsinoe. There may have been later Ptolemaic additions, for we believe no Roman interfered with the old royal cult of deified rulers, the ancient state religion of Egypt.

The floors of the great Hall were encrusted with myriad gems of many colored glass and stone and rare metals which formed a mosaic Book of the mythi of Greco-Egyptian cults, a veritable Bible of the Pantheon of Egypt.

The primal impression of the great Temple Hall (the vastness of the place, its sombre lights, its atmosphere of deep mystery) was doubtless more suggestive of the ancient East than of the modern West. As one ascended the great aisle running through a mighty forest of stone, the farthest end of the Hall seemed incredi-

bly remote. At that end were the low marble altars for the sacrificial rites. Some distance behind, there hung a tapestry of
unbelievable looms, for it appeared as if all the threads of silk
from the unknown East (Ind and Cathay), of Tyrian dyed linens
of Sidon and Egypt, of subtle colors known to temple-crafts of
the Nile and Phoenician guilds, of traditional skills of Babylonian
and Persian weavers, had by some stroke of magic or wondrous
act of the jinn been synchronized into a fabulous painting out-
ranking the efforts of pencil and brush. Pictorially it represented
the deified Alexander in the garb of Osiris-Pharaoh, ruler of
Upper and Lower Egypt, but also ruler of the two worlds with
the symbols of earthly power and the instruments of eternity.
Only absolute dominion could have obtained, with priestly
acquiescence, so complete an apotheosis. And yet it was not the
subject of the tapestry, but the perfection of design and composition, the wondrous scheme of harmony as one color melted
into another, and the imperceptible blending of light and shadow, that arrested the spectator as a thing most wondrous to
behold. This pictured fabric covered a recess or large semi-circu-
lar alcove at the extreme end of the Temple Hall. The artistic
beauty of this tapestry was a daring example of the sure dramatic
instinct of the Greek and Egyptian temple-priests. Now all the
elaborate ceremonial, the ritual, the vestments, the incense, the
rites of sacrifices, the endless paraphernalia of sacerdotal pomp,
the vast temple-area with all its instrumentalities, the great
temple itself, were all mere religious steps for the glorification
of the god Serapis. After all the power of government, the wisdom and ingenuity of hierophant, the judicious employment
of all the arts – architecture, music, painting, song and letters –,
the Alexandrians were willing to attempt the perfect climax with
sculpture, and with it all to prefix the culmination of all their
religious ceremonies a masterpiece of pictorial art, believing,
with their keen, perfect sense of art-effect and human reaction
to beauty, that their statue of Serapis would indeed be the apogee
of their worship of the god. The statue had been marvelously
wrought by a master sculptor of the fourth century, who, though
endeavoring to retain much of the serenity of the perfect form
of Phidias, emancipated himself from earlier restraint, and bravely sought to portray the feeling, sentiment, and spirituality of

man, seeking for freedom and a norm of destiny. It was of the school of Praxitales, Scopas, and Lysippus, who so closely touched the greater awakening, the glory of the Italian Renaissance. The figure was colossal, of marble, with ivory and gold-plate in the manner of the great Greek temple gods. It represented the god in profound majesty, serene, self-centered, in celestial glory. The god was seated, dressed in the manner of the Greeks, holding in his left hand the wand or scepter of awful power and with his right hand restraining the three-headed hounds of the underworld. The face of the god was of ivory, gem-chiselled and polished, with beard and hair modeled with the attractive freedom of fourth century art, crowned with a peculiar measure of abundance, but with all a countenance of much dignity and beauty.

As the great tapestry curtain was raised, to the soft strands of cithara and softer note of the pipes and the triumphal blast of cymbals and trumpet, the serene figure of Bryaxis, Plutonian-Zeus, the great god Serapis was exhibited to the expectant and joyous crowd of worshippers, amid the harmonies of sound, the odors of incense, and the eye beheld the perfect vision of the god.

The Serapeum was a museum of the arts and the treasure-house of the wealth of centuries; gold, silver, and marble vases, masterpieces of marble and bronze figures stood between the pillars of the Hypostyle Hall and around the ornate walls of the resplendent sanctuary.

The Serapeum was a world-in-little of all the arts and sciences and learning of pagan antiquity, and the home of the great national deity of Greco-Roman Egypt.

From its lofty pedestal in Rhakotis it surveyed the famous city, built to the glory of the great Alexander, and especially did it look down on the royal and memorable palaces, Museum and Library of the Brucheion. It had beheld much in its long seven centuries since the days of Soter: the panorama of the fabulous Ptolemies, the conquering Romans, the hectic visits of the emperors, countless scenes of its turbulent and restless people, the rise of a new religion and civilization, and now the fatal days of Theodosius.

The Serapeum had suffered by fire under Marcus Aurelius and in the second year of Commodus (183 A.D.), but "we hear of no loss of books; and two hundred years later the Library of the Serapeum had risen" if not to the "number of seven hundred thousand volumes"[1], at least to a vast collection, well-representative of its ancient glory.

Throughout most of the centuries the worship and cult of Serapis was that of the general run of idolatry that appealed to the masses and was condescendingly tolerated by the classes. But with the rapid progress of Christianity the hierarchy of the Temples and the civil leaders of government realized that the exalted teaching of the Church, and the dynamic zeal of its ministers would soon destroy the conventional and traditional worship of the gods. So paganism tried to reform, or at least provide doctrines and rites that would appeal to its more serious and sober followers who were yearning for the spiritual food of an exalted moral faith. Brotherhoods, mysteries, and sacerdotal societies and orders were organized to meet the growing danger, and this no doubt induced a fine scholar[2] to assert of the cult of Serapis, "into whose worship more and more of symbolism and of mysticism entered, until the Egyptian religion seemed to the pagans of the third century of our era no unworthy rival of Christianity."

The philosophic schools, however, were doing work which compelled the respect of tolerance, and Theon, the mathematician, the last known member of the Museum, and his gifted daughter Hypatia[3] sincerely labored in the vineyard of philosophy and learning, and were scholars of high character, and the devoted victims on the dying altar of paganism.

But the Edict of Theodosius was the knell of the gods. To Alexandria came the Pretorian prefect of the East, Cynegius, whether an officer of the empire reluctantly doing his duty, or a notorious pagan baiter we do not know, but to Theophilus, Patriarch of Alexandria (385–412), the real ruler of the city, he came.

1. Samuel Sharpe: *op. cit.* II, 196. This most certainly is involved with the confusion of Ammianus.
2. Percy Gardner: *New Chapters in Greek History* (p. 225), London, 1892.
3. *Hypatia* by Charles Kingsley. That exquisite story of the unfortunate Hypatia will abide with our language. The effect it had on the mind of a lover of antiquity was enduring. After forty years he has reread the novel, he believes, with all his original youthful wonder and enthusiasm.

Of Theophilus we are well-informed. Ordinarily, in such a particular instance, the zealous rhetoric of Gibbon might be taken *cum grano salis*:

> The perpetual enemy of peace and virtue; a bold, bad man, whose hands were alternately polluted with gold and with blood[1].

That he was a man of violent passion and without scruples is well-known. His infamous conduct toward St. John Chrysostom puts him among those prelates that the Church in her wisdom and rectitude does not choose to defend[2].

The populace of Alexandria, equally willing to riot about the dress and affectations of an insane Roman emperor or the sacred incarnation of the Godhead, anticipating the coming final conflict, for days had filled the streets of the city with wild, turbulent mobs tearing at each other in semi-oriental fashion, and many persons had been killed. The imperial authorities, agnostic or tolerant, were beside themselves to keep a reasonable peace between the warring factions. But, with Theophilus, the overshadowing and dominant figure, the virtual dictator of Alexandria, the spirit of havoc was abroad.

There was a secession of strife, an appeal was made to the emperor, and the dread decision announced that the temples, idols, and pagan sacrifices must be destroyed. The howling mob rushed to the devoted Serapeum, all under control of Theophilus, the genius of destruction. The frenzied people rushed through the street of Brucheion, the Greek royal quarter, pouring into Rhakotis along the Canopic way, turning into the short street that led to the temple-area of Serapis, meeting other crowds there, up the great flight of marble steps, led by Theophilus[3], through the Propylaeum, across the stone platform and into the temple, where the mass was held by imperial troops that had anticipated the final tragedy. Man, the most destructive of the human forces in the universe, took little heed of the gold and silver ornaments, the precious jewels, the bronze and marble statues, the rare murals and tapestries of priceless weave, the carved and painted pillars, the wealth of malakite, alabaster,

---

1. Gibbon: *op. cit.* Ch. XXVIII (ed. Bury).
2. Chrys. Baur: *Catholic Encyclopedia* (s.v. *John Chrysostom* and s.v. *Theophilus*).
3. Theodoret: *The Ecclesiastical History* (Ch. XXII).

granite, and of many marbles, of ebony and scented woods, of ivory and exotic furniture from unknown lands, all into the vortex of ruin were poured, as up ladders, axes in hand, Lilliputian men labored with demoniac delight, destroying the masterpieces of Bryaxis which had been wrought with such patient care and devoted labor to create a thing of beauty for all time. At last the deed was done; rubble and ruin occupied at least the interior of the great temple, the site where a few hours before a noble structure graced the earth – a building that could have been used for government, culture, or as a Christian Church, in spite of man's insensate destructiveness. Yet it is true the gods were dead, by violence the pagan way of life was forever past; and now amid the scene of desolation, where the jackal may haunt, and the moon, that for eons had viewed the plains of havoc, this night looked down on the things of death.

From the time of the destruction of the Serapeum, the city of Alexandria, naturally a place that reveled in mobs, was the scene of constant tumult between the Christian sectarians, the Jews, and the pagans. The violent zealotry of Theophilus was constantly abroad. His nephew Cyril succeeded him in 412. Both of these prelates were violent controversialists. Trouble arose between the Jews and Christians, and Cyril was for expelling the Jews altogether. The Prefect Orestes opposed this. Frequent conflicts took place, uncontrollable mobs paraded the city, the streets were unsafe due to the natural recklessness of the Alexandrians and the conflict between the Bishop and the Prefect. Modern historians say that Cyril and his followers thought that Hypatia was advising Orestes the Prefect[1]. If this be so, then Cyril was in some way morally responsible for the terrible crime committed by his adherents, who shamelessly murdered Hypatia.

Hypatia, daughter of Theon, last fellow of the Museum, who was a famed mathematician and philosopher and who had succeeded to the school of Plato and Plotinus, was a woman of great learning and highest character.

Socrates, the Church historian, described her:

The daughter of the philosopher Theon, who was so learned that she surpassed all contemporary philosophers. She carried on the

1. E. W. Brooks: in Ch. *The Eastern Provinces from Arcadius to Anastasius* in *C.M.H.*, Vol. 1, 463.

Platonic tradition derived from Plotinus, and instructed those who desired to learn in all philosophic discipline. Wherefore all those wishing to work at philosophy streamed in from all parts of the world, collecting around her on account of her learned and courageous character. She maintained a dignified intercourse with the chief people of the city. She was not ashamed to spend time in the society of men, for all esteemed her highly, and admired her for her purity[1].

Damascius, the last of the Neo-Platonic teachers, the last who taught in the cathedra of Platonic philosophy at Athens, praises her beauty and chastity, and Philostorgius, the Arian, says she was superior to her father in astronomy. Indeed her genius seems to have excelled in the mathematical sciences. She was the "August Mistress", the divine teacher of Synesius, and, like many a worldteacher, none of her writings survive.

As this distinguished woman was driving in her chariot, the mob dragged her from the car into the church, formerly the Caesarium, and, subjecting her to every indignity, foully murdered her[2]. The Christian historian Socrates tells how "all men on account of her extraordinary dignity and virtue admired her" and confesses that the hideous "affair brought not the least opprobrium, not only upon Cyril, but also upon the whole Alexandrian Church"[3].

After the generous and honorable comment of the Christian historians, we can well understand the enthusiasm of poor Palladas, one of the last of the pagan poets:

Thee when I view, thyself and thy discourse
I worship, for I see thy virgin-home
Is in the stars, thy converse is in heaven,
Adorable Hypatia, Grace of speech,
Unsullied Star of true philosophy[4].

Was the Library of the Serapeum (the "daughter" branch of the

1. Tr. of Augustine FitzGerald.
2. "The maiden philosopher was torn to pieces by a mob of Christian fanatics in an orgie worthy of the ancient temple of Saturn" (Dr. Butler: *op. cit.* p. 374).
3. Socrates: *The Ecclesiastical History*, VII–15 (ed. A. C. Zenos, in *Nicean and Post Nicene Fathers*, New York, 1890).
4. *Greek Anthology*, IX, 400; quoted from Sandys (p. 370) who refers to Alfred Franke: *Dissertation*, 1899 (p. 101); and T. R. Glover: *Life and Letters in the Fourth Century*, Cambridge, 1901 (pp. 303–19).

Alexandriana) totally, partially, or not involved in the great catastrophe?

We have sound reason to believe that the Library of the Serapeum was there before as well as after the destruction of the pagan worship of the Serapeum, because it certainly appears to be mentioned by Aphthonius, the Greek rhetorician, who lived at the end of the fourth century and the early part of the fifth century[1].

1. Gibbon:

> The valuable library of Alexandria was pillaged or destroyed; and, near twenty years afterwards, the appearance of the empty shelves excited the regret and indignation of every spectator whose mind was not totally darked by religious prejudice[2].

He refers to Orosius, whose mind, although religious, was not prejudiced, and who was most probably not referring to the Serapiana.

2. Susemihl:

> Omar fand 642 schwerlich noch Bücher in Alexandreia zu verbrennen[3].

3. Sandys:

> Under Theodosius I (391 A.D.) the temple of Serapis which had been partly burnt in 183 A.D. was demolished, and transformed into a Church and monastery, by Theophilus, the patriarch of Alexandria, and the lesser library of the Serapeum can hardly have survived this destruction[4].

4. Frederick I. Teggart, in *The Nation*, sustains Gibbon's view[5].

5. But Dr. Bury believes otherwise; after noting that Gibbon failed to distinguish between the Greater Library in the Museum and the Lesser Library in the Serapeum, and that this Library, at least, was *not* burnt down when Caesar was in Alexandria, Dr. Bury says:

1. Alfred Croiset: *Histoire de la Littérature Grecque*, Paris (Vol. V, p. 983):
Élève de Libanios, il vécut et enseigna à la fin du IVe siècle et dans la première partie du Ve siècle.
2. Gibbon: *op. cit.* Ch. XXVIII (Bury ed.).
3. Susemihl: *op. cit.* p. 344.
4. Sandys: *op. cit.* p. 113.
5. *The Nation*, July 7, 1898 – *The Destruction of the Alexandrian Library*.

But is it an attested fact that the lesser or daughter library was destroyed in A.D. 391? The sanctuary of Serapis was demolished, but does that imply the demolition of all the buildings connected with the Serapeum? The only evidence on which Gibbon's statement rests is the sentence which he quotes from Orosius. But Orosius does not mention the Serapeum or speak of a large library. He merely says that he has seen book-cases in temples (which he does not name); and that, since then, he had been informed that the temples had been pillaged and the book-cases emptied. It seems to me highly improbable that Orosius is thinking either of the Alexandrian Library or of the Serapeum. There is no reason to suppose that the library was *in* the temple. I conclude then that there is no evidence that the library of the Serapeum did not survive till the Saracen conquest notwithstanding the verdict of Susemihl[1].

And so the belief in the tenaciousness of fragile papyrii and stronger parchments to survive incredible hardship is still strong in men of letters.

And thus it becomes our task to sustain the conclusion of Dr. Bury, that there is no evidence that the Library of the Serapeum was destroyed when the Temple of Serapis was devastated, or to use Dr. Bury's own words:

> I conclude that there is no evidence that the library of the Serapeum did not survive until the Saracen conquest.

We will conclude this chapter with an attempt to show that there *is* no evidence of the destruction of the Library of the Serapeum at the time that the Christians destroyed the worship and sanctuary of Serapis at Alexandria (391 A.D.).

Though we do not believe that the books of the Lesser ("Daughter") Alexandrian Library were ever kept *in* the Temple of Serapis, we likewise do not believe that the Temple (i.e. the great building) was totally demolished or destroyed. Of course, its contents, furniture, statues, paintings, works of art, and the great idol of the god Serapis were reduced to bits of wood, ivory, marble, metal, stone by the frenzied mob. The mob were armed with sticks, spears, swords, axes, and miscellaneous weapons of the day, but these, though they could destroy the utensils and things of sacerdotal use, and the fragile works of art, were not sufficient to totally destroy the second greatest building of the ancient

1. J. B. Bury, in his edition of *Gibbon* (Appendix, note 3).

world, that had been built in the most solid and almost indestructible manner. Was the building not converted into a church
and monastery? One may condemn the zeal, but never doubt
the intelligence of Theophilus. His purpose was not to destroy
a building, but to destroy *a worship*. When the idol of the false
god was smashed and all the instruments of his worship destroyed,
the triumph of Christianity over paganism was for all practical
purposes complete. No one knew this better than Theophilus.
Why attempt to destroy the massive walls, the stone roof, and
the deep foundations which could be converted into a church
for the worship of God?

Does not John of Nikiu say:

> Theophilus who destroyed the temple named Serapis and converted
> it into a church (LXXVIII–45).

And again (although perhaps with a different context):

> And there was a temple of Serapis in the city, and he converted it
> into a church and named it after the name of his (Theodosius's)
> younger son Honorius (LXXXIII–38).

And Dr. Butler does not hesitate to quote as most worthwhile
Philo's description of The Caesarion:

> That temple of Caesar's in Alexandria under the name of Sebastian
> (Augustus) is a piece incomparable above all others. It stands
> situate over against a most commodious harbour; wonderful high
> and large in proportion; an eminent sea-mark; full of choice
> painting and statues, with donatives and oblation in abundance;
> and then it is beautiful all over with gold and silver; the model
> curious and regular in the disposition of the parts, as galleries, librar-
> ies, porches, courts, halls, walks and consecrated groves, as glorious
> as expense and art could make them, and everything in the proper
> place[1].

And then he quotes John of Nikiu as saying it "was changed by
Constantine the Great into a Christian church and dedicated
to St. Michael" (p. 374). And Dr. Butler records in a note:
"The church stood until the Muslims came, and then was destroyed" (p. 374, note 1).

1. Philo's Embassy from the Jews of Alexandria to Caligula in *Josephus*, ed. Sir. R.
L'Estrange, London, 1902, p. 1087; Butler: *op. cit.* 373.

This valuable description of the Sebastian (The Caesarion) should teach us much. First, that great sanctuaries, such as The Caesarion and The Serapeum, were not just one building, but great temple groups or piles, having courts, colonnades, porticoes, libraries, walks and consecrated groves, etc. Of course, all these appendages were not *in* the Temple or Sanctuary proper, but separate. Certainly the walks, groves and libraries were not *in* The Caesarion. Yet the whole area was called The Caesarion.

So in the case of The Serapeum the porticoes, annexes and libraries were not *in* the Temple or Sanctuary proper, but separate appendages, forming a part of the whole harmonious area, and, in speaking, were all referred to as The Serapeum.

The second lesson is that the Christians did not usually destroy mighty buildings of the pagan cults, but after destroying the heathen sanctuaries, their idols and utensils of worship they turned the structures into churches.

Throughout the whole of the Roman empire was not this the usual, reasonable and sane policy of the Church? Indeed, in the later days of advanced culture and civilization of the Arabs, did not the Moslems follow our example? Sadly have we looked upon the great Santa Sophia, now the famous Mosque, called by the Turks Ayiah Sofia.

Besides, the complete destruction of the well-built buildings and the cities of antiquity were not easy to accomplish. The Romans were unable to completely obliterate Carthage in 146 B.C., and when, after Caesar, it was rebuilt, it was not difficult to follow the actual ancient architectural lines of the famous capital of Rome's earliest great antagonist in rebuilding Roman Carthage. We know that there are some writers who have reported the total destruction of the Temple (Serapeum) (*building*), but charity compels us to attribute these accounts to their earnest zeal, or certainly to rhetorical embellishment. Indeed, to represent a major disaster as complete is the natural inclination of man.

And finally Dr. Butler[1] frankly tells us:

Makrizi's account of the Serapeum, quoted from Mas'udi, is truthful enough:

1. Alfred J. Butler: *The Arab Conquest of Egypt and the Last Thirty Years of the Roman Domination*, Oxford, 1902 (p. 387).

There was in Alexandria a great palace without equal on earth, standing on a mound opposite the gate of the city. It was 500 cubits long and 250 broad with a huge massive gateway, each pier of which was a monolith and the lintel a monolith. In the palace were about 100 pillars, and in front of it a great pillar, of unheard-of size, surmounted by a capital (i.e. the Pillar of Diocletian, the famous "Pompey's Pillar"[1].

Now this was the great Serapeum temple-area itself. Al Mas'udi flourished c. 960. Al Mas'udi, Dr. Butler reminds us, was a most careful observer and a valuable authority for the monuments of Alexandria. Al Makrizi was an Egyptian (1365–1441), an indefatigable writer; "he had access to a vast number of authorities, the greater part of whose works have absolutely perished"; he is the most important of our authorities, though lacking in critical judgment[2].

In 1167 Saladin's governor of Alexandria, a man named Karaja, had all the columns broken down, and taken away and cast into the sea[3].

And much more might be brought forth to strenghten the view that the Temple of Serapis (i.e. the *building*) was not totally destroyed under Theophilus.

Now if the building was not totally destroyed, why should we *assume* that the Alexandrian Library situated on the acropolis or temple-area, but separated from the Temple, in the Halls of its vast Porticoes (which Porticoes were not destroyed) ? Why should we assume that in some way the Library was also destroyed ? Now in justice to Theophilus, we freely admit that he was a man of intelligence, a man of learning and culture. He zealously sought to destroy paganism, in this instance, the worship of the god Serapis. We have no reason to believe that he was bent on obliterating all the writings of the past. That was not the attitude

1. Dr. Botti: *Fouilles à la Colonne Théodosienne.* We cannot follow this distinguished scholar, who believes it was erected after the destruction of the Serapeum, and who calls it the Theodosian Column.
2. Butler: *op. cit.* Preface XIX.
3. Makrizi: *Khitat* (I, p. 159) 'Abd al Latif, however, who says he saw about 400 large columns broken into pieces and lying on the edge of the shore, thinks that Karaja's intention was either to deaden the force of the waves which were undermining the city walls, or to keep off the enemy's fleet – in any case, a childish piece of mischief, he adds (p. 113), quoted by Dr. Butler: *op. cit.* (p. 388 N.). The reflection certainly does credit to 'Abd al Latif.

of his masters in Constantinople who were collecting great libraries of Christian and pagan books at that time. Certainly he had received no orders from Theodosius to destroy libraries or books. Theophilus may have been "a bold, bad man", but he certainly was an able leader and not an ignorant man. The mob was his mob and within all human possibilities under his control[1]. That he would not have let them destroy the Library is our honest, if charitable, belief. We hold no brief for the mob itself, or for any mob, be it Alexandrian Christian fanatics or French revolutionary sansculottes. If objection is made that he could not have prevented the destruction, our answer is that we believe he could and did, and that his lieutenants knew well how to lead the mob to the citadel, or temple-area, and to the temple itself (the Sanctuary), where within they had a saturnalia of destruction with the smashing of statues, pictures, works of art, utensils of the pagan worship, and the great climax when the mighty idol was smashed with axes by the Roman soldiery. To carry the remains of the once serene and beautiful pagan idol through the streets of Alexandria to be burned in the Hippodrome, was not all this enough even for the most frenzied of men to attain a triumph.

After writing the above, we crossed the opinion of a fine scholar, who declares that among his contemporaries, Theophilus

excelled most of them in scientific and literary taste. But he has incurred the odium which attaches to every religious persecutor who has not the mitigating plea of personal fanaticism.
Theophilus was himself a man of learning and culture, electic in taste, diplomatic in schemes. He had used his mathematical knowledge to make an elaborate table of the Easter cycle. He could read and enjoy the works of writers whose teaching he was publicly anathematising[2].

But have we forgotten Synesius of Cyrene? This distinguished Lybian Hellene, descendant of the Heracleidae, soldier, sportsman, diplomat, orator, poet, but essentially a man of letters:

My life has been one of books[3].

1. How a little incident supports this view: The great measuring gauge was not destroyed, but was moved from the Temple of Serapis to a church for safety (*Cam. Medieval History*, I, 489).
2. A. Gardner: *Religious Disunion in the Fifth Century* (in *C. Med. H.* I, pp. 489–490).
3. Synesius: *De Insomniis*.

This philosopher, half a pagan, that is at least a lover of ancient culture, and half a Christian; this brilliant pupil of Hypatia, who in his last *Hymn* recommended himself to Christ. It is his prayer that "his sins may be forgiven and that he may behold the glory of the Savior"[1].

His last letter was to Hypatia:

> I am dictating this letter to you from my bed, but may you receive it in good health, mother, sister, teacher, and withal benefactress, and whatsoever is honoured in name and deed[2].

Yet knowing Synesius's literary flare, his philosophy, in fact knowing him intimately, Theophilus forced him to accept the office of Bishop of Ptolemais.

Synesius, a man of courage and character, would never have been the friend of the gratuitous destroyer of the Alexandrian Library, which event, had it taken place, he never would have forgotten. Synesius survived Theophilus, but fortunately died before Hypatia and was spared the sorrow of her dreadful murder.

Is Theophilus the man whom we should accuse of gratuitously destroying the Alexandrian (Serapeum) Library? We say gratuitously because he led and controlled the mob, and Theodoret, an eye-witness of the destruction of the Temple, never mentions the Library.

It is curious that in the long career of the Alexandrian Library its destruction has been definitely reported but twice – once at the time of Caesar's visit (B.C. 47), and finally at the conquest of Alexandria by the Arabs under 'Amr (A.D. 642–6). The first report, we hope, has been shown, in the first chapter of Book IV of this treatise, to have been at least greatly exaggerated, and the second will be treated in the following and concluding chapter of this work.

Dr. Butler, who believes the library of the Serapeum was destroyed when the great temple of Serapis was, as he believes, "destroyed" or that it did not exist in 416, when Orosius wrote, produces the testimony of two writers to sustain his view –

1. F. J. Bacchus: s. v. *Synesius* in *Cath. Encyc.*
2. Synesius: *The Letters of Synesius of Cyrene* (Ep. 16 (157)), tr. Augustine FitzGerald, Oxford, 1926 (p. 99).

Aphthonius and Rufinus, a pagan and a Christian witness. Aphthonius of Antioch, pupil of Libanius, the last of the important Greek rhetors, lived at the end of the fourth and the beginning of the fifth century[1]. He wrote a little book, *Preparatory Exercises*, which has preserved his fame. It was used as a text-book in the Middle Ages, in the Byzantine period, and as late as the seventeenth century. It is so aptly described by Saintsbury:

> One of the most craftsmanlike crambooks that ever deserved the encomium of the epithet and the discredit of the noun (I, p. 92).

In this book he describes the elevated Serapeum area which he calls the "acropolis" of Alexandria. In this *Progymnasmata* Aphthonius gives a comparison between the acropoli of Athens and Alexandria, and much interesting information. Now the first fact to endeavor to ascertain is the date of Aphthonius's visit to Alexandria. The exact date is unknown. Dr. Butler says: "Aphthonius visited Alexandria c. 315 A.D."[2]. M. Matter places the visit as *after* 391[3].

Dr. Butler's date, c. 315, for the visit of Aphthonius is, of course, impossible. Assuming that he was then 30 years of age, it would place his birth 285 A.D. As he lived to the first part of the fifth century (say only to 410), he would have been 125 years old. However, we believe Dr. Butler did not mean this early date, for later in his work (p. 415) he says: "We have the testimony of Aphthonius who visited the Serapeum in the fourth century *some time before* its destruction."

Now Matter meant his date – after 391.

Sandys merely says: "It is this Library [i.e. Serapeum] which is doubtless intended by the rhetorician Aphthonius (end of cent. IV), when he mentions it in the course of his glowing description of the "acropolis" of Alexandria"(p.108).

Aphthonius mentions the Library, but in all the "glowing description" of the acropolis or temple-area – he does not mention the Temple or Sanctuary of Serapis, the most magnificent build-

1. Sandys: *op. cit.* p. 108; p. 381; Croiset: *op. cit.* V-983; Christ: *op. cit.* par. 546[4]; Suidas: s.v. *Aphthonios*; Pauly-Wissowa: Brzoska, art. Aphthonios I; Shaefer: *De Aphthonio Sophista*, Breslau, 1854; Walz: *Rhetores Graeci*, I-54.
2. Butler: *op. cit.* p. 382 (note 2).
3. Matter: *op. cit.*

ing in all the world (perhaps the Capitol of Rome excepted), the interior of which was a veritable Museum of Art. How could this cultured pagan lover of the beautiful have failed to mention the Temple of Serapis? Dr. Butler sees this dilemma and thinks it "very curious". Could it not have been merely reasonable, that the temple was not there, if it had been so completely "destroyed" as Eunapius and Theodoret report[1], or that its beauty and purpose were indeed destroyed, and that all its wonders in ivory, marble, bronze, its fabulous paintings and tapestries were gone.

Aphthonios was a highly cultured pagan – a philosopher who may well have felt that there was nothing that he could say that would properly express his sentiments – pride and a philosophic appreciation of human conduct and of the difficult age in which he lived, all compelled him to treat with silence the great tragedy that had befallen his cause. But as a teacher writing a book for the schools, he did describe or mention the great site and all that he saw was there.

Now Dr. Butler, our most formidable antagonist, a fine scholar of high integrity and ability, tries to present his case fairly. He says:

Since, however, there is no specific evidence that the Library perished in the destruction of the temple, one must show one of two things in order to prove the ruin of the Library – either (1) that the Library was housed in the temple, or (2) that the whole of the

1. As a fact, Dr. Butler admits that Eunapius is guilty of exaggeration (p. 414); and as for Theodoret, this is his description of the "destruction" of the temple:
Moreover he [Theophilus] went up into the temple of Serapis, which has been described by some as excelling in size and beauty all the temples in the world. There he saw a huge image of which the bulk struck beholders with terror, increased by a lying report which got abroad that if any one approached it, there would be a great earthquake, and that all the people would be destroyed. The bishop.... told a man who had an axe to give Serapis a good blow with it. No sooner had the man struck, than all the folk cried out, for they were afraid of the threatened catastrophe. Serapis, however, who had received the blow, felt no pain, inasmuch as he was made of wood, and uttered never a word, since he was a lifeless block. His head was cut off... Serapis was broken into small pieces of which most was committed to the flame, but his head was carried through all the town in sight of his worshippers, who mocked the weakness of him to whom they had bowed the knee.
Thus all over the world the shrines of the idols were destroyed.
Theodoret: *The Ecclesiastical History* (Ch. XXII) tr. Rev. Blomfield Jackson, *Nicene and Post Nicene Fathers* (2nd Series), London, 1892.

buildings on the acropolis were wrecked by the Christians under Theophilus[1].

He adds:

> Of these alternatives the second is easily refuted. I have already shown that as late as the twelfth century there were remains of considerable magnificence still standing[1].

However, he promptly, argumentatively, says that as their [the other buildings on the temple-area – the acropolis] exact position and their original purpose are unknown:

> Accordingly their survival proves nothing except that, if the Library was in these buildings, it may have survived with them (p. 415).

And then he produces his two witnesses: Aphthonios, the pagan, and Rufinus, the Christian, to prove his case.
Aphthonios:

> Now it is admitted that Aphthonius saw the Library, and Sandys has no doubt that what he saw was the Serapeum (or "daughter" library of the great Alexandriana).

When and *where* did he see the library?

The exact date of his visit is unknown. We have already argued *a priori* that his visit was *after* the destruction of the temple. If Matter and others are correct about this, the survival is proven and the case is closed.

But Dr. Butler argued that those who believe this cannot escape the difficulty in which the language of Aphthonios puts them. Aphthonios, he says, distinctly states:

> that the annexes of the temple are built adjoining the colonnades on the inner sides, some used for the library and open for students, others devoted to the service of the ancient gods (p. 415, note 2).

Taking the above literally as Dr. Butler gives it, what does it show?

1. That the library was *not in* the temple.
2. That there were "annexes", rooms, halls, within the great porticoes, which were, of course, adjoining their columns, and were on the inner sides (of their columns or colonnades) and

1. Dr. Butler: *op. cit.* p. 414.

that *these* "annexes" rooms, halls, were some of them used for the library, lecture rooms, and open to students; and others for purposes devoted to the ancient gods.

Why is it unreasonable to assume that the library and its rooms untouched in the destruction of the worship of Serapis were now in charge of appointees of the cultured, literary Theophilus. Some of the other rooms that had been used for the pagan service, we may be sure were now empty or were warehouses for the refuse of the destroyed temple contents, or used for other purposes. Why should we expect Aphthonios, an intellectual traveler, interested in things of culture, to have actually visited *every* room of the vast porticoes or annexes on the acropolis. It may be well to summarize that this vast area, this "acropolis", was occupied by a Propylaeum, by vast porticoes, prostyle, having columns in front with "annexes", rooms or halls on the inner sides of the colonnades, that the area had vast courts, colonnades, the mighty single column (of "Pompey", Diocletian, or "Theodosius", etc.), fountains, and finally the great Temple or Serapis.

We believe that if the great temple itself was *totally* destroyed, in medieval phrase, "from turret to foundation stone", it was the most wonderful exhibition of demolition in all antiquity, presaging indeed the atomic age. But its destruction is of no consequence in this inquiry, because it was not the custom of the Greeks to keep their libraries *in* the temples of their gods. The Library of Aristotle was housed in the Museum on the campus of the Lyceum. When the great Alexandrian Library was founded under Ptolemy Soter, through Demetrios of Phaleron, in a separate building connected with the Museum (itself perhaps connected with the Palace piles), it had no connection with a *temple* of the gods.

When the rolls increased to so vast a number, perhaps under Ptolemy II, the Serapiana was established on the "acropolis" or temple-area (within the annexes of its vast porticoes), under the shadow of the Serapeum, certainly not in the temple proper. There was no reason then or at any subsequent time to actually put the books *in* the temple, but they were placed in the temple-area, on the vast acropolis in convenient rooms or halls, or annexes in the vast porticoes.

There was nothing begging the question when old Matter said[1]

1. M. Matter: *Histoire de l'École d'Alexandrie* (2nd ed.), Paris, 1840, I, p. 321.

over a hundred years ago (we quote Dr. Butler's own translation and his comment):

> Matter justly says: "To make the destruction complete, not only must the sanctuary of Serapis have been destroyed, but also its vast annexes – the courts, porticoes, dwellingrooms and the library which had been established *there* over six centuries" (*École d'Alexandrie*, t. I, p. 321): but the word "there" rather begs the question. He thinks the damage to these buildings was slight and soon repaired; and his conclusion is that, as the remembrance of the older Museum faded, the Serapeum took the place in tradition as well as in fact and that "the new establishment so prospered that at the time of the Arab conquest the Serapeum still possessed a considerable library" (p. 414, note 1).

We agree with Dr. Butler that Matter "justly says" the above, but do not believe that he in any way "begs the question".

In the first chapter of Book IV of this treatise, we felt bound to show what poor knowledge Ammianus had of things Egyptian, particularly of Alexandria. We remember that he spoke of *"libraries* of inestimable value" of the Serapeum. It is true he says that they were destroyed under Caesar, which, of course, is nonsense. But his use of the plural for the Serapeum libraries would at least be correct in tradition and in fact – as this library of the Serapeum seems to have occupied many "annexes" or rooms in the porticoes, as was actually seen by Aphthonios. That Ammianus says they were in the Serapeum should be of little concern, as it is well known that the whole area of the "acropolis" was called the "Serapeum." But it was the sanctuary of the god, the temple proper that Theophilus devastated or "destroyed", not the porticoes where the *libraries* or library *rooms* were.

And now for the second witness, Rufinus the Christian.

Tyrannius Rufinus, presbyter and theological writer and translator was born near Aquileia. He was a man of good lineage, substance and learning. He was not baptised until his twenty-fifth year. Soon afterwards he joined the pilgrimage to the East of Melania, a wealthy Roman lady, a widow and great benefactress of the Church, living some time in Egypt, mostly in Palestine. He was ordained by John, Bishop of Jerusalem, in 390. A great lover of Origen, he translated many of his works and rendered great service to the West by translating the Greek father into Latin.

Early friend of St. Jerome, they quarreled over the Origen controversy. He made a free translation of Eusebius's *Ecclesiastical History* to which he added two books of his own, bringing it down to his time. He was a pupil of Didymus, head of the catechetical school, and of Theophilus who was to become Bishop of Alexandria. He appears to have been a witness of the destruction of the Temple or sanctuary of Serapis, and as he was friendly with Theophilus, he may have marched with him or at least seen him march at the head of his mob, as he led his forces into the Temple to destroy the idol of Serapis and his worship.

Now Rufinus is the sole eyewitness of the destruction of the Sanctuary of Serapis. Dr. Butler feels that, in some way:

> The two accounts help each other out: yet it is very curious that while Aphthonius does not directly mention the temple, Rufinus is totally silent about the Library (p. 416).

And then, in a sort of desperate last resort, Aphthonios is again referred to and the author says: "Moreover, either these shrines(?) were in the temple, or they were in the great exterior range of buildings. But of the latter [the great exterior range of buildings] Rufinus says that they comprised lecture-room or abode for the priest, or for the staff of custodians, or for the monks or ascetics or the like" (p. 416, note 1). Now this merely shows that Rufinus was perfectly aware of *"the great exterior range of buildings"*, even if he was confused as to the miscellaneous uses to which they were put[1].

And so, after all this travail, we have only two facts: that Aphthonios *saw* the Library in "the great exterior range of buildings" and that Rufinus who was a man of letters, who loved books[2], and who alone saw the destruction of the Sanctuary of Serapis, does not say one word about the destruction of the Library.

1. Rev. William Henry Fremantle, Canon of Canterbury, may have meant this when he said of Rufinus's *Ecclesiastical History* that which he relates is "told with little sense of proportion" (*Prolegomena on Life and Writings of Rufinus, Nicene and Post Nicene Fathers*, New York, 1892, III, p. 411).
2. Macarius describes Rufinus as returning to Italy some years before Alaric's sack of Rome (A.D. 385–410) "like a ship laden with the merchandise of the East, an Italian who lived some 25 years in Greek lands, and sufficiently equipped for the work of a translator"; and St. Jerome satirically records how Rufinus dramatically gave his lectures, where "he had a pile of tomes upon the table" before him (Jerome: *Letter to Rusticus* (CXXV–18).

When there is not a single writer or authority, good, bad or indifferent, that infers or says that the Library was destroyed by the Christians in 391, how can there be a doubt as to the soundness of Dr. Bury's dictum:

> There is no reason to suppose that the library was *in* the temple. I conclude then that there is no evidence that the library of the Serapeum did not survive till the Saracen conquest.

CHAPTER XVIII

ISLAM, THE LAST PHASE

> With the first library in the world Alexandria retained at the
> same time, through the whole imperial period, a certain pri-
> macy of scientific work, until Islam burnt the library and killed
> the ancient civilization[1].

———————

IN the preceding chapter, we have endeavored to maintain
that the Library of the Serapeum survived the fatal destruction
of the worship and sanctuary of Serapis by Theophilus in 391
A.D. As not a single writer has shown or a scrap of evidence exists to
record its destruction, and as the long and varied history of the
Alexandrian Library has at least demonstrated its peculiar
quality to survive disaster, it is indeed strange that such a conflict exists among scholars as to its survival to the seventh century
and its final passing, together with the very civilization whose
living muniments it had preserved and guarded, through good
and ill, for nigh a thousand years[2].

Taking Dr. Butler as the foremost protagonist of the Arab
cause, we quote fully from him and shall endeavor to meet his
arguments.

> Granting for a moment that the destruction of the Library took
> place as related, we have to believe that instead of being made
> into a bonfire on the acropolis, the books were laboriously put into
> baskets and taken down to the city; that they were then laboriously
> distributed among the countless baths (Butler, p. 404).

We have to believe nothing about baskets, labor or baths,

1. Theodor Mommsen: *The Provinces of the Roman Empire*, London, 1909, Vol. II,
page 271.
2. We would have liked to begin and also end this chapter with the words of Cardinal
Newman:
> After lasting nearly a thousand years, this noblest of dynastic monuments was
> deliberately burned, as all the world knows, by the Saracens, on their becoming
> masters of Alexandria (*Macedonian and Roman Schools*, p. 93).
This would have satisfied great scholarship nearly a hundred years ago. Curious
it is the Moslems have no quarrel with this statement, but western oriental scholars,
all non-Moslems, have made this chapter necessary.

nothing about six months or seventy days to consume the books; these are the not unusual trimmings of an oriental narrative. Neither have we to be annoyed as to whether the Greek scholar who interceded for the preservation of the residium of the Alexandrian Library was Johannes Philoponus, or some one of another name, or if any known person ever interceded with 'Amr. These too may be embellishments of an early Muslim annalist – we say Muslim, for you must remember that it was a Muslim writer, a man of refinement, character and learning who first refers to the fact of the burning of the books, and he did so as if it, the fact, were commonly known. When we say first, we mean the oldest written authority which we have yet discovered. We do believe that the Christian Copts, who were almost autochthonic, were perfectly aware, as their fathers had been, of the burning of the books.

Now let us leave the amusing features of the controversy aside – such as the proportion of vellum manuscripts to papyrus rolls or documents and whether after deducting the vellum MSS. (because Dr. Butler says: "Now vellum is a material which will not burn as fuel, and all the Caliph's orders could not make it burn: what then became of all these manuscripts?", p. 405) from the mass, there was not enough material to heat the four thousand baths, which one of our Latin scholars tells us the Muslims required at a temperature of at least sixty degrees, and which another has curiously calculated with arithmetical ingenuity that it would require fourteen million[1], or even seventy-two million volumes to properly heat the baths of the devoted city.

By-passing the hyperbole of our Eastern authorities, we find that Dr. Butler lays down that "there are two points presumably vital – the existence of John Philoponus at the time of the conquest and the existence of the Library" (p. 405).

We believe we have said enough about the date of birth and death, the existence or non-existence of Philoponus, although it is curious that the Arabs believe that Philoponus did live until the conquest[2]. Of course, the only question is the existence of the Library.

1. Chauvin: *Le livre dans le monde arabe*, Bruxelles, 1911 (p. 5); quoted in M. Casanova: *L'incendie de la Bibliothèque d'Alexandrie par les Arabes* (Académie des Inscriptions et Belles-Lettres, Séances 1923, Paris, 1923); 14,000,000 was the estimate of M. Chauvin and 72,000,000 of M. Casanova.

2. The celebrated *Fihrist (Index)* (988 A.D.), Flugel–Rodiges ed. Leipzig, 1871, p. 254.

In the previous chapter we have considered the vital question as to whether the Library of the Serapeum was destroyed, when the worship and sanctuary of Serapis were overthrown. We hope we have shown that there is not a particle of evidence to prove its destruction and that it survived to meet its final destiny.

Now it might be said that, although it survived the mobs of Theophilus, at least twenty years afterwards, at the time of the visit of Orosius, it had disappeared. Orosius (*Hist.* VI–15–31), after telling about the burning of books in Caesar's time, which were stored in a building which happened to be nearby, says:

> In regard to this, however true it may be that in some of the temples there remain up to the present time book-chests, which we ourselves have seen, and that, as we are told, these were emptied by our own men in our own day when these temples were plundered – this statement is true enough – yet it seems fairer to suppose that other collections had later been formed to rival the ancient love of literature[1].

But the pleasure of dealing with a scholar as fair and honorable as Dr. Butler makes it unnecessary to elaborate on this point. Suffice to record Dr. Butler:

> Matter is also justified in insisting that Orosius says nothing about the Serapeum... When Prof. Bury adds 'It is highly improbable that Orosius was thinking either of the Alexandrian Library or the Serapeum', in regard to the empty shelves, I agree with him (p. 421, note 1).

And so Sir John Sandys said:

> Orosius at the time of his visit, saw only empty book-cases in 'the temples' of the city, but his evidence is very vague[2].

We feel it is unnecessary to say more about the passage of Orosius, remembering Casaubon's comment that no dependence could be placed on Orosius unless his statement is confirmed by other or trustworthy writers.

However, Dr. Butler is still reluctant to let Orosius rest and says:

1. Paulus Orosius: *Seven Books of History Against the Pagans* (tr. I. W. Raymond), New York, 1936, p. 298.
2. Sandys: *op. cit.* p. 113.

It is simply inconceivable that Orosius in following the train of thought which I have set out, should have passed it over in silence. Orosius therefore is really a witness not to the destruction of the Serapeum Library in 391, but to its non-existence in 416 (p. 422).

This is, of course, another reliance upon an *argumentum e silentio*, of which we shall hear much in marshalling Christian and Muslim, Greek, Syrian, Coptic, and Ethiopian texts, to take the place of simple statements by writers who actually mention our subject. The argument will be treated fully under our examination of John of Nikiu.

Dr. Butler:

> Of course no one supposes that even in the great wars upon books – such as the war made by Diocletian upon Christian books and the war made by Theophilus upon pagan books – all the books in Alexandria perished (p. 422).

But Diocletian did not make war on Christian books, but on the works of necromancers on alchemy and of the pseudo-philosophers who wrote on transmutation of metals – the makers of synthetic gold. Certainly he did not destroy pagan books, and, although we hold no brief for Theophilus, candor compels us to record his zealous and implacable war against pagan worship and pagan sanctuaries, but not against books, pagan or otherwise.

Dr. Butler admits that:

> The very fact that Alexandrian learning was not extinguished proves the use of books (p. 422).

And then he mentions that *before* the conquest John Moschus and his friend Sophronius, two bookish men, visited Egypt and did not mention the Library. Again the negative argument of silence, unfortunate in this place for we know that Aphthonios, also a bookish man, visited Alexandria after, or if you will, just before the destruction of the sanctuary of Serapis, and he does mention the Library.

And then he advances an argument almost ad hominem: if everything that has been heretofore said does not shake the belief in the survival of the Serapeum Library, this should prove that the Arabs did not destroy it – that the Arabs did not enter Alexandria until eleven months after its capture (armistice expiring Sept. 28, 642) and that "not only might the Romans themselves depart, but that they might carry off all their movable possessions and valuables" (p. 423), according to the terms of the Armistice or Surrender Treaty.

Dr. Butler then assumes that "a large number of persons with intellectual interests" would have saved the Library and made "the fabled zeal of John Philoponus" unnecessary! Is there any justification in all history for the assumption that a people in the dreadful situation of the Alexandrians, surrounded by the wild tribesmen of Islam, would have thought of or been able to save more than themselves, their children, their family, their coin and jewels, and their most sacred household souvenirs? Would they have deserted these, and rushed up the steep steps of the acropolis into the rooms of books to save a Clement, an Origen, or some frail classic of ancient Hellas! If in the Great War, the unthinkable should have happened, and London were captured during the Battle of Britain, and the conqueror have given the people an opportunity to leave the devoted city with their personal belongings, how many, in the greatest book centre in the world, how many, in this most cultured city of a cultured age, would have hastened to the British Museum to save some precious muniment of time from the ruthless invader?

And finally, we are told, the *silence* that prevailed in the fifth and sixth century *before*, and during the seventh and eighth century *after* the taking of Alexandria by 'Amr should settle the controversy; particularly when John of Nikiu, the Coptic bishop who wrote at the end of the seventh century, does not mention the Library.

So curious is the mind of man in the spoken and the written word, that the omission, the silence, an hiatus of person, event, or thing, in the literature of any age or clime, should now be recognized as a natural phenomenon. Indeed "it is dangerous to argue from silence", as a fine classical scholar admits[1].

Homer nods, Herodotus, most curious of the curiously-minded Greeks, fails to tell us of the mysterious Sphinx, and Pausanias, the Baedeker of ancient Greece, did not see Lycabettus, that finely shaped hill, which dominates the best views of Athens. Old Timon of Phlius shoots his satiric barb at the bird-cage of the Muses, but misses the opportunity of ridiculing the mountains of

1. W. Rhys Roberts: Demetrius, *On Style* (L.C.L.), p. 272.

books in the Library, as Seneca would hardly have let pass.

Herodes, the writer of mimes, who lived in the days of Ptolemy II (certainly in the third century B.C.) and who knew Alexandria, mentions all the wonders of Alexandria, including the *Museum*, but not a word about the Library[1]. And remember it has been said of Herodes by Dr. Knox that:

> He [Herodes] must at all costs be bookish and removed wholly from common life and common idiom[2].

And yet he does not mention the Library then in the perfect flower of its bloom!

But Herodes, one might say, was a careless writer of light verse.

Yet how will we explain Strabo, a very serious writer of prose, a great traveller and scholar, who wrote "a philosophy of geography". He lived more than five years in Alexandria, being in Egypt when Augustus was still in Samos (20 B.C.) His late distinguished editors do not hesitate to say: "we may infer that it was in the Alexandrian Library that he made from the works of his predecessors those numerous excerpts with which his book is filled"[3].

Now Strabo, as is well known, describes the buildings of Alexandria, one by one, in great detail and in order: the structures along the famous harbors, mentioning structure after structure; and then he mentions the Palaces and the Museum, but not a word about the Library, where he may possibly have been writing his actual text. And let no one imagine that the Library had been "destroyed" under Caesar some twenty-seven years past, for first we believe the most careful study has shown that this is not so, but, even if it were the fact, there was still the great branch (daughter) Library of the Serapeum of thousands of single books and then the 200,000 rolls, single, unmixed, and magnificent collection that had been brought from Pergamum to Alexandria in Cleopatra's day – none of these vast collections

---

1. Herodes: *The Bawd or Matchmaker* (Mime I–21), ed. and tr. by A. D. Knox (L.C.L.), London, 1929.
2. *Herodes, Cercidas and the Greek Choliambic Poets* (L.C.L.) by A. D. Knox, London, 1929, p. XXI.
3. Dr. J. R.S. Sterrett: *The Geography of Strabo* (L.C.L.). Dr. Horace Leonard Jones who has edited and translated the L.C.L. fine edition of Strabo very graciously says that the Introduction was substantially written by Dr. Sterrett before his death.

could have been affected by a fire on the harbor front, when the Serapeum Library was situated on the acropolis of Rhakotis beyond all reach of the flames and, of course, the Pergamene Library was then in Caesar's time still in Pergamum, in the possession of its rightful owners, the princes of the House of Attalus.

Strabo is indeed the perfect example of the fallacy of the argument that the failure of an author to mention a person, an event, a thing or a place is proof that the person, the event, the thing or the place never existed or did not exist at the time of the author's visit or writing. And yet to be fair with Strabo in his omission or silence, he was with the vast majority of ancient writers who most rarely mention the Alexandriana or any library. Did not Polybius fail to record his indebtedness to the Alexandrian Library? We know that Athenaeus later did, although it is thought that he used 1500 rolls of its precious stores in writing *The Deipnosophists*[1].

And this same failure to note, this silence, is likewise a trait of most modern writers, and even when it is mentioned by modern authors, the merest student of this subject can see that it is a casual reference without any claim to research.

Now the main if not the sole argument – as most of the others seem to be trivial – that the Arabs did not destroy the books at Alexandria at the time of the conquest is the silence of certain Greek, Coptic and Ethiopian Christian writers, and certain Arabic Muslim authors of the seventh and eighth centuries.

At the beginning it is well to remember that almost all of these writers have come down to our time in defective manuscripts and that there is hardly a single text in its initial integrity.

As most of the Arabian apologists in this controversy seem to feel that the silence on this subject, in the *Chronicle* of Joannes, Bishop of Nikiu, gives the coup de grâce to the claim of those who believe that there were the remains of the Alexandrian (Serapeum) Library at Alexandria at the coming of the Muslims and that they destroyed books in the devoted city, it may be well to at once examine the book of the Coptic Bishop of Nikiu.

Joannes of Nikiu, an Egyptian town in the Delta, on the Nile, on "the western or Bolbitic main", was a Copt. He became

1. J. Bidez: *Literature and Philosophy in the Eastern Half of the Empire – C.A.H.*, Vol. XII, p. 620.

Bishop of Nikiu and toward the end of the seventh century he wrote a Chronicle. The original work was in Greek, with parts in Coptic. It is lost. It was translated into Arabic. The Arabic version is lost. In 1602 Gabriel, an Egyptian, translated the Arabic version into Ethiopic. There are two manuscripts of the Ethiopic version known, one in the Bibliothèque Nationale and the other in the British Museum, acquired during the British Abyssinian expedition. It has been translated into French by Zotenberg[1] and into English by Dr. Charles[2].

Dr. Charles says "the Ethiopic translators were using an unpointed Arabic text, and were largely ignorant of the historical persons and events described in John of Nikiu's *Chronicle*"[2].

Dr. Butler[3] says:

His [John's] evidence therefore is of extreme value, as far as it goes, though unfortunately parts of the history are entirely wanting, while others are in such lamentable disorder that the sense cannot be followed. But notwithstanding the state of the Ethiopic MS., it gives some fresh dates of remarkable precision and these dates give fixed bases for the construction of a scientific chronology.

And again Dr. Butler in his Preface (p. IX) says of John's book:

Where it is clear and uncorrupted it is of extreme value; but most unhappily it is almost a complete blank from the accession of Heraclius to the arrival of the Arabs before Babylon: thus the story of the Persian conquest and the recovery of Egypt has dropped out, and the history of the later stages of the Arab conquest is in such a tumbled and topsy-turvy state that the true order and meaning of the narrative are almost past the power of criticism to reconstitute.

Now John of Nikiu was an annalist, who wrote in the ecclesiastical manner. He was a Jacobite. His work opens: "In the name of the Father and of the Son and of the Holy Spirit, one God." It ends with a prayer that it may serve to the salvation of the soul and the preservation of the body. "And praise be unto Him, who has given us power to begin and to finish (this work), for ever and ever. Amen. So be it."

This book is in 122 short chapters:

1. Zotenberg: *Chronique* du Jean, Évêque de Nikiou, Paris, 1883.
2. Dr. R. H. Charles: *The Chronicle* of John, Bishop of Nikiu, London, 1916, p. VI.
3. Dr. Butler: *op. cit.* p. 532.

Beginning with Adam and Eve (I); Cronus was a giant of the race of Shem, the first-born of Noah (VI); Zeus was the first to take his sister to wife (VII). Of Alexander he says that when Candace discovered Alexander among the spies sent to her country, she seized him. But he said to her: "Henceforth I will preserve thee unharmed (even) thee and thy children, and I will make thee my wife." And when she heard these words she cast herself at his feet and made alliance with him, and he made her his wife. And therefore the Ethiopians submitted to him (LIX–6).

The following quotations from the text of John of Nikiu are made merely to give some idea of the character of the *Chronicle*, as it has come down to us:

And Diocletian, he went down into Egypt and made it subject to him, and as for the city of Alexandria he destroyed it (LXXVII). Theophilus who destroyed the temple named Serapis and converted it into a church (LXXVIII–45).

And in those days there appeared in Alexandria a female philosopher, a pagan named Hypatia, and she was devoted at all times to magic, astrolabes and instruments of music, and she beguiled many people through (her) Satanic wiles. 88. And the governor of the city honoured her exceedingly; for she had beguiled him through her magic. And he ceased attending church as had been his custom. But he went once under circumstances of danger. And he not only did this, but he drew many believers to her, and he himself received the unbelievers at his house. 89. And on a certain day when they were making merry over a theatrical exhibition connected with dancers, the governor of the city published (an edict) regarding the public exhibitions in the city of Alexandria: and all the inhabitants of the city had assembled there (in the theatre).

And thereafter a multitude of believers in God arose under the guidance of Peter the magistrate – now this Peter was a perfect believer in all respects in Jesus Christ – and they proceeded to seek for the pagan woman who had beguiled the people of the city and the prefect through her enchantments. 101. And when they learnt the place where she was, they proceeded to her and found her seated on a (lofty) chair; and having made her descend they dragged her along till they brought her to the great church, named Caesarion. Now this was in the days of the fast. 102. And they tare off her clothing and dragged her [till they brought her] through the streets of the city till she died. And they carried her to a place named Cinaron, and they burned her body with fire. 103. And all the people surrounded the patriarch Cyril and named him 'the new Theophilus'; for he had destroyed the last remains of idolatry in the city (LXXXIV–87 to 103).

12. And the chief of the faction who was with Jeremiah informed the Moslem troops of the Roman soldiers who were hidden. And so these took them prisoners and put them to death (CXI).

And people began to help the Moslem (CXIII).

6. Then a panic fell on all the cities of Egypt, and all their inhabitants took to flight, and made their way to Alexandria, abandoning all their possessions and wealth and cattle (CXIII).

And he gave them all the booty which he had taken from the city of Alexandria (CXV).

11. Indeed, all the inhabitants of the province submitted to the Moslem, and paid them tribute (CXV).

He attacked the general Domentianus. 5. But when the latter learnt of the approach of the Moslem troops, he embarked on a ship and fled [in a ship] and abandoned the army and their fleet (CXVIII).

1. And Egypt also had become enslaved to Satan. A great strife had broken out between the inhabitants of Lower Egypt, and these were divided into two parties. Of these, one sided with Theodore, but the other wished to join the Moslem. 2. And straightway the one party rose against the other, and they plundered their possessions and burnt their city. But the Moslem distrusted them (CXIX).

9. And Domentianus mustered a large force of the 'Blues'. And when Menas was apprised of this movement, he too mustered

a large force of the 'Greens' and of the troops in the city. And thus these two kept up their hostility (CXIX).

It has been said that this strife and tumult originated in religious dissensions (CXIX).

22. And subsequently he (Pyrrhus) appointed him [Cyrus] a second time to the city of Alexandria, and the priests who were with him. He gave him power and authority to make peace with the Moslem and check any further resistance against them, and to establish a system of administration suitable to the government of the land of Egypt (CXIX).

4. And some of them gave over warring against the Moslem, and turned their hostilities against their own countrymen (CXX).

17. And subsequently the patriarch Cyrus set out and went to Babylon to the Moslem, seeking by the offer of tribute to procure peace from them and put a stop to war in the land of Egypt. And 'Amr welcomed his arrival, and said unto him: 'Thou hast done well to come to us.' And Cyrus answered and said unto him: 'God has delivered this land into your hands: let there be no enmity from henceforth between you and Rome: heretofore there has been no persistent strife with you.' 18. And they fixed the amount of tribute to be paid. And as for the Ishmaelites, they were not to intervene in any matter, but were to keep to themselves for eleven months. The Roman troops in Alexandria were to carry off their possessions and their treasures and proceed (home) by sea, and no other Roman army was to return. But those who wished to journey by land were to pay a monthly(?) tribute. 19. And the Moslem were to take as hostages one hundred and fifty soldiers and fifty civilians and make peace. 20. And the Romans were to cease warring against the Moslem, and the Moslem were to desist from seizing Christian Churches, and the latter were not to intermeddle with any concerns of the Christians. 21. And the Jews were to be permitted to remain in the city of Alexandria (CXX).

36. Now the patriarch Cyrus was greatly grieved on account of the calamities which had befallen the land of Egypt. For 'Amr

had no mercy on the Egyptians, and did not observe the covenant they had made with him, for he was of a barbaric race (CXX).

69. And the general Valentine and his troops were not able to give any assistance to the Egyptians; but the latter, and particularly the Alexandrians, were very hard pressed by the Moslem. And they were not able to bear the tribute which was exacted from them. And the rich men of the city (country?) concealed themselves ten months in the islands (CXX).

72. On the twentieth of Maskaram, Theodore and all his troops and officers set out and proceeded to the island of Cyprus, and abandoned the city of Alexandria. And thereupon 'Amr the chief of the Moslem made his entry without effort into the city of Alexandria. And the inhabitants received him with respect; for they were in great tribulation and affliction (CXX).

10. And now many of the Egyptians who had been false Christians denied the holy orthodox faith and lifegiving baptism, and embraced the religion of the Moslem, the enemies of God, and accepted the detestable doctrine of the beast, this is Mohammed, and they erred together with those idolaters, and took arms in their hands and fought against the Christians. 11. And one of them, named John, the Chalcedonian of the Convent of Sinai, embraced the faith of Islam, and quitting his monk's habit he took up the sword, and persecuted the Christians who were faithful to our Lord Jesus Christ (CXXI).

1. (Herewith) ends this blessed book which John the rector bishop of Nikius composed for the profit of the soul (CXXIII).

Now we have quoted in extenso from the *Cronicle* of John to give some idea to the reader as to this work and how it has come down to us. The excellent labors of Dr. Charles in translating this work, which is out of print and most difficult to obtain, need no commendation at this date.

Now John of Nikiu does not mention the burning of the books or the Library. But in all fairness, must we not admit that there are hundreds of other events which the worthy bishop has failed to mention, as well as hundreds of items that he has erroneously described. Perhaps if we had his original text, it would appear, perhaps not. Of course, we make no point as to this. A statement of John of Nikiu that the Arabs did not destroy the books would be of great importance, though unreasonable to understand, because it was and is to this day the traditional belief of his own people, the Copts, that the books of the Library were destroyed by the Arab conquerors.

And it is important that we remember Dr. Butler's own opinion of the historic value of Coptic writers and documents (p. X):

> But the historical value of these Coptic documents is not very great.
>
> The writers were set upon recording matters of Church interest – the more miraculous the better – and their minds were almost closed to the great movements of the world about them. It is useless lamenting that, where they might have told us so much, they furnish only a few scanty and incidental allusions to contemporary history.

Still the concluding statements of Dr. Butler (p. 425) are:

> That if the Library had been removed, or if it had been destroyed, the almost contemporary historian and man of letters, John of Nikiou, could not have passed over its disappearance in total silence.
>
> The conclusion of the whole matter can be no longer doubtful. The suspicion of Renaudot and the scepticism of Gibbon are more than justified. One must pronounce that Abû'l Faraj's story is a mere fable, totally destitute of historical foundation.

These final statements of Dr. Butler, though sound in rhetoric, are hardly founded in logic. They merely show that in his very able treatment of a negative case he has convinced himself that the Arabs are entitled to an acquittal, if not to a Scotch verdict.

Of course, we know that John of Nikiu was not an historian[1] and could hardly be classed as a man of letters, and that the "suspicion" of even a Renaudot or the "scepticism" of even a Gibbon could hardly take the place of common proofs of the fact. And then we know that the story of the burning is not Abû'l

---

1. Dr. R. H. Charles in his *The Chronicle* of John, Bishop of Nikiu (London, 1916), says: "John of Nikiu is merely an annalist." (p. XI.)

Faraj's "fable", but that that distinguished historian and scholar most certainly derived it from the Muslim diplomatist and scholar, Ibn al Kifti, who wrote about 1227.

If in the foregoing pages we have utterly failed in our attempt to meet the arguments of Dr. Butler, then it would seem appropriate for the reader to end his travail here. If, however, we have at least thrown grave doubts on the case as presented by Dr. Butler, then it becomes our duty to advance our proofs and arguments in support of our belief that there were the remnants of the Alexandrian (Serapeum) Library at the coming of the Muslims and that they destroyed the books that were there – even if but the last modicum of the famed Alexandriana.

Our case rests on at least the following principal points:

1. The Coptic Tradition.
2. The Oriental flavor of the story of the burning.
3. The known historic character and conduct of Omar.
4. 'Abd al Latîf.
5. Ibn al Kifti.
6. Gregory, Abû'l Faraj, bar Hebraeus.
7. Abû'l Fidâ.
8. Makrîzî.
9. Hadji Khalifa.
10. Jurji Zaydan.
11. The "silence", if we must consider a negative, of any writer denying the Destruction.

1. *The Coptic Tradition*

The unshakable tenacity of Coptic tradition is proverbial. How well Dr. Butler says:

> To the Copts Alexandria was always known less by the name oɩ its great founder than by that of the fishing-village [Rakoti] which existed for ages before Alexander – a curious instance of their time-defying conservatism (p. 380).

If it is so that in the various parts of the works which have survived to our time of writers known to us from John of Nikiu to Abu Salih, there is no reference to the Library, may we not at least urge that the fact survived for several centuries as an unwritten tradition? Dr. Butler here says:

And this view may be held to receive conformation from the undoubted fact that the tradition lives to this day among the Copts, although they give seventy days, instead of six months for the burning (p. 403).

And it must be remembered that all of our history of the past is a composite of unwritten tradition, written statements of writers and a few monuments.

Should we not repeat here, Sir Frederick Kenyon's masterful dictum of Tradition:

> Tradition is a bad master, but is a useful guide and the scholar must teach himself not to be afraid of it. It is by no means always to be accepted, but it should always be scrutinized with respect; and it should be realized that the early Christian centuries were not wholly credulous, not deficient in critical ability[1].

And so, at all events, a tradition that was old in 1200, in 'Abd al Latíf's day[2], may be as well assumed to have originated naturally with the fact of the destruction, as to assume that it started at some unknown date, out of some whim of imagination.

2. *The Oriental Tone of the Story*

Dr. Butler says:

> It is undeniably picturesque, and the reply of Omar has the true Oriental flavour. This really is the strongest point about it (p. 403).

Perhaps the very cause of the modern doubt and disbelief of the story is the oriental embellishments. Just to destroy books is a matter of ordinary interest, but to use them to heat the 4000 baths of the imperial city of Alexandria; to drown in the water, as well as burn in fire, the books of the fire-worshippers of Persia; and to make a veritable bridge of books across the Tigris, which all the while ran black with the blood of the priceless manuscripts of Muslim Baghdad – these are stories to excite the interest of the oriental mind. But because the literary enthusiasms, the poetic licenses, taken by every chronicler or historian of the East, are not to be considered literally does not likewise mean that the kernel of the story, the statement of fact – the *destruction* of books –

---

1. Sir Frederick G. Kenyon: *The Bible and Modern Scholarship*, London, 1948.
2. Dr. Butler is mistaken when he says that there is nothing to show this Coptic tradition as being older than Abû'l Faraj. Certainly it was common knowledge when 'Abd al Latíf wrote.

is also to be disbelieved. If you apply this rule to the general run of oriental literature, you might, indeed, as well burn or drown all their books.

Does not the oriental writer in extolling the fabulous wealth that fell into the lap of the Moslem conquerors of Alexandria and of Egypt, in describing the endless line of camels bearing the treasures of the soil and the treasury of spoil to the Caliph at Medina, say that when the first camel of the unbroken line of beasts of burden entered the Gate of Medina, the last camel of the line had not yet left Egyptian soil. Now because this description of the line of camels is preposterous, it does not also mean that the produce and spoil of Egypt were not sent to Medina. In describing the city of Cairo:

He who hath not seen Cairo hath not Seen the World.
Her Soil is Gold;
Her Nile is a Marvel;
Her Women are as the bright-eyed Houris of Paradise;
Her Houses are Palaces, and her Air is soft, with an Odour above Aloes, refreshing the Heart;
And how should Cairo be otherwise, when she is the Mother of the World?[1]

3. *The known historic character of Omar*

Omar was a convert-fanatic to the cause of Islam. He was an energetic and ruthless warrior. A distinguished oriental scholar, M. Casanova, Arabic apologist, who does not believe in the burning of the Alexandrian Library[2], has set forth clearly the tradition as to Omar's dictum: "No other book but the book of God", and he admits that the legend reflects a state of mind which had really existed among the first Muslims. And then he gives the famous account which shows that Omar was fanatically a man of *One* Book – the *Koran*.

Toward the middle of the ninth century, the two principal traditionists of Islam, Bouharî and Mouslim, relate that, according to Ibn 'Abbas, the cousin of Mohammed, the prophet feeling the approach of death, wanted to write a book that would protect the Muslim from error. Omar was present and loudly

1. Stanley Lane-Poole: *The Story of Cairo*, London, 1902, p. VI.
2. M. Casanova: *L'incendie de la Bibliothèque d'Alexandrie par les Arabes* (*Académie des Inscriptions et Belles-Lettres* – Séances, 1923, Paris, 1923).

cried out: "Pain makes our prophet delirious; we have the book of God, that will suffice us." Those who were present divided into two groups, those who believed like Omar and those who wanted to obey the prophet. The latter did not want a quarrel to take place in his presence, and Ibn 'Abbas retired disconsolate[1].

The tradition is believed by the Muslim, and certainly Omar was successful in preventing his co-religionist from receiving a second text.

M. Casanova says:

> His lieutenant 'Amr must have shared this opinion, if we believe a curious Syriac document with which M. l'abbé Nau has acquainted us[2]. In fact, he ['Amr] had the pretention to impose it on the Christians: summoning the Jacobite patriarch of Syria, John I he asked him: "If there is a single Gospel, without any diversity, which all those who are Christians believe in.... Why, since the Gospel is one, is the faith different?" The patriarch endeavored to show that the Christians could have other books than the Gospel, and M. l'abbé Nau remarks: 'Amr's pretention to bring the Christian back to one book, the Gospel, prepares us for the dilemma in consequence of which, following Omar's advice, he would have burned, some years later, the library of Alexandria.

And Herr Ludolf Krehl[3], also an Arab apologist, says:

> The character of Omar, a convert enthusiast Muslim, rigorous in life and manners, a dictator by nature, willing it is true to admit an error in religious decision if shown, was just the man to do a thing like the burning of the library (p. 436). A collection of writings in which nothing was mentioned of the religion which to him was the sole truth, could but appear to him as a dangerous infection – a focus of harmful influence – he well could have thought it necessary to destroy.

From the above, from those who oppose our view, certainly the characters of both Omar and 'Amr are shown to be such that they would destroy the Library.

1. M. Casanova: *op. cit.*, who cites authorities.
2. M. l'abbé Nau: *Un colloque du Patriarche Jean avec l'émir des Agaréens*, in *Journal Asiatique*, 11th series, Vol. V (1915), pp. 225–279.
3. Ludolf Krehl: *Ueber die Sage von der Verbrennung der alexandrinischen Bibliothek durch die Araber* (in International Congress of Orientalist held in Florence, 1878 (Firenze, 1880, p. 436).

And to the late contentions that though the Persian books were destroyed by order of Omar[1] but not the Greek books, and that the Muslim would not have destroyed any book containing the name of God, we submit that the early Muslim had a perfect horror of the written word, and that certainly Omar nor his lieutenants had the knowledge of tongues that would have enabled them to distinguish the books of Zarathushtra from the *Theogony* of Hesiod, the commentaries of the Fathers, not to mention the numerous classics of Hellenic literature.

4. *'Abd al Latîf*

'Abd al Latîf (1160–1231) of Baghdad, a celebrated physician, writer and traveller, was a seeker after knowledge who journeyed throughout the East with letters of commendation from the wazir of Salah ed-Din, in order to meet the great scholars of his age and visit the seats of learning. He was a man of high talent, keen, with an eagerness to learn, who with judgment used books, travel, and contemporary scholars as his university, and from these sources acquired a vast fund of knowledge which in his profession of medicine he employed to correct the anatomy of Galen, and in his profession of letters to illustrate the geography and history of Egypt. He taught philosophy and medicine at Damascus and Cairo and enjoyed a distinguished place among the illuminati that graced the court of Salah ed-Din at Jerusalem.

He was a versatile Arab scholar, and "his numerous writings cover almost the whole domain of the knowledge of those days"[2].

In his long, active intellectual life, he wrote many books; we are told of a charming *Autobiography*, which unfortunately we

1. Ibn Khaldun of Tunis (1332–1406) in his *Prolegomena*, "the most remarkable product of Islamic thought", in discussing what has perished of the ancient sciences, does not hesitate to ask:
Where, for instance, is the learning of the Persians, which Omar ordered to be destroyed at the Arab conquest? (Vol. I, p. 61).
Now this work of Ibn Khaldun has been declared by Prof. Toynbee: "He has conceived and formulated a philosophy of history which is undoubtedly the greatest work of its kind that has ever yet been created by any mind in any time or place." We believe we should note that Mr. Charles Issawi in his fascinating selections from the *Prolegomena, An Arab Philosophy of History*, London, 1950 (p. 36), says on the authority of Dr. Butler: "There is no historical basis whatsoever for the often repeated legend that Omar ordered the destruction of Greek and Persian books." Yet Ibn Khaldun thought that there *was* such an historical basis for his statement, like many of the Muslim and Arabic writers who had preceded or followed him.
2. M. Th. Houtsma: *The Encyclopaedia of Islam*, Leyden (1913) s.v. *'Abd al-Latîf*, p. 47.

do not know, and of his vivid *Account of Egypt* which is known to the West[1].

Now 'Abd al Latîf was a Muhammadan, a man not only of note and learning, but of unassailable patriotism. In speaking of Alexandria, he tells of:

> The academy erected by Alexander when he built this city, and in which he deposited the library consigned to the flames, with the permission of Omar, by 'Amr ibn el-As.

This at present is the earliest account that we have of the burning of the Library by 'Amr by authority of Omar. And this account is written not by a Christian who was a Greek scholar, by but a reliable Muhammadan man of letters.

We say "at present" because it is but reasonable to assume that accounts of the destruction may be found in other writers or in better manuscripts of known writers which may be later discovered. When Dr. Butler wrote (1902), the next writer, Ibn al Kifti was apparently unknown.

Now 'Abd al Latîf mentions this burning under Omar quite incidently and as a matter of well known fact. There is not the faintest indication that he felt that he was stating anything new. It would seem an unsafe assumption of scholarship to say that 'Abd al Latîf is the *first* author to refer to the destruction of the books under Omar, because for years it has been stated that the Abû'l Faraj, bar Hebraeus, was the *first* author to report the "fable" of the details of the burning of the books, for which he had no authority, but now we know that this is not so and that he had good Muslim authority for his account[2].

5. *'Ali ibn al Kifti*

Ibn al Kifti (1172–1248) was born at Kift (old Coptos) Upper Egypt, of a family of pure Arab origin. His father and grandfather had held high official positions under the Aiyubids, Salah ed-Din, and other Muslim rulers. He unable to escape the traditions of his family, likewise held various high diplo-

---

1. 'Abd al Latîf: *Relation de l'Egypte*, tr. Silvestre de Sacy, Paris, 1810, p. 183; J. White: *Abdollatiphi Historiae Aegypti compendium*, Oxford, 1800, p. 114.
2. Dr. Butler: *op. cit.* Dr. Butler thought even the Coptic tradition could not be older than Abu 'l Faraj, because he was, as it was then thought, the first writer to tell the full story (p. 403; also p. 425).

matic and political positions, "but his inclinations were rather towards scholarship"[1]. He wrote many literary and historical works, many of which are lost. His *History of the Seldjuks* is considered an important loss to historical scholarship. There is a posthumous work on the poets that has survived; a synopsis of his *History of the Grammarians*; but the most valuable of his literary labors that have survived is his *Kitab Ikhbar al-'Ulama bi-Akhbar al-Hukama (History of the Wise)* (and that through an extract made from it in 1249), which is "our most important source for the history of the exact sciences and Hellenistic tradition in Islam"[2].

On account of the major importance of Ibn al Kifti in this inquiry, we are privileged to give a new, literal and complete translation of all the passages on Yahyā (John, the grammarian), and the full text of the burning of the books, as found in his *Ta'rikh al-Hukama*[3]:

> (p. 354) The Egyptian from Alexandria, disciple of Shawari [Aristotle]. He was a bishop in the Church of Alexandria in Egypt. He was originally a Jacobite. But after reading the books of philosophy, he changed his mind and believed no more of the Christian creed of the Trinity, as he thought it impossible to make "Three" of the "One" and "One" of the "Three". When the Bishops of Egypt knew of the change occurring to him and were sure of that, they found this too much for them to accept, and held a meeting to discuss the matter with him. They beat him in the discussion and proved the falsehood of his creed. They nevertheless felt sorry for his ignorance. They thus pleaded with him and assured him of their sorrow and sympathy, and then asked him to change his mind and to stop proclaiming the ideas which he declared and which were the subject of his discussion with them. He refused, and upon that they deprived him of his dignities and caused him to suffer much adversity.

> Yahyā lived until 'Amr ibn al-'As conquered Egypt and Alexandria. He went to see 'Amr, who was well informed about his vast knowledge, his creed and what happened between him and the Chris-

---

1. C. Brockelmann: *The Encyc. of Islam*, s.v. *al-Kifti*.
2. Idem, p. 1004.
3. This translation, especially made for this book, is the work of the distinguished scholar, Dr. Hussein Monés, assistant professor of history at Fouad I University, Cairo, Egypt.

tians. 'Amr respected him highly and saw that he was really worthy of great honour. He heard his arguments against the Trinity and admired them. He also listened to him speaking about the end of the world and was charmed with it. 'Amr was greatly astonished as he heard his logical arguments and his philosophical expressions which the Arabs did not know before.

'Amr was a wise man and enjoyed listening, and was of a fine mind; he thus kept Yahyā so near to him that he rarely parted with him.

One day Yahyā said to him: "You have already put all the depots of Alexandria under your control and sealed everything in it. (p. 355) I have no objection as to the things which may be of any use to you, but as for those other things of which you and your people can make no use, we should rather have them. Please give orders to set them free." 'Amr said: "What are the things that you need?" He answered: "The books of wisdom [hikma may be *philosophy* too] which are in the royal treasuries. You have laid hands upon them and we need them. You cannot make ány profit of them." 'Amr said: "And who collected these books and what is their story?" Yahyā said: "When Ptolemy Philadelphus, king of Alexandria, ascended the throne he became very fond of knowledge and learned men. He searched for books of knowledge and ordered them to be gathered and bought however high their prices might be and offered the merchants the best conditions which would make them bring their books over there. All this was done, and in a short while 54,000 books were gathered. When the king took notice of that he said to Zamira [this may be one of his counselors i.e. Demetrios of Phaleron]: 'Do you think there are still on earth books of knowledge out of our hands?' Zamira said: 'Yes, there are still multitudes of them in Sind [North India], India, Persia, Jurjān [Georgia approximately], Arman [Armenia], Babylonia, Musil and in the lands of Rūm [the Greeks].' The king was astonished to hear that and said to him: 'Continue gathering them.' In that way he went till he died. These books continued to be well preserved and guarded by the kings and their followers till our days." 'Amr felt that what Yahyā said was important and kept wondering about it and said: "I cannot dispose of these books without the permission of 'Umr ibn al-Khittāb." He then wrote to 'Umar, telling him all that Yahyā said and asked him to instruct him as to what he should do with them. 'Umar in his answer said "...and as for the books you mentioned: if their contents agree with the Book of

Allāh [the Korān] we can dispense with them, as the Book of Allāh is — in this case — more than enough. If they contain anything against what is in the Book of Allāh, there is no need to keep them. Go on and destroy them." 'Amr began, upon receiving these instructions, to distribute them among the baths of Alexandria to be burnt in their stoves [also heaters]. The number of these baths was well known (p. 356), but I forget it. It is related that the baths took six months to burn them. Hear what happened and wonder!

Now, M. Casanova, in his learned study[1], says:

About 1227 Ibn al Kifti wrote a *Histoire des Savants*[2]. Speaking of Yahyā al Nahawi[3], he relates that he described to 'Amrou, the conquering Arab general of Egypt about 640, the literary treasures contained in the library of Alexandria. The latter amazed replied that he could do nothing without receiving instructions from the caliph 'Oumar. "He wrote then to 'Oumar reporting Yahyā's story, and asked him how he was to proceed. 'Oumar's reply was as follows: "Regarding the books of which you have told us, if they contain any thing which conforms to the Book of God (the Koran), the Book of God permits us to eliminate them; if they contain any thing which is contrary, they are useless; proceed then to destroy them." 'Amrou distributed them among the baths of Alexandria and ordered them burned in the warming-rooms"[4].

Now M. Casanova considers as a matter of serious importance that the account which Ibn al Kifti has attributed to Jean the Grammarian appears in the celebrated bibliographical treatise known as the *Fihrist* (Index)[5] drawn up in 988 by Abû'l Faraj Muhammed al Nadim, known as al Warraq (the bookseller of Baghdad). Al Warraq merely tells us that Jean lived until the conquest of Egypt by 'Amr, with whom he was in great favor. Of course, the *Fihrist* was a catalogue of many precious, rare and lost books, but it was not an epitome of the works recorded.

1. M. Casanova: *op. cit.*
2. Ibn al-Qifti: *Ta'rikh al-Hukama*, ed. Julius Lippert, Leipzig, 1903, p. 8 of the Introduction.
3. Jean le Grammairien, who is identified as Jean Philoponus. See Leclerc, *Histoire de la médecine arabe*, Paris, 1876, 2 vols. Vol. I, p. 56–60, who first pointed out the text of Ibn al Kifti.
4. Ibn al Kifti: *op. cit.* pp. 355–356.
5. Edition Flugel-Rodiges, Leipzig, 1871, p. 254.

M. Clément Huart, the distinguished Secretary-Interpreter for oriental language to the French government, has here a very valued comment:

> It is a catalogue of books, most of which have now disappeared, either because they did not survive the great catastrophes which overtook the Baghdad Libraries (destroyed by the Mongols in the thirteenth and by Tamerlane in the fifteenth century) – disasters which may compare, as regards the Arab Middle Ages, with the various destructions of the Alexandrian Library in ancient times... or they may have been epitomized in more recent works[1].

One can well understand the disaster to scholarship in the loss of all these precious or at least valuable books, any number of which might have settled for all time the present controversy.

But Ibn al Kifti survives and he reports the destruction. Either we have to accept it as an account of a reliable writer – a good source – as most of the accounts of ancient writers are received and which go to form the mass of history, or we have to reject it on some reasonable ground.

All the ingenuity and brilliant scholarship of M. Casanova has been brought to bear to find a "reasonable" explanation for rejecting Ibn al Kifti. At the outset, let us disencumber ourselves of all the oriental trimmings, the romantic setting, for the story, and consider merely the essence of the account, the thing alone which can be of concern to scholarship – *the destruction of books at Alexandria by the Arab conquerors*. All other questions are trivial. The friendships of 'Amr may have a romantic aspect; certainly the number of books required to heat 4000 baths for a definite time can only be of interest to plumbers or heating contractors.

The case of M. Casanova vs. Ibn al Kifti:

1. It is Ibn al Kifti who has invented (or added) this episode, probably embellishing a story which was current in Egypt in his day. We must assume that "this episode" means the *baths*, not *the destruction of the books*.

However, if inventing or adding "this episode", that is if "this episode" means the destruction of the books, the baths, and

1. Clément Huart: *A History of Arabic Literature*, N.Y., 1915, p. 186.

the whole story, then M. Casanova realized that Abd al Latîf had already written of the burning of the books as a matter of common knowledge.

2. As he seems to desire to have the dubious honor of originating this story to belong to Ibn al Kifti or at least to his family, M. Casanova surmises that as Abd al Latîf visited Jerusalem, he may have met the father of Ibn al Kifti, who was the cadi, that it was from his contemporary. Ibn al Kifti's father, the cadi, that Abd al Latîf obtained the first account to which he briefly alludes in his *Account of Egypt*, and that it was Ibn al Kifti, the cadi's son, who later related the story in full.

Be this as it may, M. Casanova is convinced that the first author of the story belonged to Salah ed-Din's entourage, and that he *created or revived the anecdote* in order to flatter the new ruler of Egypt.

3. Indeed, the whole theory of M. Casanova is based upon the supposition that Ibn al Kifti in order to flatter Salah ed-Din compares his master – the Second Conqueror of Egypt – with 'Amr, the First Conqueror. And as Salah ed-Din, after abolishing the Fatimite dynasty, was guilty of dispersing at auction the treasures of the Fatimite palaces and particularly the extensive and valuable libraries of these princes[1], it would be well to show that the great 'Amr also not only dispersed, but destroyed books.

It is with some embarrassment that we attempt to defend Ibn al Kifti against the arguments of this distinguished oriental scholar. It is our belief that Ibn al Kifti was an aristocrat of purest Arab stock, that he was the scion of a line of distinguished ancestors who were holders of great place and men of character and intellect, and that he, himself, was an historian, a man of

---

[1]. Stanley Lane-Poole in *Saladin and the Fall of the Kingdom of Jerusalem*, New York, 1898 (p. 115), however says:
Of all the treasures that he found, Saladin, kept nothing for himself. Some he distributed among his followers, or presented to Nur-ed-din; the glorious library of 120,000 manuscript volumes he gave to his learned chancellor the Kady ed-Fadel; the rest of the treasures was sold for the public purse.
And in a note the author says the library was reported by some as 2,600,000 volumes, including 1220 copies of one book, the History of At-Tabari. Mr. Lane-Poole reminds us that in number and statistics Oriental writers are to be hardly trusted. This is but another example of the exaggeration of the East.
This work of Lane-Poole is characterized by Sobernheim (*Encyc. of Islam*: s.v. *Saladin*) as that "brilliant and lucid" study.

letters and a bookman, and that it is unthinkable that he could have permitted his pen to malign one of the great heroes of his race and faith.

It is well known that he disliked public office, which was thrust upon him, due to his distinguished family connections. He became governor of Aleppo (1214) much against his will. When Malek al Zahir died, he quickly gave up the post. Twice again fate seemed to force upon him public duties, but his true flare was that:

> He was a great lover of books, and had turned his back on all other eartly delights, so as to indulge his favourite passion[1].

Was this the scholar who would invent, add to, or trifle with a subject representing an act, that not only racially, spiritually, intellectually, but personally, must have been abhorrent to him?

The most reasonable conclusion is that he wrote the account, deriving it from some earlier authority which he considered good, and to assume that he or someone in the entourage of Salah ed-Din invented or built up the story is as sound as the old suspicion or belief held for years that Abû'l Faraj, bar Hebraeus, may have invented or built up the story, when we now know that he merely derived it from this Muslim scholar, Ibn al Kifti.

6. Gregory, Abû'l Faraj, bar Hebraeus

Many pages we wrote, in former years, to defend Gregory, when now we know that he needs no defense. He is the sole Christian of former ages, of whom we know up to now, who has given a description of the destruction of the books.

Abû'l Faraj, bar Hebraeus (1226–1286 or 1287), Arab historian, son of a Jewish physician convert to Christianity and last great classical author in Syriac literature, was a universal scholar of profound erudition and a man of high character and integrity[2]. He was a grammarian, Biblical commentator, theologian, philosopher, physician, poet and historian, with the most useful advantage of the gift of tongues. In the course of his episcopal duties, he made many journeys, in which he never failed to advantage

---

1. Clément Huart: *A History of Arabic Literature*, N.Y., 1915, p. 196.
2. It is refreshing in the annals of history to meet with an historian who has the suffrages of Christian, Jew, Muhammadan and agnostic.

his scholarly vocation by visits to convents, libraries, and seats of learning. How delightfully does he tell us of his method of historical research:

> Therefore, according to what time has brought I, having entered the Library of the City of Maraghah of Adharbaidjan, have loaded up this my little book with narratives which are worthy of remembrance, from many volumes of the Syrians, Saracens (Arabs) and Persians which are (preserved) here[1].

How we used to grieve that he had not mentioned his source. Even the most daring, outspoken Arabic apologists, however, did not venture to openly accuse him of inventing the details of the story of the burning of the books – it was too unreasonable that he should gratuitously insult his Muslim friends, besides that the known high character of the man and the scholar precluded such an attack. But a fine orientalist thought we could at least blame it on the Byzantines! Dr. Krehl[2] says:

> Faraj who wrote in Mesopotamia and who probably used Byzantine authorities... It is quite probable that the whole story was made up by Byzantines to make the Muslims barbarians.

Of course, no one thought to inquire why we do not find it in the Byzantine writers. And why should a scholar imagine that something had to be done to make the early Muslims of the conquest barbarians?[3] But in the eleventh-twelfth century, Ibn al Kifti and his associates were scholars and gentlemen. And we do not believe that he, Ibn al Kifti, invented the details of the story.

Faraj, in his numerous journeyings, sought converse with wise and cultured men, all in furtherance of the acquisition of an enormous fund of learning which he seemed to pursue with enthusiasm and a technical sense of good bibliography. He wrote an extensive history called the *Chronicon*, from the creation to his day.

At the request of prominent Muhammadan friends and admirers[4], he translated into Arabic an abridgment of his work,

1. *The Chronography* of Gregory, Abul Faraj (Bar-Hebraeus), *op. cit.* I, Introduction.
2. Krehl: *op. cit.* p. 448.
3. Were not the ancestors of most Europeans in the time of Caesar barbarians?
4. C. Brockelmann in *The Encyc. of Islam*, s.v. *Bar Hebraeus*.

under the title *History of the Dynasties*[1]. It was not merely an epitome of his larger work, but partly an original treatise. It is in this work that this serious and usually reliable historian tells the famous story of the final destruction of the Alexandrian Library:

> John the Grammarian, a famous peripatetic philosopher, being in Alexandria at the time of its capture, and in high favor with Amr, begged that he would give him the royal library. Amr told him that it was not in his power to grant such a request, but promised to write to the caliph for his consent. Omar, on hearing the request of his general, is said to have replied that if those books contained the same doctrine with the Koran, they could be of no use, since the Koran contained all necessary truths; but if they contained anything contrary to that book, they ought to be destroyed, and therefore, whatever their contents were, he ordered them to be burnt. Pursuant to this order, they were distributed among the public baths, of which there was a large number in the city, where, for six months they served to supply the fires.

He must have known of 'Abd al Latîf's earlier brief account. We now know that he certainly knew of Ibn al Kifti's fuller account, and perhaps other authorities. Certainly he must have considered these authorities sound and worthy of respect, particularly when he puts this story in the epitome of his larger *Chronicon* which he actually translated in Arabic at the request of Muhammadan friends. He could hardly have included this account except that he knew that his Muslim friend had heard of it and would deem it proper that it should be recorded by him.

7. *Abû'l Fidâ*

Abû'l Fidâ (1273–1331) was an Arabian prince born in Damascus. Although he was a distinguished soldier and when he died was Sultan of Hamat, where his court was the resort of scholars and artists, his fame is as a man of letters. He wrote two outstanding works: *Universal History* (pre-Islamic history and Islam to the year 729); and his *Geography*, of which the Library of Leyden possesses the MS. corrected with his own hand[2].

1. a. *Specimen Historiae Arabum* sive Gregorii Abul Farajii: opera and studio, Edward Pocock, Oxford, 1650. b. *Specimen Historiae Arabum*, Edward Pocock, edited by Josephus White, Oxford, 1806. c. There is an edition by Rev. Father Salhani (Beyrout); and a translation in German by Herr Bauer, which we have not seen.
2. Brockelmann: *The Encyc. of Islam*, s.v. *Abu 'al-Fida*, I, p. 85.

He made his reputation by his *Universal History*, which was known to the West before the texts of Ibn al-Athir and al-Tabari. It is considered an abridgment of Ibn al-Athir's (b. Kurdistan 1160–d. Mosul 1234) *Complete Chronology* (to year 1231). Now al-Athir's work is muchly abridged from Tabari (838–923) (that is the portion from the Creation to the tenth century), although Herr Brockelmann has shown that al-Athir added information from other sources[1].

Abû'l Fidâ gives the account of the burning of the books, and is one of "the other Arab authors who have only repeated what their predecessors have said"[2].

8. al-Makrîzî

al-Makrîzî (1364–1442) was born at Cairo. He was an Arabian historian of prodigious output and unlimited plans for vast literary and historical writings. He was thoroughly educated by his grandfather, became the head of the al-Hakimiya mosque and was a teacher of tradition. He went to Damascus for some time, spent five years in Mecca, and then returned to Cairo, where he retired to a private station and devoted his life entirely to literary labors. He died at Cairo the 27th of Ramadan (Febr. 9, 1442)[3].

He began his great activities as a writer of history, with his own local community and country; then extended it to neighboring lands, such as Abyssinia. He wrote essays on historical questions and kindred subjects. He planned a supplemental work to his famous *Khitat* which was to contain the biographies of all the rulers and famous men who had lived in Egypt. It was to be in 80 volumes. There are three authographic volumes at Leyden and one at Paris. He then planned a work to begin with the Creation, to give a general geography, and to contain the genealogies of all the tribes of Arabia, including a history of Persia down to the Sassanians. He was actually laboring at this tremendous work in 1441.

His great and principal work was his *al-Khitat* (*The Survey*). It is a history and geography of Egypt, with special treatment of the topography of Fustat and Cairo. After a long historical and

1. Huart: *op. cit.*, p. 206.
2. Casanova: *op. cit.*
3. Brockelmann: *The Encyc. of Islam*, s.v. *al-Makrîzî*, II, p. 175.

geographical introduction, he begins his description of the country with Alexandria[1]. It was this work that gives him the title of Historian of Muslim Egypt[2].

Now he reports the account of the burning of the Library. When speaking of the Serapeum, he says:

> Some think that these columns upheld the Porch of Aristotle who taught philosophy here: that it was a school of learning: and that it contained the library which was burnt by 'Amr on the advice of the Caliph Omar[3].

Now what fault can be found with this statement. Makrîzî was an historian, he was writing the history of his country, when on the subject of Alexandria, he speaks of the Serapeum, referring to the Porch of Aristotle (sic), but remember that Aristotle, the scholar, and Alexander, the warrior, were the two Greeks best known to the Arabs. And exactly in this place (the Serapeum), most appropriately, he refers to the burning of the Library by 'Amr on the order of Omar. He must have thought this to be his duty, to state at least the cold fact without the fancy trimmings. And why should he have left it out, when all the Copts as well as well as the Muslims know of it?

9. Hadji Khalifa

Mustafa Hadji Khalifa (d. 1658) was a Turk of Constantinople where his father was an attaché of the War office. He followed the army to the siege of Erzeroum, to Baghdad, Hamadhan and Aleppo. He made the Pilgrimage (hence Hadji), and an influential friend of his youth had him appointed to the post of Khalifa (lieutenant at the War office), so that he is known solely by his two titles: Hadji Khalifa.

Hadji Khalifa, besides his Turkish writings, "left a great encyclopaedic and bibliographic treatise, the basis of all inquiry into Arabic, Persian and Turkish literature, called the *Kashf al-Zunun (Doubts Cleared Up)*"[4]. This work has been edited and

1. Brockelmann: *op. cit.*
2. Makrîzî "was a most voluminous writer, and he had access to a vast number of authorities the greater part of whose works have absolutely perished. Accordingly he is, in mere point of matter, the most important of our authorities." Butler: *op. cit.* p. XIX.
3. al-Makrîzî: *Khitat*, Vol. I, p. 159. See Butler: *op. cit.* p. 402, note.
4. Huart: *op. cit.* p. 383.

translated into Latin by Gustav Flugel, which he calls *Lexicon Bibliographicum*.

Now Herr Krehl[1] states that Hadji Khalifa was an authority of the first rank and that no matter how late he may have written he gave a clear and concise picture of his early co-religionist (p. 434).

Now Hadji Khalifa says[2]:

> That their antagonism against other cultures and religions was to keep their religion pure. They recognized only the law of the Koran and medicine.

> And Hadji Khalifa is quoted as saying that they burned all non-Arabic books (p. 434) which they found in the countries which they overran[3].

10. *Jurji Zaydan*

Finally, Jurji Zaydan (1861–1914), our contemporary, in writing in Arabic his *Ta'rikhu 'l-Tamaddun al-Islami* (*History of Islamic Civilization*), after making a most careful investigation of this controversy, did not hesitate to throw the weight of his scholarship in favor of the destruction of the books in Alexandria at the Arab Conquest. He frankly admits that in one of his earlier works, *Modern History of Egypt*, he followed other writers in exonerating the Arabs from the burning of the books, but that from his "constant research in studies of Islamic history and Islamic civilization" he is of the opinion that it is more probable that the Arabs did burn the books, and the truth of this can be proven by Arabian texts.

As we found the study of this writer when this work was ready for the press, we have had his discussion translated into English and printed in full in an Appendix (I).

The opinion of Zaydan completes a presentation of Arabic texts from 'Abd al Latîf and 'Ali ibn al Kifti to Zaydan, without an Arab dissent, that should within reason settle this controversy.

11. *The "silence", if we must consider a negative, of any writer denying the destruction.*

1. Krehl: *op. cit.* pp. 433–434.
2. Hadji Khalifa: *Lexicon Bibliographicum*, I, 78.
3. Krehl: *op. cit.* p. 434 and ch. foregoing note. All of which had been seriously maintained by the great Ibn Khaldun (1332–1406) in his epoch-making *Prolegomena* (Vol. I, p. 61). See page 388 of this treatise.

The chief argument of those who wish to believe that there were no books in Alexandria, or that at least none were destroyed by the Arabs at the time of the conquest, is to give a list of Christian and Muslim writings, which have all come down the hard road of the transmission of manuscripts, some in fragments, extracts, recensions, translations of translations of lost originals or of lost copies of originals, epitomes, manuscripts where certain periods of history have simply "dropped out" of the copy and are lost[1]; and some few in part or close to completion. The argument is that the failure of these writings to contain the account of the destruction of the books is fatal to the belief in the destruction and destroys every positive proof in extant writings, Muslim and Christian, to the contrary, the centuries old tradition of the occurrence and the perfect fitness of the historical characters for the roles assigned to them by historians.

And, with it all, no one seems to consider that where as it might be said that it was not the province of a Christian (of course we do not agree with this) to deny the story, that at least some patriotic Muslim, proud of his lineage and a lover of truth, would have risen to denounce the account as a slander and libel on his race and a falsification of history.

Curious it is, that this controversy seems to have been born of the playful scepticism of the agnostic Gibbon and the suspicion of M. Renaudot.

In conclusion, we believe it is fair to assert that the negative side has not produced a single piece of evidence, good or bad. That for those who believe that there were books in Alexandria at the time of the conquest and that they were destroyed by the Arabs, we have produced this array of evidence to prove their case:

1. That the Coptic Tradition of the occurence is centuries old, and that there is nothing to show that it did not begin at the conquest.

2. The Oriental flavor of the story is admitted.

1. Such as John of Nikiu (see Butler: *op. cit.* p. IX; and one can never forget Dr. Butler's frank scholarship, when, after enumerating his authorities, he says: "Not one of them contains a clear, a connected, or, as I am bound to say, an accurate account of the Arab conquest. This confusion of dates, of events, and of persons almost passes belief" (p. XXI). Now if this is the case as to the great central fact of the narrative – the conquest itself – why should we expect so much from them on any matter of detail? And the marvel is that Dr. Butler has written the best book on the subject.

3. The historic character of Omar (and perhaps 'Amr) are in perfect keeping with the event described.

4. That Abd al Latîf, Muslim physician and scholar, mentions the burning as if it was common knowledge.

5. That Ibn al Kifti, Arab aristocrat and scholar, gives the oriental details of the burning.

6. That Gregory, Abû'l Faraj, bar Hebraeus, Christian historian and scholar, writing for his Muslim friends, in Arabic, gives the same story.

7. That Abû'l Fidâ, Arabian prince and historical scholar, does likewise.

8. That Makrîzî, the Historian of Muslim Egypt, gives the account as a matter of common knowledge.

9. That Hadji Khalifa, Muslim encyclopaedist, frankly shows that the early conquerors destroyed books and gives reasons which cannot be successfully contradicted, agreeing in this with Ibn Khaldun.

10. That Zaydan, writing in Arabic, in this age, has not hesitated to advance his scholarship in favor of the destruction of the books.

11. That not a single writer, Muslim or Christian, denies the story.

12. That the history of the survival of the Alexandrian Library to the Arab Conquest is merely in perfect keeping with its long known history of endurance for over nine hundred years.

And finally, if there is one outstanding characteristic of the Alexandrian Library revealed by this investigation, it is its genius in surviving "destruction". After every disaster, buildings and books arise, phoenix-like[1] from their ashes to serve the mind of men and to meet the next catastrophe! How often in this history of the destructions of the Library have we beheld this phenomenon repeated. It is the story of glory constantly enveloped in chaos and ruin and, apparently, constantly reborn.

Through the genius of Demetrios and the ambition of Ptolemy (Soter) the glorious idea of the Alexandriana was conceived[2].

1. Glorious mythus of the Phoenix, Egyptian in origin, passing through the alambic of Greek genius, serving the realism of Rome and actually embedded in the Epistle to the Corinthians of Clement, as a symbol of the Resurrection.

2. James Gow, Headmaster of Westminster School, in *A Companion to Greek Studies*, ed. by L. Whibley, Cambridge, 1936 (3rd ed.), par. 282, p. 233:
On Alexander's death it (Alexandria) fell to the portion of Ptolemy Legi (322 B.C.), who founded the famous library and schools. These continued to exist till the city

Zenodotus, Callimachus, Eratosthenes, Aristophanes of Byzantium, and Aristarchus, and doubtlessly others, added to and perfected the great collection. In the third century before Christ, the Alexandrian Library, the heart of the famous Museum, was not only the glory of fabulous Alexandria, but was indeed the chief wonder of the ancient world. It embraced the Library in the Museum for scientists and scholars, and the Branch Library at the Serapeum for the priests of the temple and for the public, or as a repertory for a select but duplicate collection. For 239 years it grew and prospered under the Ptolemaic kings, good and bad, and had reached the amazing distinction of literary arbiter of the world, with over 700,000 manuscript rolls, when the shadow of Rome fell athwart the sun-land of the Nile.

With the ambition of Cleopatra and the passion of Caesar begins the long history of the vicissitudes or so-called "destructions" of the Alexandrian libraries.

In Caesar's visit (48–47 B.C.) the Library was not destroyed. Some books may have been burned, perhaps Seneca's 40,000.

The infatuated Antony ruthlessly raped from Pergamum its great library of 200,000 manuscript rolls, the pride of its Attalid kings, which he gave to Egypt's queen. This gift was balm for Cleopatra, balm for whatever bibliophilic sins she may have been guilty of during Caesar's visit.

Certainly at this time, with the addition of the rich parchment-papyrus manuscripts of its only rival, the Alexandriana must have achieved its ultimate height.

The Ptolemaic dynasty began and closed in greatness – the amazing genius of Alexander whose vision founded Alexandria, the highest talents of Soter, soldier, diplomat, builder, founder of the Museum-Library, and the sunset genius of the fabulous Cleopatra, who may well have been the greatest of the successors of Alexander[1], as she was certainly one of the two greatest antagonists of Rome[2].

was taken by the Arabs in A.D. 640, and almost every scientific man of any note in the intervening centuries either was a professor or had been a student in Alexandria.
1. H. Idris Bell: *Egypt from Alexander the Great to the Arab Conquest*, Oxford, 1948, p. 62. A most delightful little book crammed with distinguished scholarship.
2. Dr. Tarn: *C.A.H.* (X, p. 111): "Rome, who has never condescended to fear any nation or people, did in her time fear two human beings; one was Hannibal, and the other was a woman." (Cf. contemporary Propertius (*Elegies*, III, 58) on which much might be written).

Incidentally – for such would be the attitude of most writers – she left the greatest cultural institution of antiquity at its apogee[1]. She won the affection of Caesar, the utter devotion of Antony, and when the cold Augustus came, she was without power or help, yet her intellect soared above human hopelessness, and with the last resources of a queen and heroine, she achieved her final victory over Rome.

Augustus Caesar ruled the world, the sun of Egypt had set. As a province of the Empire she is subject to every whim or policy of the extraordinary successors of Augustus.

The incredible punishment inflicted upon the Alexandrines for their folly by the beast Caracalla and the vast destruction in the Brucheion or Royal quarter (where were situated the main ("Mother") Alexandrian Library and the Museum) under Gallenius seem to have by-passed the Library, or it was again reborn and confronted the violence of Aurelian. Yet after the short military conquest by Aurelian of an unworthy opponent and the long siege, burning and sack of Alexandria by Diocletian, the almost indestructible Library is able to furnish books in the special field of alchemy and magic to be burned, again apparently retaining the substantial mass of the collection for perhaps a major disaster.

From now on the few cryptic references to libraries seem to indicate the Branch Library at the Serapeum, and the "Mother" Library of the Museum in the Brucheion quarter fades deeper into the unknown, but does not knowingly entirely disappear, for we are inclined to the belief that the Museum somehow existed in the days of Theon, and if the Museum, why not its indispensable Library?

At this very time (end of the 4th and beginning of the 5th century) Synesius, philosopher and bishop of Ptolemais, who had been a favorite pupil of Hypatia and who delighted in all proper things of life, in his witty skit in praise of baldness, tells us:

> You may look at the pictures in the Museum, I mean those of
> Diogenes and Socrates, and whomsoever you please of those who

1. If Demetrios of Phaleron collected 200,000 rolls for Soter, if Ptolemy II did as well, and Euergetes about the same, plus those of their successors, certainly Cleopatra added also the most valuable 200,000 (even if they were wrongfully taken by Antony from the then Roman city of Pergamum).

in their age were wise, and your survey would be an inspection of bald heads[1].

And he adds that as for the portrait of Apollonius (of Tyana) and his flowing hair, this merely confirms him as "a wizard and an adept in demoniac practices".

For a moment let us follow the career of the famous "Daughter" or Outer, or Branch of the Alexandriana, situated within the spacious porticoes of the sacred precinct of the Temple of the great god Serapis. From the beginning it was endowed with 42,800 carefully selected assorted rolls arranged in order. Whatever damage may have occurred in Caesar's time, the Serapeum branch was untouched. If it received the Pergamene books or any part there of, it was greatly enriched.

It was from within the safe precincts of this hallowed Temple that Caracalla viewed the bloody tragedy of his infamous revenge and even dedicated the fratricidal sword that had slain his brother Geta. From this great pagan stronghold Gallenius, Aurelian, and certainly Diocletian (note his "Pompey's Pillar") must have beheld with varied emotion the havoc wrought upon the main quarter of the city, its centre, the Brucheion or Royal Greek-Macedonian quarter. We remember that the Temple of Serapis was injured by fire in the days of Marcus Aurelius (162–181); but we know that the good Marcus visited Alexandria, after the disaffection of the prefect Cassius, that he forgave everyone, mixed with the people in their city and Temple and associated with the philosophers and pundits of the Museum and Libraries in their schools and studies, not as their military master, but as their intellectual companion or father; that his statue, which he erected in Alexandria, exhibited to the Alexandrian, as it does to the visitor of the British Museum, this mild and philosophic ruler. There is here no indication of a loss of books. Again in the second year of the reign of his wicked son Commodus (181–194), the temple was injured by fire. Again we hear of no loss of books, and as we believe the Library of the Serapeum was not located within the Temple proper, but separated from it in one of the porticoes of its vast precincts, there is no reason to insist on a disaster, particularly when as late as the age of Julian (361–363), Ammia-

1. Synesius: *An Eulogy of Baldness* (1176), *Calvitii Encomium*, tr. A. FitzGerald (*The Essays and Hymns of Synesius*, II, p. 250, London, 1930).

nus, with all his lack of knowledge of things Egyptian, does know of libraries of the Serapeum; and, more significant, the sophist Aphthonius, who visited Alexandria (c. after 391), describes the Serapeum temple area and speaks of the compartments within the temple porticoes, which were used as book-rooms for the library or collection which made Alexandria the center of learning[1].

Be this as it may, the immortal books and library were there in A.D. 391 for the Christian mob to destroy, according to Sandys and Susemihl, not to mention Gibbon[2].

But again the imagery of the Phoenix holds true when Prof. Bury's deliberate conclusion is considered:

> I conclude then that there is no evidence that the library of the Serapeum did not survive the Saracen conquest notwithstanding the verdict of Susemihl[3].

Omar fand 642 schwerlich noch Bücher in Alexandreia zu verbrennen[4].

Alexandria was essentially ever a city of books. Not only the Alexandriana, with its Serapiana, but always scholars and bookmen must have had small or large personal collections. In Roman times when Alexandria was recognized as the library center of the world, the emperors flattered their cultural vanity by bookish gestures towards or literary recognition of the Museum and Library. The great Caesar, alone, may have attempted to appropriate a small section of the Alexandriana, but his successors did not employ such methods, but rather recognizing the the Museum-Library as the fountain of learning, they sent to it for copies of the classical texts (such as Diocletian's commission for copies of the great Alexandrian editions) for the growing libraries of the imperial capital. To the Caesarium, there was attached a temple library; the whimsical Claudius even added his own Museum to the great Alexandrian and provided that in one his *Etruscan History* in 20 books and in the other his *History of*

---

1. Aphthonius: *Progymnasmata*, XII, p. 107.
2. Dr. Frederick J. Teggart, in his letter on *The Destruction of the Alexandrian Library*, in *The Nation*, July 7, 1898 (Vol. 67, p. 11), believes that "the Christian rabble made bonfires of all the books they could lay hands on in Alexandria".
3. Prof. J. B. Bury in appendix 3 to Ch. XXVII of Gibbon.
4. Susemihl: *op. cit.* I-344.

Carthage in 8 books should be completely read yearly in public recitals[1]; the gentle Marcus lingered amidst the scholarly book-men and teachers of the Muse's precincts, where the dilettante Hadrian could not have failed to have bestowed rich gifts, literary and artistic, upon the great institution of a people which, although he did not respect, he wished well and upon whom he had bestowed every favor[2].

To these imperial libraries and individual Greek-Macedonian collections, pagan in their content, we must add the books of the Jews, which must have been numerous and valuable, among the great population occupying the third section of the city, indeed a second Jerusalem, forming one of the three great Jewish cities in history. The libraries and collections of the Christians must have been vast and important, and we have the particular account of that of George, Arian bishop of Alexandria, who was literally torn to pieces by a city mob (Dec. 24, 361) and the extant *Letters of the Emperor Julian*[3], denouncing the outrage, and commanding that the Bishop's fine library of philosophy, rhetoric history, and theology be sought and sent to him. Within a genera-tion, another Alexandrian mob (this time Christian) destroyed the sanctuary and idol of Serapis (391). Now the library of the Serapeum was not in the temple but in one of the numerous porticoes or builders of the temple area. There is not the slightest evidence that the Library was then destroyed.

Alexandria, we repeat, was essentially a city of books. After the fall of paganism, the greater mass of book accumulation in public and private libraries must have been biblical and patristic literature with much theological polemics.

With the reign of Constantine (A.D. 323–37) the sun of Chris-tianity rose and that of paganism entered into its final eclipse. With Theodosius (379–394) Christianity was proclaimed the religion of the empire, the pagan temples closed, and the worship and rituals of the gods forbidden. Yet the theosophical schools

---

1. Suetonius (*Vit. Claud.* 42).
2. Flavius Vopiscus: *Vita Saturnini* (in *Scriptores Historiae Augustae*) VIII, *The Letter* of Hadrian doubtless apocryphal.
3. Julian: *Letters* (21–23–28), Julian remarks: "and I know what books George had, many of them, at any rate, if not all; for he lent me some of them to copy, when I was in Cappadocia (when Julian was interned at Macellum) and these he received back" (Ep. 23). Ammianus describes the murder of the bishop (XXII-11-3-10).

still taught philosophy and science, and many had respect and apology for the ancient religion. But the reign of Justinian (527–566) witnessed the death of the pagan cults and the fall of ancient learning:

> Justinian confiscated the property of the Platonic Academy and forbade at the University of Athens teaching in philosophy and law (529 A.D.)[1].

With the suppression of the Greek philosophical and cultural foundations, the last flicker of the dying flame of pagan thought and practice expired. The last disciples of Plato and the Hellenic schools, the last teachers of the pagan cult of beauty, the last protagonists of a civilization that had created the perfect canons of every type of literary and artistic expression, in intellectual bewilderment sought asylum with Chosroes in the Persian court, under the vain delusion that amidst the environs of the ancestral enemy of Hellas they might find a simulacrum of the Republic of Plato. Of course, the distressed scholars were soon disillusioned and returned precipitately to what they considered the lesser evils, their own land, not, however, before Chosroes, to his enduring fame, exacted of Justinian that his Grecian guests should be exempted from the effect of the laws against the pagan subjects of the empire. What a curious turn of fate, that the Greek should have received in the late hours of ancient pagan Hellenism this gracious gesture at the hands of the Persian barbarian[2].

Though the schools were closed and the teachers dead, yet more than a modicum of the teaching lived on in other systems, in many lands, in many ages, by many thinkers taught. All this meant books, books became collections and, by natural accumulation, libraries. The pagan schools were indeed gone, but the Christian schools were reorganized institutions most alive and combative not only in violent physical conflict, but in the endless battle of the controversial written page. The new and current theological literature was immense and constantly growing, while the

1. Vide: Krumbacker, *Gesch. der byz. Litteratur* (ed. 2) p. 6 and Gelser, ib. p. 940, as above.
2. Agathias, the lawyer-scholar, a Christian, an impartial historian and an honest man, who was born about the time (c. 536), tells the story. He regarded these last teachers of the schools with respect, indeed as the "flower" of the philosophy of his age. Vide: Gibbon, Ch. XL.

old literature in verse and prose survived in spite of every deterrent of the surrounding new world.

About fifty years after the death of Justinian (A.D. 618), during which time his successors precariously held Egypt, a Persian interlude was added to the varied and eventful history of the Alexandrians. Due to the unfortunate constant conflict between the Greek and Coptic churches, the Copts enabled Chosroes to effect an easy conquest, which lasted ten years during which period the difficult Egyptians had a Jacobite patriarch as the price of their assisting the invaders of their country. The Persian decade was peaceful, and the Alexandrian and visiting ecclesiastics again demonstrated that Alexandria was a seat of learning and of books: a Syrian bishop, Thomas, came to Alexandria in order to correct the Syrian version of the New Testament of Philoxenus. Here he found abundant Greek manuscripts, and made the corrections to the Syrian version conform to the Greek, and we have his labors at this day; Paul of Tela, in Mesopotamia, another Syrian scholar, was translating the Old Testament from the famous Septuagent in the Alexandrian Monastery of St. Zacchaeus; in the library of the Augustines at Rome there is a Syrian New Testament manuscript written at this time. If these be all labors in the field of theology, we know that in medicine, Aaron of Alexandria was recording in Syriac the medical researches which the Arabs afterwards greatly cherished. So that during the Persian interlude the city was at least faithful to its intellectual renown.

The Muslims under 'Amr ibn al-As, with the disaffection of the Copts, affected the easy conquest of Alexandria (642-646).

As the first occupation of the city was by capitulation, the city must have obtained the most favorable terms of complete freedom for those who accepted Islam and the head tax or tribute for those who would not conform. But in a short while (A.D. 645) the Byzantines, under Manuel, returned and recovered the city for Constantine, the son of Heraclius. But 'Amr with a large army quickly returned; he:

> Made a heavy assault, set the ballistae and destroyed the walls of the city. He pressed the fight so hard until he entered the city by assault, killed the fighters and carried away the children as captives. Some of its Greek inhabitants left to join the Greek somewhere else: and

Allah's enemy, Manuwil (Manuel), was killed. 'Amr and the Muslims destroyed the wall of Alexandria in pursuance to a vow 'Amr had made to that effect, in case he reduced the city[1].

This was the final scene of destruction (A.D. 646), and Alexandria, under the shadow of Islam, joins her sister Hellenic cities of forlorn Asia, sinking below the historical horizon, as the philosophic travelers, Muslim and Christian, beheld the wreck of her former glory, the seat of ancient wisdom and the treasure-house of the classic beauty and thought of ancient Hellas. Upon the coming of the Arabs, the city entered upon its period of final decay and degradation[2]. For us, that should be the last phase of our rather long and perhaps tedious investigation of the "destructions" of Alexandria's cultural institutions, the Museum and particularly its far-famed Library.

We venture but little more.

It is most reasonable that a city, such as Alexandria, which for over eight centuries (from the coming of Demetrios of Phaleron (c. 295 B.C.) to the closing of the School of Athens by Justinian (529 A.D.) had been so library-minded, would continue to possess books and libraries for the remaining century between Justinian's suppression of the schools and the conquest of Egypt by the Saracens. The armies of the Muslims were composed mostly of poor, wild, illiterate, dauntless warriors, barbarians, zealous in Islam's cause, for whom Muhammad and the Koran sufficed for all terrestial and celestial needs. The raw recruits of the Prophet from desert and mountain were spreading over the plains and conquering the cities and countries of the East in Allah's name and consolidating these vast domains into the empire or kingdoms of Islam. Their chiefs were men of action, warriors of the new faith and builders of the foundations of a new empire. It was the era of violent action and religious enthusiasm, all embraced in the cry of Allah il Allah and Muhammad his Prophet. The softer and more liberal days when Baghdad, Cordo-

1. Al-Baladhuri: *Kitab Futuh al-Buldan, History of the Moslem Conquest* (tr. by Philip Khuri Hitti (Columbia Un. New York) 1916, p. 348. This Arab historiographer was, like al-Tabari, of Persian stock. He died 892, mentally deranged from an overdose of the juice of the anacardia, an Indian fruit thought to strengthen the memory. His name was from this curious Marahnut (Baladhur). The destruction of the walls of Alexandria enabled 'Amr to say "that men could go in at every side as to the house of a harlot". (Lane-Poole: *op. cit.* 21).
2. Does not Mommsen describe Islam as "the executioner of Hellenism"?

va, and Cairo were the seats of Arabian learning, as well as citadels of spiritual and temporal power, were yet to come.

Why is it unreasonable for these same wild zealots to have consumed by fire the books of the Greeks?

The specious plea of the modern apologists for Islam is that the Muslims could not have destroyed the manuscripts of Alexandria because they contained the name of God. But the men of the Museum could assure us that the poems of Sappho, Alcaeus and Archilochus, the comedies of Aristophanes, Cratinus and Eupolis, the works of Athenaeus and the wits of Alexandria, the mimes of Herodas, the Memoirs of Ptolemy Soter, and the vast range of pagan literature could hardly claim this protection. If Prof. Bury's opinion is sound that the Library of the Serapeum at least survived the Muslim conquest, then it is reasonable to assume that the pagan or classical manuscripts bore a high relative position to the more modern works of theology and patristic learning. And certainly the Greek works of classical antiquity were not entitled to better treatment than that accorded the Avestic literature of the Persians.

There is every reason to believe, as we have fully shown in the greater part of this chapter, that there were books, the remains of the Alexandrian Library in Alexandria at the time of the conquest, and that there is good and sufficient historical Muslim and Christian authority that they were burned by 'Amr by order of Omar.

This is the end of our theme. The magnificent Hellenic queen-city of Antiquity, wrought in marble, seat of the arts and sciences, guardian of the accumulated culture and learning of the ancient world, with all the fabulous glories of her Museum and Library, now under the blight of Islam, has finally ceased to be[1].

Thus we reach the denouement, and the curtain falls on the tragic history of man's greatest original creative effort in preserving for time the precious records of mystery, beauty and wisdom of the divine-human mind.

The white stone roof of the Muses' Hall
Has fallen and is no more;

[1]. For the curious reader, in an Appendix, we have excerpted the impressions of travelers and others who have witnessed the ruins of Alexandria (Appendix B).

Here, on frail papyrus writ, was all that man
Had dreamed and thought and from the heavens caught
Of wisdom's truth and beauty's fleeting glory.
 Now, the sacred and awful treasures of the mind
 Are scattered by the winds of yore.

Laus Deo

The Burning of the Books at the Library of Alexandria and Elsewhere

by Gergy Zeydan[1]

The Ptolemies founded a library in Alexandria, in the third century B.C., into which they gathered books of knowledge from all parts of the then civilized world, as you will see below. This library suffered many ups and downs from the days of the Romans till the Islamic conquests. It was destroyed by fire and looting.

Arab historians and others disagree as to how the library was destroyed. Some attribute its burning to 'Amr bin al 'Ass by orders from Umar bin al Khattab, and they prove it by Arab texts, the most famous of which are the writings of Abû'l Faraj of Malatya, Abd al Lateef of Baghdad, al Maqureezy, and Hajj Khalfah. Others exonerate the Arabs of this act and refute and attempt to weaken these stories. We ourselves, in our book *Modern History of Egypt*, were of this latter group a few decades ago. From our constant research in studies of Islamic history and Islamic civilization, we have later come to hold the former opinion as more probable, for reasons which we shall give herewith, in order to make the truth clear.

First – You have noticed from what has preceeded the desire of the Arabs at the beginning of Islam to destroy every book except the Quran, as encouraged by the sayings of the Prophet and the outspoken statements of his preeminent companions[2].

Second – In his book of history, *Mukhtassar al Duwal*, Abû'l Faraj of Malatya discussing the occupation of Egypt by 'Amr bin al 'Ass says:

And Yahya al Grammatiquy lived till 'Amr bin al 'Ass took the city of Alexandria. He paid a visit to 'Amr, who knew his intellectual standing and was gracious to him and listened to his discourses on

1. Jurji Zeydan: *Ta'rikhu 'l-Tamaddun al-Islami* (*History of Islamic Civilization*), Part III, pp. 40–46.
2. *History of Moslem Civilization*, Vol. 3, p. 6, 4th ed.

Philosophy. As the Arabs had then no acquaintance with philosophy he was awestricken. 'Amr was a wise man, both a good listener and a good thinker, and he became Yahya's close friend and constant companion.

One day Yahya said to him: "You have surrounded yourself with all the wealth of Alexandria, and you have put your seal on all its literary works. We do not mind your keeping all that is of use to you, but what you cannot use we ought to have more than you". "What do you need?" questioned 'Amr. Yahya replied: "Books of learning that are in the Royal Libraries". "This I cannot order", said 'Amr, "Except with the approval of the Caliph Umar bin al Khattab".

So he wrote to Umar telling him of Yahya's request and received a letter saying: "And as for the books that you mention, if their contents agree with the Book of God, then having the Book of God we are wealthy without them, and if they contradict the Book of God we have no need for them, so start destroying them".

Thereupon 'Amr bin al 'Ass proceeded to distribute them among the sections of Alexandria and burned them in the fireplaces, so that they were exhausted within six months. When he (the Caliph translators note) was told what had happened, he was pleased[1].

There is no possibility of misunderstanding in the meaning intended by this text. Those who would free the Arabs from the charge of burning this library refute the story, however, and attribute religious bias to its relators, among whom were many European historians who have written books and papers to fix the guilt.

Their arguments are summarized thus: The Abû'l Faraj mentioned above is the first to attribute the burning of the library at Alexandria to 'Amr bin al 'Ass. He did so because of his bias towards Christianity and also because he wished to humiliate Islam. He lived during the seventh century. His father had been a Jew but was converted to Christianity, hence Abû'l Faraj was raised a Christian. He rose through the ranks of the priesthood to become a Bishop. He first wrote a book of history in the Syriac tongue which he extracted from books in Greek, Persian, Arabic, and Syriac. Later he wrote a summary of this book in Arabic and called it *Mukhtassar al Duwal*. It is

1. *Mukhtassar al Duwal*, p. 180. Pub. Bukuk, Eskonia, 1663 A.D. but the edition published by the Jesuit Fathers in Beirut has cancelled all the statements for some reason.

claimed, "And this is the first book in which this story is mentioned, and the Europeans have copied the story from it for this
purpose". Furthermore, what is related by the Moslem historians Abd al Lateef of Baghdad, al Maqureezy, and Hajj Khalfah
cannot be taken as independent sources because al Maqureezy
copied his account *verbatim* from Abd al Lateef, and Hajj Khalfah did not even mention the city of Alexandria but merely
pointed out that the Arabs paid so little attention to scholarship, except for their language and law, that it was said of them,
"And it is said that the Arabs burned all the books that came
their way during their conquests of the countries". Abd al Lateef
of Baghdad mentioned the burning of the library, moreover, in
connection with 'Amood as Sawary, without giving proofs. The
holders of this opinion assume that the Alexandrian Library was
burned by the Romans before the coming of Islam. They believe
that if the Arabs had burned it, then Arab historians would have
mentioned it, especially the book *Kitab al Futooh ual Maghazy*.

We do not deny that part of this library was burned before the
coming of Islam, but that does not preclude the burning of the
remaining part under Islam.

As for the quotations concerning this burning, Abû'l Faraj is
not the first to relate it, as some have mistakenly thought. More
than twenty years before Abû'l Faraj was born, Abd al Lateef of
Baghdad visited Egypt, and, writing about its sights and relics,
mentioned that the Arabs burned the library. Abû'l Faraj was born
622 H. (1226 A.D.) and Abd al Lateef visited Egypt towards the end
of the sixth century H. Here is the quotation from Abd al Lateef:

And I saw around 'Amood as Sawary, one of the pillars, a good
amount of remains, some of which were intact and others broken.
From their condition it seemed that there had been a roof which
the pillars held, but there was a dome on 'Amood as Sawary. Then
I realized that this was the porch where Aristotle and his followers
studied and furthermore that this was the school building which
Alexander built when he built his city, and in it had been the treasury of books which 'Amr bin al 'Ass burned by permission from
Umar bin al Khattab, may God be pleased with him[1].

True, the statement of the man from Baghdad is brief and incidental, but it is related in a sure manner, as though he took it

1. *al Ifada wa al I'tibar*, p. 28.

from a well known and reliable source of that age, resembling the source from which Abû'l Faraj quotes.

As for Abû'l Faraj, he completed his Arabic book *Mukhtassar al Duwal* towards the end of his life and he died in 684 H. The book is not an exact summary of his history book in Syriac except for the description of the conquests, for the Arabic text has much additional material about Islam, the Mongols, and the history of Roman and Arabic sciences and literature. The book in Syriac recounts the conquests only and its failure to mention the burning of the library does not mean that this was foreign to the Arabic text or was stealthily slipped in later, as some have mistakenly believed. The mention occurs in the Arabic text simply because it has to do with Roman and Arabic culture, which the author included in this work, as already stated.

After study and research it became apparent to us that Abû'l Faraj copied the story from a Moslem historian, the Wazir of Aleppo who was known as "The Generous Judge", who died about forty years before him, Jamal ad Deed Abu al Hasan 'Ali, son of Yousif, son of Ibrahim from Qaft. He was born in Qaft on the soil of Egypt in 565 H. and died in Aleppo in 646 H. This judge wrote a book *Tarajim al Hukama*, a copy of which, written in 1197 H., we accidentally found in the Sultan's library. In it we read about Yahya al Nahawy and the account is very similar to that given by Abû'l Faraj except that it was written in greater detail. It also contains something of the history of the library from its foundation. Here is the account as he gives it:

> Yahya al Nahawy lived till 'Amr bin al 'Ass conquered Egypt and Alexandria, and he visited 'Amr who knew his reputation in learning and knew his faith and knew what took place between him and the Christians. 'Amr welcomed him and respected him. He listened to his beliefs concerning the Trinity and was pleased. He also listened to his views concerning the end of time and liked him extremely. Not only was he impressed by his great eloquence, but also he was awe stricken with his philosophical ideas which the Arabs had not been acquainted with. Moreover, 'Amr was a wise man, a good listener as well as a good thinker, and he liked Yahya and kept him close to himself.
>
> One day Yahya said to him: "You have gathered all the wealth of Alexandria and you have put your seal on everything describable

in it. Now what you have use for I will not mind your keeping, but what you have no use for, we deserve more to have."

'Amr asked him: "What do you need?"

Yahya replied: "The books of learning which you are holding in the Royal Treasury, which we need and for which you have no use".

Upon being asked: "Who collected the books and what is their story?", Yahya told him: "When Ptolemy Philadelphus, one of the kings of Alexandria, ruled, he attracted to himself knowledge and learned men, and he searched for books of wisdom and gave orders to have them brought to him, and he set apart for them libraries where they were to be collected. And he put in charge of them a man called Zumayra, the son of Murra, who was very enthusiastic in their collection and procurement, and who paid high prices for the books and encouraged merchants to bring them to him. As a result, this elaborate collection in time amounted to fifty thousand one hundred and twenty books. When the King learned of the number collected and the provision for them, he asked Zumayra, saying: "Do you suppose that there are other books of wisdom on this earth that we do not have?" And Zumayra told him: "There are some books in China, India, Persia, Jirgan, Arman, Babylon, and Mosul, and also some among the Romans that we do not have." And the King was pleased and told him to keep collecting, which he did until he died. These books have been guarded and protected by every Ruler and King and King's household until our time."

'Amr thought that Yahya's knowledge was great, and he liked him. And he told him: "I cannot do anything with the books without the permission of the Caliph Umar bin al Khattab".

He wrote to Umar, told him what Yahya had said, and asked his permission to do what he was planning.

A letter came back from Umar, saying: "As for the books you mentioned, if they contain that which agrees with the Book of God, then having the Book of God we are wealthy without them, and if they contradict the Book of God Almighty then we have no need for them. Proceed to destroy them."

Thereupon 'Amr bin al 'Ass proceeded to distribute the books among the sections of Alexandria and burned them in their fire-places. Many of these sections mention that the books were exhausted within six months. And when he was told what took place he was pleased[1].

1. *Tarapim al Hukama* (mss.).

In comparing this paragraph with the text of Abû'l Faraj, it becomes apparent that Abu al Faraj summarized the story of Ibn al Qafty. If one reads both books, it will be noticed that Abû'l Faraj copied much of the additional material in the Arabic book from Ibn al Qafty's book; for example, when talking about Theodoc, the physician of al Hajjaj[1], he copied word for word from the *Tarajim al Hukama.*

It remains for us now to examine the source from which Ibn al Qafty copied, and this is most probably the same source as that from which Abd al Lateef of Baghdad copied, because they were contemporaries, though Abd al Lateef was the senior, having been born in 557 and died in 629 H. Unfortunately these sources are among the other lost works of the Arab writers.

If we consider what Ibn an Nadeem relates in his book *Al Fahrist* about the philosophers of Nature and their stories about the establishment of the library at Alexandria, it becomes apparent that among the sources from which these stories were copied was a history written by a man known as Iassa the Monk, a student of Greek and Roman culture. Among the passages which they copy from this work is the description of the founding of the library at Alexandria by Zumayra, and here is the passage:

> When Ptolemy Philadelphus, one of the kings of Alexandria, ruled he searched for books of learning, and put them in charge of a man named Zumayra. Zumayra collected fifty four thousand one hundred and twenty books and informed the king that there were still other books in China, India, Persia, Jirjan, Arman, Babylon, Mosul and among the Romans[2].

This passage is the same thing that Ibn al Qafty relates. Therefore it seems likely that he took the founding of the library from the Isaac noted above, and the account of its burning from someone else. Had it not been for the quotation of Ibn an Nadeem from Isaac the Monk about the philosophers, we would not have known of its existence, and we would have supposed that he had said nothing, just as we had supposed that the Moslems had mentioned nothing about the burning of the Alexandrian Library by 'Amr.

Therefore it seems from what has preceded that the story about

1. *Mukhtassar al Duwal*, p. 194, Beirut.
2. *Al Fahrist*, p. 239.

the burning of the library at Alexandria was not made up by
Abû'l Faraj because of his religious bias, nor was it inserted by
others later on, but that he quoted it from Ibn al Qafty who was a
Moslem judge well versed in jurisprudence, Hadeeth, Qur'anic
theology, language, grammar, philosophy, history, surgery,
surveying, and engineering. We mean that Ibn al Qafty who
died 646 H. mentioned it in the book *Tarajim al Hukama*, which
was a fruitful source. He had collected an indescribable number
of books. People brought books to him from far off countries;
his library was worth fifty thousand dinars, and he loved books
more than anything else in the world. There are many strange
tales about him and his love of books. Since he had no heir he
left his library to Nassr ad Dawla, the Governor of Aleppo. He
had many books of history, grammar, and literature, and among
them is the book *Akhbar Massr* in six volumes, covering the period
from the beginning of Egypt to the time of Salah ed Din (Saladin)[1].
It is his book *Tarajim al Hukama* that is the topic of our discussion.

Both Ibn al Qafty and Abd al Lateef of Baghdad copied from
a lost source, but the fact that the histories of the conquests
do not mention the burning probably has a reason. Probably it
was mentioned, but was cancelled later on; that is, after the
maturation of Islamic civilization, or after the Moslems had
become interested in learning and had come to know the importance of books, they cancelled out the incident in the time
of the Orthodox Caliphs.

There may be some other reason. At any rate, we think the
story of Abû'l Faraj to be very likely.

Third – From many sources of Moslem history there come reports
of the burning of libraries in Persia and other places, which the
author of *Kashf ath Thunun* has summarized in his presentation of
knowledge of the ancients. He says:

> When the Moslems conquered Persia and got hold of their books,
> Sa'd bin Aby Waqqas wrote to Umar bin al Khattab, asking his
> permission to send these books to the Moslems. Umar, may God be
> pleased with him, wrote: "Throw them into the water, for if they
> contain guidance, we already have been guided by Almighty God
> with a Greater Guidance; and if they lead astray, then God Almighty

1. *Fawat al Wafiyat*, vol. 2, p. 99.

is sufficient for us." And they threw them into the water or fire, and thus the learning of the Persians was lost with them[1].

In his discussion of the Moslems and their learning, he (the author of *Kashf ath Thunun*, translators note) says: "They burned what books they found during their conquests of the countries"[2]. There must be a source from which the author of *Kashf ath Thunun* copied, and Ibn Khaldoon likewise points to it in his question: "And where is the learning of the Persians which Umar, may God be pleased with him, ordered to be destroyed, upon their conquest?"[3]

Fourth – The burning of books was a matter of course in that time as a way to take revenge upon the enemy or simply to torment him, and people of every sect and creed used to burn the books of others. 'Abd Allah bin Tahir did so with the books of the Persians, and with those of the Magi, which had remained until his day (213 H.), for when he knew of their contents, he ordered them to be thrown into the water, and sent word to all parts of the world that whosoever found any books of the Magi should destroy them[4]. Moreover, when Hulako conquered Baghdad in 656 H., he ordered that the books of learning that were in the library should be thrown into the River Tigris, and these were uncountable beside the books of Persian wisdom destroyed by the Arabs early in the conquests[5]. Some said besides that they built stables and mangers too with these books instead of with mud[6], but most likely the majority were destroyed by water for revenge against the Sunnis.

When the Europeans conquered Tripoli in Syria during the wars of the Crusades they burned its libraries upon orders from Count Bertram Saint Jeal. Having entered a room wherein were many volumes of the Qur'an, he thereupon ordered the entire library to be burned; the estimate was three million books[7]. The Spaniards did the same thing with the libraries of Andalusia,

1. *Kashf ath Thunun*, vol. 1, p. 446.
2. *Idem*, vol. 1, p. 25.
3. *Ibin Khaldoon*, vol. 1, p. 32.
4. *Browne's Literary History of Persia*, p. 347.
5. *Ibin Khaldoon*, vol. 3, p. 537, and vol. 5, p. 543.
6. *Ibin as Saa'ee*, p. 127.
7. *Gibbon's Roman Empire*, 11, 505; *Ibin Khellikan*, vol. 2, p. 128.

when they reclaimed it from the hands of the Arabs in the latter part of the fifteenth century.

Fifth – In those days, people of the various religions believed that destroying the ancient temples and burning the books of the worshipers was a necessary step towards the establishment of a new religion. The Roman emperors, as soon as they had been converted to Christianity, ordered the destruction of the pagan temples in Egypt and the burning of whatsoever they contained, books and otherwise. The Moslem Caliphs, when they wished to persecute the Seceders and philosophers, burned their books. It was in danger of death that the Seceders used to avoid this; they would hide and hold secret conclaves, while the Caliphs would trace them and burn their books. The most famous incident of this sort occurred when the Sultan Mahmood al Ghaznawy conquered Alree and other places in 420 H., for he killed the Batinites, a secret sect, and exiled the Seceders, and burned their books, and the books on philosophy and astrology[1].

Sixth – In Moslem history there have been a number of Moslem leaders who burned their own books of their own accord. Among them was Ahmad bin Abi al Hawary, for when he had finished his studies, an idea came to him one day, and he took his books to the River Euphrates. He sat down and cried for an hour, then said, "You have been an excellent guide to me for finding my God, but now that I have found Him, to spend time on the guide is absurd!" He thereupon threw his books into the water. There is also mentioned Suffyan al Thawry, who left in his will instructions to have his books buried, and Abu 'Amr Ibin al 'Ala, whose books filled the house clear to the ceiling, until he became an ascetic and burned them[2].

From what has gone before, it seems probable that in the beginning the Arabs, in order to establish the Moslem faith, burned the books of ancient wisdom where they encountered. After they were established and had become interested in learning, they made up to the world many times over for what they had burned, as will appear later.

1. *Ibin Khaldoon*, vol. 4, p. 478.
2. *Kashf ath Thunun*, vol. 1, p. 40. *Al Bayan*, vol. 1, p. 123.

A List of Writers who do not mention the Burning of the Books

―――――――

1. John, Jacobite Bishop of Nikiu, who lived to end 7th or beginning of 8th century A.D.

2. Theophanes (d. 817), a continuator of his friend George the Syncellus (i.e.: Secretary of the Patriarch Tarasius), was a man of a noble and wealthy family, an ascetic, who founded an abbey known as "the great acre", near Cyzicus, in Mysia, Asia Minor.

He wrote a *Chronography* (from 284 to 813), arranged as annals, adopting the unfortunate and necessarily confused tripartite systems of chronology: the Annus Mundi, the regnal years of the Roman Emperors, the Persian Kings and (later) the Moslem Caliphs, and the Episcopal years of the Five Great Sees.

His authorities were known to him through intermediate sources, but he had for the seventh and part of the eighth century some unknown source. His work is inaccurate and uncritical, though it ranks well among the Byzantine chronicles.

Theophanes does not mention the burning of the books or library, but "the silence of the chronicles of Theophanes and Nicephorus does not count for much, as they are capricious and unaccountable in their selection of facts"[1].

3. Nicephorus (c. 758–829), Patriarch of Constantinople (806–815) was the great champion of orthodoxy in the bitter theological feuds concerning the veneration of images.

He was an able theologian who wrote against the Iconoclastic fanatics and to this he devoted the major part of his intellectual labors. However, he wrote two small historical tracts: the *Chronographis* ("Concise lists of dates") and the *Breviarum* ("Concise History"). The History is a very poor composition; the author "selects what is likely to interest an illiterate public and disregards the relative importance of events"[2]. Like Theophanes, he does seem to have unknown sources. He does not mention the

1. Prof. Bury in Gibbon: *op. cit.* IX, p. 185.
2. Idem: VIII, p. 185.

burning of books or library, yet his silence, like that of Theophanes, counts for little[1].

4. Ibn Abd al Hakam (d. 871 at Old Cairo) was an Arabian
historian, who wrote *History of the Conquest of Egypt, North Africa
and Spain,* still in MS. in the Bibliothèque Nationale. The work has
been partly used by de Slane, J. Karle, and John Harris Jones.
Ibn Abd al Hakam is silent on the burning of books and libraries,
which is important, but not decisive perhaps because Hakam
was most loyal to the faith and reputation of Islam, he being a
son of the Malikite qudi in Egypt, a follower of Malik, one of the
four sects of the Sunni, orthodox of the orthodox.

5. Abu-Jafar Muhammad ibn Jarir (839–923) called al Tabari,
a Persian who taught, wrote and died in Baghdad. His opus, the
most ancient extant and extensive universal history in Arabian,
the *History of the Prophets and Kings,* contains the prodigious and
valuable accumulations of a host of earlier writers. His work,
although it has attained to great fame, is uncritical, but of real
importance because he has preserved the vast body of Arabian
historiography, a veritable mine of lost authorities, from which
his successors have dug not only rare nuggets but great segments
of material for embellishment, if not for the substance, of their
narratives. He was a student of learning from youth, and the
years of his productive scholarship have recorded his intellectual
labors as having written forty pages a day for forty years
(584,000 sheets!)[2].

The silence of al Tabari as to the burning of books or libraries
is of much importance, but yet not decisive. In the selection of
his materials al Tabari, although he was unsparing in his efforts
of accumulation, did not seem to possess the necessary sense of
historical critical judgment. More important still, we should remember that in spite of the monumental edition of his *Ta'rikh al
Rusul wa'l Muluk,* his *History of the World,* as published in Leyden
in over 12 volumes, even this is only an abbreviated text of this
prodigious work which is said to have been ten times as long as the
Leyden edition, referred to as a synopsis[3].

1. Prof. Bury in Gibbon: *op. cit.,* VIII, p. 185, to whom we are so much indebted.
2. How modest our own voluminous Gibbon, with only 3904 pages, text and notes
(editio princeps: 6 vols., London, 1776–1788).
3. R. Paret in *The Encyclopaedia of Islam* (s.v. *al–Tabari*), London, 1928 (fasciculus J).

6. Abu'l Hasan Ali, Masudi (900–956), a brilliant and witty raconteur, scion of the family of Masud, a companion of the Prophet, was born at Baghdad, then the university of Islam. At its schools and in its libraries, he took all learning for his portion and to his native Moslem studies his curious mind added inquiries into the history and traditions of the Persians, the civilizations of the alien lands of Rome (Byzantium) and India, the theocracies of Jew and Christian, the cultures of the ancient pagan and his modern world. Extensive and intelligent travel added its unique polish to his general scholarship.

He wrote a great historical work in 30 volumes of which but one volume is extant, at Vienna. He made an abridgment of this work, and further an extract of his opus which he called *The Golden Meadows*. This delightful work, a picture of Eastern life, with its anecdotes of the Caliphs and its amusing stories of the manners and customs of Moslem men, is reminiscent of *The Thousand Nights and a Night*, which he tells us was a Persian book translated into Arabic from the Pehlevi, and which we now believe the Persians took from India.

Now here was a writer of universal learning and liberal scholarship, doubtless a lover of books, with all the gifts of the teller of tales, from whom you might have expected some account of the burning of the books and libraries. Yet Masudi is silent. This silence, of course, is significant, but yet not decisive, because *The Golden Meadows* is but an Extract of an Epitome of his great work of universal history, now 29/30th lost.

Masudi died in Egypt, at Old Cairo, at the age of 56.

7. Said ibn al-Batriq (876–940), known as Eutychius, was an Egyptian Arab Christian physician born at Old Cairo. He became Melchite (Orthodox) Patriarch of Alexandria in 933, when he adopted the name Eutychius. He wrote a universal history in Arabic (from Adam to 938) called *Chaplet of Pearls*. The work was translated by Pocock[1] into Latin and used by Gibbon as an authority.

Eutychius does not mention the burning of books or libraries. This is important, but not decisive, because although he was a good student of history, his works have been only partly preserved. Eutychius is till to be studied.

---

1. Translated under the title of *Annales* (Oxford, 1658–1659. See Adrian Fortesque in *Cath. Encyc.* (s.v. *Eutychius*).

8. al-Makin (1205–1273) was a Christian employed in the War Office at Cairo, where he was born. He wrote a history of the world which he called, in florid eastern style, *The Blessed Collection*, and which Gibbon calls the *Saracenic History of Elmacin*. al-Makin used Eutychius and al-Tabari.

He makes no mention of the burning of books or libraries. Again the position is purely negative.

9. Murtadi of Cairo. And finally there is Murtadi, an obscure authority of Gibbon, who notes that Muradi wrote a book in the 13th century, the Arabic MS. of which belonged to Cardinal Mazarin (published by Pierre Vatier, Paris, 1666), translated in a small volume entitled *Des Merveilles etc. de l'Egypte*. He, also, does not mention the burning of books or libraries, but the author of the Decline and Fall does not fail to remark that "the silence of Abulfeda, Murtadi and a crowd of Moslems is less conclusive from their ignorance of Christian literature".

Comments of Christian and Moslem Travelers of Post-Hellenic Alexandria

a. The Rabbi Benjamin of Tudela (1160–1173) speaks:

> Without the city a great and beautiful building is yet to be seen, which is reported to have been the college of Aristotle, the master of Alexander, wherein there are almost twenty schools, which were frequented in former times by the learned men of the whole world[1].

One would think the Jewish traveler had beheld the Museum-Library of the Ptolemies.

b. Lewis Barthema (1503):

> Wee arrived at the Citie of Alexandria in Egypt: where the desire wee had to know things more strange and farther off, would not permit us to tarrie long[2].

c. Martin Baumgarten (1507):

> So that at length, according to some, it became the most glorious city in the world.... anciently in this city many eminent scholars and divines flourish'd.... At this time it looks very glorious without.... but within, instead of a city, there's nothing to be seen but a prodigious heap of stones. There are to be seen still at Alexandria several Christian churches, among the rest.... that of St. Mark. Behind the altar of that church are to be seen ancient manuscripts containing the works of Athanasius, Cyrillus, Irenaeus, and several others, all rotten and moth-eaten and some of them almost quite burnt[3].

d. Leo Africanus (before 1526):

> The great citie of Alexandria in Egypt founded by Alexander the great... was in times past, till it grew subject unto the Mahumetans, most sumptiously and strongly built, as divers and sundry authors beare record. Afterward this citie decaying many years

---

1. *The Travels of Rabbi Benjamin* (in Jno. Pinkerton collection (Vol. VII, p. 18).
2. *The Travels of Lewis Barthema* (in Purchas *His Pilgremes*), Glasgow, 1905 (Vol. IX, p. 55).
3. *The Travels of Martin Baumgarten* (in the Churchill Collection, London, 1744, Vol. I, p. 324).

together, was deprived of the ancient renowe and honour, and remained in manner desolate[1].

e. John Fox (1577):

The valiant and resourceful John Fox was too occupied devising means of escape from his imprisonment as a galley-slave at Alexandria to tell of the town, but he did better, by delivering 266 Christians out of the terrible captivity of the Turks[2].

f. John Sanderson (1585):

That citie (Alexandria) and land standeth so lowe that, except the Pharos and some sight of topps of the palme trees, you may be uppon it before ye be ware.... Alexandria is built uppon admirable marble pillours, all vaulted underneth, evry house havinge his sondry sesterns.... Within the waules is an ould ruine of the castel whear Cleopatra was stonge to death.

The last may have been the Caesareum, begun by Cleopatra, or one of the palace of the Ptolemies[3].

g. John Evesham (1586):

The said citie of Alexandria is an old thing decayed or ruinated, having bene a faire and great citie neere two miles in length, being all vauted underneath for provision of fresh water, which water commeth thether but once every yeere, out of.... the Nilus. There is within the walls of said Citie.... another marble pillar, being round, called Pompey his pillar: this pillar standeth upon a great square stone, every square is fifteene foote, the same stone is fifteene foote high, and the compasse of the pillar is 37 foote, and the height of it is 101 feete, which is a wonder to thinke how ever it was possible to set the said pillar upon the said square stone[4].

h. M. Laurence Aldersey (1586):

This traveler stayed at the English House in Alexandria and daily was shown its monuments:

Hee brought mee first to Pompey his pillar, which is a mighty thing

1. Al-Hassan ibn-Mohammed al-wezaz al-Fasi, known as Leo Africanus: *His Historie of Africa* (tr. John Pory, ed. Hakluyt Society, London, 1896, Vol. III, 861).
2. The worthy Enterprise of John Fox, an Englishman (in *The Principal Navigations, Voyages and Discoveries of the English Nation*, by Richard Hakluyt, Glasgow, 1904, Vol. V, p. 153).
3. *The Travels of John Sanderson in the Levant* (1584–1602), Hakluyt Society, London, 1931, pp. 39–41.
4. John Evesham, Gentlemen: *The Voyage passed by Sea into Aegypt* (in Hakluyt: *op. cit.* Vol. VI, p. 35).

of grey marble, and all of one stone in height by estimation above 52 yards, and the compasse about sixe fadome. The Citie hath three gates. He brought mee to a stone in the streete of the citie whereupon S. Marke was beheaded: to the place where S. Katherine died.... The Citie standeth upon great arches or vawtes.... It hath three Castles and a hundred Churches: but the part that is destroyed of it, is sixe times more than that part which standeth[1].

i. Captain John Smith (1596):

The Captain merely sailed along the African shoare for Alexandria in Egypt. There having delivered their fraught they sailed by Cypress and Rhodes, the coast of Graecia, on to "the entrance of the Adriaticke sea, till they mette with an Argosie of Venice" which acting unfriendly they faught, captured, rifled, then let her go with her companie and much good Merchandize[2].

j. George Sandys (1610):

In times past reputed the granary of the world, insomuch as it was not thought possible for the Romane Empire to subsist if not assisted by the affluence of Aegypt.

Queene of Cities and Metropolis of Africa: (Alexandria) who now hath nothing left her but ruines; and those ill witnesses of her perished beauties: declaring that Townes as well as men, have their ages and destinies. Only those wals remaine which were founded (as some say) by Ptolomie... The buildings now being, are meane and few, erected on the ruines of the former: that part that lieth along the shoare inhabited only, the rest desolate.... Inhabited by Moores, Turkes, Jewes, Copties and Grecians.... Wee lodged in the house of the French Consul[3].

k. Master Henry Blount (1634):

Alexandria, first built by Alexander the Great, was after beautified by many, especially by Pompey; it bears yet the monuments of its ancient glory, pillars in large number and size, both above ground and below, most of porphiry and other marble as fine... the ruin of Cleopatra's palace, high upon the shore with the private gate

1. *The Second Voyage of M. Laurence Aldersey* to the Cities of Alexandria and Cayro in Aegypt (in Hakluyt: *oḃ. cit.* Vol. VI, p. 39).
2. *Travels and Adventures of Captaine John Smith* (in Purchas: *op. cit.* Vol. VIII, p. 324).
3. Master George Sandys: *Relations of Africa* (in Purchas: *op. cit.* Vol. VI, p. 173–186).

whereat she received her Mark Antony after their overthrow at Actium. The town is now almost nothing but a white heap of ruins, especially the east and south parts[1].

l. Dr. John Francis Gemelli Careri (1693):

Alexandria built by Alexander the Great according to the form drawn by Dinocrates, 322 years before the birth of Christ. The old City is much disinhabited and the ancient spot serves to preserve the rain-water for the use of the citizens. The new city is but ill peopled.... It was formerly a city of 15 miles in compass: It was reduced to the miserable, ruinous condition it is now in by falling under several masters and enduring many bloody sieges; but above all by the destruction made in it by Antoninus Caracalla, who filled it with blood and dead bodies, not to mention what Maximilianus Herculeus did to it[2].

m. M. de Maillet, French Consul at Cairo (1692):

When he landed at Alexandria, he found that the city had scarcely any inhabitants. M. Savary[3] found the town in ruins, of small extent with perhaps six thousand people.

The place had become a desert and robber hole in the early 18th century, with little to remind one of the great imperial metropolis under Augustus of nearly a million souls (300,000 citizens and about 600,000 slaves)[4].

1. Master Henry Blount: *A Voyage into the Levant* (in Harleian Collection of Voyages and Travels, from the curious Library of the Earl of Oxford, London, 1745, Vol. I, p. 523).
2. Dr. John Francis Gemelli Careri: *A Voyage round the World* (in Churchill Collection of Voyages and Travels, London, 1745, p. 12).
3. Savary: *Letters on Egypt*, Vol. I, pp. 337–384.
4. *Description de l'Egypte* (ed. by L'Abbé Le Mascrier, 1740, Vol. I, p. 186; vide notes to Book VIII of Pory's tr. of Leo Africanus, ed. by Dr. Robert Browne, Vol. III, p. 906, Hakluyt Society, London, 1896).

ACKNOWLEDGMENTS

The writer feels that he would have liked to have expressed his appreciation to the numerous scholars of the past and present whose works in many fields of classical philology have been freely used by him, and it is hoped that the attempt to be meticulous in referring to their labors will be considered as a mark of his appreciation.

Although we feel that this work has the benediction of the great American Hellenist, Dr. Charles Burton Gulick of Harvard, it is our deepest regret that that distinguished scholar was physically prevented from giving us that attention which would have greatly enhanced whatever merit this work may possess.

To Dr. Evaristo Breccia of the Instituto d'Storia Antica of the University of Pisa, formerly of the Alexandrian Museum, who has been most generous of his knowledge of ancient Alexandria, and particularly for his service in our effort to rediscover the Plautine Scholium, we are most grateful.

Dr. Ernest H. Wilkins, President Emeritus of Oberlin College, has been most gracious in obtaining for us the versions of the Tzetzes Commentary on Aristophanes and has permitted us to use his rendering of the Plautine Scholium.

Cardinal Mercati of the Biblioteca Apostolica Vaticana graciously permitted the Plautine Scholium to be reproduced in this work.

We wish to thank Mr. Saul Levin of the Society of Fellows, Harvard University, for his version of the Commentary on Aristophanes. We would also thank Rev. J. B. Bassich, S.J., of Loyola University, for courtesies.

We are deeply indebted to Mr. Henry Hans Frenkle who so generously contributed his time in lessening the considerable linguistic labors involved.

In our considered effort to learn the true import of the Indian Mission to the Hellenic powers at the time of Ptolemy II, we were most kindly helped by the Honorable R. H. Hadow of the British Embassy at Washington, who interested in our behalf the Department of Coins and Medals, British Museum, the Indian Office, the Embassy of India, who in turn referred us to Dr. Tara Chan,

Vice Chancellor, Allahabad University, and Prof. Dr. K. A. Nilakanta Sastri, University of Madras.

Dr. Hussein Monés, Professor of History, Fouad I University, Cairo, has graciously made the translation of the important Arabic text of 'Ali ibn al–Kifti, for wich we are grateful.

For the most liberal loan of valuable books, we want to thank Dr. Luther H. Evans, Director of the Library of Congress; Dr. Keyes De Wit Metcalf, Director of the Harvard University Library; Dr. Julian P. Boyd, Librarian of Princeton University; Dr. Warner G. Rice, Director of the University of Michigan Library; Dr. Emelia E. Wefel, Librarian of the Cleveland Public Library; Dr. Garland F. Taylor, Librarian of the Tulane University Library; and Miss Nelle C. Davidson, Librarian of the New Orleans Baptist Theological Seminary.

The vast number of books referred to within this work are the copies in the Bibliotheca Parsoniana.

In the many years of this study, it may well be that we have failed to remember kindnesses shown by friends and scholars who may have in any way helped us in these labors.

BIBLIOGRAPHY[1]

ABÛ'L-FARAJ, Bar-Hebraeus, Gregory:
   The Mukhtasar al-duwal (Historia Dynastiarum):
   a. *Specimen Historiae Arabum*, sive Gregorii Abul Farajii: opera and studio,
      ed. Edward Pocock, Oxford, 1650; also pub. Bukuk, Eskonia, 1663;
   b. *Specimen Historiae Arabum*. Edw. Pocock, ed. Josephus White, Oxford,
      1806;
   c. Edition by Rev. Father Salhani, Beyrout.
   The Chronography of, tr. (with Syriac text) by Ernest A. Wallis Budge, 2
      vols., Oxford, 1932.
ABÛ'L FIDA. *Annales Muslemici arabice et latine.* J. J. Reiske, 5 vols., Hafniae,
      1789–94.
—, Géographie. Text, 1840; tr. from Arabic, Reinaud & Guyard, 3 vols.,
      Paris, 1848–83.
ABÛ SÂLIH. *Churches and Monasteries of Egypt*, ed. Evetts and Butler, Oxford,
      1895.
ACHILLES TATIUS. See Tatius.
ADRIANI, A., s.v. *Alessandria* in *Enciclopedia Italiana Appendice*, 1938–48.
—, *Annuaire du Musée Gréco-Romain*, 1932 et seq.
AELIAN. *Varia Historia; De Natura Animalium*, ed. R. Hercher, Teubner, 1864.
AELIUS SPARTIANUS. See *Historiae Augustae.*
AESCHYLUS, H. W. Smyth, 2 vols. – L.C.L.
AFRICANUS, LEO. *The History and Description of Africa*, tr. John Pory, 1600
      (The Hakluyt Society), 3 vols., London, 1896.
AFRICANUS, SEXTUS JULIUS. *Chronicle.* Vide: Eusebius, Syncellus, Cedrenus
      Paschale Chronicon, Gelzer, H. *Sextus Julius Africanus.* 2 vols.
AGATHIAS. *Histories*, ed. Niebuhr, Bonn, 1828.
ALCIPHRON. *Letters.* Athens (Pseudo), 1896.
—, *The Letters* of Alciphron, Aelian and Philostratus. A. R. Benner & F. H.
      Fobes – L.C.L.
Alexandrian Library, The, in *The Eclectic Magazine*, New Series, IX, Apr. 1869.
ALFÖLDI, A. *The Crisis of the Empire*, in *C.A.H.*, Vol. XII, Cambridge, 1939.
ALLEN, T. W. *The Ancient and Modern Vulgate of Homer*, *Classical Review*, Vol.
      13, 1899.
—, *Ludwich's Homervulgata, Clas. Rev.*, Vol. 13, 1899.
—, *The Nature of the Ancient Homeric Vulgate, Clas. Rev.*, Vol. 15, 1901.
—, *The Eccentric Editions and Aristarchus, Clas. Rev.*, Vol. 15, 1901.
AMÉLINEAU, E., *Géographie de l'Egypte à l'Epoque Copte.* Paris, 1893.
—, *Histoire des Monastères de la Basse Egypte.* Paris, 1894.
Amherst Papyri, The. Grenfell and Hunt, London, 1901.

---

1. The rendering of Greek and Latin names and those of oriental tongues are usually
those of the authors quoted, and no attempt has been made for attaining a system
of uniformity.

434 BIBLIOGRAPHY

AMMIANUS MARCELLINUS. The Surviving Books of *The History of.* J. C. Rolfe, 3 vols. – L.C.L.
—, *The Roman History.* C. D. Yonge, 2 vols., London, 1894.
ANATOLIUS. *The Canons on the Pascha* in Eusebius. *Ecclesiastical History.*
Anecdota Oxoniensia, Semetic Series, Vol. I, pt. VI, *Mediaeval Jewish Chronicles,* II (Neubauer's ed.), Oxford, 1895 (from Thackeray).
ANGUS, S. *The Sources of Augustine's De civitate Dei.* Princeton Un., 1906.
Annales du Service des Antiquités de L'Egypte. Cairo.
Antigonos of Karystos. See Wilamowitz.
Antioch on-the-Orontes. Princeton Un. Press, 3 vols., 1934-38-41.
APHTHONIOS. *Progymnasmata* in Walz's *Rhetores Graeci.*
—, Brzoska in Pauly-Wissowa, s.v. *Aphthonios.*
—, Shaefer. *De Apthonio Sophista.* Breslau, 1854.
APOLLONIUS OF PERGA. *Treatise on Conic Sections,* ed. in modern notation, T. L. Heath, Cambridge, 1896.
—, See *Greek Mathematics.*
APOLLONIUS OF RHODES:
 The Argonautica. R. C. Seaton, 1912 – L.C.L. Fragments: ap. *Collectanea Alexandrina.* J. U. Powell, 1925.
 Scholia Vetera. C. Wendel, 1935.
 Commentary. G. W. Mooney, 1912.
 Kraack, Gr. s.v. *Apollonius,* ap. Pauly Wissowa, II.
Apostolic Fathers, The. Kirsopp Lake, 2 vols. – L.C.L.
APPIAN OF ALEXANDRIA. *The Civil Wars.* Horace White, 2 vols. – L.C.L.
—, *Roman History.* Horace White, 4 vols. – L.C.L.
APULEIUS. *The Golden Ass,* tr. Adlington, 1566, rev. S. Gaselee – L.C.L.
ARATUS, G. R. Mair. – L.C.L.
ARCHIMEDES. *The Works of,* ed. in modern notation, T. L. Heath, Cambridge, 1897.
—, See *Greek Mathematics.*
ARISTARCHUS OF SAMOS. See *Greek Mathematics.*
ARISTARCHUS OF SAMOTHRACE:
 Lehrs, L. *de Aristarchi studiis Homericis,* 1882.
 Ludwich, A. *Aristarchs homerische Textkritik,* 1884-5.
 Römer, A. *Die Homerexegese Aristarchs,* ed. E. Belzer, 1924.
 Cauer, P. *Grundfragen der Homerkritik,* 1923.
 Monro, D. B. *Homer's Odyssey,* Appen., 1901.
ARISTEAS. Text, P. Wendland, Teubner series, Leipzig, 1900.
—, *The Letter of,* tr. H. St. J. Thackeray, London, 1918.
—, *La Lettera di Aristea a Filocrate,* tr. R. Tramentano, 1931.
—, *Pseudo Letter to his brother Philocrates,* ed. prin. Simon Schard, Basil, 1561.
ARISTIDES, AELIUS. *Orations,* ex recensione G. Dindorfii, 3 vols., Leipzig, 1829.
ARISTOBULUS (Pseudo). See Eusebius. *Preparation for the Gospel* (XIII–12).
ARISTOPHANES. *The Comedies of,* ed. tr., & com. Benjamin Buckley Rogers, 6 vols., London, 1902–16.
—, Van Leeuwen, J. The Complete Works of Aristophanes, 1893–1906. *Prolegomena ad Aristophanem,* 1909.
—, White, John Williams. *The Scholia on the Aves of Aristophanes,* Boston, 1914.

ARISTOPHANES. Tzetzes, Johnnes. *The Prolegomena to Aristophanes*, ed. H. Keil, 1847; ap. Lexicon Vindobonensi, 1867; Kaibel, 1899.
ARISTOPHANES OF BYZANTIUM.
    Nauck, A. *Aristophanis Byzantini grammatici Alexandrini fragmenta*. Halle, 1848.
    Wagner, I. *Die metrische Hypotheseis zu Aristophanes*, 1908.
    Grenfell & Hunt. *Amherst Papyri*, II, 1901.
    Oxyrhynchus Papyri, II, 1899.
    Wilamowitz-Moellendorff, U. von. *Textgeschichte der griechischen Lyriker*, 1900.
    Vide: Aristarchus.
    Vide: Aristophanes.
    Vide: Tzetzes.
ARISTOTLE. L.C.L. for text, 16 vols., various eds. & trs., London, v.d. *The "Art" of Rhetoric*. J. H. Freese – L.C.L.
—, *Oeconomica*. G. Cyril Armstrong – L.C.L.
—, *On the Constitution of Athens*, ed. F. G. Kenyon, ed. pr., London, 1891.
—, *The Works of*, tr. & ed. W. D. Ross & others, 11 vols., Oxford, 1908–1931.
ARRIAN. *The Anabasis of Alexander*, tr. E. J. Chinnock, London, 1893.
—, *Anabasis of Alexander: Indica*. E. Ileff Robson, 2 vols. – L.C.L.
ATHENAEUS. *The Deipnosophists*. Charles Burton Gulick, 7 vols., London, 1927–41. L.C.L.
AUGUSTI, DIVI. *Res. Gestae* (Monumentum Ancyranum). Fredrick W. Shipley – L.C.L.
AUGUSTINE, SAINT. *Confessions*. Wm. Watts, 2 vols. – L.C.L.
—, *Select Letters*. J. H. Baxter – L.C.L.
—, *City of God*. Marcus Dods, 2 vols. New York, 1948.
AUSFELD. *Neapolis und Brucheion in Alexandria*. Philologus, 63, 1904.
—, *Der griech. Alexanderroman*. 1907.
AUSONIUS. *The Order of Famous Cities; Epistles*. Hugh G. E. White, 2 vols. – L.C.L.
AXON, W. E. A. *On the Extent of Ancient Libraries*. Roy Soc. Lit., ser. 2, X, 1874.
BACCHUS, F. J. s. v. *Synesius* in *Cath. Ency*.
BAEDAE. *Opera Historica*. J. E. King, 2 vols. – L.C.L.
BAEDEKER, KARL. *Egypt and the Sûdân*. 8th ed., Leipzig, 1929.
—, *Palestine and Syria*. 4th ed., Leipzig, 1906.
—, *Greece*. 3rd ed., Leipzig, 1905.
BAGNINI, G. *Hellenistic Sculpture from Cyrene, Jour. Hell. Studies*. XLI, 1921.
BAIKIE, JAS. *Egyptian Papyri and Papyrus-Hunting*. London, 1925.
BALÂDHURÎ, AL. *Kitab Futûh al-Buldan, History of the Moslem Conquest*, tr. Philip Khuri Hitti, Columbia Un., New York, 1916.
BANERJEE, GAURANGA NATH. *Hellenism in Ancient India*. 2nd ed., Calcutta, 1920.
BARBER, E. A. s.v. *Alexandrian Literature* in *Cambridge Ancient History*.
—, s.v. *Alexander of Pleuron in Aetolia* in *Oxford Classical Dict*.
—, s.v. *Apollonius* in *Oxford Classical Dictionary*.
BARBER, E. A. See Powell, J. A.
BARTHEMA, LEWIS. *The Travels of*, in Purchas *His Pilgremes*, Glasgow, 1905.
BASIL, SAINT. *The Letters*. Roy J. Deferrari, 4 vols. – L.C.L.

BAUMGARTEN, MARTIN. *The Travels of*, in the Churchill Collection, London, 1744.

BAUR, CHRYS. s.v. *John Chrysostom* and s.v. *Theophilus* in *Cath. Ency.*

BAYNES, NORMAN H. and Moss, H. St. L. B. (ed.) *Byzantium.* Oxford, 1948.

BEAZLEY, C. R. *The Dawn of Modern Geography.* 3 vols., London, 1897, Oxford, 1906.

BECK, JOHANNE GUILIELMO. *Specimen Historiae Bibliothecarum Alexandrinarum.* Lipsiae, 1779.

BECKER, W. A. *Charicles.* 6th ed., London, 1882.

—, *Gallus.* 8th ed., London, 1886.

BELL, H. *Early Codices from Egypt*, in *The Library*, n.s., X, 1909.

BELL, H. Idris. *Egypt from Alexander the Great to the Arab Conquest*, Oxford, 1948.

—, *Jews and Christians in Egypt* (British Museum), 1924.

BELOCH, KARL JULIUS. *Griechische Geschichte.* 2nd ed., Berlin-Leipzig, 1922–27.

—, *Zur Chronologie der ersten Ptolemäer. Archiv fuer Papyrusforschung*, VII (1924) and VIII (1926).

—, *Die Bevölkerung der griechisch-römischen Welt.* Leipzig, 1886.

BENJAMIN, RABBI. *The Travels of*, in Jno. Pinkerton Collection.

BENTIVICH, NORMAN. *Hellenism.* Philadelphia, 1919.

BENTLEY, RICHARD. *Remarks on a Late Discourse of Freethinking by Philelentherius Lipsensis.* 1713.

BÉRARD, VICTOR. *Did Homer Live?*, tr. Brian Rhys, New York, 1931.

BERNHARDY, G. *Eratosthenica.* Berol, 1822.

BERNHARDY, G. *Grundriss der griechischen Litteratur.* Halle, 1892 (1872,3 vols.)

BEVAN, EDWYN ROBERT. *A History of Egypt under the Ptolemaic Dynasty.* London, 1914–27.

—, *The House of Seleucus.* 2 vols., London, 1902.

—, s.v. *Hellenism* in *Ency. Brit.* 11th ed., Vol. 13.

BEZOLD, S. *Catal. of the Cuneiform Tablets.* British Museum 5, 1899.

—, See Pauly-Wissowa, II, 1762.

Bible, The Hexaglot, ed. E. Riches de Levante, 6 vols., New York, 1906.

Bible, The Holy, tr. from the Latin Vulgate (*The New Testament*), Rheims, 1582.

Bible, The Holy, tr. from the Latin Vulgate (*The Old Testament*), Douay, 1609.

Bible, The Holy, conteying the Old Testament and the New, newly translated out of the Originall Tongues. Imprinted at London by Robert Barker, Anno Dom. 1611.

The New Testament of Our Lord and Saviour Jesus Christ, newly tr. from Vulgate Latin. Mgr. Ronald A. Knox, New York, 1944.

The Old Testament, tr. from the Latin Vulgate by Mgr. Ronald A. Knox, 2 vols., London, 1949.

Bible, The Holy. See Septuagint.

BIDEZ, J. s.v. *Literature and Philosophy in the Eastern Half of the Empire* in *Cambridge Ancient History*, Vol. XII.

BIRT, THEODOR. *Des Antiken Buchwesens.* Munich, 1913.

BLANKENHORN, MAX. *Geologie Aegyptens.* Berlin, 1911.

BLOMFIELD, R. MASSIE. *Map of Alexandria* in *Bulletin de la Société Archéologique d'Alexandrie* No. 8, 1905.

BLOMFIELD, R. MASSIE. *L'emplacement du Musée et de la Bibliothèque des Ptolémées* in *Bulletin No. 6*, Alexandrie, 1904.

—, *The Arsinoeum and its Obelisk* in *Bull. de la Soc. Arch. d'Alexandrie*, No. 8, Alexandrie, 1905.

BLOUNT, MASTER HENRY. *A Voyage into the Levant* in Harleian Collection of Voyages and Travels, from the library of the Earl of Oxford, London, 1745.

BOECKH, AUGUSTE. *The Public Economy of Athens*. 2nd ed., London, 1842.

BOETHIUS. *The Theological Tractates; The Consolation of Philosophy*. H. F. Stewart, E. K. Rand – L.C.L.

BOISSIER, GASTON. *Atticus* in *Revue Archéologique*, n.s., VII.

—, *Roman Africa*. New York, 1898.

BOLLING, GEORGE MELVILLE, s.v. *Alexandrian Library* in *Cath. Ency.*

BONAMY. *Dissertation historique sur la Bibl. d'Alexandrie* in *Mém. de l'acad. des Inscript.*, Vol. IX.

BOTFIELD, BERIAH. *Praefationes et Epistolae (Preface to the First Editions of the Greek and Roman Classics and of the Sacred Scriptures*. Cambridge, 1861.

BOTSFORD, GEORGE WILLIS. *Hellenic History*. New York, 1926.

BOTTI. *L'acropole d'Alexandrie et le Sérapeum*. Alexandrie, 1895.

—, *Fouilles à la colonne Théodosienne*. Alexandrie, 1897.

—, *Plan d'Alexandrie à l'époque ptolémaique*. Alexandrie, 1898.

BOUCHÉ-LECLERCQ, A. *Histoire des Lagides*. 4 vols., Paris, 1903–07.

—, *Histoire des Séleucides*. Paris, 1913–14.

BOYD, C. E. *Public Libraries and Literary Culture in Ancient Rome*. Chicago, 1915.

BRADY, THOMAS ALLEN. s.v. *Serapis* in *The Oxford Classical Dictionary*.

BREASTED, JAMES HENRY. *Ancient Records of Egypt*. 5 vols., Chicago, 1906.

—, *A History of Egypt from the Earliest Times to the Persian Conquest*. New York, 1905.

BRECCIA, EVARISTO. *Alexandrea ad Aegyptum*. Bergamo, 1922.

—, s.v. *Alessandria* in *Enci. Ital.*, Vol. I, 1929.

—, *Les fouilles dans le Sérapeum d'Alexandrie en 1905–1906 (Annales du Service des antiquités* VIII).

—, *La Nécropoli de l'Ibrahimieh (Bull. Soc. Archéol.* 9, n.s. T I fasc. I).

—, *La Nécropoli di Sciatbi*.

BROCKELMANN, CARL. s.v. *Abu 'al-Fida* in *Ency. of Islam*.

—, s.v. *al-Kifti* in *Ency. of Islam*.

—, s.v. *al-Makrizi* in *Ency. of Islam*.

—, *History of the Islamic Peoples*. New York, 1947.

BROOKS, E. W. *The Arabs in Asia Minor (641–750) from Arabic Sources* (apud. J. H. S. Vol. XVIII).

—, *The Eastern Provinces from Arcadius to Anastasius* in *C.M.H.*, Vol. I.

—, *On the Chronology of the Conquest of Egypt by the Saracens*, in *Byzantinische Zeitschrift* for 1895.

BROWN, JAMES DUFF. See Tedder, H. R.

BROWNE, EDWARD G. *A Literary History of Persia*. 4 vols., London, 1929.

BRUGSCH-BEY, HEINRICK. *Egypt under the Pharaohs, a History derived entirely from the Monuments*. London, 1891, new, revised, and condensed ed.

BRZOSKA. *De canone decemoratorium atticorum*, 1883.

438 BIBLIOGRAPHY

BUDIK, P. A. *Die Bibliothek zu Alexandria.* Serapeum, XI, 1850.
BULLE, H. *Der Leichenwagen Alexanders. Jahrbuch der deutschen archäologischen Institute.* 1906.
Bulletin de la Société archéologique d'Alexandrie. (Various.)
BUNBURY, EDWARD HERBERT. *A History of Ancient Geography among the Greeks and Romans.* 2 vols. London, 1879.
BUNSEN, BARON CHRISTIAN C. J. *Egypt's Place in Universal History,* ed. S. Birch, 5 vols., London, 1848–67.
BURCKHARDT, JACOB. *Griechische Kulturgeschichte.* 4 vols., Berlin, 1899–1931.
BURY, J. B. *A History of Greece to the Death of Alexander the Great.* London, 1911.
—, *History of the Later Roman Empire.* 2 vols., London, 1923.
—, s.v. *Homer* in *Cambridge Ancient History.*
—, Editor. *Decline & Fall.* See Gibbon.
BURY, J. B., BARBER, E.A., BEVAN, E.A., and TARN, W.W. *The Hellenistic Age.* 2nd ed. Cambridge, 1925.
BUSCH, GUILELMUS, *De Bibliothecariis Alexandrinis qui feruntur primis.* Leipzig, 1884.
BUSHNELL, G. H. *The World's Earliest Libraries.* London, 1930.
—, *The Alexandrian Library* (in *Antiquity* 2, 1928).
BUTCHER, E. L. *Story of the Church of Egypt.* 2 vols., London, 1897.
BUTLER, ALFRED J. *The Arab Conquest of Egypt and the Last Thirty Years of the Roman Domination.* Oxford, 1902.
—, *Ancient Coptic Churches of Egypt.* 2 vols., Oxford, 1884.
CAESAR. *The Civil Wars.* A. G. Peskett – L.C.L.
— (Hirtius). *The Alexandrian War.* Philadelphia, 1837.
CAHEN, EMILE. Supplement chapter, *The Elegies of Callimachus, etc.* in Couat's *Alexandrian Poetry,* tr. Jas. Loeb, London, 1931.
CALDERINI, ARISTIDE. *Bagni publici nell'Egitto Greco-Romano,* Milano, 1919.
—, *Dizionario dei nomi geografici e topografici dell'Egitto Greco-Romano.* 3 vols., Cairo, 1935.
Callimachus and Lycophron. A. W. Mair – L.C.L.
CALLIMACHUS OF CYRENE:
  WILAMOWITZ-MOELLENDORFF, U. VON. *Callimachi Hymni et Epigrammata.* 1925.
  SCHNEIDER, O. *Callimachea.* 1870, 1873.
  COUAT, A. *La poésie alexandrine sous les trois premiers Ptolémées.*
  CAHEN, E. *Callimaque et son oeuvre poétique.* 1929.
  —, *Les Hymnes de Callimaque.* 1930.
  HERTER, H. s.v. *Kallimachos.* ap. Pauly-Wissowa, Supp. V.
  PFEIFFER, R. *Callimachus-Fragmenta.* 2 vols., 1949–1950.
  WESSELY. ap. *Studies, Griffith,* London, 1932.
  MAIR, A. W. *Callimachus.* – L.C.L.
  Oxyrhynchus Papyri, XVII (1927).
  STUART, REED DUANE. *The Prenuptial Rite in the New Callimachus* (ap. *Classical Philology,* VI, Chicago, 1911).
  BONNER, CAMPBELL. *The Prenuptial Rite in the Aetid of Callimachus.* (ap. *Class. Phil.* VI, Chicago, 1911).
CALLISTHENES, PSEUDO-. Text: W. Kroll. *Historia Alexandri Magni,* 1926.
CALLISTRATUS. *Descriptions.* Arthur Fairbanks – L.C.L.

CALLIXENUS OF RHODES. *Description of Alexandria* (in Athenaeus, V, 196–203).

Cambridge Ancient History. 12 vols., London, 1926–40.

Cambridge Medieval History. 8 vols., London, 1911–1936.

CAMPBELL, DONALD. *Arabian Medicine and its Influence on the Middle Ages.* 2 vols., London, 1926.

CARAPANOS, CONSTANTIN. *Dodone et ses Ruines.* 2 vols., Paris, 1878.

CARDINALI, G. *Il regno di Pergamo.* Turin, 1906.

CARERI, JOHN FRANCIS GEMELLI. *A Voyage round the World* in Churchill Collection of Voyages and Travels, London, 1745.

CARYSTIUS OF PERGAMUM. *Notes* (ap. Athenaeus, XII).

CASANOVA, MONS. P. *L'incendie de la Bibliothèque d'Alexandrie par les Arabes* (in *Académie des Inscriptions et Belles-Lettres, Séances,* 1923, Paris, 1923.

Catholic Encyclopedia, The. 15 vols., New York, 1907–12.

CATULLUS, GAIUS VALERIUS. *The Poems of.* F. W. Cornish – L.C.L.

CEDRENUS, GEORGE. *The Historical Synopsis.* Bonn ed., 2 vols., 1838–9.

CELSUS. *De Medicina.* W. G. Spencer, 3 vols. – L.C.L.

CESSI, C. *La poesia ellenistica.* Bari, 1912.

CHAMPOLLION, J. F.:

    a. *Lettre à M. Dacier relative à l'alphabet des hiéroglyphes phonétiques.* Paris, 1822.

    b. *Précis du système hiéroglyphique.* Paris, 1824.

    c. *Grammaire égyptienne.* Paris, 1834.

CHASTEL, E. *Les Destinées de la Bibl. d'Alex.* (Rev. Hist., 1876).

CHAUVIN, M. *Le livre dans le monde arabe.* Bruxelles, 1911.

CHEVALLIER, E. See Lenormant, François.

CHRIST, WILHELM VON, and SCHMID. *Geschichte der griechischen Litteratur.* 6th ed., Munich, 1920.

Chronicon Paschale (or Alexandrinum), ed. Dindorf in the Bonn series[1].

CHRYSOSTOM. See Dio.

CICERO. *Works* text & tr. var. eds., 25 vols. continuing – L.C.L.

—, *Letters to Atticus.* E. O. Winstedt, 3 vols. – L.C.L.

—, *De Finibus, Bonorum et Malorum.* H. Rackham – L.C.L.

—, *Epistulae ad familiares.* W. G. Williams, 3 vols. – L.C.L.

—, *De Oratore.* E. W. Sullon & H. Rackham, 2 vols. – L.C.L.

—, *Pro Archia Poeta.* N. H. Watts – L.C.L.

—, *Tusculan Disputations.* J. E. King – L.C.L.

CLARK, J. W. *The Care of Books.* London, 1909.

CLARKE, EDWARD DANIEL. *The Tomb of Alexander: a Dissertation on the Sarcophagus brought from Alexandria and now in the British Museum.* Cambridge, 1805.

CLEMENT OF ALEXANDRIA. G. W. Butterworth – L.C.L.

—, *The Stromata* or *Miscellanies.* 2 vols., Edinburgh, 1872.

CLÉMENT, P. *Etude sur les droits des auteurs chez les Grecs et chez les Romains.* Grenoble, 1867.

CLINTON, HENRY FYNES. *An Epitome of the Civil and Literary Chronology of Greece.* Oxford, 1851.

1. "When the Paschal Chronicle deserts us in A.D. 627, we have no contemporary historians or chroniclers for the general course of the Imperial history until we reach the end of the eighth century" – J. B. Bury.

CLINTON, HENRY FYNES. *Fasti Hellenici, The Civil and Literary Chronology of Greece* (to LVth Olympiad), 3 vols., Oxford, 1834.

COBHAM, CLAUDE DELAVAL. *Excerpta Cypria*. 5th ed., Cambridge, 1908.

COPERNICUS. *De Revolutionibus orbium coelestium libri VI*. Nurimbergae, 1543.

Corpus Inscriptionum Graecarum, ed. Boeckh (also Berlin).

Corpus Inscriptionum Indicarum, ed. E. Hultzsch, new ed., Oxford, 1925.

Corpus Inscriptionum Latinarum. 1863 foll.

Corpus Scriptorum Historicorum Byzantinorum. W. Dindorf, 1829.

CORY, ISAAC PRESTON. *Ancient Fragments*. Pickering ed., London, 1832.

COUAT, AUGUSTE. *Alexandrian Poetry under the First Three Ptolemies*, tr. James Loeb, London, 1931.

—, *Le Musée d'Alexandrie sous les premiers Ptolémées*. Ann. Bordeaux I, 1879.

CRAMER, JOHN ANTONY. *Anecdota graeca e codd. manuscriptis Bibliothecae Regiae Parisiensis*. 4 vols., Oxford, 1835–37.

CROISET, ALFRED and MAURICE. *Histoire de la littérature grecque*. 5 vols., Paris, 1901 (especially Vol. V).

CRUNI, W. E. *Coptic Ostraka*. London, 1902.

CTESIAS OF CNIDOS. See Mc Crindle. *Ancient India as described by Ktesias, etc.*

CUMFE, K. *Beiträge zu einigen das Museum und die Bibliotheken zu Alex. betreffende Fragen*, in Listy. Filil., 1885.

CURTIUS, ERNEST. *The History of Greece*. 5 vols., London, 1868–73.

CURTIUS RUFUS QUINTUS. *History of Alexander the Great of Macedon*. Jno. C. Rolfe, 2 vols. – L.C.L.

CYPRIAN. *Hept. Exod.*

CYRIL, SAINT. Arch. of Jerusalem. *The Catechetical Lectures*. Oxford, 1872.

DAHL, SVEND. *Geschichte des Buches*. Leipzig, 1928.

DALTON, O. M. *The Letters of Sidonius*. Oxford, 1915.

D'ANVILLE. *Mémoires sur l'Egypte*. Paris, 1766.

DAREMBERG ET SAGLIO. *Dictionnaire des Antiquités Grecques et Romaines*. Paris, 1877–1918.

DECHARME, PAUL. *Euripides and The Spirit of his Dramas*, tr. Jas. Loeb, N.Y., 1906.

DE COULANGES, FUSTEL. *La cité antique*. 1893.

DEDEL, JOHN. *Historia critica bibliothecarum alex.* Lugduni Batav., 1823.

DE GOEJE, M. J. *Bibliotheca Geographica Arabicorum*. Leyden, 1870–79 (especially al Mas'udi).

DEISSMANN, ADOLF. *Light from the Ancient East*. New & Rev. Ed., N.Y. & London, n.d.

DELAMBRE, JEAN BAPTISTE. *Histoire de l'astronomie ancienne*. 2 vols., Paris, 1817.

DELAPIERRE, O. *Le canard de la biblioth. d'Alexandrie*. London, 1862.

DEMETRIOS OF PHALERON:

　Demetrios von Phaleron (ap. *Die Schule des Aristoteles*). Texte und Kommentar, von Fritz Wehrli, Basel, 1949.

　Fragmenta Historicorum Graecorum. Karl Muller, Paris, 1841-70.

　BAYER, E. *Demetrios Palereus der Athener*, Tübinger Beiträge zur Altertumswissenschaft XXXVI, 1942.

　COHN, D. *De Demetrios Phalereo, Mnemosyne*, N.S. 54, 1926.

　DOHRN, H. *De vita et rebus Demetrii Phalerei Peripatetici*. Kiel, 1825.

Dow, Sterling and Travis, Albert H. *Demetrios of Phaleron and his Lawgiving*. Hesperia 12, 1943.

HERWIG, TH. *Ueber Demetrios Phalereus*, Gymnasialprogramm, Rinteln, 1850.

JACOBY, F. *Die Fragmente der griechischen Historiker* II, 1929–1930.

LACROIX, J. *Demetrios de Phalère*, Thèse de licence, Université de Liége, 1942–43.

MARTINI, E. s.v. *Demetrios* in Pauly-Wissowa, No. 85.

OSTERMANN, CHR. *Commentatio de Demetrii Phalerei vita, rebus gestis et scriptorum reliquiis*. Herfeld und Fulda, 1847 und 1857.

PAPASIS, K. A. *Demetrius und die Stadt Athen*, Dissertation. Erlangen, 1893.

DEMETRIUS. *On Style*. W. Rhys Roberts – L.C.L.

DEMOSTHENES. J. H. Vince and others, 7 vols. – L.C.L.

—, *Against Dionysodorus* – L.C.L. *Private Orations*. A. T. Murray, 3 vols., 1936–39.

DENNISTON, J. D. s.v. *Hypotheses* in *Ox. Class. Dic.*

DEPHI LIBRARY. See *Rhein. Mus.*, XVIII.

Dictionnaire d'Archéologie chrétienne et de liturgie, s.v. *Alexandrie* by Dom Leclercq.

Dictionnaire d'histoire et de géographie ecclésiastiques. Paris, 1912, s.v. *Alexandrie* by Père J. Faivre.

DIEHL, CHARLES. *History of the Byzantine Empire*. New York, 1945.

—, *L'Afrique Byzantine*. Paris, 1896.

DIENER, BERTHA. *Imperial Byzantium*. Boston, 1938.

DIEUCHIDAS. *Megarian History* (ap. Athenaeus I).

DILL. *Roman Society from Nero to Aurelius*. London, 1904.

DIMITRIADIS. Ἱστορ.δοχίμτῶν᾿Αλεξ.ΒιΒλ. Leipzig, 1871.

DINDORF, W. in *Rheinisches Museum*, IV, 1830. (See Tzetzes).

DIO's *Roman History*. E. Cary on H.B. Foster, 9 vols. – L.C.L.

DIO CHRYSOSTOM. J. W. Cohoon & H. Lamar Crosby, 5 vols. – L.C.L. a. *The Corinthian Oration*; b. *The Thirty-Second Discourse*.

—, *Homilies on the Gospel of St. Matthew*. 3 vols., Oxford, 1876.

—, See Migne – *P. G.* Vols. 47–64.

DIODORUS SICULUS. C. H. Oldfather & Russel M. Geer, 12 vols. – L.C.L.

DIOGENES LAERTIUS. *Lives of Eminent Philosophers*. R. D. Hicks, 2 vols. – L.C.L.

DIONYSIUS OF CYZICUS. See Bunsen's *Egypt*.

DIONYSIUS OF HALICARNASSUS. *The Literary Letters*, ed. W. Rhys Roberts, Cambridge, 1901.

—, *The Roman Antiquities* of. E. Cary on Edw. Spelman, 7 vols., London, 1937 – L.C.L.

DITTENBERGER, W. *Orientiz Graeci Inscriptiones Selectae*. Leipzig, 1905.

DODGE, THEODORE AYRAULT. *Alexander (Art of War to Battle of Ipsus, B.C. 301)*, 2 vols., Boston, 1890.

—, *Caesar (Art of War to End of the Roman Empire)*, 2 vols., Boston, 1892.

DODWELL, EDWARD. *A Classical and Topographical Tour through Greece during the years 1800-5-6*. 2 vols., London, 1819.

DONALDSON, JNO. WM. *Continuation of K. O. Muller's History of the Literature of Ancient Greece*. 3 vols., London, 1858.

DONNE, WM. BODHAM. s.v. *Alexandreia* in *Smith's Dict. Gr. & Roman Geography*, London, 1854.

DOUGHERTY, R. P. *Writing upon Parchment and Papyrus among the Babylonians and Assyrians*, in *Jour. Am. Oriental Soc.*, XLVIII, 1928.

DRAPEYRON, L. *L'Empereur Héraclius*. Paris, 1869.

DROYSEN, JOHAN GUSTAV. *Geschichte des Hellenismus*. Hamburg, 1836; 2nd ed. Gotha, 1876.

—, *Geschichte Alexanders des Grossen*. Berlin, 1917.

—, *Die Demokratie*. Leipzic, 1882.

DUDDEN, F. H. *Gregory the Great*. 2 vols. London, 1905.

DURANT, WILL. *Caesar and Christ*. New York, 1944.

—, *The Life of Greece*. New York, 1939.

DURIS OF SAMOS. *Histories* (ap. Athenaeus XII).

DZIATZKO, KARL. *Antikes Buchwesen*. Leipzig, 1900.

—, s.v. *Pergame* in Pauly-Wissowa under *Bibliotheken*.

—, s.v. *Buch*. s.v. *Buchhandel* in Pauly-Wissowa.

—, s.v. *Alexandrinische Bibliotheken* in Pauly-Wissowa.

—, Jno. Tzetzes and das Plautus scholion über die Alex. Bibliotheken (in *Rh. Mus.* 46, 1891).

EBERS, GEORG. *Egypt: Descriptive, Historical and Picturesque*. 2 vols., London.

—, *Serapis*. New York, 1885.

EDWARDS, EDWARD. *Memoirs of Libraries*. London, 1859.

EGGER, E. *Callimaque considéré comme bibliographe* in *Annuaire de la Société des études grecs*. Paris, 1876.

—, *Essai sur l'Histoire de la Critique chez les Grecs*. 2nd ed. rev. Paris, 1886.

Egypt: Description de l'Egypte ou recueil des observations et des recherches qui ont été faites en Egypte pendant l'Expédition de l'Armée Française. Paris (de l'Imprimerie Impériale) 1809–13; (de l'Imprimerie Royale) 1817–30. Texte 9 vols. folio; Plates, hand-painted, 11 vols. Elephant folio; 3 vols. Atlas folio (23 vols.).

Elegy and Iambus. Being the Remains of all the Greek Elegiac and Iambic Poets from Callimachus to Crates, excepting the Choliambic Writers; The Anacrontea. 2 vols. J. M. Edmonds – L.C.L.

ELGOOD, Lt. Col. P. G. *The Ptolemies of Egypt*. London, 1938.

EMERSON. *Quotation and Originality*. Boston.

EMPERICUS, SEXTUS. R. G. Bury, 3 vols. – L.C.L.

—, *Adversus Mathematicos*. R. G. Bury – L.C.L.

Enciclopedia Italiana. 35 vols. and Supp. vols., Milano-Roma, 1929–1937.

Encyclopaedia Britannica. 11th ed., Cambridge, 1910; 1949 ed., 24 vols. Chicago.

Ephesus. Inscriptions of (Jahreshefte des Österreichischen Arch. Institu. 8–1905).

EPICTETUS. *The Discourses as reported by Arrian, the Manual and Fragments*. W. A. Oldfather, 2 vols. – L.C.L.

EPIPHANIUS. *De Ponderibus et Mensuris*. See tr. Gr. & Syriac Version in Thackeray's *Aristeas*.

ERATOSTHENES OF CYRENE:

   BERNHARDY, G. *Eratosthenica*. Berol, 1822.

   OLIVIERI, A. ap. *Mythographi Graeci III*, 1897.

   POWELL, J. U. *Collectanea Alexandrina*. 1925.

   STRECKER, C. *De Lycophrone Euphronio Eratosthene comicorum interpretibus*. 1884.

—, *Fragments on Chronology*. See Didot. *Herodotus*. Paris, 1844.

ERATOSTENES OF CYRENE. *Die geographischen Fragmente des Eratosthenes* by H. Berger, Leipzig, 1880.
—, See *Greek Mathematics.*
Etymologicum Magnum, ed. T. Gaisford, 1848.
EUCLID. *The Thirteen Books of Euclid's Elements*, tr. & com. by T. L. Heath, 2nd ed., 3 vols., Cambridge, 1926.
EUNAPIUS. *Vita Aedesii.*
EURIPIDES. Arthur S. Way, 4 vols. - L.C.L.
EVRIPIDIS. *Tragoedie septendecim, ex quib, quaedam habent commentaria, etc.*, Venetiis apud Aldvm mense febrvario MDIII, 2 vols,. 1503, ed. pr.
EUSEBIUS. *The Ecclesiastical History.* Kirsopp Lake & J. E. L. Oulton, 2 vols. - L.C.L.
—, *Preparation for the Gospel.*
—, *Cronicorum*, ed. A. Schöne, 1875.
EUSTATHIUS. *Commentary on the Iliad and Odyssey*, ed. Stallboum, 1825-30.
EUTYCHIUS. *Annales*, tr. by Pococke, Oxford, 1658-59.
—, *Annales* (ap. Migne, *Patr. Gr.*, the Latin series LVII).
EVESHAM, JOHN. *The Voyage passed by Sea into Aegypt*, ed. Hakluyt Society.
FARAJ. See Abû'l-Faraj.
FARRAR, J. A. *Literary Forgeries.* London, 1907.
FERGUSON, W. S. *Greek Imperialism.* London, 1913.
—, *Hellenistic Athens.* London, 1911.
—, *The Hellenistic Monarchies and the Rise of Rome.* Cambridge, 1928.
—, *The Leading Ideas of the New Period* in *C.A.H.*, Vol. VII, Ch. I. See also for *Demetrios of Phaleron.*
FERRERO, GUGLIELMO. *The Greatness and Decline of Rome.* 5 vols., New York, n.d.
Fihrist. See Warraq, al.
FINLAY, GEORGE. *A History of Greece from its Conquest by the Romans to the Present Time* (B.C. 146 to A.D. 1864), ed. H. F. Tozer, 7 vols., Oxford, 1877.
FLACH. *Peisistratos und seine literarische Thätigkeit.* 1885.
FLORUS, LUCIUS ANNAEUS. *Epitome of Roman History.* E. S. Forester - L.C.L.
FORBES, P. B. R. s.v. *Tzetzes* in *The Ox. Class. Dic.*
FORSTER, A. M. *Alexandria - a History and a Guide.* 2nd ed., 1938.
FORTESQUE, ADRIAN. s.v. *Eutychius* in *Cath. Ency.*
—, s.v. *Theodosius* in *Cath. Ency.*
FOWLER, H. W. & F. G. *The Works of Lucian of Samosata.* 4 vols., Oxford, 1905.
FOWLER. W. Warde. s.v. *Sibyllini Libri* in *Smith's Dictionary of Greek and Roman Antiquities.*
FRANKE, ALFRED. *Dissertation.* ref. Palladas. *Gr. An.* IX-400 on *Hypatia.* Leipzig, 1899.
FRASCHETTI, STANISLAO. *Il Bernini.* Milano, 1900.
FREEMAN, E. A. *A History of Sicily.* 4 vols., Oxford, 1891.
FRITZE, M. *Die Ersten Ptolemaer und Griechenland.* Halle, 1917.
FRONTINUS, SEXTUS JULIUS. *The Stratagems of.* Chas. E. Bennett. - L.C.L.
FROUDE, JAMES ANTHONY. *Caesar, A Sketch.* London, 1896.
FRUMANTLE, Wm. HENRY. *Prolegomena on Life and Writings of Rufinus* in *Nicene and Post-Nicene Fathers*, New York, 1892.
FURLANI, G. *Sull'incendio della biblioteca di Alessandria* (in *Aegyptus* 5, 1924).

FURLANI, G. *Giovanni il Filosofo e l'incendio della biblioteca di Alessandria* (in B.S.A.A. 21–1925).

FURTWÄNGLER, ADOLF. *Masterpieces of Greek Sculpture.* 2 vols., 1895.

GALEN. *Opera.* (ed. Kuhn) Leipzig, 1830.

—, *On the Natural Faculties.* A. J. Brock – L.C.L.

GARBELLI, FILIPPO. *Le Biblioteche in Italia.* All'Epoca Romana con un'appendice sulle Antiche Biblioteche di Ninive ed Alessandria, Milano, 1894.

GARDINER, H. ALAN. *The Nature and Development of the Egyptian Hieroglyphic Writing (Jour. of Egyptian Archaeology* II, 1915).

GARDNER, ALICE. *Religious Disunion in the Fifth Century* in *Cambridge Medieval History.*

GARDNER, E. A., HOGARTH, D. G., JAMES, M. R., SMITH, R., ELSEY. *Excavations in Cyprus, 1887–1888* in *The Journal of Hellenic Studies.* Vol. IX, London, 1888.

GARDNER, PERCY. *New Chapters in Greek History.* London, 1892.

—, *The Seleucid Kings of Syria.* British Mus. Cat. 1878.

GARDTHAUSEN, VICTOR. *Die alexandrinische Bibliothek.* Leipzig, 1922.

—, *Bibliothekskunde.* Leipzig, 1920.

GELENIUS, JOHN. *Programma de bibliotheca alex.* Dresden, 1710.

GELLIUS, AULUS. *The Attic Nights.* John C. Rolfe, 3 vols. – L.C.L.

GEORGE MONARCHUS. Ed. E. de Muralt. St. Petersburg, 1859; Migne. *Patro. Script.*

GEORGE PISIDES. ap. Migne, *Patr. Gr.* XCII; the *Historical Poems,* ed. Bekker, in Bonn series, 1836.

GEORGE, THE SYNCELLOS, ed. W. Dindorf, 2 vols., *Corp. Script. his. byz.,* Vol. 11 – 12, Bonn, 1829.

GIBBON, EDWARD. *The History of the Decline and Fall of the Roman Empire,* ed. by J. B. Bury. 7 vols., London, 1896. Also, same: 12 vols., New York, 1906. Also, editio princeps – 6 vols. fol., London, 1776–88.

GLADSTONE, Wm. E. *Studies on Homer and The Homeric Age.* 3 vols., Oxford, 1858.

GLANVILLE, S. R. K. ed. *The Legacy of Egypt.* Oxford, 1942. Especially: *The Greek Papyri* by C. H. Roberts, *Egypt and Rome* by J. H. M. Jones.

GLOVER, T. R. *Life and Letters in the Fourth Century.* Cambridge, 1901.

GOLDZIHER, IGNAZ. *Muhammedanische Studien.* Halle, 1888–90.

GÖLL, HEINRICH HERMANN. *Das alexandrinische Museum.* Planen, 1868.

GOMPERZ, TH. *Greek Thinkers: a History of Ancient Philosophy.* 4 vols., 1901–12.

GORIS, JAN–ALBERT. *Furore Teutonico Diruta* (apud. *News from Belgium,* Oct. 21, 1944).

GORRINGE, H. *Egyptian Obelisks.* London, 1885.

GOW, JAMES. In *A Companion to Greek Studies,* ed. L. Whibley, Cambridge, 1936, 3rd ed.

GRAETZ, H. *History of the Jews.* 5 vols., Philadelphia, 1891.

GRAINDOR, PAUL. *La Guerre d'Alexandrie.* Le Caire, 1931.

Greek Anthology, The. W. R. Paton, 5 vols. – L.C.L.

Greek Bucolic Poets, The. J. M. Edmonds – L.C.L.

Greek Literary Papyri. D. L. Page, 2 vols. – L.C.L.

Greek Mathematics. Ivor Thomas, 2 vols – L.C.L.

GREGOROVIUS, FERDINAND. *The Emperor Hadrian.* London, 1898.

GREGORY, C. R. *The Canon and Text of the New Testament.* New York, 1907.
GREGORY OF NYSSA. Tr. Moore and Wilson, Oxford, 1893.
GRENFELL, BERNARD P., and Hunt, Arthur S. *The Hibeh Papyri,* 1906.
—, *The Amherst Papyri.* London, 1901.
GRENFELL, B. P., HUNT, A. S. and BELL: *The Oxyrhynchus Papyri.* 17 vols., London, 1898–1927 (Especially Vol. X, No. 1241).
GRENFELL, B. P., HUNT, A. S., HOGARTH, D. G. *Fayûm Towns and their Papyri.* London, 1900.
GRENFELL, B.P., HUNT, A. S., and SMYLY, J. GILBERT. *The Tebtunis Papyri.* 2 vols., London, 1902.
GRIFFITH, FRANCIS LLEWELLYN. s.v. *Manetho* in *Enc. Brit.,* 11th ed.
GRIFFITH, LL. *Stories of the High Priests of Memphis.* Oxford, 1900.
GRINFIELD, E. W. *An Apology for the Septuagint.* London, 1850.
GRONINGEN, B. A. VAN *Short Manuel of Greek Palaeography.* Leiden, 1940.
GROTE, GEORGE. *Aristotle.* 2 vols., London, 1872.
—, *History of Greece,* 2nd ed., 12 vols., London, 1849–57.
—, *Plato and the other Companions of Sokrates.* 2nd ed., 3 vols., London, 1867.
GUEST, RHUVON. s.v. *al-Iskandariya* in *Ency. Islam.*
GUHL, E., and KONER, W. *The Life of the Greeks and Romans.* London, 1889.
GULICK, CHARLES BURTON. *The Life of the Ancient Greeks.* 1909.
—, See Athenaeus.
HAARHOFF, THEODORE JOHANNES. s.v. *Museum* in *The Ox. Class. Dic.*
HADJI KHALIFA. See Khalifa.
HAKLUYT, RICHARD. *The Principal Navigations, Voyages and Discoveries of the English Nation.* 12 vols., Glasgow, 1904.
HALL, F. W. *A Companion to Classical Texts.* Oxford, 1913.
HALL, H. R. s.v. *Manetho* in *Cambridge Ancient History.*
HALLEAUX, M. *Ptolemaios Epigonos, Jour. Hell. Studies,* XLI, 1921.
HANNAK, E. *Das Museum und die Bibliotheken in Alexandria.* Vienna, 1867.
Harper's Dictionary of Classical Literature and Antiquities, ed. Harry Thurston Peck, 2 vols., New York, 1897.
HARRISON, FREDERIC. *Among My Books.* London, 1912.
HARVEY, PAUL. *The Oxford Companion to Classical Literature.* Oxford, 1940. Especially: *The Alexandrian Library.*
HASTINGS. *Encyclopaedia of Religion and Ethics.* Edinburgh, 1908.
HAVET, ERNEST. *Mémoire sur les écrits qui portent les noms de Bérose et de Manéthon.* Paris, 1873.
HEATH, T. L. *Aristarchus of Samos; The Ancient Copernicus.* Oxford, 1913.
HEEREN, A. H. L. *A Manual of Ancient History.* Oxford, 1840.
HELIODORUS. tr. Underdowne and Wright, London, 1925.
Hellenica Oxyrhynchia. E. M. Walker, Oxford, 1913.
HERODES. *Mimes and Fragments* in *Herodes, Cercidas and The Greek Choliambic Poets (except Callimachus and Babrius).* A.D. Knox – L.C.L.
HERODIAN. Ed. Mendelssohn, Leipzig, 1883.
—, *Herodiani ab excessu divi Marci libri octo.* I. Bekker, Leipzig, 1855.
HERODOTUS. A. D. Godley, 4 vols. – L.C.L.
—, *The History of.* Tr. Geo. Rawlinson, with commentary by Sir Henry Rawlinson & J. Gardner Wilkinson, 4 vols., New York, 1889.

HERZ, MAX. *Les citernes d'Alexandrie* in *Monuments de l'art Arabe*. 1898.
HESIOD. *The Homeric Hymns and Homerica*. H. G. Evelyn-White – L.C.L.
Hibeh Papyri, The. Grenfell and Hunt. Oxford, 1906.
HILD, J. J. A. s.v. *Pan* in Daremberg et Saglio *Dict*.
HIPPOCRATES. W. H. S. JONES, 4 vols. – L.C.L.
HIRSCHFELD, O. *Die kaiserlichen Verwaltungsbeambten*. 1905.
Historiae Augustae: Scriptores Historiae Augustae. David Magie, 3 vols. – L.C.L.
HITTI, P. *History of the Arabs*. London, 1942.
HODGKIN, THOMAS. *Italy and her Invaders*. 2nd ed., 7 vols., Oxford, 1892–99.
HOGARTH, DAVID, G. *Devia Cypria*. London, 1889.
—, *Philip and Alexander of Macedon*. New York, 1897.
—, *Report on Prospects of Research in Alexandria* from Archæological Report of the Egypt Exploration Fund, 1894–95.
—, s.v. *Alexander in Egypt* in *Journal of Egyptian Archeology*, II, 1915.
—, See Grenfell and Hunt.
HOLM, ADOLPH. *The History of Greece*. 4 vols., London, 1894–1911.
HOMER, *The Iliad*. Tr. Wm. Benjamin Smith & Miller, New York, 1944.
—, *The Iliad*. Tr. A. T. Murray, 2 vols. – L.C.L.
—, *The Odyssey*. Tr. W. C. Bryant, Boston, 1871.
—, *The Odyssey*. A. T. Murray, 2 vols. – L.C.L.
—, *Galleria Omerica o raccolta di Monumenti antighi*. Cav. Francesco Inghirami, Poligrafia Fiesolana, 4 vols., 1831.
HORACE. *Satires*; *Epistles, Ars Poetica*. H. R. Fanclough – L.C.L.
—, *The Odes and Epodes*. C. B. Bennett – L.C.L.
HOUTSMA, M. TH. s.v. *'Abd al-Latif* in *Ency. Islam*, Leyden, 1913.
HUART, CLÉMENT. *A History of Arabic Literature*. New York, 1915.
HUIT, C. *Les bibliothèques, d'Alexandrie et de Pergame* in *L'instr. pub*. 1876 (Febr.-March).
HUNT, ARTHUR S. See Grenfell.
HYVERNAT, H. *Actes des Martyrs de l'Egypte*. Paris, 1886.
IBN AL ATHÎR. *Faultless Chronicle*. Ed. C. J. Tornberg, Leyden, 1868–74.
IBN BATTUTA. *Travels in Asia and Africa* 1325–54, tr. H. A. R. Gibb, London, 1929.
IBN DUKMÂK. *Description de l'Egypte*. Ed. K. Vollers, Cairo, 1893.
IBRAHIM-HILMY, H. H. PRINCE. *The Literature of Egypt and The Soudan*. 2 vols., London, 1886 (s.v. *Alexandrian Library*).
IDRÎSÎ, AL. *Nuzhat al-Mushtâg* (*Geographia Nubiensis*, Paris, 1609).
—, *Geographie*. Tr. fr. Amédée Jaubert, 2 vols., Paris, 1836–40.
IHNE, W. s.v. *Homerus* in *Smith Dict*.
IRENAEUS. English tr. Alex. Roberts & W. H. Rambant in *Ante-Nicene Library*, 2 vols., Edinborough, 1868–69.
—, *Five Books of S. Irenaeus Against Heresies*. John Keble, Oxford, 1872.
—, *Against Heresies* (*Contra omnes haereses*). Ed. W. W. Harvey, 2 vols., Cambridge, 1857.
Islam, The Encyclopaedia of, Leyden, 1913–27.
ISOCRATES, G. Norlin, 3 vols. – L.C.L.
ISODORUS HISPALENSIS. *Etymologiae or Origines*. Ed. Wm. Lindsay, 2 vols., London, 1911.

JACOBY, F. *Die Fragmente der griechischen Historiker*. Berlin, 1923.

JANKO, J. *Das Delta des Nil*. Buda-Pest, 1890.

JASTROW, M. *Did the Babylonian Temples Have Libraries?* in *Proc. Am. Oriental Soc*. I, 1906.

JEBB, RICHARD CLAVERHOUSE. *Homer*. 3rd ed., 1888.

JEROME, SAINT. *Letters*. F. A. Wright – L.C.L.

—, *Preface to the Book of Hebrew Questions* in *Library of Nicene and Post Nicene Fathers*, 2nd series, Oxford, 1893.

—, *Preface to the Pentateuch*.

—, *Commentary* on Ezekiel II–5.

—, *Chronicon E. C*. Ed. Helm.

Jewish Encyclopedia, The. 12 vols., New York, 1901–6. s.v. *Alexandria* by E. Schürer and Eli-Hazan.

JOHANN. ANTIOCH. fragment: F. H.G. IV 599.

JOHN OF NIKIU. *Chronique* du Jean, Evêque de Nikiou, tr. into Fr. by Zotenberg, Paris, 1883.

—, *The Chronicle* of John, Bishop of Nikiu, tr. into English by Dr. R. H. Charles, London, 1916.

JOSEPHUS, FLAVIUS. H. St. J. Thackeray and Ralph Marcus, 9 vols. – L.C.L.

—, *Contra Apionem*. H. St. J. Thackeray, 1 vol. – L.C.L.

—, *Jewish Antiquities*. H. St. J. Thackeray & Ralph Marcus, 6 vols. – L.C.L.

—, *The Jewish War*. H. St. J. Thackeray, 2 vols. – L.C.L.

—, *Philo's Embassy from the Jews of Alexandria to Caligula*, ed. Sir R. L'Estrange, London, 1902.

JOUGUET, PIERRE. *Macedonian Imperialism and the Hellenization of the East*. New York, 1932.

Journal of Egyptian Archaeology.

Journal of Hellenic Studies.

JULIAN. *The Works of the Emperor Julian*, tr. W. C. Wright, 3 vols. – L.C.L.
a. *Letters*.
b. *Panegyric in Honour of Constantius*.
c. *Misopogon*.

JUSTIN, *Apology* (from Thackeray).

JUSTIN (Pseudo). *Exhortation to Greeks* (from Thackeray).

KAERST, J. *Geschichte des Hellenismus*. 2nd ed., Leipzig, 1917–26.

KAIBEL, G. *Comicorum Graecorum Fragmenta*. Berlin, 1899.

KEIL, H. *The Prolegomena to Aristophanes* by Johnnes Tzetzes in *Rheinisches Museum*, VI, 1847.

KENRICK, JOHN. *Phoenicia*. London, 1855.

KENYON, FREDERICK G. *The Bible and Modern Scholarship*. London, 1948.

—, *Books and Readers in Ancient Greece and Rome*. Oxford, 1932.

—, *Palaeography of Greek Papyri*. Oxford, 1899.

—, *The Library of a Greek of Oxyrhynchus* in *Journal of Egyptian Archeology*, VIII, 1922.

—, s.v. *Libraries* in *The Ox. Class. Dic*.

KHALDÛN, IBN. *Histoire des Berbères et des Dynasties Musulmanes de l'Afrique Septentrionale*. Tr. M. le Baron Mac Guckin de Slane, 4 vols., Ager, 1852–56.

KHALDÛN. *An Arab Philosophy of History.* Selections from the *Prolegomena* of Ibn Khaldûn. Tr. Chas. Issawi. London, 1950.

—, *Prolégomènes.* Tr. Baron de Slane, 3 vols., Paris, 1863–68.

KHALIFA, HAJJI. *Lexicon bibliographicum et encyclopaedicum.* Arabic text and Latin tr., G. Fluegel, 7 vols., Leipzig and London, 1835–58.

KHALLIKAN, IBN. *Biographical Dictionary.* Tr. Baron Mac Guckin de Slane, 4 vols., Paris, 1842–71.

KIEPERT, HEINRICH. *A Manual of Ancient Geography.* G. A. Macmillan, London, 1881.

—, *Zur Topographie der alten Alexandria.* Berlin, 1872.

KIFTI, IBN AL. See Qifti, Ibn al.

KING, LEONARD, W. *A History of Babylon.* London, 1915.

—, *A History of Sumer and Akkad.* London, 1916.

KINGSLEY, CHARLES, *Hypatia.* 2 vols., New York, 1895.

—, *Alexandria and her Schools.* Cambridge, 1854.

KLIPPEL, GEORGE HEINRICH. *Ueber das alexandrinische Museum,* Göttingen, 1838.

KNAACK, G. s.v. Apollonios (ap. Pauly-Wissowa).

KOCK, TH. *Comicorum Atticorum Fragmenta.* 3 vols., Leipzig, 1880.

KONER, W. See Guhl, E.

KREHL, LUDOLF. *Gli Arabi e le biblioteche d'Alessandria* in *Bibliofilia,* XV.

—, *Ueber die Sage von der Verbrennung der alexandrinischen Bibliothek durch die Araber* (in International Congress of Orientalist held in Florence, 1878), Firenze, 1880.

KREMER, A. VON. *Culturgeschichtliche Streifzüge auf dem Gebiete des Islams.* Leipzig, 1873; also Engl. tr. by S. Khuda Bukhsh in *Contribution to the History of Islamic Civilization.* Calcutta, 1905.

KRUMBACHER, CARL. *Geschichte der byzantinischen Literatur.* 2nd ed. 1897.

KUIPER, K. *Proceedings* of the Utrecht Society of Letters for 1894.

LAFAYE, GEORGES. s.v. *Liber* in *Dict. des Antiq.* of Daremberg et Saglio.

—, s.v. *Serapis* in *Dict. des Antiq.* of Daremberg et Saglio.

—, *Histoire du Culte des Divinités d'Alexandrie hors de l'Egypte.* Paris, 1884.

LANCIANI, R. A. *Ancient Rome in the Light of Recent Discoveries.* New York, 1889.

LANE-POOLE, STANLEY. *The Mohammadan Dynasties.* London, 1894.

—, *Saladin and the Fall of the Kingdom of Jerusalem.* N.Y., 1898.

—, *The Story of Cairo.* London, 1902.

LANG, ANDREW. *Homer and the Epic.* London, 1893.

LANGIE. *Les bibliothèques publiques dans l'ancienne Rome et dans l'empire Romain.* 1908.

LAQUEUR, RICHARD. s.v. *Manetho* in Pauly-Wissowa.

LATIF, 'ABD AL. *Historia Aegypti Compendiosa.* Ed. J. White, Oxford, 1800.

—, *Relation de l'Egypte.* Tr. Silvestre de Sacy, Paris, 1810.

LAYARD, AUSTIN HENRY. *Nineveh and its Remains.* 3rd ed., 2 vols., London, 1849.

LEAF, WALTER. ed. *The Iliad.* 2 vols., London, 1886.

LEAKE, Wm. Martin. *The Demi of Attica.* London, 1841.

—, *The Topography of Athens.* 2nd ed., London, 1841.

LE BEAU, C. *Histoire de Bas Empire.* Ed. de St.-Martin, 21 vols., Paris, 1824–38.

LECLERC. *Histoire de la médecine arabe.* 2 vols., Paris, 1876.

Le Clercq, Dom. ed. *Dictionnaire d'Archéologie Chrétienne*, s.v. *Alexandrie* and *Bibliothèque.*

Le Fort, L. *La bibliothèque d'Alex.*, et sa destruction. Paris, 1875.

Legrand, Ph. E. *The New Greek Comedy*, tr. James Loeb, London, 1917.

—, *La poésie alexandrine.* Paris, 1924.

Lehrs, K. *De Aristarchi studiis Homericis.* 1882.

Le Mascrier, L'Abbé. ed. *Description de l'Egypte.* Vol. I, 1740. (Also 1735).

Lempriere's *Classical Dictionary.* 4th ed., 3 vols, London, 1843.

Lenormant, François. *Histoire Ancienne de l'Orient.* 6 vols., Paris, 1881–88.

Lenormant, François, and Chevallier, E. *A Manual of the Ancient History of the East.* 2 vols., Phila., 1871.

Le Pere, Gratien. *Mémoire sur la ville d'Alexandrie* in *Description de l'Egypte,* Vol. XVIII.

Lepsius, Karl Richard. *Chronologie der Ägypter.* 1849.

—, *Denkmäler aus Ägypten und Äthipien.* 12 vols. 1859.

Lesquier, J. *L'armée romaine d'Egypte à Auguste à Dioclétien.* Cairo, 1918.

—, *Les institutions militaires de l'Egypte sous les Legides.* Paris, 1911.

Le Strange, Guy. *Baghdad during the Abbasid Caliphate.* Oxford, 1900.

Letronne, Jean Antoine. Recueil des Inscriptions Grecques et Latines de l'Egypte *étudiées dans leur rapport avec l'histoire politique, l'administration intérieure, les institutions civiles et religieuses de ce pays, depuis la conquête d'Alexandrie jusqu'à celle des Arabes.* Paris, 1842–48.

Lewis, G. C. *Roman Book Trade under the Empire* in *Fraser's Magazine,* LXV.

Libanius. Ed. R. Foerster. Leipzig, 1903.

Livingstone, R. W. *The Legacy of Greece.* Oxford, 1924.

Livy. *Ab Urbe Condita.* B. O. Foster, G. T. Moore, E. T. Sage and Alfred C. Schlesinger, 13 vols. – L.C.L.

Loeb Classical Library. 388 Volumes, London, 1912–1950. Continuing.

Long, George. *The Decline of the Roman Republic.* 5 vols., London, 1874.

Longinus, Dionysius. *On the Sublime* in Dr. Wm. Smith's *Dionysius Longinus.* London, 1819.

—, *On the Sublime.* W. H. Fyfe – L.C.L.

Longus. *Daphnis and Chloe.* Geo. Thornley. rev. J. M. Edmonds – L.C.L.

Lucan. *The Civil War.* J. D. Duff – L.C.L.

Lucian. A. M. Harmon, 8 vols. – L.C.L.

—, *The Ignorant Book-Collector.*

—, *Works of Lucian of Samosata.* H. W. & F. G. Fowler, 4 vols., Oxford, 1905.

Lucretius. *De rerum natura.* W. H. D. Rouse – L.C.L.

—, *On Life and Death.* Tr. W. H. Mallock, New York, 1900.

Ludwich, Arthur von. *Aristarchs Hom. Textkritik.* 1885.

—, *Die Homervulgata als voralexandrinische erwiesen,* Leipzig, 1898.

Lumbroso, G. *L'Egitto dei Greci e dei Romani.* 2nd ed., Rome, 1896.

—, *L'Egitto al tempo dei Greci.* Rome, 1895.

—, *Recherches sur l'économie politique de l'Egypte sur les Lagides.*

Lycophron. See Callimachus.

Lyra Graeca. Being the Remains of all the Greek Lyric Poets from Eumelus to Timotheus, excepting Pindar. J. M. Edmonds, 3 vols. – L.C.L.

MACAIRE, S.B. MONS. KYRILLOS. *Le Temple du Cesareum* (in *Bulletin de la Société Khédiviale de Géographie*, Ve série, No. 6, Feb. 1900 (Le Caire).

—, *Nouvelle Étude sur le Serapeum d'Alexandrie* (in *Bulletin de la Soc. Khédiviale de Géographie, série VII*, No. 8, Le Caire, 1911).

MADVIG, JOHAN N. *Adversaria Critica ad Scriptores Graecos et Latinos.* 3 vols., Hanan, 1871–84.

MAGDI BEY, M. *Observations on the Fate of the Alexandrian Library* (in *Bull. de la Soc. Khédiviale de Geo.*, VIIe série, No. 10, Le Caire, 1911).

MAGNIEN, VICTOR. *Les Mystères d'Eleusis.* Paris, 1938.

MAHAFFY, JOHN PENTLAND. *Alexander's Empire.* London, 1889.

—, *The Empire of the Ptolemies.* London, 1895.

—, (Ed. with Smyly) Flinders Petrie Papyri. Dublin Academy, 3v. 1890–1894.

—, *Greek Life and Thought from the Death of Alexander to the Roman Conquest.* 2nd ed., London, 1896.

—, *A History of Classical Greek Literature.* 2 vols. in 4, London, 1895.

—, *A History of Egypt under the Ptolemaic Dynasty.* London, 1898.

—, *The Silver Age of the Greek World.* London, 1906.

MAHMOUD-EL-FALAKI. *Mémoire sur l'ancienne Alexandrie.* Copenhagen, 1872.

MAKÎN, AL. *Historia Saracenica.* Ed. T. Erpenius, Leyden, 1625.

MAKRÎZÎ, AL TAKI-EDDIN AHMED. *Histoire des Sultans Mamlouks de l'Egypte.* Tr. in Fr. Etienne Quatremère, 2 vols., Paris, 1845.

—, *Khitat.* 2 vols. Bûlâq (Text) Fr. tr. U. Bouriant in *Mémoires de l'École du Caire.*

MALALAS, JOANNES. *Chronicle of John Malalas.* Tr. M. Spinka and G. Downey, Chicago, 1940.

MANETHO. Text.

See Muller. *Frag. Hist. Grae.*

The *Epitome.* ap. *Chronologie des Manetho* (G. F. Unger), Berlin, 1867.

Greek text of *King's Lists* ap. *Königsbuch der alte Ägypter* (R. Lepsius), Berlin, 1858.

Greek text of Religious writings: ap. *Fontes Historiae Religionis Aegyptiacae* (Th. Hopfner), 1922–25.

Manetho. Tr. W. G. Waddell – L.C.L., London, 1940.

MARCUS AURELIUS ANTONINUS. *The Communings with himself of; His Speeches and Sayings.* C. R. Haines – L.C.L.

MARIETTE, AUGUSTE. *Outlines of Ancient Egyptian History.* Tr. Broderick, New York, 1892.

MARTIAL. *Epigrams.* Walter C. A. Ker, 2 vols. – L.C.L.

MASPERO, HENRI. *Les Finances de l'Egypte sous les Lagides.* Paris, 1905.

Masseketh Sopherim (The Tractate of the Scribes). Ed. Joel Muller, Leipzig, 1878.

MAS'UDI, ABÛ'L – HASAN 'ALI. *Collection d'ouvrages orientaux.* Ed. Barbier de Maynard, Paris, 1863.

See *The Golden Meadows*, an extract of his *Akhbâr al-Zâman.*

—, *Tanbih wa'l-ishraf (Notice and Review).* Text pub. by De Goeje & Fr. tr. by Baron Carra de Vaux.

MATTER, M. *Histoire de l'École d'Alexandrie comparée aux Principales Écoles Contemporaines.* 3 vols., 2nd ed., Paris, 1840–44.

MATTINGLY, H. *The Imperial Recovery* in *C.A.H.*, Vol. XII.

MC CRINDLE, J. W. *Ancient India as described by Megasthenes and Arrian, etc.*, Calcutta, 1926.

MC DOWALL, KATHARINE A. *Some Greek Portraits, Jour. Hellenic Studies*, Vol. XXIV (1904).

Mediaeval Jewish Chronicles. Oxford, 1895.

MEGASTHENES. See MC CRINDLE; also SCHWANBECK.

Megillath Taanith (Roll of Fasting). See Anecdota Oxon. Semitic Series.

MEMNON OF HERACLEA. (ap. Photius.)

MENANDER. *The Principal Fragments.* F. G. Allinson, rev. ed. – L.C.L.

MÉNARD, RENÉ (dessins par Cl. Souvageot). *La Vie Privée des Anciens.* 4 vols. Paris, 1880–83. (Especially Vol. *Les Institutions de l'Antiquité.*)

MERIVALE, CHARLES. *History of the Romans under the Empire.* 5th. ed., 7 vols., London, 1864.

MEYER, ERNEST. *Untersuchungen z. Chronologie d. erst. Ptolemy.* 1925.

MEYER, J. J. *Das Arthacastra des Kautilya.* Leipzig, 1925.

MICHAEL OF MELITENE. *Chronicle* (in Syriac); Armenian Version; Fr. tr. of pts. See *A Syriac Chronicle of the year 846*, text & tr. E. W. Brooks (This author used many of the same sources as Michael).

MIGNE, JACQUES PAUL. *Patrologia Graeca.* Paris, 1860 sq. ap. *Patrologiae curcus completus.* 386 vols. (Latin series, 221 vols., 1844–1855; 2nd ed. 1878 seq.; Greek series 165 vols., 1857–1866).

MILNE, J. GRAFTON. *A History of Egypt under Roman Rule.* London, 1898.

Minor Attic Orators. K. J. Mardonent, 2 vols. – L.C.L.

Minor Latin Poets. J. Wright Duff & Arnold M. Duff – L.C.L.

MINUCIUS, FELIX. *Octavius.* Gerald H. Rendall - L.C.L.

MOMMSEN, THEODOR. *The History of Rome.* 5 vols., London, 1866.

—, *The Provinces of the Roman Empire from Caesar to Diocletian.* 2 vols., London, 1909.

MOSCHION. (ap. Athenaeus V).

MULLER, KARL & THEODOR. *Fragmenta Historicorum Graecorum.* 5 vols., Paris, 1841–70. Especially: *Demetrios of Phaleron.*

MULLER, K. O. and DONALDSON, J. W., *A History of the Literature of Ancient Greece*, 3 vols., London, 1858.

MÜLLER-GRAUPE. s.v. *Museion* in Pauly-Wissowa.

MURE, WILLIAM. *A Critical History of the Language and Literature of Ancient Greece.* 5 vols., London, 1850.

MURRAY, GILBERT. *A History of Ancient Greek Literature.* New York, 1897.

MUSAEUS. Tr. E. E. Sikes, London, 1920.

NAU, M. L'ABBÉ. *Un colloque du Patriarche Jean avec l'émir des Agaréens* (in *Journal Asiatique*, 11th series, Vol. V), 1915.

NAUCK, AUGUST. *Aristophanes Byzantii Grammatici Alexandrini Fragmenta.* Halle, 1848.

—, *Lexicon Vindobonense.* St. Petersburg, 1867.

—, *Tragicorum Graecorum fragmenta.* 2nd. ed., Leipzig, 1889.

NEALE, JOHN MASON. *A History of the Holy Eastern Church. The Patriarchate of Alexandria.* 2 vols., London, 1847.

NEGRI, GAETANO. *Julian the Apostate.* 2 vols., London, 1905.

NEROUTSOS-BEY, TASS. *L'ancienne Alexandrie*. Paris, 1888.

NEWMAN, JOHN HENRY CARDINAL. *Macedonian and Roman Schools* in *Rise and Progress of Universities* in *Historical Sketches*. London, 1899.

NICANDER, NICANDREA. O. Schneider, Leipzig, 1856.

NICEPHORUS, CALLISTUS XANTHOPOULOS. *Historica Ecclesiastica* (ap. Migne, *Pat. Gra.*).

NICEPHORUS, PATRIARCHA. *Historicum Breviarium (Concise History)*; *Concise Lists of Dates*; ed. C. de Boor, 1880.

NICHOLS, CHARLES L. *The Library of Rameses the Great and some of its Books*. Boston, 1909.

NICHOLSON, REYNOLD A. *A Literary History of the Arabs*. London, 1914.

NIEBUHR, BERTHOLD GEORGE. *The History of Rome*. 5 vols., London, 1844.

—, *Lectures on Ancient History*. London, 1852.

NIESE, B. *Geschichte der griechischen und makedonischen Staaten* (1–3), 1893–1903.

NOACK, F. *Neue Untersuchungen in Alex*. Athen-Mettteil, 1900.

NOLDEKE, Th. *Sketches from Eastern History*, tr. J. S. Black, London, 1892.

NONNOS. *Dionysiaca*. W. H. D. Rouse, 3 vols. – L.C.L.

NORDEN, E. *Die antike Kunstprosa*. 2 vols., Leipzig, 1898.

NOURRISSON, V. *La Bibliothèque des Ptolémées*. Alexandrie, 1893.

NUCHTER, FRIEDRICH. *Albrecht Dürer*. Ansbach, 1911.

OCKLEY, S. *History of the Saracens*. London, 1847.

OLDFATHER, W. A. *The Maintenance of Ancient Greek Public Libraries* in *Library Quarterly*, VIII, April, 1935.

ORIGEN. *Origenis opera omnia;* J. P. Migne. *Patrologia Graeca*. Vols. 11–17, Paris, 1857.

OROSIUS, PAULUS. *Seven Books of History against the Pagans*, tr. I. W. Raymond, New York, 1936.

—, *Historiarum adversus paganos, Libri Semptem*. Venice, 1499.

OSBURN, WILLIAM. *The Monumental History of Egypt*. London, 1854.

OTTO, WALTER. *Priester und Tempel im hellenistischen Aegypten*. 2 vols., Leipzig, 1903–8.

OUSSANI, GABRIEL, S.V. *Berosus* in *Catholic Ency*.

OVID. *Metamorphosis: The XV Books of P. Ouidius Naso entytuled Metamorphosis,* tr. Arthur Golding, London, 1567.

—, *Metamorphoses*. Fr. J. Miller. 2 vols. – L.C.L.

—, *Heroides* and *Amores*. Grand Showerman – L.C.L.

—, *Tristia; Epistulae ex Ponto*. A. L. Wheeler – L.C.L.

—, *The Art of Love and Other Poems*. Vide: *The Ibis*. J. H. Mozley – L.C.L.

OVIDII NASONIS, PUBLII. *Festorum libre six* (ed. tr. com.), James George Frazer, 5 vols., London, 1929.

Oxyrhynchus Papyrus. See Grenfell & Hunt.

PAGE, T. E. *Letter to James Loeb* in *Alexandrian Poetry under the First Three Ptolemies* by Auguste Couat, tr. Jas. Loeb. London, 1931.

PAGENSTECHER, R. *Alexandrinische Studien*. Heidelberg, 1917.

PALLADAS OF ALEXANDRIA. See *Gr. Anthology*, IX–400; Franke Alf.

PALMER, WILLIAM. *Egyptian Chronicles*. London, 1861.

Papyri Collections. Vide List in Calderini. Dizionario.

Paradise or Garden of the Holy Fathers being Histories of the Anchorites... and Ascetic

Fathers of the Deserts of Egypt (from A.D. 250) compiled by Athanasius, Archbishop of Alexandria; Palladius, Bishop of Hellennopolis; St. Jerome & others, tr. out of the Syriac by Ernest A. Wallis Budge, 2 vols., London, 1907.

PARET, R. s.v. *al-Tabari* in *Ency. Islam.*

PARTHENIUS. *The Love Romances of* & other Fragments. S. Gaselee – L.C.L.

PARTHEY, G. *Das alexandrinische Museum.* Berlin, 1838.

PASQUALI, GIORGIO. s.v. *Biblioteca* in *Enci Ital.* Vol. VI, Milano-Roma, 1930.

PATERCULUS, C. VELLERIUS. *The Roman History.* F. W. Shipley – L.C.L.

PAULY, WISSOWA, KROLL, MITTELHAUS, ZIEGLER. *Real-Encyclopädie der klassischen Altertumswissenschaften.* 64 vols. continuing, 1893–1950.

PAUSANIAS. *Description of Greece,* tr. with commentary J. G. Frazer, 6 vols., London, 1913.

—, *Description of Greece.* W. H. S. Jones, 6 vols. – L.C.L.

PERRAULT, CHARLES. *Parallèle des Anciens et des Modernes,* 1692.

PETRIE, WM. FLINDERS. *A History of Egypt from the Earliest Times to the XVIth Dynasty.* New York, 1895.

—, *Social Life in Ancient Egypt.*

PETRONIUS, TITUS (Arbiter). *Satyricon; Fragments; Poems.* Michael Haseltine – L.C.L.

PHILO. F. H. Colson & G. H. Whitaker, 10 vols. – L.C.L.

—, *In Flaccum.* F. H. Colson – L.C.L.

—, *On the Life of Moses.* F. H. Colson – L.C.L.

—, *The Biblical Antiquities of Philo,* tr. fr. old Latin Version, M. R. Jones, London, 1917.

PHILO BYBLIUS. *Sanchuniathonis Historiarum Phoeniciae libros novem Graece versos a Philone Byblio edidit Latinaque version donavit Fr. Wagenfeld.* Bremae, 1837, ex officina Caroli Schunemanni.

PHILOSTRATUS. *The Life of Apollonius of Tyana,* F. C. Conybeare, 2 vols. – L.C.L.

PHILOSTRATUS, THE YOUNGER. *Imagines.* Arthur Fairbanks – L.C.L.

PHOTIUS. *Librorum quos legit,* ed. pr., Augsburg, 1601.

—, *Myriobiblion seu Bibliotheca,* tr. J. H. Freese, 6 vols., London, 1920.

Pinakes (πιναξ) by Regenbogen ap. Pauly-Wissowa, Vol. XX–2 (*Pigranes bis Plautinus*), 1950.

PINDAR. *The Odes of, including The Principal Fragments.* John Sandys – L.C.L.

PINNER, H. L. *The World of Books in Classical Antiquity.* Leiden, 1948.

PLATO, 12 vols. and various ed. & tr. – L.C.L.

—, *Hipparchus.* W. R. M. Lamb – L.C.L.

—, *The Republic.* Pauly Shorey, 2 vols. – L.C.L.

PLAUTUS. Aldus, 1522.

—, Nixon, Paul, 5 vols. – L.C.L.

—, *Scholia to.* See Ritschl. *Opuscula philologica,* and especially Tzetzes.

PLINY, THE ELDER (Gaius Plinius Secundus). *The Natural History.* H. Rackham, 10 vols. – L.C.L.

PLINY, the YOUNGER. Wm. Melmoth, 2 vols – L.C.L.

PLOTINUS. TR. S. M'KENNA, London, 1927.

PLUTARCH. *Moralia.* F. C. Babbitt et als. Vols. I–VI and X – L.C.L. especially:

454   BIBLIOGRAPHY

Non posse suaviter vivi secundum Epicurum – Isis and Osiris – De Defectu Oraculorum – The Apophthegms of Kings and Commanders.
PLUTARCH. *Parallel Lives.* Bernadotte Perrin, 11 vols. – L.C.L. Especially: Aemilius Paulus – Alexander – Alcibiades – Antony – Caesar – Demetrius – Lycurgus – Solon.
PLUTARCH, PSEUDO-. *Lives of the Ten Orators,* Plutarch's *Moralia.* H. N. Fowler – L.C.L.
POLLIO, THEBELLIUS. *Tyranni Triginta* in Scrip. Hist. Aug. – L.C.L.
POLLUX JULIUS OF NAUCRATIS. Ed. Bekker, 1846.
POLYBIUS. *The Histories.* W. R. Paton, 6 vols. – L.C.L.
POOLE, R. S. *The Ptolemies, Kings of Egypt.* British Mus. Cat. 1883.
POSIDONIUS OF APAMIA. *Histories* (ap. Athenaeus).
POWELL, J. U. *Collectanea Alexandrina.* Oxford, 1925.
POWELL, J. U. and BARBER, E. A. *New Chapters in the History of Greek Literature.* 1st series, Oxford – 2nd series, Oxford, 1929 (*Catalogue of a Library at Rhodes*). – 3rd series, Oxford, 1933.
PRAT, J. M. *Histoire de l'Eclectisme Alexandrin, Considéré dans sa Lutte avec le Christianisme.* 2 vols., Paris, 1843.
PROCOPIUS OF CAESAREA. *History of the Wars* – 5 vols. – *The Anecdota or Secret History* – 1 vol. – *Buildings* – 1 vol. – tr. H. B. Dewing – L.C.L.
PROPERTIUS, SEXTUS. *The Elegies of.* H. E. Butler – L.C.L.
PROSPER, TIRO. *Chronicle.* Ed. Mommsen in *Mon. Germ. Hist.* IX, Berlin, 1892.
PROTAGORIDES. *Fragments* (ap. Athenaeus).
PRUDENTIUS. H. J. Thomson, 2 vols. – L.C.L.
PTOLEMY, CLAUDIUS. *Tetrabiblos.* F. E. Robbins – L.C.L.
PUCHSTEIN, s.v. *Alexandreia* in Pauly-Wissowa.
PUECH, A. *Histoire de la Littérature Grecque Chrétienne.* Vols. 1 & 2, Paris, 1928.
PUTNAM, G. H. *Authors and their Public in Ancient Times.* New York, 1894.
QIFTI, IBN AL-. *Ta'rih Al-Hukama.* Ed. Julius Lippert, Leipzig, 1903.
—, C. Brockelmann in The Encyc. Islam, s.v. *al Kifti.*
QUATREMÈRE, E. *Mémoires Géographiques et Historiques sur l'Egypte.* 2 vols., Paris, 1811.
QUINTILIAN. *Institutio Oratoria.* H. E. Butler, 4 vols. – L.C.L.
QUINTUS SMYRAEUS. *The Fall of Troy.* A. S. Way – L.C.L.
RABIOU, M. G. s.v. *Bibliotheca* in Daremberg & Saglio *Dict.*
RADIN, MAX. *The Jews Among the Greeks and Romans.* Philadelphia, 1915.
RAMSAY, W. M. *Letters to the Seven Churches.* 1904.
RANKE, LEOPOLD VON. *Weltgeschichte.* 1880–86.
RAU, R. VASUDEVA. *Did Omar Destroy The Alexandrian Library?* (*Nineteenth Century,* October, 1894.)
RAWLINSON, GEORGE. *History of Ancient Egypt.* London, 1881.
—, *History of Phoenicia.* London, 1889.
RAWLINSON, H. G. *Bactria, The History of a Forgotten Empire.* London, 1912.
REINACH, A. J. *On the Three Volumes of Dioscurides* in *Bull. Soc.* A.A. II (1909), p. 350.
REINACH, S. *Répertoire des Vases Grecs et Etrusques.* 2 vols., 2nd ed., Paris, 1923.
REINACH, TH. *La charte ptolémaique de Cyrène* in *Revue Archéologique* XXVI, 1927.
REINHARD. *Ueber die jüngsten Schicksale der alexandr. Bibliotheken.* Göttingen, 1792.

REITZENSTEIN, R. *Epigram und Skolion.* Giessen, 1893.
Remains of Old Latin with *Archaic Inscriptions.* E. H. Warrington, 4 vols. – L.C.L.
RENAUDOT, EUSÈBE. *Historia Patriarcharum Alexandrinorum jacobitarum, a. D. Marco usque ad finem saeculi XIII.* Paris, 1713.
RHONÉ ARTHUR. *Résumé chronologique de l'histoire d'Egypte,* Paris, 1877.
RICHARDSON, C. *The Beginnings of Libraries.* Princeton, 1914.
RITSCHL, FRIEDRICH WILHELM. *Die alexandrinischen Bibliotheken unter den ersten Ptolemäern.* Breslau, 1838.
—, *Opuscula philologica.* Leipzig, 1866.
ROBERT, C. H. *The Greek Papyri* (ap. *The Legacy of Egypt*), Oxford, 1942.
ROBINSON, E. S. G. *Cyrenaica.* British Museum Cat. 1883.
ROBINSON, G. W. *The Librarian of Julian the Apostate* in *Harvard Studies in Class. Philol.,* XXVI.
ROBIOU. *Mémoire sur l'économie politique de l'Egypte au temps des Lagides.* Paris, 1876.
ROGERS, R. W. *History of Babylonia and Assyria,* ed. 6, New York, 1915.
ROHDE, E. *Der griechische Roman und seine Vorläufer.* 3rd ed., Leipzig, 1914.
ROSTAGNI, A. *Bibliotecari alessandrini nella cronologia della letteratura ellenistica,* Atti della R. Accad. di Torino, I, 1914–15.
—, *Poeti alessandrini.* Torino, 1916.
—, See *Rev. di fil.,* 1928.
ROSTOVTZEFF, M. *A Large Estate in Egypt in the Third Century B.C.,* Madison, 1922.
—, *A History of the Ancient World.* 2 vols., Oxford, 1926.
—, s.v. *Ptolemaic Egypt* in *Cambridge Ancient History.*
ROUSE, W. H. D. *Greek Votive Offerings.* Cambridge, 1902.
ROWE, A. *Discovery of the Famous Temple and Enclosure of Serapis at Alexandria;* Annales du Service des Antiquités de l'Egypte, Cahier No. 12, 1946.
RUBENSOHN, O. *Elephantine-Papyrus.* Berlin, 1907.
RUFINUS. *Vitae Patrum.*
—, *Historia Ecclesiastica* in *Nicene and Post Nicene Fathers,* New York, 1892.
RUSKIN, JOHN. *The Works of,* ed. Cook and Wedderburn, 39 vols., London, 1909. See: *Arrows of the Chace,* Vol. 34; original ed., London, 1908.
SAINT–GENIS. *Description des Antiquités d'Alexandrie et ses environs* in *Description de l'Egypte,* Vol. V.
—, *La Colonne Dioclétienne* in *Description de l'Egypte,* Vol. V.
SALLUST. Especially *The Historiae.* J. C. Rolfe – L.C.L.
SALVIAN. *The Writings of Salvian, the Prysbyter,* tr. J. F. O'Sullivan, New York, 1947.
SANDERSON, JOHN. *The Travels of John Sanderson in the Levant (1584–1602).* Hakluyt Society, London, 1931.
SANDYS, JOHN EDWIN. *A History of Classical Scholarship.* 3 vols. (3rd ed.), Cambridge, 1921.
SARTON, GEORGE. *Introduction to the History of Science.* 5 vols., Carnegie Institute of Washington, Baltimore, 1927.
SAYLE, C. *The Vatican Library* in *The Library,* VI, 1894.
SCHANZ, M. *Zur Stichometrie* in *Hermes,* XVI, 1881.
SCHEDEL, HARTMANN. *Libri Chronecarum* – The Nuremberg Chronicle. Wood-

cuts by Wolgemuth and Pleydenwurff, Nuremberg, end 15th Century.

SCHLUMBERGER, GUSTAVE. *L'Epopée Byzantine.* 3 vols., Paris, 1900–05.

SCHMID. See Christ.

SCHMID, W. -STAHLIN, O. *Geschichte der griechischen Literatur.* 2 vols., 8 pts, 1920–48.

SCHMIDT, Fr. *Die Pinakes des Kallimachos.* Berlin, 1922.

SCHNEIDER, OTTO. *Callimachia.* 2 vols. Leipzig, 1870–73.

SCHOELL, M. *Histoire de la Littérature Grecque Profane.* 8 vols., Paris, 1825.

SCHUBART, W. *Das Buch bei den Griechen und Römer.* Berlin, 1907.

—, *Aegypten von Alexander bis Mohammed.* 1924.

SCHURER, E. and ELI-HAZAN, s.v. *Alexandria* in *The Jewish Encyclopedia,* New York.

SCHURER. *History of the Jewish People.* 1897.

SCHWABE. See Teuffel.

SCHWANBECK, E. A. *Megasthenis Indica.* Bonn, 1864.

SCHWARCZ. *Die Demokratie.* Leipzig, 1882.

SCOTT, JOHN A. *The Unity of Homer.* 1921.

—, *Athenian Interpolations in Homer* (*Classical Philology* VI, Chicago, 1911).

SÉDILLOT. *Histoire Générale des Arabes.* 2nd ed., Paris, 1877.

SEEMAN, OTTO. *De primis sex bibliothecae Alexandrinae Custodibus.* Essen, 1859, in *Jahresbericht über das Königliche Gymnasium,* 1858–59.

Select Papyri. A. S. Hunt & C. C. Edgar, 2 vols. – L.C.L.

SEMONIDES OF AMORGUS. See *Lyra Graeca.*

SENECA, LUCIUS ANNAEUS. *Ad Lucilium. Epistulae Morales.* Richard M. Gummere, 3 vols. – L.C.L.

—, *Moral Essays.* John W. Basore, 3 vols. – L.C.L. (Especially: *De Tranquillitate Animi.*)

—, *Apocolocyntosis.* W. H. D. Rouse – L.C.L.

Septuagint (The LXX):
   1. Aldine edition (commenced by Aldus Manucius), Venice, 1518, *ed. prin.*
   2. The Complutensian, printed at Alcalá, Spain, 1514–18, published in 1520, when it appeared in the *Polyglot* of Cardinal *Ximenes.*
   3. Codex Alexandrinus, one of 6 exemplars on vellum: *Vetus Testamentum Graecum e Codice MS. Alexandrino* (with Letter of Cyril) and volume *Prolegomena et Notae,* published by H. H. Barber, 6 vols., London (Ricardi & Taylor), 1816–28, also *Novum Testamentum Graecum e Codice MS. Alexandrino* (C. G. Woide), London (Joannis Nichols), 1786 – one of 7 exemplars on vellum.
   4. Codex Vaticanus (B): *Bibliorum S. S. Graecorum Cod.* Vat. 1209, Cod. B, denuo phototypice expressus, jussu et cura praesidum Bibliothecae Vaticanae, Milan (Hoepli), 1904–06, 3 vols.

SEYFFERT, OSKAR. *A Dictionary of Classical Antiquities.* London, 1906.

SHAEFER. *De Aphthonio Sophista.* Breslau, 1854.

SHARPE, SAMUEL. *The History of Egypt.* 2 vols., London, 1885; & later eds. Especially Notes in German ed.

SIDONIUS. *Poems and Letters.* W. B. Anderson, 2 vols. – L.C.L.

SIMON, J. ed. *Histoire de l'Ecole d'Alexandrie.* 2 vols., Paris, 1843.

SIMONIDES OF CEOS. See *Lyra Graeca*.

SMITH, CAPTAIN JOHN. *Travels and Adventures of,* in Purchas.

SMITH, VINCENT A. *History of India.* New York, 1906.

—, *Asoka,* 1901.

SMITH'S *Dictionary of Greek and Roman Biography and Mythology,* ed. Wm. Smith, Wayte-Marindin. London, 1867 and 3rd ed., 1891 – 3 vols.

—, *Dictionary of Greek and Roman Geography.* ed. Wm. Smith, 2 vols., London, 1854.

—, *A Dictionary of Greek and Roman Antiquities,* ed. Wm. Smith, Wm. Wayte, G. E. Marindin, 3rd ed. rev., 2 vols., London, 1891.

SMYLY, J. GILBERT. See GRENFELL.

SOBERNHEIM. s.v. *Saladin* in *Ency. Islam.*

SOCRATES. *The Ecclesiastical History,* ed. A. C. Zenos in *Nicene and Post Nicene Fathers.* New York, 1890.

SOPHOCLES. F. STORR, 2 vols. – L.C.L.

—, *The Plays and Fragments,* text, tr. & commentary, R. C. Jebb, 6 vols., Cambridge, 1907.

SOPHRONIUS. *Opera* (ap. Migne. *Patr. Gr.*).

SOTION. *Succession of the Philosophers* in Diogenes Laertius.

SOZOMEN. *Historia Ecclesiastica,* tr. Hartranft (in *Nicene and Post Nicene Fathers,* II s., New York, 1890).

SPARTIANUS, AELIUS, in *The Life of Antoninus Caracalla (Historiae Augustae)* – L.C.L.

STAQUET, J. J. *César à Alexandrie. L'incendie de la bibliothèque (Nova et Vetera,* XII, 1928).

STATIUS. *Silvae.* J. H. Mozley, 2 vols. – L.C.L.

STEFANINI, GIOVANNI, s.v. *Alessandria* in *Enci. Ital.,* Vol. I, 1929.

STOBAEUS, JOANNES. *Collectiones Sententiarium.* Venice, 1536, ed. pr.

—. *Florilegium,* ed. Wachsmuth & Hense, 5 vols., Berlin, 1884–1912.

STOFFEL, E. *Histoire de J. César, Guerre Civile.* 2 vols., Paris, 1887.

STRABO. *The Geography of.* Horace Leonard Jones, early part unfinished version by J. R. S. Sterrett, 8 vols., London, 1917–32.

—, H. C. Hamilton & W. Falconer, 3 vols., London, 1892–3.

STRACK, M. L. *Die Dynastie der Ptolemäer.* Berlin, 1897.

—, *Kleopatra (Historische Zeitschrift,* CXV, 1916).

STUDNICZKA, F. *Das Symposion Ptolemaios II.* Leipzig, 1914.

SUETONIUS. *The Lives of the Caesars.* J. C. Rolfe, 2 vols. – L.C.L. – *The Deified Julius – The Deified Claudius – Domitian.*

Suidas, eds. 1. Demetrios Chalcondyles, Milan, 1499 (ed. princeps); 2. Gottfried Bernhardy, 2 vols. in 4, Halle, 1834–53; s.v. *Aphthonius – Aristarchus – Aristonicus of Alexandria – Diocletian – Homer – Lycophron.*

SUSEMIHL, FRANZ. *Geschichte der griechischen Litteratur in der Alexandrinerzeit.* 2 vols., Leipzig, 1891.

SUYÛTÎ, AS. *History of the Caliphs,* tr. H. S. Jarrett, Calcutta, 1881.

SWETE, HENRY BARCLAY. *An Introduction to the Old Testament in Greek.* Cambridge, 1902.

SYMEON MAGISTER AND LOGOTHETE (probably S. Metaphrastes). *The Chronicle of.* See in two redactions, in names of Leo Grammaticus (Bonn series,

1842) and Theodosius of Melitene (1859). Migne. *Gr. Patr.* (114–116).
SYMONDS, JOHN ADDINGTON. *Studies of the Greek Poets.* 2 vols., London, 1873–76.
SYNESIUS OF CYRENE. *The Essays and Hymns of*, tr. Augustine FitzGerald, 2 vols., Oxford, 1930.
—, *The Letters of*, tr. Augustine FitzGerald, Oxford, 1926.
TABARI, AT–, ABU DJAFAR MOH. IBN DJARIR. *Annales*, ed. Barth, Nöldeke, de Jong, Guidi, de Goeje, Houtsma. 15 vols., Leyden, 1879–1901.
TACITUS, PUBLIUS CORNELIUS:
   The Histories. Clifford H. Moore, 2 vols. – L.C.L.
   The Annals. John Jackson, 2 vols. – L.C.L.
   The Dialogues of. Wm. Petterson – L.C.L.
   Agricola and *Germania.* Maurice Hutton – L.C.L.
Talmud, The Babylonian. 2nd rev. ed., tr. Michael L. Rodkinson, 13 vols., Boston, 1918.
Talmud of Jerusalem (Palestinian Talmud). Megilla I 71 d. – from Thackeray.
TARN, W. W. *Antigonos Gonatas.* Oxford, 1913.
—, *Hellenistic Civilization.* London, 1927.
—, s.v. *Cleopatra* in *Cambridge Ancient History.*
—, *Alexanders's ʽὑπομνήματα* and *the 'World-Kingdom', Jour. Hell. Studies,* XLI, 1921.
TATIUS, ACHILLES. *Clitophon and Leucippe.* S. Gaselee – L.C.L.
TEDDER, H. R. and Brown, James Duff, s.v. *Libraries* in *Enc. Brit.*, 11th ed.
TEGGART, FREDERICK I. *The Destruction of the Alexandrian Library* in *The Nation*, July 7, 1898, Vol. 67.
—, *Caesar and the Alexandrian Library* in *Zentralbl. f. Bibl.* XVI, 1899.
TERTULLIAN. *The Book of Apology Against The Heathen.* Oxford, 1854.
—, *Apologeticus; De Spectaculis.* T. R. Glover – L.C.L.
TEUFFEL AND SCHWABE. *History of Latin Literature.* London, 1891.
THAUSING, MORIZ. *Albert Durer, His Life and Works.* London, 1882.
THEBELLIUS, POLLIO. See *Historiae Augustae.*
THEOCRITUS, BION AND MOCHUS, tr. Andrew Lang. London, 1906.
THEOCRITUS, ed., tr. & com. by A. S. F. Gow, 2 vols., Cambridge, 1950.
THEODORET. *The Ecclesiastical History*, tr. Rev. Blomfield Jackson in *Nicene and Post Nicene Fathers.* 2nd series, London, 1892.
THEON OF ALEXANDER. *Ep. ad Lucianum cubic*, ap. *Patro. Grae.*
THEOPHANES. *Chronography* (A.D. 284–813); ed. C. de Boor, 2 vols., 1883–85.
THEOPHRASTUS. *The Characters of.* J. M. Edmonds – L.C.L.
—, *Enquiry into Plants* & *Minor Works.* A. Hort, 2 vols. – L.C.L.
THIERSCH, H. *Die alexandrinischen Königsnekropolen* in *Jahrbuch d. K.D. Archaeol. Instituts*, 1910, Vol. XXV.
—, *Der Pharos Antike Islam und Occident.*
THIRLWALL, CONNOP. *The History of Greece*, new ed., 8 vols., London, 1855.
THOMPSON, JAMES WESTFALL. *Ancient Libraries.* Berkeley, 1940.
THORNDIKE, LYNN. *History of Magic and Experimental Science.* 6 vols., New York, 1923–1941.
THUCYDIDES. C. FOSTER SMITH, 4 vols. – L.C.L.
TILLEMONT, SEBASTIEN LE NAIN DE. *Histoire des Empereurs.* Paris, 1701–38.
—, *Mémoires Ecclésiastiques*, 1693.

TIMON OF PHLIUS. *On the Alexandrian Museum*, in Sandy's *History of Classical Scholarship*.

TIMOTHEOS. *Die Perser*, ed. Ulrich von Wilamowitz-Moellendorff, Leipzig, 1903.

TOYNBEE, ARNOLD J. *A Study of History*, 6 Vols., London, 1934.

TZETZES, JOHNNES. *The Plautine Scholium*:
 a. MEINEKE. *Quaest. Scen. Sepec.*, III-3.
 b. DINDORF, W. ap. *Rheinisches Museum*, IV-232, 1930.
 c. RITSCHL, Dr. FRIEDRICH. *Die alexandrinischen Bibliotheken unter den ersten Ptolemaern*. Breslau, 1838.
 d. RITSCHL, Dr. FRIEDRICH. *Opuscula philologica*. Vol. I-124-5, Leipzig, 1866.
 e. CRAMER, J. A. *Anecdota graeca* etc., I-3, Oxford, 1839.
—, *The Prolegomena*.
 a. *The Prolegomena to Aristophanes* by J. Tzetzes, ed. H. Keil, in *Rhein. Mus.*, VI, 1847.
 b. ed. by Nauck. *Lexicon Vindobonense*. St. Petersburg, 1867.
 c. ed. by Kaibel ap. *Comicorum Gr. Frag.*, Berlin, 1899.

ULLMAN, B. L. *Ancient Writing and its Influence*. New York, 1932.

—, *American Journal of Archaeology*, XXXI, 1927.

USTICK, W. LEE. '*Parchment*' and '*Vellum*', in *The Library*, 4th series, Oxford, 1936.

VACHEROT, E., ed. *Histoire Critique de l'École d'Alexandrie*. 3 vols., Paris, 1846.

VAILHE, S. s.v. *Pergamus* in *Cath. Enc.*

VAILLANT, J. *Historia Ptolemaeorum Aegypti regum, ad fidem numismatum accomodata*. Amsterdam, 1701.

VALERIUS, FLACCUS GAIUS. *Argonautica*. H. H. Mozley – L.C.L.

VANDER HEEREN, A. s.v. *Septuagint* in *Cath. Enc.*

VAN GRONINGEN, B. A. *Short Manual of Greek Palaeography*. Leyden, 1940.

VAUNJANY (DE). *Recherches sur l'anc. Alex.* 1888.

VERGIL. *Eclogues*.

—, *Georgics*.

—, *Aeneid*.

—, *The Minor Poems*.
 H. RUSH FAIRCLOUGH, 2 vols., rev. – L.C.L.

VICO, GIAMBATTISTA. *Il Vero Omero* ap. *Opera* di Vico, Milan, 1836, Vol. V.

VISCONTI, E. I. *Iconographie Romaine*. 4 vols., Paris, 1817.

—,*Iconographie Grecque*. 3 vols., Paris, 1817.

VITRUVIUS. *De Architectura*. Fr. Granger, 2 vols. – L.C.L.

VOPISCUS, FLAVIUS. *Divus Aurelianus*. See *Historiae Augustae*.

—, *Vita Saturnin*. See *Historiae Augustae*.

WACHSMUTH, C. *Die pinakographische Thätigkeit des Kallimachus* in *Philologus*, Volume XVI.

—, *Zur Geschichte Alex*. (*Rhein. Museum*, 35).

—, *Zur Topog. Alex*. (*Rhein. Museum*, 42).

WAKIDÎ, AL. *Kitâb Futûh Misr*. ed. Hamaker, Leyden, 1825.

WARRAQ, AL (ABUL FARAJ, MUHAMMED AL NADIN) *Fihrist* (*Index*), ed. Flugel-Rodiges, Leipzig, 1871.

WEHRLI, FRITZ. *Demetrios von Phaleron.* Basel, 1949.
WEIGALL, ARTHUR. *The Life and Times of Cleopatra.* rev. ed., New York, 1926.
WEIL, G. *Geschichte des Abbasiden-Chalifats in Egypten.* 2 vols., Stuttgart, 1860–62.
—, *Geschichte der Chalifen.* 3 vols., Mannheim, 1846.
WEITZMANN, KURT. *Illustrations of Euripides and Homer in the Mosaics of.* Antioch, 1941. See *Antioch on-the-Orontes.*
WELLES, C. BRADFORD. *Royal Correspondence in the Hellenistic Period.* New Haven, 1934.
WENDLAND, P. *Die hellenistisch–römische Kultur.* 3rd ed., Tübingen, 1912.
WENIGER. *Das alexandrinische Museum.* Berlin, 1875.
WENSINCK, A. J. *A Handbook of Early Muhammadan Tradition.* Leyden, 1927.
WHEATLEY, L. A. *Was the Alexandrian Library burnt by the Mohometans?*, in *The Bibliographer*, No. 25, Vol. 5, Dec., 1883.
WHIBLEY, LEONARD. Ed. *A Companion to Greek Studies.* 3rd ed., Cambridge, 1916 (especially s.v. *Science* by James Gow).
WHITE, JOHN WILLIAMS. *The Scholia on the Aves of Aristophanes.* Boston, 1914.
WILAMOWITZ–MOELLENDORFF, U. VON. *Antigonos von Karystos.* Berlin, 1881.
—, *Die Ilias und Homer.* Berlin, 1916.
—, *Hellenistische Dichtung in der Zeit des Kallimachos,* 2 vols., Berlin, 1924.
—, *Herakles.* 1899.
—, *Homerische Untersuchungen.* Berlin, 1884.
WILBUR, DONALD N. *The Plateau of Daphne* in *Antioch on-the-Orontes,* Princeton University, 1938.
WILCHEN, U. *Griechische Ostraka aus Ägypten und Nubien.* Leipzig, 1899.
—, *Griechische Geschichte,* 1924.
—, *Urkunder der Ptolemäerzeit.* Berlin-Leipzig, 1922 (*Einleitung B, Das Serapeum von Memphis*).
—, *Zum alexandrinischen Antisemitismus.* Leipzig, 1909.
—, *Alexander der Grosse.* Leipzig, 1931.
WILCKEN, U. AND MITTERS, L. *Grundzüge und Chrestomathie der Papyruskunde.* Berlin-Leipzig, 1912.
WINKELMANN, JOHN JOAKIM. *A History of Ancient Art,* tr. G. Henry Lodge, 5 vols., Boston, 1880.
WRIGHT, F. A. *A History of Later Greek Literature* (323 B.C. – 565 A.D.), London, 1932.
—, *The Poets of the Greek Anthology.* London, 1925.
WUNSCH, s.v. *Charta* in Pauly-Wissowa.
XENOPHON, *Anabasis.* C. L. Brownson, 2 vols. – L.C.L.
—, *Cyropaedia.* Walter Muller, 2 vols. – L.C.L.
—, *Hellenica.* C. L. Brownson, 2 vols. – L.C.L.
—, *Memorabilia Oeconomicus.* E. C. Marchant – L.C.L.
—, *Scripta Minora.* E. C. Marchant – L.C.L.
—, *Symposium; Apology.* O. J. Todd – L.C.L.
YA'KUBI, AL. *Ibn Wâdhih qui dicitur Al Ya'kubi Historiae.* Ed. M. T. Houtsma. 2 vols., Leyden, 1883.
YÂKÛT. *Mu'jám al Buldán (Geographical Dictionary).* Ed. Wustenfeld, 6 vols., Leipzig, 1866–73.
ZACHARIAH OF MITYLENE. *Chronicle,* tr. Hamilton and Brooks. London, 1889.

ZAYDÁN, JURJI. *History of Islamic Civilization,* being Fourth Part, *Umayyads and 'Abbasids,* tr. D. S. Margoliouth. London, 1907.

—, *Ta'rikhu 'l-Tamaddun al Islami* (Arabic). See tr. in App. A. of this work.

ZELLER. Ed. *Die Philosophie der Griechen.* 3 vols., 6 parts.

ZENODOTUS OF EPHESUS:

DÜNTZER, H. *De Zenodoti studiis Homericis.* 1843.

ROMER, A. *Über die Homerrezension des Zenodot.* 1886.

(See also authorities under other 6 great librarians).

Zenon Papyri. Ed.Westermann, N.Y., 1934; also Un. Mich., ed. C. C. Edgar, Ann Arbor, 1931.

ZERVOS, SKEVOS GEORGES. *Rhodes Capitale du Dodécanèse.* Paris, 1920.

ZOGHEB, A. DE. *Etudes sur l'ancienne Alexandrie.* Paris, 1910.

—, *Le tombeau d'Alexandre.* 1896.

ZONARAS, JOANNES. *The Epitome of History* (ed. Pinder & Büttner–Wobst, in Bonn, *Corpus Scriptorium Hist. Byz.* (1841–1897).

ZOSIMUS. *Historiae* (Reitemeier-Hayne). Leipzig, 1784.

ZSCHIETZSCHMANN, W. s.v. *Pergamon,* ap. Pauly–Wissowa, XIX–p XI (1937).

INDEX

The writer is greatly indebted for work on this index to Mrs. Gloria Shearin Smith